RESEARCH
METHODS
IN FORENSIC
PSYCHOLOGY

RESEARCH METHODS
IN FORENSIC
PSYCHOLOGY

Edited by

BARRY ROSENFELD
STEVEN D. PENROD

WILEY

John Wiley & Sons, Inc.

This book is printed on acid-free paper. ⊗

Copyright © 2011 by John Wiley & Sons, Inc. All rights reserved.

Published by John Wiley & Sons, Inc., Hoboken, New Jersey.
Published simultaneously in Canada.

No part of this publication may be reproduced, stored in a retrieval system, or transmitted in any form or by any means, electronic, mechanical, photocopying, recording, scanning, or otherwise, except as permitted under Section 107 or 108 of the 1976 United States Copyright Act, without either the prior written permission of the Publisher, or authorization through payment of the appropriate per-copy fee to the Copyright Clearance Center, Inc., 222 Rosewood Drive, Danvers, MA 01923, (978) 750-8400, fax (978) 646-8600, or on the web at www.copyright.com. Requests to the Publisher for permission should be addressed to the Permissions Department, John Wiley & Sons, Inc., 111 River Street, Hoboken, NJ 07030, (201) 748-6011, fax (201) 748-6008. *10 0646838 1*

Limit of Liability/Disclaimer of Warranty: While the publisher and author have used their best efforts in preparing this book, they make no representations or warranties with respect to the accuracy or completeness of the contents of this book and specifically disclaim any implied warranties of merchantability or fitness for a particular purpose. No warranty may be created or extended by sales representatives or written sales materials. The advice and strategies contained herein may not be suitable for your situation. You should consult with a professional where appropriate. Neither the publisher nor author shall be liable for any loss of profit or any other commercial damages, including but not limited to special, incidental, consequential, or other damages.

This publication is designed to provide accurate and authoritative information in regard to the subject matter covered. It is sold with the understanding that the publisher is not engaged in rendering professional services. If legal, accounting, medical, psychological or any other expert assistance is required, the services of a competent professional person should be sought.

Designations used by companies to distinguish their products are often claimed as trademarks. In all instances where John Wiley & Sons, Inc. is aware of a claim, the product names appear in initial capital or all capital letters. Readers, however, should contact the appropriate companies for more complete information regarding trademarks and registration.

For general information on our other products and services please contact our Customer Care Department within the U.S. at (800) 762-2974, outside the United States at (317) 572-3993 or fax (317) 572-4002.

Wiley also publishes its books in a variety of electronic formats. Some content that appears in print may not be available in electronic books. For more information about Wiley products, visit our Web site at www.wiley.com.

Library of Congress Cataloging-in-Publication Data:

Research Methods in Forensic Psychology/Edited by Barry Rosenfeld, Steven D. Penrod.
    p. cm.
  Includes index.
   ISBNs 978-0-470-24982-6; 978-0-470-93338-1; 978-0-470-93340-4; 978-0-470-93339-8
  1. Forensic psychology. I. Rosenfeld, Barry, editor of compilation. II. Penrod, Steven D., editor of compilation. III. Rosenfeld, Barry. Overview of forensic research.
   RA1148.R47 2011
   614'.15—dc22
                                                                    2010045677

Printed in the United States of America

10 9 8 7 6 5 4 3 2 1

Contents

Contributors

Kathryn Byars, MA
John Jay College of Criminal Justice

Debra Chen, BS
The University of Alabama

Lawrence D. Cohn, PhD
University of Texas, El Paso

Anna Coward, MA
Fairleigh Dickinson University

Keith R. Cruise, PhD
Fordham University

Tarika Daftary-Kapur, PhD
Vera Institute of Justice

Stephanie Davidson, JD, MLS
University of Illinois

Kevin S. Douglas PhD, LLB
Simon Fraser University

John Edens, PhD
Texas A&M University

Eric B. Elbogen, PhD
University of North Carolina

Robert E. Emery, PhD
University of Virginia

Solomon M. Fulero, PhD, JD
Sinclair College

Michele Galietta, PhD
John Jay College of Criminal
Justice

Nathan D. Gillard, MS
University of North Texas

Gail S. Goodman, PhD
University of California, Davis

Sarah Greathouse, PhD
Iowa State University

Debbie Green, PhD
Fairleigh Dickinson University

Ross D. Grimes, MA
The University of Alabama

Jennifer Groscup, JD, PhD
Scripps College

Maria Hartwig, PhD
John Jay College of Criminal
Justice

Larry Heuer PhD
Barnard College, Columbia
University

Charles R. Honts, PhD
Boise State University

John C. Kircher, PhD
University of Utah

Margaret Bull Kovera, PhD
John Jay College of Criminal Justice

Raina Lamade, MA
Fairleigh Dickinson University

Elise C. Landry, JD, MA
John Jay College of Criminal Justice

Zina Lee, PhD
University of the Fraser Valley

Sara Lowmaster, MA
Texas A&M University

Kelly McWilliams, MA
University of California, Davis

Mindy B. Mechanic, PhD
California State University, Fullerton

Elizabeth Nicholson MA
Simon Fraser University

J. Gregory Olley, PhD
University of North Carolina at Chapel Hill

Steven D. Penrod JD, PhD
John Jay College of Criminal Justice

Margaret-Ellen Pipe, PhD
Brooklyn College

Ekaterina Pivovarova, MA
Fordham University

Robert A. Prentky, PhD
Fairleigh Dickinson University

Jennifer K. Robbennolt JD, PhD
University of Illinois

Richard Rogers PhD
University of North Texas

Barry Rosenfeld, PhD
Fordham University

Karen Salekin, PhD
The University of Alabama

Randall T. Salekin, PhD
The University of Alabama

C. Gabrielle Salfati, PhD
John Jay College of Criminal Justice

David A. Sbarra, PhD
University of Arizona

Diane Sivasubramaniam, PhD
University of Ontario Institute of Technology

Jennifer L. Skeem, PhD
University of California, Irvine

Lisa Spano, PhD
PhaseOne Communications

Siegfried L. Sporer, PhD
University of Giessen, Germany

Gary L. Wells Ph.D.
Iowa State University

Cathy Spatz Widom, PhD
John Jay College of Criminal Justice

Patricia Zapf, PhD
John Jay College of Criminal Justice

Acknowledgments

Barry Rosenfeld:

For Cara, Jane, Kate, and Anna, who put up with far too many nights when I'm at the computer.

Steve Penrod:

To Joan

The Importance of Appropriate Research Methods

BARRY ROSENFELD AND STEVEN D. PENROD

FOR MORE THAN a century, since the publication of Hugo Munsterberg's seminal book *On the Witness Stand*, psychologists have been actively engaged in research aimed at addressing and informing legal questions. Although Munsterberg's work was largely ignored in his lifetime, important developments in legally relevant aspects of psychology have continued to emerge in the decades that followed. In 1917, William Marston published the first of many papers (as part of his dissertation research) examining the utility of autonomic nervous system arousal as a measure of deception. This work eventually culminated in the modern-day polygraph test, but also formed the basis for the U.S. Supreme Court's decision in *Frye v. U.S.* (1923), which defined the "general acceptance" standard for admissibility of scientific testimony—a standard that still plays a part in admissibility decisions in almost all jurisdictions. But without question, the "breakthrough" application of psychological research to legal proceedings occurred in the landmark case of *Brown v. Board of Education* (1954), in which the research of Kenneth and Mamie Clark was cited in support of the argument that racially segregated educational systems were inherently unequal.

However, much of this seminal research, like Munsterberg's early writings, has been ignored by the legal community. For example, Marston's precursor to the polygraph test was deemed inadmissible in *Frye* because it was not "generally accepted" by scholars in the field. Many such examples exist, including Supreme Court decisions in *Barefoot v. Estelle* (1983) and *Lockhart v. McCree* (1986), both of which effectively ignored decades of published research (regarding the accuracy of predictions of violence and the impact of death qualification on jury verdicts, respectively). In some cases, judicial fact-finders and policymakers have cited limitations in the published research, noting that the published research does not directly answer the specific legal issue at hand; in other instances, however, concerns relate to the study methodology used. Indeed, the rigor of psycholegal research methodology is a critical element underlying legal and policy decisions about the relevance and implications of published research.

The importance of a rigorous research methodology grew exponentially with the Supreme Court's decision in *Daubert v. Merrill Dow Pharmaceutical* (1993). In outlining the factors that should be considered in deciding whether scientific testimony should be admissible, the Court, in *Daubert*, focused on the quality of the scientific research that underlies expert opinions. Although no specific prescription exists for determining when a research study is "good enough," there is little doubt that stronger research is more likely to yield data upon which policymakers can rely. Indeed, *Daubert* called on judges to make determinations about whether research is sufficiently reliable as to warrant admissibility under the label of "scientific" or "expert" testimony.

The benefits of rigorous and systematic research are perhaps best exemplified by the widespread acceptance, by the U.S. Department of Justice, of the findings from eyewitness researchers. Based on the large and rigorous body of research demonstrating the problems associated with traditional eyewitness lineup procedures, as well as the existence of multiple procedures for reducing inaccurate lineup identifications, the Department of Justice (DOJ) recommended a number of modifications to traditional police procedures. Although changes to existing practice are no doubt slow to achieve, the DOJ's acceptance of the input of psychology researchers was clearly based on the respect for, and indisputable quality of the scholarship that underlay the recommendations.

In short, during the past century the potential impact of psycholegal research in guiding policy and practice has been repeatedly demonstrated. Yet these advances could not have been possible without the application of rigorous research methods. For many scholars, learning these "tricks of the trade" is simply a part of the graduate school experience, with mentors educating their students in the nuances of research in their area of expertise. But not all learning follows this prototypical approach. Particularly given the rapid expansion of forensic psychology graduate programs and journals, the need for guidance in developing methodologically rigorous research studies has far outstripped the resources of the profession. Quite simply, not all budding research scholars can have the opportunity to learn from a well-established and widely recognized authority. Hence, the impetus for the present book: to fill this void in mentorship and guidance by providing concise summaries of the principal methodological issues that pervade psychology/law research.

AN OVERVIEW OF THIS BOOK

When we initiated this project, a number of people asked why such a book was needed. Who is the intended audience? Aren't there already enough resources out there for anyone who is interested in learning research methodology? Of course, a knee-jerk reaction might be to reply "because there isn't a book like it" or "*everyone* who conducts psychology/law research could benefit from this book." But the reality may be slightly more humble. We hoped that this book would serve as a comprehensive resource for a wide range of scholars, ranging from novice researchers who have relatively limited guidance to draw upon within their own institutions, to established researchers who are expanding their research focus and seek to avoid the pitfalls that might jeopardize their initial forays. Almost every researcher, no matter how well established, has had the experience of conducting a research study and writing up the results, only to discover that the journal reviewers have identified "fatal flaws" that limit its utility—perhaps even to the point of it's being unpublishable. Our hope is that a book such as this one will help avoid the wasted time, money, and energy that go into research projects that ultimately fall short because of methodological naiveté.

Attorneys, too, may find this book useful, particularly when they struggle to understand the research that an expert might draw on in forming an expert opinion. Experts routinely testify about published research, yet few attorneys have sufficient familiarity with research methodology to understand, let alone cross-examine, psychologists on their work or the work they reference. At present, there is little by way of guidance for attorneys or policy-makers who need to differentiate between rigorous scholarship and the "junk science" that occasionally makes its way into the courtroom.

To provide the most comprehensive overview of research methodology, we invited leading scholars in each of the primary psychology/law arenas to contribute chapters. Authors were charged with a simple task: to summarize the primary methodological issues and common problems encountered in their respective areas of study. The result is a succinct overview of the field of psychology/law, as viewed by some of the world's leading experts.

As evident from the Table of Contents, the topics encompassed by these chapters are diverse and represent the breadth of the field. Although many chapters address topics related to the criminal law, there are also a number of chapters that demonstrate the application of psychology/law research to civil law, family law, and unique subgroups of the population. Part I addresses broad methodological topics, including how to conduct legal research, a basic primer on statistics, and more detailed coverage of important topics such as meta-analysis, measure development, and Internet-based data collection. These topics represent more general issues that are often applied to the more specific content areas addressed in subsequent chapters.

Part II of this volume addresses a range of pre-trial issues in the criminal law arena, including the polygraph, competence to stand trial, malingering, criminal profiling, and false confessions and interrogations. Trial-related psycholegal issues comprise Part III, including jury decision making and litigation consultation, the accuracy of eyewitnesses and children, and procedural justice research. Part IV addresses post-trial issues and special populations, including violence risk assessment and psychopathy research, as well as sex offenders, juvenile offenders, and mentally retarded offenders.

Each of these populations presents unique challenges that are often over-looked by novice researchers. The final set of chapters addresses topics primarily related to civil and family law, including informed consent and decisional competence, child custody and divorce mediation, intimate partner violence, and child abuse. In short, this volume is intended to provide guidance for researchers who seek to study virtually any conceivable topic in the field of psychology/law.

This book is not, however, intended to replace a more general research methodology textbook. Readers will be far better able to digest and use the information in this volume if they already have a working knowledge of the "basics" of research methodology. Clearly, outlining all aspects of research design, sampling, and statistical methods is beyond the scope of this text. Rather, we have attempted to provide a comprehensive supplement that will enable the psychology/law researcher to apply the principles gleaned from a more general text or course on research methodology to the nuances of law/psychology research. Of course, these nuances differ depending on the nature of the psycholegal questions being investigated, and hence, the large volume of chapters, each of which covers distinct research areas and provides the insights and guidance of leading researchers.

There is little doubt that psychology and law has grown exponentially during the past few decades. Since the initial development of the American Psychology-Law Society in 1978, and the subsequent emergence of Law and Human Behavior as the flagship journal of the Society, research scholarship around issues related to legal and policy issues has exploded. From a small society with a single journal, psychologists today have numerous scholarly outlets for their work and multiple professional organizations that address issues of relevance to psychology/law researchers. Yet the variability of scholarship continues to be wide, indicating an ever-growing need for expert guidance. We hope that this book can represent one step toward filling this void and improving the quality of scholarship that will be produced by the next generation of researchers.

PART I

GENERAL ISSUES IN FORENSIC RESEARCH

CHAPTER 1

Legal Research Techniques for Social Scientists

JENNIFER K. ROBBENNOLT AND STEPHANIE DAVIDSON

INTRODUCTION

The range of legal topics into which psychology can offer insight is enormous. Similarly, psychologists can occupy a variety of roles as they contribute to the analysis of these legal questions. However, whether a psychologist is conducting research, working as a practitioner, or serving as an expert, a detailed knowledge of the substantive law, the operation of the legal system and its processes, and the content of legal policy debates is critical. Indeed, knowledge of the law has been identified as one of the core competencies of psycholegal scholars, with basic competence including knowledge of "the basic tools of law (e.g., legal processes, evidence), sources of law (e.g., common law, statutory law, constitutional law, administrative law), and the core substance of law itself (e.g., civil, criminal)" (Bersoff et al., 1997, p. 1305).

Skill in performing legal research is central to gaining this requisite legal knowledge. As Grisso and his colleagues (1982) have argued, proficiency with legal research is of particular importance for those

> who will be performing psychological research on legal issues, since the relevance of their research will often depend on the care with which their studies are grounded conceptually in matters of law and legal precedent. Similarly, it is unlikely that professionals will stay abreast of the law that controls their practice unless they know where to "find" the law, how to interpret it, and how to keep abreast of any amendments to it. (p. 272)

To help legal psychologists attain this necessary competence with the law and legal materials, this chapter provides an introduction to the sources of law and the processes of legal research. Before probing the particulars of the structure of the law and how to do legal research, we describe in more detail the importance of legal research for legal psychologists.

KNOWLEDGE OF THE LAW

Across legal issues, areas of psychology, and professional roles, a working knowledge of the law that is relevant to one's area of research or practice is indispensable.

> While it may not be essential for every legal psychologist to have extensive training in law, it is important that psychologists who work in the legal psychology area have an in-depth understanding of the law that pertains to their own areas of work.
>
> *(Ogloff, 2001, p. 11)*

Without such an understanding of the relevant law, legal psychologists cannot be effective. In order to acquire this meaningful understanding of the law, researchers, practitioners, and experts all need to be able to conduct legal research. Effective legal research enables psychologists to design research programs that will be relevant to law and legal decision making, to frame and disseminate the results of psycholegal research in ways that will have meaning for legal actors, to identify broader questions that are of interest to the law and into which psychology can offer important insights, and to comply with ethical guidelines that call for an understanding of the law related to the relevant research or practice area.

DESIGNING RESEARCH WITH RELEVANCE TO LAW

A primary reason why psychologists working on legal topics must be familiar with the sources of law and how to do legal research is that it is difficult to design research that will be of relevance to legal doctrine, legal process, or policy debates in law without a grounding in the relevant law and practice. In order to design sophisticated research that addresses important legal questions in ways that are attuned to nuances in the law, researchers need to be aware of the relevant law and how it operates.

Wiener and his colleagues (2002) reviewed the research submitted to and published in *Law and Human Behavior* and found that the most common independent variable was the manipulation of a legal rule—with many studies examining the effect of a particular legal rule on judgments and decisions—and that almost all the studies published included some legal measure as a dependent variable. To design such studies well, it is important to know the relevant legal rules, their nuances and exceptions, and how they are applied. Similarly, it is important to know the legal meanings of the pertinent legal constructs. For example, without a working knowledge of how line-ups are conducted and of the legal rules governing them, it is difficult to design a study of eyewitness identification that will have relevance to such procedures. Indeed, it has been by careful attention to such details that research on eyewitness identifications has had an impact on the legal system (Wells et al., 2000).

Unfortunately, legal psychologists have not always operated with a highly developed sense of the law—either its substance or the relevant procedure (Ogloff, 2001; Weiten & Diamond, 1979). To the extent that the measures that are created or the research procedures that are employed diverge from their legal counterparts, the research may be difficult to apply to the legal context. Research that employs measures and procedures that differ from the corresponding legal constructs and procedures should not be dismissed out of hand, nor, however, should such research be accepted uncritically. Instead, a more careful analysis is required. The key to this analysis is to examine whether the departure from the particular legal constructs or context at issue is a departure that has important implications for the interpretation and application of the research results.

Of particular concern would be instances in which the departure is likely to lead to different patterns of effects (see Robbennolt, 2002). For example, if an impoverished measure of a legal construct is likely to lead to a different set of results than a measure that is more legally informed—such as finding an effect when the impoverished measure is used, but not when the legally informed measure is used, or vice versa, or obtaining effects that point in opposite directions when using the two measures—application of the results obtained using the impoverished measure in the legal context cannot be done with a great deal of confidence. Similarly, naïve mistakes about the law—for example, conflating measures of guilt on the one hand and sentencing on the other (Weiten & Diamond, 1979) or misunderstandings of the factors that are relevant to a particular legal decision task—present problems for application of the research to the legal context.

On the other hand, there may be some departures that are less troubling. For example, imagine a set of studies that produce a pattern of results suggesting that people have trouble understanding jury instructions (see Ogloff & Rose, 2005, for a review). Imagine further that these studies used college students— who are collectively more highly educated than the typical jury pool—as study participants. One might have a relatively high level of confidence in concluding that jurors have difficulty understanding such instructions, because one would predict that actual jurors would demonstrate even lower levels of comprehension. Indeed, studies that have examined this issue have found that jury-eligible participants evidence even lower levels of jury instruction comprehension than do college student participants (Lynch & Haney, 2000).

As a practical matter, it is worth noting that deviations from the strictures of the substantive law or the practice setting—whether or not the particular deviation is likely to have significant implications for the interpretation and application of the results to the legal context—may have implications for how legal actors respond to the research findings. While decision makers ought to be most concerned with the external validity or generalizability of psycho-legal research, they may instead focus on departures from the law as a proxy for external validity or as a convenient way in which to reject the research. Indeed, a representativeness heuristic may operate such that decision makers discount the usefulness of research that does not fully replicate the law or legal context (Kovera, McAuliff, & Herbert, 1999). Using the representativeness heuristic, decision makers make categorizations based on the degree to which the object of the evaluation is representative of the category to the neglect of other relevant considerations (Kahneman & Tversky, 1971). Accordingly, courts and other legal actors may dismiss research that, for example, does not use measures that are completely in accord with the legal constructs, that is not sensitive to exceptions to a rule, or that does not incorporate particular aspects of the relevant procedure.[1] While such an automatic rejection of otherwise useful research is problematic (Robbennolt, 2002), psychologists can address such tendencies by designing research that attends to the law and by critically justifying any deviations.

Of course, none of this analysis is possible if the ways in which the variables, measures, and context depart from the law and the legal context are not identified, and the relevant departures are unlikely to be recognized unless the researcher has become familiar with the relevant law.

Framing and Disseminating Results

A second and related reason that psychologists ought to become skilled at finding and understanding the law is that familiarity with the law and legal considerations will help psychologists to present research results in ways that speak to lawyers and other legal actors (Bersoff et al., 1997). At a basic level, this follows from the previous argument—the results of psychological research will find more credibility among those in the legal system when they address questions of relevance to law. As Ogloff (2002) has argued,

> psychologists who attempt to have their findings make their way into the legal system must be willing to meet legal professionals on their own terms . . . this requires having psychologists frame their work in legal terms and to ensure that it is legally relevant and valid. (p. 27)

---

1. Such criticism can be on the basis of substantive law or procedure. In *Lockhart v. McCree* (1986), the U.S. Supreme Court rejected the body of work on the death qualification of jurors because the participants "were not actual jurors sworn under oath to apply the law to the facts of an actual case involving the fate of an actual capital defendant." Courts have rejected empirical studies of the comprehensibility of capital phase jury instructions on similar grounds (see, e.g., *State v. Deck*, 1999). Similarly, legal scholars have debated whether particular legal constructs have been operationalized in ways that sufficiently capture the underlying legal construct. For a recent debate in the context of the Fourth Amendment, see Kahan, Hoffman, and Braman (2009) and comments at http://volokh.com/posts/1199994070.shtml and http://www.concurringopinions.com/archives/2008/01/whose_eyes_in_s.html.

Beyond issues of research design, the choice of research questions, or the structure of particular measures, however, psychologists working on legal topics ought to be able to write or testify about their findings or the findings of others in ways that demonstrate some degree of sophistication with the relevant legal constructs. Researchers, practitioners, or expert witnesses who can explain how the psychological research fits into the substance of the law or has relevance for legal procedure, and who are sensitive to the relevant nuances in the law will likely be more successful in communicating with the relevant legal players. For example, to the extent that the substantive law varies across jurisdictions, a legally sophisticated psychologist will be aware of the variation, the policy judgments behind the different approaches, and the implications of such variation for the applicability of the research.

IDENTIFYING QUESTIONS OF INTEREST TO LAW

A third reason for psychologists working on legal topics to become more familiar with how to research the law is that a more sophisticated knowledge of the law can lead to the identification of a broader range of legal topics to which psychology and psychological research can make interesting contributions (Ogloff, 2002).

Many commentators have noted that psychologists have not conducted research about the full range of topics afforded by the law (Melton, Monahan, & Saks, 1987; Ogloff, 2002; Rachlinski, 2000; Saks, 1986; Wiener et al., 2002). While a great deal of excellent research has examined issues related to jury decision making, eyewitness testimony, and psychological assessment (Wiener et al., 2002), far less attention has been paid to how psychology might contribute to analyses of tax policy, contracts, property law, torts, estates and trusts, corporate and commercial law, health policy, civil procedure, elder law, labor law, environmental law, and many other legal topics. Similarly, while the focus of psychologists has been primarily, though not exclusively, on the behavior of jurors, witnesses, and criminals, the decisions of many other legal actors (e.g., judges, attorneys, litigants, corporate actors, physicians, and consumers) also present a host of interesting questions about law and human behavior. Although some first-rate research has started to address this broader range of topics and actors, this research has only begun to scratch the surface.

Relatedly, skill in finding the law can lead both to ideas for new research projects and to unique sets of materials for use in such studies. Enterprising researchers did just this in response to the U.S. Supreme Court's recent decision in *Scott v. Harris* (2007), a case that involved the assessment of whether a police officer used excessive force when he rammed his vehicle into the car of a fleeing suspect with whom he was engaged in a high-speed chase. In conjunction with its opinion, the Court posted a copy of the video footage from one of the police cruisers involved in the chase. Researchers who were attendant to such legal developments were able to capitalize on the availability of such evidence for use in constructing stimulus materials (Kahan, Hoffman, & Braman, 2009).

As noted, however, legal psychologists have not always engaged fully with a broad range of legal issues, actors, and materials. As Michael Saks (1986) put it,

> My warning is that our usefulness, both as scholars of the behavioral aspects of law and as applied researchers producing knowledge that can enlightened policy and practice, will be limited by the range of topics and issues we address. To be a field that studies law and human behavior is a grand and noble enterprise. To be the field that knows more than anyone would ever want to ask about a narrow assortment of issues is, to put it mildly, less grand. (p. 279)

In order to identify a broad range of promising areas for research, legal psychologists need to find and engage with an increasingly wide ranging set of legal resources. Without the ability to delve deeply into the law, contribution to an extensive range of legal topics will continue to be elusive.

ETHICS

A final reason for psychologists to become familiar with the law related to their area of research or practice is that it is ethically appropriate to do so. As a general matter, the American Psychological Association's Ethical Principles of Psychologists and Code of Conduct provides that "psychologists provide services, teach, and conduct research only within the boundaries of their competence" (Standard 1.04 Boundaries of Competence).

With regard to psychologists working on legal issues more specifically, the 1991 Specialty Guidelines for Forensic Psychologists provide that "forensic psychologists have an obligation to maintain current knowledge of scientific, professional, and *legal* developments within their area of claimed competence" (Guideline VI.A; Committee on Ethical Guidelines for Forensic Psychologists, 1991). More recently, the Third Proposed Draft of the Revised Specialty Guidelines for Forensic Psychology (§ 4.04; Committee on the Revision of the Specialty Guidelines for Forensic Psychology, 2008) provides that

> [f]orensic practitioners are responsible for a fundamental and reasonable level of knowledge and understanding of the legal and professional standards, laws, rules, and precedents that govern their participation in legal proceedings and that guide the impact of their services on service recipients.

Having a fundamental knowledge of the relevant law is aided by an ability to find and understand the applicable legal rules.

FINDING AND UNDERSTANDING THE LAW

It is clear that it is important for legal psychologists to have an understanding of those aspects of the law that are relevant to their research or practice. However, the law can be elusive, difficult to locate, and resistant to clear or concise answers. In addition to helping the researcher reach an answer to a question about the law, legal research can reveal the complexity of questions regarding substantive or procedural legal rules. Therefore, good legal research requires both mastery of basic skills and careful analysis of the results.

In the U.S. legal system, law is the written product of several different governmental bodies. Most law takes the form of statutes, court opinions, and agency regulations, which are issued by legislatures, courts, and executive agencies, respectively. All of these texts overlap and intersect with each other to produce what we know as law. Finding the law on any given issue may require using all these sources in conjunction with each other, reading and interpreting the texts along with secondary sources that provide analysis and commentary.

THE INTERCONNECTEDNESS OF LAW

Consider one example. The Americans with Disabilities Act (ADA), a statute passed by the U.S. Congress, includes the general provision that no covered employer "shall discriminate against a qualified individual with a disability because of the disability of such individual in regard to job application procedures, the hiring, advancement, or discharge of employees, employee compensation, job training, and other terms, conditions, and privileges of employment" (§ 12112(a)). Under the ADA, "disability" is defined as "a physical or mental impairment that substantially limits one or more of the major life activities of such individual" (§ 12012(2)(A)).

The Equal Employment Opportunity Commission, an administrative agency, was authorized (42 U.S.C.A. § 12116) to promulgate the regulations necessary to implement the ADA. These regulations contain more detailed provisions related to how the general prohibition against disability discrimination will be carried out and enforced. One of the regulations issued permits an employer to defend against a claim of discrimination under the ADA by arguing that the worker's disability poses "a direct threat to the health or safety of the individual or others in the workplace" (29 C.F.R. § 1630.15(b)(2)). The regulations further provide that a "direct threat" is one that involves "a significant risk of substantial harm to the health or safety of the individual or others that cannot be eliminated or reduced by reasonable accommodation." The determination of whether there was a significant risk of substantial harm is to be based on "(1) the duration of the risk; (2) the nature and severity of the potential harm; (3) the likelihood that the potential harm will occur; and (4) the imminence of the potential harm" (29 C.F.R. § 1630.2(r)).

When specific disputes arise between employers and employees under these statutory and regulatory provisions, the courts are called on to interpret the provisions and apply them to the particular facts of the cases. In one case, for example, the plaintiff, who worked for a contractor at an oil refinery, had hepatitis C, a disease of the liver. The refinery's doctors concluded that exposure to the chemicals at the refinery would aggravate the plaintiff's liver condition, and the refinery asked that he be reassigned to a job in which he would not be exposed or that he be removed from the refinery. The plaintiff was subsequently laid off. In considering the plaintiff's claim against the refinery, the courts had to determine (among other things) whether or not the plaintiff's medical condition posed a "direct threat" to his own health given the conditions in the workplace (Chevron U.S.A., Inc. v. Echazabal, 2002). The precise details of the worker's medical condition and the particular toxins at issue in the case were not specifically contemplated by the legislature when the statute was enacted or by the regulatory agency when the regulations were promulgated; therefore, the courts were needed to determine the outcome of this specific case under the relevant provisions.

Note that to have a nuanced sense of the operation of the ADA, one would need to become familiar with the general provisions of the statute, the details of the administrative regulations, and the relevant case law. This familiarity would need to extend well beyond the individual provisions and cases described here. In addition, a range of secondary sources can provide additional insight into the policies underlying the rules, how the rules have been applied, proposed alternatives, and so on. Of course, not all legal questions will directly implicate all of the sources described here. For example, some areas of law are predominantly characterized by case law and involve little statutory regulation. In any case, the relevant legal question should be investigated thoroughly to determine the range of applicable law.

JURISDICTION, STARE DECISIS, AND TYPES OF AUTHORITY

While the mechanics of finding the law are relatively straightforward, the process of legal research requires making decisions about the scope and direction of the search and analyzing the results. This decision making and analysis continue to drive the research process until the search is concluded and requires an understanding of several important concepts: *jurisdiction, stare decisis,* and *authority.* Jurisdiction refers to the power of a governmental body such as a court to exercise its power. Some courts have jurisdiction over certain types of cases, such as bankruptcy filings or estate settlements; others have more general jurisdiction. Most governmental bodies also have a geographical boundary that defines and limits their power, and the term *jurisdiction* can be used to describe that boundary. For example, the Supreme Court of Michigan has jurisdiction over cases arising in the state of Michigan, and Michigan statutes apply in Michigan.

Another concept that is important in the United States and other common law systems is the doctrine of *stare decisis* ("to stand by things decided"), which binds courts to follow law that has been previously settled. The requirement of adherence to the authority of prior decisions, or *precedent,* ensures a certain measure of consistency in the interpretation of law. Practitioners and researchers can use judicial decisions, therefore, to understand how a court will be bound in the future. The decisions of courts and the legal authority they represent are massive; when considered in conjunction with the law created by legislatures and agencies, the magnitude and complexity of the law becomes apparent.

The process of legal research involves examining a variety of texts to determine the legal rules governing a given issue. But not all texts have equal value in this process—some have more *authority* than others. A researcher must always pay close attention to the source of the text (e.g., a court, a legislative body, or a scholar) as well as to the hierarchical relationship between governmental bodies. When called upon to resolve a dispute between parties, a court is bound only to follow *primary authority*—texts that are the law, as opposed to commentary on or analysis of the law. While the commentary of a legal scholar is useful as a resource for finding relevant law, for understanding the shape of the current law, or for insight into how the law may change in the future, such commentary is not binding on a court. Primary authority consists of the statutes, cases, and administrative regulations that come from lawmaking bodies.

Not all primary authority is binding, or *mandatory* authority, however. Statutes in a particular jurisdiction are mandatory in that jurisdiction; the court must recognize and follow them. Similarly, cases from the highest court in a jurisdiction are binding on courts within that jurisdiction. But cases from a neighboring state, or from lower courts—even one in the same jurisdiction—are not mandatory. They may, however, be used as *persuasive* authority.

SOURCES OF LAW: STATUTES, COURT DECISIONS, AND REGULATIONS

The primary sources of law in the United States can be organized according to the three branches of government that produce them: legislative, judicial, and executive. Each of these governmental bodies creates a different type of law: legislation, case law, and regulations.

The legislative branch (e.g., the U.S. Congress in the federal system) creates statutes such as the Americans with Disabilities Act (ADA), or the Civil Rights Act. The legislative process is formal and forward-looking and requires participation by the members of the legislative bodies in the jurisdiction, as well as signature by the Executive.

The judicial branch interprets the law by hearing and resolving disputes between parties. Courts in the judicial branch issue opinions that become binding on future parties according to the doctrine of stare decisis.

The executive branch enforces the law, and the administrative agencies that report to the executive branch implement legislation by issuing regulations and managing legislative programs. For example, the Social Security Administration is charged with the responsibility of managing the Social Security program.

The 51 parallel systems of lawmaking in the United States (one federal system, and 50 state systems) all create law. The U.S. Constitution delegates specific powers to the federal government and outlines the creation of the relevant governmental bodies. Those powers not delegated to the federal government by the U.S. Constitution are left in the hands of each of the states. Each state's constitution provides for the organization of the three branches of the state's government.

While they operate relatively independently, state and federal law may both operate to affect a legal problem. For example, while federal legislation provides protections to disabled persons under the ADA, state law may impose additional responsibilities on employers. Consider any current societal issue, such as the psychiatric treatment of mentally ill prisoners or the regulation of schools; both state and federal law from all three branches of government will likely be at work in defining the relevant rights and responsibilities. It is the complex interaction of all of these sources of lawmaking that can make certain aspects of legal research challenging.

The examples throughout the rest of this chapter are drawn from the federal system, but note that the structure of lawmaking bodies is mirrored for the most part in each of the 50 state systems.

Statutes

Statutes, also referred to as legislation, or simply "laws," are laws drafted by a legislative body, such as the U.S. Congress. Statutes such as the Americans with Disabilities Act or the USA Patriot Act set out the rights and responsibilities of individuals and the government in a particular area. Such statutes define such things as the type of conduct prohibited or the category of people who are affected, and may provide for remedies if the statute is violated.

Statutes passed by the U.S. Congress are published individually and then assembled into the current legislative *Code*, which contains the current law in force. Codes are organized by subject with related statutes clustered together. The broadest subject categories in the Code are called *Titles*, and each Title of the Code is numbered. Within each Title, statutes are organized by topical chapters and subchapters, facilitating efficient research.

Reading and Using Statute Citations   Citations to statutes are generally given in the following form:

Health Insurance Portability and Accountability Act, 42 U.S.C. §1301 (2000).

Similar to the format of most legal publications, this citation provides the statute's name, the volume number and the name of the publication where it can be found, the specific page or section number referred to, and the date. Most legal publications follow a highly condensed citation format based on a style guide called *The Bluebook*,[2] using standard abbreviations for legal

---

2. *The Bluebook* is the citation manual for legal publications; it also contains a list of abbreviations for court reporters and law journals, as well as the titles of official and unofficial publications of statutes and cases in the federal and state systems.

publications. The first number in a citation to a statute refers to the numbered Title. Since each Title of the Code represents a particular subject area, the Title's number is meaningful—a reader familiar with health care law would recognize this citation as being in the public health part of the Code. The next part of the citation is an abbreviation for the U.S. Code (U.S.C.). This is the publication to look for in the library's catalog, or to ask the librarian for help finding. Next, the citation refers to a particular section within Title 42—i.e., section 1301. And finally, the date in parentheses refers to the date of the particular *edition or update* of the U.S. Code that was used—*not* the date the statute came into effect.

In addition to the Code, two additional forms of legislation can be important: *session laws* and *bills*. Both of these represent earlier versions of a statute. When the idea for a law is first introduced in Congress, it is known as a *bill*. The bill is considered and debated, and if it is successfully voted in both houses and is signed by the President of the United States, it becomes law. The first publication of this new law is in a form known as the *session laws*, representing the collected laws of the Congressional session, arranged in the order in which they were signed into law. If you wish to research the background of a statute and its enactment in more detail, several sources in the library can help you explore the statute's *legislative history*.

Legislative history refers to a broad category of materials that are produced during the legislative process. These include Committee Reports, the transcripts of Hearings, and debates in Congress. For laws passed before 1972, most of these documents will be available only in print in your library. For laws passed after 1972, however, the online source LexisNexis Congressional (also known as Congressional Universe) is useful. Begin your work in Congressional Universe with the Public Law Number of the statute, e.g., P.L. 104-191.

Finding Statutes   The Code is issued by three publishers, and each version has a slightly different name: The *United States Code*, abbreviated *U.S.C.*, is published by the Government Printing Office (GPO). It is the "official" version of the code and contains only the text of the statutes. It is updated slowly and is generally more than a year out of date.

The two dominant legal publishers, Thomson West and LexisNexis, each produce their own editions of the Code. West's edition is called the *United States Code Annotated* and is abbreviated U.S.C.A. The LexisNexis edition is called the *United States Code Service*, and is abbreviated U.S.C.S. Although the *United States Code* contains the official version of the federal statutes, these two private publications are better suited to research and are held in print by most law libraries. In addition, the U.S.C.S. is available online through LexisNexis Academic, also known as Academic Universe, which is available at most universities. While they do not alter the text of the Code itself, both of the commercial publishers add substantial editorial enhancements to their editions, adding reference materials and notes called *annotations* to aid researchers, such as citations to cases that have interpreted the statute.

The commercial publishers also provide better and more detailed indexes for finding statutes, and they update their versions of the Code to reflect new legislation much more quickly than the GPO's official version.

Federal statutes are also available in several free, online forms. One of the oldest is Cornell University's Legal Information Institute, at http://www.law.cornell.edu/uscode/. It is compiled from the House of Representatives' official version and allows simple searching and browsing. The *United States Code* is also available on the House Web site at http://uscode.house.gov, as well as the West-owned Findlaw at http://caselaw.lp.findlaw.com/casecode/uscodes/toc.html (which is supported by advertising). None of these free online versions contain the same level of editorial enhancement found in the privately published editions of the Code, but they are helpful for beginning research in an area or simply to look for the text of a particular Code section.

To find a relevant statute, use an index for the print versions or search one of the online databases previously described. It is important to consider particular statutory provisions in their proper context, reading neighboring sections as well as the headings for the subchapter and chapter that the sections fall under. The sections of a statute may work in tandem, and the operation of a particular section may be influenced by surrounding provisions. In addition, the first section of a subchapter or chapter is often a "purpose statement" for the statute and may also include definitions of terms as they are to be used in that statute. To find out how the statute has been applied and interpreted, look for relevant cases in the annotations, or search for cases through other means (see the following text).

Updating Statutes   The *United States Code* is a snapshot of the laws in force at a particular date. To understand the current law, it is important to consider any amendments to the statute passed after that date. While the online versions are updated more frequently than print, you should still check the revision date (generally found at the top of the page) to determine how current that version is, as the Code is not updated in real time with the passage of new laws.

To check for current legislation that might affect the statute, examine the current *session laws*. These are published by GPO in a set of books called the *Statutes at Large*, but they are also available online on LexisNexis Academic and on the free site Thomas http://thomas.loc.gov, a service of the Library of Congress.

To check for current legislation on Thomas, for instance, use the Public Laws section of the site and search within the most current group of laws. Note that Public Laws are numbered consecutively, using a format that includes both the number of the Congressional term and the number of laws passed thus far in the term. Thus, the citation P.L. 107-1 means that it was the first public law passed in the 107th Congress. Search for the citation to the statute as a phrase (e.g., "42 U.S.C. 1301") or search by keyword using words from the heading of the statute. Sort through the results to look for any laws that indicate that they will amend the statute.

Even when statutes are written carefully, the drafters can not anticipate precisely what their effects will be until they become law. The courts will then be called upon to help interpret the statute and resolve conflicts.

CASES

The legal authority of cases is unique to common law systems and is closely linked to the doctrine of stare decisis. In the majority of the world's legal systems, laws are written in legislative codes and judges merely interpret those codes to resolve the dispute in front of them. In the United States, England, and other common-law countries, the courts have a different role—their decisions are given legal weight, or *precedent*. The tradition of recording precedent over time has created a substantial body of recorded, judge-made law.

Cases generally begin with a trial, heard in the designated *trial court* for the jurisdiction. Appeals are taken to the appropriate *intermediate appellate court*. Final appeals, if granted, are taken to the *court of last resort*. State courts of last resort have the last word on matters of state law, but matters of federal or U.S. constitutional law may be appealed to the U.S. Supreme Court. The Court has discretion to choose which cases to hear, and a very small number of these petitions are granted each year.

Courts make decisions in actual disputes between parties, whether civil or criminal.[3] The trial court is responsible for resolving both issues of fact (e.g., "Did the driver run a red light?") and issues of law (e.g., "Did the driver's actions meet the standards for vehicular manslaughter under the relevant state statute?"). In jury trials, the judge is responsible for ruling on the admissibility of evidence and for instructing the jury on the relevant law, and the jury hears the evidence presented and issues its decision, which resolves issues of fact and applies the law to the facts found. In a bench trial, the judge takes on the fact-finding role. The fact-finding role of the trial court is important and is treated with deference by appellate courts; once the trial is concluded, parties generally do not have another opportunity to make any arguments regarding factual issues.

At the conclusion of a trial, the losing party may appeal the decision, arguing that the court made an error of law—that the judge excluded or admitted evidence erroneously, that the instructions that were given to the jury incorrectly stated the law, that the sentence was unconstitutional, and so on. Each jurisdiction has procedural rules that govern the filing of appeals, including the proper format for written petitions and *briefs*, which are written arguments that the parties present to the court. If the petition for appeal is accepted, the parties will generally submit written briefs to the court and

---

3. Not all disputes between parties result in consideration by a court, and not all trials result in decisions on the merits or in appeals (Felstiner, Abel, & Sarat, 1980-81; Guthrie, 2002). Thus, it is important to recognize that court opinions are not necessarily representative of the complete body of disputes.

present *oral arguments* before the judge or panel of judges.[4] The appellate court issues a decision contained in a written opinion, summarizing the history of the case, the arguments made, and the basis for the court's decision. In cases before a group of judges, such as the U.S. Supreme Court, individual judges may agree or disagree with the result, and they may also file opinions to express reasoning separate from the opinion of the court. These are called *concurring* or *dissenting* opinions.

Only the opinion of the court has precedential value, but these concurring and dissenting opinions may offer useful insight into legal debates. In addition, within a lengthy appellate opinion, a variety of statements may be made about the law. The only part of the court's opinion that is binding on future parties, however, is the *holding*, which is that part of the opinion that was necessary to resolve the case for the parties and that articulates the legal principle or principles for which the case stands. Many other portions of the court's opinion may look like new law, but statements in the case that go beyond the facts presented by the case are called *dicta* and are not binding. Careful reading of court opinions is necessary to recognize the holding and dicta.

In the federal system, the three levels of courts are structured as follows:[5]

1. The U.S. Supreme Court, the court of last resort.
2. Twelve regional Circuits, each with a court of appeals that hears appeals from the trial courts.
3. Multiple district courts (trial-level) within each of the Circuits. The regions are divided up along state borders, so that the 7th Circuit, for example, covers Illinois, Wisconsin, and Indiana. District courts sit in each of those states, so that there is a U.S. district court for the Southern District of Illinois, another in the Northern District of Illinois, and another in the Central District of Illinois.

Federal cases begin in district court. Following trial, the losing party may appeal the decision of the district court to the court of appeals for the relevant Circuit. The decision of the court of appeals is binding on district courts within that Circuit, as well as on itself. Over time, courts of appeal in the various circuits may interpret a provision differently, leading to a "split" in interpretation. Out of an interest in maintaining some uniformity in federal law, the U.S. Supreme Court is often called upon to resolve circuit splits by hearing an appeal from one or more of the courts of appeal.

---

4. These briefs and oral arguments are also relevant to legal psychologists—psychologists may author a brief as an amicus curiae or "friend of the court" (see Roesch et al., 1993) or get research ideas from briefs, may use oral arguments for research purposes (see, e.g., Wrightsman, 2008), and so on.
5. For more information about the federal court system, see the Administrative Office of the U.S. Courts, http://www.uscourts.gov/.

Each state also has its own court system, largely modeled on the federal system. In each state, there is a court of last resort (often, but not always, called the state's "Supreme Court"), a group of intermediate appellate courts, and a network of trial courts and other courts that hear specific kinds of cases.

Reading and Using Case Citations   Citations to cases are nearly always to the opinions of appellate courts—the decisions that have precedential value. Citations follow the typical volume/publication/page number pattern found in legal citations:

Addington v. Texas, *441 U.S. 418 (1979).*

After the name of the case is given, the citation indicates the volume number, the publication where the case may be found, and the page where the court's opinion begins. The abbreviation "U.S." stands for the United States Reports, which is the official reporter for U.S. Supreme Court decisions. The date in a case citation refers to the year the opinion was handed down.

With legal citations, the greatest challenge can be figuring out the publication abbreviations. Table 1.1 lists the major federal and state case reporters. For additional help, see a copy of *The Bluebook* or *Bieber's Dictionary of Legal Citations.* Note that most cases are published in more than one reporter and U.S. Supreme Court cases are published in at least three reporters. Citations to

Table 1.1
Federal and State Case Reporters

Jurisdiction	Reporters	Abbreviations
United States Supreme Court	United States Reports	U.S.
	West's Supreme Court Reporter	S.Ct.
	Supreme Court Reports, Lawyers' Ed.	L.Ed.
United States courts of appeal	Federal Reporter (and 2nd series, and 3rd series)	F., F.2d, F.3d.
United States district courts	Federal Supplement (and 2nd series)	F. Supp, F. Supp.2d.
Highest court of each state (grouped geographically)	Atlantic Reporter	A., A.2d
	North Eastern Reporter	N.E., N.E.2d
	Northwestern Reporter	N.W., N.W.2d
	Pacific Reporter	P., P.2d
	South Eastern Reporter	S.E., S.E.2d
	Southwestern Reporter	S.W., S.W.2d
	Southern Reporter	So., So.2d.

alternative reporters are often provided in parentheses at the top of the opinion; these are called *parallel citations*.

Finding Cases   Finding relevant case law requires paying close attention to both jurisdiction and the hierarchy of courts. The system of courts in the United States is vast; it ranges from the U.S. Supreme Court down to the traffic court in a particular city. Before beginning a search, take some time to decide whether federal or state cases are relevant and whether to limit the search to a particular circuit or state or to search for cases from any jurisdiction. Obviously, the wider the net is cast, the more time it will take to sort through the results. On the other hand, to get a broader sense of the case law and to catch circuit splits or differing approaches among states, a more expansive search might be appropriate.

A search for case law is typically a search for mandatory authority in the relevant jurisdiction. This may mean that a decision of the U.S. Supreme Court is most appropriate (for example, on a U.S. Constitutional issue), but for some issues state supreme court decisions are most relevant. If decisions from the highest court in the jurisdiction are not available, decisions from intermediate appellate courts may be appropriate, though it is important to be aware of their more limited applicability. Finally, note that because trial court cases have limited weight and often have limited *precedential value*—that is, they do not set out any new law for the courts to follow—they are not as routinely published.[6]

Research on cases can be done effectively on a database such as LexisNexis Academic or Westlaw Campus.[7] These databases provide coverage of appellate case law (federal and state) and should serve the needs of most researchers. In addition to their availability via subscription databases, U. S. Supreme Court cases are available from numerous sources, including the Court's own Web site (http://www.supremecourtus.gov) and Findlaw (http://www.findlaw.com). The Web sites of most courts of appeal provide access to recent opinions issued by those courts, but state case law can be more difficult to access in electronic form without access to a subscription service.

It is possible to do effective research using print sources, but doing so is admittedly more time-consuming and requires access to a well-stocked law library.

Updating Case Law   When a case is decided, it represents legal authority that must be followed by lower courts in the jurisdiction. Consider the possibility,

---

6. Selected decisions of the U.S. District Courts are published in the Federal Supplement, but many more are designated not for publication. State trial court decisions are also typically not published. The office of the clerk of the court may allow copying of unpublished materials, such as trial court rulings, court briefs, or trial transcripts.

7. While Westlaw Campus and LexisNexis Academic are available at many universities, check with the librarian for availability of these and any alternative resources.

however, that a decision was later appealed and overturned. Case reporters and online databases are not updated directly when later action by a case or statute affects its validity. To be sure that the case is still binding, it is important to update it using something called a *citator*. The original citator, which was initially developed in print, is called *Shepard's Citations*, and it is available on Academic Universe as well as on LexisNexis' pay-per-use service (via credit card).

The purpose of *Shepard's Citations* is twofold: to determine whether the holding in the case has not been overturned (i.e., that it is still "good law") and to provide additional research references related to the case. Two pieces of information are relevant to determining whether the case is good law: the subsequent procedural history of the case itself, which indicates whether any part of the court's holding was reversed on an appeal and the treatment of the case by other cases, which indicates whether the holding has been *overruled*. A court can overrule one of its earlier cases, such as the U.S. Supreme Court's overruling of *Bowers v. Hardwick* (1986), with its decision in *Lawrence v. Texas* (2003).

When a citation is entered into *Shepard's*, the service returns the procedural history of a case, gathering together the citations for opinions from the lower appellate court, any petitions for appeal, and opinions issued at later appeals. In addition, *Shepard's* returns a list of cases that have *cited* the case. When a court issues an opinion, the text is heavily footnoted to provide support for each point being expressed. *Shepard's* tracks this network of citations between cases so that the researcher can see how often later cases have cited to earlier cases. *Shepard's* also keeps track of the manner in which a case was cited by noting the court's attitude towards the cited case—whether it *questioned* the case's holding, *distinguished* the case, *overruled* it, or *followed* it.

REGULATIONS

The third source of lawmaking is the executive branch,[8] which makes law through the rulemaking activity of administrative agencies.[9] Agencies such as the Department of Health and Human Services or the Internal Revenue Service report to the executive branch, but their power to make law comes from the legislature. Thus, Congress will pass statutes—such as the Health Insurance Portability and Accountability Act (HIPAA) or the Internal Revenue Code—that maps out the basic contours of the law, but will charge the relevant agencies with making the more detailed *regulations*, also known as *rules*, that are necessary to implement the statutes and carry out any reporting or enforcement requirements.

8. The executive branch also produces law in the form of signed Treaties with foreign nations, Presidential Proclamations, and Executive Orders.

9. Note that administrative agencies also have a quasi-judicial function, in that they hold hearings and issue decisions, but the decisions do not bear the weight of authority that decisions from the judicial branch have.

Administrative regulations have a constant and significant effect on people's daily lives, as they cover everything from airline safety to the release of new medicines to broadcast television standards. In researching legislation, it is important to pay attention to the mention of the role of any executive agencies with respect to the statute. Even if the statute itself does not mention an agency or implementing regulations explicitly, it is useful to conduct research to find out whether there are any regulations that affect the legal issue.

Regulations from federal agencies are published in the Code of Federal Regulations (CFR), which is published by the Government Printing Office (GPO). The CFR is organized much like the U.S. Code, using subject groups called Titles, with further division underneath the Titles that correspond to particular agencies—called chapters and parts. The numbered titles very roughly correspond to the subjects contained in the same numbered Titles of the United States Code, but all similarities between the two publications end there.

Each of the 50 states also has its own administrative agencies, which make regulations such as building codes and professional licensing regulations. These are generally contained in a separate publication called an administrative code.

Reading and Using Regulation Citations   Federal regulations are cited as follows:

28 C.F.R. 549.43 (2007)

Like most other legal citations, the first number refers to the volume. In this case, it refers to *Title* 28, because the CFR is arranged in numbered titles. The abbreviation CFR stands for the *Code of Federal Regulations,* the official source for federal regulations that are currently in force. The number 549.43 refers to the Part and section number within Title 28. Finally, the number in parentheses refers to the year of the CFR (*not* the year when the regulation was issued).

Finding Regulations   The only print publication of the CFR is the one printed by the GPO. However, there are numerous sources for the CFR online, including the subscription database LexisNexis Academic and the free site GPO Access, http://www.gpoaccess.gov/cfr/index.html, which offers both text and pdf images.

To find regulations governing a particular topic, one can either browse the list of agencies and their regulations or search the CFR by keyword. For example, to find regulations dealing with involuntary psychiatric care for prison inmates, one might search for "involuntary AND psychiatric AND prison." Browse the list of results, choosing the summary for a quick view of the regulation. To view a more complete picture of this area of the CFR, go back to the search screen and choose "browse," and browse the relevant

Title—in this case, Title 28, Judicial Administration—and the table of contents for the Part, reading the appropriate regulation in context. For more information on the organization of each agency, and the scope of their delegated lawmaking authority, see the United States Government Manual.

Updating Regulations The CFR is updated in parts, each at one of four scheduled times during the year. Online editions of the CFR are updated more frequently than print editions; the date at the top of the regulation indicates how current it is. In the interim, proposed and final rules are printed in the *Federal Register*, which is published daily. To update a regulation, check the table in the *Federal Register* called "List of CFR Sections Affected," either in print or on GPO Access online (http://www.gpoaccess.gov/fr/index.html).

SECONDARY SOURCES

In addition to the primary sources of the law mentioned previously, another group of sources can be helpful for legal research: secondary sources. While they are not themselves law, the analysis and research references they offer can save considerable time. Some secondary sources are written specifically for law students, some for practitioners, some for other scholars, and some for laypersons. Note that some of these resources are available online, including law review articles, but many others are available only in print. If you have limited time to spend in the law library, these are the resources to focus on, as most others can be found electronically.

Treatises, Encyclopedias, and Other Books   *Treatises* provide a detailed treatment of a broad area of the law, such as criminal procedure or family law. They can be used as a guide to this area of law throughout your research, or they can be used for a quick reference to something more specific, like the operation of the Federal Sentencing Guidelines or the best interests of the child standard. The best treatises are written by scholars who are the top experts in their field, and treatises are cited often in law review articles. Examples include *Prosser on Torts* and *Tribe's Constitutional Law*. For treatises that are regularly updated, the publisher typically issues *pocket parts*, which are unbound pamphlets filed in the back of the book with any changes listed by page or section number. Researchers should be sure to check these.

Looseleafs are a specialized type of legal publication that integrates statutes, regulations, case law, expert commentary, and news about developments in a particular area of the law. They are generally the starting point and anchor resource for practitioners. But while looseleafs are intended primarily for attorneys, they can be useful for anyone seeking an integrated view of a particular problem in the law. They are published in binders that can be disassembled so that updated pages can be shipped and interfiled frequently.

To identify major and authoritative treatises and looseleafs in a particular area, ask the librarian for a recommendation, or browse the area of the library where materials on that topic are shelved. Be sure to ask whether treatises and looseleafs are shelved in a special area; in some law libraries they are kept in an area dedicated to high-use materials and can be checked out for only a few hours at a time. The constantly changing nature of these resources makes them prime candidates for well-designed online services, but not all publishers currently offer this service. A limited number of looseleaf titles are available online, some through databases such as LexisNexis Academic, and others through the publisher's own platform. Check with your librarian to see whether you have access to databases from BNA, CCH, Matthew Bender, or RIA, the leading looseleaf publishers.

For each state, additional resources such as *practice books, pattern jury instructions, CLE materials*, and *formbooks* are available and may be useful for gaining insight into practice issues or in developing stimulus materials. Practice books are published as a set for general practice in the state, or by subject such as family law. They attempt to synthesize law in the state and provide guidance for attorneys. Pattern jury instructions offer sample language for the court to use when instructing the jury about the law. They vary by type of case, and are often separated into two volumes: one for criminal trials, and one for civil trials. Continuing legal education (CLE) materials are produced by the state Bar Association or Bar Examiner's office and are designed for use with continuing education courses for practicing attorneys. Formbooks include basic general forms for procedural use (e.g., motions and orders) or for contracts or other legal transactions. There are many of these, including sets that are specific to major states and sets that are developed for specialized areas of practice. While they can be illustrative, users must be sure that a sample form published in one of them is consistent with current law.

Legal encyclopedias are specialized sets of books that provide an overview of all areas of the law. The national encyclopedias, *American Jurisprudence, 2d* and *Corpus Juris Secundum*, attempt to cover all the law in the United States, but they are too large and provide very shallow coverage. The encyclopedias include very detailed commentary on law across the country, and provide extensive references to statutes and cases, but the complexity and volume of U.S. law makes it impossible to adequately cover everything, and national coverage can be of limited use when jurisdiction matters. Some states have their own legal encyclopedias, and they provide better treatment of the law of the state.

Legal dictionaries such as *Black's Law Dictionary* define words and phrases as they are used in the legal context. Dictionaries can be helpful resources as you read cases and encounter Latin words or other unusual phrases. Legal dictionaries may also prove useful when assembling keywords to use in searching databases. Many terms have very specific meanings as they are used in the law, and their legal meanings can be quite different from the ways in which the terms are more commonly used in standard English or in the social sciences.

Law reviews, or *law journals*, contain articles that comment on, theorize about, or analyze law and legal topics. Some journals are published by law schools, others by professional societies. The law school journals are edited by law students, who solicit articles from leading scholars. Shorter pieces are provided by selected student editors, commenting on recent cases or analyzing a particular area of the law. Law journal articles form the body of scholarly discussion about existing and developing law. While much of the work suggests new ways of analyzing legal issues, many articles also document and analyze settled law. And since legal writing tends to be heavily footnoted to provide foundation for the statements that an author is making, the footnotes in law review articles are valuable resources for research purposes. The quality of the article as a research resource, however, depends on the quality of the underlying primary authorities that the author cites. You *must* check the currency of the cases, statutes, and regulations cited in it to be sure that they reflect current law (see the preceding discussion).

The citation to a law review article consists of the author's name, the title of the article, the volume, journal name (abbreviated), the page number on which the article begins, and the date. Again, deciphering a publication's abbreviation can be tricky. See Table 1.2 for some standard abbreviations, and consult your library's copy of *Bieber's Dictionary of Legal Abbreviations* for a full list.

Relevant law review articles can be identified either by using specialized legal indexes such as Legaltrac or the Index to Legal Periodicals or resources such as LexisNexis Academic, Westlaw Campus, JSTOR, or even Google Scholar. In addition, the Social Science Research Network (SSRN; http://www.ssrn.com) provides access to recent and forthcoming scholarship.

FINAL COMMENT ON THE RESEARCH PROCESS

Be critical. When you choose a source, be aware of its purpose, its creator or publisher, and the intended audience. With single- and multi-volume treatises and other books, many of these questions can be answered by reading the introduction or the "how to use this publication" statement near the front of the first volume. For online databases, look for a descriptive statement about the database in your library's list of electronic resources. Similarly, it is important to learn the limits of a database's contents. Searching a database for a type of resource that is not contained there is a bit like fishing for salmon in your backyard pond. Find out whether the database is limited to materials published during the past 20 years or to materials published by the database's vendor or its parent company. Constantly challenge the comprehensiveness of the sources you are using; rarely will one source serve your legal research needs completely.

Be critical during the search process, as well, and use connectors like "AND" and "OR" when possible to narrow the search. Check the help section of the database to determine whether additional connectors or symbols are available. Proficient use of these connectors will eliminate

Table 1.2
Standard Abbreviations

L. Rev.	Law Review
L.J.	Law Journal
U.	University
Behav.	Behavior
Forensic	Forensic
Hum.	Human
Interdisc.	Interdisciplinary
Just.	Justice
Psychol.	Psychology; Psychological
Psychiatry	Psychiatry
Res.	Research
Sci.	Science; Sciences; Scientific
Soc.	Social

irrelevant material from the search results, facilitating greater precision. At the same time, it is important not to sacrifice relevant materials in a quest for precision.

Finally, when the search results are returned, critically analyze them against the search query. Are there too many irrelevant items? Why? Keep in mind that with non-Google searching, the best results might not be at the top of the list. Most systems are still not capable of understanding plain English language requests; you may have to be creative with the terms you enter.

CONCLUSION

While the law can be complex and elusive, it can also be fascinating and enlightening. Legal psychologists who are equipped to do effective legal research have the tools with which to decipher the intricacies of the law. Armed with the skills of legal research, psychologists will be better positioned to undertake and communicate important empirical research that is relevant to the law.

RESOURCES FOR LEGAL RESEARCH

The Bluebook: A Uniform System of Citation (18th ed). (2005). Cambridge, MA: Harvard Law Review.

Cohen, M. (2007). *Legal research in a nutshell*, 5th ed. Eagan, MN: Thomson West.

Eis, A. (2008). *Legal looseleafs in print* (annual). Teaneck, NJ: Infosources Publishing.

Fine, T. M. (1997). *American legal systems: a resource and reference guide.* Cincinnati, OH: Anderson.

Garner, B. A. (2009). *Black's law dictionary* (9th ed). St. Paul, MN: West Group.

Prince, M. M. (2001). *Bieber's dictionary of legal citation* (5th ed). Buffalo, NY: W. S. Hein.

REFERENCES

Bersoff, D. N, Goodman-Delahunty, J., Grisso, J. T., Hans, V. P., Poythress, N. G., & Roesch, R. G. (1997). Training in law and psychology: Models from the Villanova Conference. *American Psychologist*, 52, 1301–1310.

Bowers v. Hardwick, 478 U.S. 186 (1986).

Chevron U.S.A., Inc. v. Echazabal, 536 U.S. 73 (2002).

Committee on Ethical Guidelines for Forensic Psychologists (1991). *Specialty guidelines for forensic psychology, Guideline VI.A. Law and human behavior*, 15, 655–665.

Committee on the Revision of the Specialty Guidelines for Forensic Psychology (2008). *Specialty guidelines for forensic psychology*, § 4.04. Last retrieved on November 12, 2010, from http://www.ap-ls.org/links/22808 sgfp.pdf

Felstiner, W. L. F., Abel, R. L., & Sarat, A. (1980-1981). The emergence and transformation of disputes: Naming, blaming, and claiming. *Law & Society Review*, 15, 631–654.

Grisso, T., Sales, B. D., & Bayless, S. (1982). Law-related courses and programs in graduate psychology departments. *American Psychologist*, 37, 267–278.

Guthrie, C. (2002). Procedural justice research and the paucity of trials. *Journal of Dispute Resolution*, 2002, 127–130

Kahan, D. M., Hoffman, D. A., & Braman, D. (2009). Whose eyes are you going to believe? *Scott v. Harris* and the perils of cognitive illiberalism. *Harvard Law Review*, 122, 837–906.

Kahneman, D., & Tversky, A. (1971). Belief in the law of small numbers. *Psychological Bulletin*, 76, 105–110.

Kovera, M. B., McAuliff, B. D., & Herbert, K. S. (1999). Reasoning about scientific evidence: Effects of juror gender and evidence quality on juror decisions in a hostile work environment case. *Journal of Applied Psychology*, 84, 362–375.

Lawrence v. Texas, 539 U.S. 538 (2003).

Lockhart v. McCree, 476 U.S. 162 (1986).

Lynch, M., & Haney, C. (2000). Discrimination and instructional comprehension: Guided discretion, racial bias, and the death penalty. *Law & Human Behavior*, 24, 337–358.

Melton, G. B., Monahan, J., & Saks, M. J. (1987). Psychologists as law professors. *American Psychologist*, 42, 502–509.

Ogloff, J. R. P. (2001). Jingoism, dogmatism, and other evils in legal psychology: Lessons learned in the 20th century. In R. Roesch, R. R. Corrado, & R. Dempster (Eds.), *Psychology in the courts: International advances in knowledge* (pp. 1–17). London, England: Routledge.

Ogloff, J. R. P. (2002). Two steps forward and one step backward: The law and psychology movement(s) in the 20th century. In J. R. P. Ogloff (Ed.), *Taking psychology and law into the twenty-first century* (pp. 1–33). New York, NY: Kluwer Academic/Plenum.

Ogloff, J. R. P. & Rose, V. G. (2005). The comprehension of judicial instructions. In Neil Brewer & Kipling D. Williams (Eds.), *Psychology and law: An empirical perspective* (pp. 407–444). New York, NY: Guilford Press.

Rachlinski, J. J. (2000). The "new" law and psychology: A reply to critics, skeptics, and cautious supporters. *Cornell Law Review*, 85, 739–766.

Robbennolt, J. (2002). Evaluating empirical research methods: Using empirical research in law and policy. *Nebraska Law Review*, 81, 777–804.

Roesch, R., Golding, S. L., Hans, V. P., & Reppucci, N. D. (1991). Social science and the courts: The role of *amicus* curiae briefs. *Law and Human Behavior*, 15, 1–11.

Saks, M. J. (1986). The law does not live by eyewitness testimony alone. *Law and Human Behavior*, 10, 279–280.

Scott v. Harris, 127 S.Ct. 1769 (2007).

State v. Deck, 994 S.W.2d 527 (Mo. 1999).

Weiten, W., & Diamond, S. S. (1979). A critical review of the jury simulation paradigm: The case of defendant characteristics. *Law & Human Behavior*, 3, 71–93.

Wells, G. L., Malpass, R. S., Lindsay, R. C. L., Fisher, R. P., Turtle, J. W., & Fulero, S. M. (2000). From the lab to the police station: A successful application of eyewitness research. *American Psychologist*, 55, 581–598.

Wiener, R. L., Winter, R. J., Rogers, M., Seib, H., Rauch, S., Kadela, K., Hackney, A., & Warren, L. (2002). Evaluating published research in psychology and law: A gatekeeper analysis of law and human behavior. In J. R. P. Ogloff (Ed.), *Taking psychology and law into the twenty-first century* (pp. 371–405). New York, NY: Kluwer Academic/Plenum.

Wrightsman, L. (2008). *Oral arguments before the Supreme Court: An empirical approach*. New York, NY: Oxford University Press.

CHAPTER 2

Measure Development in Forensic Psychology

BARRY ROSENFELD, JOHN EDENS, AND SARA LOWMASTER

URING THE PAST few decades, forensic psychologists have developed and published numerous psychological tests and instruments specifically targeting psycholegal issues. Beginning with Lipsitt's Competency Screening Test (1971), researchers and clinicians have increasingly attempted to develop reliable, valid, and psychometrically sound instruments for assessing psycholegal constructs. Indeed, the importance of tests designed for or adapted to forensic populations and issues, particularly when applied to clinical forensic settings, cannot be overstated. Although "traditional" psychological measures can often provide important data that are useful in forensic settings, many specific issues arise in forensic evaluations (e.g., malingering, competence to stand trial, and violence risk assessment) that are simply not addressed by more general psychological inventories—if they are addressed at all. Moreover, when measures that have been developed for clinical settings do have relevance for forensic issues, normative data often provide an inappropriate basis for comparison and can lead to misleading or erroneous conclusions.

Yet the methodological rigor used in the development of measures designed for forensic settings has varied tremendously, with many researchers using an extremely thorough and systematic approach whereas others have, unfortunately, "shortcut" some of the critical steps that are needed before a novel instrument can be considered ready for applied use. This chapter is intended to provide a useful, albeit deliberately broad starting point for researchers interested in developing or adapting instruments for forensic settings. Those interested in specific topics such as competence to stand trial, malingering, or psychopathy will also benefit from consulting the relevant chapters in this volume, although many of the issues that arise in measurement development and validation cut across multiple topics. It should be noted that most of the examples used in this chapter are grounded in clinical forensic psychology (reflecting the background of the authors), but the issues are no less relevant to measure development in experimental, social, or developmental psychological research.

ASSESSING "FORENSIC" CONSTRUCTS

Theorists have distinguished between two "types" of instruments used in forensic assessment: *forensically relevant instruments* (FRI) and *forensic assessment instruments* (FAI). The distinction between these two categories hinges on the extent to which the instrument directly targets a specific legal issue. Heilbrun, Rogers, and Otto (2002) characterized FAIs as being "directly relevant to a specific legal standard and its included capacities that are needed for the individual being evaluated to meet that legal standard" (Heilbrun et al., 2002, p. 128). On the other hand, FRIs are those tools that provide information relevant to forensic evaluators or practitioners; without directly targeting a legal standard per se, they "address clinical constructs that are sometimes pertinent to legal standards" (Heilbrun et al., 2002, p. 128). Examples of the latter include measures such as the Psychopathy Checklist-Revised (PCL-R; Hare, 2003) or any of the measures of malingering currently available, whereas examples of the former include the many instruments designed to address competence to stand trial.[1]

Perhaps the seminal FAI that initiated the trend of rigorously researched, psychometrically sound assessment tools is Tom Grisso's set of instruments for understanding and appreciating Miranda Rights (1998). This measure, originally developed in the late 1970s, applied a multimethod approach to assessing a range of functions and abilities that are theoretically and conceptually related to the waiver of Miranda rights. Although the measure was initially developed for and validated with juvenile offenders, normative data were collected (and compared with) samples of adult criminal offenders and juveniles with no history of criminal behavior to provide appropriate reference groups. This early measure may well be considered an exemplar for instrument development, including the application of a broad-based theory supporting the instrument's elements and foci, a multistage development process, the use of multiple comparison groups to establish appropriate normative data, and considerable attention devoted to developing adequate evidence of reliability and validity. Of course, even an optimal approach to instrument development does not guarantee that the end result will be either useful or accepted by the legal system, but there is little doubt that these (and other) positive outcomes are far more likely when adequate attention has been paid to scale development.

---

1. It is worth noting that the distinction between an FRI and an FAI can be blurry at times. For example, sexually violent predator statutes in Texas require that an assessment of "psychopathy" be conducted as part of the civil commitment evaluation process. In such a context, the PCL-R might arguably be considered an FAI.

THE IMPORTANCE OF THEORY

DeVellis (2003) writes that "theory plays a key role in how we conceptualize our measurement problems" (p. 6). Although the division between FAIs and FRIs is not always readily apparent, FAIs are typically grounded in legal theory and case law whereas FRIs are typically grounded in psychological theory. Regardless of the origin of the underlying theory, a thorough analysis of theory can and should guide the conceptualization of a measure. Broad, multifaceted constructs should require a multifaceted or even multimethod measurement approach whereas narrow constructs may be adequately captured by a more singular measurement approach.

A clear example of the importance of legal and psychological theory is reflected in the evolution of measures to assess competence to stand trial. Although early measures focused on a narrow band of knowledge and/or abilities, many of which drew directly from the *Dusky* standard, more recent measures such as the MacCAT-CA (Poythress et al., 1999) tap a wide range of abilities that correspond to the distinct theoretically relevant elements that constitute the construct of competence. Hence, the developers of the MacCAT were able to generate a collection of instruments (MacCAT-CA, MacCAT-CR, MacCAT-T), all of which tap the core elements identified by both case law and theoretical formulations of competence, but differ in the context for decision making (clinical treatment decisions, clinical research participation, and competence to stand trial). These multidimensional scales are premised on the underlying assumption that impairment in one domain (understanding, appreciation, and rationality) may not correspond to impairment in another (i.e., although not uncorrelated, the different constructs require different assessment approaches and may yield only modest correlations across domains). Still, impairment in *any* domain should be sufficient to raise questions about a defendant's competence. On the other hand, constructs such as psychopathy are conceptualized as a more unified or psychologically coherent construct; thus, items that tap elements of psychopathy tend to correlate more highly with one another.

Theory can also guide the researcher's decisions regarding scale format— whether a Likert-type scale is preferable to a true/false scale, or whether the construct is better rated by objective evaluators or through self-report. Of course, these decisions are often made without regard to the underlying theory (i.e., many researchers simply choose a response format that suits them or that is most convenient, with little analysis as to whether one format is preferable to another), and different assessment approaches may be appropriate for the same construct. For example, although the clinician-rated PCL-R (Hare, 2003) has been argued to be the "gold standard" for assessing psychopathy, many interesting and informative studies have been published that rely on the self-report Psychopathic Personality Inventory (PPI; Lilienfeld & Andrews, 1996). The latter may have somewhat less clinical utility, as the potential for distortion is particularly high in adversarial legal contexts, but in research settings the scale has a number of advantages (e.g., ease of administration to large numbers of individuals, ability to use the scale with research assistants who lack clinical training or expertise). Moreover, self-report measures such as the PPI typically include scales designed to tap various forms of response bias (e.g., "faking good" or "faking bad"), which may obviate some concerns about examinees' propensities toward response distortion. On the other hand, many constructs, such as cognitive impairment, simply may not be adequately assessed through a self-report inventory, and performance-based measures are then critical. Thus, in addition to exploring the underlying construct and/or theory a scale is intended to address, consideration of the setting in which research will be conducted is also beneficial in determining the optimal nature and composition of an assessment instrument.

NORMATIVE DATA

One of the core elements of any psychological test is the development of normative data against which to compare individual performance. However, this seemingly simple task masks a number of complexities, including determination as to who makes up the normative sample and how performance should be measured. Many of these questions have no simple answer, but different approaches have different implications for the interpretation of a scale or instrument. Take, for example, the development of the MMPI F scale, a widely studied index used to identify symptom exaggeration or feigning. Originally created by identifying items rarely endorsed by the general population (less than 10%), subsequent research revealed that genuinely impaired psychiatric patients often endorsed these same symptoms, necessitating a dramatic increase in the cut-off score used to identify probable exaggeration. Yet even this accommodation has proven insufficient, and identification of feigning was substantially improved by identifying items that are rarely endorsed by *psychiatric patients* (i.e., the F(p) scale). Thus, identifying the appropriate sample for development of normative data is a critical step in measure development.

However, this seemingly obvious requirement of conceptualizing the appropriate comparison group is surprisingly absent in many measure-development studies, where undergraduate college students form the normative sample and deviations from this "norm" are considered aberrant. Even when "clinical" comparison samples are used, questions may exist as to how elevations or deviations should be interpreted. For example, in the development of the MacCAT-CA, normative data were based on samples of competent and incompetent criminal defendants, including both jail inmates who were receiving mental health treatment and those who were not. Yet determining that an individual's score is comparable to a "typical" (e.g., 50th percentile) incompetent defendant does not necessarily indicate that the individual should be considered incompetent. Indeed, the scale's authors recognized this issue and provide normative data purely for descriptive purposes rather than recommending cut-off scores for classification of competent or incompetent defendants. Ideally, of course, the distribution of scores for contrasting normative samples will overlap only minimally (e.g., suspected malingerers will all score above the range of genuinely ill patients), allowing for a high degree of classification accuracy, but in practice this ideal is not often realized.

Thus, a primary consideration in the development of adequate normative data is the population with which the instrument will be used (i.e., the target population). Even simple distinctions such as age can have important ramifications for scale interpretation. For example, a measure of impulsivity that is "normed" on a sample of adults may yield inaccurate results when applied to adolescents, who generally display considerably more impulsivity than adults. Hence, a "typical" adolescent may appear highly impulsive when compared with a sample of adults. Likewise, some constructs may be expected to differ across ethnic groups or between men and women. Not only should validation studies examine the existence of such differences (and factor these differences into scale interpretation), but potential sources of scale bias should ideally be resolved or minimized through the choice of terminology or scale composition decisions.

Another approach to the problem of differing "norms" is to develop normative data for multiple populations. For example, a computerized interpretive report has been developed for the Personality Assessment Inventory (PAI; Morey, 2007) for use in correctional settings to aid in the identification of inmates who may have mental health problems and/or be prone to adjustment difficulties (Edens & Ruiz, 2005). A large normative sample was collected for this project, including data from offenders in several prison systems, such that the performance of an inmate could be evaluated against the "typical" prisoner. Because criminal offenders may show different patterns of responses than the general public and/or psychiatric populations (with whom the scale was originally developed and normed), many interpretations of the scale are enhanced by a comparison to these inmate norms.

Consider, for example, an index of antisocial behavior. In comparison with non-offender samples, even modest elevations on this index might appear highly pathological; yet when compared with the typical criminal offender, the same responses may seem quite modest or even low. Decisions such as eligibility for parole may hinge on a comparison of a particular individual to the typical offender. On the other hand, some interpretations (e.g., the presence of psychotic symptoms requiring treatment) may be largely irrelevant to the population under investigation. Thus, the need to tailor scales and develop normative data for multiple populations will differ depending on the construct under investigation and the purpose for which a measure in intended.

Care should be taken to not overgeneralize across individuals being assessed at different stages within the legal/criminal justice system. For example, although the PAI prisoner norms appear to be highly relevant for inmates within prison settings (i.e., post-adjudication), the applicability of these norms to pre-trial settings (e.g., forensic examinations for competence or sanity) is largely unknown and is an empirical question that should be scrutinized rather than assumed (although preliminary data identified relatively few differences in PAI scores across these two settings, Douglas, Hart, & Kropp, 2001). Prisoner norms are certainly likely to represent a more valid basis for comparison than the community norms on which PAI scale scores were originally based, but there are obvious reasons to question whether normative data from a post-incarceration sample would be representative of individuals who are referred for a mental health evaluation in the context of pending criminal charges. For example, the Positive Impression Management scale is likely to be far higher in a prison sample whereas the Negative Impression Management scale is more relevant for criminal defendants pursuing a mental health defense. As a general rule, one should always consider the relevance of contextual factors in judging the appropriateness of any comparison or normative group and not assume that "all offenders are alike."

For self-report questionnaires and structured interviews, the language used may also need to be tailored for the intended population, whether by simplifying the language for individuals who may have relatively limited education (e.g., correctional populations) or by avoiding terminology that is prone to misinterpretation or confusion. For example, despite the strengths of Grisso's Miranda instruments, this measure has been criticized for, among other things, assessing the subject's familiarity with specific, and often overly sophisticated terms (e.g., "attorney" rather than "lawyer" or "interrogation" rather than "interview" or "questioning"). Ideally, any scale under development will be pilot tested with samples drawn from the intended population(s) in order to assess comprehension and the appropriateness of terminology used.

Another critical question that must be addressed by researchers is whether a scale is intended to generate a classification or simply to provide a comparison to normative group. Many researchers deliberately avoid the problem of classification and instead choose to develop scales for descriptive purposes (i.e., comparison with one or more normative groups), whereas other scales (e.g., measures of symptom exaggeration or feigning) are intended specifically to generate a group classification. This decision should be grounded in theory, but it also hinges on the expected distribution of scores on a measure. For example, some measures of symptom exaggeration are intended to generate a deliberately skewed distribution of scores, with the vast majority of honest responders obtaining perfect or near-perfect scores, whereas a subset (i.e., malingerers) are expected to perform more poorly. In fact, the distribution of scores for the subset of malingerers *may* approach a normal distribution, whereas the distribution for honest responders will be quite different (e.g., a J-shaped distribution). This scenario is often optimal for the development of cut-off scores, whereas less extreme differences (e.g., partially overlapping distributions) typically yield a large number of in-determinate or erroneous classifications.[2]

Scale interpretation, particularly when classification accuracy is a critical metric, is also highly dependent on the base rate of the construct being assessed. The impact of base rates is widely acknowledged (see Rosenfeld, Sands, & Van Gorp, 2000, for example) and is discussed elsewhere in this volume (e.g., Chapter 10 on malingering). Nevertheless, consideration of the expected base rate of the construct being assessed *in the population for which a scale will be applied* is critical to accurately estimating the classification accuracy of an instrument. Of course, for many forensic issues, the base rate will vary dramatically across populations. For example, although an instrument may perform well in terms of identifying violent behavior among samples in which the rates of violence are high (e.g., a violent recidivism rate of 50%), the same instrument will generate a much higher rate of false positives when applied in settings where base rates are much lower (e.g., 5%). Although certain statistical methods allow one to ignore the impact of base rates when considering the relationship between a test and a criterion measure, they do not obviate the fact that such predictive errors will occur in low (or high) base rate settings.

In sum, interpretation of any scale or instrument developed, particularly when forensic applications are intended, should be limited to those groups for which adequate normative data exist.

RELIABILITY AND VALIDITY ARE DIFFERENT

Perhaps the most obvious element of scale development is the assessment of reliability and validity. Although every introductory psychology textbook provides definitions of reliability and validity, many research studies seem to confuse these basic constructs or fuse "reliability" into a unitary construct without regard to the distinctions among different types of reliability. For example, researchers must consider which types of reliability are appro-priate for a given instrument and how each type is best assessed.

---

2. Scale classification is typically evaluated through the use of four indices: sensitivity, specificity, positive predictive accuracy (PPA), and negative predictive accuracy (NPA). Sensitivity is defined as the proportion of a relevant group that is identified by the test or technique, whereas specificity is the proportion that does not belong to the group who are so identified by the test. For example, in violence "prediction," sensitivity refers to the proportion of violent individuals who are identified as likely to be violent on a particular test, whereas specificity is the proportion of nonviolent individuals who are classified as not likely to be violent on that test. PPA and NPA, on the other hand, refer to the proportion of individuals classified by the technique who actually do have a particular characteristic. For example, PPA would refer to the proportion of individuals classified as likely to be violent on a given test who actually do engage in violence, whereas those who are misclassified by the test are typically termed "false positive" predictions. Similarly, NPA refers to the proportion of individuals classified as not likely to be violent who do not engage in violence and those who are misclassified (i.e., wrongly predicted to be nonviolent) are termed "false negative" predictions.

Important distinctions exist between inter-rater reliability, test-retest reliability, and internal consistency, with some of these indices being more relevant than others for a particular type of scale or measure. Similarly, with validity, important differences exist across predictive, concurrent, discriminant, and face validity, and researchers must consider which are most relevant for their particular purposes. Each of these issues is discussed in brief, with examples of settings and measurement techniques in which each has greater or lesser utility.

WHAT FORMS OF RELIABILITY ARE NECESSARY?

The issue of reliability is intimately intertwined with decisions as to what type of scale or instrument one is attempting to develop. For example, a scale in which the goal is to develop a method for quantifying the extent to which a relatively narrow construct is present should demonstrate substantial internal consistency *within* the scale. Similarly, within a large, multiscale inventory such as the PAI, each individual scale is typically intended to assess a construct that should have some coherent structure. Thus, individuals who endorse some of the scale items should be more likely to endorse other items, resulting in a relatively high degree of internal consistency within a construct. On the other hand, measures of ability are not necessarily intended to tap a unitary construct per se but rather are intended to assess the extent to which abilities are intact versus impaired; thus, establishing internal consistency may not be as essential a component of scale development.

A far more confusing issue, particularly for novice researchers, pertains to inter-rater reliability. In our experience, inter-rater reliability continues to be one of the most pervasive sources of confusion, in part because novice researchers often fail to realize that inter-rater reliability is *a property of a specific research team and study, not a property of a scale*. Despite this seemingly obvious fact, many researchers present inter-rater reliability from earlier research as though it applied to the scale itself and assume that by simply using the scale one would necessarily achieve the same level of reliability. Of course, the repeated demonstration that inter-rater reliability *can* be established with a given scale is useful—and perhaps critical—to demonstrating the adequacy of a measure that requires subjective judgments. However, the demonstration of high inter-rater reliability does not indicate that the raters are correct in their ratings, merely that they are consistent with one another. Thus, many researchers will establish inter-rater reliability against an external criterion to demonstrate accuracy in their own ratings (e.g., analyzing ratings of a videotaped interview in which an "official" rating has already been established). From a statistical perspective, inter-rater reliability is typically estimated using kappa coefficients (for categorical data) that correct for chance responding or intraclass correlation coefficients (for continuous data) that address mean differences, not simply consistency in rank order. Fortunately, inter-rater reliability applies only to clinician-rated instruments, inasmuch as no rater differences should exist with self-report type measures. That is assuming, of course, that examiners do not make scoring or data entry errors when generating summary information, which is an assumption that is at least occasionally incorrect.

A third form of reliability that may have relevance for instrument development is test-retest reliability. However, test-retest reliability is relevant only for instruments that purport to measure a trait that is expected to have some degree of consistency over time. For example, measures of psychopathy, which is presumed to reflect a long-standing personality style, *should* have a high degree of test-retest reliability even over a relatively long period of time. Measures of ability, on the other hand, may have varying degrees of stability, particularly in the context of a mental disorder that might impact performance only for limited periods of time. Still other measures are intended to vary considerably over time, and demonstrations of test-retest reliability have little merit and may actually raise questions about the scale (if insufficient variability is observed).

VALIDITY CONSIDERATIONS

The nature of the construct or criterion under investigation has equally important ramifications for determining the type of validity necessary. For example, instruments designed to quantify violence risk should demonstrate predictive validity, not simply differentiate individuals known to have a history of violence. On the other hand, measures that assess more transient states, such as malingering, are better described by concurrent validity (i.e., discriminating between groups), not predictive validity. Failure to appreciate this important distinction can lead to unwarranted criticism of a measure, such as labeling a measure inadequate for failing to "predict" an outcome that arguably should not be expected. Just as one would not necessarily expect a malingering measure to "predict" future behavior (e.g., malingering following a subsequent arrest), measures of personality constructs (e.g., psychopathy) may not be associated with legal system constructs such as trial competence. Unfortunately, because establishing predictive validity requires longitudinal research, which presents its own unique set of challenges, some researchers interpret "prediction" models based on cross-sectional or retrospective data as though it established predictive rather than concurrent validity.

Discriminant validity is another important, but often misunderstood, aspect of validation research. Identifying variables or outcomes that should *not* be associated with a measure is often challenging, particularly for constructs that are broad or multifaceted. For example, studies demonstrating that measures of sexual violence risk are better predictors of future nonviolent and non-sexual offending than with future actual sexual violence raise questions about the extent to which the instrument actually measures sexual violence risk (versus risk factors for general offending). Moreover, if civil commitment statutes specifically indicate that future acts of *sexual* aggression are the types of criminal acts that the commitment laws are intended to prevent, then validity data concerning non-sexual violent behavior arguably has no legal relevance to determining whether an examinee meets the legal criteria for commitment (Amenta, Guy, & Edens, 2003).

Although the determination of most forms of validity relies heavily on objective data, face validity is a rather subjective interpretation of an instrument's or an item's relevance to the construct it purports to measure (Murphy & Davidshofer, 2005). Face validity is not of great importance psychometrically, but it is likely to play an important role in most legal settings. Judges, attorneys, and juries who do not see the direct relevance of an instrument may be more likely to disregard its importance. This, in fact, has been the case, and several psychological measures have been deemed inadmissible solely on the basis of a lack of face validity (see Kleiman & Faley, 1978, for issues related to personnel testing). Development of measures for forensic settings should thus take into account the face validity of its contents (e.g., the MacCAT) as they are likely to prove beneficial when subjected to scrutiny in legal settings (Bartholomew, Badger, & Milte, 1977).

Perhaps the most important element of instrument validation is the separation of measure development from validation. Many researchers short-cut this process, by generating a single dataset, identifying variables or items that correlate with a desired outcome, and labeling that item set a "scale." Although this process is likely to generate the appearance of validity, it also capitalizes on chance to an unacceptably high degree. That is, derivation samples optimize the magnitude of the relationship between the scale and the criterion by statistically ensuring that the best predictive model is identified *in that particular data set*. This does not indicate that the scale will perform similarly in cross-validation samples, and in fact, it should be expected that there will be evidence of "shrinkage" in new samples.

Thus, at a minimum, researchers should utilize separate datasets for the initial scale development (e.g., item analysis and refinement) from the validation process. Of note, this problem is *not* resolved by conducting cross-validation research within the same data set (e.g., using a bootstrapped classification approach), as the degree of "shrinkage" obtained in a subsequent study is usually far more than observed through a bootstrapped classification analysis. Without replication, preferably even from an independent research team but certainly in a separate research study, validity data can only be considered preliminary.

A final general comment is worth highlighting regarding validity. It is not uncommon to observe clinicians or researchers describe a test as "valid" (or "invalid"). Although such statements may reflect summary opinions about the extent to which the construct validity of a measure has generally been supported (e.g., the PCL-R is widely considered to be a valid *measure* of the psychopathy *construct*), we would argue that these are overly broad conclusions that ignore the fact that validity is not a static property of a test (DeMatteo & Edens, 2006). Rather, it reflects the extent to which inferences drawn from test scores are useful and accurate (Messick, 1995). Consequently, the validity of any instrument is an open question that must be considered in the context in which the instrument is being used; evidence of validity in relation to one issue (e.g., malingered psychotic symptoms) may have little or nothing to do with validity for another purpose (e.g., malingered cognitive impairment).

In sum, linking validity research methods to the nature of the construct being assessed is critical to demonstrating an instrument's validity. Without such data, a measure is vulnerable to criticisms, perhaps even resulting in an instrument that does not meet the criteria for admissibility as scientific evidence. Although this outcome may be irrelevant in many settings, for an FAI that is intended to measure a legally relevant construct, this outcome is far more problematic.

DATA-ANALYTIC APPROACHES

A thorough analysis of statistical approaches used in measure development could itself easily fill an entire volume and is thus far beyond the scope of this chapter. However, a number of approaches are sufficiently important—yet often neglected in the process of measure development and validation—as to warrant a brief review here. The topics discussed in the following text are clearly selective and represent important additions to the "standard" statistical approaches that most researchers have been taught and put to use (e.g., correlational models), some of which are reviewed elsewhere (see Chapter 5) and are discussed in detail in numerous textbooks on research methodology. Similarly, the interested researcher will need to seek additional guidance for a sufficiently detailed explanation as to how these analyses are best conducted and interpreted, as explaining in depth even one of the topics that follow is beyond the scope of this chapter.

THE ROLE OF FACTOR ANALYSIS

Although factor analysis is a well-established statistical approach and is widely used in measurement, a number of important applications are infrequently used in measure development. Factor analysis is a central element of classical test theory and is frequently used as a means of identifying test items that are more or less closely related to the underlying construct, or covary in a way that facilitates clinical interpretation. Indeed, a central tenet of classical test theory is that the construct being measured is represented by an underlying latent variable (i.e., factor), and that identifying scale items that are stronger or weaker indicators can be facilitated by factor analysis. This process can be particularly useful in the preliminary stages of measure development as a way to identify a subset of test items that are most strongly associated with the construct (i.e., to narrow an initial item pool). Of course, decisions regarding which items should be retained in a scale must be based on more than just inter-item correlations, because infrequently endorsed items (e.g., "I plan to kill myself in the next 24 hours") may have considerable clinical significance, despite appearing to detract somewhat from a scale's reliability due to low endorsement rates.

Another important use of factor analysis focuses on confirmatory models to identify potential sources of bias in individual items, item subsets (factors), or even scales. The crux of this approach involves assessing the extent to which factor solutions remain consistent (termed factorial invariance) across different groups. This method of analysis can be used to assess for gender or ethnic/racial differences (or any other potentially relevant sociodemographic variable) in a measure or even to assess whether comparable reliability exists for translated versions of a scale or when different administration approaches are used. For example, comparing the factor structure across genders might identify scale items that are associated with the underlying construct for men but not women, or for Caucasians but not for African Americans. These differences may reflect a source of bias or simply differences in the meaning and interpretation of a scale item across groups. In either case, such findings have important implications for scale interpretation and applicability to new populations or settings.

Along these same lines, factor analysis simply reflects patterns of covariance among variables and cannot resolve issues concerning the nature or causes of the relationships among those variables. For example, some researchers have attempted to use factor analysis to demonstrate that criminal activity is a core element of psychopathy, arguing that an "antisocial" factor can be demonstrated among the items comprising the PCL-R. Others have argued that such patterns of relationships, even if statistically demonstrated (cf. Cooke, Michie, & Skeem, 2007), have no bearing on determining the role of criminality in conceptualizing psychopathy, because such criminal acts may simply reflect downstream behavioral consequences of psychopathy—consequences that also may be caused by numerous other etiological factors irrelevant to the construct of psychopathy. In short, while there are clearly important benefits to incorporating factor analysis into instrument development, this approach in itself does not answer ultimate questions about how to best construct or interpret an instrument.

ITEM RESPONSE THEORY

During the past few decades, item response theory (IRT) has emerged as an important supplement to classical test theory. Rather than conceptualizing a scale score as simply the sum of an underlying true score and error, as is true of classical test theory, IRT attempts to differentiate sources of error by analyzing item characteristics. In particular, two primary elements of scale items form the source of IRT: item difficulty and discriminatory power. The term item difficulty is grounded in ability testing and refers to the level of an attribute that is associated with item endorsement (or correct responding, in

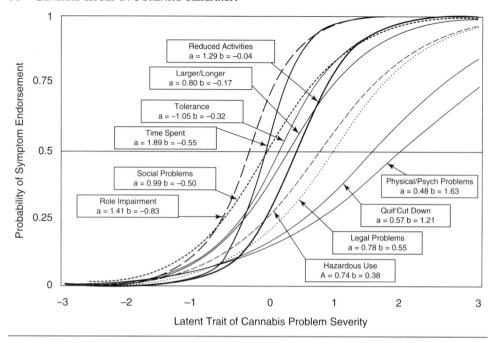

Figure 2.1   Item-response curve example

an ability test). For a test measuring propensity to abuse cannabis, a very difficult item would be one that is endorsed only by individuals with a history of abuse, whereas an "easy" item would be endorsed by even mild cannabis users. Figure 2.1 depicts item difficulty curves for a range of different test items, each of which has greater or lesser item difficulty.

In some settings it is optimal to have items with a wide range of difficulty, although in other settings one might select only items with a relatively high level of difficulty. Discrimination, on the other hand, focuses on the clarity with which an item can distinguish high versus low scorers on an item. For example, an item predicting likelihood of cannabis abuse with high discrimination would indicate that an individual with such a disorder would be much more likely to endorse the item than an individual who does not abuse cannabis, who would very rarely endorse the item (note that this explanation becomes increasingly complex, but no less accurate, as the number of possible response options increases).

Another application of IRT that can be useful for measure development and validation is the comparison of difficulty and discriminatory power across different groups (e.g., men and women, or using different administration formats such as self-report versus interview-based; referred to as differential item functioning or DIF). Identifying items that are more difficult (less often endorsed or rated) for women as compared with men can be a powerful technique for detecting scale biases. In fact, this approach can be far more powerful than classical test theory approaches (e.g., factor analysis), given that the precise nature of the bias is more directly identifiable rather than being inferred through differing factor structures.

Although IRT provides a useful complement to classical approaches to item selection or scale reduction, the interpretation of item characteristic curves (a graphical representation of the item's difficulty and discrimination) is not straightforward. Identifying better or worse items, like deciding on the appropriate number of factors or the optimal factor extraction or rotation method in factor analysis, requires considerable familiarity with the underlying theory, the resulting output, and the advantages and disadvantages of alternative approaches. Clearly, these topics are beyond the scope of this chapter. A final point of concern is that IRT approaches to data analysis typically require extremely large sample sizes (i.e., several hundred subjects), which frequently may be unavailable, particularly during the initial stages of instrument development. Despite the complexity involved in applying IRT, the potential advantages for instrument development are profound.

RECEIVER OPERATING CHARACTERISTIC (ROC) CURVE ANALYSIS

Another statistical approach that plays an important but often underutilized (and misunderstood) role in measure development is the use of ROC curve analysis. ROC curves are a graphical representation of classification accuracy, plotting the sensitivity of a measure against its specificity (1 minus specificity, actually) across all possible cut-off scores. Because sensitivity and specificity are a function of the cut-off score chosen, ROC curves provide an overall index of classification accuracy and enable the researcher to identify optimal cut-off scores in a particular data set. A test or classification approach that cannot improve upon chance would be represented by a 45-degree line; however, as the test improves upon chance, the line begins to depart from this reference line (often referred to as the line of no information). As a classification approach becomes more accurate, the line departs further from the reference line, taking on an increasingly curved appearance.

Predictive accuracy, represented by ROC curves, typically is quantified by the "area under the curve" (AUC) value (see Figure 2.2).

In its simplest form, the AUC value can be interpreted as the likelihood that a randomly selected individual who is positive for the criterion of interest (e.g., was or will be violent) would obtain a higher score on the predictor test than would a randomly selected person who is negative for the criterion (e.g., would not be violent). An AUC value of .5 indicates that the test is useless; the odds are 50/50 across groups. An AUC value of 1.0 indicates perfect accuracy, with all violent individuals scoring higher on the test than non-violent individuals. AUCs below .50 also indicate that the test works—but in the wrong direction (e.g., violent individuals score lower than non-violent individuals). Because the AUC statistic reflects an effect size, the magnitude of the coefficient is often more important than statistical significance (which is dependent on sample size); in general, AUCs in excess of .80 are considered to represent "good" predictive accuracy. As can be seen in Figure 2.2, the HCR-20 (a widely used risk-assessment instrument, with an AUC of .82 in this study)

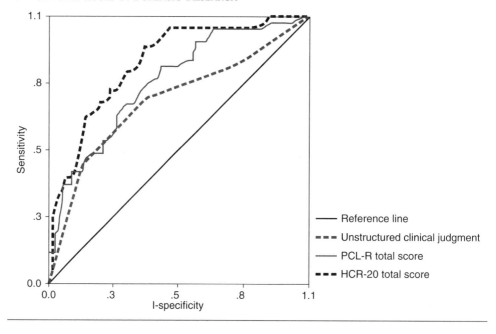

Figure 2.2 ROC curves for HCR-20, PCL-R, and unstructured clinical judgment for violent re-offending ($N = 119$)

outperformed the PCL-R (AUC = .75) and unstructured clinical judgment (AUC =.68) in the prediction of violence in this study (de Vogel, de Ruiter, Hildebrand, Bos, & van de Ven, 2004).

Of course, the determination of what is "optimal" in prediction research is a value judgment that does not necessarily correspond to the point at which the curve most departs from the axis, although that point may represent the greatest overall classification accuracy from a purely statistical perspective. For example, in many settings researchers will deliberately maximize either sensitivity (e.g., in a screening instrument, designed to identify any individuals who might possibly warrant some intervention or further testing) or specificity (e.g., where "false positives" have tremendous negative consequences, such as in the assessment of malingering). Nevertheless, the ROC curve provides a method for determining the optimal cut-off score regardless of whether the goal is to maximize either or both of these indices of classification accuracy.

It is worth noting that ROC curves have been widely touted in various areas of research, and particularly in violence risk research (e.g., Quinsey, Harris, Rice, & Cormier, 2005), as a means of assessing predictive validity that is superior to other indicators of effect size (e.g., correlations, odds ratios). This argument largely stems from the fact that AUC values, unlike many other effect-size indicators, are not tied to the base rate of the criterion of interest. Because, for example, violent acts have been rare in many outcome studies of risk-assessment instruments, correlations between risk instruments and these scales are necessarily attenuated. Although AUC values can be extremely informative, we would argue that they do not solve the "low base rate" problem as much as they simply ignore it (Amenta, Guy, & Edens, 2003).

Even with relatively high AUC values (e.g., .80), predictions of the occurrence of low base rate events (e.g., 10% base rate or lower) will almost always result in a very large number of false positives or cases in which a person not actually positive for the criterion (e.g., did not engage in violence) is misidentified as being so (e.g., predicted to be violent). That is, the positive predictive power (or PPP) of a cut score that might be reasonably effective at a .50 base rate will decrease substantially at much lower base rates simply because there are so few "true positives" in the sample. For a detailed and highly informative analysis of this issue using a widely researched risk assessment instrument, see Streiner (2003).

SUMMARY

Development of legally relevant assessment instruments is of critical importance, both in improving the process of forensic assessment and for facilitating important forensic research agendas. Although there are numerous challenges to this process, measure development can be greatly enhanced through attention to the many issues that complicate instrument development, including the conceptual and psychometric. Only with careful attention to these issues can researchers ensure that their efforts will generate measures that can and should withstand judicial and clinical scrutiny.

REFERENCES

Amenta, A. E., Guy, L. S., & Edens, J. F. (2003). Sex offender risk assessment: A cautionary note regarding measures attempting to quantify violence risk. *Journal of Forensic Psychology Practice, 3,* 39–50.

Bartholomew, A. A., Badger, P., & Milte, K. L. (1977). The psychologist as an expert witness in the criminal courts. *Australian Psychologist, 12,* 133–150.

Cooke, D. J., Michie, C., & Skeem, J. L. (2007). Understanding the structure of the Psychopathy Checklist-Revised: An exploration of methodological confusion. *British Journal of Psychiatry, 190,* s39–s50.

DeMatteo, D., & Edens, J. F. (2006). The role and relevance of the Psychopathy Checklist-Revised in court: A case law survey of U.S. courts (1991-2004). *Psychology, Public Policy, and Law, 12,* 214–241.

DeVellis, R. F. (2003). *Scale Development: Theory and Applications* (2nd ed.). Newbury Park, CA: Sage.

de Vogel, V., de Ruiter, C., Hildebrand, M., Bos, B., & van de Ven, P. (2004). Type of discharge and risk of recidivism measured by the HCR-20. A retrospective study in a Dutch sample of treated forensic psychiatric patients. *International Journal of Forensic Mental Health, 3,* 149–165.

Douglas, K. S., Hart, S. D., & Kropp, P. R. (2001). Validity of the Personality Assessment Inventory for forensic assessments. *International Journal of Offender Therapy and Comparative Criminology, 45,* 183–197.

Edens, J. F., & Ruiz, M. A. (2005). *Personality Assessment Inventory Interpretive Report for Correctional Settings (PAI-CS) professional manual.* Odessa, FL: PAR, Inc.

Grisso, T. (1998). *Instruments for assessing understanding & appreciation of Miranda rights.* Sarasota, FL: Professional Resource Press/Professional Resource Exchange.

Hare, R. D. (2003). *The Psychopathy Checklist—Revised technical manual* (2nd ed.). Toronto, Canada: Multi-Health Systems.

Heilbrun, K., Rogers, R., & Otto, R. K. (2002). Forensic assessment: Current status and future directions. In J. R. P. Ogloff (Ed.), *Taking Psychology and law into the twenty-first century* (pp. 119–146). Secaucus, NJ: Kluwer.

Kleiman, L. S., & Faley, R. H. (1978). Assessing content validity: Standards set by the court. *Personnel Psychology, 31,* 701–713.

Lilienfeld, S. O., & Andrews, B. P. (1996). Development and preliminary validation of a self-report measure of psychopathic personality traits in noncriminal populations. *Journal of Personality Assessment, 66,* 488–524.

Lipsitt, P. D., Lelos, D., & McGarry, A. L. (1971). Competency for trial: A screening instrument. *American Journal of Psychiatry, 128,* 105–109.

Messick, S. (1995). Validity of psychological assessment: Validation of inferences from persons' responses and performances as scientific inquiry into score meaning. *American Psychologist, 50,* 741–749.

Morey, L. C. (2007). *The Personality Assessment Inventory (PAI): Professional manual* (2nd ed.). Lutz, FL: Psychological Assessment Resources.

Murphy, K. R, & Davidshofer, C. O. (2005). *Psychological testing: Principles & applications. 6th Ed.* Upper Saddle River, NJ: Pearson Education.

Poythress, N. G., Nicholson, R. A., Otto, R. K., Edens, J. F., Bonnie, R. J., Monahan, J., & Hoge, S. K. (1999). *The MacArthur Competence Assessment Tool-Criminal Adjudication (MacCAT-CA) professional manual.* Odessa, FL: Psychological Assessment Resources.

Quinsey, V., Harris, G., Rice, M., & Cormier, C. (2005). *Violent offenders: Appraising and managing risk* (2nd ed.). Washington, DC: American Psychological Association.

Rosenfeld, B., Sands, S. A., & Van Gorp, W. G. (2000). Have we forgotten the base rate problem? Methodological issues in the detection of distortion. *Archives of Clinical Neuropsychology, 15,* 349–359.

Streiner, D. L. (2003). Diagnosing tests: Using and misusing diagnostic and screening tests. *Journal of Personality Assessment, 81,* 209–219.

CHAPTER 3

Meta-Analysis

SIEGFRIED L. SPORER AND LAWRENCE D. COHN[1]

A S THE FIELD of psychology and law has grown tremendously during the past decades, so has the number of articles within its subfields. For individual researchers and even more for the disparate "consumers" of this literature (legal scholars and policy makers), it has become increasingly difficult to keep abreast of the growing body of research. One consequence of this growth is that it is difficult for narrative reviews to summarize findings from the large number of studies; moreover, two narrative reviews of the same body of research have sometimes reached different conclusions (e.g., the literature on "recovered memories" or the "false memory syndrome"). Reviews that yield contradictory conclusions raise questions about the scientific status of a field. Yet courts have demanded that only "reliable" evidence in the form of peer-reviewed publications should be presented as part of expert testimony (*Daubert v. Merrell Dow Pharmaceuticals*, 1993).

In medicine, so-called "systematic reviews," often in connection with meta-analytic integrations of the literature, have been recommended to assure "evidence-based policy." Research centers have been created to collect and document systematic reviews following an initiative called the Cochrane Collaboration in medicine (Higgins & Green, 2008), followed by the Campbell Collaboration in the social sciences (see White, 2009). These centers, and the publications derived from them, have provided guidelines for conducting and reporting systematic reviews. These efforts have increased the number of published meta-analyses and have led to an ever-increasing number of books and articles as well as computer programs on more advanced statistical techniques for conducting meta-analyses.

The field of psychology and law has also witnessed the growth of meta-analytic reviews that summarize findings in specific areas. This chapter

---

1. We are indebted to Colin Tredoux, Jane Goodman-Delahunty, and Maike M. Breuer for their diligent comments on portions of this manuscript and Valerie Hauch for her help in locating some of the references and preparing the reference list.

provides an introductory guide on how to conduct a meta-analysis. We introduce the novice to different indices of effect size, and we outline the major steps involved in conducting a meta-analysis. At the same time, we draw researchers' attention to pitfalls, problems, and emerging statistical issues in the burgeoning art of meta-analytic synthesis.

GOALS OF META-ANALYSES AND TYPES OF RESEARCH QUESTIONS ADDRESSED BY QUANTITATIVE REVIEWS

The major goal of a meta-analysis is to summarize the current state of knowledge regarding a specific research question in a mathematical way. Narrative reviews often focus on "significant" results ($p < .05$) while ignoring effect sizes and sample sizes. In contrast, a meta-analytic synthesis estimates the population effect size, weighting individual effect sizes as a function of sample sizes. In general, the relationship between a test statistic, effect size, and study size can be characterized as follows:

$$\text{Test of significance} = \text{effect size} * \text{size of study}$$

By rearranging this simple formula, we arrive at a general characterization of an effect size:

$$\text{Effect size} = \text{test of significance}/\text{size of study}$$

The size of a study determines the precision with which an effect size can be estimated. Thus, for each individual effect size (ES), a 95% confidence interval can be constructed, $CI = ES \pm 1.96 * SE$, with 1.96 [2.56] corresponding to the normal distribution Z value associated with $p = .05$ [.01]. If the CI does not include zero, the null hypothesis that the ES is zero can be rejected.

While the precision of an estimate is primarily a function of sample size, other factors such as study design (e.g., between-participants vs. within-participants designs) also affect precision and need to be taken into consideration when performing a research synthesis. Since sample effect sizes vary from study to study, meta-analysts are interested in both an average effect size and the variability of the sample effect sizes. The variance, standard error, and confidence intervals for population effect sizes are estimated, and one or more methods are used to analyze the homogeneity of effect sizes. When sample effect sizes are heterogeneous, or for a priori theoretical reasons, moderator analyses are conducted to account for this variability. Alternative models for conducting meta-analytic syntheses (fixed-effect, random-effect, or mixed-effect model) are available. Researchers should be aware of the different underlying assumptions of these models and choose them appropriately.

THE CASE AGAINST VOTE COUNTING

Some research reviews incorporate summary tables of studies that have yielded significant positive, significant negative, or null findings. For several decades, meta-analysts have criticized such practices as "crude, flawed, and worthless" (Bushman & Wang, 2009, p. 208). The major problem is that vote-counting tallies the number of significant findings in a body of research while ignoring issues of sample size and statistical power. Studies with small sample sizes and low statistical power are less likely to detect significant population effects than studies with large sample sizes and high power. Thus, research reviews based on vote counting can inadvertently reach erroneous conclusions if they contain studies with low statistical power. In contrast, meta-analytic reviews are based on computations that include sample size information. Indeed, one of the most frequently cited reasons for conducting meta-analytic reviews is the increased statistical power that accompanies the procedure (Cohn & Becker, 2003). More recently, methods for constructing confidence intervals based on vote-counting procedures, as well as maximum likelihood estimators of various effect sizes, have become available (see Bushman & Wang, 2009). Also, there are now methods to integrate vote counts and effect size estimates for r and d when insufficient information is available from studies (see Bushman & Wang, 1995, 1996, 2009).

Although many measures of effect sizes are available, we focus here on the most frequently used effect sizes r, d, and *OR*. Figure 3.1 provides an overview of these three classes of effect sizes. Note that formulae are available for converting different effect-size measures among each other, but these may not be as interchangeable as previously thought (e.g., Ray & Shadish, 1996; Sánchez-Meca, Marín-Martinez, & Chacón-Moscoso, 2003). Estimates of the population variance—and hence standard errors and confidence intervals—are highly dependent on the effect size metric. Consequently, meta-analytic summaries may depend on the effect size used, specifically with respect to testing homogeneity and the detection of outliers. Also, using some of these conversion formulae simplistically, in particular with complex

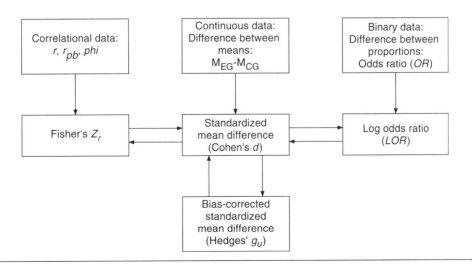

Figure 3.1 Classes of effect sizes for correlations, mean differences, and binary data and their bias corrections

experimental designs and with repeated measurements, can lead to serious errors (see Cortina & Nouri, 2000; Dunlap, Cortina, Vaslow, & Burke, 1996; Morris, 2008; Morris & DeShon, 2002; Viechtbauer, 2007).

Although Rosenthal (1991, 1994) has argued that the (point-biserial) correlation r and its transform, Fisher's Z_r, could be used for any type of effect size, this may be too simplistic. There seems to be consensus today that meta-analyses should be conducted using an effect size index that is most appropriate for the type of statistical relations that are tested in a given domain of studies; that is, for studies focusing on comparisons between treatment or experimental and control groups measured on continuous variables meta-analysts should use d, for correlations between continuous variables with other continuous variables r, and with dichotomous variables r_{pb}, and for comparisons of frequencies or proportions of binary variables *odds ratios* (even if primary researchers may have reported different effect sizes). These effect sizes should preferably be calculated from the original data reported (like means and standard deviations or proportions, and the respective ns), rather than the F, t, or chi^2 values and dfs. Conversions of effect sizes should be used only to compare results with findings reported in other domains (or previous meta-analyses) that have used different effect size indices (see Cooper, Hedges, & Valentine, 2009).

We will discuss only the effect size indices r, d, and the odds-ratio (OR), but additional indices are discussed in Cooper and Hedges (1994), Lipsey and Wilson (2001) and Cooper et al. (2009). Note that many of the calculations performed in a meta-analysis require that the effect sizes be normalized; when reporting results, however, the findings are transformed back to the original effect-size index (see Figure 3.1).

STEPS IN CONDUCTING A META-ANALYSIS

Defining a Research Hypothesis

The first step in a meta-analysis involves clearly defining a research hypothesis that incorporates precise operational definitions of all constructs of the relationship under investigation. Reading past narrative reviews or representative articles in a given domain will give a first impression of the kinds of operationalizations researchers have used. As the search for relevant studies continues, the constructs may have to be more precisely defined to arrive at clear rules for including and excluding studies from the review. Often, more than one dependent variable is assessed in a study, and meta-analysts need to decide which dependent variable best represents the target construct and then conduct the analysis using the latter dependent variable. In some instances, it is appropriate to compute the average of several effect sizes in a single study rather than selecting one of the effect sizes to represent the outcome of a given study (see the excellent discussion of stochastically dependent effect sizes and possible solutions by Gleser & Olkin, 1994, 2009).

Making these choices requires the meta-analyst to be well grounded in the theories and research issues under study. The meta-analyst must also formulate a directional hypothesis, and the results of each study are coded according to the presumed direction of a relationship. For example, if we want to compare the memory ability of police officers with the memory ability of civilians, then we may find some studies that report the amount of correct recall that is displayed by both groups, whereas other studies may report the number of errors displayed by both groups. If we hypothesize that memory ability is greater in police than civilians (e.g., due to their prolonged experience or their ability to handle stress), then positive effect size values (e.g., *more* items recalled correctly, or *fewer* errors) would always indicate superior police performance. Familiarity with the research literature in a given domain is also necessary to identify a priori hypotheses regarding potential moderators of the observed relationships (see Sporer & Schwandt, 2007, for an example of such a theory-based meta-analysis).

FINDING RELEVANT PUBLICATIONS

The conclusiveness of a meta-analytic synthesis depends on the comprehensiveness of the population of studies included in the review. Ideally, every study that meets previously defined inclusion criteria should be included in the review. Several strategies have been proposed for searching a body of literature. White (2009) provided an integration of these approaches, distinguishing five major modes of searching which are further detailed into substrategies:

- Footnote chasing
- Consultation with colleagues
- Searching in subject indices
- Browsing
- Citation searches

We briefly discuss the relative advantages and disadvantages of each approach, paying special attention to the role of reference databases when searching citations and subject indices (see Reed & Baxter, 2009, who provide an illuminating example from the eyewitness literature).

A good starting point for the literature search involves consulting reference lists of previous narrative review articles. This strategy is sometimes referred to as either the *ancestry approach*, or *footnote chasing*. The advantage of this approach is that one gains a good overview of the theoretical and practical issues surrounding the research question, as well as the different operationalizations, measurement strategies, and potential moderator variables. In addition, the references culled from review articles are likely to be empirical studies (hits) that can be included in the meta-analysis.

Traditionally, researchers have consulted subject indices (called *thesauri*) such as *Psychological Abstracts*. Portions of these indices have been retrospectively indexed with subject terms and can be searched electronically in databases such as PsycINFO. However, index terms always lag behind, change over time, or vary by "indexers" (the library personnel whose task it is to systematically index a literature); moreover, authors themselves vary in their use of natural or technical index terms to characterize certain topics (Reed & Baxter, 2009; White, 2009).

In the experience of the first author, without proper instruction in search strategies, large numbers of relevant studies are missed when PsycINFO is used exclusively. Therefore, we strongly recommend complementing such searches with *prospective* citation searches conducted with the Science Citation Index or the Social Sciences Citation Index. In a prospective search, a key article is initially identified and then the meta-analyst searches for all subsequent papers that cite the original article. Although this strategy often generates a fairly comprehensive list of relevant articles, it may also yield many non-empirical articles or articles that report research that is not directly relevant to the meta-analytic review.

Writing to authors may seem to be a prudent and convenient strategy for identifying relevant research, but reviewers should not assume that busy primary researchers will provide them with complete reference lists of their work on specific topics.

Finally, we do not recommend using Google, Google Scholar, Yahoo, or other search engines, except perhaps as an initial strategy for identifying a few relevant articles. Most people using these search engines do not use them to their full potential, and focusing only on the first couple of hits (out of some thousands or tens of thousands; see Cooper, 2010) is not likely to be productive.

CODING OF STUDY VARIABLES

After meta-analytic hypotheses have been formulated and primary studies have been obtained, the relevant information from these studies has to be extracted. On the one hand, this involves extracting information needed to calculate effect sizes (e.g., means and standard deviations, sample sizes, tests of statistical significance). On the other hand, study descriptors have to be coded for use in subsequent analyses. For example, a reviewer may code the type of research design that was employed in a study (e.g., randomized control group design vs. quasi-experiment, number of independent variables), or the type of participants in a study (e.g., age, numbers of males and females, students vs. community participants, remuneration), or the naturalness of the setting (e.g., laboratory vs. field studies). Coding of study characteristics is also essential for defining the boundary conditions for a research synthesis and identifying potential moderator variables. Boundary conditions refer to potential limitations of contextual or methodological variables, information that is important for practitioners and policy makers.

For example, in reviews of eyewitness research, studies should be coded for the type of face recognition paradigm employed or the use of filmed materials or staged live events. Similarly, studies of jury research should be coded for the type of sample recruited (e.g., students vs. adults who are eligible for jury duty); moreover, studies involving program evaluation should code whether the program was evaluated by the researchers or by a team of independent researchers.

We recommend organizing these different sets of values in different files that can later be combined on the basis of study identification numbers (and thus quickly accessed to test hypotheses regarding moderator variables).

Coding some variables is straightforward, such as sample size or the gender composition of a sample; coding other variables, however, is more difficult, such as the experimental paradigm, or instructional content, or the type of stimulus materials employed. Coding the latter variables is often subjective. Hence, it is essential that a coding manual be developed a priori, with precise definitions of the respective codes, operationalizations, and examples of the application of coding rules (see Wilson, 2009).

A frustrating experience for meta-analytic reviewers involves coding missing data. Data may be unavailable for inclusion in a meta-analytic review for several reasons, including (a) the findings may be unpublished and unavailable, (b) the findings were presented at a conference but are no longer accessible, (c) the relevant study is published but the authors fail to report effect-size information and fail to report statistics that could be used to compute effect sizes, or (d) an article is missing descriptor information (e.g., insufficient details about the methods and procedures involved in the study). Meta-analysts also distinguish between data missing completely at random (MCAR), missing at random (MAR), and not missing at random (NMAR), according to Pigott (1994, 2009). Studies may have to be excluded from the review, which could introduce systematic biases in results. Different methods for imputing missing values are available based on regression techniques for randomly missing data, and model-based methods based on maximum-likelihood estimation (see Pigott, 2009, for illustrative examples). In case of NMAR data, publication bias may play a prominent role and will be discussed in more detail subsequently (see Sutton, 2009).

Reliability of Coding   The ultimate goal of a coding manual is replicability—that is, coding criteria must be transparent and well documented to ensure that researchers and research consumers can evaluate the adequacy of the database and subsequent analyses. Coding should be undertaken by more than one coder, codings should be compared across raters, inter-coder reliabilities should be calculated and reported, and discrepant codings should be integrated (Orwin & Vevea, 2009). However, simply reporting that "discrepancies were resolved by discussion" or reporting the average inter-coder agreement are usually not sufficient.

When coding is undertaken in different locations (as is increasingly common with collaborations across laboratories), evaluating inter-coder reliability is particularly crucial. Intra-class correlation coefficients and Pearson correlations can be used to assess coding reliability of continuous variables. When coding categorical variables, such as type of study design. Cohen's *kappa* should be used for assessing inter-coder reliability. because *kappa* controls for chance agreement (in contrast, computing the percentage agreement rate between coders does not control for chance agreement (see Fleiss, Levin & Paik, 2003; Orwin & Vevea, 2009).

CALCULATING EFFECT-SIZE MEASURES

TYPES OF EFFECT SIZE

Several indices are available to express the strength of a relationship, including the correlation coefficient (r), the standardized mean difference (d), and the odds ratio (OR). Studies that address the same hypothesis may not report their results using the same effect-size index. When these studies are included in a meta-analysis, however, the effect sizes must be converted to a common metric. The meta-analyst must decide which metric or effect-size index is most appropriate for characterizing the relationship under review (see Figure 3.1).

Correlations and Fisher's Z_r Transformation   The strength of a relationship between two continuous variables is usually assessed using Pearson correlation coefficients (r). When one of the variables is dichotomous, the point-biserial correlation r_{pb} is used, which is the Pearson correlation between a dichotomous variable and a continuous variable. However, in meta-analysis the raw correlations are not used due to undesirable statistical properties (Borenstein, 2009; Hedges & Olkin, 1985; Rosenthal, 1994). Therefore, Fisher's Z_r transformation is used for all analyses, including the calculation of its variance, standard error, and inverse variance weight respectively; see Lipsey & Wilson, 2001). All calculations are performed with Fisher's Z_r. When reporting results such as the weighted mean effect size and its confidence intervals, the Z_r values are back-transformed to their respective equivalents of r or r_{pb}.

Standardized Mean Difference   Several additional effect size indices have been developed to assess the magnitude of association between two variables. One commonly used index is Cohen's d (1988). Cohen's d is defined as the difference between two means expressed in standard deviation units (hence the phrase "standardized mean difference"). The computation of d is straight-forward: the mean of Group 2 (e.g., the control group, M_{CG}) is subtracted from the mean of Group 1 (e.g., an experimental group, M_{EG}) and the result is divided by the standard deviation (SD) of the individual scores. The SD of individual scores is typically obtained by pooling the standard deviation of scores within each of the two groups; the latter value is referred to as the "pooled within-groups standard deviation."

Primary research studies do not always report values for d. If a paper reports the means and standard deviations for an experimental group and a control group, 0 the d-value can be computed directly from equations provided by Lipsey and Wilson (2001) or other standard meta-analytic texts. When the ns for the experimental groups differ, formulae that take the respective ns into account are to be preferred over those that assume them to be equal. If a study reports only the value of a t-test, a simple algebraic manipulation can be used to convert the t-value into a d-value (provided in standard meta-analytic texts). If authors report a significant difference between the means of two groups but fail to report the means, standard deviations, or t-value, the meta-analyst can adopt a conservative strategy for estimating the sample effect size: determine the minimum t-value that would be considered significant for the stated degrees of freedom and then use standard equations for converting the t-value into a d-value. All the statistical functions necessary for these conversions are available in Excel spreadsheets and can be easily programmed to make these transformations.

We have already noted the particular problems of calculating appropriate effect sizes for complex ANOVA designs, particularly those involving repeated measures. For these designs, simple conversion formulae for obtaining d- or r-values as effect sizes are often inappropriate, and meta-analysts should consult the specific literature (see Cortina & Nouri, 2000; Dunlap, Cortina, Vaslow, & Burke, 1994; Morris, 2008; Morris & DeShon, 2002; Viechtbauer, 2007).

Odds Ratios Meta-analyses often synthesize research findings that are based on dichotomous outcomes (Haddock, Rindskopf, & Shadish, 1998). For example, studies of eyewitness identification may assess the impact of presentation mode (sequential vs. simultaneous lineups) on eyewitness accuracy (accurate vs. inaccurate). Similarly, studies of jury decision making may assess the impact of a defendant's language of testimony (Spanish vs. English) on juror verdicts (guilty vs. not guilty). In such studies, the findings can be reported as frequencies or "counts" in fourfold tables. For example, in the latter study investigators could report the number of jurors who cast *guilty* verdicts after listening to a defendant's testimony in English, the number of jurors who cast *not guilty* verdicts after listening to a defendant's testimony in English, the number of jurors who cast *guilty* verdicts after listening to testimony in Spanish, and the number of jurors who cast *not guilty* verdicts after listening to testimony in Spanish. The strength of association between the defendant's language of testimony and a juror's verdict can be assessed using several effect-size indices, including the *odds ratio*. Fleiss (1994) and Fleiss and Berlin (2009) have systematically compared these different effect sizes and concluded that the odds ratio is to be preferred over the other indices for various reasons, particularly desirable characteristics of the underlying distributions of the log-transformed odds ratio.

The odds ratio refers to the ratio of two odds. A meta-analysis of odds ratios proceeds in the following steps: (a) an odds ratio is retrieved or computed for each independent sample that is included in the meta-analysis; (b) each odds ratio is converted to the natural log of the odds ratio (*LOR*), because the sampling distribution of the odds ratio does not approximate a normal distribution, making it difficult for investigators to compute a 95% confidence interval around the weighted average *OR*; (c) the variance (v_i) of each *LOR* is computed; (d) each *LOR* in the meta-analysis is weighted by the reciprocal (inverse) of its variance—that is, $w_i = 1/v_i$. Finally we compute the weighted average of the log odds ratios. The latter value provides the best estimate of the population effect size, assuming that the sample effect sizes in the meta-analysis estimate the same parameter. When reporting results, the *LOR* values are back-transformed to *OR*s by taking the antilog (see Figure 3.1).

PRELIMINARY ANALYSES AND DETECTING OUTLIERS

In the following section, we briefly describe the steps in conducting a meta-analytic synthesis.

After calculating all relevant effect sizes, confidence intervals, and inverse variance weights, we recommend examining the distribution of effect sizes to detect potential outliers. At the very least, the effect sizes in each study (ordered in ascending magnitude) along with their confidence intervals should be plotted to facilitate detection of potential outliers (as an example, see Figure 3.2). With large numbers of studies in a data set, we recommend using stem-and-leaf plots or box plots (which display the median, 10th, 25th, 75th, and 90th percentiles, along with extreme values) as a quick screening device. More sophisticated methods to search for outliers have been proposed by Hedges and Olkin (1985) and Huffcutt and Arthur (1995), and should be consulted and applied routinely. Note, however, that Beal, Corey, and Dunlap (2002) recommend that the procedure recommended by Huffcutt and Arthur (1995) should not be used with *r*, but preferably with Fisher's Z_r.

Homogeneity of Effect Sizes

Researchers typically seek to estimate the population effect size based on a set of sample effect sizes. Yet it is also important to assess the variability among the sample effect sizes themselves. Can the distribution of sample effect sizes be considered homogeneous? Under the assumption of a fixed-effects model (see the following text), the observed effect size variance can be partitioned into two components, one attributable to participant-level sampling error and one to other between-study differences (Hunter & Schmidt, 1990, 2004). Ideally, a mean effect size is estimated, and the between-studies variance is fully accounted for by sampling error (see the discussion of fixed-effect vs. random-effect models that follows). As a rule of thumb, if more than two-thirds of the variance is accounted for by sampling error, it is unlikely that effect sizes will vary as a function of study characteristics (Hunter & Schmidt, 2004).

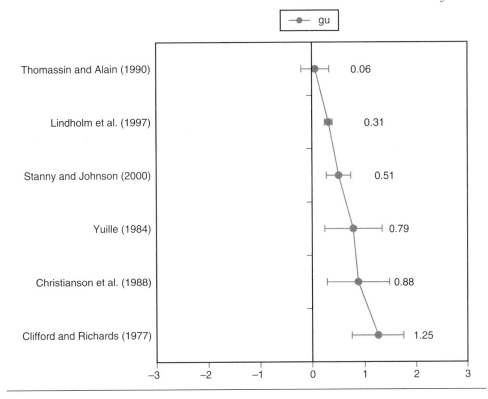

Figure 3.2 Outlier detection via visual displays of effect sizes and their confidence Intervals

A formal test for the homogeneity of effect sizes is provided by the Q statistic (Hedges & Olkin, 1985; Lipsey & Wilson, 2001). Q is distributed as a *chi-square* variable with $k - 1$ degrees of freedom and can be used to test the null hypothesis of homogeneity of variance of effect sizes. If Q is significant, the mean weighted effect size should no longer be considered a good estimate of the population effect size. In the latter situation, subgroups of studies could be formed to help identify moderator variables; in addition, random effects analyses could be conducted.

The value of Q partially depends on the number of studies sampled. Q has low statistical power when only a few studies are included in a review; thus, a nonsignificant Q does not necessarily indicate the presence of homogeneity. Low power of the Q statistic is also likely when the between-studies variance is small and the sampling error variance is large. Hence, Q should be supplemented by the descriptive statistic referred to as I^2 (Borenstein, Hedges, Higgins, & Rothstein, 2009; Higgins & Thompson, 2002).

META-ANALYTIC SYNTHESIS: INTEGRATING STUDIES

UNWEIGHTED ANALYSIS

Several procedures have been developed for combining effect sizes from independent samples. The simplest procedure entails computing an unweighted average of all effect sizes included in a review—that is, a meta-analyst calculates the sum of the individual effect sizes and then divides the latter value by k, where k equals the number of effect sizes included in the analysis (for a recent example in psychology and law, see Clark, Howell, & Davey, 2008). This strategy is problematic, however, when effect sizes are derived from studies of varying sample sizes. Intuition suggests that studies with large sample sizes yield "better" estimates of the population effect size than do studies with small sample sizes. Statistical theory confirms this intuition. Indeed, the standard error of an effect size is always a function of a study's sample size. As sample sizes increase, the standard errors of the effect sizes decrease. Effect sizes with small standard errors provide more precise estimates of the population effect size than do effect sizes with large standard errors. For this reason, meta-analyses do not typically employ unweighted analyses when estimating the population effect size.

As noted previously, a primary goal of meta-analysis involves estimating the strength of a relationship by combining sample effect sizes to estimate the population effect size. However, research synthesists should also attend to the variability of sample effect sizes in a given domain (see Borenstein et al., 2009; Cooper, Hedges, & Valentine, 2009; Hedges & Olkin, 1985; Lipsey & Wilson, 2001).

Fixed-Effects vs. Random-Effects Models

Two statistical models typically serve as the basis for analyzing meta-analytic data—a fixed-effects model and a random-effects model. Model selection can influence effect-size computations, the results of significance tests, and the interpretation of meta-analytic findings. The fixed-effects (FE) model assumes that the sample effect sizes that are included in a meta-analysis are homogeneous—that is, the model assumes that each sample effect size in a review estimates the same parameter or population value. From this perspective, each sample effect size in the meta-analysis is interchangeable with every other sample effect size included in the meta-analysis. Presumably, sample effect sizes differ in magnitude solely due to sampling error.

In contrast, the random-effects (RE) model assumes that the sample effect sizes in a meta-analysis are heterogeneous and thus *do not* estimate a single population value (Higgins, Thompson, & Spiegelhalter, 2009). Indeed, the RE model assumes that each sample effect size that is included in a review may estimate a unique parameter or population value. For example, if a reviewer retrieves 30 *sample effect sizes*, the meta-analysis may include estimates of 30 different *population effect sizes*; these population effect sizes may differ in magnitude due to countless moderator variables that influence the phenomenon under investigation. In other words, the RE model assumes that there is no single population effect size that characterizes the phenomenon; rather, there exists a distribution of population effect sizes that characterizes the general phenomenon under various conditions. Stated in the extreme, an RE analysis is appropriate when sample effect sizes are heterogeneous and the reviewer seeks to draw inferences that generalize beyond the specific set of studies and contexts under review (Hedges & Vevea, 1998; Raudenbush, 2009; Schmidt, Oh, & Hayes, 2009).

A fixed-effects analysis assumes that the sample effect sizes within a meta-analysis vary in magnitude solely due to the sampling error associated with estimating a single population value. In contrast, a random-effects analysis assumes that the variability among sample effect sizes arises from two sources: (1) variability due to sampling error associated with estimating each unique population effect size in the meta-analysis and (2) variability among the *population* effect sizes themselves (the latter variability is referred to as a *random-variance parameter*). The variance term that is used to weight each sample effect size in a random effects meta-analysis includes both sources of variability. Consequently, the variance terms that are computed in an RE analysis are always larger than the variance terms that are computed in an FE analysis. An FE analysis usually requires a larger number of studies to estimate the random variance component and to generalize to a population of studies (for a detailed discussion, see Raudenbush, 2009). Perhaps, a compromise strategy is to calculate and report results of both models and compare the resulting conclusions (Cooper, 2010).

MODERATOR ANALYSES

Either on the basis of a priori theoretical considerations or as a consequence of the observed heterogeneity, practically all meta-analyses today include a search for moderator variables. The procedure frequently used is analogous to ANOVA, with the k hypothesis tests grouped ("blocked") into two or more subgroups on the basis of some study descriptor (e.g., laboratory vs. field experiment, or student vs. community participants, or jury deliberation vs. no group discussion). For example, in a meta-analysis of studies evaluating a new interview technique for interrogating witnesses (or suspects), participants were either college students, police trainees, or experienced police officers. All participants were randomly assigned to employ either the new interview technique or a standard interview-control technique. Effect sizes that were derived from studies with student participants could be compared with effect sizes that were derived from studies with police trainees pooled together with experienced officers. Accordingly, contrasts are constructed analogous to ANOVA (in this case, using $-2, +1, +1$ as contrast parameters; see Konstantopoulos & Hedges, 2009). Such blocking or groupings can be done a priori, based on theoretical considerations, or the groupings can be constructed post hoc.

However, multiple blocked comparisons of a small set of studies are problematic because these comparisons capitalize on chance. The latter comparisons are also likely to be confounded due to the covariation among the grouping variables tested (a problem that is analogous to collinearity in multiple-regression analysis). Before engaging in such analyses, the categorical variables to be used should be checked by cross-tabulation analyses to detect such dependencies and to avoid small (or even empty) cells.

These comparisons can be used to compare groups of studies, individual studies, and an individual study with a group of studies (Konstantopoulos & Hedges, 2009).

REPORTING AND INTERPRETATION OF META-ANALYSES

Reporting

All steps in conducting a meta-analysis should be carefully documented, and databases should be kept to allow other investigators to conduct additional analyses or check the accuracy of reported ones. A consortium of meta-analysis experts has elaborated and refined the Meta-Analysis Reporting Standards (MARS; American Psychological Association, 2008; see also Clarke, 2009; Cooper, 2010) that should be used as guidelines. Lipsey and Wilson (2001), Borman and Grigg (2009), and most recently Cooper (2010) provide useful suggestions regarding the presentation of meta-analytic findings, including visual displays and graphs. The authors also provide suggestions for presenting difficult concepts within consumer-friendly interpretation formats.

Interpretation of Meta-Analyses

Several issues should be considered when interpreting the results of a meta-analysis, including the rigor of the review, the number of samples included in the analysis, the magnitude of the estimated effect size, and the practical importance of the findings. Deciding if a reported effect size should be considered small, medium, or large should not be determined solely by using Cohen's (1988) informal recommendations; the judgment depends on the dependent variable under investigation. For example, a "small" effect size may be considered highly significant when the dependent variable is the death penalty as opposed to credibility ratings of a laboratory-told story.

As more and more meta-analyses in a given domain become available, *empirical distributions* of estimated population effect sizes can be constructed, and the results of a given meta-analysis can be located with respect to these distributions. Thus, an estimate of a mean effect size for a given meta-analysis may be compared with mean effect sizes for relationships in similar research areas (see Lipsey & Wilson, 1993, for an example). Hence, the practical and theoretical importance of an effect size is not determined solely by its magnitude, and Cohen's guidelines should not be applied mechanically when interpreting effect sizes reported in meta-analytic reviews. Also, mean effect sizes should never be interpreted in isolation but always with respect to the homogeneity or heterogeneity of findings as well as the impact of potential moderators.

PUBLICATION BIAS

Reviews that rely solely on published studies may be subject to publication bias and thus may overestimate the magnitude of association under investigation. Similarly, reviews that rely on a limited number of samples may yield effect-size estimates that are unstable—that is, the effect size estimate could change with the inclusion of a few additional studies. Rosenthal (1979) and Orwin (1983) have developed procedures for estimating the number of additional studies with null findings that would need to be added to a meta-analysis to reduce the estimated effect size to zero (or to a specified value; Orwin, 1983). The latter number of studies is often referred to as the "failsafe *N*." However, more sophisticated graphical and mathematical methods are available to assess publication bias and the possible mechanisms underlying it (see Sutton, 2009).

Several studies suggest that authors are more inclined to submit significant findings for publication than nonsignificant findings. Cooper, DeNeve, and Charlton (1997), for example, tracked the publication history of 159 studies that were approved by an institutional review board. Approximately 74% of the studies that yielded significant findings were submitted for publication; in contrast, only 4% of the studies that did not yield significant findings were submitted for publication. Research journals are more likely to publish papers that report significant findings than papers that report nonsignificant findings. Jointly, these tendencies contribute to a phenomenon referred to as *publication bias*. Notably, that bias may distort the estimated effect size that is reported in a meta-analysis if the meta-analysis relies solely on published data. In the psychology and law arena, Lösel and Schmucker's (2005) meta-analysis observed larger effects for the treatment of sexual offenders in published studies ($OR = 1.62$) than in unpublished studies (1.16).

Thus, it is important that meta-analysts strive to identify both published and unpublished studies to include in their reviews.

VALIDITY OF META-ANALYTIC SYNTHESIS

As with many innovations, meta-analysis was initially greeted with skepticism, ranging from blank rejection, as in Eysenck's (1978) critique of meta-analyses as an exercise in "mega-silliness," to skepticism arising from the concern that meta-analysts combine findings from studies with disparate designs and dependent variables (the "apples and oranges" problem; see Mullen, 1989; Rosenthal, 1991). The growing sophistication in meta-analytic statistical theories and techniques may not have been accompanied by a comparably sophisticated reception and critical analysis of meta-analytic approaches and findings. Nonetheless, critical discussions of meta-analytic methods are available, and both consumers and synthesists ought be aware of these debates (e.g., Cooper, 2009, 2010; Cooper & Hedges, 2009; Lipsey & Wilson, 2001; Matt, 2003; Matt & Cook, 2009; Rosenthal, 1991). We have already discussed the problem of publication bias and its implications for psychology and law.

A particularly thorny issue is the extent to which meta-analyses allow causal conclusions, which is discussed quite controversially (see Cooper, 2009, 2010; Cooper & Hedges, 2009). Strictly speaking, meta-analyses can provide only evidence about associations between variables, not causal conclusions. Thus, meta-analyses are in essence correlational techniques, with all the pitfalls associated with their interpretation. Taking this point to the extreme would imply that even when all studies in a meta-analysis consist of well-controlled experiments, with random assignment of participants to conditions (Campbell & Stanley, 1963), causal conclusions are not possible. Here, the distinction between study-generated and synthesis-generated evidence by Cooper (2009, 2010) and Cooper and Harris (2009) may be useful. Only study-generated evidence, provided that appropriate experimental designs were used, allows causal conclusions. Synthesis-generated evidence, on the other hand, depends on the procedural variations across studies that may have contributed to the strength of the observed effect sizes. As long as we are simply concerned with main effects in our research synthesis of experimental studies that have tested the question of interest with strict random assignment (e.g., the role of group discussion on jury verdicts), causal conclusions may be drawn with some confidence. In fact, one could even hope that, by using variations in procedures, some irrelevant features may cancel each other out by virtue of multiple operationalism (e.g., variations of the duration of discussion or case complexity).

However, when moderator variables are investigated, we are no longer studying main effects but the validity of conclusions as a function of other independent variables. In other words, we are concerned about an interaction between some other variable (e.g., participants eligible for jury duty vs. college students) and the variable of interest (group discussion). The problem with the use of post-hoc (or even a priori) moderator variables is that they are often confounded with other variables characteristic of individual studies. For example, jury studies with college students may use more complex experimental designs but less realistic stimulus materials ("vignettes"). Thus, even when comparisons between subgroups of studies sharing particular procedural features may use statistical procedures to control some of these confounds (e.g., via meta-regression), our confidence in inferences regarding the effect of these moderator variables ought to be considerably reduced. Nonetheless, research syntheses may uncover complex dependencies between moderator variables associated with the effect of interest that may not yet have been investigated at all and primary studies. Hence, research syntheses can also be considered useful for generating hypotheses for future research.

Specific efforts have been taken by meta-analysts to develop lists of criteria that may threaten meta-analytic conclusions. These threats to validity were partially derived, adapted, and refined from threats to validity in primary research continually developed by Campbell and Stanley (1963); Cook and Campbell (1979); and Shadish, Cook, and Campbell (2002); which were classified into statistical conclusion validity, internal validity, construct validity of putative causes and effects, and external validity.

The specific threats to conclusions from meta-analytic syntheses are listed in Matt and Cook (2009), but space limitations do not permit discussion and potential solutions to these problems (see Cooper, 2010; Matt, 2003; Matt & Cook, 2009).

CONCLUSIONS

Meta-analyses are here to stay, and they will increase in importance. Consequently, the methodology and statistical theory and methods will be steadily improved. Researchers aspiring to conduct a meta-analysis should review these recent developments (see Borenstein et al., 2009; Cooper, 2010; Cooper & Hedges, 2009; Cooper et al., 2009). Instead of a summary, we conclude with a checklist for conducting and evaluating meta-analytic syntheses (for more thorough lists, see Cooper, 2010; Cooper & Hedges, 2009), which we formulate as questions:

1. Were the research hypotheses stated in terms of available psychological theories, and were the conceptual definitions of variables clearly operationalized? Were inclusion and exclusion criteria specified and adhered to in the review?
2. Did the literature search use multiple, complementary approaches? Were efforts made to locate unpublished studies? Were the search strategies, the search terms, and the results of the search clearly documented?
3. Was the coding of study characteristics and outcomes guided by precise operationalizations? Was inter-coder reliability established and reported for all aspects of the synthesis? How were disagreements resolved?
4. Was the choice of effect sizes appropriate for the designs of the primary studies? To what extent were data missing in the database and how were missing data handled?
5. Was the choice of statistical approach (e.g., fixed-effects, random-effects, mixed model) justified? Were the tests of associations appropriate for the questions asked? Were statistical assumptions tested and justified?
6. In addition to mean effect sizes and confidence intervals, was homogeneity tested and reported? Were moderators considered on the basis of theory-driven a priori hypotheses, or did synthesists engage in a post hoc fishing expedition?
7. Can the selection of studies be considered representative with respect to participants, treatments, interventions and constructs, outcome measures, settings, and time?
8. Were the questions originally asked answered appropriately? Did the authors discuss both the generality and the limitations of the

meta-analysis' results? Did the authors compare the findings with the magnitude of effects in comparable research domains? Did the authors distinguish between study-generated evidence (which may allow causal conclusions) and synthesis-generated evidence? Were the practical conclusions justified based on the data presented?

9. Were the results presented clearly—that is, communicated in a way to address both scientists and nonscientists? Were policy implications stated, along with cautionary statements about areas of lack of knowledge?

10. Were research deficits identified and implications for theory-building and future research spelled out?

REFERENCES

American Psychological Association. (2008). Reporting standards for research in psychology: Why do we need them? What might they be? *American Psychologist, 63,* 839–851.

Beal, D. J., Corey, D. M., & Dunlap, W. P. (2002). On the bias of Huffcutt and Arthur's (1995) procedure on identifying outliers in the meta-analysis of correlations. *Journal of Applied Psychology, 87,* 583–589.

Borenstein, M. (2009). Effect sizes for continuous data. In H. Cooper, L. V. Hedges, & J. C. Valentine (Eds.), *The handbook of research synthesis and meta-analysis* (2nd ed., pp. 221–235). New York, NY: Russell Sage Foundation.

Borenstein, M., Hedges, L., Higgins, J., & Rothstein, H. R. (2009). *Computing effect sizes for meta-analysis.* Chichester, England: Wiley.

Borman, G. D., & Grigg, J. A. (2009). Visual and narrative interpretation. In H. Cooper, L. V. Hedges, & J. C. Valentine (Eds.), *The handbook of research synthesis and meta-analysis* (2nd ed., pp. 497–519). New York, NY: Russell Sage Foundation.

Bushman, B. J., & Wang, M. C. (1995). A procedure for combining sample correlation coefficients and vote counts to obtain an estimate and a confidence interval for the population correlation coefficient. *Psychological Bulletin, 117,* 530–546.

Bushman, B. J., & Wang, M. C. (1996). A procedure for combining sample standardized mean differences and vote counts to estimate the population standardized mean difference in fixed effects model. *Psychological Methods, 1,* 66–80.

Bushman, B. J., & Wang, M. C. (2009). Vote-counting procedures in meta-analysis. In H. Cooper, L. V. Hedges, & J. C. Valentine (Eds.), *The handbook of research synthesis and meta-analysis* (2nd ed., pp. 207–220). New York, NY: Russell Sage Foundation.

Campbell, D. T., & Stanley, J. C. (1963). *Experimental and quasi-experimental designs for research.* Chicago, IL: Rand McNally.

Clark, S. E., Howell, R. T., & Davey, S. L. (2008). Regularities in eyewitness identification. *Law and Human Behavior, 32,* 187–218.

Clarke, M. (2009). Reporting format. In H. Cooper, L. V. Hedges, & J. C. Valentine (Eds.), *The handbook of research synthesis and meta-analysis* (2nd ed., pp. 521–534). New York, NY: Russell Sage Foundation.

Cohen, J. (1988). *Statistical power analysis for the behavioral sciences* (2nd ed.). Hillsdale, NJ: Lawrence Erlbaum.

Cohn, L. D., & Becker, B. J. (2003). How meta-analysis increases statistical power. *Psychological Methods, 8,* 243–253.

Cook, T. D., & Campbell, D. T. (1979). *Quasi-experimentation: Design and analysis issues for field settings.* Chicago, IL: Rand McNally.

Cooper, H., & Hedges, L. V. (1994). Research synthesis as a scientific enterprise. In H. Cooper, & L. V. Hedges (Eds.), *The handbook of research synthesis* (pp. 3–14). New York, NY: Russell Sage Foundation.

Cooper, H. (2009). Hypotheses and problems in research synthesis. In H. Cooper, L. V. Hedges, & J. C. Valentine (Eds.), *The handbook of research synthesis and meta-analysis* (2nd ed., pp. 19–35). New York, NY: Russell Sage Foundation.

Cooper, H. (2010). *Research synthesis and meta-analysis: A step-by-step approach.* Los Angeles, CA: Sage.

Cooper, H., DeNeve, K., & Charlton, K. (1997). Finding the missing science: The fate of studies submitted for review by a human subjects committee. *Psychological Methods, 2*, 447–452.

Cooper, H., & Hedges, L. V. (2009). Potentials and limitations. In H. Cooper, L. V. Hedges, & J. C. Valentine (Eds.), *The handbook of research synthesis and meta-analysis* (2nd ed., pp. 561–572). New York, NY: Russell Sage Foundation.

Cooper, H., Hedges, L. V., & Valentine, J. C. (Eds.). (2009). *The handbook of research synthesis and meta-analysis* (2nd ed.). New York, NY: Russell Sage Foundation.

Cortina, J. M., & Nouri, H. (2000). *Effect size for ANOVA designs.* Thousand Oaks, CA: Sage.

Daubert v. Merrell Dow Pharmaceuticals, 509 U. S. 579 (1993).

Dunlap, W. P., Cortina, J., Vaslow, J. B., & Burke, M. J. (1996). Meta-analysis of experiments with matched groups or repeated measures designs. *Psychological Methods, 1*, 170–177.

Eysenck, H. J. (1978). An exercise in mega-silliness. *American Psychologist, 33*, 517.

Fleiss, J. L. (1994). Measures of effect size for categorical data. In H. Cooper, & L. V. Hedges (Eds.), *The handbook of research synthesis* (pp. 245–260). New York, NY: Russell Sage Foundation.

Fleiss, J. L., & Berlin, J. A. (2009). Effect sizes for dichotomous data. In H. Cooper, L. V. Hedges, & J. C. Valentine (Eds.), *The handbook of research synthesis and meta-analysis* (2nd ed., pp. 237–253). New York, NY: Russell Sage Foundation.

Fleiss, J. L., Levin, B., & Paik, M. C. (2003). *Statistical methods for rates and proportions* (3rd ed.). Hoboken, NJ: Wiley.

Gleser, L. J., & Olkin, I. (1994). Stochastically dependent effect sizes. In H. Cooper, & L. V. Hedges (Eds.), *The handbook of research synthesis* (pp. 339–355). New York, NY: Russell Sage Foundation.

Gleser, L. J., & Olkin, I. (2009). Stochastically dependent effect sizes. In H. Cooper, L. V. Hedges, & J. C. Valentine (Eds.), *The handbook of research synthesis and meta-analysis* (2nd ed., pp. 357–376). New York, NY: Russell Sage Foundation.

Haddock, C. K., Rindskopf, D., & Shadish, W. R. (1998). Using odds ratios as effect sizes for meta-analysis of dichotomous data: A primer on methods and issues. *Psychological Methods, 3*, 339–353.

Hedges, L. V., & Olkin, I. (1985). *Statistical methods for meta-analysis.* New York, NY: Academic Press.

Hedges, L. V., & Vevea, J. L. (1998). Fixed- and random-effects models in meta-analysis. *Psychological Methods, 3*, 486–504.

Higgins, J. P. T., & Green, S. (2008). *Cochrane handbook for systematic reviews of interventions.* Chichester, England: Wiley.

Higgins, J. P. T., & Thompson, S. G. (2002). Quantifying heterogeneity in a meta-analysis. *Statistics in Medicine, 21*, 1539–1558.

Higgins, J. P. T., Thompson, S. G., & Spiegelhalter, D. J. (2009). A re-evaluation of random-effects meta-analysis. *Journal of the Royal Statistical Society Series A: Statistics in Society, 172*, 137–159.

Huffcutt, A. I., & Arthur, W. (1995). Development of a new outlier statistic for meta-analytic data. *Journal of Applied Psychology, 80*, 327–334.

Hunter, J. E., & Schmidt, F. L. (1990). *Methods of meta-analysis. Correcting error and bias in research findings* (1st ed.) Thousand Oaks, CA: Sage.

Hunter, J. E., & Schmidt, F. L. (2004). *Methods of meta-analysis. Correcting error and bias in research findings* (2nd ed.). Thousand Oaks, CA: Sage.

Konstantopoulos, S., & Hedges, L. V. (2009). Analyzing effect sizes: Fixed-effects models. In H. Cooper, L. V. Hedges, & J. C. Valentine (Eds.), *The handbook of research synthesis and meta-analysis* (2nd ed., pp. 279–293). New York, NY: Russell Sage Foundation.

Lipsey, M. W., & Wilson, D. B. (1993). The efficacy of psychological, educational, and behavioral treatment. *American Psychologist, 48*, 1181–1209.

Lipsey, M. W., & Wilson, D. B. (2001). *Practical meta-analysis.* Thousand Oaks, CA: Sage.

Lösel, F., & Schmucker, M. (2005). The effectiveness of treatment for sexual offenders: A comprehensive meta-analysis. *Journal of Experimental Criminology, 1*, 117–146.

Matt, G. E. (2003). Will it work in Münster? Meta-analysis and the empirical generalization of causal relationships. In R. Schulze, H. Holling, & D. Böhning (Eds.), *Meta-analysis: New developments and applications in medical and social sciences* (pp. 113–139). Göttingen, Germany: Hogrefe & Huber.

Matt, G. E., & Cook, T. D. (2009). Threats to the validity of generalized inferences. In H. Cooper, L. V. Hedges, & J. C. Valentine (Eds.), *The handbook of research synthesis and meta-analysis* (2nd ed., pp. 537–560). New York, NY: Russell Sage Foundation.

Morris, S. B. (2008). Estimating effect sizes from pretest-posttest-control group designs. *Organizational Research Methods, 11,* 364–386.

Morris, S. B., & DeShon, R. P. (2002). Combining effect size estimates in meta-analysis with repeated measures and independent-groups designs. *Psychological Methods, 7,* 105–125.

Mullen, B. (1989). *Advanced BASIC meta-analysis.* Hillsdale, NJ: Lawrence Erlbaum.

Orwin, R. G. (1983). A fail-safe N for effect size in meta-analysis. *Journal of Educational Statistics, 8,* 157–159.

Orwin, R. G., & Vevea, J. L. (2009). Evaluating coding decisions. In H. Cooper, L. V. Hedges, & J. C. Valentine (Eds.), *The handbook of research synthesis and meta-analysis* (2nd ed., pp. 177–205). New York, NY: Russell Sage Foundation.

Pigott, T. D. (1994). Methods of handling missing data in research synthesis. In H. Cooper, & L. V. Hedges (Eds.), *The handbook of research synthesis* (pp. 163–175). New York, NY: Russell Sage Foundation.

Pigott, T. D. (2009). Handling missing data. In H. Cooper, L. V. Hedges, & J. C. Valentine (Eds.), *The handbook of research synthesis and meta-analysis* (2nd ed., pp. 399–416). New York, NY: Russell Sage Foundation.

Raudenbush, S. W. (2009). Analyzing effect sizes: Random-effects models. In H. Cooper, L. V. Hedges, & J. C. Valentine (Eds.), *The handbook of research synthesis and meta-analysis* (2nd ed., pp. 295–315). New York, NY: Russell Sage Foundation.

Ray, J. W., & Shadish, W. (1996). How interchangeable are different estimators of effect size? *Journal of Consulting and Clinical Psychology, 64,* 1316–1325.

Reed, J. G., & Baxter, P. M. (2009). Using reference databases. In H. Cooper, L. V. Hedges, & J. C. Valentine (Eds.), *The handbook of research synthesis and meta-analysis* (2nd ed., pp. 73–101). New York, NY: Russell Sage Foundation.

Rosenthal, R. (1979). The "file drawer problem" and tolerance for null results. *Psychological Bulletin, 86,* 638–641.

Rosenthal, R. (1991). *Meta-analytic procedures for social research.* Newbury Park, CA: Sage.

Rosenthal, R. (1994). Parametric measures of effect size. In H. Cooper, & L. V. Hedges (Eds.), *The handbook of research synthesis* (pp. 231–244). New York, NY: Russell Sage Foundation.

Sánchez-Meca, J., Marín-Martinez, F., & Chacón-Moscoso, S. (2003). Effect-size indices for dichotomized outcomes in meta-analysis. *Psychological Methods, 8,* 448–467.

Shadish, W. R., Cook, T. D., & Campbell, D. T. (2002). *Experimental and quasi-experimental designs for generalized causal inference.* Boston, MA: Houghton Mifflin.

Schmidt, F. L., Oh, I. S., & Hayes, T. L. (2009). Fixed- versus random-effects models in meta-analysis: Model properties and an empirical comparison of differences in results. *British Journal of Mathematical & Statistical Psychology, 62,* 97–128.

Sporer, S. L., & Schwandt, B. (2007). Moderators of nonverbal indicators of deception: A meta-analytic synthesis. *Psychology, Public Policy, and Law, 13,* 1–34.

Sutton, A. J. (2009). Publication bias. In H. Cooper, L. V. Hedges, & J. C. Valentine (Eds.), *The handbook of research synthesis and meta-analysis* (2nd ed., pp. 435–452). New York, NY: Russell Sage Foundation.

Viechtbauer, W. (2007). Approximate confidence intervals for standardized effect sizes in the two-independent and two-dependent samples design. *Journal of Educational and Behavioral Statistics, 32,* 39–60.

White, H. D. (2009). Scientific communication and literature retrieval. In H. Cooper, L. V. Hedges, & J. C. Valentine (Eds.), *The handbook of research synthesis and meta-analysis* (2nd ed., pp. 51–71). New York, NY: Russell Sage Foundation.

Wilson, D. B. (2009). Identifying interesting variables and analysis opportunities. In H. Cooper, L. V. Hedges, & J. C. Valentine (Eds.), *The handbook of research synthesis and meta-analysis* (2nd ed., pp. 159–176). New York, NY: Russell Sage Foundation.

CHAPTER 4

Forensic Psychological Research and the Internet

TARIKA DAFTARY-KAPUR AND SARAH GREATHOUSE

SINCE THE FIRST online studies were conducted in the mid-1990s (Krantz, Ballard, & Scher, 1997; Welch & Krantz, 1996), the use of Web-based psychological research has rapidly increased; between 1998 and 1999 the number of psychological studies conducted online doubled (O'Neil, Penrod, & Bornstein, 2003). During the past decade, online data collection has been used to conduct both survey research and experimental research that allows participants to be randomly assigned to view various stimuli, including audio and video stimuli. The use of online studies has expanded researchers' access to potential participants across the world and has allowed researchers greater access to special populations that previously may have been difficult to reach in significant numbers. According to the U.S. Census Bureau, Internet usage has increased 128% from 2000 to 2008, with over 59% of the population having Internet access (www.census.gov). Due to the multiple advantages of online data collection methods and access to broader, possibly more generalizable populations, it is reasonable to assume that the use of Web-based studies will continue to grow. As the popularity of online studies increases, researchers will surely continue to develop innovative methods of collecting data online.

The Internet offers new opportunities and possible avenues for research in forensic psychology, including but not limited to research on eyewitness identifications, juror decision making, forensic assessment tools, and special populations. Although some psycholegal research has used online data collection methods (e.g., Chrzanowski, 2006; Daftary-Kapur, 2009; Levett & Kovera, 2008), it is our view that the use of Web-based studies in psycholegal research could be expanded as one of the basic methods researchers use to investigate the workings of the legal system. This chapter is designed to introduce forensic psychologists to the methods involved in conducting survey and experimental research over the Internet. This chapter covers both the various advantages and potential issues with Web-based studies that researchers using online data collection methods should consider and provides some examples of successfully conducted online research in the field of forensic psychology.

TYPES OF WEB-BASED RESEARCH

The Internet can be used for conducting research using various research methodologies that are traditionally employed in psychological studies. Two of those most often used by forensic psychologists and are discussed in detail in this chapter are survey methods and experimental methods.

Several researchers have suggested that the Internet can be an effective means of collecting survey data. Musch and Reips (2000) interviewed psychologists who had conducted Internet studies and found that some of the advantages cited included access to a larger population, lower costs, and complete voluntary participation. Given that the administration of survey tools requires very little, if any, experimenter participation, the Web is ideal for collecting data when this methodology is appropriate for a study. Despite its perceived advantages, many researchers have speculated about the pros and cons of using the Internet for research (Kraut et al., 2004; Schmidt, 1997). To address these concerns, researchers have conducted empirical analyses of the quality of Internet data—specifically survey data collected from self-selected Internet samples.

Riva, Teruzzi, and Anolli (2003) compared responses to a questionnaire collected via traditional methods to those collected over the Web. They found no differences in the psychometric properties or the internal reliability of the survey between the two samples, thus providing support to the viability of Web-based research as an alternative to traditional methods. Gosling, Vazire, Srivastava, and John (2004) conducted a comparative analysis with traditional paper-and-pencil data of six preconceptions about Web-based questionnaires. They found that Internet samples were relatively diverse and comparable to those found using traditional methods, results generalize across presentation formats, findings are not adversely affected by repeat responders, and findings are consistent with traditional methods.

A second methodology commonly used by researchers in psychology is that of random-assignment experimental design. There are a number of Web sites that allow for the use of these design procedures using the Web (e.g., studyresponse.com; psychsurveys.org). In addition, researchers familiar with HTML can design their own Web sites using various hosts (e.g., cPanel.net). Concerns have been raised regarding whether experimental data collected online are comparable to data collected in the lab. Some of these concerns involve issues such as lack of control over the experimental setting and lack of motivation on the part of the participants. Metzger, Kristof, and Yoest (2003) compared face-recognition data collected online with data collected from undergraduates in a classroom setting. They found no significant differences in the results of the two groups. O'Neil, Penrod, and Bornstein (2003) found that sample type (students vs. non-students) was related to sample character-istics, but this was moderated by other variables, such as asking for personal information. At the same time, no published research exists in the field of forensic psychology that has specifically examined the differences between traditional methods and Web-based research, although results from other fields are likely to generalize (O'Neil & Penrod, 2003).

WHY WEB EXPERIMENTS?

Traditional forms of research allow for two basic types of experiments—experiments in the laboratory and those in the field. Both these categories have inherent limitations, including but not limited to small participant pools, limited sample populations, limited external validity, questionable voluntar-iness on the part of participants (e.g., psychology students who are required to participate in experiments to fulfill course requirements), motivational confounding, experimenter bias, and organizational limitations in laboratory experiments versus limited control in field studies, (Reips, 2000). Given these limitations, there appears to be a need to validate laboratory findings using other methodologies. Web-based studies allow for this validation while allowing for experimental research into previously unexplored areas.

Some researchers believe that data collected via the Web is "better" than that collected in the lab. One reason for this belief is that participants in Web-based studies are volunteers and may have an interest in the study as compared with student participants who are required to participate for course credit (Reips, 2000). Additionally, many researchers (Birnbaum, 2004), including the authors, have received messages from Web participants expressing their interest in the findings and providing encouragement for the research. There is a sense, one that is currently untested among Web-based researchers, that Web participants are more invested in the research and take the task more seriously. On the other hand, participants may provide false information via the Internet as it is somewhat anonymous, even in situations where identifying information is requested.

Another consideration is that the Internet creates new social situations (Bargh & McKenna, 2004). People may create new identities and, feeling anonymous, respond differently than they would in person. This can lead to either more honest or more dishonest responding. If the theory that anonym-ity leads to more honest responding holds true, this would bode well for research in forensic psychology, where more often than not sensitive matters are the topic of discussion. For example, certain types of forensic assessments that cover sensitive topics may yield better data when collected over the Web than in a lab with an experimenter present.

ADVANTAGES OF WEB-BASED RESEARCH

If the design of a study allows for online data collection, there are several features of Web-based studies that researchers may find advantageous. First,

Web-based studies may address some of the common criticisms of traditional laboratory and field research, including issues of generalizability, issues of possible experimenter expectancy effects, and issues of low power. Second, the ease associated with conducting and participating in Web-based studies reduces administrative difficulties common in lab and field studies. Finally, Web-based studies may also address ethical issues researchers must consider when conducting lab or field research that require participants to be physically present for data collection.

In many psychological studies, undergraduate psychology students attending the researcher's institution serve as the participants. The predominant use of psychology student participants has sparked many debates concerning the generalizability of psychological research findings beyond the 18- to 21-year-old college student population. This is particularly relevant in the field of forensic psychology. Research conducted online presents researchers with the opportunity to collect data from a more diverse sample of the population. Although limiting the sample to individuals with access to an online computer does not reach all members of the population, research indicates that Internet samples are more diverse than traditional student populations (Reips, 1996; Best, Krueger, Hubbard, & Smith, 2001). A number of Web sites that specialize in recruiting participants (e.g., studyresponse. com) practice random sampling methods in an attempt to obtain a representative sample of the population.

It should be noted that the use of undergraduate psychology students as participants is not necessarily cause for concern (Mook, 1983). However, the legal community may perceive forensic research conducted with college student participants as nongeneralizable to the population of interest (e.g., jurors, eyewitnesses, police officers, etc). Moreover, because forensic psychological research is often driven by the goal of improving and influencing the legal system, there is additional incentive for forensic researchers to attempt to increase the ecological validity of a study by using community member participants. Although they may not result in a perfect representation of the population, Internet-based studies provide the opportunity to gather data from a wider geographic location and a more diverse sample than may be feasible with laboratory-based studies.

In addition, if researchers are seeking participants who may not be present in high enough numbers in any one specific geographic location, online studies provide researchers with more far-reaching access to a specific population. For example, one program of research examining the diagnosticity of attorneys' questions to potential jurors during jury selection required the participation of several hundred attorneys and advanced law students (Crocker, Busso, Greathouse, & Kovera, 2008; Crocker, Busso, Kennard, & Greathouse, 2009). Recruiting a large number of attorneys and law students to attend a laboratory study in a single geographic location would have been difficult. The researchers instead employed an online collection method in which the attorneys were invited to participate in a Web-based study via email. If they were interested in participating, the attorneys or law students were provided with a link to the study Web site, where they were randomly assigned to one of several experimental conditions. Across a series of studies, data was gathered from hundreds of prosecutors, defense attorneys, and law students across the country. Online data collection provided busy attorneys with the opportunity to participate in the research without having to make time in their schedules to be physically present in a lab study, and the researchers were able to gather a larger and more diverse sample than was available to them in their immediate geographic location.

In another study Chrzanowski (2006) recruited students from three states (Florida, California, and New York) to participate in a jury study that was conducted online. This study was conducted over six sessions, each 30 minutes in length, over a period of one month. The Internet provided an ideal medium to allow for data collection on a large scale, across the country, with few associated costs. Additionally, given the convenience factor for participants, who could access the study from disparate locations and did not have to come in to the laboratory for the six sessions, attrition rates were low. This design was replicated by Daftary-Kapur (2009) using community member participants in Boston and New York, for a study that lasted 10 weeks. Attrition rates were relatively low, only 12%.

Another population of interest for forensic psychologists is experts in different areas of the fields, such as eyewitness identification, sexual harassment, forensic assessments, mental health issues, and so on. Collecting data from these experts through lab-based studies would be somewhat difficult because of the limitations previously mentioned. Web-based methods provide the opportunity to conduct surveys and experimental studies with these special populations across the United States and around the world with little time investment and expense. One line of research surveyed experts on their experience with gender-intrusive lines of questioning in the courtroom (Daftary, O'Connor, & Mechanic, 2007) using a Web survey hosted on www .surveymonkey.com. Responses were received from experts around the country, as well as internationally. Self-identified experts in various forensic-related fields were queried as to their experiences with various types of questioning by attorneys in the courtroom. More than 200 responses were received within a week of posting the survey, illustrating the ease of data collection via the Internet.

The Internet also provides us with the ability to reach experts in the field quite efficiently. Daftary and Penrod (2009) conducted a survey and experimental study of eyewitness experts, completing data collection in three days, with a response rate of 77%. This is an illustration of the ease and effectiveness with which the Internet can be used for data collection.

Demand characteristics, or particular aspects of an experimental design that could clue participants to the hypotheses of the study and subsequently influence participants' behavior, have traditionally been a concern for researchers conducting laboratory and field research. Online studies provide distance and structure to a study that may help combat the presence of demand characteristics. For example, when an experimenter is physically present during a study, it is possible he or she will unconsciously emit cues to the participants that will influence the participants' behavior in the direction of the experimenter's hypotheses. The existence of experimenter expectancy effects has consistently been demonstrated in laboratory and field research (see Rosenthal, 2002, for a review). By conducting experiments over the Internet and reducing the experimenter's contact with participants, the risk of experimenter expectancy effects could be significantly reduced.

Web-based studies can also provide solutions to low power issues, another common concern in psychological experiments (Erdfelder, Faul, & Buchner, 1996). To understand the workings of the legal system, forensic researchers may want to manipulate a number of independent variables, or they may want to understand mediational processes at work in legal decision making. Both instances require a large number of participants for sufficient power, and Web-based studies may be a viable option for researchers seeking to reach a large number of participants. The traditional method of increasing power is to increase the N or sample size in the experiment; however, experiments conducted in laboratories are often limited by time, lab space, and the participant pool available at the researcher's institution. When conducting studies over the Internet, researchers have access to more potential participants and are not limited by time and space constraints.

Access to a greater number of potential participants via the Internet can also be valuable for recruitment purposes when potential participants need to be screened for particular characteristics. For example, recent research examining the efficacy of voir dire in capital cases required participants who were qualified to serve in a death penalty case (Greathouse et al., 2008). To serve as a juror in a capital case, potential jurors must be able to state that they would be able to hear the case fairly, knowing that if convicted the defendant could be sentenced to death (Haney, 1984). To increase the ecological validity of the study, the researchers were seeking only those participants who would be able to answer the qualification questions affirmatively and could, therefore, potentially serve on a capital case.

Advertisements for the study were placed online, and interested participants were directed to an online screening survey containing the standard qualification questions that potential jurors must answer to serve on a capital case. The screening survey also gathered information relevant to the general requirements for jury service, including participant age and citizenship status. The researchers were able to download the data gathered from the screening survey, and those participants who were qualified to serve as jurors on a capital case were subsequently contacted to participate in the laboratory research. The online screening process also allowed researchers to gather information about participants' attitudes toward the death penalty prior to attending the laboratory study. Before coming into the laboratory, participants completed the Death Penalty Attitudes scale (DPA; O'Neil, Patry, & Penrod, 2004) as part of the online screening process. Researchers were then able to compare the DPA scores that were collected online, well before the participants attending study, with the participants' DPA scores at the end of the experiment.

Additional ease-of-administration aspects of Web-based studies may also factor in to a researcher's decision to employ online data collection methods. Less time is required on the part of the researcher in both the data collection and the data entry processes. Compared with lab or field research that requires researchers to be physically present during data collection, once the study Web pages have been created and uploaded, considerably less time is required from the researcher to collect the data. In addition, the data does not need to be entered (and possibly reentered) by the researcher. The lack of the need for manual data entry reduces errors resulting from incorrect data input. In addition, the study Web pages can be designed to reduce errors in participants' answers—for example, by eliminating the ability to choose multiple answers to a question. There is no need for physical lab space to collect the data from participants, and the participants are often free to participate at their convenience from their own homes, at the time of their choosing, as opposed to being restricted to times when both the researcher and the participant are able to be physically present in the laboratory.

Online data collection methods may also address ethical issues concerning the voluntariness of participation. Participants in lab experiments are informed that they are free to withdraw from the study at any time, but when participants are physically present in the laboratory with the researcher, it is possible they may feel obligated to stay. Participants in online studies may feel increased freedom to discontinue the study if they no longer wish to participate. As a result, the researcher can be more confident that participation is truly voluntary. Of course, the researcher must establish that drop-out rates in an online study do not differ between one experimental condition to another. If, for example, participants perceive a particular condition to be cumbersome and consequently discontinue participation at a higher rate in that condition as compared with other conditions, the internal validity of the study would be threatened. However, if there are no differences in drop-out rates between conditions, the presence of motivated and voluntary participants in online studies is an advantage.

The question still remains as to whether data collected online produce similar results to data collected in the laboratory or in the field. Although we know of no forensic research that has manipulated data collection methods in order to compare the results of laboratory participants versus online participants, research in other areas of psychology has begun to examine whether there are differences between the two samples. Research has generally found comparable results from online participants and laboratory participants (e.g., Best, Krueger, Hubbard, & Smith, 2001; Dandurand, Shultz, & Onishi, 2008; Davis, 1999; Riva, Teruzzi, & Anolli, 2003). Results from these studies provide some evidence that online data collection methods are a viable alternative to laboratory and field research. However, we believe it would be advantageous for forensic psychologists to employ studies that collect data from both online and traditional samples to test for differences in responses. As the popularity of online data collection methods in forensic psychological research increases, it will be important to assess the generalizability of findings across study methods.

VALIDITY OF INTERNET RESEARCH

As with any innovative research method, it is necessary to establish the validity of Web-based research. Since Web experiments are conducted in environments that are less controlled than lab experiments, researchers typically believe that the data obtained from Web experiments is less valid than the data obtained from lab experiments. To address this, many researchers have suggested either comparing results from Web-based studies with those obtained via traditional methods or determining whether the results obtained are in accord with theoretical predictions (Birnbaum, 2001; Buchanan & Smith 1999; Krantz & Dalal, 2000).

In general, survey methodologists have reported similar findings between Web-based and laboratory-based studies (Miller et al., 2002; Yun & Trumbo, 2000). Best, Krueger, Hubbard, and Smith (2001) found that Internet and non-Internet users recruited through probabilistic telephone sampling came to convergent political choice decisions using similar decision-making processes. A survey by Musch and Reips (2000) reported that data from 18 Web experiments and their lab replications were highly consistent. Krantz and Dalal (2000) summarized nine psychological studies that used Web-based versus laboratory methods and found that results were comparable in terms of main effects. Across all variables manipulated and measures used, findings were consistent in that Web findings were comparable to those of laboratory studies, providing support for the validity of Web-based studies. Similar studies have been conducted using survey methodology.

Penrod and O'Neil (2000) compared Web-based and paper-and-pencil methodologies in two studies of capital jury decision making. In the first study, participants for the Web-based version were recruited through email and direct mail solicitations from Texas, and participants were solicited from Nebraska and Texas for the paper version. The second study solicited undergraduates for the paper version, and a non-student national sample for the Web-based version. They found no main effects for method or sample type or any interactions with these variables and others tested in the study. At the same time, there was greater variance in the dependent variables in the Web-based sample as compared with the student sample in the second study.

One challenge for Internet-based research is to establish better control over internal validity. One way to test this is to conduct parallel studies using both traditional and Internet-based methods. Riva, Teruzzi, and Anolli (2003) administered attitude questionnaires to college students (traditional paper-and-pencil method) and community members recruited via online advertisements and email solicitations (Internet method). They found no significant differences in the responses as a function of method.

Researchers should also pay attention to various methodological variables associated with research over the Internet to ensure that different methods of doing Web-based research do not hurt the ecological validity of the research. O'Neil and Penrod (2001) examined a number of variables, including payment incentive, sample type, and requests for personal information as well as their influence on dropout and prediction of verdicts in a death penalty case. They found that offering payments did not decrease nonresponse error. At the same time, the request for personal information such as an email address marginally increased dropout rates. Additionally, the day of the week involved was related to dropout rates and predicted verdicts.

METHODOLOGICAL SUGGESTIONS IN CONDUCTING WEB-BASED RESEARCH IN FORENSIC PSYCHOLOGY

A number of factors should be taken into consideration when designing and conducting online studies. Some of these are reviewed in the following sections.

SAMPLING

Sampling to gain data that is representative of the population as a whole is always a challenge in research, and this can become pronounced in Web-based research. The sample by its very nature is restricted to Internet users who, as a group, may not be representative of the population as a whole. According to a survey by Rainie (2010), 76% of those who identify as White, 70% of those who identify as Black, and 64% of those who identify as Hispanic are Internet users. Approximately 74% of adult men and women use the Internet. In addition, 93% of those between the ages of 18 and 29 are Internet users, and this percentage decreases as age increases. Most people who have at least a college degree are Internet users (94%), whereas only 39% of those who have less than a high school degree use the Internet.

These findings indicate that some groups remain unrepresented in the online population. Thus researchers should look for ways to increase diversity in online samples. At the same time, one must remain cognizant of the sample that would have been obtained via alternative recruitment methods. If the alternative sampling method uses undergraduates enrolled in introductory psychology classes, the Internet sample may be somewhat more diverse and representative of the population. For research in experimental forensic psychology, a representative sample is highly desirable, given that much of the work is applied to real-world settings. Additionally the Internet allows for recruitment of a more targeted sample, which is often the case in clinical studies. For example, if the goal of the study is to examine the responses of people who are experiencing symptoms of depression, it may be easier to recruit them over the Internet, as there may be more willingness to participate when the process is somewhat anonymous.

Comparison of Lab-Based and Web-Based Studies   When planning research studies that are conducted online, researchers may want to conduct the same study with their university "participant pool" by having them come into the laboratory and complete the study on computers. Although a significant number of studies have been conducted in a number of domains that show little or no significant differences between online and traditional methods of data collection (e.g., Krantz & Dalal, 2000), few studies have been conducted in the domain of forensic psychology (see O'Neil & Penrod, 2001; O'Neill et al., 2003 for exceptions). Demonstrating the lack of significant differences in Web-based and traditional research methods can circumvent reviewer criticism regarding the efficacy of Web-based research.

Dropout Rate

A serious threat to the internal validity of a between-subjects experiment occurs when there are dropouts—people who begin a study and quit before completing it. This can be even more of a concern in studies with experimental designs as compared with survey studies, especially if dropout occurrence is systematic as a function of experimental conditions (Birnbaum, 2000a). Web-based research has been found to have larger dropout rates than lab studies. In the lab, the experimenter is present and a participant would have to give a reason for walking out of a research session. On the other hand, Web-based participants are free of such social pressures and can quit with the click of a button (Birnbaum, 2003). For example, O'Neil and Penrod (2001) found that there was a significant dropout factor over the course of a study. They found that out of 791 participants who received the first page of the study, 48% did not continue to the second page, and of those who did, 31% did not continue to the third page, which was the start of the research materials. It is possible that these participants dropped out based on their assessment of whether the research was of interest to them, the time commitment required, or possible compensation. Of those who did reach the research materials, 31% dropped out, leaving a total of 193 participants who completed the study. Additionally, they found that offering payment incentives did not influence dropout rates, whereas requesting personal information (email addresses) significantly increased dropout. When conducting online studies, researchers should systematically examine whether dropout is tied to specific experimental conditions or is random. Dropout tied to experimental conditions is of concern, as it could potentially influence the outcome of the study.

INTEGRITY OF RESPONSES

It is necessary to maintain the integrity of responses by ensuring that participants do not over-represent themselves in the data set by submitting multiple responses. Thus, submissions should be monitored through various methods (e.g., monitoring of IP addresses) to ensure that there is no duplicate responding. Although multiple submissions may strike one as a major issue with Web-based research, the consensus is that this does not represent a major challenge to the integrity of the research (Birnbaum, 2000b; Musch & Reips, 2000). Additionally, multiple submissions are fairly easy to detect during the data-cleaning process. Most participants who attempt multiple submissions do so immediately after their first submission; this can be detected by examining IP addresses, date and time of submission, and length of session. Additionally, time spent by participants in completing the study should be closely monitored. Given the limited experimental control over research done over the Internet, monitoring time spent completing the study is one way to ensure that participants are invested in the process and are not responding without processing the information.

EXAMPLES OF WEB-BASED STUDIES IN FORENSIC PSYCHOLOGY

The following sections describe two recent examples of successful Web-based studies conducted by the authors.

SURVEY RESEARCH

In the following example, online data collection methods were employed to conduct a survey of experts in the area of pretrial publicity effects on juror decision making (Busso, Kennard, Zimmerman, & Kovera, 2009). In cases containing a high amount of pretrial publicity, defense attorneys sometimes file a motion with the court to move the trial venue to another geographic location that has not been inundated with pretrial publicity about the case. During a motion hearing, experts on pretrial publicity may be called by either side to testify about the effects of pretrial publicity on juror bias as well as research on the effectiveness of common remedies used by the courts to combat the potentially biasing effects of pretrial publicity. In some change of venue motions, the judge may ask whether the evidence to be presented by the expert is generally accepted in the scientific community of pretrial publicity researchers.

To examine whether the results from the existing body of literature on pretrial publicity effects were generally accepted by the scientific community, Busso, Kennard, et al. (2009) conducted an online survey with pretrial publicity experts. To recruit participants, a search was performed in PsycInfo for researchers who had published at least one article in a scientific journal or one book chapter on pretrial publicity. Internet searches were performed for the contact information of qualified individuals. Participants were emailed an invitation to participate in the online survey that included a link to the survey Web site. Participants were first directed to a page containing consent information.

Participants were able to indicate consent to participate in the survey by typing their names into a text box included at the bottom of the consent page. Participants were then directed to a page that contained a number of statements describing pre-trial publicity (PTP) phenomena (e.g., "Negative PTP causes potential jurors to prejudge a defendant to be guilty"). Participants answered a number of questions in relation to each PTP phenomenon (e.g., "How reliable is this phenomenon?"). Participants indicated their answers to each question by clicking on tab buttons located next to each answer. When participants were finished answering the survey questions, they were directed to a debriefing page that provided an explanation of the survey and the researcher's contact information.

Of the PTP experts who were emailed, 38% participated in the survey. In comparison, a paper survey of psycholegal experts on confession research yielded a response rate of 34% (Kassin et al., 2001). The use of online survey methods allowed the researchers to quickly reach PTP experts across the country. The experts who participated were easily able to complete the survey online without needing to mail a paper copy of the survey back to the researcher. In addition, the data was collected and stored in an Excel file that could be easily converted to another file format for analysis. In sum, online data collection methods provided the researcher with an efficient, cost-effective method of survey collection, seemingly without hindering the survey-participant response rate.

EXPERIMENTAL RESEARCH

In this example, online data collection methods were employed to conduct an experimental study spanning a period of eight weeks (Daftary-Kapur, 2009). The study was designed to examine the influence of PTP on juror decision making in an actual case as it progressed. To do so, the study employed participants as mock shadow jurors who followed the case in real time. Information was disseminated to participants during six half-hour sessions conducted over an eight-week period. Two weeks prior to the start of the trial, participants read newspaper articles regarding the case (slant determined by experimental condition). After the trial began, we assessed participants' knowledge about the case, their attitudes toward the criminal justice system (e.g., Perceptions of Police Scale, Hadar & Snortum, 1975), their demographics, and their opinions of the defendant. Participants then read summaries of the attorneys' actual opening statements; rated the believability, likeability, and persuasiveness of the attorneys; and indicated their verdict leanings.

In the next three sessions, participants read summaries of prosecution and defense witnesses' testimony and rated the believability, likeability, and persuasiveness of the witnesses and indicated their current guilt ratings. Finally, participants read summaries of the attorneys' closing statements and rated the strength of each argument, the strength of the case presented by each side, read jury instructions, rendered verdicts, and answered questions about the trial evidence. The attrition rate over the eight-week period was 12% and appeared to be random across the 12 experimental conditions. To participate, participants were directed to a Web site where they created an account and were given a login and password. This information was used each time participants were notified that a new session was available for them to complete.

The study Web site also captured time spent by each participant on each page of the session to provide a check on the integrity of responding. Additionally, the participant pool was quite diverse. Two samples were drawn in this study—one from New York and the other from Boston. Sample demographics for New York included 115 participants, of whom 84 (73%) were female (age $M = 36.92$, $SD = 12.53$; range 18–72). The sample was ethnically diverse, with 66 Caucasians (57.4%), 22 African Americans (19.1%), 9 Hispanics (7.8%), 7 Asian Americans (6.1%), and 11 (9.6%) who identified as other. Overall, results from the study were consistent with prior research on PTP effects. At the same time, due to the novel methodology, we were able to capture data over a much longer period of time than is typical of laboratory studies, adding to the external validity of PTP effects.

CONCLUSION

Web-based data collection is growing in popularity for a number of reasons. Online research provides many advantages, including but not limited to sample size and diversity, fidelity to protocols, lower costs and automation, and efficient data entry. The consensus among Web-based research appears to be that the advantages outweigh the disadvantages. However, before undertaking Web-based research, it is important for researchers to weigh the advantages and disadvantages of this approach and to be prepared to address the methodological and ethical issues unique to this medium. Finally, if Web-based data collection is selected as the preferred method for a particular study, researchers need to use the best application available to collect the data needed for the particular project.

REFERENCES

Bargh, J. A., & McKenna, K. Y. A. (2004). The Internet and social life. *Annual Review of Psychology, 55*, 573–590.

Best, S., Krueger, B., Hubbard, C., & Smith, A. (2001). An assessment of the generalizability of Internet surveys. *Social Science Computer Review, 19*, 131–145.

Birnbaum, M. H. (2000a). *Introduction to behavioral research on the Internet.* Upper Saddle River, NJ: Prentice Hall.

Birnbaum, M. H. (Ed.) (2000b). *Psychological experiments on the Internet.* New York, NY: Academic Press.

Birnbaum, M. (2004). Methodological and ethical issues in conducting social psychology research via the Internet. *The Sage handbook of methods in social psychology* (pp. 359–382). Thousand Oaks, CA: Sage.

Buchanan, T., & Smith, J. (1999). Research on the Internet: Validation of a World-Wide Web mediated personality scale. *Behavior Research Methods, Instruments & Computers, 31*(4), 565–571.

Busso, J., Kennard, J., Zimmerman, D., & Kovera, M. B. (2009). *General acceptance of pretrial publicity phenomenon.* Poster Paper presented at the meetings of the American Psychology-Law Society, San Antonio, TX.

Chrzanowski, L. M. (2006). *Rape? Truth? And the media: Laboratory and field assessments of pretrial publicity in a real case.* ProQuest, UMI Dissertations Publishing.

Crocker, C. B., Busso, J. B., Greathouse, S. M., & Kovera, M. B. (March, 2008). *Hypothesis testing in voir dire: Information gathering and inference.* Paper presented at the meetings of the American Psychology-Law Society, Jacksonville, FL.

Crocker, C. B., Busso, J., Kennard, J., Greathouse, S. M., & Kovera, M. B. (March, 2009). *An investigation of attorneys' questioning strategies during voir dire.* Paper presented at the meetings of the American Psychology-Law Society, San Antonio, TX.

Daftary, T., O'Connor, M., & Mechanic, M. (2007). *Gender intrusive questioning of expert witnesses.* Paper presented at the American Psychological Association conference in San Francisco, CA.

Daftary-Kapur, T. (2009). The effects of pre- and post-venire publicity on juror decision-making. *Dissertation Abstracts International, 70,* 6605.

Daftary-Kapur, T., & Penrod, S. D. (2009). *Assessing the impact of new research on the formation of a scientific consensus concerning eyewitness research findings.* Paper presented at the European Association of Psychology and Law, Sorrento, Italy.

Dandurand, F., Shultz, R. T., & Onishi, K. H. (2008). Comparing online and lab methods in a problem solving experiment, *Behavior Research Methods, 40,* 428–434.

Davis, J. (1999). Effectiveness of Internet advertising by leading national advertisers. *Advertising and the World Wide Web* (pp. 81–97). Mahwah, NJ: Lawrence Erlbaum.

Erdfelder, E., Faul, F., and Buchner, A. (1996). GPOWER: A general power analysis program. *Behavior, Research Methods, Instruments, and Computers, 28,* 1–11.

Gosling, S., Vazire, S., Srivastava, S., & John, O. (2004). Should we trust Web-based studies? A comparative analysis of six preconceptions about Internet questionnaires. *American Psychologist, 59*(2), 93–104.

Greathouse, S. M., Crocker, C. B., Busso, J. B., Austin, J., Vitriol, J., Torkildson, J., & Kovera, M. B. (March, 2008). *Do attorney expectations influence the voir dire process?* Paper presented at the meetings of the American Psychology-Law Society, Jacksonville, FL.

Hadar, I., & Snortum, J. (1975). The eye of the beholder: Differential perceptions of the police and the public. *Criminal Justice and Behavior, 2*(1), pp. 37–54.

Haney, C. (1984). On the selection of capital juries: The biasing effect of the death qualification process. *Law and Human Behavior, 8,* 121–132.

Kassin, S., Tubb, V., Hosch, H., & Memon, A. (2001). On the ''general acceptance'' of eyewitness testimony research: A new survey of the experts. *American Psychologist, 56*(5), 405–416.

Krantz, J., Ballard, J., & Scher, J. (1997). Comparing the results of laboratory and World-Wide Web samples on the determinants of female attractiveness. *Behavior Research Methods, Instruments & Computers, 29*(2), 264–269.

Krantz, J. H., & Dalal, R. (2000). Validity of web-based psychology research. In M. H. Birnbaum (Ed.), *Psychological experiments on the Internet* (pp. 35–60). New York, NY: Academic Press.

Kraut, R., Olson, J., Banaji, M., Bruckman, A., Cohen, J., & Couper, M. (2004). Psychological research online: Report of board of scientific affairs' advisory group on the conduct of research on the Internet. *The American Psychologist, 59*(2), 105–117.

Levett, L. M., & Kovera, M. B. (2008). The effectiveness of educating jurors about unreliable expert evidence using an opposing witness. *Law and Human Behavior, 32,* 363–374.

McKenna, K., & Bargh, J. (2006). Coming out in the age of the Internet: Identity. In J. M. Levine & R. L. Moreland (Eds.), *Small groups* (pp. 433–452). New York, NY: Psychology Press.

Metzger, M. M., Kristof, V. L., & Yoest, D. J. (2003). The world wide web and the laboratory: A comparison using face recognition. *CyberPsychology & Behavior, 6* (6), 613–621.

Miller, E. T., Neal, D. J., Roberts, L. J., Baer, J., Cressler, S. O., Metrik, J., & Marlatt, G. A. (2002). Test-retest reliability of alcohol measures: Is there a difference between internet-based assessment and traditional methods? *Psychology of Addictive Behaviors, 16,* 56–63.

Mook, D. G. (1983). In defense of external validity. *American Psychologist, 38,* 379–387.

Musch, J., & Reips, U. (2000). A brief history of web experimenting. In M. H. Birnbaum (Ed.), *Psychological experiments on the Internet.* New York, NY: Academic Press, 61–87.

O'Neil, K. M., & Penrod, S. D. (2001). Methodological variables in Web-based research that may affect results: Sample type, monetary incentives, and personal information. *Behavior Research Methods, Instruments, & Computers, 33,* 226–233.

O'Neil, K. M., Penrod, S. D., & Bornstein, B. H. (2003). Web-based research: Methodological variables' effects on dropout and sample characteristics. *Behavior Research Methods, Instruments, & Computers, 35,* 217–226.

O'Neil, K. M., Patry, M. W., Penrod, & S. D. (2004). Exploring the effects of attitudes toward the death penalty on capital sentencing verdicts. *Psychology, Public Policy, and Law, 10,* 443–470.

Rainie, L. (2010). Internet, broadband, and cell phone statistics. *Pew Internet and American Life Project.* Retrieved September 10, 2010, from: http://www.pewinternet.org/Reports/2010/Internet-broadband-and-cell-phone-statistics/Report.aspx

Reips, U. (1996). *Experimenting in the World-Wide Web.* Paper presented at the 1996 Society for Computers in Psychology Conference, Chicago, IL.

Reips, U-D. (2000). The web experiment method: Advantages, disadvantages, and solutions. In M. H. Birnbaum (Ed.), *Psychological experiments on the Internet.* (pp. 89–118). San Diego, CA: Academic Press.

Riva, G., Teruzzi, T., & Anolli, L. (2003). The use of the internet in psychology research: A comparison of online and offline questionnaires. *CyberPsychology and Behavior, 6,* 73–80.

Rosenthal, R. (2002). Covert communication in classrooms, clinics, courtrooms, and cubicles. *American Psychologist, 57,* 839–849.

Schmidt, W. (1997). World-Wide Web survey research: Benefits, potential problems, and solutions. *Behavior Research Methods, Instruments & Computers, 29*(2), 274–279.

Welch, N., & Krantz, J. H. (1996). The World-Wide Web as a medium for psychoacoustical demonstrations and experiments: Experience and results. *Behavior Research Methods, Instruments, & Computers, 28,* 192–196.

Yun, G.W., and Trumbo, C. W. (2000). Response comparison of a survey executed by mail, e-mail, & website. *Journal of Computer Mediated Communication.* Retrieved September 13, 2010, from http://jcmc.indiana.edu/vol6/issue1/yun.html

CHAPTER 5

Statistical Principles in
Forensic Research

JENNIFER GROSCUP

S TATISTICS ARE AN essential part of research in forensic psychology because they allow us to test our research hypotheses. It can seem as though there are an infinite number of possibilities for statistics to use in research, so how do you choose between them? The first step in choosing a statistical approach is to think about your research hypotheses and what type of relationship they are testing. For example, if your hypotheses are about an association between your variables, you should select a statistic from the group of statistics that test associations, such as a mean difference test or a correlation. If your hypotheses are about predicting the value of one variable from other variables, you should select a statistic from the group of statistics that test prediction, such as regression.

Once you have determined what type of statistical test you need, you will need to consider the variables you are interested in analyzing. If your hypothesis relates two variables to each other, you will need a bivariate statistic; if your hypothesis relates multiple variables to each other, you will need a multivariate statistic. These first two steps will get you to the right family of statistics to test your research question, but there will still be options. You will need to consider how your variables are measured in order to select an appropriate statistic. Even after this process, there may be options to consider, and there will definitely be options in how you report the results of your analyses. At this point, it is wise to consult articles published in your area of research (e.g., forensic psychology) to determine what the conventions for choosing and reporting statistics are in that area.

This chapter reviews some of the most commonly used statistics in forensic psychology and suggests when it is appropriate to use them. For each topic, there are references to useful texts in case you need more information about the individual techniques. Articles published in *Law and Human Behavior* in the years 2008 and 2009 were reviewed for their use of each technique described. Almost all of the statistics used in the articles published in

Law and Human Behavior are reviewed here, except for a few appearing in only one or two articles. This review should give you a sense of the conventions regarding statistics and the reporting of results in the field of forensic psychology. References to articles in *Law and Human Behavior* are included to provide you with examples of how these statistics are typically used in forensic psychology research. All other references are included to provide you with additional information on the statistics discussed in this chapter, in case you want to use them in your own research.

SOME DATA ISSUES TO CONSIDER PRIOR TO ANALYSIS

STATISTICAL ASSUMPTIONS

Many of the statistical tests typically used in forensic psychology research share assumptions about the data (see Tabachnick & Fidell, 2007, for a review of multivariate data issues). When these assumptions are violated, the statistics used to test the research hypotheses may be biased. Prior to conducting any particular type of analysis, the data should be examined for violations of the assumptions made by that type of analysis. For example, many statistics (including but not limited to correlations, ANOVA, MANOVA, and linear regression) assume that the data is normally distributed. Many tests can be affected by outliers in the data, such as cases with extreme high or low values on a single variable or multiple variables. Many statistics also assume that there is a linear relationship among the variables, and many multivariate statistics assume homoscedasticity.

If these assumptions are violated, there are a few options. An alternative statistic can be used to test the research hypothesis that is not affected by the same data assumptions. If the use of an alternative statistic is not desirable, the data can be modified so that it no longer violates any assumptions of the desired test. For example, transformations may be performed on non-normal variables to create normality. If outliers are present, they can be either removed or converted into a value that is more consistent with the rest of the data (Tabachnick & Fidell, 2007). However, any manipulation of the data conducted before testing the hypothesis should be reported. If no modification is done to the data and the tests are performed regardless of the presence of these violations, this decision should be reflected somewhere in the statement of the results or the limitations of the research. Unfortunately, results of data analysis investigating statistical assumptions are rarely if ever reported in published articles in forensic psychology.

MISSING VALUES

A dataset will have missing values when data for every participant is not complete. Missing data can be either random or systematic (Kline, 2005; Tabachnick & Fidell, 2007). Random missing data may be caused by random participant error, such as accidentally missing a question. Systematic missing data may be caused by participants refusing to answer particular questions because they seemed offensive, confusing, or too personal. The suggested approach for dealing with missing data depends on whether it is missing randomly or systematically (Kline, 2005; Tabachnick & Fidell, 2007). If the data is missing systematically, analysis should be performed to determine how the results regarding the research hypotheses differ, depending on whether or not the cases that have missing data are included. The results of this analysis should be reported. If the data is missing randomly, it can be analyzed "as is," but the cases with the missing data will not be included in the analysis; this is called deletion. It is an acceptable option if the ability to test the research hypothesis will not be lost along with the deleted cases because of reduced power or any unequal cell sizes that might occur in an experimental design.

The second option for randomly missing data is to replace those missing values with "created" values that can be estimated from the rest of the data, also called imputation (Kline, 2005; Tabachnick & Fidell, 2007). Imputation is appropriate if less than 5% of the data for any one variable is missing (Tabachnick & Fidell, 2007). This option would be preferred if the deletion of cases during the analysis is undesirable. There are several imputation options available, including replacement with the mean, regression-based methods, expectation maximization, and multiple imputation, the last of which is the method currently preferred (Tabachnick & Fidell, 2007). After the missing values have been estimated and replaced, the end result will be a "complete" data set.

In summary, missing data should be considered using at least the following four steps prior to any data analysis: (1) identify variables for which data is missing; (2) determine how much data is missing and why; (3) decide between doing nothing, imputing, and analyzing, and (4) if imputing, decide what method will be used and replace the missing values. Be sure to fully specify any procedure used when writing-up the results, including why the particular imputation technique was chosen, the variables affected, and the proportion of cases affected. Although missing data is very common, very few articles discuss missing data and how the authors dealt with it. Only three articles published in the 2008 and 2009 years of *Law and Human Behavior* mentioned missing data. Jehle, Miller, and Kemmelmeier (2009) did not replace their missing values, but they noted that the number of cases in each analysis they described would be different, which is appropriate information to provide when the researchers choose the "do nothing" option. Two articles discussed imputation techniques (Schwalbe & Maschi, 2009; Wright & Fitzgerald, 2009), and each of these articles provided information about the amount of missing data per variable and the imputation technique used.

Reliability and Internal Consistency

It is common in research to use preexisting scales to measure constructs of interest, and this is also true in forensic psychological research. It is particularly common to measure attitudes relevant to the legal system (see, e.g.,

Miller & Hayward, 2008; Schwalbe & Maschi, 2009; Wright & Fitzgerald, 2009) and to measure personality characteristics or experiences relevant to the legal system (see, e.g., Douglas et al., 2008; Fishbein et al., 2009; Modecki, 2009; Skeem et al., 2009; Stockdale, Logan, & Weston, 2009; Swanson et al., 2008; Wright & Fitzgerald, 2009). When a scale is used with several items that will be combined into one scale score to be analyzed, reliability analysis on those items must be conducted to demonstrate that the scale has good internal consistency (DeVellis, 2003). In other words, all the items in the scale should be measuring the same construct. Chronbach's Alpha is the test that provides information about reliability. Alpha values should be greater than .80 for the scale to have good reliability (DeVellis, 2003).

Even if no preexisting scales are used, Alpha analysis may still be required. To increase the convergent validity of their measures, many researchers measure constructs with multiple measures they create. For example, McAuliff, Kovera, and Nunez (2009) had mock jurors in a sexual harassment case evaluate the quality and credibility of the expert witness and the credibility of the plaintiff. All three of these constructs were measured with multiple questions participants had to answer; then participants' answers on those individual questions were combined to form a stronger, composite measure of the constructs (McAuliff et al., 2009). When constructing a composite variable from multiple measures in this way, the researchers should provide information about the reliability of the measure using Chronbach's Alpha at a minimum (see also, Jehle et al., 2009; Schwalbe & Maschi, 2009; Wright & Fitzgerald, 2009). Additional indicators that the variables are measuring the same construct may also be provided, such as the correlations among the variables (see, e.g., Devine, Buddenbaum, Houp, Studebaker, & Stolle, 2009; Wiley & Bottoms, 2009) or an exploratory factor analysis to determine whether all the variables in the combined measure load onto the same factor (see, e.g., Schuller, Kazoleas, & Kawakami, 2009).

INTER-RATER RELIABILITY ANALYSIS

Some research involves coding of content (e.g., jury deliberations or narratives written by participants) or behavior (e.g., observations or behavioral measures) by the researchers. The codes generated by the researchers constitute the data that is later analyzed to test the research hypotheses. To demonstrate that the coding is reliable, objective, and not biased by the researcher, inter-rater reliability information is required. To test inter-rater reliability, two or more raters must cross-code the content or behavior from some percentage of the total content or behavior to be coded so that their ratings can be compared. Inter-rater reliability statistics test the amount of agreement between two or more raters, and the researchers can be more confident in the reliability of the results when agreement between raters is high. When the data is a categorical or nominal level measurement, Kappa is the most commonly used statistic to demonstrate inter-rater reliability

(Landis & Koch, 1977). Kappa compares the amount of agreement in the categories coded by two raters. Researchers typically conclude that inter-rater reliability is excellent when Kappa is greater than .80, although values as small as .40 have been judged acceptable (Landis & Koch, 1977; see, e.g., Modecki, 2009; Swanson et al., 2008). Pearson's correlations are sometimes used to assess inter-rater reliability when the data is continuous or measured on an interval level (see, e.g., Vrij et al., 2008). However, two researchers' ratings could be positively correlated because they are varying together, but they may not have selected the same ratings.

Additionally, there may be more than two raters cross-coding. Therefore, the inter-class correlation (ICC) is also commonly used to assess the inter-rater reliability of a measure that is an interval level variable (see McGraw & Wong, 1996, for a discussion of ICC). In forensic psychology, ICC has been used to demonstrate the inter-rater reliability on forensic measures such as the MacCAT-CA (Viljoen, Slaney, & Grisso, 2009), the PCL:R (Brown, St. Amand, & Zamble, 2009; Douglas et al., 2008), the PCL:SV (Vitacco et al., 2009), the PCL: YV (Douglas, Epstein, & Poythress, 2008), and across the judgments of individual jurors on a jury (Devine et al., 2009). ICC is interpreted similarly to Kappa, such that as values approach 1.0, the reliability is higher and values under .65 indicate poor inter-rater reliability (Brown et al., 2009).

HYPOTHESIS TESTING

NULL HYPOTHESIS SIGNIFICANCE TESTING

Traditionally, psychological research uses null hypothesis significance testing (NHST) in order to test research hypotheses (see any introductory statistics textbook for a thorough review, or one specific to criminal justice research, e.g., Weisburd & Britt, 2003). In NHST, the researcher begins by assuming the null hypothesis. The null hypothesis is that there is no relationship between the variables of interest in the population of interest. Next, the researcher formulates the research hypothesis. The research hypothesis (or hypotheses) should state that there is a relationship between the variables, and it should be very specific about the direction and magnitude of the relationship that is expected. The research hypothesis should be informed by theory and/or the findings of related research (Weisburd & Britt, 2003).

Significance testing is based on the probability that a large relationship between the variables in the sample would not be found if that relationship did not exist in the population. A significance test provides information about (a) whether the relationship between the variables is large enough to permit an inference that it is likely to exist in the population and the null hypothesis should be rejected, or (b) whether the relationship between the variables is too small to permit an inference that it is likely to exist in the population and the null hypothesis should be retained. Each test of significance (e.g., t-tests, correlations, chi-square, and ANOVA) has a value that summarizes the relationship between the variables (i.e., t, r, X^2, and F, respectively) and an associated error rate (the p-value or Alpha).

To determine whether the relationship is large enough to reject the null, the p-value is examined. The traditional cut-off score for p is .05. When $p < .05$, the null is rejected, and it is inferred that a relationship between the variables in the population is likely. Next, the pattern of the relationship between the variables must be examined to determine whether it is consistent with the pattern in the research hypothesis. When the null is rejected using a $p < .05$ cut-off, there is a 5% chance that there is no actual relationship between the variables in the population. The decision to reject the null and conclude there is a relationship between the variables in the population when there is no true relationship between the variables is called a Type I error. In significance testing, a Type II error can also be made, which is the decision to retain the null based on the sample data when there is actually a relationship between the variables in the population (see generally, Weisburd & Britt, 2003).

Although NHST is the traditional approach in psychology to testing research hypotheses, alternative approaches have begun to gain favor with statisticians. Many recommend that additional information about the relationships between the variables in NHST should be provided. This includes providing effect size estimates (Cortina & Nouri, 2000) and confidence intervals (Smithson, 2003) for all hypothesis tests. Providing information about confidence intervals and effect size estimates in addition to measures of significance is recommended in the *APA Manual* and may be required for publication of articles in APA journals (APA, 2009).

CONFIDENCE INTERVALS

In addition to (or occasionally in place of) significance testing, many researchers provide information about confidence intervals. A confidence interval is a range of possible values for an estimate, such as an estimated mean, an effect size estimate, or a parameter estimate (Smithson, 2003; Weisburd & Britt, 2003). The confidence interval is the range of values of the estimate, and the confidence level is the percentage of times it is believed that estimates from the population will fall into that range. The most common confidence levels are 95% and 99%, which correspond to the $p < .05$ and $p < .01$ criteria in NHST. Generally, the more conservative level is preferred to decrease family-wise error. The benefits of confidence intervals over NHST include that confidence intervals provide a range of values for an estimate that cannot be rejected as likely, whereas NHST tests only one value. Because they provide a range of values, confidence intervals also allow for better comparisons of estimates across studies (Smithson, 2003).

Although the reporting of confidence intervals is common in other disciplines, it is not yet universal in psychology (Smithson, 2003). However, including them where possible is recommended by the APA (APA, 2009). The APA also recommends that the confidence level used to calculate them (for example, 95% or 99%) should be specified when providing confidence intervals and that effect size estimates should always be reported with their associated confidence intervals where possible (APA, 2009). Some authors in forensic psychology have followed this recommendation. For example, several articles published in *Law and Human Behavior* during 2008 and 2009 included confidence intervals around means (see, e.g., Dahl, Brimacombe, & Lindsay, 2009; Martire & Kemp, 2009). Confidence intervals were also occasionally reported around the odds ratios in logistic regression analysis (see, e.g., Levine, 2009; McEwan, Mullen, & MacKenzie, 2009; Swanson et al., 2008; Wright & Fitzgerald, 2009), and around the Area Under the Curve (AUC) estimates in Receiver Operating Characteristic (ROC) analysis (see, e.g., Douglas, Epstein, & Poythress, 2008; Hilton, Harris, Rice, Houghton, & Eke, 2008; Manchak, Skeem, & Douglas, 2008; McEwan et al., 2009; Walters & Schlauch, 2008).

EFFECT SIZE ESTIMATES

Effect size estimates are measures of the strength or magnitude of the relationship between variables (see Cortina & Nouri, 2000, for a review). Most summary statistics from NHST provide information about whether the relationship is significant. In other words, is the relationship observed between the variables large enough in the sample data to infer that the relationship between those variables exists in the population? However, these statistics do not provide information about how strong the relationship between the variables is. Effect size estimates provide this type of information—they estimate the strength or magnitude of the relationship between the variables in the population of interest. Effect size estimates have additional advantages over tests of significance. Tests of significance are dependent on the sample size used to calculate them. The larger the sample, the more power the statistical analysis will have, and it becomes more likely that significant relationships will be observed between variables when those relationships exist in the population. With very large sample sizes, even very weak relationships can be significant. Conversely, with very small sample sizes, there may not be a significant relationship between the variables even when the actual relationship between the variables in the population is quite strong. Therefore, different conclusions may be drawn in different studies because of the size of the sample, if conclusions were drawn based only on significance testing. Unlike tests of significance, effect size estimates are not dependent on sample size. Therefore, another advantage of using effect size estimates is that they provide information that permits comparisons of these relationships across studies (Cortina & Nouri, 2000).

Effect size estimates can represent either the strength of association between variables or the variance shared by the variables. The most common strength of association effect-size estimates are Pearson's r, Cohen's d, Cramer's V (V), eta (η), and omega (ω). Certain effect sizes are generally reported as a companion to various significance tests. For example, SPSS will generate Cramer's V with chi-square, and it is the most common effect size estimate reported in conjunction with chi-square in forensic psychology articles that appeared in *Law and Human Behavior* in 2008 and 2009 (see, e.g., Dahl et al., 2009; Levett & Kovera, 2008; McAuliff et al., 2009). Because Cohen's *d* is an effect size for the mean difference between two groups, it is reported with *t*-tests (see, e.g., Dahl et al., 2009) and with ANOVA when it is used for two groups (see, e.g., Vitacco et al., 2009).

The most common variance shared effect size estimates reported in forensic psychology research are Pearson's r^2, eta-squared (η^2), and omega-squared (ω^2). When "effect size estimates" is selected when conducting ANOVA or ANCOVA in SPSS, SPSS generates partial eta-squared (η^2) as the effect size. It is very common in forensic psychology research to report eta-squared or partial eta-squared with ANOVA results (see, e.g., Dahl et al., 2009; Gabbert, Hope, & Fisher, 2009; Greathouse & Kovera, 2009; Leippe, Eisenstadt, & Rauch, 2009; Martire & Kemp, 2009; McAuliff et al., 2009; McQuiston-Surrett & Saks, 2009; Wiley & Bottoms, 2009). It is APA style to report effect size estimates for all inferential statistics (APA, 2009), and many journals, like *Law and Human Behavior*, are now requiring that researchers report effect size estimates in their articles.

BASIC BIVARIATE STATISTICS

When your research hypothesis involves the relationship between two variables, a bivariate statistic will be the appropriate test of that hypothesis because it tests the association between two variables. There are several statistics that can be used to test a basic bivariate hypothesis. Bivariate hypotheses can take several forms based on the measurement of the variables involved. For example, is gender related to jury verdict? As the number of previous offenses increases, does recidivism increase? Do eyewitnesses who choose someone from a lineup report more confidence in their decisions than eyewitnesses who do not choose someone from a lineup? Each of these hypotheses could be addressed with the statistics described subsequently, and the choice between the statistics depends on how the variables in the hypotheses are measured.

CHI-SQUARE

Use when: You want to test the significance of the relationship between two nominal variables.

A chi-square is a measure of the association between two nominal or categorical variables (see Weisburd & Britt, 2003, or any introductory statistics text). This is an appropriate test to use if you have two nominal variables and you want to test the relationship between them. In forensic psychology, it can be used to test relationships between variables such as a manipulated independent variable (IV) and the accuracy of an eyewitness identification (see, e.g., Blunt & McAllister, 2009; Leippe et al., 2009; Martire & Kemp, 2009) or juror verdicts (see, e.g., McAuliff et al., 2009). When two nominal variables are compared, the unique combinations of the categories of those two variables are called cells. For example, if juror gender and juror verdicts were compared, the cells would be female jurors with guilty verdicts, male jurors with guilty verdicts, and so on. Chi-square (χ^2) compares the observed frequencies in the cells to the expected frequencies. Expected frequencies are the frequencies in the cells that would be expected in each cell if there were no relationship between the variables—in other words, if the null hypothesis were true. An example would be the number of male and female jurors that would vote guilty or not guilty if there were no relationship between juror gender and verdict.

Observed frequencies are the actual frequencies in the cells from the data. For example, the number of female jurors who actually voted guilty would be an observed frequency. Chi-square compares the observed frequencies with the expected frequencies. The value of chi-square becomes larger the more the observed frequencies differ from the expected frequencies, and the values can range from zero to infinity. Chi-square makes few assumptions about the data, but for chi-square to work well, the cells should not have fewer than five observed frequencies. When 20% of the cells have fewer than five observed frequencies, it is not appropriate to conduct a chi-square (Weisburd & Britt, 2003). When chi-square is significant and the null is rejected, the pattern of relationship between the variables must be compared with the hypothesized pattern of relationship to determine whether the research hypothesis is supported. To do this, the observed frequencies in the cells should be compared with the expected frequencies to determine where the frequencies are larger or smaller than what would be expected if there were no relationship between the variables. It is typical to report the observed frequencies (and percentages), the chi-square value, the degrees of freedom, the sample size, the p-value, and an effect size estimate such as Cramer's V or Phi (APA, 2009).

CORRELATION

Use when: You want to test the strength and significance of the relationship between two continuous variables.

A correlation is a measure of the association between two continuous variables measured on an interval-level scale (see Weisburd & Britt, 2003, or any introductory statistics text). This is an appropriate test to use if you have two interval level variables and you want to test the relationship between them. In forensic psychology, it can be used to test relationships between the dependent variables in a study, such as measures of attitudes, experiences, and evaluations of evidence in a mock trial (see, e.g., McAuliff et al., 2009; Stockdale et al., 2009). Pearson's correlation assumes that the variables have a linear relationship, are normally distributed, and are homoscedastic.

Pearson's correlation has a range of −1.0 to +1.0. A value of 0 indicates that there is no linear relationship between the variables. As the values diverge from zero (become closer to 1.0 or −1.0), the relationship between the variables is stronger. A positive correlation coefficient indicates that as values on one of the variables are increasing, the values on the other variable are also increasing. A negative correlation coefficient indicates that as values on one of the variables are increasing, the values on the other variable are decreasing.

Because correlation assumes a linear relationship between the variables, a nonsignificant or small correlation could indicate that there is no relationship between the variables, but there could be a nonlinear relationship between the variables. Therefore, if the correlation is small, the scatterplot (a graph of the data points) should be examined to determine which of these options is happening. When there is a significant correlation between two variables, the direction of that relationship should be examined and compared with the research hypothesis. If several correlations are calculated, it is typical to report them in a correlation matrix containing the means and standard deviations for all the variables (see, e.g., McAuliff et al., 2009; Stockdale et al., 2009). It is also suggested that the degrees of freedom, the sample size, and the *p*-values be reported (APA, 2009).

MEAN DIFFERENCE

Use when: You want to test the significance of the relationship between a nominal variable and a continuous variable.

A mean difference test measures the association between one nominal level variable and one variable measured on a continuous scale, usually interval or ratio level measurement (see Weisburd & Britt, 2003, or any introductory statistics text). The nominal variable is usually the IV in the research, and the continuous variable is typically the DV. When the IV is measured between groups, an independent or between groups mean difference test should be used, and when the IV is a repeated measure, a dependent or within groups mean difference test is appropriate. The IV can have two or more categories or levels. When the IV has two levels, either a t-test or an ANOVA (F-test) can be used to test the mean difference. When the result is significant ($p < .05$), there is a difference between the means of the DV between the two groups. The direction of the mean difference needs to be inspected to determine if it is consistent with the direction of the research hypothesis.

When the nominal variable has more than two levels, ANOVA must be used to test the variation across those levels. When an ANOVA testing for variation across multiple groups is significant, it indicates that there is significant variation across the groups, but it does not indicate between which groups there is significant variation. Follow-up pairwise tests are required. Multiple *t*-tests could be performed that compare all the possible pairs of groups to each other (Turner & Thayer, 2001). Obviously, this increases the number of tests that are done to test the hypothesis that the groups differ. As the number of tests increase, alpha inflation occurs. Alpha inflation is an increase in the chances that a Type I error will be made. Many multiple comparison tests have been developed to compare multiple groups that also correct for alpha inflation, ranging from less correction (i.e., more chance of making a Type I error) to more conservative correction (i.e., less chance of making a Type I error). Many options are available for multiple comparison or post-hoc tests of this kind. Among the most commonly used is Tukey's honestly significant difference (HSD), which is a conservative multiple comparison test (Weisburd & Britt, 2003). Tukey's HSD was the most frequently used post-hoc test for multiple group ANOVA in the 2008 and 2009 issues of *Law and Human Behavior* (see, e.g., Blunt & McAllister, 2009; Gabbert et al., 2009; Jehle et al., 2009; Neuschatz, Lawson, Swanner, Meissner, & Neuschatz, 2008).

A second common use for ANOVA is to test interaction effects between two or more factors or IVs (see Turner & Thayer, 2001; Weisburd & Britt, 2003). Testing for interactions is common in forensic psychology, because much research in forensic psychology uses factorial designs. Researchers often have hypotheses about how two or more IVs will affect their DVs, and how the effect of one IV might depend on another. Part of testing an interaction is examining the main effects of each IV in the interaction—in other words, the effect of each IV across the conditions of the other IV(s). An interaction tests whether the effect of one IV depends on the effect of another IV, or whether the simple effects have different patterns. A simple effect is the difference between the conditions of one IV within one condition of the other IV. A significant interaction means that the patterns of the simple effects are different. If the interaction is significant, the simple effects need to be examined to determine what the pattern of the interaction is. The most common approach to simple effects testing in the 2008 and 2009 issues of *Law and Human Behavior* was to conduct t-tests (see, e.g., Dahl et al., 2009; Neuschatz et al., 2008) or ANOVAs (see, e.g., McQuiston-Surrett & Saks, 2009; Vrij et al., 2008).

MULTIVARIATE STATISTICS

When your research hypothesis involves the relationship between more than two variables, a multivariate statistic will be the appropriate test of that hypothesis. Like bivariate hypotheses, there are several statistics that can be used to test a basic multivariate hypothesis. The choice between the available multivariate statistics depends both on the type of research hypothesis and on the type of variables in the analysis.

MANOVA: Multivariate Analysis of Variance

Use when: You have one or more categorical IVs that have two or more groups each and two or more continuous DVs and you want to test whether the responses on all the DVs together differ based on group membership in the IVs.

Multivariate analysis of variance (MANOVA) is a multivariate technique that can be used to assess the statistical significance of the effect of one or more independent variables on a set of two or more dependent variables (see Tabachnick & Fidell, 2007; Weinfurt, 1995). It requires at least one "grouping" variable (the IV) that is a categorical or nominal measure with at least two levels and multiple DVs that can be continuous or binary. MANOVA can test the hypothesis that the DVs when considered together as a set are significantly different across the levels of the IV(s). The DVs should be related to each other either statistically or theoretically to support a hypothesis that they might be affected as a set by the IVs. The benefit of MANOVA is that it takes the intercorrelations among the DVs into account, allowing for a richer analysis of the data, as opposed to testing the univariate relationships between the IV(s) and the DVs individually, as with ANOVA. Intercorrelations can indicate that some DVs are redundant because there is conceptual overlap between them. In interpreting the data, it is important to take these intercorrelations into account. If there is overlap and separate ANOVAs with significant results were conducted, it is questionable whether these tapped into two separate constructs. Examined individually, there might not be group differences, but there are group differences when the DVs are taken as a whole. Multivariate assumptions of MANOVA are multivariate normality, homogeneity of covariance matrices, and independence of observations. The univariate assumptions of MANOVA are the same assumptions of ANOVA (Tabachnick & Fidell, 2007; Weinfurt, 1995).

MANOVA generates several statistics that are typically reported (see Tabachnick & Fidell, 2007; Weinfurt, 1995). Wilks's lambda (λ) gives the proportion of variance that is not explained by the IVs; therefore, lambda is small when there is a significant effect. The Pillai-Bartlett Trace, or Pillai's Trace, is the proportion of explained variance, and Pillai's Trace should be larger when there is a significant effect. Partial eta-squared is often calculated as an effect size estimate with MANOVA and is interpreted as variance accounted for in the DVs by the IV(s). There is an F-test of the significance of the relationship between the IVs and the DVs. It is interpreted similar to a univariate F-test with $p < .05$ to indicating significance (Tabachnick & Fidell, 2007; Weinfurt, 1995). There is some variation in what is reported across articles in forensic psychology. Some researchers prefer to report the F-test and η^2 (see, e.g., Greathouse, & Kovera, 2009; McAuliff et al., 2009; Neuschatz et al., 2008; Vrij et al., 2008), while others report Pillai's Trace and η^2 (Jehle et al., 2009; Modecki, 2008) or Wilks's lambda (Connolly, Price, Lavoie, & Gordon, 2008; Levett & Kovera, 2008).

A significant MANOVA indicates that the multiple dependent measures are varying together across the conditions of the independent variable(s). MANOVA results provide information about the significance of the relationship between the IVs and the DVs and about the amount of variance in the DVs as a group accounted for by the IVs. However, MANOVA provides no information about the pattern of relationship between the IVs and the DVs.

Therefore, it is necessary to do follow-up testing when you conduct a MANOVA and get a significant result. There are several options for follow-up tests (see Tabachnick & Fidell, 2007; Weinfurt, 1995). They include

- Conducting multiple univariate ANOVAs on each of the DVs for the same set of IVs in the MANOVA.
- "Stepdown" analysis, in which a series of successive ANOVAs and ANCOVAs are performed to determine each DV's additional contribution to the multivariate effect (appropriate when there is a logical ordering to the DVs).
- Linear discriminant function (LDF) analysis, which predicts membership in a group (the IV) from multiple DVs to confirm that the groups being discriminated in the LDF are the same groups on which there are significant mean differences on the DVs in the MANOVA.
- Performing successive MANOVAs, one with all variables included and others deleting one variable from the analysis each time to determine which DVs are not contributing to the multivariate effect.
- Calculating *F*-to-remove statistics, which provide information about which variables are most essential and least essential to the model (Tabachnick & Fidell, 2007; Weinfurt, 1995).

Univariate ANOVAs are the most commonly used follow-up tests for a significant MANOVA. In fact, they are the only type of follow-up test reported in the 2008 through 2009 issues of *Law and Human Behavior* (see, e.g., Connolly, Price, Lavoie, & Gordon, 2008; Greathouse, & Kovera, 2009; Jehle et al., 2009; Levett & Kovera, 2008; McAuliff et al., 2009; Modecki, 2008; Neuschatz et al., 2008; Vrij et al., 2008). Criticisms of this approach include that it can increase the chance of Type I error if no alpha correction (e.g., Bonferroni) is used, and that it ignores intercorrelations among DVs by testing the effect of each DV individually, testing multivariate questions from a univariate perspective (Weinfurt, 1995). The other more multivariate follow-up techniques should be considered in deciding which type of follow-up analysis to conduct.

LINEAR REGRESSION

Use when: You want to predict values on a continuous DV using one or more continuous or dichotomous IVs.

Although it is informative to examine the associations among variables, researchers often want to determine whether they can predict the values of their dependent measures from other variables of interest. When researchers have predictive hypotheses, regression is the most likely statistical technique they will use to test their hypotheses. One of the most commonly used forms of regression is linear or ordinary least squares regression (for reviews, see Berk, 2004; J. Cohen, Cohen, West, & Aiken, 2003; Licht, 1995; Tabachnick &

Fidell, 2007). In linear regression, one or multiple variables called predictors are used to predict the value of one DV called the criterion. The predictors must be dichotomous or measured on an interval level, and the DV should be measured on an interval level. Categorical predictors that have multiple categories can be dummy coded or effects coded into dichotomous variables so they are suitable as predictors in linear regression (for a review of dummy coding and effects coding, see Cohen et al., 2003). The goal of regression analysis is to create a regression model in which the predictors account for as much variance in the DV as possible. Linear regression assumes a linear relationship between the predictors and the criterion variable, and it is more effective when the linear relationship between the predictors and the criterion is strong. Normality and homoscedasticity of residuals are also assumptions of linear regression. Although IVs or predictors in regression can be related to each other, they will not be effective predictors if they are highly related to each other, a problem called *multicollinearity*. Multicollinearity can be diagnosed with tolerance values that indicate which IVs are too highly related to the other predictors (see Tabachnick & Fidell, 2007). Linear regression models require many cases to test effectively, and it is recommended that there are more than 100 cases in the analysis for a simple model. The number of cases required increases as predictors are added to the model and degrees of freedom are used (Tabachnick & Fidell, 2007).

Linear regression can address several hypotheses: Do the predictors together account for a significant amount of variance in the DV? How much variance in the DV do the predictors account for? Which predictors significantly contribute to the model? How strong are each of the predictors? Therefore, the basic steps in testing multiple regression models include determining whether the model "works," how well the model works, which predictors are contributing to the model, and which predictors make the largest contribution to the model (see Cohen et al., 2003; Licht, 1995; Tabachnick & Fidell, 2007). First, an *F*-test of significance provides information about whether the predictors are accounting for a significant amount of variance in the DV. When $p < .05$, the model accounts for significant variance in the DV.

Second, to answer the question of how well the model works, R-square is inspected. R-square is an effect size estimate indicating the proportion of variance of the DV that is accounted for by the model. For example, if $R^2 = .45$, the model accounts for 45% of the variance in the values of the criterion. One minus R-square is the proportion of the DV that is not accounted for by the predictors, called the residual (see Cohen et al., 2003; Licht, 1995; Tabachnick & Fidell, 2007). Adjusted R-square corrects *R*-square for inflation from a large number of predictors relative to the sample size. Using this adjustment is recommended when there are a large number of predictors and a small sample (Tabachnick & Fidell, 2007; see, e.g., Cooper & Zapf, 2008; Modecki, 2008). Whether the model accounts for significant variance in the DV and how much variance the model accounts for are typically reported for linear regression (see, e.g., Cooper & Zapf, 2008; Douglas, Lilienfeld, et al., 2008; Fishbein et al., 2009; Modecki, 2008; Modecki, 2009; Stockdale et al., 2009).

If the regression model is significant, the predictors in the model as a group are accounting for significant variance in the DV. However, the research hypothesis might concern which of the predictors in the model are significantly contributing to it. A t-test and its associated p-value are generated for each predictor, and decisions about which predictors are significantly contributing to the model are traditionally made using the $p < .05$ cut-off (see Cohen et al., 2003; Licht, 1995; Tabachnick & Fidell, 2007). Regression coefficients or parameter estimates and the standard errors (SEs) for these estimates are also calculated for each predictor. Regression coefficients represent the unique and independent contribution of that predictor to the models, controlling for the contribution of all other predictors in the model. B-values are the unstandardized regression coefficients. Each B-value represents the expected amount of change in the criterion for a 1-unit change in that predictor while holding the value of all the other predictors constant.

Positive regression coefficients indicate that an increase in the value of the DV is expected as the value of the predictor increases, and negative regression coefficients indicate that a decrease in the value of the DV is expected as the value of the predictor increases. Beta weights (β) are the standardized version of B. Although both B and beta indicate what the independent contribution of a given predictor is to the model, interpreting beta weights is preferred to interpreting the raw regression coefficients (B), because beta weights allow for the contributions of the predictors to be compared with each other. As the value of beta diverges from zero, the predictors become stronger (see Cohen et al., 2003; Licht, 1995; Tabachnick & Fidell, 2007). It is recommended to at least report B, SE of B, and beta for each predictor (see, e.g., Cooper & Zapf, 2008; Fishbein et al., 2009; Modecki, 2008; Modecki, 2009; Stockdale et al., 2009), but the most complete information includes the results of the t-test and p-value for each predictor (see, e.g., Douglas, Lilienfeld, et al., 2008).

There are several approaches to creating regression models (see Cohen et al., 2003; Licht, 1995; Tabachnick & Fidell, 2007). In simultaneous regression, all predictor variables are entered into the model simultaneously in one group. Simultaneous regression provides information about whether the predictors account for significant variance in the DV and about which predictors are significantly contributing to the model. It does not provide information about the effect of adding or deleting predictors (see, e.g., Ferguson, Babcock, & Shane, 2008). If the research hypothesis involves the impact of adding or subtracting predictors from the model, the "full model," which includes all of the predictors of interest, will be compared with one or more "reduced models," which include some subset of the predictors. A reduced model that is "nested" contains only variables that are also in the full model and does not contain variables that are not in the full model.

A "non-nested" model is a model that shares some variables with the "full" model but has some unique or additional variables not contained in the full model. The following approaches to regression model building compare nested reduced models with full models, and it is not typical to do analysis with non-nested models. Hierarchical regression is a series of simultaneous regression analyses in which predictor variables are either added or removed from the equation to see how that affects the performance of the model, and it is the most common type of linear regression reported in the 2008 and 2009 years of *Law and Human Behavior* (see, e.g., Cooper & Zapf, 2008; Douglas, Lillienfeld, et al., 2008; Fishbein et al., 2009; Modecki, 2008; Modecki, 2009; Stockdale et al., 2009). Hierarchical regression can start either with the smallest reduced model, adding predictors in one or multiple steps or with the full model, deleting predictors in one or multiple steps. The order of entry or deletion of variables is determined by the researcher based on the research hypotheses. The amount of change in R-square resulting from the change in predictors in the model is calculated at each step, which equals the proportion of variance accounted for in the DV by the predictors that were added or removed from the model at each step. The *F*-change test is a test of the significance of the change in R-square. R-square change and *F*-change are typically reported with this type of regression analysis (see, e.g., Douglas, Lillienfeld, et al., 2008; Fishbein et al., 2009; Modecki, 2009; Stockdale et al., 2009).

When this change is significant, the predictors that were added or removed on that step of the analysis significantly change the model's performance. Note that the order in which variables are added or removed is important, because it determines which variables are being controlled for at each step. In stepwise (or statistical) regression, the entry or deletion of predictors from the model is determined one variable at a time based on which variables will have the most impact on the model's performance. There are two approaches to stepwise regression. In forward inclusion, variables are added to the model one at a time based on predictive utility. In backward elimination, the model starts with all predictors included, and variables are deleted based on lack of predictive utility. Using either approach, the analysis terminates when no additional variable either significantly increases or decreases variance accounted for in the DV, leaving the researcher with a model that includes only variables that maximize the predictive utility of the model. This final model is based on statistical decisions, not on theory or research hypotheses (see Cohen et al., 2003; Licht, 1995; Tabachnick & Fidell, 2007).

LOGISTIC REGRESSION

Use when: You want to predict values on a dichotomous DV using one or more continuous or dichotomous IVs.

Logistic regression has become popular in forensic psychology research, appearing in more than 20% of the articles in the 2008 and 2009 issues of

Law and Human Behavior, more frequently than any other multivariate statistic. In jury research, it is increasingly used to test how only the IVs and the interactions between the IVs are related to verdict (see, e.g., Levett & Kovera, 2008; Jehle et al., 2009; Schuller et al., 2009; Wiley & Bottoms, 2009). It is also used to do more complex modeling of verdicts with additional predictors (see, e.g., Devine et al., 2009; Martire & Kemp, 2009), eyewitness identifications (see, e.g., Greathouse & Kovera, 2009), violence and recidivism (see, e.g., Levine, 2009; McEwan et al., 2009; Modecki, 2009; Swanson et al., 2008), clinical symptoms and decisions (Douglas, Lillienfeld, et al., 2008; Fishbein et al., 2009; Stockdale et al., 2009), and other forensic psychology decisions (see, e.g., Ferguson, Babcock, & Shane, 2008; Miller & Hayward, 2008; Wright & Fitzgerald, 2009).

Like linear regression, logistic regression is used to predict the value of one variable (now called the "outcome" variable rather than the "criterion" variable) from the value of one or multiple other variables (the predictors) (for a review, see Pampel, 2000; Tabachnick & Fidell, 2007; Wright, 1995). Binary logistic regression is used when the outcome variable is dichotomous, and multinomial logistic regression is used when the outcome variable has more than two categories. Because binary logistic regression is far more common in forensic psychology research, multinomial logistic regression is not discussed here, but see Ferguson, Babcock, and Shane (2008) and Modecki (2009) for forensic psychology examples. Like linear regression, logistic regression analysis can test hypotheses about whether and how much the predictors account for group membership in the outcome variable, which predictors are accounting for a significant amount of membership in the outcome variable, and the expected change in odds of group membership on the outcome for observed change in the predictors.

Binary logistic regression makes several assumptions. First, the "outcome" variable is dichotomous, and the categories in the outcome variable must be independent and exhaustive (Pampel, 2000; Tabachnick & Fidell, 2007; Wright, 1995). In other words, participants must be necessarily in one or the other category, and those categories represent all possible outcomes of interest. Second, the model must be correctly specified. Excluding relevant variables from the model will lead to biased estimates, and including irrelevant variables may increase the standard error, increasing the risk of Type II error (i.e., it sabotages significance tests). Unlike linear regression, logistic regression does not make the assumption that the predictors will be interval-level measures, nor does it assume that the predictor variables will be normally distributed. Therefore, it is a useful analysis when the predictors are non-normally distributed interval-level measures and/or categorical measures (Pampel, 2000; Tabachnick & Fidell, 2007; Wright, 1995). Logistic regression requires a large sample to test hypotheses. For logistic regression, a minimum of 50 cases per predictor variable is recommended (Wright, 1995). It is also important that there is not multicollinearity among the predictor variables, as is true in linear regression (Tabachnik & Fidell, 2007).

Although the statistical approach to the model is different and better for dichotomous outcome variables (see Pampel, 2000; Wright, 1995), the basic approach to conducting the analysis is the same as for linear regression. Like linear regression, logistic regression tests whether and how well the model works, which predictors are significantly contributing to the model, the magnitude of each predictor's contribution, and whether adding additional predictors improves the model's performance. There are two statistics used to determine whether the model is significant: the −2 log likelihood and the chi-square (Pampel, 2000; Tabachnick & Fidell, 2007). Logistic regression uses maximum-likelihood estimation, in which the procedure selects estimates that are most likely to be correct given the observed values of the data, based on a series of iterations. Minimizing the log likelihood score is the criterion for estimating the parameters in logistic regression, which is called the log likelihood test for model fit.

Statistical programs multiply the log likelihood by –2, because this approximates a chi-square distribution and allows for a chi-square test of significance of the change in log likelihood resulting from adding predictors to the model. As significant predictors are added to the model, the –2 log likelihood (–2LL) decreases. Using chi-square, we can determine whether this decrease in –2LL (or increase in model fit) is significant (Pampel, 2000; Tabachnick & Fidell, 2007). The "model" chi-square is the test of the significance of the overall model fit. This is the only test of model fit you will need if you are doing simultaneous logistic regression in one block.

Most researchers in forensic psychology report the model chi-square (see, e.g., Devine et al., 2009; Fishbein et al., 2009; Levett & Kovera, 2008; McEwan et al., 2009; Modecki, 2009; Wright & Fitzgerald, 2009), and many also report the –2LL (see, e.g., Douglas, Lillienfeld, et al., 2008; Jehle et al., 2009; Miller & Hayward, 2008). In hierarchical logistic regression, model chi-square is the test of the fit of the full model at each block of entry. "Block" chi-square tests the change in model performance when a block of variables are entered (see, e.g., Devine et al., 2009), similar to the *F*-change test in linear regression. If you are doing stepwise logistic regression (see, e.g., Greathouse & Kovera, 2009), the "step" chi-square tests the change in model performance at a step of entry of variables stepwise. You will get tests for each variable that is "stepped" in or out. When these chi-squares are significant ($p < .05$), the predictor variables are significantly predicting group membership in the outcome variable (Pampel, 2000; Tabachnick & Fidell, 2007; Wright, 1995).

There are a couple of options for determining how well the model works in logistic regression. First, the classification table and the percentage of cases correctly reclassified can be examined (Pampel, 2000; Tabachnick & Fidell, 2007; Wright, 1995). The classification table summarizes the fit between the actual data and the predicted group memberships. Overall percent correct reclassified describes the number of cases correctly classified into the categories of the outcome variable based on the values of the predictors in the model. When that value is high, the match between the observed outcomes and the predicted outcomes is better, which means the model is performing better. Information about the percent correct reclassified with logistic regression models is sometimes reported in forensic psychology (see, e.g., Devine et al., 2009; Jehle et al., 2009; Miller & Hayward, 2008; Stockdale et al., 2009; Wright & Fitzgerald, 2009).

Second, although logistic regression is not testing a linear relationship or variance accounted for by the predictors, two pseudo R-squares are available in logistic regression (Pampel, 2000). The Cox and Snell's R^2 approximates what R-square does in linear regression. It is a proxy for explaining the proportion of variance explained in the model. Negelkerke's R^2 is also a pseudo R-square that approximates the linear regression R-square as with Cox and Snell. However, Negelkerke's is preferred by some because it is adjusted to be on the same scale of measurement as a linear regression R-square (Pampel, 2000). R-squares for logistic regression are also sometimes reported in forensic psychology, with some researchers reporting the Cox and Snell version (see, e.g., Fishbein et al., 2009; Wright & Fitzgerald, 2009) and others reporting the Negelkerke version (see, e.g., Devine et al., 2009; Douglas, Lillienfeld, et al., 2008; McEwan et al., 2009; Stockdale et al., 2009; Wright & Fitzgerald, 2009).

There are several pieces of information about the contribution of individual predictors to the model that are important to interpret in logistic regression. The Wald statistic is used in logistic regression as a test of significance for individual predictors (Pampel, 2000; Tabachnick & Fidell, 2007; Wright, 1995). Significance values are associated with the Wald statistic, and they are interpreted with the traditional $p < .05$ cutoff to determine whether to reject or retain the null that the individual predictor does not contribute to the model. When $p < .05$ for a predictor, that predictor is significantly accounting for group membership in the outcome variable. For each predictor, raw parameter estimates (B) and odds ratios are also calculated.

To determine the type and magnitude of the contribution of each predictor, the odds ratio is interpreted. The odds ratio, indicated as "exp(B)" in SPSS and often abbreviated as "OR" in articles, is a change in the odds of membership in the target group of the outcome variable for a one-unit change in the value of the predictor. Odds ratios represent the change in the odds of being in the target group based on changes in the value of the predictors. The target group of the outcome variable is the group with the higher value. For example, if the outcome variable is verdict and it is coded as "0 = not guilty" and "1 = guilty," "guilty" would be the target group. Values on predictors can either increase or decrease chances of being in the target group. An odds ratio of 1.0 indicates that changes in the value of the predictor make membership in the target group no more or less likely. Predictors with these values or close to them are not likely to be significant. Odds ratios that are greater than 1.0 indicate that increases in the value of the predictor increase the odds of being in the target group or make target group membership more likely. For every one-point increase in the value of the predictor, the odds of being in the target group of the outcome variable are the value of the odds ratio times more likely.

Odds ratios that are less than 1.0 indicate that increases in the value of the predictor decrease the odds of being in the target group or make target group membership less likely. For every one-point increase in the value of the predictor, the odds of being in the target group are (1– the value of the odds ratio) × 100% less likely (Pampel, 2000; Tabachnick & Fidell, 2007; Wright, 1995). For example, if verdict (as coded previously in the chapter) was predicted by the gender of the juror (coded 0 = male and 1 = female), an odds ratio of 1.0 indicates that the gender of the juror does not make a guilty verdict any more or less likely. If the odds ratio for gender as a predictor was 8.76, then female jurors as compared to male jurors make a guilty verdict 8.76 times more likely. If the odds ratio for gender was .76, then female jurors as compared with male jurors make a guilty verdict 24% less likely. The same is true for interval-level predictors, except that the increase or decrease in the odds of target group membership would be per every point increase in the value of the predictor.

All the articles in the 2008 and 2009 years of *Law and Human Behavior* using logistic regression (cited previously) reported the odds ratios. Some also reported a combination of B, the SE of B, the Wald statistic, and the exact *p*-values associated with the odds ratios (see, e.g., Devine et al., 2009; Greathouse & Kovera, 2009; Douglas, Lillienfeld, et al., 2008; Levine, 2009; Martire & Kemp, 2009; Wiley & Bottoms, 2009; Wright & Fitzgerald, 2009). Confidence intervals around the odds ratios were occasionally reported as well (see, e.g., Levine, 2009; McEwan et al., 2009; Swanson et al., 2008; Wright & Fitzgerald, 2009).

STRUCTURAL EQUATION MODELING

Structural equation modeling (SEM) is becoming more common in psychological research, and forensic psychological research is no exception. SEM is a family of statistical approaches including but not limited to path analysis, confirmatory factor analysis, and the analysis of full structural models (for a review of SEM, see Kline, 2005). Confirmatory factor analysis (CFA) permits the examination of latent variables created from observed variables (for a review of factor analysis, see Gorsuch, 1983). Path analysis and full structural models permit the prediction of multiple DVs and testing the meditational effect of multiple predictor variables (for a review of path analysis, see Klem, 2000). Path analysis tests only observed variables, whereas full structural models combine path analysis and CFA, measuring the effect of both observed and latent variables. In all types of SEM, it is typical to report on the fit of the model. Sometimes SEM is done with programs specifically designed to test SEM, and sometimes it is done using other statistics, such as the use of hierarchical linear regression to create path models (see, e.g., Wiener & Richter, 2008). Fit indices that are often reported when the model is tested using an SEM program include but are not limited to chi-square, GFI, CFI, NFI, and RMSEA (Kline, 2005). For predictive models, the parameter estimates for all of the paths are usually reported, including direct, indirect, and total effects. Figures containing the direct paths are usually included. In forensic psychology, confirmatory factor analysis is often used to test the factor structure of psychometric measures (see, e.g., Fishbein et al., 2009; Jacobs et al., 2008; Viljoen et al., 2009). Path analysis has been used to test the effect of IVs and mediators on verdict decision making (see, e.g., Wiener & Richter, 2008; Wiley & Bottoms, 2009). SEM is likely to become more commonly used in forensic psychology research, as it has in other areas of psychology.

A NOTE ON REPORTING YOUR RESULTS

Once you have selected and conducted the appropriate bivariate analysis, the *APA Manual* recommends that you report enough information about your statistical tests and the results of those tests to allow your readers to understand why you conducted those tests, to interpret the results, and to be aware of anything that might have affected those results. What is required to provide this information will vary depending on the type of tests used. However, basic descriptive information should be provided, such as means (or cell frequencies where appropriate), measures of variability around those means (such as the standard deviation), and cell sample sizes. For multivariate analyses, the correlation matrix or covariance matrix for all the variables in the analysis might be appropriate descriptive information to provide in addition to the means, standard deviations, and sample sizes. When reporting the inferential statistics described previously, it is important to provide the value and the direction of the summary statistic (such as t, r, F, X^2, etc.), the degrees of freedom associated with that statistic, a measure of error (such as the mean square error for ANOVA), and the exact p-value to provide a level of significance. Symbols for the statistics should be italicized. Numbers should be rounded where possible to two decimal places, but reporting more than two decimal places is acceptable, particularly for exact p-values. Statistics should be displayed in tables where possible. Text descriptions of the statistics should refer to those tables, but information displayed in tables should not be repeated in the text (APA, 2009).

STATISTICS: THE BOTTOM LINE

Deciding which statistics are appropriate for your study can be overwhelming. The goal is to pick statistics that allow you to test your research hypothesis. Think carefully about whether your hypothesis is associative or predictive and about whether it requires a multivariate statistic. Also carefully consider how your variables are measured so that you pick the best statistic to test their relationships. Remember that your ability to make causal interpretations of the relationships between your variables rests in your research design, not in the statistics that you use. Therefore, you must be very careful in the way you phrase your results. Finally, make sure you are careful to fully describe your analyses so that readers can fully understand your results.

REFERENCES

American Psychological Association (2009). *Publication manual of the American Psychological Association* (6th ed.). Washington, DC: American Psychological Association.

Berk, R. A. (2004). *Regression analysis: A constructive critique*. Thousand Oaks, CA: Sage.

Blunt, M., & McAllister, H. (2009). Mug shot exposure effects: Does size matter? *Law and Human Behavior, 33*, 175–182. doi: 10.1007/s10979-008-9126-z

Brown, S., St. Amand, M., & Zamble, E. (2009). The dynamic prediction of criminal recidivism: A three-wave prospective study. *Law and Human Behavior, 33*, 25–45. doi: 10.1007/s10979-008-9139-7

Bryant, F. B., & Yarnold, P. R. (1995). Principal-components analysis and exploratory and confirmatory factor analysis. In L. G. Grimm & P. R. Yarnold (Eds.), *Reading and understanding multivariate statistics* (pp. 65–98). Washington, DC: American Psychological Association.

Cohen, J., Cohen, P., West, S., & Aiken, L. (2003). *Applied multiple regression/correlation analysis for the behavioral sciences* (3rd ed.). Mahwah, NJ: Lawrence Erlbaum.

Connolly, D., Price, H., Lavoie, J., & Gordon, H. (2008). Perceptions and predictors of children's credibility of a unique event and an instance of a repeated event. *Law and Human Behavior, 32*, 92–112. doi: 10.1007/s10979-006-9083-3

Cooper, V., & Zapf, P. (2008). Psychiatric patients' comprehension of Miranda rights. *Law and Human Behavior, 32*, 390–405. doi: 10.1007/s10979-007-9099-3

Cortina, J. M., & Nouri, H. (2000). *Effect size for ANOVA designs*. (Sage University Papers Series on Quantitative Applications in the Social Sciences, 07-129). Thousand Oaks, CA: Sage.

Dahl, L. C., Brimacombe, C. A. E., & Lindsay, D. S. (2009). Investigating investigators: How presentation order influences participant-investigators' interpretations of eyewitness identification and alibi evidence. *Law and Human Behavior, 33*, 368–380. doi: 10.1007/s10979-008-9151-y

DeVellis, R.F. (2003). *Scale development: Theory and applications*. Thousand Oaks, CA: Sage.

Devine, D. J., Buddenbaum, J., Houp, S., Stolle, D. P., & Studebaker, N. (2009). Strength of evidence, extraevidentiary influence, and the liberation hypothesis: Data from the field. *Law and Human Behavior, 33*, 136–148. doi: 10.1007/s10979-008-9144-x

Douglas, K. S., Epstein, M. E., & Poythress, N. G. (2008). Criminal recidivism among juvenile offenders: Testing the incremental and predictive validity of three measures of psychopathic features. *Law and Human Behavior, 32*, 423–438. doi: 10.1007/s10979-007-9114-8

Douglas, K. S., Lilienfeld, S. O., Skeem, J. L., Edens, J. F., Patrick, C. J., & Poythress, N. G. (2008). Relation of antisocial and psychopathic traits to suicide-related behavior among offenders. *Law and Human Behavior, 32*, 511–525. doi: 10.1007/s10979-007-9122-8

Ferguson, J. R., Babcock, L., & Shane, P. M. (2008). Behind the mask of method: Political orientation and constitutional interpretive preferences. *Law and Human Behavior, 32*, 502–510. doi: 10.1007/s10979-007-9112-x

Fishbein, D., Sheppard, M., Hyde, C., Hubal, R., Newlin, D., Serin, R., . . . Alesci, S. (2009). Deficits in behavioral inhibition predict treatment engagement in prison inmates. *Law and Human Behavior, 33*, 419–435. doi: 10.1007/s10979-008-9163-7

Gabbert, F., Hope, L., & Fisher, R. P. (2009). Protecting eyewitness evidence: Examining the efficacy of a self-administered interview tool. *Law and Human Behavior, 33*, 298–307. doi: 10.1007/s10979-008-9146-8

Gorsuch, R. L. (1983). *Factor analysis* (2nd ed.). Hillsdale, NJ: Lawrence Erlbaum.

Greathouse, S. M., & Kovera, M. B. (2009). Instruction bias and lineup presentation moderate the effects of administrator knowledge on eyewitness identification. *Law and Human Behavior, 33*, 70–82. doi: 10.1007/s10979-008-9136-x

Hilton, N. Z., Harris, G. T., Rice, M. E., Houghton, R. E., & Eke, A. W. (2008). An in-depth actuarial assessment for wife assault recidivism: The domestic violence risk appraisal guide. *Law and Human Behavior*, *32*, 150–163. doi:10.1007/s10979-007-9088-6

Jehle, A., Miller, M., & Kemmelmeier, M. (2009). The influence of accounts and remorse on mock jurors' judgments of offenders. *Law and Human Behavior, 33*, 393–404. doi: 10.1007/s10979-008-9164-6

Klem, L. (2000). Structural equation modeling. In L. G. Grimm & P. R. Yarnold (Eds.), *Reading and understanding more multivariate statistics* (pp. 227-260). Washington, DC: American Psychological Association.

Kline, R. B. (2005). *Principles and practice of structural equation modeling* (2nd ed.). New York, NY: Guilford Press.

Landis, J. R., & Koch, G. G. (1977). The measurement of observer agreement for categorical data. *Biometrics, 33*, 159–174.

Leippe, M. R., Eisenstadt, D., & Rauch, S. M. (2009). Cueing confidence in eyewitness identifications: Influence of biased lineup instructions and pre-identification memory feedback under varying lineup conditions. *Law and Human Behavior, 33*, 194–212. doi: 10.1007/s10979-008-9135-y

Levett, L. M., & Kovera, M. B. (2008). The effectiveness of opposing expert witnesses for educating jurors about unreliable expert evidence. *Law and Human Behavior, 32*, 363–374. doi: 10.1007/s10979-007-9113-9

Levine, S. Z. (2009). Examining the incidence of and time to recidivism within the risk contingency framework: A 20-year follow up study. *Law and Human Behavior, 33*, 167–174. doi: 10.1007/s10979-008-9142-z

Licht, M. H. (1995). Multiple regression and correlation. In L. G. Grimm & P. R. Yarnold (Eds.), *Reading and understanding multivariate statistics* (pp. 19–64). Washington, DC: American Psychological Association.

Manchak, S. M., Skeem, J. L., & Douglas, K. S. (2008). Utility of the revised level of service inventory (LSI-R) in predicting recidivism after long-term incarceration. *Law and Human Behavior, 32*, 477–488. doi: 10.1007/s10979-007-9118-4

Martire, K. A., & Kemp, R. I. (2009). The impact of eyewitness expert evidence and judicial instruction on juror ability to evaluate eyewitness testimony. *Law and Human Behavior, 33*, 225–236. doi:10.1007/s10979-008-9134-z

McAuliff, B. D., Kovera, M. B., & Nunez, G. (2009). Can jurors recognize missing control groups, confounds, and experimenter bias in psychological science? *Law and*

Human Behavior, 33, 247–257. doi: 10.1007/s10979-008-9133-0

McEwan, T. E., Mullen, P. E., & MacKenzie, R. (2009). A study of the predictors of persistence in stalking situations. *Law and Human Behavior, 33*, 149–158. doi: 10.1007/s10979-008-9141-0

McGraw, K. O., & Wong, S. P. (1996). Forming inferences about some interclass correlation coefficients. *Psychological Methods, 1*, 20–26.

McQuiston-Surrett, D., & Saks, M. J. (2009). The testimony of forensic identification science: What expert witnesses say and what factfinders hear. *Law and Human Behavior, 33*, 436–453. doi: 10.1007/s10979-008-9169-1

Miller, M. K., & Hayward, R. D. (2008). Religious characteristics and the death penalty. *Law and Human Behavior, 32*, 113–123. doi: 10.1007/s10979-007-9090-z

Modecki, K. L. (2008). Addressing gaps in the maturity of judgment literature: Age differences and delinquency. *Law and Human Behavior, 32*, 78–91. doi: 10.1007/s10979-007-9087-7

Modecki, K. L. (2009). "It's a rush": Psychosocial content of antisocial decision making. *Law and Human Behavior, 33*, 183–193. doi: 10.1007/s10979-008-9150-z

Neuschatz, J. S., Lawson, D. S., Swanner, J. K., Meissner, C. A., & Neuschatz, J. S. (2008). The effects of accomplice witnesses and jailhouse informants on jury decision making. *Law and Human Behavior, 32*, 137–149. doi: 10.1007/s10979-007-9100-1

Pampel, F. C. (2000). *Logistic regression: A primer*. (Sage University Papers Series on Quantitative Applications in the Social Sciences, 07–132). Thousand Oaks, CA: Sage.

Schuller, R. A., Kazoleas, V., & Kawakami, K. (2009). The impact of prejudice screening procedures on racial bias in the courtroom. *Law and Human Behavior, 33*, 320–328. doi: 10.1007/s10979-008-9153-9

Schwalbe, C. S., & Maschi, T. (2009). Investigating probation strategies with juvenile offenders: The influence of officers' attitudes and youth characteristics. *Law and Human Behavior, 33*, 357–367. doi: 10.1007/s10979-008-9158-4

Skeem, J., Eno Louden, J., Manchak, S., Haddad, E., & Vidal, S. (2009). Social networks and social control of probationers with co-occurring mental and substance abuse problems. *Law and Human Behavior, 33*, 122–135. doi: 10.1007/s10979-008-9140-1

Smithson, M. (2003). *Confidence intervals.* (Sage University Papers Series on Quantitative Applications in the Social Sciences, 07–140). Thousand Oaks, CA: Sage.

Stockdale, M. S., Logan, T. K., & Weston, R. (2009). Sexual harassment and post-traumatic stress disorder. *Law and Human Behavior, 33,* 405–418. doi: 10.1007/s10979-008-9162-8

Swanson, J. W., Van Dorn, R. A., Swartz, M. S., Smith, A., Elbogen, E. B., & Monahan, J. (2008). Alternative pathways to violence in persons with schizophrenia: The role of childhood antisocial behavior problems. *Law and Human Behavior, 32,* 228–240. doi: 10.1007/s10979-007-9095-7

Tabachnick, B. G., & Fidell, L. S. (2007). *Using multivariate statistics* (5th ed.). Boston, MA: Pearson.

Turner, J., & Thayer, J. (2001). *Introduction to analysis of variance: Design, analysis, and interpretation.* Thousand Oaks, CA: Sage.

Viljoen, J. L., Slaney, K. L., & Grisso, T. (2009). The use of the MacCAT-CA with adolescents: An item response theory investigation of age-related measurement bias. *Law and Human Behavior, 33,* 283–297. doi: 10.1007/s10979-008-9154-8

Vitacco, M. J., Van Rybroek, G. J., Rogstad, J. E., Yahr, L. E., Tomony, J. D., & Saewert, E. (2009). Predicting short-term institutional aggression in forensic patients: A multi-trait method for understanding subtypes of aggression. *Law and Human Behavior, 33,* 308–319. doi: 10.1007/s10979-008-9155-7

Vrij, A., Mann, S. A., Fisher, R. P., Leal, S., Milne, R., & Bull, R. (2008). Increasing cognitive load to facilitate lie detection: The benefit of recalling an event in reverse order. *Law and Human Behavior, 32,* 253–265. doi: 10.1007/s10979-007-9103-y

Walters, G. D., & Schlauch, C. (2008). The psychological inventory of criminal thinking styles and level of service inventory—revised: Screening version as predictors of official and self-reported disciplinary infractions. *Law and Human Behavior, 32,* 454–462. doi: 10.1007/s10979-007-9117-5

Weinfurt, K. P. (1995). Multivariate analysis of variance. In L. G. Grimm & P. R. Yarnold (Eds.), *Reading and understanding multivariate statistics* (pp. 245–276). Washington, DC: American Psychological Association.

Weisburd, D., & Britt, C. (2003). *Statistics in criminal justice* (2nd ed.). Belmont, CA: Thomson Wadsworth.

Wiener, R. L., & Richter, E. (2008). Symbolic hate: Intention to intimidate, political ideology, and group association. *Law and Human Behavior, 32,* 463–476. doi: 10.1007/s10979-007-9119-3

Wiley, T. R. A., & Bottoms, B. L. (2009). Effects of defendant sexual orientation on jurors' perceptions of child sexual assault. *Law and Human Behavior, 33,* 46–60. doi: 10.1007/s10979-008-9131-2

Wright, R. E. (1995). Logistic regression. In L. G. Grimm & P. R. Yarnold (Eds.), *Reading and understanding multivariate statistics* (pp. 217–244). Washington, DC: American Psychological Association.

Wright, C. V., & Fitzgerald, L. F. (2009) Correlates of joining a sexual harassment class action. *Law and Human Behavior, 33,* 265–282. doi: 10.1007/s10979-008-9156-6

CRIMINAL LAW—PRETRIAL ISSUES: CRIMINAL INVESTIGATIONS AND PRETRIAL FORENSIC ASSESSMENT

CHAPTER 6

Research Methods for Psychophysiological Deception Detection

CHARLES R. HONTS AND JOHN C. KIRCHER[1]

FOR PURPOSES OF this chapter, we accept Vrij's (2000) definition of deception as "a successful or unsuccessful deliberate attempt, without forewarning, to create in another a belief which the communicator considers to be untrue" (p. 6). Deception is a ubiquitous human behavior. DePaulo and her colleagues (DePaulo & Kashy, 1998; DePaulo, Kashy, Kirkendol, Wyer, & Epstein, 1996; Kashy & Depaulo, 1996) studied deception in naturalistic settings and found that during interpersonal interactions of 10 minutes or longer, people lied on average twice a day. Deception is used in one quarter of interactions with others, and on average, a person lies to 34% of the people interacted with during an average week. Robinson, Shepherd, and Heywood (1998) reported that 83% of the university undergraduates surveyed said they would lie to get a job.

Although deception in daily discourse is common, the overwhelming weight of the scientific evidence indicates that without technological assistance, people are terrible lie detectors. Vrij (2008) summarized the results of 79 studies of unassisted lie detection and found that observers were barely better than chance with accuracies of 54.27% and showed a general truth bias. Professional experience at attempting to detect lies does not enable police officers to improve on the ability of average citizens to detect lies, although it does increase the confidence they have in their ability to detect deception. Unfortunately, research consistently shows that confidence in deception detection judgments is unrelated to their accuracy.

---

1. The authors would like to thank Racheal Reavy and Kimberly Markowski for their comments on the draft of this chapter. Correspondence should be addressed to Charles R. Honts, Psychology Department, Boise State University, 1910 University Drive, MS-1715, Boise, ID 83725-1715; E-mail: chonts@boisestate.edu

If deception was limited to matters of little import, our inability to detect deception might be of little concern. While many lies are innocuous, others can result in the direst of consequences. Each of the 19 terrorists who attacked the United States on September 11, 2001 lied to officials on at least three occasions: when they applied for entry visas to the United States, when they entered the United States, and when they passed through airport security on September 11. Not one of those terrorists was detected in their deception. What a different world we might live in now had some of those terrorists been detected!

Deception and deception detection are also critical factors in forensics. Criminals are highly motivated to deceive and hide their crimes, and suspects who are falsely accused of a crime are highly motivated to convince authorities of their innocence. One of the main duties of the triers of fact in the legal system is to decide who is and who is not telling the truth. The task of judicial credibility assessment is assigned to and is almost always limited to triers of fact, despite the overwhelming weight of the scientific evidence suggesting that both judges and juries are likely to perform abysmally at the task of detecting deception.

Given the frequency of deception as a human behavior, the inability of people to detect deception and the potential seriousness of successful deception, one might expect that the study of deception and deception detection would be a focal area of scientific study within psychological science. However, this is not the case. The number of active researchers in this area is quite small, and the volume of research, although growing, remains somewhat limited, given the extensive role of deception in human behavior and affairs. We will not attempt to review the existing literature here. Two excellent volumes on deception detection research were recently published, and readers are referred to Vrij (2008) and to Granhag and Strömwall (2004).

As authors of this chapter, we wish to acknowledge that we have spent most of our adult lives as applied scientists studying deception detection—and in particular, the use of autonomic measures for that purpose. One (Honts) is also a practicing polygraph examiner with more than 35 years of experience. As we are most well versed in psychophysiological deception detection (PDD) research, we concentrate our discussion on research methods within that context. However, we also have ventured into other areas of deception detection, including statement analysis, personnel screening, false confessions, and deception detection at portals. We have found that many of the methods and limitations of research on detecting deception in forensic settings are encountered in these other areas as well. Although this chapter focuses on PDD, many of the concerns we raise are applicable to research on deception detection in general.

THE COMPARISON QUESTION TEST

Although several types of polygraph tests are used worldwide, the comparison question test (CQT) is the most common technique for PDD in criminal investigations in the United States and in most other countries (Honts, 2004).

Standard field polygraph tests measure respiration, electrodermal responses, and relative blood pressure. However, other physiological measures are sometimes used and new measures are being explored. Please see the Apparatus section that follows for more detail on physiological measures. The CQT contains several types of questions, but the relative strength of physiological reactions to two types of questions is used to draw inferences about truth and deception. The CQT includes two to four accusatory questions, known as relevant questions. Relevant questions directly and unequivocally address the issue(s) to be resolved (e.g., Did you shoot John Doe?). The CQT also includes two to four comparison questions that are intended to be answered by the subject with a deceptive response (e.g., Prior to 2008, did you ever do anything that was dishonest or illegal?). In the traditional approach to the CQT, the subject is told that the comparison questions are used to determine whether the subject is the type of person who would commit the crime in question and then lie about it, or not. Thus, if the subject were to answer "Yes" to a comparison question, that subject would appear to be the type of person who committed the crime. Consequently, the subject chooses to answer "No" to the comparison questions, responses that in all likelihood are lies. The demand characteristics of this pretest review of the questions with the subject strongly influences the subject to make a deceptive answer to the comparison questions.

In a newer approach to presenting comparison questions, the examiner instructs the subject to answer them with a clearly deceptive response, saying that it is important that the examiner be able to observe appropriate physiological responses from the subject when he or she is deceptive; otherwise an inconclusive outcome will result. In either case, the CQT predicts a cross-over interaction in the physiological responses between question type (relevant, comparison) and deception status (truthful, deceptive). Subjects whose answers to relevant questions are deceptive are expected to exhibit stronger physiological responses to them than to the comparison questions. Conversely, subjects whose answers to the relevant questions are truthful are expected to react more strongly to the comparison questions to which they are lying than to the relevant questions to which they are responding truthfully.

METHODS: BASIC ISSUES

Because this is a book about research methods in forensic psychology, presumably most readers are interested in applied research. A scientist in this area must first decide whether her or his questions can best be addressed in a laboratory or a field setting. If the purpose of the research is to identify and delineate causal relationships between variables or to test for effects of specific independent variables, the controlled conditions of randomized experiments are preferred. If the primary goal of the research is to assess the generalizability of known relationships to real-world settings, field settings and quasi-natural or natural experiments are preferred.

Competition between the respective goals of experimental clarity and the desire for high generalizability has resulted in considerable debate and controversy in the literature on PDD. Some commentators have denigrated the role of randomized experiments to study deception detection, taking a general if sometimes implicit position that deception phenomena cannot be modeled in controlled settings because the real-world motivational setting cannot be brought into the laboratory (e.g., Ben-Shakhar & Furedy, 1990; Iacono & Lykken, 2005). Others have taken the position that thoughtfully designed randomized experiments can provide useful information about the phenomena in real-world settings (e.g., Kircher, Horowitz & Raskin, 1988; Honts, Raskin, & Kircher, 2005).

Research and logic now indicate that the argument against randomized experiments is specious. Support for the generalizability of results from laboratory experiments on PDD comes from several sources. Polina, Dollins, Senter, Krapohl, and Ryan (2004) compared data collected in randomized experiments with data collected from real-world polygraph examinations confirmed by confession. Although they report overall differences between the laboratory and field settings in levels of physiological activation, accuracies of classifications did not differ. The results confirmed earlier findings by Kircher, Raskin, Honts, and Horowitz (1988). Since the CQT relies on within subject comparisons of reactions to two types of questions, differences in tonic levels of activation should be relatively unimportant.

Another line of support for the generalizability of laboratory data comes from surveys of the scientific community. Although there are several surveys of the scientific community concerning issues related to the validity of polygraph examination results, only one survey directly addressed the issue of the scientific community's attitudes toward the use of laboratory data for making policy and admissibility decisions in real-world settings. In a telephone survey Honts, Thurber, Cvencek, and Alloway (2002) asked a random sample of members of the Society for Psychophysiological Research (SPR) and the American Psychology-Law Society (AP-LS) "How much weight should policy makers and the courts give to laboratory studies in estimating the validity of the polygraph in real-world tests?" Respondents were asked to use a 5-point scale that was anchored with none (1) and considerable (5). The results of that survey are illustrated in Figure 6.1. The modal response for the members of the SPR was "moderate" (4), and the modal response for the members of the AP-LS was "some" (3). Overall, 85.5% of the respondents from the AP-LS thought that polygraph examinations should be given some or more weight, while 76.4% of the SPR respondents endorsed giving some or more weight. These results indicate that a substantial majority of the members of these two scientific organizations believe that laboratory studies of the polygraph do offer valuable information for informing real-world decisions, and they support the generalizability of laboratory research.

Research on the effects of motivation on PDD also supports the use of randomized experiments in controlled settings. Critics argue that laboratory

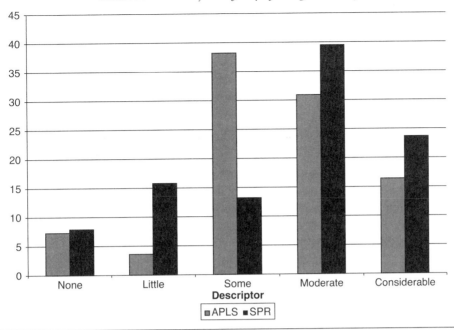

Figure 6.1 Mean Responses from Members of the American Psychology-Law Society (APLS) and the Society for Psychophysiological Research (SPR) concerning the amount of weight policy makers should give to the results of laboratory research on PDD

simulations are hopelessly flawed because they cannot achieve the high levels of motivation that are characteristic of polygraph tests in actual criminal investigations. However, the data on effects of motivation do not support that position. Honts and Carlton (1990) provided an extensive review of the literature and found that most of the research had focused on the effects of motivation on the detection of information. Although the detection of information paradigm differs in several important respects from the detection of deception (Raskin & Honts, 2002), both approaches yield inferences about deception that are based on within-subject comparisons of physiological responses to two types of test items.

Tests for the effects of motivation on the detection of information were mixed. Effects of motivation were observed in two studies, and null results were reported in three other studies. With regard to deception detection, Podlesny and Raskin (1977) stated that motivation associated with the outcome of an examination is a critical part of simulating the deceptive context of the real world in the laboratory. Others have argued that the subject must not only be motivated to deceive but also must experience actual fear of detection (Saxe, 1985). Kircher et al. (1988) provides some support for the notion that motivation is associated with the accuracy of the control question test in a meta-analysis of 14 laboratory studies. Kircher et al. found three significant predictors of increased accuracy of the CQT in those studies. Motivation was among them. Stronger incentives were associated with higher levels of accuracy, $r = .73$, although motivation shared considerable co-variance with the other two predictors in that study and could not be isolated as a unique predictor.

Two other studies directly addressed the effects of motivation on the CQT. Bradley and Janisse (1981) threatened half of their subjects with a "painful but not permanently damaging electric shock if judged guilty" (p. 309). The other half of the subjects received no such threat. Bradley and Janisse reported no effect of this manipulation on detectability. Similarly, in a mock-crime experiment, Honts and Carlton (1990) found no effects of motivation in a group of U.S. Army basic trainees who were or were not offered an afternoon off from their basic training duties if they could pass a CQT. Recently, Honts, Amato, and Gordon (2004) reported very high detection rates in a mock-crime study that used only a reward of $1.00 as the motivation for passing the CQT. As a whole, and notwithstanding critics' strong assertions, the data do not support the argument that difficulties in simulating the high levels of motivation present in real-world applications of PDD invalidate results of laboratory research in this field.

CHARACTERISTICS OF A HIGH-QUALITY LABORATORY PDD STUDY

PARTICIPANTS

Participant samples in the published PDD literature vary widely, from incarcerated male prisoners to women undergraduates at an expensive private liberal arts college. For those with a wish to make forensically relevant statements, careful attention to the participant sample would seem to be prudent. For most forensic applications, college student participants, although available and inexpensive, probably are not the best sample if the target population consists of suspects involved in actual criminal investigations (although some college students might find themselves in such situations). Moreover, Kircher et al. (1988) reported that the use of college students in CQT studies was associated with lower accuracy in CQT mock-crime studies.

Starting in the 1970s, the Utah research group took the approach of recruiting subjects from the general community with help-wanted ads (Podlesny & Raskin, 1978). Honts, Raskin, and Kircher (1985) later compared several different mock-crime subject samples on socialization scores. The mean socialization score for a prison inmate sample was 23.5, SD = 5.8. The mean socialization score for a community sample recruited by newspaper ads was about a standard deviation higher (29.3) than the sample of prison inmates, and the mean for a sample of college students was about two standard deviations higher (35.3). Although the community sample differed from the prison inmates sample, they were considerable closer to the inmates than were the college students on this theoretically relevant dimension of personality. If one wishes to generalize about the results of a laboratory study, then the use of community samples would seem prudent.

The Internet now offers additional inexpensive avenues for participant recruitment. The deception detection laboratory at Boise State University has used the job listings on Craigslist and in the online help-wanted section of a local weekly publication. The demographics of Internet samples appear similar to the ones we have previously obtained from newspaper advertisements.

STATISTICAL POWER

All of the usual recommendations for statistical power apply to research on deception and the detection of deception. However, given this chapter's focus on forensic issues, most readers will most likely be interested in clinically significant effects of substantial magnitude. If clinical significance is the criterion, statistical power is less of an issue, because large effects are detectable even in relatively small samples.

The investigator's choice of the outcome variable for analysis will affect statistical power. Virtually all of the analysis systems that compare physiological reactions to relevant and comparison questions produce a single score that is a composite of the multiple channels of physiological data and several repetitions of test questions. Those differences are measured on interval or ratio scales. Cut points are applied to the composite score that allows the case to be classified as truthful, inconclusive, or deceptive. Those cut points often are based on field practice and can be arbitrary. Nevertheless, for reasons that remain obscure, some researchers prefer to conduct analyses only at the level of the classification data (i.e., the examiner's classification of individual subjects as truthful or deceptive) and treat those data as nominal. This practice results in a substantial loss of statistical power to detect theoretically and practically meaningful effects. At the very least, classifications of outcomes as truthful, inconclusive, and deceptive can be treated as an ordinal metric and analyzed with statistics designed for such purposes with a substantial gain in statistical power over those based only on nominal measurement (for an example of this approach, see Honts, Raskin, & Kircher, 1994). However, an even more sensitive approach would be to analyze channel-specific or composite measures of differential reactivity with any of the appropriate parametric methods.

PROCEDURES

Podlesny and Raskin (1977; 1978) originated the basic mock-crime paradigm that is in widespread use in PDD research today. They discuss the importance of establishing a deceptive context in the laboratory setting. Their description of deceptive context is worth repeating:

> The deceptive context refers to the total set of circumstances surrounding a subject's possible deception. In the field, deceptive subjects have usually committed specific acts about which they are questioned, whereas

non-deceptive subjects have not. Since any subject may receive punishment if he appears deceptive, guilty subjects are typically motivated to deceive, whereas innocent subjects are motivated to be truthful. Both guilty and innocent subjects desire the same outcome, that is, a decision of "truthful" by the polygrapher. (1977, p. 783)

Two aspects of the deceptive context seem critical: (1) the guilty commit the specific acts that are the subject for deception detection, and (2) some consequence must be associated with a "deceptive" outcome for both the innocent and the guilty, although the research indicates that the consequence need not be large. A variety of experimental procedures could be used to achieve those goals and create an effective deceptive context.

In the typical Utah-style mock crime, the process proceeds as follows: A participant is recruited from the community and comes to the campus for an appointment. An envelope addressed to the participant is attached to the door. The note directs the individual to enter a private room where he or she receives informed consent and recorded instructions for his or her participation. In our present format, the participants select themselves into conditions by choosing an envelope from a large box of envelopes. Each envelope contains instructions for only one condition of the study. That way all research personnel are unaware of the subject's condition throughout the procedure. It is only during the debriefing that the condition of the subject is revealed to the research team. The participant then goes to a different location and commits the mock crime (usually a theft) and reports to the laboratory at a later time for testing. An examiner who has not previously interacted with the participant and who has no knowledge of the subject's guilt status tests the person. Following the examination, the participant is debriefed about his or her participation.

If one is interested in producing data that are relevant to field applications, efforts should be made to model the field deceptive context and use field techniques as much as possible. Unfortunately, all too often this is not done. Kircher et al. (1988) found that the accuracy of CQT classifications achieved in the laboratory increased to the extent that the testing and scoring procedures approximated those used in the field. At one time, information about the conduct of polygraph examinations was withheld from the general public. That is no longer the case. Detailed descriptions of testing methods, including those used by the government, can be obtained on the Internet with minimal effort, and detailed descriptions are available in the published literature (e.g., Raskin & Honts, 2002). Moreover, it does not take extensive training to sufficiently model field techniques for laboratory study purposes. Honts, Amato, and Gordon (2004) reported training two individuals with PhD degrees in psychology and an undergraduate research assistant to use the Defense Academy of Credibility Assessment (DACA) version of the CQT (the technique used by all U. S. Federal law enforcement) in a few hours. Videotape recordings of their tests were evaluated by DACA polygraph training personnel and were considered to be representative of the Government's testing techniques. In the experimental conditions of the Honts et al. (2000) study that most closely modeled field techniques, these "examiners" were able to achieve 96% accuracy of classifications with no formal polygraph training. Thus, the training of laboratory personnel to conduct CQT examinations is neither too difficult nor too time consuming to adequately represent current field practice.

APPARATUS

Standard field polygraph instruments measure three physiological systems. Two separate measures of respiratory activity are taken from sensors placed around the upper chest and the abdomen. Two sensors for respiration are useful, because breathing is controlled by two sets of muscles—(1) the intercostal muscles between the ribs and (2) the diaphragm. There are individual differences, with some individuals showing a predominance of activity in one or the other of the muscle groups. Typically, the two respiration recordings are scored as one. Electrodermal activity is typically measured from the tips of two fingers or the palm. Although there is still variability in the quality of the electrodermal recordings made by field instruments, there are commercially available instruments that would meet current scientific standards that use constant voltage circuits and nonpolarizing electrodes. Field polygraph instruments also take a measure of relative blood pressure from a partially inflated low-pressure cuff on the upper arm. The recording that results from this cuff sensor system contains both fast and slow components. The fast component reflects the pulse wave associated with each heart cycle; the slower component correlates with changes in blood pressure (Podlesny & Kircher, 1999). Laboratory and field research indicate that it is the slower blood pressure component that provides the most useful information for deception detection (Honts et al., 2005).

Many modern instruments contain additional channels. Peripheral vasomotor recordings from a sensor placed on the palmar surface of the thumb were shown to contain useful information for deception detection in some laboratory studies of the CQT. Little is known about the diagnostic validity of the peripheral vasomotor activity in the field, as field polygraph examiners have only recently begun to record it. It also is now common for field instruments to record body movement from a device placed under the subject's chair or in the seat of the chair. Movement sensors can be used to indicate whether changes in other channels are artifacts or whether the subject attempts to use movements to distort the recordings and defeat the test.

Research in the laboratory certainly should not be limited to either field instruments or standard field measures. In fact, considerable effort is being expended by the U.S. Government to discover alternative or complementary measures. However, researchers who wish to draw data-based conclusions that are relevant to policy or practice should include the standard field measures in addition to any new or untested measures of deception.

CHARACTERISTICS OF A HIGH-QUALITY FIELD PDD STUDY

Whereas laboratory experiments offer more control over extraneous and confounding variables, they may be less externally valid than field studies. Field studies use polygraph tests conducted on actual criminal suspects, witnesses, or victims of real crimes. Although field studies are subject to many threats to validity (Shadish, Cook, & Campbell, 2002), the most significant difficulty in field studies of PDD is establishing ground truth. That is, some method that is independent of the outcome of the test is needed to determine who in fact told the truth and who did not. Although a number of approaches have been attempted, it is generally agreed that confessions are the best available criterion for ground truth (their real-world status as truthful or deceptive) in these studies. Honts et al. (2005) reported that scientists who conduct research on PDD generally agree that field validity studies should have all the following characteristics:

- Subjects should be sampled from the actual population of subjects in which the researcher is interested. If the researcher wants to make inferences about tests conducted on criminal suspects, it is criminal suspects who should be the subjects studied. If the researcher wants to make statements about victim verification statement, victims should be sampled.
- Subjects should be sampled using a random process. Cases must be accepted into the study without reference to either the accuracy of the original deception detection test outcome or the quality of the physiological recordings obtained in that test.
- Persons trained and experienced in the field-scoring techniques about which inferential statements are to be made must evaluate the resulting physiological data. Independent evaluations by persons with access to only the physiological data are useful for evaluating the information content of those data. However, the decisions rendered by the original examiners probably provide a better estimate of the accuracy of deception detection techniques as they are actually employed in the field.
- The real-world credibility status of each subject must be determined by information that is independent of the deception detection test outcome. Confessions substantiated by physical evidence are presently the best criterion available.

Unfortunately, there are very few studies in the literature that meet these criteria (Honts et al., 2005), and it is an area in need of additional research. Sadly, it has been argued that the process of conducting field studies on PDD is fatally flawed. Iacono (1991) presents one of the most often repeated of those attacks, but his argument through thought experiment is based on a series of highly implausible hypothetical conditions (for a detailed critique of the thought experiment, see Honts, Raskin, & Kircher, 2005). Kraphol, Shull, and Ryan (2002) conducted an extensive analysis of field polygraph data in a direct effort to test Iacono's hypotheses and failed to find any support for his conclusions.

DATA REDUCTION

The various physiological waveforms that are recorded in a PDD examination present a number of data analytic challenges. The difficulties of data analysis are mitigated to some extent if computers are used to digitize and store the polygraph charts. The usual approach is to program the computer to extract discrete features, such as the amplitude and the duration of the physiological response to relevant and comparison questions. However, this approach also has challenges. The number of discrete features that could be extracted from these analog waveforms is quite large. A stepwise multivariate statistical procedure may be used to identify an optimal subset of diagnostic features. The measurements of those features are weighed and combined into a single score that places the subject on a truthful-deceptive continuum. The features are selected and weighted so as to maximize the separation between groups of known truthful and deceptive subjects.

A naive approach to this problem would be to extract as many features as possible and submit them to the stepwise algorithm to see what results. The Johns Hopkins/Applied Physics Laboratory (JHU/APL), under non-competitive U.S. Government contract, took such an approach. It is reported that they examined at least 9,911 features in a relatively small sample of data that was only partially confirmed (Porges, Johnson, Kircher, & Stern, 1996). Not surprisingly this effort, although still endorsed by the U.S. Government, was strongly criticized by a review panel of scientific experts (Porges et al., 1996). The greatest problem with this approach is that stepwise multivariate classifiers are notoriously unreliable; they capitalize on chance and yield highly inflated estimates of discrimination (Hocking, 1983). The inflation problem is compounded if the number of variables provided to the stepwise variable selection algorithm is large relative to the number of cases. Under these conditions, random numbers would yield perfect or near-perfect discrimination between groups, which was precisely what the JHU/APL investigators reported (Olsen, Harris, & Chiu, 1984).

Kircher and Raskin (1988; 2002) described a more reasonable approach to this problem. Their approach was to select a small subset of features that were standard measures from psychophysiological research and had been shown to be useful predictors in other psychophysiological problems. They maintained a minimum recommended ratio of subjects to variables and cross-validated their classifier with an independent sample of cases that had not been used to develop the model. Cross-validation or jackknife procedures that can provide indications of the bias present in the developed model are a requirement in this type of research (McNemar, 1969; Pedhazur, 1997). Unfortunately, in our experience such analyses are all too often submitted for publication without this necessary additional statistical step having been taken.

USEFUL DATA PRESENTATION

While we advocate using the highest information content data possible for hypothesis testing and statistical analysis, we realize that policy makers and courts may be primarily interested in questions concerning the accuracy of classification. As a result, there is utility in including such information in publications of research with generalizability to forensic or other applied settings. We favor the presentation of a classification cross-table that simply presents *guilt status* crossed with *test outcome*. Kircher et al. (1988) presented a simple and elegant statistic to describe such classification tables. These researchers coded actual guilt and innocence as –1 and 1, respectively. Test outcomes—deceptive, inconclusive, and truthful—were coded –1, 0, and +1, respectively. The resultant data vectors were then correlated. They referred to the resultant statistic as a detection-efficiency coefficient. That coefficient could vary from 0.0 when there was no relationship between test outcome and guilt status, to 1.0 when the test outcome correlated perfectly with guilt status.

Following the publication of the National Research Council's (2003) report on polygraph validity, it has become the vogue to describe polygraph accuracy with methods and language of signal detection theory (SDT) using receiver operating characteristic curve (ROC) analysis. Although this is a technically correct and potentially useful way to examine PDD, the technique is often poorly understood by readers, and a thorough understanding of the resulting statistics is usually held only by those who have had graduate-level exposure to psychophysics or decision-making theory. As a result, many of the presentations that currently appear in the literature are often facile and report the incorrect statistics for these data. For example, as the NRC (2003) noted, the correct index of accuracy for PDD is the statistic A, the ROC accuracy index, rather than the more commonly reported d', because the assumptions of d' usually cannot be met in these data. Technical issues aside, few forensic scientists are adequately trained in SDT, and very few lawyers or judges have any working knowledge of SDT technology. The presentation of SDT statistics in policy and judicial forums has a great potential for generating misrepresentation and misunderstanding.

Accessibility issues aside, all point-statistical indices of accuracy have one problem when they are presented in policy and judicial forums: they do not incorporate information about the impact of base rates nor do they account for the interaction of base rates with differential accuracy rates for innocent and guilty individuals (few studies have produced equal accuracy rates with both criterion conditions). The confidence that one has in any single test outcome depends on both the accuracy of the technique within each classification and the frequency of occurrence of the target condition in the population being studied.

Although these problems have been discussed in the PDD literature (e.g., Honts, 1991), such discussions have generally been set in the context of individual examples. Honts (1991) describes a hypothetical situation in which 1,000 people are evaluated with a test that is 90% accurate with both innocent and guilty subjects. However, 990 of the individuals being tested are innocent while only 10 are guilty. In this case, virtually all truthful outcomes will be correct (891/892), but few of the deceptive outcomes will be correct (9/108). Such examples have been presented in courts with mixed outcomes, sometime in the same case. In *Lee et al. v. Martinez et al.* (2004), a hearing concerning the admissibility of polygraph results was ordered by the New Mexico Supreme Court subsequent to the court's adoption of the Daubert standard. Base rates issues occupied a significant portion of the week-long hearing. The judge who administered the hearing opined that base-rate issues were an important factor in making the Daubert judgment and included base-rate issues as one of the factors in his conclusion that polygraph results did not meet the Daubert standard. However, the New Mexico Supreme Court subsequently concluded that polygraph test results did meet the Daubert standard and were therefore admissible in New Mexico. The court specifically rejected the relevance of base-rate issues for a Daubert analysis and noted that they were a matter of the weight of the evidence to be evaluated by the trier of fact.

The ultimate result of *Lee* highlights the need for an understandable presentation of the impact of base rates on validity. Fortunately, Gary Wells and his associates developed an elegant and easily understandable metric for such problems, known as the information gain index (IGI; Wells & Lindsay, 1980; Wells & Olson, 2002). The IGI uses Bayesian statistical logic and is ideally suited to address the translation of traditional inferential statistics and point estimates into information that is easily interpreted and used by practitioners and policy makers and in legal situations. In the PDD, information gain is simply the difference between the probability that the subject is the guilty party before the polygraph test has been administered and the probability that the suspect is the guilty party after the polygraph has been administered (a posterior probability). The PDD outcome matrix differs from the original problem of eyewitness identification described by Wells and his colleagues. In the PDD, there are only six possible outcomes, whereas in the Wells and Olsen (2002) eyewitness identification problem, there were eight possible outcomes. However, adaptation of the IGI to PDD is a simple matter of adjusting the equations for a smaller outcome matrix.

Honts and Schweinle (2009) presented the first adaptation of IGI to PDD. They examined several settings and presented IGI graphs that represented the information gained across the range of base rates in those situations. In Figure 6.2 (adapted from Honts & Schweinle, 2009), the two curves labeled Lay illustrate the information gain over chance (the x axis) when lay people

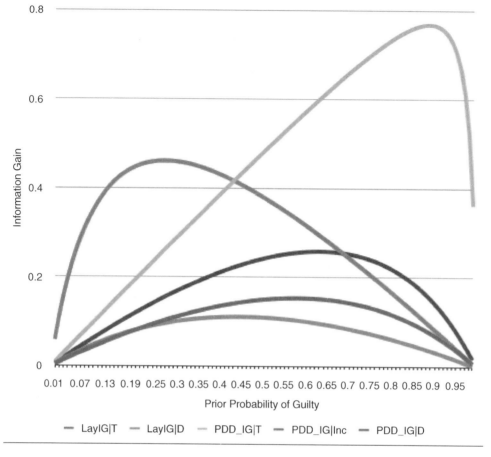

Figure 6.2 Information gain curves for decisions of truthful and deceptive for unassisted laypersons and for PDD test outcomes of truthful, inconclusive, and deceptive

make unassisted judgments of credibility for guilty and innocent targets. The Lay data are adapted from the comprehensive meta-analysis by Vrij (2008). Vrij's estimated accuracy for laypersons in a neutral base rate situation demonstrated a truth bias with 48% correct for guilty and 63% for innocent. Those data might be expected to be the upper end of performance for the average juror attempting to assess the credibility of a witness in court.

The three curves labeled PDD represent the information gain for polygraph outcomes of deceptive, inconclusive, and truthful outcomes. Generation of the IGI curves required estimates of test accuracy for truthful and deceptive individuals. Accuracy estimates for deceptive and truthful subjects were obtained from independent judgments by chart evaluators who had had no contact with the tested individuals in five high-quality field studies reviewed by Honts and Schweinle (2009). The IGI curves provide information of direct relevance to policy makers and jurists. That is, the polygraph provides substantial information gain over that of the average unassisted person, across almost the entire range of prior probability for both deceptive and truthful outcomes. In other words, the polygraph provides helpful information to jurors, judges, and other decision makers at all base rate conditions likely to be encountered in forensic settings. Thus, the polygraph should be useful in increasing the accuracy of decisions made by triers of fact. However, the IGI curves also reveal that truthful outcomes are more informative than deceptive ones. Interestingly, inconclusive outcomes also are informative, in that they generally occur more often with truthful suspects.

SUMMARY AND CLOSING COMMENTS

PDD represents an important and widespread application of psychology in the real world. Valid techniques for the detection of deception are needed to protect both individuals and society at large. Considering the importance of these techniques, it is surprising how little research has been conducted in this area. To illustrate, Honts (2006) conducted a set of PsychInfo searches. He recorded the number of publications returned for the search terms "deception detection" as compared to "attention," "schemata," and "semantic priming." Only 637 publications were returned for deception detection, 94,959 for attention, 1,952 for schemata, and 1,994 semantic priming. While we would not denigrate the importance of study in any of these areas, given the critical role of deception detection in everyday life, in the criminal justice system, and in national security, it is odd and disconcerting that psychological science has devoted so little effort to this topic. We encourage readers to involve themselves in this important area of applied psychology.

REFERENCES

Ben-Shakhar, G., & Furedy, J. J. (1990). *Theories and applications in the detection of deception.* New York, NY: Springer-Verlag.

Bradley, M. T., & Janisse, M. P. (1981). Demonstrations, threat, and detection of deception: Cardiovascular, electrodermal, and papillary measures. *Psychophysiology, 18,* 307–315.

DePaulo, D. M., & Kashy, D. A. (1998). Everyday lies in close and casual relationships. *Journal of Personality and Social Psychology, 74,* 63–79.

DePaulo, D. M., Kashy, D. A., Kirkendol, S. E., Wyer, M. S., & Epstein, J. A. (1996). Lying in everyday life. *Journal of Personality and Social Psychology, 70,* 979–995.

Granhag, P. A., & Strömwall (Eds., 2004). *The detection of deception in forensic contexts.* Cambridge, England: Cambridge University Press.

Hocking, R. R. (1983). Developments in linear regression methodology: 1959–1982. *Technometrics, 25,* 219–230.

Honts, C. R., (1991). The emperor's new clothes: Application of polygraph tests in the American workplace. *Forensic Reports, 4,* 91–116.

Honts, C. R. (2004). The psychophysiological detection of deception. In P. Granhag & L. Strömwall (Eds.), *Detection of deception in forensic contexts* (pp. 103–123). London, England: Cambridge University Press.

Honts, C. R. (2006, April). *Deception and deception detection: The unwanted psychology.* Presidential address delivered at the annual meeting of the Rocky Mountain Psychological Association, The Canyons, UT.

Honts, C. R., Amato, S., & Gordon, A. (2004). Effects of outside issues on the control question test. *The Journal of General Psychology, 151,* 53–74.

Honts, C. R., & Carlton, B. (1990) *The effects of incentives on the detection of deception: Report No. DoDPI90-R-0003.* Department of Defense Polygraph Institute, Fort McClellan, AL, DTIC# ADA305810.

Honts, C. R., Thurber, S., Cvencek, D., & Alloway, W. (2002, March). *General acceptance of the polygraph by the scientific community: Two surveys of professional attitudes.* Paper presented at the American Psychology-Law Society biennial meeting, Austin, TX.

Honts, C. R., Raskin, D. C., & Kircher, J. C. (1985). Effects of socialization on the physiological detection of deception. *Journal of Research in Personality, 19,* 373–385.

Honts, C. R., Raskin, D. C., & Kircher, J. C. (2005). Scientific status: The case for polygraph tests. In D. L. Faigman, D. Kaye, M. J. Saks, & J. Sanders (Eds.), *Modern scientific evidence: The law and science of expert testimony (Volume 4): Forensics 2005-2006 Edition* (pp. 571–605). Eagan, MN: Thompson West.

Honts, C. R., & Schweinle, W. (2009). Information gain of psychophysiological detection of deception in forensic and screening settings. *Applied Psychophysiology and Biofeedback, 34,* 161–172.

Iacono, W. G. (1991). Can we determine the accuracy of the polygraph tests? In J. R. Jennings, P. K. Ackles, & M. G. H. Coles (Eds.), *Advances in Psychophysiology* (pp. 202–208). London, England: Jessica Kingsley.

Iacono, W. G., & Lykken, D. T. (2005). Scientific Status: The case against polygraph tests. In D. L. Faigman, D. Kaye, M. J. Saks, & J. Sanders (Eds.), *Modern scientific evidence: The law and science of expert testimony (Volume 4): Forensics 2005-2006 Edition* (pp. 605–655). Eagan, MN: Thompson West.

Kashy, D. A., & DePaulo, D. M. (1996). Who lies? *Journal of Personality and Social Psychology, 70,* 1037–1051.

Kircher, J. C., Horowitz, S. W., & Raskin, D. C. (1988). Meta-analysis of mock crime studies of the control question polygraph technique. *Law and Human Behavior, 12,* 79–90.

Kircher, J. C., & Raskin, D. C. (2002). Computer methods for psychophysiological detection of deception. In M. Kleiner (Ed.), *Handbook of polygraph testing* (pp. 287–326). London, England: Academic.

Kircher, J. C., Raskin, D. C., Honts, C. R., & Horowitz, S. W. (1988, October). *Generalizability of mock crime laboratory studies of the control question polygraph technique.* Paper presented at the annual meeting of the Society for Psychophysiological Research, San Francisco, CA.

Kraphol, D. J., Shull, K. W., & Ryan, A. (2002). Does the confession criterion in case selection inflate polygraph accuracy estimates? *Forensic Science Communications, 4*(3). Retrieved November 13, 2010, from http://www2.fbi.gov/hq/lab/fsc/backissu/july2002/krapohl.htm

Lee et al. v. Martinez et al. (2004-NMSC-027).

McNemar, Q. (1969). *Psychological Statistics,* 4th ed. New York. NY: Wiley.

Olsen, D. E., Harris, J. C., & Chiu, W. W. (1984). The development of a physiological detection of deception scoring algorithm. *Psychophysiology, 31,* S11–12.

Pedhazur, E. J. (1997). *Multiple regression in behavioral research.* New York, NY: Harcourt.

Podlesny, J. A., & Kircher, J. C. (1999) The Finapres (volume clamp) recording method in psychophysiological detection of deception examinations: Experimental comparison with the cardiograph method. *Forensic Science Communication, 1*(3), 1–17.

Podlesny, J. A., & Raskin, D. C. (1977). Physiological measures and the detection of deception. *Psychological Bulletin, 84,* 782–799.

Podlesny, J. A., & Raskin, D. C. (1978). Effectiveness of techniques and physiological measures in the detection of deception. *Psychophysiology, 15,* 344–358.

Polina, D. A., Dollins, A. B., Senter, S. M., Krapohl, D. J., & Ryan, A. H. (2004). *Journal of Applied Psychology, 89,* 1099–1105.

Porges, S. W., Johnson, R., Kircher, J. C., & Stern, J. (1996). *Report of peer review of Johns Hopkins University/Applied Physics Laboratory.* Unpublished U.S. Government Report.

Raskin, D. C., & Honts, C. R. (2002). The comparison question test. In M. Kleiner (Ed.), *Handbook of polygraph testing* (pp. 1–49). London, England: Academic.

Robinson, W. P., Shepherd, A., & Heywood, J. (1998). Truth, equivocation/concealment, and lies in job applications and doctor-patient communications. *Journal of Language and Social Psychology, 17,* 149–164.

Saxe, L. (1985). Liars and lie detection: Umpiring controversy. *Transaction/Society, 22*(6), 39–42.

Shadish, W. R., Cook, T. D., & Campbell, D. T. (2002). *Experimental and quasi-experimental designs for generalized causal inference.* Boston, MA: Houghton Mifflin.

Vrij, A. (2000). *Detecting lies and deceit: The psychology of lying and implications for professional practice.* New York, NY: Wiley.

Vrij, A. (2008). *Detecting lies and deceit: Pitfalls and opportunities,* 2nd ed. Hoboken, NJ: Wiley.

Wells, G. L., & Lindsay, R. C. L. (1980). On estimating the diagnosticity of eyewitness nonidentifications. *Psychological Bulletin, 88,* 776–784.

Wells, G. L., & Olson, E. A. (2002). Eyewitness identification: Information gain from incriminating and exonerating behaviors. *Journal of Experimental Psychology: Applied, 8,* 155–167.

CHAPTER 7

Criminal Profiling

C. GABRIELLE SALFATI

INTRODUCTION

Criminal profiling, also known as offender profiling, is the process of linking an offender's actions at the crime scene to their most likely characteristics to help police investigators narrow down and prioritize a pool of most likely suspects (Salfati, 2007). Profiling is a relatively new area of forensic psychology that during the past 20 years has developed from what used to be described as an art to a rigorous science. Part of a subfield of forensic psychology called *investigative psychology*, criminal profiling is based on increasingly rigorous methodological advances and empirical research.

HISTORICAL BACKGROUND

Although there have been cases of criminal profiling going back as far as Jack the Ripper in the 1880s and the Mad Bomber in New York in the 1950s, criminal profiling developed as a field of study during the 1970s through the 1990s. Early work on profiling focused on interviewing offenders to access the information about what happened at the crime scene and combined this with an analysis of the evidence left by the offenders at the crime scenes themselves. The earliest and most quoted work was that published by people associated with the FBI's Behavioral Science Unit (see, e.g., Ressler, Burgess, & Douglas, 1988). These first studies attempted to systematically identify patterns and subtypes in the offender's crime scene behavior and were instrumental in laying the foundations for future work by alerting researchers to the fact that crime scenes are rich sources of behavioral information for analyzing the psychology of homicide. However, as the authors themselves stated, "at present there have been no systematic efforts to validate these profile derived classifications" (Ressler et al., 1992, p. 22), stressing that their work was in the pilot stage and had not been thoroughly empirically tested.

Despite these cautions, the FBI along with other practitioners and academics used this model as a base for much of the early training and practice in profiling. As this original model grew in popularity and started being integrated in other work (see Meloy, 2000, for an overview), authors (e.g., Bateman & Salfati, 2007; Canter, 1994; Canter, L. J. Alison, Alison, & Wentink, 2004; Salfati & Bateman, 2005; Salfati & Canter, 1999) started highlighting that, although the approach of using the crime scene as a starting point was indeed a very useful one, there was now the need not only to test the validity of crime scene profiling models but to test many of the early assumptions in the literature regarding differences between offenders (see Canter, 2000).

As highlighted by Alison, Bennell, Mokros, and Ormerod (2002), few studies or theoretical reviews had considered the process itself or the premises on which analysis are founded. Also in reviewing the validity of the assumptions integral to the process, they highlight that few studies or theoretical reviews demonstrated much of what was considered standard practice in the analysis of behavioral consistency as it pertains to criminal behavior, and many fell short of current understanding of key psychological processes and principles. Thus much of the work did not meet basic expert witness standards under Federal Rule of Evidence 702 or the Daubert criteria for admissible scientific evidence.

A number of other studies were done to evaluate various aspects of profiling. One of these studies (Risinger & Loop, 2002) reviewed the history of crime analysis. What the study found was that the analysis of criminal behavior has not very often been based on empirical and scientific evidence. Essentially what they found was that people were giving their opinions about what they thought an offender's behavior was an indication of, rather than using solidly founded scientific knowledge of human behavior. Another study evaluated international case law (Meyer, 2007), and also concluded that the analysis of criminal behavior methods was failing the legal tests for admissible expert evidence due to little valid empirical basis. Alison, Smith, Eastman, and Rainbow (2003) specifically examined the practical implications of these issues, including testing the reliability and validity of 21 actual investigative profiles provided by experts, which sought to provide the police with identifiable characteristics of suspects based on behavioral indices at the crime scene. Their study showed that of nearly 4,000 claims regarding the characteristics of offenders present in the 21 profiles, as much as 80% of the information provided was not supported by evidence. The authors concluded by providing guidelines that stressed the importance of backing up any claims about the characteristics of the offender and the importance of basing profiles on empirically validated research regarding the link between the actions of an offender at the crime scene and their corresponding characteristics.

The need to move the field from an "art" towards an empirical science thus became the key focus in the next stage of the development of the field of criminal profiling. Investigative psychology, with its emphasis on the development of rigorous empirical and methodological approaches to research relating to the application of psychological principles to police investigations, aimed to do just this, and has since the early 1990's developed and established a continued development of a rigorous methodology to underpin studies of criminal behavior in the context of criminal investigations.

INVESTIGATIVE PSYCHOLOGY

Along with the increased popularity of crime scene profiling that occurred in the 1970s through the 1990s and the increasing questions regarding its validity as a field, came an increasing need to demonstrate its validity in identifying differences in types of crime scenes and the characteristics of the offender responsible for the crime. It was because of this need that the field of investigative psychology emerged in the late 1980s (see Canter, 1994, for an early historical overview). Early researchers began looking at how psychology may help in understanding the various inference processes used in offender profiling. Studies endeavored to distinguish between different types of criminals and the way they commit their crimes, in hopes that this greater understanding of criminal behavior as it applies to the crime scene could be used to substantiate the conclusions made in offender profiles.

Ultimately, the goal of this research is practical—to help identify the most likely offenders for further investigation by the police. But underpinning this applied work are key theoretical and methodological issues. The research field has generated three interlinked areas that have been the focus of recent profiling research: individual differentiation, behavioral consistency, and inferences about offender characteristics (Canter, 2000; Salfati, 2007).

1. *Individual differentiation* aims to establish differences between the behavioral actions of offenders and uses this information to identify subgroups of crime scene types.
2. *Behavioral consistency* is used for understanding both the development of an offender's criminal career and an individual's consistency across a series of crimes (e.g., whether the same subsets of actions are displayed at each crime scene over a series, linking serial crimes).
3. *Drawing inferences about offender characteristics* uses consistency analysis as its main focus in establishing the link between subgroups of crime scene actions and subgroups of offender background characteristics to make predictions about an offender based on the offender's criminal actions at the crime scene. This can, in theory, be used by the police to narrow their suspect pool down to the most likely offender.

This chapter outlines each of these aspects of profiling and discusses the most pertinent methodological issues as they have been identified to date, as well as key avenues and foci of study the field will move toward during the following decade.

INDIVIDUAL DIFFERENTIATION

The first step in profiling is to devise a method for determining individual differentiation or for comparing individuals in terms of conceptual categories. This step in profiling is normally referred to as determining the *actions* of the offender during the crime in question. The idea behind this process is that offenders engage in various ways of acting at the crime scene. These conceptual categories generally include subgroups of behaviors with the same underlying psychological theme or significance for the offender. As an example, in the first paper ever published in investigative psychology, Canter and Heritage (1990) analyzed 66 stranger rapes committed by 27 offenders in order to determine whether the behaviors that had occurred at crime scenes displayed any coherent patterns of co-occurrences. Their results indicated several subtypes of offending styles, including the *pseudointimate* type, in which offenders engaged in behaviors such as kissing or complimenting the victim, and the *controlling* type, in which offenders engaged in behaviors such as binding and gagging the victim. Being able to use the information regarding the crime taken from actual police files to empirically differentiate subtypes of crime scene styles was an important step towards establishing a methodological basis for investigative psychology and provided a stepping stone from which to explore further methodological issues regarding the data source itself. Other studies in investigative psychology have continued to focus on, and develop, robust methodological approaches to be used in this type of analysis.

REAL WORLD RESEARCH

Real world research refers to research that deals with the world as it is rather than with experimental laboratory settings. Instead of identifying, isolating, and analyzing individual variables, we observe events as they happen or collect information from events that have already happened and have been recorded in ways that were meant to document the original event (e.g., a police file, where all the information contained in it was collected for the purpose of prosecution). This type of research has a great deal of ecological validity, but it is also fraught with methodological issues that must be carefully considered.

There are many types of real world research approaches, including observation, trace evidence, and archival data; however, this chapter focuses primarily on *archival data* (for a review of different types of real world research methods, see Robson, 2002, and Webb, Campbell, Schwartz, & Sechrest, 1966). Examples of archival data that are relevant to criminal profiling research include police files, court records, prison files, mental health records, and medical examiner reports, as well as crime scene photos, interviews, information in books and the media (e.g., newspapers), and most recently, the Internet. Retrieving information from archival data sources is often referred to as *content analysis*. Analyzing the content of police files is an indirect rather than direct form of measurement, in that the data has been produced for purposes other than our research.

Information collected specifically for police investigations, which can be found in a police file, is most often used in research linked to offender profiling and crime scene analysis. The idea behind this approach is that researchers will use information that is available to actual investigators in their analyses so that the results are most applicable to the investigative context. Information in police files includes the original police report that was written by the responding officer(s), witness reports, suspect interviews, photographs, and information regarding the victim, as well as the medical examiner's report (in cases of violent crimes such as rape, assault, and homicide), and forensic reports (e.g., DNA testing, ballistics reports, blood spatter analysis, trace evidence analysis, etc.). Because this information was not gathered for the purpose of scientific research, however, a number of methodological issues must be kept in mind when using such police files as a basis for research.

The clear *advantage* of this approach is that the data is not affected by people being involved in a study (i.e., participant effect), nor is the data abstract or experimentally manipulated. Instead it is a reflection of events in the real world outside the research laboratory.

The main *limitations* relate to the nature of the information collected and how the police investigation will have influenced what information was collected and documented. The information contained in the police file is intended to help obtain a conviction; consequently, it may contain information related to solving and prosecuting a case. It is therefore important that the context in which information was recorded be taken into account when interpreting this information. In addition, researchers must take into account information that is not present in the file and what implications *these omissions have*. For example, information that psychologists normally would analyze, such as (in cases of solved crimes) pertinent psychological information about the offender (e.g., information regarding the personal background of the offender) *may be unavailable*. This does not mean that the offender does not have certain characteristics that would be important correlates of crime scene behavior, but rather that the information is absent from the file. This distinction is crucial given that assumptions can spin the resulting analysis in different directions and lead the researcher to false conclusions.

A related point is whether information in the file can be seen as reliable and valid. Alison, Snook, and Stein (2001) specifically discussed how information in police files may be distorted due to its link to the court process, noting that "police officer(s), offender(s), victim(s) and witness(es) are likely to construct different accounts of an offense because of the different motives for giving the account. Moreover, accounts may vary over time and are likely to be strongly influenced by whom they are given to." (p. 249) Ultimately, to increase the reliability and validity of the information collected, it is crucial to establish what information in the police files can be considered a reliable and valid account of the events as they happened.

INFORMATION RETRIEVAL AND CODING

Coding refers to the process whereby qualitative information is transferred into numerical data that lends itself to empirical and statistical analysis. For the coding process to be both reliable and valid, the researcher needs to go through a number of steps and at each stage deal with a different set of methodological questions. The first step is identifying the *research question* itself. The research question guides the collection of information, in that it requires the specific information that allows the question that is to be answered to be collected. If the researcher is aiming to conduct an analysis of individual differentiation in ways of killing a victim (level of aggression, types of weapon, etc.), information relating to this process needs to be the focus of the data. Collecting information not relevant to the process under investigation may muddy the results.

The next step is to establish the *sampling strategy*, if such a process is even possible. In real world research, the researcher often deals with small, unrepresentative samples. For this data to be generalizable, the nature of the sample itself becomes crucial. The context of where the sample was obtained must be at the forefront at this stage of the methodological outline.

The next step is to define the recording unit. The nature of recording units will partly depend on the material that is being analyzed. For example, in interviews or written records it may be individual words used as the unit of analysis; in photographs it may become the visual image that needs to be interpreted and coded. Early classifications used in profiling research were often based on internal psychological processes, and different types of offenders were distinguished based on presumed motivation. Motivations, however, are not only difficult to measure (particularly at the crime scene) but involve a great deal of subjective interpretation (see a discussion of this in Canter et al., 2004; Canter & Wentink, 2004). At the first methodological stages of developing an empirical model, this subjectivity could create biases that would render the resulting models unreliable and invalid. Thus, in at least the first stages of model construction, there is a need to develop models that are not only valid but are based on more reliable units of analysis, such as observable—and thus testable—actions at the crime scene. Models focusing on observable behaviors also use data that are more readily available during investigations and are typically accessible to investigators. When motivations are the focus of interest, such as to understand the dynamics of the crime, they need to be reconceptualized as behaviors in order to be measured more reliably. If the researcher can ascertain how certain motivations are exhibited at crime scenes, we may ultimately be able to explain why the offender committed the crime, which in turn can be used to interpret behaviors and make assertions about the type of offender responsible.

Whatever the source material (police files or other sources of data), the process by which data is coded is a sensitive stage. Variables at this step need to be operationalized, which is often done through the process of developing a *coding dictionary*. The importance of this coding process becomes clear when, as an example, we examine how one might define the criminal action of what is often termed "overkill." "Overkill" often refers to when a victim has been killed in a way that indicates violence that goes beyond what is needed to kill the victim. However, this term also refers to the emotional element of the crime, indicating an offender who is out of control or in a stage of intense anger. Therefore, when multiple stab wounds are present, especially if they are located in one area of the victim's body, practitioners often label this action as overkill.

However, the researcher needs to determine exactly how many stab wounds are required for the definition of overkill to be applicable. If a victim dies after the first stab wound and the offender stabs the victim several more times, is this the same as the offender stabbing the victim repeatedly in a less lethal part of the body before stabbing the victim once in a more lethal place? At what point do multiple stab wounds become overkill? When variables require too much interpretation and questioning, the risk of unreliability increases. A more objective way of defining "overkill" would be to re-conceptualize this variable as the number and distribution of stab wounds, along with depth of wounds to indicate force. By conceptualizing variables in this way, one can obtain more reliable variables, and the interpretation of this data as a case of "overkill" can be done during a second phase. Finally, researchers need to empirically test and measure the reliability of their measurements by examining whether different coders interpret the variable in the same way and ultimately code the information similarly (for a detailed discussion of interrater reliability and coding dictionary construction in crime scene analysis, see Salfati, 2006), and by so doing, establishing that each variable reliably measures what it sets out to measure.

Currently, there are many approaches to collecting data. However, many of the existing data collection tools that have been used to create the data sets on which studies have been based do not have clear definitions of what con-stitutes each of the items or variables contained within the tool. This ambi-guity has led to problems with the reliability of research based on these tools (for a discussion of these issues, see Canter, L. J. Alison, Alison, & Wentink, 2004; Canter & Wentink, 2004; Salfati, 2006). In an effort to rectify this methodological problem, much of the research in investigative psychology has aimed to develop reliable coding frameworks by creating objective measurement tools to measure the actions that occur at the crime scene.

Once the information has been collected, the next stage involves the con-struction of units for the actual *analysis*. This stage is explored in the following section, which reviews the use of *individual behaviors* versus *psychological themes*.

INDIVIDUAL DISCRIMINATION

Canter, L. J. Alison, Alison, and Wentink (2004), in their study evaluating the FBI's proposed two subtypes of sexual homicide, found that many of the behaviors that were originally used to differentiate between the two proposed types were actually common to most offenders (i.e., they were behaviors that occurred at a high frequency across the sample as a whole and therefore could not be used to differentiate subtypes).

Salfati (2003) has further helped identify the parameters of what we can and what we cannot profile. This study on homicide identified four behaviors that were of high frequency (i.e., occurred in more than 50% of the whole sample), and as such defined what was common to the sample rather than what could be used to differentiate *between* crime scenes. Of more crucial importance to the issue of how useful such models are for profiling, further analysis showed that 57% of the sample had a higher percentage of variables present in this (four variable) high frequency band than for the rest of the 32 "low frequency" variables analyzed. Essentially what this indicates is that more than half of this sample showed a pattern that is common to most homicides and thus could not be profiled, because they do not constitute a specific subgroup of offenders. Rather, they exemplified the most common type of homicide. These studies highlight how important it is to identify the commonalities in the sample before attempting to identify the variables that are most effective in differentiating between subtypes of homicide. The study by Salfati (2003) is the only one to date that highlights this simple yet important issue by providing data to determine which types of homicide can more easily be profiled; it also supports what Canter (2000) outlined in his review of theoretical and methodological issues relating to individual differentiation. Thus, it is the less common subgroup of behaviors that may prove more useful in differentiating between types of crime scenes.

ESTABLISHING TYPE

Another key issue that has been highlighted in work relating to individual differentiation is determining what constitutes a "type" or "theme." Much theoretical and methodological work has outlined models composed of different subtypes of offending (individual differentiation in the use of behaviors at the crime scene). However, until recently few studies provided guidelines on establishing how an individual can be classified and what the criterion or unit of analysis should be.

In the first published study on the profiling of homicide crime scenes in investigative psychology, Salfati and Canter (1999) proposed a framework for classification criteria that established three basic types or themes of homicide. They also provided some basic guidelines for how each individual crime scene could be allocated to a theme in their discussion of the issue of dominant themes. For each case in their sample, they calculated the number of behaviors present in each of the three themes. They suggested that a crime scene displayed a "dominant" theme if one theme contained more behaviors than the other two themes combined. This calculation enabled them to establish a "count" of theme dominance and showed that 65% of their cases could be assigned to one of the dominant styles while 36% were considered "hybrids" (i.e., there was no single dominant theme but rather a combination of themes). By providing criteria for establishing theme dominance, their model could be used not only to classify an individual case but in terms of methodology, could also be used to test the robustness and inclusiveness of the model itself in order to identify the areas that need further refinement.

In a subsequent study, Salfati (2000) analyzed 247 cases and calculated the number of behaviors present in each of the two homicide themes she studied. These themes were converted into a *proportion* of behaviors present in each theme. By dealing with a percentage rather than an actual number, this method allowed for a more precise calculation. In addition, the level of stringency for identifying a dominant behavioral type was increased by requiring that one theme display at least twice the percentage as in the other theme. These methods provide a systematic basis for establishing which offenders show a dominant crime scene behavioral type. On a practical level, they may also allow crime scene investigators to use such models to identify the type of offender they are dealing with, which can then be used to prioritize suspects for questioning.

In terms of methodology, one key question is what criteria should be applied for establishing whether a crime scene displays a dominant pattern type (theme). Trojan and Salfati (2009) recently reviewed the literature that has applied different criteria and made an in-depth comparison of how these criteria influence classification. At the start of any scientific endeavor, it is important to establish stringent criteria, even if it does not allow the model to fully classify all cases, inasmuch as this process provides a benchmark of stringency and highlights the need for further study and exploration of how to refine the model to allow more cases to be classified. Indeed, identifying the percentage of cases that *cannot* be allocated to a dominant theme allows researchers to evaluate the theoretical reasons for this underidentification and explore ways to refine their models. As Salfati (2000) and Salfati and Bateman (2005) have highlighted, the reasons cases do not show a dominant theme may be situational, affecting an offender's behavioral consistency (described subsequently). By evaluating which variables are stable and intrinsic to the *offender* versus behaviors that are easily influenced by the *situation* or the *context*, researchers can apply more stringent criteria for selection of behaviors in the construction of robust models, which, in turn, can be used with a higher degree of reliability in the classification of offenders. This issue of consistency across situations is explored further in the following section.

BEHAVIORAL CONSISTENCY

Behavioral consistency is critical to differentiating individuals and is the second key issue in empirical studies of offender profiling. Behavioral consistency comprises two separate yet interrelated fields of study. The first aims to look at the consistency *across* an individual's series of crimes; this is typically referred to as "linking." The second aims to look at the consistency between what offenders do at the crime scene and what they do in *other* aspects of their lives, including both criminal (i.e., their previous criminal activities and how this relates to their current crime) and noncriminal (i.e., personal) aspects. This second aspect of behavioral consistency is what is normally referred to as the "actions to characteristics" link or the A-to-C equation (Canter, 2000).

To test whether offenders are consistent across offenses (i.e., whether there is a link between their different crime scenes), the researcher needs to examine whether offenders engage in the same behaviors across their series of offenses. More importantly, however, before testing whether an offender is consistent, it is critical to define the *unit of measure* to be used in making this determination. More specifically, researchers must define whether they are examining *individual* behavior (e.g., binding or gagging), or the psychological *type* of behavior, or *theme* (e.g., controlling). Depending on the unit of analysis used, the researcher will need different methodologies, and ultimately this will affect the nature of the results obtained. The first question before identifying a methodology, therefore, becomes the theoretical one of which way of looking at behavior is the most valid. We can use Canter and Heritage's (1990) pseudointimate and controlling types of rape as an example to illustrate these interlinked theoretical and methodological issues.

Consider a situation in which a number of rapes have been committed and have been linked because in each case the offender used the single identifying behavior of gagging his victim. Similarly, another series has been identified by the offender's binding the victim. By using a single behavior, two series have been identified. However, focusing on the individual behavior excludes a possible link between these two series through their underlying adherence to the same psychological theme—notably *control*. By moving from *the individual behavior* to the *thematic*, one can expand the unit of analysis from the *descriptive* to the *psychological*, thereby increasing the chance of linking. This decision becomes important when the individual level of analysis is affected by the situational factors (e.g., the offender may bind the victim in situations where she tries to run away or gag her in situations where she screams). In both situations, although the individual behaviors are different, they illustrate the offender's attempt to control the situation.

The remainder of the chapter reviews studies that specifically focus on serial crimes, and further examines what is needed methodologically to develop studies in the field of behavioral consistency to further lend validity and reliability to empirical studies of linking in the field of offender profiling.

CONSISTENCY IN SERIAL CRIMES

The key research questions in the area of linking are whether we can link crime scenes to *each other* and thereby identify an *individual series* while also identifying how it differs from other series. Specifically, an important question is *which* behaviors are the most reliable to focus on when making this determination. Running through all these questions is the key question of what is meant by *consistency* and how this may be *displayed*.

Much of the criminological literature conceptualizes legally separate crimes based on interpretations of crime seriousness rather than any criminological or psychological theory. For example, sexual homicide and rape are treated as two unrelated crimes, set apart by different psychological mechanisms and motivations. As a consequence, research adhering to legal distinctions accepts a restricted perspective for examining patterns in offenders' behavior and may consequently overlook important similarities and differences across the various forms (e.g., sexual violence). To fully understand crimes such as sexual violence, it is thus necessary to extend beyond a research perspective shaped by *legal classifications* and instead identify the actual *psychological variations* in crime scene actions that will differentiate between sexually violent offenses.

Salfati and Taylor (2006) analyzed a sample of 37 sexual homicides and 37 rapes to determine whether these two types of offenses represent two separate types of crime or could be understood as part of a more general theory of violent sexual crime. This study first identified key behaviors of crime scenes containing a sexual element and then compared these behaviors in terms of their relative importance in sexual homicide and rape offenses. Their analysis indicated that offender–victim interactions in sexual homicide and rape were predominantly distinguished by the degree of violence, such that behaviors associated with each type of offense were found to occur in two discrete areas along a single continuum.

This methodological point becomes especially important when examining the progression of an offender's crime development and its consistency pattern, such as in cases where an offender progresses from sexual assaults, to rapes, to sexual homicides. Each one of these crimes is separate and legally defined, but psychologically, the offender is committing a series of sexual assaults, which shows psychological consistency. In addition, the offender is showing development and change in the escalation in both physical invasion of the victim and in violence.

The issue of development becomes more important when selecting specific samples on which to conduct analyses and draw conclusions, such as occurs when linking serial crimes. In addition to clearly defining the crime under investigation, it is important to put the crimes in a timeline of an offender's criminal activities. Normally in crime research, researchers select "subjects" based on what is termed the "index" crime (i.e., the most recent crime the offender committed). In this way, a "homicide offender" is one whose most recent crime was a homicide, and a "rape offender" is one whose most recent crime was a rape. This approach is consistent with the way offenders are identified in the criminal justice system—by their most recent crime. But we must bear in mind that this practice influences all consequent analysis and conclusions about patterns in criminal behavior.

Table 7.1

Potential Consistency Trends in Criminal Histories and Index Crimes

Offender	Criminal History	Crime in series				
		1	2	3	4	5 (Index offence)
1	Previous violent convictions	Rape	Rape	Rape	Rape	Rape
2	Previous sexual convictions	Rape	Rape	Rape	Rape	Rape
3	Previous sexual convictions	Sexual assault	Sexual assault	Sexual homicide	Sexual homicide	Sexual homicide

(Adapted from Salfati, 2008.)

An illustrative example from Salfati (2008) is presented in Table 7.1. These data outline three pictures of violent offenders, in terms of their index offense (crime 5 in the series), the previous four crimes in their series, and the nature of their criminal history prior to the current series. As can be seen in this example, series 1 depicts an offender who is clearly a serial rapist and who has a previous criminal history of violent convictions. Because the start of the offender's rape series has been identified, researchers can examine the series in its entirety and make assertions about the link between the offender's current crime and his previous crime types. In this case, the offender has shown a development from general violence to sexual violence. This pattern differs from that of offender 2, who has committed a series of five rapes but also has a previous criminal history of sexual convictions.

In comparing offenders 1 and 2, one may draw conclusions about the differences between rapists who have previous convictions for violence and those who have previous convictions for sexual assaults. However, this distinction is made because of the arbitrary assignment of certain crimes to the offender's past and certain crimes to the offender's present series. Although some people may argue that the series of rapes committed by offender 2 is a distinctly linked series, the fact remains that the offender has previous sexual assaults in his background and the only apparent basis for separating his current series from his previous ones is the fact that the offender was arrested in the midst of the series. By allocating some crimes to the past and some to the present and by starting the analysis at crime 1 in the current series rather than by starting at the first sexual crime, researchers may miss important factors that could help them to understand the development in this offender's consistency patterns.

A similar logic applies to the data for offender 3, who was convicted for a series that included three homicides. If one examines the homicides, all are sexual in character, and indeed the two crimes committed before the homicides were defined as sexual assaults. Without considering these three sexual assaults, one may miss an important element of this offender's development over time. Indeed, depending on where one decides to draw the line between a current crime series and previous crimes, it will affect determinations regarding the A-to-C link (i.e., the link between the offender's current crime and his previous crimes). It is therefore essential that before considering methodologies for identifying linking and consistency patterns in an offender's "series," the researcher must clearly define what a series is.

CONCLUSION

This chapter has aimed to give a brief overview of how work in the area of criminal profiling from the perspective of investigative psychology has developed since its beginning, and how recent developments have attempted to establish a more reliable and solid methodological framework for applying psychological and methodological principles to the analysis of offending behavior as it applies to police investigations. These principles provide a way to establish a baseline of good research practice in the area of criminal profiling.

REFERENCES

Alison, L., Bennell, C., Mokros, A., & Ormerod, D. (2002). The personality paradox in offender profiling: A theoretical review of the processes involved in deriving background characteristics from crime scene actions. *Psychology, Public Policy, and Law, 8*(1), 115–135.

Alison, L., Smith, M. D., Eastman, O., & Rainbow, L. (2003). Toulmin's philosophy of argument and its relevance to offender profiling. *Psychology, Crime & Law, 9*, 173–183.

Alison, L., Snook, B., & Stein, K. L. (2001). Unobtrusive measurement: Using police information for forensic research. *Qualitative Research, 1*, 241–254.

Bateman, A. L., & Salfati, C. G. (2007) An examination of behavioral consistency using individual behaviors or groups of behaviors in serial homicide. *Behavioral Sciences and the Law, 25*(4), 527–544.

Canter, D. (1994). *Criminal Shadows*. London, England: HarperCollins.

Canter, D. V. (2000). Offender profiling and criminal differentiation. *Legal and Criminological Psychology, 5*, 23–46.

Canter, D. V., Alison, L. J., Alison, E., & Wentink, N. (2004). The organized/disorganized typology of serial murder: Myth or model? *Psychology, Public Policy, & Law, 10*(3), 293–320.

Canter, D., & Heritage, R. (1990) A multivariate model of sexual offence behavior: Developments in "offender profiling" I. *Journal of Forensic Psychiatry, 1*(2), 185–212.

Canter, D. V., & Wentink, N. (2004). An empirical test of Holmes and Holmes's serial murder typology. *Criminal Justice & Behavior, 31*(4), 489–515.

Meloy, J. R. (2000). The nature and dynamics of sexual homicide: An integrative review. *Aggression and Violent Behavior, 5*(1), 1–22.

Meyer, C. B. (2007) Criminal profiling as expert evidence? An international case law perspective. In R. N. Kocsis (Ed.), *Criminal profiling: International theory, research, and practice* (pp. 207–248). Totowa, NJ: Humana Press Inc.

Ressler, R. K., Burgess, A. W., & Douglas, J. E. (1988). *Sexual homicide: Patterns and motives.* Lexington, MA: Lexington Books.

Risinger, D. M., and Loop, J. L. (2002). Three card monte, Monty Hall, modus operandi and "offender profiling": Some lessons from modern cognitive science for the law of evidence. *Law Review, 24,* 193–286.

Robson, C. (2002). *Real-world research: A resource for social scientists and practitioner researchers* (2nd ed.). Oxford, England: Blackwell Publishers.

Salfati, C. G. (2000). Profiling homicide: A multidimensional approach. *Homicide Studies, 4*(3), 265–293.

Salfati, C. G. (2003). Offender interaction with victims in homicide: A multidimensional analysis of frequencies in crime scene behaviors. *Journal of Interpersonal Violence, 18*(5), 490–512.

Salfati, C. G. (2006). The homicide profiling index (HPI)—A tool for measurements of crime scene behaviors, victim characteristics, and offender characteristics. In C. G. Salfati (Ed.), *Homicide research: Past, present and future.* Proceedings of the 2005 Meeting of the Homicide Research Working Group. Chicago, IL: Homicide Research Working Group.

Salfati, C. G. (2007). Profiling. *Encyclopedia of Psychology and Law.* SAGE Publications. Retrieved October 14, 2010, from http://www.sage-ereference.com/psychology-law/Article_n251.html>.

Salfati, C. G. (2008). Offender profiling: Psychological and methodological issues of testing for behavioural consistency. *Issues in Forensic Psychology: Investigative Psychology, 8,* 68–81. British Psychological Society, Division of Forensic Psychology Publications.

Salfati, C. G., & Bateman, A. (2005) Serial homicide: An investigation of behavioral consistency. *Journal of Investigative Psychology and Offender Profiling, 2*(2), 121–144.

Salfati, C. G., & Canter, D. V. (1999). Differentiating stranger murders: Profiling offender characteristics from behavioral styles. *Behavioral Sciences and the Law, 17,* 391–406.

Salfati, C. G., & Taylor, P. (2006). Differentiating sexual violence: A comparison of sexual homicide and rape. *Psychology, Crime and Law, 12*(2), 107–126.

Trojan, C., & Salfati, C. G. (2009). Methodological considerations of determining dominance in multidimensional analyses of crime scene behaviors and offender characteristics. Special issue: Debates and critiques within investigative psychology. In D. V. Canter (Ed.), *Journal of Investigative Psychology and Offender Profiling, 5*(3), 125–146.

Webb, E. J., Campbell, D. T., Schwartz, R. D., & Sechrest, L. (1966). *Unobtrusive measures: Nonreactive research in the social sciences.* Chicago, IL: Rand McNally.

CHAPTER 8

Methods in Deception Detection Research

MARIA HARTWIG

MISCLASSIFICATIONS OF INNOCENT SUSPECTS

Recent developments in the evaluation of criminal evidence have revealed that wrongful convictions of innocent people occur with some regularity, suggesting serious flaws in the methods employed by the criminal justice system (Scheck, Neufeld, & Dwyer, 2000). Case studies show that miscarriages of justice sometimes begin with the misidentification of innocent suspects and the subsequent exposure of such suspects to manipulative and psychologically coercive interrogation tactics that can elicit false confessions (Drizin & Leo, 2004; Gudjonsson, 2003; Kassin & Gudjonsson, 2004). During the course of criminal investigations, suspects are chosen for interrogation on the basis of a variety of evidence, including witness information and other extrinsic evidence. However, sometimes suspects are targeted for interrogation because of little more than an investigator's hunch based on the impression that a person is displaying a guilty or deceptive demeanor (Kassin, 2005).

To illustrate this sequence of errors, consider the case of 14-year-old Michael Crowe. He and his friend Joshua Treadway were subjected to lengthy interrogations during which they were induced into confessing to the murder of Michael's sister, Stephanie. The charges against the boys were later dropped when another person who was seen in the area at the night of the murder was found with the victim's blood on his clothing. It seems these boys were targeted because the detectives working on the case believed that Crowe had reacted to his sister's death with an inappropriate absence of emotion (Johnson, 2003).

Consider further the case of Jeffrey Deskovic. In late 1989, a 15-year-old girl was found beaten, raped, and strangled to death, prompting an investigation. The 16-year-old Deskovic, who was a classmate of the victim, became a suspect in the case and was led to produce self-incriminating statements during lengthy and coercive interrogations. One of the reasons for the targeting of Deskovic for interrogation was the detectives' impression that he was behaving suspiciously; he was thought to be overly emotional and distraught at the victim's death, visiting her wake three times. On the basis of the flawed evidence produced during the interrogations, Deskovic was convicted for the murder, even though it was known all along that the semen found at the crime scene did not match his. It took nearly 16 years and the confession of another inmate (whose semen did match that found at the scene of the crime) before Deskovic was exonerated and released from prison.

RESEARCH QUESTIONS IN THE STUDY OF DECEPTION

These tragic cases point to a problem of broad impact for the legal system: investigators' first impression of credibility and truthfulness can be a critical factor in determining the fate of a person under suspicion. A substantial body of scientific literature employing a variety of methodologies has examined human ability to make lie and truth judgments on the basis of behavior, providing answers to a number of questions of relevance for deception detection in forensic settings. For example, what behaviors do people generally associate with deception? That is, what are subjective cues to deception and to what extent do such beliefs match the patterns of behavior observed in research on objective (i.e., actual) indicators of deception? Further, how skilled are people at distinguishing between truthful and deceptive statements? And of particular relevance for forensic settings, how accurate are criminal investigators and other legal professionals in detecting deception?

As will be discussed in some detail, empirical research has shown that human ability to make judgments of deception and truthfulness is limited (Bond & DePaulo, 2006) and that even presumed experts at the task, such as criminal investigators, fall prey to a number of judgmental and decision-making errors when they attempt to establish veracity (Granhag & Strömwall, 2004). However, such research has also been criticized on methodological grounds, in particular with regard to external validity (i.e., the generalizability of the findings to relevant non-laboratory settings; see Inbau, Reid, Buckley, & Jayne, 2001). This chapter provides a review of the features of some main paradigms of relevance for assessments of deception and truth in criminal investigations and discusses the methodological strengths and weaknesses of each paradigm with regard to its application to forensic settings.

SELF-REPORT AND SURVEY STUDIES ON DECEPTION AND ITS DETECTION

In the words of philosopher Michel de Montaigne, "The reverse of truth has a hundred thousand faces and an infinite field" (Bok, 1999). It is not surprising that many academic domains have focused on deception, including moral philosophy, psychiatry, and communication research. This chapter focuses on the empirical psychological research founded in the tradition of social psychology, which views deception as an interpersonal phenomenon serving the purpose of regulating social life (DePaulo et al., 2003). In this research, lying is defined as "an act that is intended to foster in another person a belief or understanding which the deceiver considers to be false" (Zuckerman, DePaulo, & Rosenthal, 1981, p. 3).

An important question studied by social psychologists is how frequent lies are in everyday social interactions. Such data is also of interest to the forensic domain because of its implications for lie catching; if lies are common in everyday life, we can expect people to be good liars as a simple effect of practice. Although it might seem straightforward at first glance to study the prevalence of deception, establishing the base rate of lies and truth in everyday social life is associated with serious methodological challenges. The observational method, which has been used extensively to study social behavior, cannot be employed to study the frequency of lies in social life because of the problem of establishing *ground truth*. That is, when observing social interactions researchers typically cannot establish with satisfactory degrees of certainty whether the statements people provide are in fact truthful or deceptive. The issue of ground truth is central in deception research, and we will return to it in relation to the discussion about laboratory and field approaches.

As an alternative strategy to obtain data on how common lies are, social psychologists have relied on self-reports. In some studies people have been asked how many lies they told during a given period of time (e.g., Jensen, Arnett, Feldman, & Cauffman, 2004; Vrij, Floyd, & Ennis, 2003). In other studies people have been asked to keep a diary in which they recorded all their social interactions and the lies they told during these interactions (DePaulo & Bell, 1996; DePaulo & Kashy, 1998). These methods might yield unreliable results for a variety of reasons. First, there might be errors in reporting, because people might not remember all the lies they told. Second, these studies might yield underreports because people might not be willing to provide information about all the lies they told or they might systematically leave out more serious lies.

It has long been known to social psychologists that people are concerned about the impressions they give to others and that people consequently might not respond truthfully to questions about socially undesirable behavior. Ironically, the fact that self-reports might not yield reliable measures stems from the very same psychological mechanism that provides the impetus for many lies: people care about what others think of them and will sometimes transgress the boundaries of the truth to maintain a positive image in the eyes of others (DePaulo, 1992; DePaulo et al., 2003). Despite the intrinsic problems of self-reports, studies employing this method to map the frequency of lies consistently reveal that lies are common and that people on average tell between one and two lies each day. Analyses of introspective data collected in self-report studies reveal that most people are not plagued by feelings of discomfort and guilt as a result of lying—an interesting finding given the commonsense notion that lying is an immoral act, reserved for con-men and criminals (Vrij, 2008).

While research on deception in interpersonal settings offers an informative perspective on the social context of deceptive behavior, most everyday lies are of a trivial rather than a serious nature. Obviously, as lies become increasingly serious, the problems of self-reports become increasingly untenable. This does not preclude the possibility of approaching the subject with alternative research strategies (DePaulo, Ansfield, Kirkendol, & Boden, 2004). We will return to research on serious lies told under high-stake conditions in the discussion of field studies on deception.

SUBJECTIVE CUES TO DECEPTION

Although self-report data might be limited for the study of the most serious forms of deception, the methodology has yielded important evidence on the question of *subjective* (i.e., believed) *cues to deception*. To appreciate the importance of subjective beliefs about the characteristics of deceptive behavior, recall the examples of police investigators misinterpreting the behavior of innocent suspects with devastating outcomes. Even though failure to make appropriate attributions of behavior does not always end in miscarriages of justice, misclassifications of deceptive and truthful statements nevertheless cause considerable problems (DePaulo & Morris, 2004). Precious time and resources might go to waste, and costly errors might ensue if legal professionals systematically rely on misleading behavior.

More than a dozen surveys on subjective cues to deception have been conducted, primarily in the United States, the United Kingdom, and Sweden. In most of these studies, respondents were provided with a list of verbal and nonverbal behaviors and asked how, if at all, these behaviors are related to deception (e.g., Colwell, H. Miller, Miller, & Lyons, 2006; Lakhani & Taylor, 2003; Taylor & Hick, 2007). In contrast to this closed-ended approach, some studies have employed an open-ended approach in which respondents are asked what behavioral cues they associate with deception. In at least one large survey, respondents were first asked an open-ended question about cues to deception ("How can you tell when people are lying?"). On the basis of the responses to this open-ended question, a closed-ended questionnaire was developed and distributed to other respondents (The Global Deception Research Team, 2006).

Regardless of the sample and measurement characteristics, strikingly similar results have emerged from this research. Most commonly, people report the belief that gaze aversion is indicative of deception. In a worldwide study surveying beliefs about cues to deception in 58 countries, in 51 of these the belief in a link between gaze behavior and deception was the most frequently reported cue. Survey results also show that people believe that increased body movements, fidgeting, and posture changes are associated with deceit, as along with a higher-pitched voice and speech hesitations and errors. In general, it seems that people associate deception with nonverbal behavior rather than verbal content cues (Mann, Vrij, & Bull, 2004). A possible explanation for this is that in many social situations, nonverbal behavior provides useful information about the characteristics of others—for example, about their social status and personality traits (Vrij, 2008). Nonverbal behavior is also an important tool in interpersonal communication (DePaulo, 1992). When judging veracity, people might rely on the same social inference strategies they employ in other domains. Alternatively, people might overestimate the extent to which nonverbal behavior is prone to leakage (Hale & Stiff, 1990). People might assume that nonverbal channels of communication are less regulated than verbal channels and therefore that it is more informative to pay attention to the former.

Overall, the pattern of subjective cues suggests that people expect liars to experience nervousness and discomfort and that this nervousness is evident in behavior (Vrij & Semin 1996). The tendency to make judgments of the probability of group membership on the basis of superficial similarity to a stereotype is an example of the representativeness heuristic, a rule of thumb used by social perceivers in a range of situations (Tversky & Kahneman, 1974). Importantly, the belief that liars experience and display signs of nervousness is not supported by laboratory research on objective (i.e., actual) indicators of deception. In fact, surprisingly few of the subjective cues to deception are reliably related to deception (DePaulo et al., 2003). Gaze aversion is unrelated to deception, and people endorse an incorrect view of body movements during lying; if anything, liars make fewer movements including fewer hand/finger and leg/feet movements (Vrij, 2008). In addition, speech hesitations and errors are not reliably related to deception. In summary, the surveys on subjective cues to deception consistently show that people endorse a myth about psychological processes that indicate lying that has little basis in reality.

There are some limitations to the validity of these surveys. We cannot be certain that the behaviors people report explicitly as criteria for forming judgments of veracity are those that best capture their decision-making strategies (Nisbett & Wilson, 1977). Because impression formation is partly automatic and implicit (Fiske & Taylor, 2008), it is quite possible that people are unaware of the basis for their veracity assessments. As an alternative approach to self-reports, some studies have coded the behavior of liars and truth tellers and correlated these behaviors with the veracity judgments made by lie-catchers. This correlational method has revealed a finding not observed in self-report studies: People make lie judgments when behavior deviates from norms and expectations (Bond et al., 1992). For example, both gaze aversion and staring is associated with deception judgments (Desforges & Lee, 1995; Levine et al., 2000). Similarly, while intermediate delays between question and response are associated with truth judgments, both overly long and overly brief delays are associated with deception judgments (Baskett & Freedle, 1974; Boltz, 2005).

Studies of lay people's beliefs about cues to deception have been criticized on the basis of limited generalizability to populations in legal and forensic settings (Strömwall, Granhag, & Hartwig, 2004). The commonsense argument holds that people who make judgments about veracity on a professional basis (e.g., police and customs officers) ought to have more insight into the psychology of deception as a function of training and on-the-job experience and that such professionals will endorse more correct beliefs about the behavioral characteristics of deception. A number of surveys have explored this possibility by mapping the beliefs of presumed lie experts such as police officers, prosecutors, judges, customs officers, prison guards, and immigration board officers (Akehurst, Köhnken, Vrij, & Bull, 1996; Granhag, Strömwall, & Hartwig, 2004; Masip & Garrido, 2001; Strömwall & Granhag, 2003). The consistent finding from these surveys is that presumed lie experts endorse the same stereotypes of deceptive behavior as lay people. In fact, none of the studies comparing lay people's beliefs with those of legal professionals observed differences between the groups (Strömwall, Granhag, & Hartwig, 2004).

The robust finding of stereotypical and flawed beliefs about cues to deception begs the question of the origin of these misconceptions and why incorrect beliefs are not corrected over time even with professional experience of veracity judgments. There are several possible explanations. First, people rarely receive outcome feedback about whether their impressions of veracity were correct. Absence of such outcome feedback prevents people from adjusting faulty decision-making strategies and can serve to perpetuate false beliefs over time (DePaulo & Pfeifer, 1986; Hartwig, Granhag, Strömwall, & Andersson, 2004; Hogarth, 2001). Second, social inference and hypothesis testing is prone to confirmation bias, meaning that people tend to seek and receive support for their beliefs rather than to falsify them (Darley & Gross, 1983; Hill, Memon, & McGeorge, 2008; Nickerson, 1998). Third, by processes of belief perseverance, beliefs might be conserved even in the face of disconfirming information (Anderson, Lepper, & Ross, 1980). For a further discussion of the origin of false beliefs about deception, see Strömwall, Granhag, and Hartwig (2004).

In sum, results from surveys do not provide the basis for much optimism about deception detection in forensic contexts. Research consistently shows poor understanding of the psychology of deception, even for legal professionals with extensive experience of high-stake veracity judgments. Self-report instruments have obvious limitations. Most importantly, since they do not study deception directly (rather, people's perception of it), we cannot derive information about objective indicators of deception or about judgment accuracy. These research questions demand experimental research for reasons that will be made clear. We will now turn to the substantial body of laboratory research on deception and review some of its main methodological features and results.

LABORATORY RESEARCH ON DECEPTION

Most studies on deception have been conducted in the laboratory. In this research, participants (typically college students) are randomly assigned to an experimental or a control condition. Participants in the experimental group are asked to provide an intentionally false statement about a topic, while the participants in the control condition provide a truthful statement. The deceptive and truthful statements in these studies are typically subjected to various analyses, including coding and comparison of the verbal and nonverbal characteristics. In addition, the videotaped statements are typically shown to other participants serving as lie-catchers whose task is to make judgments about the veracity of the statements they have seen. An alternative to the laboratory approach is the field approach, in which real-life lies and truths are studied—for example, statements of politicians (Vrij, 2002) or crime suspects denying transgressions (Mann, Vrij, & Bull, 2002).

A main advantage of the laboratory approach is that it offers ground truth: since the assignment of participants to the deceptive or truthful condition is under the control of the researcher, establishing the actual veracity of the statement does not present a problem. In field research, establishing ground truth is a serious problem. If a suspect in a police investigation denies committing a particular crime, how are we to gauge whether this statement is truthful or deceptive? Independent case evidence unambiguous enough to allow us to establish veracity is rarely available for field data (Mann, Vrij, & Bull, 2004). Even if we know that a crime suspect was actually guilty on the basis of independent case evidence, it might not be possible to gauge the veracity of all the details provided in the statement.

A second advantage of the laboratory method is that it offers experimental control over extraneous variables and therefore greater internal validity. If behavioral differences between liars and truth-tellers are found in laboratory studies, we can be reasonably certain that these are not due to preexisting differences in the personality or other characteristic of the participants, as random assignment to conditions serves to distribute such characteristics evenly across the conditions. In contrast, in field research we cannot establish the origin of such differences with certainty. Since participants in field research have self-selected to different conditions, we cannot rule out that other systematic differences than veracity between the participants are responsible for differences in the dependent variables.

A third advantage of the laboratory approach is the presence of *comparable truths*—a control condition that is similar to the deceptive condition in all other respects than veracity. Such comparable truths are often absent in the case of real-life lies. Even if we manage to obtain unambiguous ground truth about the veracity of a denial of a crime suspect in a police interrogation (e.g., by CCTV footage showing his actions), it is not clear what we are to compare this statement with. We cannot compare his deceptive statement in the police interrogation with a truthful statement given in a different context (e.g., when talking to his spouse or colleagues) as there is substantial variation between the characteristics of these settings, which may influence behavior. In addition, we cannot compare his deceptive statement given in response to questions about the crime with truthful statements given in response to more neutral questions (e.g., where he lives), as we then are facing a confound between veracity and question type.

In sum, laboratory studies on deception have a clear advantage in terms of internal validity. Since the deceptive and truthful statements are generated by means of random assignment, we obtain both ground truth and the ability to establish causal links between the independent and dependent variable.

In experimental studies, the topics people are asked to lie or tell the truth about vary. In some studies, people tell lies about opinions, attitudes, and emotions (Porter & ten Brinke, 2008). These statements are misrepresentations of a person's state of mind but do not concern any factual matter (e.g., whether it is raining; whether I walked to work this morning or rode the train) outside the mind of the communicator. These are therefore *subjective lies*, as they concern matters for which there is no objective truth. In a second group of studies, people tell lies about episodic memory—actions and events they have participated in or witnessed, such as mock crimes. For these lies we can objectively evaluate veracity of the statement (e.g., by comparing the statement of the participant with a videotaped documentation of his or her actions during the experiment).

For applications of research to forensic settings, objective lies might be of more relevance. This is because in the majority of cases in the legal system, the statements evaluated for veracity concern assertions of facts rather than assertions of a specific mental state. For example, a guilty suspect who denies involvement in a particular crime is primarily concealing factual information (that he committed the crime and how it happened). Similarly, a person providing intentionally false testimony in court is concerned with the concealment of factual details about a course of events. We are not suggesting that laboratory research on subjective lies is irrelevant for all applied purposes. Research on intentional distortions of one's state of mind are relevant both for clinical and everyday, interpersonal settings. However, since distorting or fabricating episodic events may entail different psychological tasks than distorting one's state of mind, caution should be employed when generalizing from one type of deception to the other.

OBJECTIVE CUES TO DECEPTION

As we have already mentioned, analyses of verbal and nonverbal behavior of lies and truths in laboratory research show that cues to deception are scarce and that many subjective cues to deception are unrelated to deception. A meta-analysis covering 120 studies and 158 cues to deception showed that most of these cues are only weakly related to deception, if at all (DePaulo et al., 2003; see also DePaulo & Morris, 2004). The simple heuristic that liars are more nervous is not supported by the meta-analysis, as many of the overt indicators of nervousness such as fidgeting, blushing, or speech disturbances are not systematically linked to deception. The meta-analytic pattern does suggest that liars are more tense than truth-tellers: Their pupils are more dilated and their pitch of voice is higher (DePaulo et al., 2003). Moreover, the results show that there are some verbal indicators of deception. Liars talk for a shorter time and include fewer details as compared with truth tellers. In addition, liars' stories make less sense in that their stories are less plausible, less logically structured, and more ambivalent.

Liars also sound more uncertain and appear less vocally and verbally immediate than truth-tellers, meaning that observers perceive liars to be less direct, relevant, and personal in their communication. There are some differences in terms of specific details between deceptive and truthful accounts: Liars spontaneously correct themselves and admit not remembering less often than truth-tellers, indicating that liars' stories may lack some of the so-called ordinary imperfections of truthful accounts (this is in line with some predictions and findings from the research on statement validity analysis; see Köhnken, 2004; Ruby & Brigham, 1997; and Vrij, 2005).

The pattern of cues to deception is moderated by several factors. In support of our proposed distinction between subjective and objective lies, it has been found that cues to deception are more readily available for objective lies than for subjective lies. Objective lies typically result in fewer foot and leg movements (DePaulo et al., 2003), possibly because of cognitive load (Vrij, 2000). Similarly, the differences between truth-tellers and the liars in terms of the degree of tenseness are larger when the issues concern transgressions rather than opinions or emotions. This is not surprising; objective lies present a more cognitively taxing task in that they entail the distortion or fabrication of episodic information. In addition, when the motivation for lying is identity relevant rather than, for example, monetary, cues to deception generally increase in strength. Motivations for getting away with a lie are identity relevant when the consequences of getting caught are personal and may harm others' perception of oneself and the characteristics one possesses (DePaulo et al., 2003). The finding that cues to deception are often more salient when someone is lying about transgressions and when the motivation is identity relevant is practically beneficial. In legal settings, lies almost exclusively aim at covering up transgressions, and the consequences of getting caught are far-reaching for the person's personal life and social relations.

It is possible that the lack of cues to deception is partly a function of the coding procedures used. For example, when comparing liars and truth-tellers with regard to pauses in their speech, no differences emerge if the duration and frequencies of pauses are combined. If frequency and duration of pauses are analyzed separately, it can be shown that liars' pauses differ somewhat in duration but not in frequency (Vrij, 2008). Similarly, one study found that when all kinds of illustrators (hand movements illustrating a particular aspect of the statement) were collapsed into one category, no differences between liars and truth-tellers emerged. In contrast, when hand movements were divided into meaningful subtypes, truth-tellers made more deictic (pointing gestures) movements but fewer metaphoric gestures (Caso, Maricchiolo, Bonaiuto, Vrij, & Mann, 2006).

Ekman and colleagues made a distinction between genuine and false smiles. The former are displayed in response to the experience of positive emotion whereas the latter are produced voluntarily in the absence of a felt emotion (Ekman, Davidson, & Friesen, 1990). Felt smiles often involve the automatic activity of the *orbicularis oculi* muscle (producing the characteristic crow's feet around the eyes). Since the *orbicularis oculi* muscle is not typically under conscious control, action of this muscle might be missing in voluntarily orchestrated displays of emotion (Ekman & Friesen, 1982). In support of this, Ekman and colleagues have found that liars and truth-tellers do not differ in smiling when the distinction between felt and false smiles is not made. However, when felt and false smiles are analyzed separately, truth-tellers make a greater number of felt smiles than liars (Ekman, Friesen, & O'Sullivan, 1988). These findings point to the need for theory-driven coding schemes in which psychologically meaningful aspects of behavior are analyzed. Research suggests that clearer behavioral differences between liars and truth-tellers will emerge if the search for cues to deception is guided by theory.

DECEPTION DETECTION ACCURACY

On the basis of research showing that objective cues to deception are scarce, it will come as no surprise that deception detection is generally mediocre. A meta-analysis of lie judgment accuracy showed an average accuracy rate of 54% (Bond & DePaulo, 2006). Given the fact that a 50% accuracy rate can be expected by chance alone, this is not an impressive performance. Moreover, research suggests that people lack insight into the accuracy of their decision making. When analyzing judgments of confidence in relation to veracity assessments, it is typically found that confidence is only weakly related to accuracy, if at all (DePaulo, Charlton, Cooper, Lindsay, & Muhlenbruck, 1997). This means that a confident lie-catcher is as likely to be inaccurate as a less confident lie-catcher. Poor metacognitive calibration is not unique to deception judgments. People display poor calibration in a range of situations, including social judgments and judgments about the quality of one's own memory (Allwood & Granhag, 1999; Dunning, Griffin, Milojkovic, & Ross, 1990).

Analyzing accuracy for truthful and deceptive accounts separately reveals that truthful statements are identified with greater accuracy than are deceptive ones. This phenomenon, called the *veracity effect* (Levine, Sun Park, & McCornack, 1999), stems from the fact that people are prone to a judgment bias; they make more truth than lie judgments. The *truth bias* (Buller & Burgoon, 1996) may be an effect of the availability heuristic (Tversky & Kahneman, 1974); people encounter more truthful than deceptive statements in everyday life, and the inference of truth is therefore more readily available. Further, social and conversational rules prevent people from being suspicious in social interaction. In the absence of obvious indications of deceit, people might prefer the safe and polite assumption of veracity (DePaulo, Jordan, Irvine, & Laser, 1982).

DEPENDENT MEASURES

Most research employs *explicit judgments* of veracity (i.e., participants are simply asked whether the person they observed making a statement was lying or telling the truth). This research consistently shows poor accuracy rates in distinguishing between truthful and deceptive statements. On the basis of the consistency of this finding, we might conclude that there is no difference in how truthful and deceptive statements are perceived and processed. However, interesting evidence to the contrary has emerged from research employing *implicit* or indirect judgments of veracity—that is, where observers were asked to judge the message on some dimension other than veracity. For example, people are better able to discriminate between liars and truth-tellers when they are asked whether the person is thinking hard as compared with when they are explicitly asked whether the person was lying or not (Vrij, Edward, & Bull, 2001). The explanation is plausibly that explicit veracity judgments are based on stereotypical and incorrect notions about the characteristics of deception, so that observers who are asked to make such judgments attend to nondiagnostic aspects of the message such as posture, fidgeting, or gaze aversion.

In contrast, when asked whether the person is thinking hard, observers are led to attend to the diagnostic aspects of the target's behavior (recall the results from the meta-analysis on objective cues showing that liars are more tense and have a more rigid demeanor). Further, a meta-analysis on the relation between accuracy and confidence in deception judgments showed that confidence is indirectly related to veracity: regardless of what explicit veracity judgment they made, people were more confident when they saw a truthful statement (DePaulo et al., 1997). A study by DePaulo and colleagues on deception detection in close relationships also provided evidence that observers perceive truthful and deceptive messages differently. Even though the explicit veracity judgments were not accurate, observers reported feeling more suspicious when they watched a deceptive statement than when they watched a truthful statement (DePaulo & Morris, 2004).

Finally, in a study on veracity assessments of mock witnesses, it was found that while observers could not make accurate explicit judgments of veracity, their memory reports of the statements differed depending on veracity: Truthful statements were better remembered than deceptive ones (Granhag, Landström, & Hartwig, 2005). It is possible that the logical structure and coherence of truthful statements made them easier to encode and retrieve. In summary, this research shows some hope for lie detection. Even though observers are generally unable to explicitly distinguish between deceptive and truthful statements, they nevertheless process and perceive true and false statements differently. It is a challenge for future research to investigate how, if at all, implicit judgments of veracity can improve deception detection in forensic settings.

CRITICISM OF LABORATORY RESEARCH

We have argued that the laboratory approach offers clear advantages over field research, in particular with regard to internal validity. However, the laboratory approach has been subject to criticism, most frequently on the basis of lack of external validity. The typical argument is that laboratory research does not justify the conclusion that lie detection is flawed in forensic or other settings (Miller & Stiff, 1993). The source of such criticism can be summarized as follows. First, critics have argued that laboratory research on cues to deception suffers from lack of generalizability to forensic settings in that liars and truth tellers are not sufficiently motivated to accomplish a truthful impression. That is, whereas liars and truth-tellers in many forensic settings might be extremely motivated by the desire to escape the punishment of the legal system, ethical considerations prevent the simulation of such stakes for the purpose of laboratory research (DePaulo & Morris, 2004).

It has been argued that cues to nervousness and arousal, which do not appear in lower-stake settings, may appear as the stakes increase (Vrij, 2008). This criticism focuses on the external validity of the stimulus material (i.e., the truthful and deceptive statements) used in deception research. A second type of criticism pertains to the characteristics of the lie-catchers in the laboratory paradigms. Critics have argued that laboratory research on college students' ability to make classifications of truthful and deceptive statements does not necessarily generalize to lie-catching in forensic settings. The argument holds that professional lie-catchers might be both more motivated and capable of making accurate judgments of veracity and that they therefore might be equipped with more functional decision-making criteria. Indeed, both lay people and professionals believe that professional lie-catchers are more accurate in establishing veracity than lay people (Garrido, Masip, & Herrero, 2004).

Third, critics have argued that the judgment situation in laboratory research is unrealistic and that non-laboratory settings might allow for more accurate judgments. For example, lie-catchers in laboratory studies are typically exposed to brief segments of behavior; they rarely receive any background information about the case or about the target, and they are restricted to passively watching a tape of the person without the possibility of asking questions (Hartwig, Granhag, Strömwall, & Vrij, 2004; Park, Levine, McCornack, Morrison, & Ferrara, 2002). A number of studies have been conducted to address these concerns of limited external validity in laboratory research.

RESEARCH ON HIGH-STAKE LIES

Liars and truth-tellers in the typical laboratory paradigm attempt to deceive primarily for the sake of the experiment and often receive just a small monetary incentive to act convincingly. Consequently, the stakes of the situation are not very high. In a real-life police investigation, the stakes are considerably higher for the person whose veracity is questioned (Vrij, 2004). If his or her demeanor is not considered credible, he or she may become the target of a suspect-driven investigation (Wagenaar, van Koppen, & Crombag, 1993), which may lead to a conviction (see Dwyer, Neufeld, & Scheck, 2000). The question of whether cues to deception are more pronounced in higher-stake settings has been explored both in laboratory studies, where motivation to be believed was manipulated experimentally (DePaulo, Kirkendol, Tang, & O'Brien, 1988; DePaulo, LeMay, & Epstein, 1991; Vrij, Harden, Terry, Edward, & Bull, 2001), and in field studies of high-stake lying and truth telling in police investigations where it was possible to establish ground truth (Mann, Vrij, & Bull, 2002; Vrij & Mann, 2001, 2003).

Results from these studies do not support the commonsense notion that cues to deception in the form of nervousness and arousal (e.g., fidgeting and gaze aversion) appear when the stakes are high. Instead, findings from laboratory research are corroborated: Liars in high-stake situations display signs of cognitive load in the form of absence of peripheral body movements (e.g., hand/finger movements) and fewer eye blinks (Vrij, 2008). In general, the data suggests two possible effects of increased stakes. First, cues to deception in the form of cognitive load may become more pronounced as the stakes increase (DePaulo et al., 2003). This ought to be beneficial for lie-catching, as behavioral differences between liars and truth-tellers are magnified. Indeed, a meta-analysis on veracity judgments shows that accuracy is higher for motivated than unmotivated targets (Bond & DePaulo, 2006).

Second, as the stakes of the situation increase, people may fall prey for a *paradoxical performance effect*—a counterproductive effect of fear of failure, which may affect both liars and truth-tellers (Baumeister & Showers, 1986). In support of this, the meta-analysis on veracity judgments shows that when targets are motivated to be believed, they are perceived as deceptive regardless of whether they are, in fact, lying or telling the truth. This finding makes sense; if lie-catchers associate cues to nervousness and arousal with deception, they ought to pass lie judgments when they see a target displaying signs of such discomfort. In reality what they perceive might as well be the behavioral traces of an appraisal of the seriousness of the situation affecting both liars and truth-tellers (see Ekman, 2001, for a discussion on this so-called *Othello error*). The latter finding casts doubt on a simplistic notion that more motivated targets will make for better lie-catching.

PROFESSIONAL LIE-CATCHERS' ACCURACY

We have already seen that professional lie-catchers report the same faulty heuristic as lay people that liars display more nervous demeanor. This ought to temper optimism about professional lie-catchers being more in tune with the psychological processes at play during deception. However, it remains possible that police officers and other professional lie-catchers are more accurate lie-catchers when faced with an actual judgment task. A number of studies have explored this possibility by mapping police officers' lie-detection accuracy when judging laboratory (Ekman & O'Sullivan, 1991; Ekman, O'Sullivan, & Frank, 1999; Kassin, Meissner, & Norwick, 2005; Meissner & Kassin, 2002; Vrij & Graham, 1997) and real-life lies and truths (e.g., Mann, Vrij, & Bull, 2004; Vrij & Mann, 2001a). The results show that with few exceptions (Mann, Vrij, & Bull, 2004), presumed lie experts obtain similar hit rates as lay people (around the level of chance), rebutting the objection that laboratory studies using lay people as lie-catchers lack relevance for forensic settings (Miller & Stiff, 1993).

However, professional lie-catchers differ from lay people in two respects. First, police officers do not display a truth bias and are instead prone to make a disproportionate amount of lie judgments. In other words, while lay people might be chronically credulous, police officers err in the direction of excessive suspicion, a tendency that has been labeled the *investigator bias* (Meissner & Kassin, 2002). This bias is most likely a function of the environment shaping decision making (Hogarth, 2001); plausibly, police officers encounter a higher proportion of lies than lay people, and they are probably more aware and wary of the possibility of being duped. This is supported by research showing that the tendency for a lie bias becomes more pronounced with increasing experience of police work (Masip, Alonso, Garrido, & Anton, 2005). Second, police officers differ in the confidence estimates they make in relation to veracity judgments. While their accuracy levels are similar, police officers express significantly more confidence in the accuracy of their veracity judgment than lay people, producing a pronounced overconfidence effect (e.g., DePaulo & Pfeifer, 1986).

PASSIVE VS. ACTIVE DECEPTION DETECTION

In the majority of studies on police officers' deception detection ability, the participating police officers watched a videotaped interview after which they were asked to make a veracity judgment of the suspect they had observed (e.g., Mann, Vrij, & Bull, 2004). In other words, they were restricted to passively watching the suspects without the possibility of asking questions. This judgment situation is quite different from the one in which police officers normally assess veracity (Granhag & Strömwall, 2001). Although research in the interpersonal communication domain has shown that active conversation partners are not better lie-catchers than passive observers (if anything, active lie-catchers perform worse than passive lie-catchers; see Buller, Strzyzewski, & Hunsaker, 1991; Burgoon, Buller, White, Afifi, & Buslig, 1999; Feeley & deTurck, 1997), it is still possible that police officers possess special skills in how to elicit cues to deception during questioning. Indeed, a substantial part of the practical training of police officers pertains to eliciting cues to deception—for example, by asking behavior-provoking questions (Inbau, Reid, Buckley, & Jayne, 2001; see Vrij, Mann, & Fisher, 2006, for an objective test of this approach).

This possibility was tested in a study by Hartwig and colleagues (2004), in which experienced police officers armed with some case information were allowed to question a mock suspect in the manner of their own choice. The results did not support the notion that police officers know how to elicit cues to deception; accuracy when interviewing was compared to that obtained when watching a videotape of an interview conducted by a colleague. In fact, lie detection accuracy was at chance level in both conditions, and analyses of the demeanor of the suspects showed that liars and truth-tellers behaved similarly (even though liars and truth-tellers expressed different strategies prior to the interview; see Strömwall, Hartwig, & Granhag, 2006). In light of the results from other research on police officers, this may come as no surprise; police officers endorse stereotypes about deceptive processes, and their decision making about veracity differs from that of lay people only in self-assessed accuracy (Masip et al., 2005), not in objective accuracy. Taken together, the results suggest that presumed lie experts might not be sufficiently in tune with the psychology of deception to make accurate judgments of veracity, even when allowed to interact with the target.

ELICITING CUES TO DECEPTION

We have reviewed literature showing that deception detection is associated with a substantial error rate. Both lay people and presumed lie experts endorse incorrect views about the psychology of deception, and they fall prey to a number of judgment errors when facing the task of assessing veracity. It seems that the major challenge facing scientific research on deception detection is how to overcome these shortcomings in favor of more accurate lie detection. Given the importance of veracity assessments in forensic settings and the limitations of commonly employed techniques (Vrij, Mann, & Fisher, 2006), it is surprising how little research has focused on generating constructive guidelines for assessing veracity.

Recently, an emerging body of research has taken on this task with promising results. First, research based on the theoretical notion that lying might be more cognitively demanding than truth telling has attempted to increase cues to deception by imposing a further cognitive load on targets. The idea is that liars would be more hampered by such cognitively demanding tasks in that their resources are already preoccupied with the cognitive challenge of lying. In one study, liars and truth-tellers were asked to tell the story in reverse order. It was found that cues to deception were more pronounced when suspects told the story in reverse order, and lie-catchers were more accurate when judging these statements as compared with the control condition (in which the statement was told in chronological order; Vrij, Mann, Fisher, Leal, Milne, & Bull, 2008).

Based on similar theoretical premises postulating cognitive differences between liars and truth-tellers, a second line of research has focused on the possibility of eliciting verbal cues to deception by using the available case evidence strategically. The assumption is that liars who aim to get away with a transgression face cognitive challenges in manufacturing a denial, and that lie-catchers can capitalize on this by withholding the known case facts. The idea is straightforward and intuitively appealing; it is easier to fabricate a plausible alibi if you know the evidence against you. Traditionally, however, police officers present the evidence at the beginning of an interview, possibly to overwhelm the suspect and thereby elicit a confession (Leo, 1996). However, in this situation, liars know what they can and cannot say, and they can spin a persuasive story incorporating the evidence but maintaining innocence.

Using a mock theft paradigm in which both liars and truth-tellers touched a briefcase (from which liars then stole a wallet), Hartwig and colleagues (2005) found that when the information that their fingerprints had been found on the briefcase was disclosed in the beginning of the interview, liars and truth-tellers both gave plausible explanations for being in contact with the briefcase (e.g., that they just moved it while looking for something). Lie-catchers could not distinguish between these true and false denials. In contrast, when the evidence was strategically withheld and the interviewer posed questions about it (e.g., "Did you see or touch a briefcase?"), liars gave their guilt away by proposing denials that violated the evidence (e.g., by saying they were not close to the briefcase). In a follow-up study, police trainees who were taught these simple guidelines before questioning a mock suspect obtained hit rates of more than 85% with no evidence of a judgment bias (Hartwig et al., 2006).

A third approach drawing on cognitive differences between liars and truth tellers is the *assessment criteria indicative of deception* (ACID) approach, outlined and studied by Colwell and colleagues (Colwell, Hiscock-Anisman, Memon, Taylor, & Prewett, 2007). In this approach, targets are questioned using an interview style inspired by the cognitive interview (CI). The CI was developed to improve the accuracy and completeness of eyewitness memory reports; it uses mnemonic techniques firmly based in cognitive psychology. The ACID approach uses such mnemonics with the assumption that they will enhance verbal differences between liars and truth-tellers. More specifically, they may provide richer details from truth-tellers by probing for specific details (for whom the mnemonics serve as cues to recall) while increasing the problems for liars who have to fabricate information in response to these probes. Research on the ACID technique has shown that verbal differences between liars and truth-tellers become more pronounced when the technique is used (Colwell et al., 2007), and that it is possible to train observers in attending to relevant cues with substantial increases in accuracy as a result (Colwell et al., in press).

CONCLUSIONS AND FUTURE DIRECTIONS

Lie-catching is an enterprise fraught with error, as substantial research efforts have established. The results generalize to forensic settings. There is no

Pinocchio's nose, even for high-stake lies in police investigations, and not even experienced police officers are capable of assessing veracity at a substantially higher than chance level. This is problematic inasmuch as judgments of veracity play important roles in police investigations and other legal settings. However, there is hope for lie-catchers stemming from emerging research on the elicitation of cues to deception. The common theme of this research is that cues to deception might not be available by default and that lie-catchers must take on a more active and informed role in the process of catching lies (Granhag & Hartwig, 2008). On the basis of theoretically sound notions about cognitive differences between liars and truth-tellers, it may be possible to elicit cues to deception by strategically exploiting the challenges facing liars.

REFERENCES

Akehurst, L., Köhnken, G., Vrij, A., & Bull, R. (1996). Lay persons' and police officers' beliefs regarding deceptive behaviour. *Applied Cognitive Psychology, 10,* 461–471.

Allwood, C. M., & Granhag, P. A. (1999). Feelings of confidence and the realism of confidence judgments in everyday life. In P. Juslin & H. Montgomery (Eds.), *Judgment and decision making: Neo-Brunswikian and process-tracing approaches* (pp. 123–146). Mahwah, NJ: Lawrence Erlbaum.

Anderson, C. A., Lepper, M. R., & Ross, L. (1980). Perseverance of social theories: The role of explanation in the persistence of discredited information. *Journal of Personality & Social Psychology, 39,* 1037–1047.

Baskett, G., & Freedle, R. (1974). Aspects of language pragmatics and the social perception of lying. *Journal of Psycholinguistic Research, 3,* 117–131.

Baumeister, R. F., & Showers, C. J. (1986). A review of paradoxical performance effects: Choking under pressure in sports and mental tests. *Journal of Personality and Social Psychology, 16,* 361–383.

Bok, S. (1999). *Lying: Moral choice in public and private life.* New York, NY: Pantheon.

Boltz, M. G. (2005). Temporal dimensions of conversational interaction: The role of response latencies and pauses in social impression formation. *Journal of Language and Social Psychology, 24,* 103–138.

Bond, C. F., Jr., & DePaulo, B. M. (2006). Accuracy of deception judgments. *Personality and Social Psychology Review, 10,* 214–234.

Bond, C., Omar, A., Pitre, U., Lashley, B., Skaggs, L., & Kirk, C. (1992). Fishy-looking liars: Deception judgment from expectancy violation. *Journal of Personality and Social Psychology, 63,* 969–977.

Buller, D. B., & Burgoon, J. K. (1996). Interpersonal deception theory. *Communication Theory, 6,* 203–242.

Buller, D. B., Strzyzewski, K. D., & Hunsaker, F. G. (1991). Interpersonal deception: II. The inferiority of conversational partners as deception detectors. *Communication Monographs, 58,* 25–40.

Burgoon, J. K., Buller, D. B., White, C. H., Afifi, W., & Buslig, A. L. S. (1999). The role of conversational involvement in deceptive interpersonal interactions. *Personality and Social Psychology Bulletin, 25,* 669–685.

Caso, L., Maricchiolo, F., Bonaiuto, M., Vrij, A., & Mann, S. (2006). The impact of deception and suspicion on different hand movements. *Journal of Nonverbal Behavior, 30,* 1–19.

Colwell, K., Hiscock-Anisman, C., Memon, A., Taylor, L., & Prewett, J. (2007). Assessment criteria indicative of deception (ACID): An integrated system of investigative interviewing and detecting deception. *Journal of Investigative Psychology and Offender Profiling, 4,* 167–180.

Colwell, K., Hiscock-Anisman, C. K., Memon, A., Colwell, L., Taylor, L., & Woods, D. (in press). Training in assessment criteria indicative of deception (ACID) to improve credibility assessments. *Forensic Psychology Practice.*

Colwell, L., Miller, H., Miller, R., & Lyons, P. (2006). US police officers' knowledge regarding behaviors indicative of deception: Implications for eradicating erroneous beliefs through training. *Psychology, Crime & Law, 12*, 489–503.

Darley, J., & Gross, P. (1983). A hypothesis-confirming bias in labeling effects. *Journal of Personality and Social Psychology, 44*, 20–33.

DePaulo, B., Ansfield, M., Kirkendol, S., & Boden, J. (2004). Serious lies. *Basic and Applied Social Psychology, 26*(2), 147–167.

DePaulo, B. M. (1992). Nonverbal behavior and self-presentation. *Psychological Bulletin, 111*, 203–243.

DePaulo, B. M., & Bell, K. L. (1996). Truth and investment: Lies are told to those who care. *Journal of Personality and Social Psychology, 70*, 703–716.

DePaulo, B. M., Charlton, K., Cooper, H., Lindsay, J. L., & Muhlenbruck, L. (1997). The accuracy-confidence relation in the detection of deception. *Personality and Social Psychology Review, 1*, 346–357.

DePaulo, B. M., Jordan, A., Irvine, A., & Laser, P. S. (1982). Age changes in the detection of deception. *Child Development, 53*, 701–709.

DePaulo, B. M., & Kashy, D. A. (1998). Everyday lies in close and casual relationships. *Journal of Personality and Social Psychology, 74*, 63–79.

DePaulo, B. M., Kirkendol, S. E., Tang, J., & O'Brien, T. P. (1988). The motivational impairment effect in the communication of deception: Replications and extensions. *Journal of Nonverbal Behavior, 12*, 177–202.

DePaulo, B. M., LeMay, C. S., & Epstein, J. A. (1991). Effect of importance of success and expectations for success on effectiveness at deceiving. *Personality and Social Psychology Bulletin, 129*, 74–118.

DePaulo, B. M., Lindsay, J. J., Malone, B. E., Muhlenbruck, L., Charlton, K., & Cooper, H. (2003). Cues to deception. *Psychological Bulletin, 129*, 74–118.

DePaulo, B. M., & Morris, W. L. (2004). Discerning lies from truths: Behavioral cues to deception and the indirect pathway of intuition. In P. A. Granhag & L. A. Strömwall (Eds.), *The detection of deception in forensic contexts* (pp. 15–40). Cambridge, England: Cambridge University Press.

DePaulo, B. M., & Pfeifer, R. L. (1986). On-the-job experience and skill at detecting deception. *Journal of Applied Social Psychology, 16*, 249–267.

Desforges, D., & Lee, T. (1995). Detecting deception is not as easy as it looks. *Teaching of Psychology, 22*, 128–130.

Drizin, S. A., & Leo, R. A. (2004). The problem of false confessions in the post-DNA world. *North Carolina Law Review, 82*, 891–1007.

Dunning, D., Griffin, D. W., Milojkovic, J. D., & Ross, L. (1990). The overconfidence effect in social predictions. *Journal of Personality and Social Psychology, 58*, 568–581.

Dwyer, J., Neufeld, P., & Scheck, B. (2000). *Actual innocence: Five days to execution and other dispatches from the wrongly convicted.* New York, NY: Doubleday.

Ekman, P. (2001). *Telling lies: Clues to deceit in the marketplace, politics and marriage.* New York, NY: W. W. Norton.

Ekman, P., Davidson, R. J., & Friesen, W. V. (1990). The Duchenne smile: Emotional expression and brain physiology II. *Journal of Personality and Social Psychology, 58*, 342–353.

Ekman, P., & Friesen, W. V. (1982). Felt, false, and miserable smiles. *Journal of Nonverbal Behavior, 6*, 238–253.

Ekman, P., Friesen, W. V., & O'Sullivan, M. (1988). Smiles when lying. *Journal of Personality and Social Psychology, 54*, 414–420.

Ekman, P., & O'Sullivan, M. (1991). Who can catch a liar? *American Psychologist, 46*, 913–920.

Ekman, P., O'Sullivan, M., & Frank, M. G. (1999). A few can catch a liar. *Psychological Science, 10*, 263–266.

Feeley, T. H., & deTurck, M. A. (1997). *Perceptions of communications as seen by the actor and as seen by the observer: The case of lie detection.* Paper presented at the International Communication Association Annual Conference, Montreal, Canada.

Fiske, S. T., & Taylor, S. E. (2008). *Social cognition: From brains to culture.* Boston, MA: McGraw-Hill.

Garrido, E., Masip, J., & Herrero, C. (2004). Police officers' credibility judgements: Accuracy and estimated ability. *International Journal of Psychology, 39*, 254–275.

Global Deception Research Team (2006). A world of lies. *Journal of Cross-Cultural Psychology, 37*, 60–74.

Granhag, P. A., Andersson, L. O., Strömwall, L. A., & Hartwig, M. (2004). Imprisoned knowledge: Criminals' beliefs about deception. *Legal and Criminological Psychology, 9*, 103–119.

Granhag, P. A., & Hartwig, M. (2008). A new theoretical perspective on deception detection: On the psychology of instrumental mind reading. *Psychology, Crime and Law, 14*, 189–200.

Granhag, P. A., Landström, S., & Hartwig, M. (2005). Witnesses appearing live vs. on video: Effects on observers perception, veracity assessments and memory. *Applied Cognitive Psychology*, 19, 913–933.

Granhag, P. A., & Strömwall, L. A. (2001). Deception detection: Interrogators' and observers' decoding of consecutive statements. *The Journal of Psychology—Interdisciplinary and Applied*, 135, 630–620.

Granhag, P. A., & Strömwall, L. A. (2004). *The detection of deception in forensic contexts*. Cambridge, England: Cambridge University Press.

Gudjonsson, G. H. (2003). *The psychology of interrogations and confessions: A handbook*. Chichester, England: Wiley.

Hale, J. L., & Stiff, J. B. (1990). Nonverbal primacy in veracity judgments. *Communication Reports*, 3, 75–83.

Hartwig, M., Granhag, P. A., Strömwall, L. A., & Andersson, L. O. (2004). Suspicious minds: Criminals' ability to detect deception. *Psychology, Crime, and Law*, 10, 83–95.

Hartwig, M., Granhag, P. A., Strömwall, L. A., & Vrij, A. (2004). Police officers' lie detection accuracy: Interrogating freely versus observing video. *Police Quarterly*, 7, 429–456.

Hill, C., Memon, A., & McGeorge, P. (2008). The role of confirmation bias in suspect interviews: A systematic evaluation. *Legal and Criminological Psychology*, 13, 357–371.

Hogarth, R. M. (2001). *Educating intuition*. Chicago, IL: University of Chicago Press.

Inbau, F. E., Reid, J. E., Buckley, J. P., & Jayne, B. C. (2001). *Criminal interrogation and confessions*. Gaithersburg, MD: Aspen Publishers.

Jensen, L., Arnett, J. J., Feldman, S. S., & Cauffman, E. (2004). The right to do wrong: Lying to parents among adolescents and emerging adults. *Journal of Youth and Adolescence*, 33, 101–112.

Johnson, M. B. (2003). The interrogation of Michael Crowe: A film review focused on education and training. *American Journal of Forensic Psychology*, 21, 71–79.

Kassin, S., Meissner, C., & Norwick, R. (2005). "I'd know a false confession if I saw one": A comparative study of college students and police investigators. *Law and Human Behavior*, 29, 211–227.

Kassin, S. M. (2005). On the psychology of confessions: Does innocence put innocent at risk? *American Psychologist*, 60, 215–228.

Kassin, S. M., & Gudjonsson, G. H. (2004). The psychology of confession evidence: A review of the literature and issues. *Psychological Science in the Public Interest*, 5, 35–69.

Köhnken, G. (2004). Statement validity analysis and the "detection of the truth." In P. A. Granhag & L. A. Strömwall (Eds.), *The detection of deception in forensic contexts* (pp. 41–63). Cambridge, England: Cambridge University Press.

Lakhani, M., & Taylor, R. (2003). Beliefs about the cues to deception in high- and low-stake situations. *Psychology, Crime & Law*, 9, 357–368.

Leo, R. A. (1996). Inside the interrogation room. *Journal of Criminal Law and Criminology*, 86, 266–303.

Levine, T., Anders, L., Banas, J., Baum, K., Endo, K., Hu, A., & Wong, N. C. H. (2000). Norms, expectations, and deception: A norm violation model of veracity judgments. *Communication Monographs*, 67, 123–137.

Levine, T. R., Sun Park, H., & McCornack, S. A. (1999). Accuracy in detecting truths and lies: Documenting the "veracity effect." *Communication Monographs*, 66, 125–144.

Mann, S., Vrij, A., & Bull, R. (2002). Suspects, lies and videotape: An analysis of authentic high-stake liars. *Law and Human Behavior*, 26, 265–376.

Mann, S., Vrij, A., & Bull, R. (2004). Detecting true lies: Police officers' ability to detect suspects' lies. *Journal of Applied Psychology*, 89, 137–149.

Masip, J., Alonso, H., Garrido, E., & Anton, C. (2005). Generalized communicative suspicion (GCS) among police officers: Accounting for the investigator bias effect. *Journal of Applied Social Psychology*, 35, 1046–1066.

Masip, J., & Garrido, E. (2001, June). *Experienced and novice officers' beliefs about indicators of deception*. Paper presented at the 11th European Conference of Psychology and Law, Lisbon, Portugal.

Masip, J., Garrido, E., & Herrero, C. (2003). When did you conclude she was lying? The impact of the moment the decision about the sender's veracity is made and the sender's facial appearance on police officers' credibility judgements. *Journal of Credibility Assessment and Witness Psychology*, 4, 1–36.

Meissner, C. A., & Kassin, S. M. (2002). "He's guilty!": Investigator bias in judgments of truth and deception. *Law and Human Behavior*, 26, 469–480.

Miller, G. R., & Stiff, J. B. (1993). *Deceptive communication*. Newbury Park: Sage.

Nickerson, R. (1998). Confirmation bias: A ubiquitous phenomenon in many guises. *Review of General Psychology, 2,* 175–220.

Nisbett, R., & Wilson, T. (1977). Telling more than we can know: Verbal reports on mental processes. *Psychological Review, 84,* 231–259.

Park, H. S., Levine, T. R., McCornack, S. A., Morrison, K., & Ferrara, M. (2002). How people really detect lies. *Communication Monographs, 69,* 144–157.

Porter, S., & ten Brinke, L. (2008). Reading between the lies: Identifying concealed and falsified emotions in universal facial expressions. *Psychological Science, 19,* 508–514.

Ruby, C. L., & Brigham, J. C. (1997). The usefulness of the criteria-based content analysis technique in distinguishing between truthful and fabricated allegations. *Psychology, Public Policy and the Law, 3,* 705–737.

Scheck, B., Neufeld, P., & Dwyer, J. (2000). *Actual innocence.* Garden City, NY: Doubleday.

Strömwall, L. A., & Granhag, P. A. (2003). How to detect deception? Arresting the beliefs of police officers, prosecutors and judges. *Psychology, Crime, & Law, 9,* 19–36.

Strömwall, L. A., Granhag, P. A., & Hartwig, M. (2004). Practitioners' beliefs about deception. In P. A. Granhag & L. A. Strömwall (Eds.), *The detection of deception in forensic contexts* (pp. 229–250). Cambridge, England: Cambridge University Press.

Strömwall, L. A., Hartwig, M., & Granhag, P. A. (2006). To act truthfully: Nonverbal behaviour and strategies during a police interrogation. *Psychology, Crime and Law, 12,* 207–219.

Taylor, R., & Hick, R. (2007). Believed cues to deception: Judgments in self-generated trivial and serious situations. *Legal and Criminological Psychology, 12,* 321–331.

Tversky, A., & Kahneman, D. (1974). Judgment under uncertainty: Heuristics and biases. *Science, 185,* 1124–1131.

Vrij, A. (2002). Telling and detecting lies. In N. Brace and H. L. Westcott (Eds.), *Applying psychology* (pp. 179–241). Milton Keynes, England: Open University.

Vrij, A. (2004). Why professionals fail to catch liars and how they can improve. *Legal and Criminological Psychology, 9,* 159–181.

Vrij, A. (2005). Criteria-based content analysis: A qualitative review of the first 37 studies. *Psychology, Public Policy and the Law, 11,* 3–41.

Vrij, A. (2008). *Detecting lies and deceit: Pitfalls and opportunities* (2nd ed.). Chichester, England: Wiley.

Vrij, A., Edward, K., & Bull, R. (2001). Police officers' ability to detect deceit: The benefit of indirect deception detection measures. *Legal and Criminological Psychology, 6,* 185–196.

Vrij, A., Floyd, M., & Ennis, E. (2003). Telling lies to strangers or close friends: Its relationships with attachment style. In S. P. Shohov (Ed.), *Advances in psychological research, Vol. 20* (pp. 61–74). New York, NY: NovaScience.

Vrij, A., & Graham, S. (1997). Individual differences between liars and the ability to detect lies. *Expert Evidence: The International Digest of Human Behaviour Science and Law, 5,* 144–148.

Vrij, A., Harden, F., Terry, J., Edward, K., & Bull, R. (2001). The influence of personal characteristics, stakes and lie complexity on the accuracy and confidence to detect deceit. In R. Roesch, R. R. Corrado, & R. J. Dempster (Eds.), *Psychology in the courts: International advances in knowledge* (pp. 289–304). London, England: Routledge.

Vrij, A., & Mann, S. (2001). Telling and detecting lies in a high-stake situation: The case of a convicted murderer. *Applied Cognitive Psychology, 15,* 187–203.

Vrij, A., & Mann, S. (2003). Deceptive responses and detecting deceit. In P. W. Halligan, C. Bass, & D. Oakley (Eds.), *Malingering and illness deception: Clinical and theoretical perspectives* (pp. 348–362). Oxford, England: Oxford University Press.

Vrij, A., Mann, S., & Fisher, R. (2006). An empirical test of the behavior analysis interview. *Law and Human Behavior, 30,* 329–345.

Vrij, A., Mann, S., Fisher, R., Leal, S., Milne, R., & Bull, R. (2008). Increasing cognitive load to facilitate lie detection: The benefit of recalling an event in reverse order. *Law and Human Behavior, 32,* 253–265.

Vrij, A., & Semin, G. R. (1996). Lie experts' beliefs about nonverbal indicators of deception. *Journal of Nonverbal Behavior, 20,* 65–80.

Wagenaar, W. A., van Koppen, P. J., & Crombag, H. F. M. (1993). *Anchored narratives: The psychology of criminal evidence.* New York, NY: St. Martin's Press.

Zuckerman, M., DePaulo, B. M., & Rosenthal, R. (1981). Verbal and nonverbal communication of deception. In L. Berkowitz (Ed.), *Advances in experimental social psychology, Vol. 14* (pp. 1–57). New York, NY: Academic Press.

CHAPTER 9

Competency to Stand Trial and Criminal Responsibility Research

PATRICIA ZAPF, DEBBIE GREEN, AND BARRY ROSENFELD

THIS CHAPTER EXAMINES the methods that have been used in competency to stand trial (CST) and criminal responsibility (CR) research during the past several decades. The chapter begins with a brief introduction to competency and criminal responsibility; however, the reader who is unfamiliar with the general nature of these topics is referred to additional sources (i.e., Melton, Petrila, Poythress, & Slobogin, 2007; Zapf, Viljoen, Whittemore, Poythress, & Roesch, 2002) for more detailed background and foundational information. The bulk of this chapter focuses on methodological issues in studying CST and CR. In addition to a discussion of the research and methods that have been used, it identifies directions for future research and methods appropriate to these future lines of inquiry. It should be noted that considerably more research has focused on CST, and thus the chapter is disproportionately weighted towards this topic, with issues unique to CR integrated whenever relevant. However, because both CST and CR are trial-related legal issues having to do with a defendant's mental state, many of the methodological issues discussed in one context will apply to both types of research.

HISTORY AND LEGAL BACKGROUND

Competency and criminal responsibility (insanity) are two legal issues that pertain to a defendant's mental state. *Present* mental state is at issue in determinations of competency whereas mental state *at the time of the offense* is at issue in criminal responsibility determinations. Legal standards for competency and criminal responsibility vary from state to state, but one standard in particular—the *Dusky* standard—is almost universally accepted for competency determinations, and two (similar but slightly different) standards—the *M'Naghten* standard and the American Law Institute's standard proposed in the Model Penal Code (1962)—are the most commonly used standards for determining criminal responsibility throughout the United States.

The legal standard for competency to stand trial (CST; also referred to as adjudicative competence, competency to proceed, or fitness to proceed) is open textured (not subject to a specific, defined set of abilities) and context dependent. That is, the standard for CST may vary as a function of the capacities required of the particular defendant, in his or her particular situation, facing his or her specific charges, and working with his or her particular defense attorney. Thus, although CST can most often be defined by one legal standard (*Dusky*), the application of this standard often varies from case to case. In addition, there are at least three ways to conceptualize the *Dusky* standard, each of which has been used in research and scholarly writings regarding CST: as a three-prong discrete abilities model, as a two-prong syntactical analysis model, and as a two-prong cognitive complexity model (Rogers, 2001).

The three-prong discrete abilities model operationalizes each component of *Dusky*: rational ability to consult with one's attorney, factual understanding of the charges and courtroom proceedings, and rational understanding of the courtroom proceedings. The two-prong syntactical analysis model breaks *Dusky* into two components on the basis of sentence structure: rational ability to consult with one's attorney, and factual and rational understanding of the charges and proceedings. The two-prong cognitive complexity model breaks *Dusky* into two components on the basis of cognitive abilities: factual understanding and rational abilities. Much of the research on CST has focused either on identifying demographic, cognitive, and psychological characteristics that impair one or more of these domains of competence or on the development and validation of assessment instruments to assist in evaluating these various domains of competency.

The early CST research was mainly descriptive in nature, examining the characteristics of defendants referred for competency evaluation and comparing competent and incompetent defendants. Some of this early research focused on the evaluation process and the utility of screening evaluations (as opposed to more formal evaluations of competency). The development of a number of instruments designed to assist in the evaluation of competency (described later in the chapter) has allowed researchers to address more sophisticated research questions, such as evaluating domains of competency rather than simply evaluating competency as a dichotomous construct. Thus, the evolution of measures of competency has directly impacted the research methodology used and the sophistication of the research questions analyzed. A smaller but steadily growing body of literature has also addressed evaluator processes, such as inter-evaluator reliability, report quality, and the utility of competency-assessment instruments. More recently, researchers have begun to focus on questions related to the restoration of competency for defendants found incompetent, such as the prediction and enhancement of restorability.

Unlike the consistency that defines the legal standard for CST, multiple legal standards have been developed and used for criminal responsibility (CR). As noted previously, two legal standards are used by the majority of jurisdictions in the United States, but other legal standards and issues exist (e.g., diminished capacity defenses, *mens rea* issues in the absence of a formal insanity defense). Adding to this complexity are the changes in legal standards for CR that have taken place during the past several decades (most notably following the successful insanity defense of John Hinckley; Steadman et al., 1993), which have provided frequent opportunities to study changes at the policy level such as occurred with the abolition of the insanity defense in several states and the enactment of the *guilty but mentally ill* plea in others.

Thus, unlike most CST research, research on CR is typically less concerned with conducting in-depth examinations of legal standards or assessment instruments (which are largely absent in the CR literature) and is more focused on a broad examination of legal and policy changes and their impact on individuals found not criminally responsible (insane). However, many researchers and theorists have identified an analogous breakdown of CR into two domains that typically characterize most statutory definitions of insanity: ability to understand the nature, character, and consequences of one's actions; and ability to distinguish right from wrong). But unlike CST, much of the research on CR has focused on examining actual outcomes for individuals found not criminally responsible, as opposed to predicting treatment response. It should be noted that the CR literature also includes numerous studies of juror decision making, but because this literature is largely experimental rather than clinical, it is better addressed elsewhere in this volume (see Chapter 11 for a detailed analysis of methodological issues in jury decision-making research).

METHODOLOGICAL ISSUES

CLINICAL AND COMPARISON SAMPLES

Two types of "clinical" samples have been used in the vast majority of CST and CR research: defendants who have been referred for a forensic evaluation and defendants who have been adjudicated incompetent or not criminally responsible. Sampling a group of defendants referred for evaluation allows for comparisons between those considered competent or criminally responsible and those considered incompetent or not responsible, whereas sampling a group of defendants already found incompetent or not responsible allows only for an examination of within-group differences. In the latter instance, some researchers have chosen to use a non-referred comparison group (i.e., defendants for whom the issue of CST or CR has not been raised, usually from either a criminal justice or a psychiatric population) to allow for the examination of differences between those found incompetent or not responsible and a more general criminal justice sample or psychiatric sample. Ideally, defendants in the non-referred comparison sample will be matched to the incompetent or not-responsible sample on criminological, psychiatric, or demographic characteristics in order to minimize group differences on potentially important variables. Advantages and limitations of each of these sample types are discussed in detail in the following sections.

Defendants Found Incompetent or Not Responsible   Sampling defendants found incompetent or not responsible allows for aggregate descriptions as well as the identification of within-group differences useful for predicting treatment outcome. For example, Mossman (2007) examined the characteristics of 351 incompetent defendants and identified two groups with a low probability of being restored: those whose incompetence was a result of irremediable cognitive disorders and those who were chronically psychotic (i.e., with a history of lengthy inpatient hospitalization). In addition, focusing on the population of interest allows for analysis of trends over time. For example, Zonana, Wells, Getz, and Buchanan (1990) monitored changes in the psychiatric composition of defendants found not responsible in relation to statutory changes over a 20-year time span.

Focusing on the population of interest also allows for exploration of the heterogeneity within that group that would otherwise be obscured when offenders with a different legal status are compared. For example, Thompson, Stuart, and Holden (1992) divided a sample of defendants found not responsible into groups on the basis of presence and type of hallucinations, allowing for the identification of several additional clinical differences between the groups. The limitations of this approach, however, include the inability to determine whether findings are unique to incompetent or not-responsible defendants rather than a characteristic of all criminal offenders or all offenders referred for mental health evaluation. Without an appropriate comparison group, it is impossible to analyze issues such as referral bias, discrepancies in clinical practices, or other potentially relevant criminological, demographic, or psychiatric characteristics.

Use of a non-referred comparison group may be appropriate when the research question pertains to differences between the population of interest and the general population of criminal defendants or psychiatric patients. For example, in their validation research, the developers of the *MacArthur Competence Assessment Tool—Criminal Adjudication* (MacCAT-CA; Poythress, Bonnie, Monahan, Otto, & Hoge, 2002, described later in the chapter) used comparison samples of both incarcerated offenders and defendants deemed competent by their attorneys. The use of these comparison groups facilitated an analysis of how the MacCAT-CA might distinguish between incompetent defendants and non-referred defendants with or without a mental health history.

Of course one of the limitations in using a general criminal justice sample or a general psychiatric sample (but not both) as a comparison group is that either of these two groups captures only half of the issues (either the psychiatric issues or the criminal justice issues). In addition, a criminal justice sample generally has a low rate of severe psychiatric symptomatology, thereby limiting its utility as a "clinical" comparison group. Conversely, a psychiatric sample, while reflecting a more complete range of psychiatric symptomatology, will necessarily encompass only individuals who are moderately symptomatic, as those who are too mentally ill to participate in research will inevitably be excluded.

Another limitation of using non-referred comparison groups is that systematic differences in processing by the criminal justice system may occur between the population of interest and the comparison sample (non-referred offenders) that may be relevant. For example, Zonana, Wells, Getz, and Buchanan (1990) observed that their sample of defendants found not responsible appeared to have committed a significantly higher proportion of violent offenses as compared with the general offender population; however, rather than indicating that mentally individuals are more likely to commit violent offenses, these authors noted that non-referred defendants often plead guilty to (and thus are convicted of) lesser offenses than those originally charged at the time of arrest or indictment. In addition, defendants with less severe offenses may avoid an insanity defense given that it could lead to a lengthier period of hospitalization than would be spent incarcerated if convicted, resulting in an overrepresentation of violent offenders among those found not responsible.

Defendants Referred for Evaluation Sampling all defendants referred for CST or CR evaluation allows for the comparison of groups on the basis of legal outcome (competent vs. incompetent; responsible vs. not responsible) as well as for comparisons between the referred group and non-referred defendants. With respect to CST research, sampling referred defendants allows for evaluation of the demographic and clinical characteristics that differentiate those found competent from those found incompetent (e.g., Nicholson & Kugler, 1991; Rosenfeld & Wall, 1998), or the psychometric properties and discriminatory power of competency assessment instruments (e.g., Zapf, Roesch, & Viljoen, 2001).

For example, Nicholson and Kugler (1991) reviewed 30 studies that contrasted incompetent and competent defendants and concluded that defendants with psychotic disorders and several specific psychiatric symptoms were significantly more likely to be found incompetent to stand trial, as were older, female, and racial minority defendants. A smaller, but similar literature has emerged comparing defendants considered not responsible from those considered criminally responsible (e.g., Warren, Fitch, Deitz, & Rosenfeld, 1991). However, unlike CST evaluations, in which the court typically accepts the opinion of expert evaluators, CR evaluations are routinely contested and only a small subset are ultimately found not guilty by reason of insanity (NGRI). Thus, important differences might exist between defendants considered by the evaluating clinician to be responsible as opposed to not responsible compared with defendants actually found NGRI as opposed to those convicted after an unsuccessful NGRI defense. Little research, however, has been performed to examine this important question.

OUTCOME/CRITERION VARIABLES

As noted previously, clinician ratings of competency are a common criterion variable or outcome measure against which to evaluate predictor variables and assessment measures in CST research. Nicholson and Kugler (1991) determined that clinician opinions regarding competency status constituted the outcome variable used in 87% of the studies they reviewed. Although several studies have found high rates of judicial acceptance of clinician opinions (often approaching 99%; Zapf, Hubbard, Cooper, Wheeles, & Ronan, 2004), particularly in jurisdictions where evaluators are court-referred rather than retained by counsel, there are still limitations to the use of this outcome measure. The most obvious concern with relying on clinician opinions regarding competency, particularly in studies seeking to validate competency assessment instruments, is that the validity of clinicians' decisions is entirely unknown. Of course, judicial determination does not provide a better "gold standard," as nonclinical factors (e.g., public scrutiny) may impact judicial conclusions. Moreover, because competency can change rapidly over time, either with treatment or during incarceration without access to treatment, opinions regarding competency reflect mental status at a particular point in time rather than a fixed outcome. Therefore, it is important that CST research using clinician opinion regarding competency status as an outcome measure use the opinion that is closest in time to the actual court determination regarding competency or alternatively, closest in time to the remainder of study procedures (e.g., administration of a CST measure).

Perhaps the single most important limitation of CST and CR research is the lack of a true gold standard or ultimate criterion for competency or criminal responsibility. That is, while clinical opinions and legal determinations regarding a defendant's competency are often closely aligned, there is no absolute determination of competency against which to compare clinical opinions or judicial decisions. Defendants who are considered incompetent are never allowed to proceed with trial, so there is no way to determine whether a determination of incompetence was accurate. As Roesch and Golding (1980) noted more than 30 years ago, a provisional trial wherein incompetent defendant were allowed to proceed until their deficits compromised their trial-related abilities is the only means by which to evaluate the validity of legal or clinical determinations of competency. To date, no jurisdiction allows for such provisional trials, forcing continued reliance on clinical opinions or legal determinations.

One method of circumventing the potential limitations of, and discrepancies between, clinical opinions and legal determinations of competency and criminal responsibility is the use of a "blue ribbon" panel of experts. Golding, Roesch, and Schreiber (1984) used this approach in their study of competency evaluations, asking experts to review all data collected by the court clinics, hospital staff, and the research interviewers and evaluators and to arrive at a determination regarding competency status to be used as the criterion variable. Grisso (1992) recommended another approach to avoiding reliance on dichotomous clinical opinions, suggesting that researchers use observations of defendants enacting relevant competency-related behaviors as a criterion for evaluating competency-assessment instruments. Thus, defendants' scores on competency assessment instruments could be compared to observations of their interactions with the attorney or participation in a legal proceeding.

Grisso cited as an exemplar a study by Gannon (1990), which compared scores on the *Competency Assessment Instrument* to items on a behavioral rating scale assessed during the course of a mock hearing. Rosenfeld and Ritchie (1998) also implemented a unique approach to competency assessment, asking clinicians to rate the degree of a defendant's competency along a 0-to-10 numerical rating scale as well as generating dichotomous ratings of competence in general and for each of the two cognitive domains (ability to consult and understanding of proceedings). This methodology allowed for an analysis of the degree of competency (based on the numerical rating scale) required in felony versus misdemeanor charges, as well as an analysis of the clinical characteristics that corresponded to each domain of competency.

Research on the restoration of defendants found incompetent also suffers from limitations in the outcome variable. Much of this research has also focused on identifying characteristics that correspond to whether a defendant is ultimately restored to competency. Discrepancies may exist between clinical opinion as to restorability and actual judicial findings of competency for a defendant previously found incompetent. Although clinician predictions of restorability are likely to be less reliable than clinical opinions of competency, reliance on actual restoration cases or clinician opinions as to whether a defendant has been restored are also subject to biases. For example, institutional policies may result in an overly lenient standard for determining a defendant restored. Although limitations in these outcome variables cannot necessarily be resolved, careful attention to these potential sources of bias can alert the researcher to important considerations in the interpretation of study findings.

Concerns regarding the appropriateness of outcome measures or criterion variables are even more pronounced in CR research. As with CST, common outcome variables in CR research include legal determinations regarding criminal responsibility as well as type of disposition (e.g., release, conditional release, hospitalization) and length of detainment. Since CR cases are much more likely than CST cases to have opposing experts, clinician opinions regarding criminal responsibility are used less often in research, and the outcome variable of choice is the actual legal determination regarding criminal responsibility. Nevertheless, interesting data have emerged regarding the variables that impact clinical opinions of criminal responsibility (e.g., Warren et al., 1991), revealing expected patterns of demographic and clinical characteristics that correspond to legal disposition. Moreover, CR evaluations provide a similar opportunity for distinguishing between the components of criminal responsibility (i.e., ability to understand the nature, character, and consequences of one's actions vs. ability to distinguish right from wrong). Case outcome, on the other hand, while allowing for a more accurate understanding of the factors that result in an actual finding of NGRI, may obscure potentially interesting analyses of differences between these two domains of CR.

PREDICTOR VARIABLES

Independent or predictor variables that have dominated the CST and CR research literatures can be divided into one of three categories: demographic, criminological, and psychiatric variables. The analysis of demographic variables is, of course, not unique to CST and CR research; like most psychology research, such analyses are often relatively simplistic, focusing on broad categorical distinctions even when analyzing relatively complex constructs. For example, ethnicity is typically treated as a dichotomous (white or non-white) or trichotomous (white, black, Hispanic) variable reflecting one's race; however, more information may be gleaned by examining this variable in a way that takes into consideration its components, such as race, acculturation, and language. Similarly, variables such as socioeconomic status are often more informative than simplistic categorizations based on educational attainment (e.g., years of education completed or a dichotomous comparison of those with less than high school education to those with high school equivalency or greater).

Criminological variables used in CST and CR research typically include type of crime and whether the defendant has a history of criminal behavior. As with demographic variables, criminological variables are typically coded in a categorical fashion, often hindering an analysis of trends within these variables. Improvement on the predictive utility of criminological variables may be achieved in future research by examining the nature and quality (and quantity where appropriate) of the criminal behavior, rather than simply the type of crime, or the nature and extent of a defendant's criminal history rather than simply analyzing whether the defendant had such a history. Coding systems such as the *legal dangerousness scale* (LDS; Cocozza & Steadman, 1974), which combines length and severity of criminal history, or the *Cormier-Lang system* (Quinsey, Harris, Rice, & Cormier, 1998), which weights different types of offenses and scores defendants according to how many times they have been arrested for each form of weighted offense, may assist in this regard. Likewise, Rosenfeld and Ritchie (1998), in their analysis of competency evaluations, converted current criminal charges into a continuous variable reflecting the median possible sentence, allowing for an analysis of offense severity as a continuous variable rather than contrasting different offense categories, as is typical of CST and CR research (e.g., homicide, sex offenses, assault, property crimes, etc).

Psychiatric or psychological variables are, of course, central to most CST and CR research. Common variables studied include clinical diagnosis, history of mental health treatment, and history of psychiatric hospitalization. As is the case with the demographic and criminological predictors described previously, diagnosis is usually treated as a categorical variable. More recently, investigators have begun analyzing performance on cognitive or neuropsychological measures to assess the relationship between specific cognitive functions and competency or criminal responsibility. Moreover, recent research has begun to emphasize the presence or severity of psychiatric symptoms as predictor variables rather than simply recording a defendant's diagnosis (e.g., Rosenfeld & Wall, 1998; Viljoen, Zapf, & Roesch, 2003). The use of standardized assessment instruments (e.g., Brief Psychiatric Rating Scale, Structured Clinical Interview for the DSM-IV, Symptom Checklist—90), while still uncommon in CST and CR research, represents a substantial and important advance in the literature.

In addition to facilitating an analysis of symptoms rather than broad diagnostic categories, standardized assessment instruments ensure that mental health information is obtained and scored in a similar manner by multiple raters, thus improving the overall quality and reliability of the predictor variables. Similarly, application of cognitive assessment instruments can facilitate a much more sophisticated analysis of the impact of cognitive functioning or impairment on CST or CR outcomes. Although rarely applied to forensic research, the growing availability of increasingly sophisticated assessment techniques (e.g., functional magnetic resonance imaging) holds considerable promise for better understanding critical elements of CST and CR cases, such as identifying the patterns of cognitive functioning that correspond to impaired ability to differentiate right from wrong or ability to consult with one's attorney.

FORENSIC ASSESSMENT MEASURES

Although largely limited to CST research, the emergence of assessment measures specifically designed to measure the construct, in this case CST, represents the most important and increasingly common methodological advancement. Performance on assessment measures can be conceptualized as either a "predictor" variable (such as when analyzing the specific capacities that differentiate competent from incompetent defendants or incompetent defendants who are restored to competence versus those who cannot be restored) or as an outcome variable (as in analyses focusing on the symptoms or cognitive abilities that correspond to impaired domains of competence). Given the proliferation of forensic assessment instruments developed over the past four decades to assist in the evaluation of CST, it is beyond the scope of this chapter to describe each instrument in detail. The interested reader is referred to additional sources (e.g., Grisso, 2003; Melton, Petrila, Poythress, & Slobogin, 2007; Zapf & Roesch, in press; Zapf & Vilojoen, 1998). Instead, we focus primarily on three instruments commonly used in CST research, each of which has demonstrated levels of reliability acceptable to justify its use: the MacCAT-CA (Hoge, Bonnie, Poythress, & Monahan, 1999; Poythress et al., 1999), the *Evaluation of Competency to Stand Trial-Revised* (ECST-R; Rogers, Tillbrook, & Sewell, 2004), and the *Fitness Interview Test-Revised* (FIT-R; Roesch, Zapf, & Eaves, 2006; Roesch, Zapf, Eaves, & Webster, 1998).

Early assessment measures took the form of checklists, self-report questionnaires, and sentence-completion tasks, typically presenting a range of questions considered relevant to CST (e.g., the *Competency Assessment Instrument*, McGarry & Curran, 1973 and the *Georgia Court Competency Test*, Wildman et al., 1978). As the literature on CST developed, legal commentary about the definition of competency and the standards to be used in evaluating a defendant's competency led to the development of measures reflecting those legal criteria and standards (e.g., the *Interdisciplinary Fitness Interview*, Golding, Roesch, & Schreiber, 1984, and the *Fitness Interview Test*, Roesch, Webster, & Eaves, 1984), which allowed researchers to examine the domains of competency in addition to competency as a dichotomous variable. Accordingly, more complex research questions and more complex data analytic techniques could be applied to CST research.

Although each of these early competency assessment instruments is interview based, none of them uses criterion-based scoring (i.e., scoring on the basis of explicit, standardized criteria) for its items or domains. In response to this limitation, the MacCAT-CA and the ECST-R were developed. These two interview-based measures use standardized administration and criterion-based scoring, allowing for specific comparisons between defendants.

The MacCAT-CA and ECST-R are nomothetic in nature; thus, the scores achieved by a particular defendant can be compared to the scores of the larger population of defendants. The FIT-R, on the other hand, is idiographic in nature and is, therefore, intended to contextualize decisions based on individual symptoms and functioning. Researchers must consider the inherent trade-off that applies when choosing between a standardized (normative) assessment and a more individualized (idiographic) approach. Standardized assessment instruments that use criterion-based scoring allow for comparisons of a particular defendant with a larger group of defendants with respect to instrument scores. This enables researchers to treat competency and its domains as a continuous variable reflecting the gradations in ability observed; it may be optimal in research where competency domains are conceptualized as predictor variables or when the extent of competency-related abilities are conceptualized as the outcome variable.

However, by their very nature, standardized assessment instruments sacrifice the ability to evaluate specific concerns for a specific defendant facing specific charges. This, of course, is the advantage of a more individualized assessment approach; the disadvantage being an inability to evaluate instrument scores normatively. An individualized approach is often advantageous when standardized instruments are used to make clinical determinations about whether a defendant is competent or incompetent. Researchers must select assessment instruments carefully with a full consideration of the purpose of the research and the ecological validity of the design.

In contrast to the attempts that have been undertaken to standardize the assessment of competency to stand trial, criminal responsibility evaluations remain largely unguided. Only one published measure, the *Rogers Criminal Responsibility Assessment Scales* (R-CRAS; Rogers, 1984), exists to facilitate CR evaluations, and little research has systematically applied this measure. Nevertheless, this measure is also briefly reviewed in order to identify appropriate settings and questions that might be facilitated by its inclusion.

MacArthur Competence Assessment Tool-Criminal Adjudication   The MacCAT-CA represents the first competency assessment instrument to apply both standardized administration and criterion-based scoring. The MacCAT-CA consists of 22 items divided into three sections corresponding to the abilities underlying the *Dusky* standard: understanding, appreciation, and reasoning. A particular strength of the MacCAT-CA is that the administration technique for the understanding section allows the evaluator to assess the defendant's *capacity* to understand apart from his or her *actual* or preexisting understanding. In addition, the reasoning section includes several questions that assess aspects of a defendant's decisional competence. Finally, the appreciation section allows for the standardized assessment of information specific to the individual case.

The most significant limitation of the MacCAT-CA is that the majority of items (16 of 22 items) are based on a hypothetical vignette, thus limiting its utility for a contextualized evaluation of competency. In addition, several potentially key aspects of competency, such as the defendant's memory for individual case-relevant information and psychiatric symptoms that might impair communication with an attorney, are not evaluated by the MacCAT-CA (Melton et al., 2007). Finally, the understanding and reasoning sections (those based on the hypothetical case vignette) may be less able to differentiate competent from incompetent defendants than the appreciation section (Melton et al., 2007). On the other hand, by using a hypothetical vignette approach, two of the three MacCAT-CA sections (understanding and reasoning) can be administered to individuals who are not facing criminal charges, which is particularly useful for assessing psychiatric (non-offender) comparison samples.

Evaluation of Competency to Stand Trial-Revised   The ECST-R is composed of 18 items yielding scores on four different scales, three of which directly correspond to the abilities delineated in *Dusky*: factual understanding of the courtroom proceedings, rational understanding of the courtroom proceedings, and ability to consult with counsel; the fourth scale represents overall rational ability by combining scores from two of these scales. In addition, the ECST-R contains 28 items that yield scores on several response-style scales designed to screen for feigned incompetency, enabling an evaluation of malingering at the same time that competency is assessed.

The ECST-R has demonstrated high concurrent validity with the MacCAT-CA (Rogers et al., 2004) and covers an equally broad range of competency domains. In addition, administration is standardized but still flexible enough to allow evaluators to follow up or clarify when obtaining additional information appears warranted. Finally, its structure allows for clear delineation of the three abilities set out in *Dusky*. Each item on the ECST-R is scored on the basis of ratings (which can range from zero to four for each item), and scale scores are obtained by summing the raw scores for each relevant item. The most significant limitation of the ECST-R concerns the method of scoring and, hence, the internal validity. Although each item is rated along a scale for degree of impairment, only the most severe rating of impairment is considered to adversely affect competency. Thus, in essence, each item is rated dichotomously (impaired vs. not impaired). In addition, incongruence between item ratings and scale interpretations can occur when, as a result of the mathematical calculations for the scale scores, the scale score indicates severe impairment but none of the individual item scores suggest clinically significant impairment in any specific domain. Thus, several ratings indicative of subthreshold impairment can yield scale total scores suggesting severe impairment.

Fitness Interview Test–Revised   The FIT-R (Roesch, Zapf, & Eaves, 2006) is a semi-structured interview consisting of 70 questions encompassing 16 competency domains. The FIT-R and its domains are divided into three sections, paralleling the competence-related abilities set out in the *Criminal Code of Canada* as well as the federal standard for competency to stand trial used in the United States (U.S. Code Annotated, Title 18, Part III, chapter 13, section 4241): the ability to understand the nature or object of the proceedings (i.e., factual knowledge of criminal procedure), the ability to understand the possible consequences of the proceedings (i.e., appreciation for one's personal involvement in and importance of the proceedings), and the ability to communicate with counsel. Each domain is scored on a 3-point rating scale for level of capacity or impairment.

One of the strongest assets of the FIT-R is that it requires evaluators to attend to both the legal abilities of the defendant as well as the cause of any deficits, thus clarifying the linkage between any noted impairments and mental disorder or cognitive deficit. In addition, the FIT-R has demonstrated utility as both a screening instrument and a formal assessment instrument. Further, a recent study found high concurrent validity between the FIT-R and the MacCAT-CA (Zapf & Roesch, 2005). However, as noted previously, one limitation of the FIT-R is that because it is intended to contextualize decisions based on individual symptoms and functioning, it is impossible to compare individual scores on the FIT-R with those of a normative reference group.

Rogers Criminal Responsibility Assessment Scales   The R-CRAS (Rogers, 1984) is the only forensic assessment instrument developed to assist in the evaluation of criminal responsibility. The R-CRAS was designed to parallel the components of the ALI standard but includes additional assessment criteria for the *M'Naghten* and guilty but mentally ill (GBMI) standards. The R-CRAS is composed of 30 items divided into six domains: malingering, presence of organicity, presence of major mental disorder, loss of cognitive control, loss of volitional control, and causal relationship. Although it was developed to structure the evaluation of criminal responsibility, little research has been conducted with the R-CRAS. This instrument has also been criticized for its lack of guidance as to how to score the items and how to weigh items to score each of the domains (Melton et al., 2007). In addition, the six domains have been "validated" primarily against ultimate decisions rendered by the R-CRAS, thus likely inflating its predictive validity.

DATA ANALYSIS

As the research questions examined by CST and CR researchers have increased in sophistication, the statistical methods that have been applied to these questions have similarly evolved. Early research on CST and CR was primarily descriptive in nature and provided information regarding the characteristics of defendants referred for evaluations as well as those found incompetent or not responsible. Aside from simple descriptive statistics, comparisons between competent and incompetent or responsible and not responsible defendants typically relied on nonparametric statistics such as Pearson's chi-square test or Student's t-test. Although less common among the early studies, some researchers have applied multivariate models (e.g., logistic regression) to examine how multiple predictor variables could optimally predict outcome (competency status, competency restoration, or criminal responsibility determinations).

   As the research on CST and competency assessment measures developed, it became possible to examine the various domains of competency and to use either multiple criterion/outcome variables for competency status (e.g., the various domains measured by the instrument) or to consider competency as a continuous rather than a categorical variable (by using multiple-point rating scales or by summing item or scale scores on a particular instrument). Thus, more complex data analytic techniques, including analysis of variance

(ANOVA), analysis of covariance (ANCOVA), multiple analysis of variance (MANOVA), multiple analysis of covariance (MANCOVA), and multiple regression analysis became increasingly common methods for analyzing this type of data. Likewise, analysis of the domains of competency has increasingly applied factor analytic techniques to understand the interrelationships among domains of competency. These approaches are still rarely, if ever, applied to CR research.

Recently, CST research has begun to use additional statistical techniques that have not been used previously in CST or CR research. Techniques such as receiver operating characteristic (ROC) curve analysis for predicting restorability (Mossman, 2007) and confirmatory factor analysis (CFA) for examining the hypothesized factor structure of competency assessment instruments (Zapf, Skeem, & Golding, 2005) or the construct of competency across measures (Zapf & Roesch, 2005) have been used. Other methods that have yet to be applied to CST or CR research but have considerable importance as the research questions investigated become more complex include item response theory (IRT) and structural equation modeling (SEM). Researchers studying competency restoration or release following a finding of nonresponsibility might apply survival analysis (e.g., Cox Proportional Hazards models), but to date such methods have been rarely applied. Clearly even a simplistic explanation of these various statistical techniques is beyond the scope of this chapter (see Chapter 5 for an overview), but researchers must consider which of these analytic approaches is most appropriate for addressing their research questions to ensure that the data collected can fulfill the needs of the statistical model.

ETHICAL CONSIDERATIONS

A number of important ethical issues complicate CST and CR research and warrant brief review. The two broad issues discussed here include confidentiality (i.e., ensuring that data collection does not compromise a defendant's legal situation) and issues related to informed consent (particularly when the decisional competence of study participants is questionable). Although other issues may certainly arise, such as the disclosure of intent to harm oneself or others, these issues are not unique to CST or CR research and are not addressed here.

Ensuring Confidentiality   In recent years, stricter guidelines have been implemented for the protection of incarcerated and special populations with respect to their research participation (e.g., National Institutes of Health, Part 46, Subpart C, 2005). Participation in research must be voluntary (noncoerced) and must involve no more than minimal risk. To minimize undue pressure to participate, researchers must clearly inform participants that neither their consent nor refusal to participate in a study has any effect on their legal case. In addition, it is common for researchers to promise that a participant's study data will remain confidential. This promise of confidentiality can sometimes become difficult to keep, such as when the institution at which the research is being conducted becomes interested in obtaining participants' responses on competency assessment instruments. How then can researchers protect their participants' confidentiality and ensure that the data collected does not impact the participants' legal cases?

One of the first protective measures that can be undertaken is an open and frank discussion with the institution's administrators regarding the necessity of keeping the research data confidential. This may take the form of an educational process wherein the researcher must set out for the institution the reasons why it would be inappropriate to share test data (e.g., potential impact on the defendant's legal case, breach of confidentiality). It is helpful for the researcher to share this information with the institution before beginning the research so as to avoid any potential misunderstandings as the research gets underway.

A second protective measure that can be taken is for the researcher to apply for a Certificate of Confidentiality, issued by the National Institutes of Health (42 USC 242a), in advance of starting a study. A Certificate of Confidentiality applies to research settings in which sensitive information, including information about illegal activities, is likely to be revealed and the possibility of future legal action or economic or other harm exists. The Certificate protects researchers from being compelled to reveal information gathered during the course of a study that might cause harm to study participants or other identified individuals. To qualify for such protection, the researcher must demonstrate that the risk of harm to the participant or to the integrity of the study outweighs the importance of such disclosures. The Certificate does not, however, exempt researchers from mandatory reporting requirements, such as for child and elder abuse, risk of self-harm, or explicit threats against an individual that fall under federal and state regulations.

Obtaining Informed Consent   Involving psychiatric patients in research is further complicated by ambiguity regarding whether they are actually competent to give consent. This concern is particularly relevant when studying the issue of competency to stand trial, as the argument may be made that if the defendant was found incompetent to stand trial, he or she is also likely incompetent to give consent to participate in research. In general, however, the threshold for competency to consent to psychological research is lower than that for competency to stand trial given that the risks of participating in research are generally lower than those associated with proceeding to trial. What precautions might be taken to ensure the competency of psychiatric patients to consent to research?

In some instances, the institution may be able to provide informed consent for patient participation. Therefore, researchers need only obtain informed assent from patients to have them participate. In other instances, it may be possible for the researcher to negotiate assistance from the institution in obtaining informed consent from the patients as a separate procedure. For example, Zapf and colleagues (2004) were able to elicit the assistance of admitting psychiatrists, who evaluated each patient's competency to consent to research upon admission, thus allowing for an independent assessment of competency that did not involve the researchers.

Another strategy that has been used to circumvent the issue of obtaining informed consent is for the institution to adopt certain procedures as part of institutional practice. For example, a particular competency assessment instrument may be adopted as part of the standard procedures at an institution and used routinely for any competency evaluation. In this situation, it becomes possible for researchers to obtain the results of the competency assessment instrument as archival data, eliminating the necessity of obtaining informed consent from the defendants. Of note, concerns about competence to consent are often less pronounced in CR research, as these individuals may have already been determined competent to proceed to trial and may have had the benefit of extended psychiatric treatment.

FUTURE DIRECTIONS

Inherent in the discussion of CST and CR research and methodology presented in this chapter is the acknowledgment of how far the field has progressed during the past several decades. Examining the past leads naturally to questions about what the future might hold. This final section highlights some of the potential directions for future research in this area.

As noted previously, CST and CR research appears to be at a stage ripe for the use of more advanced data-analytic techniques. This is particularly true of CR research, which has remained at a far more nascent stage than CST research. However, the use of ROC analyses in CST research has only recently begun, and techniques such as SEM, IRT, and survival analysis appear to have considerable potential for advancing even further our understanding of competency and criminal responsibility.

In addition to the use of more sophisticated data-analytic techniques, CST research could benefit from longitudinal research designs that examine the construct of *incompetence* and how it changes over the course of treatment. To date, all the research on CST has been cross-sectional in nature. Longitudinal designs in both CST and CR research would allow for a greater understanding of these constructs over time and with the provision of mental health treatment. In addition, this type of design would allow for repeated measurements of cognitive and symptom function across time, thereby allowing for the use of more sophisticated data-analytic techniques.

A focus on "gray-area" cases is another critical next step in both CST and CR research. With respect to CST, in most instances a defendant is either clearly competent or clearly incompetent; however, it is those few gray-area cases, where ability and context make the issue ambiguous, that challenge clinical evaluators and have the potential to inform researchers about the construct of competency. Similarly, studying large samples of *incompetent* defendants will also certainly improve our knowledge of the construct of competency/incompetency. Research that focuses on the interactions between attorneys and defendants is also critical to understanding the contextual nature (interactional component) of competence. In addition, examining how attorneys navigate with (potentially) incompetent clients may serve to highlight potential intervention strategies.

As a final note to this chapter, we encourage researchers to carefully consider the purpose of their research—that is, to think about the implications of one's research as well as its limitations. Consideration of the ecological validity of the design and procedures provides an indication of the generalizability of the research findings as well as the ways in which the research could be improved to increase its real-world utility. Research on CST and CR should ultimately provide useful information for dealing with these issues in the real world.

REFERENCES

American Law Institute. (1962). *Model penal code*. Philadelphia, PA: American Law Institute.

Cocozza, J. J., & Steadman, H. J. (1974). Some refinements in the measurement and prediction of dangerous behavior. *American Journal of Psychiatry, 131*, 1012–1014.

Gannon, J. (1990). Validation of the competence assessment instrument and elements of competence to stand trial. *Dissertation Abstracts International, 50-B*, 3875.

Golding, S. L., Roesch, R., & Schreiber, J. (1984). Assessment and conceptualization of competency to stand trial: Preliminary data on the interdisciplinary fitness interview. *Law and Human Behavior, 8*, 321–334.

Grisso, T. (1992) Five-year research update (1986-1990): Evaluations for competence to stand trial. *Behavioral Sciences and the Law, 10*, 353–369.

Grisso, T. (2003). *Evaluating competencies: Forensic assessments and instruments* (2nd ed.). New York, NY: Kluwer/Plenum.

Hoge, S. K., Bonnie, R. J., Poythress, N., & Monahan, J. (1999). *The MacArthur Competence Assessment Tool—Criminal Adjudication*. Odessa, FL: Psychological Assessment Resources.

McGarry, A. L., & Curran, W. J. (1973). *Competency to stand trial and mental illness*. Rockville, MD: National Institutes of Mental Health.

Melton, G. B., Petrila, J., Poythress, N. G., & Slobogin, C. (2007). *Psychological evaluations for the courts: A handbook for mental health professionals and lawyers* (3rd ed.). New York, NY: Guilford Press.

Mossman, D. (2007). Predicting restorability of incompetent criminal defendants. *The Journal of the American Academy of Psychiatry and the Law, 35*, 34–43.

National Institutes of Health. (2005, June). *Regulations and ethical guidelines: Title 45 CFR Part*. Retrieved March 1, 2008, from http://ohsr.od.nih.gov/guidelines/45CFR46.html

Nicholson, R. A., & Kugler, K. E. (1991). Competent and incompetent criminal defendants: A quantitative review of comparative research. *Psychological Bulletin, 109*, 355–370.

Poythress, N. G., Bonnie, R. J., Monahan, J., Otto, R., & Hoge, S. K. (2002). *Adjudicative competence: The MacArthur studies*. New York, NY: Kluwer/Plenum.

Poythress, N. G., Nicholson, R. A., Otto, R. K., Edens, J. F., Bonnie, R. J., Monahan, J., & Hoge, S. K. (1999). *The MacArthur Competence Assessment Tool—Criminal Adjudication*. Odessa, FL: Psychological Assessment Resources.

Quinsey, V. L., Harris, G. T., Rice, M. E., & Cormier, C. A. (1998). *Violent offenders*. Washington, D.C.: American Psychological Association.

Roesch, R., & Golding, S. L. (1980). *Competency to stand trial.* Chicago: University of Illinois Press.

Roesch, R., Webster, C. D., & Eaves, D. (1984). *The fitness interview test: A method for examining fitness to stand trial.* Toronto, Canada: Research Report of the Centre of Criminology, University of Toronto.

Roesch, R., Zapf, P. A., & Eaves, D. (2006). *Fitness Interview Test—Revised: A structured interview for assessing competency to stand trial.* Sarasota, FL: Professional Resource Press.

Roesch, R., Zapf, P. A., Eaves, D., & Webster, C. D. (1998). *Fitness interview test* (revised ed.). Burnaby, Canada: Mental Health, Law and Policy Institute, Simon Fraser University.

Rogers, R. (1984). *Rogers criminal responsibility assessment scales.* Odessa, FL: Psychological Assessment Resources.

Rogers, R. (2001). *Handbook of diagnostic and structured interviewing.* New York, NY: Guilford Press.

Rogers, R., Tillbrook, C. E., & Sewell, K. W. (2004). *Evaluation of competency to stand trial—Revised professional manual.* Lutz, FL: Psychological Assessment Resources.

Rosenfeld, B., & Ritchie, K. (1998). Competence to stand trial: Clinical reliability and the role of offense severity. *Journal of Forensic Sciences, 43,* 151–157.

Rosenfeld, B., & Wall, A. (1998). Psychopathology and competence to stand trial. *Criminal Justice and Behavior, 25,* 443–462.

Steadman, H., McGreevy, M., Morrissey, J., Callahan, L., Robbins, P., & Cirincione, C. (1993). *Before and after Hinckley: Evaluating insanity defense reform.* New York, NY: Guilford Press.

Thompson, J. S., Stuart, G. L., & Holden, C. E. (1992). Command hallucinations and legal insanity. *Forensic Reports, 5,* 29–43.

Viljoen, J. L., Zapf, P. A., & Roesch, R. (2003). Diagnosis, current psychiatric symptoms, and the ability to stand trial. *Journal of Forensic Psychology Practice, 3,* 23–37.

Warren, J., Fitch, L., Dietz, P., & Rosenfeld, B. (1991). Criminal offense, psychiatric diagnosis, and psycholegal opinion: An analysis of 894 pretrial referrals. *Bulletin of the American Academy of Psychiatry and the Law, 19,* 63–69.

Wildman, R. W., Batchelor, E. S., Thompson, I., Nelson, F. R., Moore, J. T., Patterson, M. E., & de Laosa, M. (1978). *The Georgia Court Competency Test: An attempt to develop a rapid, quantitative measure of fitness for trial.* Unpublished manuscript, Forensic Services Division, Central State Hospital, Milledgeville, GA.

Zapf, P. A., Hubbard, K. L., Cooper, V. G., Wheeles, M. C., & Ronan, K. A. (2004). Have the courts abdicated their responsibility for determination of competency to stand trial to clinicians? *Journal of Forensic Psychology Practice, 4,* 27–44.

Zapf, P. A., & Roesch, R. (2005). An investigation of the construct of competence: A comparison of the FIT, the MacCAT-CA, and the MacCAT-T. *Law and Human Behavior, 29,* 229–252.

Zapf, P. A., & Roesch, R. (in press). *Guide to best practices for forensic mental health assessments: Competency to stand trial.* New York, NY: Oxford.

Zapf, P. A., Roesch, R., & Viljoen, J. L. (2001) Assessing fitness to stand trial: The utility of the fitness interview test (revised edition). *Canadian Journal of Psychiatry, 46,* 426–432.

Zapf, P. A., Skeem, J. L., & Golding, S. L. (2005). Factor structure and validity of the MacArthur Competence Assessment Tool—Criminal Adjudication. *Psychological Assessment, 17,* 433–445.

Zapf, P. A., & Viljoen, J. L. (1998). Issues and considerations regarding the use of assessment instruments in the evaluation of competency to stand trial. *Behavioral Sciences and the Law, 21,* 351–367.

Zapf, P. A., Viljoen, J. L., Whittemore, K. E., Poythress, N. G., & Roesch, R. (2002). Competency: Past, present, and future. In J. R. P. Ogloff (Ed.), *Taking psychology and law into the twenty-first century* (pp. 171–198). New York, NY: Kluwer/Plenum.

Zonana, H. V., Wells, J. A., Getz, M. A., & Buchanan, J. (1990). Part I: The NGRI registry: Initial analysis of data collected on Connecticut insanity acquittees. *Bulletin of the American Academy of Psychiatry and the Law, 18,* 115–128.

CHAPTER 10

Research Methods for the Assessment of Malingering[1]

RICHARD ROGERS AND NATHAN D. GILLARD

C LINICAL OBSERVATIONS AND case studies have historically formed the foundation for the assessment of malingering. The seminal article by Geller, Erlen, Kaye, and Fisher (1990) catalogs in detail the nineteenth-century literature on various malingering indicators. While extreme measures (e.g., electric shock and whirling chairs) are likely to capture our attention, most indicators focused on feigned presentations (e.g., calling attention to symptoms), atypical symptoms (e.g., nonsensical responses), and areas of intact functioning (e.g., normal facial expressions, good eye contact, and undisturbed sleep patterns). Unlike their modern counterparts, nineteenth-century practitioners often used specific interventions for the detection of malingering. When asked to repeat their disordered verbalizations, genuine patients typically failed, whereas malingerers were often adept at the same task, sometimes even providing verbatim accounts. Clinical observations of the nineteenth and early twentieth century were valuable in generating potential indicators of malingering. Some of their insights, such as unexpected patterns of intact functioning, need to be rediscovered and researched.

Most case studies, limited by their methodology, become in effect tautological exercises. As observed by Rogers (1997), clinicians *identify* malingerers by certain salient characteristics. Once identified, clinicians *describe* these same characteristics as indicators of malingering. Therefore, case studies and clinical observations should be considered useful only as hypothesis-generating methods.

---

1. Portions of this chapter were presented in a keynote lecture at the Third International Congress of Psychology and Law, Adelaide, Australia (see Rogers & Correa, 2007).

The second phase of malingering research started in the mid-twentieth century with Minnesota Multiphasic Personality Inventory (MMPI) research on group differences. Early MMPI studies were focused more on invalid responses than on malingering per se. For instance, Meehl's (1946, p. 517) early description of the F scale was simply as a measure of "carelessness and misunderstanding." In reviewing its original development and early validation, Dahlstrom, Welsh, and Dahlstrom (1972) concluded that F-scale elevations could result from problems with confusion, literacy, or pathological interpretations of life experiences. More recent research often overlooks this broad conceptual basis of the MMPI F scale.

Rogers (1984) conducted the first extensive review of malingering indicators, which yielded 44 research studies of varying sophistication. As expected, the majority of studies (26 or 59.1%) examined the MMPI. In general, these studies tested the usefulness of specific scales with comparatively little attention to the systematic investigation of their underlying principles or detection strategies within specific domains.

MALINGERING DOMAINS AND DETECTION STRATEGIES

Rogers and Bender (2003) maintained that malingering indicators should be congruent with the malingerer's efforts and objectives. For instance, a person feigning posttraumatic stress disorder (PTSD) is unlikely to also simulate mental retardation. Malingering should not be naively viewed as pervasive, because most efforts are targeted at specific conditions geared to particular objectives. Rogers (2008a) advanced the idea of conceptualizing three general domains of malingering: feigned mental disorders, feigned cognitive impairment, and feigned medical complaints. For feigned mental disorders, malingerers must make a series of decisions regarding (a) their symptoms and associated features, (b) the onset and course of these symptoms, (c) their own awareness and insight into these symptoms, and (d) the purported effect of these symptoms on their daily functioning. For feigned cognitive impairment, the malingerers' tasks are quite different. They must convincingly fail on neuropsychological measures in a way that shows effort and a credible performance. For feigned medical complaints, malingerers have several major alternatives. They can focus on common ailments (e.g., headaches and sleeping disturbances) that have a myriad of etiological possibilities. Alternatively, they can specialize in a single symptom (e.g., pain) or a complex syndrome (e.g., chronic fatigue). Their tasks as malingerers will vary widely depending on the alternative they select. To further the discussion of malingering domains, we introduce detection strategies.

Rogers (2008a, p. 16) defined detection strategies for response styles as follows: "A detection strategy is a standardized method, which is conceptually-based and empirically-validated, for systematically differentiating a specific response style (e.g., malingering or defensiveness) from other response styles (e.g., honest responding)." Of critical importance for scale development, the detection strategy should be a well-defined clinical construct. The general notion that malingerers will "do worse" on a particular test than genuine patients is impermissibly vague. Instead, a clear conceptual basis allows researchers to carefully operationalize items. These items can be systematically reviewed for their conceptual match with the resulting scale.

Detection strategies must be tested on multiple scales across various measures. However positive, good results on a single scale may reflect a "happy accident" rather than a well-defined and carefully operationalized construct. Ideally, detection strategies should be tested across diverse samples with an array of measures that vary substantially in their format from self-report to interview based.

Rogers (2008a) provides a comprehensive coverage of detection strategies that are organized, as previously noted, into three general domains (feigned mental disorders, feigned cognitive impairment, and feigned medical complaints). For each domain, the subsequent subsections illustrate how detection strategies can be understood and applied to malingering research.

DETECTION STRATEGIES IN THE DOMAIN OF FEIGNED MENTAL DISORDERS

For feigned psychopathology and mental disorders, detection strategies can be conceptualized into two general categories: unlikely and amplified. Unlikely detection strategies focus on the *presence* of very unusual and atypical presentations. In contrast, amplified detection strategies emphasize *frequency* and *intensity*. For instance, use of clang associations for malingering determinations capitalizes on an unlikely detection strategy, whereas the counting of all reported symptoms reflects an amplified detection strategy. Beyond their empirical basis (Rogers, Jackson, Sewell, & Salekin, 2005), these general categories are useful to malingering researchers to ensure that their detection strategies are not constrained to only one general category.

Feigning research has often trod the same well-worn path using the same detection strategy with designs similar to those used in past research. In the domain of feigned mental disorders, the research rut for rare symptoms (i.e., very infrequent in genuine populations) is very deep. For example, the plethora of MMPI-2 research on the F scale family (F, Fb, Fp, Fptsd) exemplifies this abiding interest. As noted in Table 10.1, however, a number of effective detection strategies have been virtually ignored. Besides the MMPI-2, erroneous stereotypes have been largely overlooked. Similarly, symptom combinations could be adapted to multiscale inventories. Specifically, what symptom pairs are almost never observed among genuine patients on the MMPI-2 and PAI? Also, which

Table 10.1

Overlooked Detection Strategies for the Domains of Feigned Mental Disorders
and Cognitive Impairment

Domain	Detection Strategy	Description and Commentary
Mental disorders	Erroneous stereotypes	Many feigners have common misperceptions about mental disorders and psychological impairment. The MMPI-2 Ds scale provides an excellent example of how this detection strategy can be highly effective, even among individuals with mental health training.
	Symptom combinations	Many feigners are simply unaware that certain symptom pairs are very common whereas others are rarely observed. Focusing on the latter, the SIRS Symptom Combination (SC) scale has proven highly effective.
	Symptom severity	Many feigners markedly overreport the frequency and intensity of their symptoms. This straightforward strategy has been effective on multiple measures.
Cognitive impairment	Magnitude of error	Many feigners focus simply on failing items and pay little attention to how items should be failed convincingly. Potential strategies include near-misses and gross errors. This effective strategy is likely to be less vulnerable than others to coaching.
	Performance curve	Many feigners neglect to consider item difficulty and fail a greater-than-expected level of comparatively easy items when compared with their performance on medium and difficult items. This approach can be adapted to standard cognitive tests.
	Symptom frequency	Many feigners exhibit a large number of associated psychological problems that occur at a much higher-than-expected rate. This strategy has not been extensively evaluated for feigned cognitive impairment.

extreme ratings on PAI items (i.e., most pathological) are common to feigners but not genuine patients?

The development of malingering measures for feigned cognitive impairment is also deeply rutted in tradition. Most researchers are content to develop yet another scale using the floor-effect (i.e., too easy to miss) detection strategy. Going beyond the familiar, the magnitude-of-error detection strategy shows great potential for detecting cognitive feigners. Two other strategies, performance curve and symptom frequency, should also be used in developing effective detection strategies. The critical point is that important advances in the assessment of malingering require an open-minded investigation of multiple strategies rather than a tradition-bound veneration of past approaches.

STUDY DESIGNS

Study design is the foundation on which all other methodological issues rest. The choice of design should therefore be careful and deliberate. Each design that has been used in dissimulation research has unique advantages and disadvantages, and each has been criticized for methodological flaws (Shadish, Cook, & Campbell, 2002). Two main considerations must be considered when evaluating the choice of research design: (1) clinical relevance and (2) experimental rigor. Often these two dimensions are inversely related (Rogers, 2008b).

Four designs are used in the vast majority of research on dissimulation. The simulation design is the most popular of these designs; it uses analog research with clinical comparison samples. Other designs are categorized as quasi-experimental (Rogers, 1997). Each design is critically evaluated in the following subsections, beginning with known-groups comparisons.

Known-Groups Comparisons

Known-groups comparison design uses individuals that have been independently classified by the best available external sources. Traditionally, known-groups comparisons have relied on mental health professionals with specific expertise on malingering. Critically important, these malingerers are identified as part of extensive evaluations, conducted in a clinical or forensic context. A clinical comparison group of individuals with only genuine disorders is also identified by the best available external sources.

The greatest challenge for known-groups design is the use of the best available external sources. Researchers are sometimes tempted to substitute expediency for rigor. For example, Edens, Poythress, and Watkins-Clay (2007) attempted to use routine consults by prison psychiatrists as an expedient proxy for a known-groups comparison. They failed to meet the rigorous standards required by known-groups comparisons by exhibiting the following limitations: (a) using evaluators who were not experts on malingering but simply practitioners given rudimentary training by the researchers, (b) relying on inaccurate detection strategies (e.g., inconsistent reporting), and (c) using overly broad classification with any instance of any strategy classified as suspected malingering (see Rogers, 2008b). To avoid questionable research designs, the following guidelines should be implemented:

1. *Expertise.* Do the evaluators have specialized training and experience to be considered malingering experts? Only with the use of experts can we improve clinical practice rather than simply replicate it.
2. *Research-quality determinations.* Do the evaluators use state-of-the-art methods for their classifications of malingering? Routine assessments, even by experts, are insufficient.
3. *Decision rules.* Are decision rules or cut scores used that produce well-defined groups of probable malingerers and probable genuine patients? Well-validated measures, such as the Structured Interview of Reported Symptoms-2 (SIRS-2; Rogers, Sewell, & Gillard, 2010), can be used to classify clinical populations with low to very low false-positive and false-negative rates.
4. *Indeterminate classifications.* To ensure a high level of accuracy, does the research design eliminate marginal cases (i.e., indeterminate classifications), for which classificatory errors are more likely? This corollary of "decision rules" is frequently omitted in otherwise sound research studies.

The major strength of the known-groups comparison is its external validity. Care must be taken to eliminate only a narrow band of indeterminate cases; otherwise, the generalizability of the results will be limited by the use of extreme cases. With careful application of the preceding four guidelines, this design can achieve moderate experimental rigor and excellent clinical relevance.

Bootstrapping Design

Bootstrapping designs were first used in neuropsychological studies of feigning. Individual indicators of feigning were frequently inaccurate in traumatic brain injuries non-litigating samples (12.5% to 63.6%). However, the combined use of indicators often produced more accurate results (see Meyers & Volbrecht, 2003, p. 271, Table 4). For example, Boone et al. (2000) categorized suspected malingerers using two or more from a list 12 feigning indices. Even with multiple indicators, the bootstrapping design lacks the precision of known-groups comparisons because the accuracy of multiple indicators has not been tested for each combination. Therefore, Rogers (2008a) recommended it be used to evaluate detection strategies by means of effect sizes but that it not be applied to utility estimates.

Researchers using the bootstrapping design should observe the following guidelines:

1. Objective criteria should be implemented that maximize accurate group membership. These criteria typically rely on specific cut scores that

increase the probability that feigning and genuine clinical groups have minimal misclassifications.

2. Relevant clinical populations should be employed to ensure the generalizability of the results.

For example, Rogers et al. (2009) made use of bootstrapping design in a study of feigned disability referrals. To test the clinical usefulness of the SIRS in disability contexts, stringent MMPI-2 and cognitive feigning rules were implemented. Differences based on diagnostic groups and referral sources were systematically evaluated.

DIFFERENTIAL PREVALENCE DESIGN

Differential prevalence design is a simplistic method that ineffectually attempts to equate the referral issue with response styles. In its most common form, all litigation-based cases are blithely assumed to be feigning, and all non-litigation cases are naively assumed to be genuine. Stated simply, one potential motivation for feigning (e.g., unwarranted gains from a personal injury suit) is often confused with actual motivation and erroneously assumed to be the *only* motivation (e.g., non-litigating cases could not possibly have other motivations for feigning). As an analog, most consulting psychologists and psychiatrists have the potential opportunity to "pad" their professional hours; using the same slipshod logic, we should assume all consulting professionals engage in fraud.

Beyond its conceptual bankruptcy, different prevalence design for malingering is untestable. Most research convincingly demonstrates that only a minority of any referral group is malingering. Rogers et al. (1998) found that estimated base rates of malingering in forensic settings varied widely but were typically less than one-third of forensic referrals ($M = 17.44\%$, $SD = 14.44\%$). Thus, assuming that the rate of malingering is 100% in this population leads to an extremely large false-positive rate. To highlight another aspect of the same problem, let's assume that an experimental feigning scale is given to forensic referrals and one-third of the protocols are "elevated." What does this mean? The answer is absolutely nothing. The sensitivity could vary from 0% (none of the malingerers were elevated) to 100% (all the malingerers were elevated). Likewise, the specificity could vary from 0% to 100%.

Historically, differential prevalence design served a limited purpose as the initial testing of feigning measures. Even in that context, its usefulness focused primarily on the elimination of ineffective strategies by means of contrary findings (e.g., higher elevations for genuine than feigning groups), rather than the validation of effective strategies. For current research, the differential prevalence design should be simply avoided as an ineffective expediency lacking in experimental rigor.

SIMULATION DESIGN

Simulation design is by far the most common design used in feigning research today. In a simulation design, random assignment is used to distribute participants between either an experimental (i.e., feigning instructions) or a control (i.e., standard instructions) group. For malingering, a fundamental error would be to rely solely on "normal" or unimpaired samples. The comparison of feigning vs. unimpaired groups completely misses the key question: Do these detection strategies effectively discriminate *feigned* from *genuine* psychopathology? Unless this question can be addressed, simulation research on malingering has no clinical relevance.

Use of the MMPI-2 F scale for feigned mental disorders is an instructive example of what can happen when clinical comparison groups are not included. As previously noted, the F scale was not originally intended to evaluate feigning and, therefore, cannot be faulted for its scale development, which used items endorsed by less than 10% of the normative sample. In the absence of clinical comparison samples, F scale items can reflect either genuine or feigned psychopathology. As a result, genuine patients with schizophrenia and PTSD exhibit extreme elevations on the F scale, with mean T scores of 80 and 86 respectively (Rogers, Sewell, Martin, & Vitacco, 2003). When considering the $M + 1 SD$ as a benchmark, it is quite possible for genuine patients to exceed 100T with diagnoses of schizophrenia (i.e., 80T + 23T = 103T) and PTSD (i.e., 86T + 22T = 108T). In summary, the F scale clearly illustrates how the absence of clinical comparison samples in its development confounds its interpretability.

Simulation designs vary in whether clinical samples are used for group assignment or are added as a comparison sample. The advantages of using clinical samples for random assignment are twofold: they maintain the experimental design and use clinical simulators with first-hand knowledge of mental disorders. The potential disadvantages of using clinical simulators include two related issues: capacity to simulate and ceiling effects. Early research by Rogers (1988) found that a substantial minority of inpatients could not maintain the instructional set under the feigning condition because of their psychological impairment. On a related issue, feigning instructions typically assume that greater levels of psychopathology are relatively easy to dissimulate. This assumption becomes tenuous when clinical simulators already experience severe impairment or total disability.

Simulation designs commonly opt for the random assignment of non-clinical sample to control and experimental conditions, which is supplemented with a clinical comparison sample (i.e., genuine patients that are not randomly assigned) to ensure clinical relevance. Care must be taken that groups are similar in their backgrounds. As an egregious example, a study of feigned cognitive impairment would be misguided if the performance of college-student simulators were contrasted with that of a clinical comparison sample with limited education. Obviously, the interpretation of the results would be confounded by educational level.

The simulation design is often criticized due to concerns about external validity (Haines & Norris, 1995; Rogers, Bagby, & Dickens, 1992). It can be limited by problems in approximating the motivation and incentive to feign that are found in professional settings. This limit is sometimes referred to as the "simulation-research paradox" (Rogers & Cavanaugh, 1983): Participants are asked to comply with instructions to fake to study examinees who fake when they are asked to comply.

Researchers using the simulation design should observe the following guidelines:

1. Pretest clinical simulators to ensure that they have the capacity and motivation to feign for the duration (e.g., 1–2 hours) of the study. This precaution is especially important with inpatients.
2. Design studies so that clinical simulators are asked to feign relevant clinical conditions in a realistic scenario. Asking clients to "feign" their own situation (e.g., being disabled and unable to work) is a serious flaw.
3. Use clinical comparison groups that are relevant to the experimental scenarios and share a similar background to the participants being assigned to experimental and control conditions.

Simulation designs also require careful consideration about how key elements of its research are addressed. The following section outlines the key issues related to instructions, incentives, and manipulation checks.

ELEMENTS OF SIMULATION DESIGNS

Simulation research on malingering is often limited in its clinical relevance by the questionable level of preparation and commitment by participants. While malingerers in real-life circumstances may have plenty of motivation and time to prepare, simulation studies are often limited in both these aspects. Rogers (2008b) has recommended several improvements in simulation design to address these limitations. The primary goal is to motivate and educate simulators so that they are invested in both the preparation and the outcome and most importantly in their effectiveness at foiling malingering measures.

INSTRUCTIONAL SET

Participants in simulation research are instructed to feign some form of psychological impairment in response to a hypothetical situation. In many studies, they are provided with little motivation to succeed at the task; the incentives are nominal and their level of psychological engagement is minimal. Moreover, the instructions are often unhelpful, with an emphasis on *what* to malinger (e.g., symptoms of a disorder) rather than *why* they should malinger. Most simulation studies simply assume there will be adequate motivation (Rogers & Cruise, 1998).

Researchers should use multiple methods to begin to approximate real-world motivation. One method is to directly challenge the participant's ability to "beat the test." Participants are more likely to be psychologically engaged if they feel they have something personal at stake. Rogers (2008b) recommended that simulators can be challenged to see whether "they are good enough" to foil a psychological measure designed to detect feigners.

Researchers can also attempt to engage simulators by stressing the personal relevance of feigning research. With billions spent each year on fraudulent insurance claims and bogus disabilities, the question can be asked whether sufficient funds will be available when these research participants or their parents have legitimate illnesses. Alternatively, in the age of managed-care pre-approval procedures, many potential participants have experienced firsthand some questioning of their "legitimate medical need" for specific procedures. For example, simulators may feel a personal investment if the scenario involved denied care of needed treatment for their own parent. Different scenarios could be pilot-tested for their levels of psychological engagement.

Motivation can be improved by developing specific scenarios with which simulators can identify. As an egregious example, college-student simulators have been asked to feign insanity by acting as if they had been arrested and faced trial for a serious felony. Their ability to "take seriously" this improbable event is called into question. Although challenging, researchers must consider which scenarios have the most relevance for their simulating group. For college-student simulators, feigning a medical or psychiatric condition to excuse a missed exam is more likely to be relevant to their experiences than pretending to be on trial for a felony.

Motivation to feign must also take into account negative consequences. As a far-fetched analogy, would-be racecar drivers have no concerns about spectacular crashes in simulation games. To avoid this illusion of invulnerability, the consequences of "getting caught" at unsuccessful feigning must be made an important part of the feigning scenario. In approximating real-world conditions, simulators must understand the risk-reward equation in deciding what and how much to feign.

COACHING

Early research implicitly assumed that malingerers would not avail themselves of readily available resources in preparing for feigning. This may have been true then, but now information about diagnoses and assessment measures is easily obtained from the Internet. Ruiz, Drake, Glass, Marcotte, and van Gorp (2002) found hundreds of Web sites that informed individuals about diagnostic information and a limited number that provided direct information about test scales and test items or how scales work. Professionals may also play a role in educating examinees about malingering methods. Psychologists may provide information about test taking via informed consent. Of much more concern is the role of attorneys in forensic cases. Wetter and Corrigan (1995) found that more than 50% of lawyers believe that they would be doing their clients a disservice by *not* coaching them on the presence of validity scales.

Coaching about detection strategies appears to significantly enhance the ability to feign convincingly whereas information about diagnostic criteria has understandably little effect (Lamb, Berry, Wetter, & Baer, 1994; Rogers, Bagby, & Chakraborty, 1993). Interestingly, Johnson and Lesniak-Karpiak (1997) found a decreased prevalence of malingering on some neuro-psychological tests when examinees were cautioned about the use of feigning indicators. While the authors concluded that cautions decreased malingering, an alternative explanation is that such information enabled many malingerers to go undetected. Similar findings were obtained when using the MMPI-2 (Bagby et al., 1997; Lamb et al., 1994; Rogers et al., 1993; Storm & Graham, 2000), and the PAI (Baer & Wetter, 1997).

INCENTIVES

Incentives for successful feigning, while typically nominal, are often included in simulation studies. However, their effects have gone mostly uninvestigated (Rogers, 1997; Rogers, Harrell, & Liff, 1993). The increased size of the incentive has produced generally positive results on feigning performances. Recent studies (Frederick, Sarfaty, Johnston, & Powel, 1994; Orey, Cragar, & Berry, 2000; Shum, O'Gorman, & Alpar, 2004) of feigned cognitive impairment have found that simulators have generally performed better when given appreciable incentives in the $20 to $25 range. Empirically untested is whether the size of the incentive has a linear or curvilinear relationship. Available studies suggest that simulators have an increased motivation when their incentives are more than symbolic (e.g., just course credit). Empirically untested is whether very large awards increase or decrease performance. Anecdotally, cases in dire circumstances (e.g., death row evaluations) sometimes produce extremely poor malingering efforts. In summary, appreciable incentives may improve feigning performances, but no extrapolations to high-incentive circumstances are limited.

The relationship of incentives to performance is complex, even in presumably genuine compensation cases. A meta-analysis by Binder and Rohling (1996) found that the magnitude of the monetary reward was correlated with higher scores on neurological measures in actual compensation cases despite less severe injuries in many cases. Does this mean that examinees were incentivized by the higher stakes to produce more pathology? On the other hand, were high stakes warranted because examinees might have other impairments (e.g., comorbid disorders) that were affecting neurological performance? Finally, had examinees with high stakes become more invested in their disability status because of the lexogenic effects (see Rogers & Payne, 2006) of protracted litigation? From an empirical perspective, simulation research is ill-equipped to examine these competing hypotheses, which are likely to be best addressed with a bootstrapping design. To date, this dose–response relationship between monetary amount and higher scores does not seem to hold in experimental settings, possibly due to the necessarily smaller scale of rewards in research (Bianchini, Curtis, & Greve, 2006).

The most pervasive omission in simulation research is the absence of negative incentives. As previously noted, simulators must consider the negative consequences of failed malingering. In disability contexts, such failures can lead to the cessation of all treatment and other benefits. Moreover, claimants may be required to repay unwarranted compensation and may even face criminal charges of fraud. Rogers and Cruise (1998) conducted one of the few investigations of negative incentives. They told participants that the names of failed simulators would be posted publicly on a bulletin board. Importantly, simulators facing even this mild negative consequence improved their performances. For purposes of generalizability, it is recommended that simulation designs include a negative consequence.

MANIPULATION CHECKS

Simulation designs cannot be effective if participants do not adopt their experimental condition or take seriously standard instructions for the control condition. Manipulation checks are used to ensure that participants understood and followed the instructions they were given. At the most basic level, simulators must be able to recall the experimental instructions and be able to paraphrase them in their own words. Additional inquiries should address the participants' compliance and psychological investment in the study. Participants may also limit their participation due to factors such as a moral conviction against lying, true psychological problems, or distrust of the experimenter (Rogers, 2008b). All inquiries should take into account social desirability, because many participants want to appear that they performed well and deserve whatever incentives are being provided.

Manipulation checks can be applied to preparation materials as well to test their effectiveness in preparing simulators. A study of coached feigning is unlikely to be successful if the simulators are unable to remember most of the presented material on detection strategies. Finally, as part of the manipulation check, researchers can inquire about the relevance of the scenario and what elements of the study (e.g., incentive or direct challenge) were the most successful at motivating simulators; these inquiries can improve future research.

CONCLUSIONS

Researchers should seek to integrate research designs and not allow expediency to diminish experimental rigor. In particular, results of simulation research with strong internal validity must be further tested with designs (known-groups comparisons and bootstrapping designs) that emphasize external validity. Only through a convergence of findings across designs can researchers and practitioners have confidence in their results.

The assessment of malingering must extend beyond individual scales to evaluate detection strategies specific to feigning domains. For existing and future measures, efforts must take into account a careful delineation of the applicable detection strategy and its relationship to other strategies. Group differences constitute an insufficient means of establishing discriminant validity. Researchers must focus instead on the magnitude of differences via effect sizes (Cohen's d) and the accuracy of individual classifications. For classificatory accuracy, the popular trend toward applying geometry (i.e., area under the curve) to receiver operator analysis (ROC; Swets, 1973) should be avoided because of (a) its untenable assumption that every data point must be considered a cut score and (b) its general neglect of positive and negative predictive powers (PPP and NPP). Rather, classification efforts should be concentrated on extensive cross-validation of cut scores and the potential integration of these cut scores for incremental accuracy.

In closing, this brief chapter summarizes the basic components for malingering research. Importantly, it provides specific cautions about common pitfalls and expediencies in conducting such research. Rogers (2008b) provides more extensive guidelines for the design and implementation of malingering research.

REFERENCES

Baer, R., & Wetter, M. (1997). Effects of information about validity scales on underreporting of symptoms on the personality assessment inventory. *Journal of Personality Assessment, 68*, 402–413.

Bagby, R. M., Rogers, R., Nicholson, R. A., Buis, T., Seeman, M. V., & Rector, N. A. (1997). Does clinical training facilitate feigning schizophrenia on the MMPI-2? *Psychological Assessment, 9*, 106–112.

Bianchini, K. J., Curtis, K. L., & Greve, K. W. (2006). Compensation and malingering in traumatic brain injury: A dose-response relationship? *The Clinical Neuropsychologist, 20*, 831–847.

Binder, L. M., & Rohling, M. L. (1996). Money matters: A meta-analytic review of the effects of financial incentives on recovery after closed head injury. *American Journal of Psychiatry, 153*, 7–10.

Boone, K. B., Lu, P., Sherman, D., Palmer, B., Back, C., Shamieh, E., . . . Berman, N. G. (2000). Validation of a new technique to detect malingering of cognitive symptoms: The b test. *Archives of Clinical Neuropsychology, 15*, 227–241.

Dahlstrom, W. G., Welsh, G. S., & Dahlstrom, L. E. (1972). *An MMPI handbook: I. Clinical interpretation* (rev. ed.). Oxford, England: University of Minnesota Press.

Edens, J. F., Poythress, N. G., & Watkins-Clay, M. M. (2007). Detection of malingering in psychiatric unit and general population prison inmates: A comparison of the PAI, SIMS, and SIRS. *Journal of Personality Assessment, 88*(1), 33–42.

Frederick, R. I., Sarfaty, S. D., Johnston, J. D., & Powel, J. (1994) Validation of a detector of response bias on a forced-choice test of nonverbal ability. *Neuropsychology, 8*(1), 118–125.

Geller, J. L., Erlen, J., Kaye, N. S., & Fisher, W. H. (1990). Feigning insanity in nineteenth century America: Tactics, trials, and truth. *Behavioral Sciences and the Law, 8*(1), 3–26.

Haines, M. E., & Norris, M. P. (1995). Detecting the malingering of cognitive deficits: An update. *Neuropsychology Review, 5*(2), 125–148.

Johnson, K. L., & Lesniak-Karpiak, K. (1997). The effect of warning on malingering on memory and motor tasks in college samples. *Archives of Clinical Neuropsychology, 12*(3), 231–238.

Lamb, D. G., Berry, D. T. R., Wetter, M. W., & Baer, R. A. (1994). Effects of two types of information on malingering of closed head injury on the MMPI-2: An analog investigation. *Psychological Assessment 6*(1), 8–13.

Meehl, P. E. (1946). Profile analysis of the Minnesota Multiphasic Personality Inventory in differential diagnosis. *Journal of Applied Psychology, 30*(5), 517–524.

Meyers, J. E., & Volbrecht, M. E. (2003). A validation of multiple malingering detection methods in a large clinical sample. *Archives of Clinical Neuropsychology, 18,* 261–276.

Orey, S. A., Cragar, D. E., & Berry, D. T. R. (2000). The effects of two motivational manipulations on the neuropsychological performance of mildly head-injured college students. *Archives of Clinical Neuropsychology, 15,* 335–348.

Rogers, R. (1984). Toward an empirical model of malingering and deception. *Behavioral Sciences and the Law, 2*(1), 93–111.

Rogers, R. (1997). *Clinical assessment of malingering and deception* (2nd ed.). New York, NY: Guilford Press.

Rogers, R. (2008a). Detection strategies for malingering and defensiveness. In R. Rogers (Ed.), *Clinical assessment of malingering and deception* (3rd ed.). New York, NY: Guilford Press.

Rogers, R. (2008b). Researching response styles. In R. Rogers (Ed.), *Clinical assessment of malingering and deception* (3rd ed.). New York, NY: Guilford Press.

Rogers, R., Bagby, R. M., & Chakraborty, D. (1993). Feigning schizophrenic disorders on the MMPI-2: Detection of coached simulators. *Journal of Personality Assessment, 60*(2), 215–226.

Rogers, R., Bagby, R. M., & Dickens, S. E. (1992). *Structured interview of reported symptoms professional manual.* Odessa, FL: Psychological Assessment Resources.

Rogers, R., & Bender, S. D. (2003). Evaluation of malingering and deception. In A. Goldstein & I. B. Weiner (Eds.), *Handbook of psychology* (Vol. 11, Forensic Psychology, pp. 109–129). Hoboken, NJ: Wiley.

Rogers, R., & Cavanaugh, J. L. (1983). 'Nothing but the truth' . . . A reexamination of malingering. *Journal of Psychiatry & Law, 11*(4), 443–459.

Rogers, R., & Correa, A. A. (2008). Determinations of malingering: The evolution from case-based methods to detection strategies. *Psychiatry, Psychology and Law, 15,* 213–223.

Rogers, R., & Cruise, K. R. (1998). Assessment of malingering with simulation designs: Threats to external validity. *Law and Human Behavior, 22*(3), 273–285.

Rogers, R., & Payne, J. W. (2006). Damages and rewards: Assessment of malingered disorders in compensation cases. *Behavioral Sciences and the Law, 24,* 645–658.

Rogers, R., Harrell, E. H., & Liff, C. D. (1993). Feigning neuropsychological impairment: A critical review of methodological and clinical considerations. *Clinical Psychology Review, 13*(3), 255–274.

Rogers, R., Jackson, R. L., Sewell, K. W., & Salekin, K. L. (2005). Detection strategies for malingering: A confirmatory factor analysis of the SIRS. *Criminal Justice and Behavior, 32,* 511–525.

Rogers, R., Payne, J. W., Correa, A. A., Ross, C. A., & Gillard, N. D. (2009). A study of the SIRS with severely traumatized patients. *Journal of Personality Assessment, 91,* 429–438.

Rogers, R., Sewell, K. W., & Gillard, N. D. (2010). *Structured Interview of Reported Symptoms-2 (SIRS-2) and professional manual.* Odessa, FL: Psychological Assessment Resources.

Rogers, R., Sewell, K. W., Martin, M. A., & Vitacco, M. J. (2003). Detection of feigned mental disorders: A meta-analysis of the MMPI-2 and malingering. *Assessment, 10,* 160–177.

Ruiz, M. A., Drake, E. B., Glass, A., Marcotte, D., & van Gorp, W. G. (2002). Trying to beat the system: Misuse of the Internet to assist in avoiding the detection of psychological symptom dissimulation. *Professional Psychology: Research and Practice*, 33(3), 294–299.

Shadish, W., Cook, T., & Campbell, D. (2002). *Experimental and quasi-experimental designs for generalized causal inference*. New York, NY: Houghton Mifflin.

Shum, D. H., O'Gorman, J. G., & Alpar, A. (2004). Effects of incentive and preparation time on performance and classification accuracy of standard and malingering-specific memory tasks. *Archives of Clinical Neuropsychology, 19,* 817–823.

Storm, J., & Graham, J. (2000). Detection of coached general malingering on the MMPI-2. *Psychological Assessment, 12,* 158–165.

Swets, J. A. (1973). The relative operating characteristic in psychology. *Science, 182* (4116), 990–1000.

Wetter, M. W., & Corrigan, S. K. (1995). Providing information to clients about psychological tests: A survey of attorneys' and law students' attitudes. *Professional Psychology: Research and Practice, 26*(5), 474–477.

PART III

CRIMINAL LAW—TRIAL ISSUES

CHAPTER 11

Jury Research Methods

STEVEN D. PENROD, MARGARET BULL KOVERA, AND JENNIFER GROSCUP

T HE UNITED STATES is famous for its jury system, though in fact only a small percentage of criminal and civil cases are actually resolved with jury trials. The majority of civil cases are resolved through settlements agreed to by the parties, and the majority of criminal cases are resolved through plea bargaining, in which defendants plead guilty in exchange for agreed-on sentences. Because there are millions of criminal and civil cases every year, juries do decide many thousands of cases annually. Furthermore, the jury looms large in settled and plea-bargained cases, because parties resolve those cases in light of their predictions about how juries might decide their cases if there were no settlement and the case proceeded to trial. As a consequence, jury trials are of critical importance in the law, and it is not surprising that juries have attracted the attention of research psychologists. As will become clear in this chapter, juries provide an interesting laboratory for research, ranging from the theoretical to the applied. In this chapter, we focus on important methodological issues relating to jury research.

Research that focuses on *jury decision making* (a term we shall use to encompass individual juror decision making as well) has developed in many ways during the past 50 years. Although researchers have used a set of standard methods over that period (Bornstein, 1999), arguably there has been a strengthening of research methods and the adoption of new methods, such as meta-analysis, in which the results of many studies are combined to aid analysis (see Chapter 3 by Sporer and Cohn in this book for further background on meta-analytic methods). The research questions addressed by researchers have expanded dramatically, and the number of researchers and the volume of research have grown as well. Over time, sustained bodies of research have developed around a number of topics, such as the effects of pretrial publicity, comprehension of jury instructions, and death-penalty decision making. And although early jury research concentrated on criminal cases, during the past two decades there has been rapid growth in studies of civil juries.

EARLY JURY RESEARCH

Although most jury studies have been conducted during the past 50 years, the first jury research was launched 90 years ago with experimental studies of whether particular products confused buyers about trademarks (Burtt, 1931; Burtt & Dobell, 1925; Paynter, 1919. Burtt was probably the first psychologist involved in systematic jury research. During the same period, law professors Hutchins and Slesinger (1928, 1929a, 1929b) wrote articles in which they applied psychological findings to evidence law (a tradition that endures to this day).

Despite these early endeavors, psychologists were not quick to adopt juries as the focus of their research. The first sustained program of research on the jury was the University of Chicago Jury Project of the 1950s and 1960s. The Chicago Jury Project was headed by law professor Harry Kalven and sociologist Hans Zeisel. These two researchers and a team of colleagues generated a number of empirical jury studies (the most important being Kalven and Zeisel's *The American Jury*, 1966), which arguably inspired most of the jury research that has been conducted during the past 50 years. Other important jury research was generated by Chicago Jury Project researchers (Broeder, 1958; James, 1959; Strodtbeck, James, & Hawkins, 1957; Strodtbeck & Mann, 1956).

The Chicago Jury Project research was strongly influenced by the legal, sociological, and political science training of the researchers, but the research also reflected matters of great interest to psychologists (such as influences on individual and group decision making and group interactions), and psychologists began generating distinctly psychological bodies of jury research during the 1970s. This early jury research often grew from topics then popular in social and cognitive psychology, such as social status and social influence in group processes and the influence of juror attitudes, jurors' stereotypes of defendants, and the physical attractiveness and race of defendants on juror decisions (for a review, see Gerbasi, Zuckerman, & Reis, 1977). The bulk of this new psychologically oriented research employed jury simulations (generally using student "mock jurors" exposed to short trial summaries, often without group deliberations) coupled with experimental methods in which mock jurors were randomly assigned to experimental conditions.

These studies had relatively little relevance to the law and were published predominantly in psychology journals. However, despite the possible limitations of the simulation methods used by researchers, it is clear that the early jury studies conducted by psychologists were intended to address legal questions. Weiten and Diamond (1977), in their critical review of these early jury studies, noted that researchers "have generally not been very timid about discussing practical implications" despite typically "provid[ing] some caveat that their findings are merely suggestive regarding the practical realities of jury functioning" (1977, p. 75). Even with the limitations of these early studies, jury research conducted by psychologists quickly acquired a higher degree of legal relevance, facilitated, in part, by collaborations between psychologists and lawyers and by individuals trained in both disciplines (e.g., Padawer-Singer & Barton, 1975; Penrod & Hastie, 1979, 1980; Sales, Elwork, & Alfini, 1977; Thompson, Cowan, Ellsworth, & Harrington, 1984).

EARLY JURY RESEARCH TOPICS

Jury research conducted between 1977 and 1994 reflected a rich mix of psychologically oriented and legally oriented topics (Nietzel, McCarthy, & Kern, 1999). During that time, jury research publications included

- Twenty articles devoted to the effects of various types of witnesses on jury decisions, including expert witnesses, child witnesses, and eye-witnesses (e.g., Wells & Leippe, 1981).
- Eighteen articles devoted to litigation strategies such as "stealing thunder," joinder of charges against defendants, the effects of opening statements, and the efficacy of voir dire (e.g., Pyszczynski, Greenberg, Mack, & Wrightsman, 1981).
- Eleven articles on the evaluation of various types of evidence such as stricken evidence and statistical evidence (for a recent review of this research see Steblay, Hosch, Culhane, & McWethy, 2006).
- Eleven studies on capital punishment, the process of "qualifying" jurors for death penalty cases (essentially excluding jurors who have moral reservations about the death penalty), and sentencing decisions (e.g., Cowan, Thompson, & Ellsworth, 1984).
- Ten studies each on juror and defendant characteristics, which yielded 10 articles each (e.g., Sigall & Landy, 1972).

Other common topics from this era include models of juror and jury decision making (e.g., Penrod & Hastie, 1979, 1980), jurors' comprehension of standards of proof (e.g., Kagehiro & Stanton, 1985), jurors' comprehension of substantive instructions about the law (e.g., Elwork, Sales, & Alfini, 1977), and the influence of alternative insanity standards on jury decisions (e.g., Finkel, Shaw, Bercaw, & Koch, 1985).

METHODOLOGICAL CRITIQUES OF JURY RESEARCH

During the late 1970s and early 1980s, jury researchers began to critically assess their research methods. In 1979, the relatively new journal *Law and Human Behavior* published a special issue devoted to jury simulations and the law. Papers included in the issue offered critiques by leading jury researchers of the jury simulation methods commonly employed by early jury researchers. The critiques focused on the ecological characteristics of jury research—characteristics that make simulations look more or less similar to actual trials. The general assumptions behind these critiques were that low ecological validity imperiled the external validity or generalizability of jury simulation findings as compared with actual juries and undermined the perceived validity of simulation findings among possible consumers of the research, such as lawyers and judges.

A number of ecological features were highlighted by critics (e.g., Bray & Kerr, 1979; Weiten & Diamond, 1979) who stressed the importance of increasing the ecological validity of jury research by

- Sampling jury-eligible community members as jury-simulation participants, as opposed to the fairly standard use of undergraduate students.
- Developing rich and extensive trial simulations such as videotaped mock trials, as opposed to relying on brief written trial summaries.
- Including jury deliberations, as opposed to relying on individual juror judgments.
- Using procedures that reflect actual trials, such as questioning and qualifying prospective jurors (the jury-selection process known as voir dire).
- Adopting legally appropriate dependent measures such as dichotomous judgments of guilt/innocence rather than measuring defendant responsibility for the crime or recommended sentences (generally not a decision made by jurors).
- Making efforts to address concerns about participants' likely understanding that their decisions had no significant consequences.

Of course it is one thing to assert that low ecological validity imperils the generalizability of jury simulation research and another thing to demonstrate that ecological validity actually affects the external validity of research findings. It was for this reason that Bray and Kerr (1979) called for researchers "to conduct a series of careful studies that systematically explore the range of actors, behaviors, and contexts over which results of simulation studies will hold" (p. 109).

Were these admonitions apt? Were they heeded? What lessons have we learned with respect to the research practices we should employ in jury research? In a recent consideration of the research methods employed in jury research, Vidmar (2008) has argued that methods—specifically ecological validity—matter because "If research is to have its best chance of having an impact on judges and other policy makers, more ecologically valid research is needed" (p. 36). Vidmar draws on an argument by Brewer (2000): "The question of whether an effect holds up across a wide variety of people or settings is somewhat different than asking whether the effect is representative of what happens in everyday life. This is the essence of ecological validity—whether an effect has been demonstrated to occur under conditions that are typical for the population at large" (Vidmar, 2008, p. 37). The thrust of Vidmar's argument is that jury research has occurred within too narrow a range of settings and people and has not captured the richness of real juries. By implication, the admonitions from the late 1970s would seem to have been ignored. Is that true? Does it matter?

What did early experimental jury research look like and has it changed? Bray and Kerr (1982) examined 72 simulation studies published before 1979 and found that students served as jurors in 67% of the studies. Bornstein (1999) took a fresh look at research methods 20 years later—analyzing 113 jury simulation studies published in *Law and Human Behavior* between 1977 and 1996. Interestingly, he observed a drop in the percentage of research articles using jury simulations in the early 1980s—perhaps a product of the 1979 critiques. With respect to specific research methods, Bornstein reported that 65% of the jury simulation studies had students as participants—essentially the same percentage reported by Bray and Kerr in 1982. With respect to trial materials, Bray and Kerr (1982) reported that 54% of pre-1979 studies used written materials and 89% used abbreviated fact summaries. Live or videotaped presentations were used in about 17% of studies, and 29% presented trials using audiotape. Twenty years later, Bornstein (1999) found that 55% of the simulation studies he examined used written trial materials. Although a higher percentage (33%) of published studies used videotapes in the 1977–1996 period than in the pre-1979 period, Bornstein concluded that videotaped trials were actually becoming less common over time (even though one might expect increased use of videotape due to reductions in cost and increased availability). He also concluded that the use of students as mock jurors was increasing over time.

In short, despite the methodological criticisms offered in the late 1970s, jury research methods changed relatively little during the following two decades; the use of students and short written trial summaries still predominated, and research was not increasing in ecological validity.

WHY WOULD RESEARCH METHODS NOT CHANGE?

Why would research methods not change and grow more ecologically similar to actual trials, and what, if anything, does this tell us about the research methods that should be employed in jury studies? There are a number of possible answers to that question. First, increased ecological validity comes at a cost—actually, a number of costs. Student jurors are often readily available to serve as mock jurors in jury simulations; often they are afforded an opportunity to participate as research participants for extra credit in introductory-level psychology classes (and it is generally expected that they will be "debriefed" about their research participation to ensure that their experiences are educational in nature). In contrast, recruiting jury-eligible adults to participate as research participants can be time-consuming (how do you find such research participants?) and expensive (who is willing to give up an evening or a weekend day to assist researchers unless compensation is involved?). Similarly, composing a short written trial summary (even several variations that reflect the experimental conditions specified in one's research design) is relatively quick and easy as compared with developing a videotaped trial, which may require constructing or adapting a complete trial transcript, recruiting and videotaping actors, and then editing the recordings into a set of videos that reflect the various experimental conditions.

Deliberations similarly impose costs on the researchers. Participants must be recruited in groups; there must be a space where the "jury" can deliberate; and if the researcher intends to analyze the deliberations (possibly very time-consuming and difficult), the deliberation room must be equipped with appropriate (and preferably, nonintrusive) recording equipment. The most interesting unit of analysis in deliberations is the jury, and it takes multiple participants (usually between 4 and 12) to create a jury. Because the data from groups of individuals is interdependent, it violates the statistical assumptions of analyses of variance that the error in the data is independent. The types of statistical methods (e.g., nested analyses, hierarchical linear modeling) that can handle these interdependent data require data from many more participants to achieve the same statistical power to detect effects that would be present if the same study were run with individual jurors. Thus, studies that include jury deliberations require a large number of participants. Recruiting groups of students can be vexing, but recruiting large numbers of community members to participate in groups poses a much greater challenge.

Given the various costs involved in constructing research studies that bear a stronger ecological resemblance to real juries, it is easy to see why researchers might hesitate to do so or even find it impossible; if all jury research resembled actual juries, there likely would be far less jury research. A second reason why jury research methods may not have changed despite questions about the extent to which low ecological validity might imperil the external validity/generalizability of research findings, is that many researchers are not persuaded that low ecological validity imperils generalizability.

DO RESEARCH METHODS MATTER?

Does the low ecological validity of the preponderance of jury simulation research matter? The most effective way to answer that question was highlighted in Bray and Kerr's (1979) call for studies that systematically explore variations in "actors, behaviors, and contexts" over which simulation researchers want to generalize their research conclusions. Do variations in research methods produce differences in research conclusions? Such differences can appear in two forms. First, there might be a difference between jury verdicts rendered based on different research methods. For example, there might be a difference in jury verdicts rendered by students as opposed to community members exposed to identical trial materials. This is a "main-effect" difference—students and community members differ from one another. A strong case can be made that differences of this sort are relatively unimportant with respect to most jury research, because the focus is not on juror types but on other variables such as pretrial publicity effects or the effects of different types of expert testimony.

Of course differences in verdicts across types of jurors can be important. Although no one is proposing that jury trials be held in front of students rather than community members, if someone (with a wild imagination) did propose such a change in actual jury practice, any differences in verdicts rendered by students as opposed to community members would become much more interesting. More realistically, whether different types of jurors render different verdicts is a central question when it comes to jury selection, an issue discussed in the following text.

From a research methods point of view, the much more interesting differences that jury researchers and policymakers who rely on jury research should be concerned about emerge in "interactions" between a factor such as students versus non-students and substantive variables that researchers are interested in. For example, do students and community members respond differently to experimental manipulations such as exposure to different types of pretrial publicity? If they do, there is an interaction between juror type and pretrial publicity. In other words, juror type moderates the relationship between exposure to pretrial publicity and verdicts in that different types of jurors react differently to pretrial publicity, which is reflected in their verdicts. But is that what happens? Do variations in the ecological validity of research methods interact with substantive variables to influence outcomes in jury simulation research?

An interaction difference is much more important than a main-effect difference, because it indicates that research methods may limit the external validity/generalizability of research conclusions. If, for example, students are highly sensitive to variations in whether pretrial publicity suggests the guilt of the defendant but community members are not, it would be an error to conclude on the basis of simulation research with students that actual jurors drawn from the community would be similarly sensitive. As noted by Bray and Kerr (1979), the only way we can detect such interactions is by testing students and community members using the same pretrial publicity manipulations. In other words, whether ecological validity influences external validity is an empirical question subject to research investigation.

WHAT DOES RESEARCH REVEAL ABOUT METHOD EFFECTS?

Bornstein (1999) aptly observed that with respect to the question of whether different types of jurors (e.g., students vs. community members) produce similar judgments, three general analytic strategies can be employed: (1) correlational studies that investigate relationships between various demographic and attitudinal variables and verdicts, (2) experimental studies that directly compare different types of jurors, and (3) sets of studies that replicate empirical results using jury samples that differ across studies. These often take the form of meta-analyses in which sets of studies look at a common independent variable (e.g., attractive versus unattractive defendants; pro-prosecution versus pro-defense pretrial publicity; or standard, jargon-ridden legal instructions versus simple English instructions).

Each of these methods *permits* investigation of both the main effects of method type (e.g., students vs. community members) and interactive effects of methods with substantive variables of interest). However, correlational studies are not designed to test for such interactions; researchers use them primarily to test for main-effect relationships between juror characteristics (e.g., student vs. community member) and verdicts. Jury experiments in which juror type is systematically varied or measured (e.g., student participants vs. participants sampled from the community) permit direct comparisons of verdict preferences as a function of juror type and have the advantage that some other variables of substantive interest can be systematically manipulated within the same experiment to test for interactions between method (juror type in our illustration) and substantive variables (e.g., pro-defense vs. pro-prosecution pretrial publicity). The presence of different juror types and substantive variables in the same study allows experimental researchers to address the generalization question: Do different types of jurors respond in the same way to variations in the substantive variables?

The third technique for assessing methods is not as powerful as within-experiment comparisons. Sometimes studies looking at a common independent variable (e.g., pretrial publicity) will have participants drawn from different populations. This similarity of independent variables combined with differences in method permits meta-analysts to test whether different types of jurors have responded in the same way to the manipulated substantive variable. The weakness of such comparisons—as opposed to the comparisons allowed by experiments in which juror type is systematically varied—is that comparisons of, say, students versus community members in the meta-analytic approach are necessarily comparing studies that may also vary in the ways in which the substantive variables are manipulated (which, by itself, could produce different effects across studies). The studies may differ from one another in numerous other ways (videotaped trials vs. written trials, criminal cases vs. civil cases, etc.) and those differences, rather than differences in juror type, might produce differences, across studies, in the impact of independent variable manipulations.

We now have meta-analyses examining leniency biases (MacCoun & Kerr, 1988); race and sentencing (Sweeney & Haney, 1992); authoritarianism (Narby, Cutler, & Moran, 1993); defendant characteristics (Mazzella

& Feingold, 1994); jury size (Saks & Marti, 1997); gender (Schutte & Hosch, 1997); the influence of juror death penalty attitudes on verdicts (Allen, Mabry, & McKelton, 1998; Nietzel et al., 1999, O'Neil, Patry, & Penrod, 2004), the influence of pretrial publicity on guilt judgments about a defendant (Steblay, Besirevic, Fulero, & Jimenez-Lorente, 1999); racial bias (Mitchell, Haw, Pfeifer, & Meissner, 2005); and inadmissible evidence (Steblay et al., 2006). One informative analysis that can often be undertaken in a meta-analysis is to test whether the substantive variable of interest interacts with the methodological features studies that examine the same substantive variables. Nietzel et al. (1999) used meta-analysis to examine the effects of judicial instructions on juror comprehension, the influence on jury decision making of expert psychological testimony, the influence on jury decision making of joinder of criminal charges, and, most pertinent to our concerns in this chapter, to test for interactions among these variables and methodological variables. We will examine in detail the results flowing from these meta-analytic studies.

In the following sections we consider, in some detail, research on the relationship between juror characteristics and verdict. We go into some detail as well to fully explore the ways in which the methodological questions we have posed can be and have been addressed. In subsequent sections, we briefly consider the results of studies that have examined the impact of other jury-method variables on the generalizability of findings from existing jury research.

ARE JUROR CHARACTERISTICS RELATED TO JUROR VERDICTS?

One source of our knowledge about main-effect differences in judgments rendered by different types of jurors is research on jury selection. At the start of trials, attorneys, judges, or both have an opportunity to question (or *voir dire*) prospective jurors to gauge whether the prospective jurors are biased in some way that will impair their ability to fairly evaluate trial evidence. Jurors may be challenged (unseated) for cause by either side if questioning reveals juror bias and the trial judge agrees with the attorney's assessment that the juror is biased. Attorneys also have available a limited number of peremptory challenges to unseat jurors whom they prefer not to have on the jury, though peremptory challenges may not be used, for example, to exclude a particular racial group from a jury. There are many books dedicated to providing attorneys guidance on how to select jurors.

Typically, the advice takes the form of seeking out (or avoiding) jurors with certain backgrounds or attitudes. From an empirical point of view, the question is whether juror characteristics or attitudes actually predict or are correlated with verdict preferences. Attorneys want to know about such differences because they can use the information for jury selection, but from a methodological point of view we want to know whether different types of jurors render different verdicts, because this can help inform our judgments about the generalizability of research findings generated by particular types of research participants. An interesting nonmythological issue is whether juror characteristics are related to decision quality and whether challenges of some types of prospective jurors might produce higher-quality jury decisions.

RESEARCH WITH ACTUAL JURORS

A number of researchers have surveyed actual jurors, looking for relationships between juror characteristics and the verdicts they rendered in the cases on which they sat. Although this method clearly has the advantage of drawing on real jurors who have decided real cases, the cases on which jurors sat could have varied quite dramatically and might have activated very different attitudes or responses based on prior experiences. In addition, the verdicts rendered by juries reflect input from all jurors, which might dampen the relationship between individual differences and verdicts. Such case variability would make it impossible to detect specific attitude–verdict relationships unique to particular types of cases. Nonetheless, it is possible for general patterns of relationships to emerge from this type of research, and it is even possible that the relationships are strong (i.e., that juror attitudes and characteristics could account for a substantial portion of the variability in jury verdicts). In their detailed review of jury selection research, Fulero and Penrod (1990) described an early study of 432 experienced jurors who served in trials in Louisiana from 1959 to 1961 (Reed, 1965). Reed found that in criminal cases, education and occupational level were related to verdicts; higher-status jurors were more likely to vote "guilty." No relationship was found for marital status, age, religious preference, or church attendance. In civil cases, no significant relationships were detected.

In a study of 197 jurors in Baltimore, jurors who were female, less educated, black, and older were more conviction prone (Mills & Bohannon, 1980). A multiple regression analysis combining these variables in one analysis showed that between 10% and 16% of the variance in verdicts in their cases was predicted by a combination of these variables. A survey of 319 Dade County, Florida felony jurors found somewhat complicated relationships that turned on juror gender (Moran & Comfort, 1982). Among men, guilty verdicts were associated with lower income and more children. For women, guilty verdicts were associated only with higher scores on a scale measuring beliefs about a just world. For men, the variables accounted for less than 11% of the variance in verdicts, and for women less than 6% of the variance in verdicts. In a second study, Moran and Comfort (1986) surveyed attitudes and demographics among more than 600 jurors across two studies. Overall, juror death penalty attitudes correlated with individual pre-deliberation verdicts.

As is evident from the examples provided here, there really is no common pattern of findings across these studies. This inconsistency may result from the fact that jurors heard very different types of cases, may be a product of regional differences, or may simply indicate that there are no widespread attitudinal/juror characteristic relationships with verdicts, and that some or many of the "relationships" that emerge may be a result of analyzing many possible relationships. We would expect 1 in 20 such tests to be significant at $p < .05$ by chance alone!

MOCK TRIAL STUDIES

A more focused research method that can examine juror characteristic and verdict relationships does so in the context of jury simulations. There are many such studies (in a sense, any jury simulation affords an opportunity to look at such relationships). Studies specifically reporting on the relationship between juror characteristics and verdict have investigated the effects of a wide variety of characteristics, and their findings have been mixed. In one of the earliest studies of this type, Simon (1967) examined the relationships among juror characteristics and verdicts in two insanity cases. She found no significant relationships for juror occupation, gender, income, religion, or age. However, jurors with less than a high school education acquitted more frequently than jurors with a college education, and blacks voted to acquit more often than jurors of other races. Although she found no relationship between gender and insanity verdicts, Simon (1967) reported that women were more likely to convict in an incest case than were men. Later research indicates that women are more likely to convict in cases involving sexual crimes against women and children (e.g., Brekke & Borgida, 1988; Kovera, Gresham, Borgida, Gray, & Regan, 1997; Kovera, Levy, Borgida, & Penrod, 1994).

Later studies have also investigated the characteristics examined by Simon and have expanded the investigation of juror traits. For example, Saks (1976), in a study of jury-size effects, looked at 27 juror variables and found the best predictor of verdicts—attitudes about crime as a product of "bad people" or "bad social conditions"—accounted for 9% of the variance in juror verdicts, but oddly jurors who believed crime was a product of bad social conditions were more likely to convict. The four best predictors, when combined, explained 13% of the variance.

Hepburn (1980) collected demographic and attitudinal information from 305 people chosen for jury duty in St. Louis and obtained their verdicts in a hypothetical murder case. Verdicts were associated with age and prior military service but not with race, military status, education, or prior criminal victimization. Nine variables combined to explain 8% of the variation in verdict. Hastie, Penrod, and Pennington (1983) reported modest links between demographics, attitudes, and verdict preferences among

828 jurors who had reported for jury duty. While in the courthouse, these jurors viewed and deliberated on a videotaped reenactment of an actual murder trial. There were weak relationships between verdict preference and employment status, gender, and prior jury service, but these variables accounted for a total of just 3.2% of the variance in verdict preference. Penrod (1979) collected data from 367 jurors on jury duty in Boston and tried to account for their verdicts in four simulated trials. The overall variance explained in verdict explained by 21 attitudinal and demographic items ranged from 4.9% to 14.1% across the four cases. No single predictor was significant in more than two of the cases, and the verdicts themselves were weakly related to one another.

It should be evident from this review of studies with actual jurors that there are no demographic or attitudinal variables that frequently produce statistically significant relationships with verdicts—results vary substantially across studies. In their review, Fulero and Penrod (1990) note that the relationships between demographic or attitudinal variables and verdict are modest, with the variance explained in verdicts ranging from 5% to 15%. They further observe that mock-trial studies that focus on a single type of case and therefore control for the "noise" introduced by case variations typically find stronger relationships. This pattern of results suggests that relationships may be case specific and do not generalize across cases, which could also explain why survey studies with former jurors tend to find smaller relationships.

We investigated whether individual juror characteristics might be systematically related to jury verdicts, because we wanted to know whether research based on particular types of (typically, mock) jurors would generalize to other types of jurors. The results suggest that when juror characteristics are systematically related to verdicts, those relationships may depend largely on the type of case being considered. We might also note that none of the findings reported up to this point would seem to indicate any pervasive differences between student jurors and real jurors.

MORE SPECIFIC ATTITUDES AND VERDICTS

Another approach to the question of whether different types of jurors produce appreciable differences in verdicts focuses on particular characteristics that, for theoretical or pragmatic reasons, researchers think might be related to verdict preferences. One area of jury research where this question has received substantial research attention relates to the death penalty. In one widely cited study (Cowan et al., 1984), a representative cross-section of California adults watched a videotaped murder trial used in previous research (Hastie, Penrod, & Pennington, 1983), including 258 death-qualified jurors and 30 jurors whose opposition to the death penalty was strong enough to disqualify them from jury service (so-called "excludables"). Death-qualified subjects were significantly more likely to vote guilty than were the excludables; the excludables were more likely to be female and Catholic than the qualified jurors.

Among the demographic and attitudinal measures examined by these researchers, attitude toward the death penalty and scores on a measure of "legal authoritarianism" were the strongest predictors of verdict severity. Much jury research has been devoted to the so-called authoritarian personality. A meta-analysis of the literature examining the relationship between the authoritarian personality and verdict underscored that compared with jurors who are less authoritarian, authoritarian jurors are significantly more likely to convict (Narby et al., 1993). Individual differences on a particular type of authoritarian personality (legal authoritarianism) had an even stronger relationship with verdict (Narby et al., 1993).

A meta-analysis of the death qualification research indicated that there is a modest but reliable correlation between death penalty attitudes and verdict (Nietzel et al., 1999). More recently, research using a new measure of death penalty attitudes has strongly linked death penalty attitudes to verdict preferences in cases when jurors must decide between the death penalty and a life sentence. Across a series of 11 experimental studies in which they refined their measure of death penalty attitudes, O'Neil and his colleagues (2004) found a very large effect of general support for the death penalty on sentencing. General support was measured by items such as "I think the death penalty is necessary" and "It is immoral for society to take a life regardless of the crime the individual has committed" (recoded).

All of these juror attitude/juror demographic studies are an indirect way of addressing the core question: Do the results of jury simulation research using students generalize to actual juries? The studies indicate that some attitudinal measures and some demographic measures are sometimes associated—generally rather weakly—with verdicts (with death penalty attitudes showing somewhat stronger effects). But few of the characteristics that have occasionally been linked to verdict preferences are characteristics that would systematically differentiate students from community members. Students are generally younger and possibly better educated, but a quick review of the research findings reported here will underscore that these two characteristics are rarely associated with differences in verdict preferences.

Experimental Studies Comparing Students With Non-Student Jurors

Bornstein (1999) has provided us with the most exhaustive summary of results from experiments that compare the decisions made by students with those made by other types of jurors. Researchers obtained the non-student samples in the experiments that Bornstein examined in a number of ways: sampled from voter registration lists, recruited from potential jurors before or after their jury duty, or sampled from a variety of community locales. In all instances, the non-student sample was older and more varied demographically. To illustrate the point, Bornstein cited studies by Finkel and colleagues (Finkel & Duff, 1991; Finkel & Handel, 1989; Finkel, Hughes, Smith, & Hurabiell, 1994; Finkel, Hurabiell, & Hughes, 1993a, 1993b; Finkel, Meister, & Lightfoot, 1991; Fulero & Finkel, 1991) in which student research participants were each asked to recruit non-student participants over 21 years of age. Both groups then rendered verdicts in hypothetical trials. In one study, Finkel and Handel (1989) compared students with an average age of 20 with a non-student sample with an average age of 45, all of whom gave decisions in a number of insanity defense cases. The verdicts from students and the older group did not differ. This, of course, is a main-effect analysis.

Finkel and Handel's finding is typical of studies that have compared students with other types of jurors. Bornstein examined 26 such studies employing a wide variety of trial types, including murder, insanity defense, assault, and civil cases. More critically for our purposes, the studies also included a wide variety of substantive manipulated variables that permit an examination of interactions between juror type and the substantive variables. Manipulated variables include variations in expert and hypnotically refreshed testimony, alternative definitions of insanity, and variations in pre-trial publicity and defendant characteristics. There was a main effect of juror type in 5 of the 26 studies that Bornstein examined, and there were no consistent differences in the judgments of different mock juror samples. When there were differences, Bornstein concluded that the general pattern is that student jurors have a "softer touch"—they more commonly favor criminal defendants and civil plaintiffs, a pattern he attributed to students' greater idealism, political liberalism, and education (Sears, 1986).

INTERACTIONS BETWEEN JUROR TYPE AND SUBSTANTIVE VARIABLES

Bornstein (1999) reported finding only two studies containing interactions between juror type and other variables. One study showed that the presence or absence of a weapon during the commission of a crime and whether the witness had searched through mug shots influenced experienced jurors' guilt judgments more than these variables influenced student jurors' guilt judgments (Cutler, Penrod, & Dexter, 1990); however, these moderator effects were tempered by the fact that juror type did not interact with eight other factors manipulated in the same study. In a second study using a simulated product-liability case, juror type interacted with two variables— jurors' race and characteristics of the plaintiff's injury (Bornstein & Rajki, 1994). Bornstein concluded that, "such interactions are the exception rather than the norm. The remaining 24 studies reported no significant interactions involving the mock juror sample, providing strong evidence that factors at trial affect students and nonstudents in the same way" (p. 80).

Nietzel et al. (1999) took a slightly different approach to these questions. They looked for interactions between methods factors and other variables by comparing the effect sizes produced by a manipulated variable under conditions that varied in ecological validity (e.g., when it was presented to students vs. non-students). They did this in several jury research domains. In the death penalty arena, they found that death penalty attitudes were more strongly related to jury decisions among non-students ($r = .19$) than among students ($r = .10$). With respect to the effect of judicial instructions on juror decisions, they found no clear pattern. Standard instructions (as compared with no instructions) had a slightly larger effect on students' decisions than on non-students' decisions, but enhanced instructions had stronger effects on non-students' decisions. Expert testimony had a slightly greater effect on students ($r = .17$) than on non-students ($r = .14$), and the effects of joinder of multiple criminal charges against a defendant yielded identical effect sizes for both groups ($r = .26$). The one consistent finding was that death penalty attitudes were more strongly related to judgments for non-students than for students—perhaps a reflection of more stable and well-elaborated attitudes among the (typically) older non-student group.

Other research has also yielded juror-type differences at times. For example, a review of 11 new studies of the relationship between death penalty attitudes and verdicts found differences in attitudes between students and non-students (O'Neil et al., 2004). Because some of those attitudes were substantially related to verdicts, one would expect verdict differences (main effects) for students as opposed to non-students. Although the authors did not examine interactions, their findings are consistent with the differences reported by others (e.g., Nietzel et al., 1999). Similarly, a meta-analysis of 34 studies of the effects of race on jurors' decisions found that racial bias (reflected in disparate treatment of racial out-group defendants) had a stronger relationship to sentencing (but not guilt) decisions among community members as opposed to students (Mitchell et al., 2005), results that are similar in form to the death penalty attitude effects (Nietzel et al., 1999). All of the relationships were relatively small (average $d = .09$).

In contrast, there is evidence of racial bias among both students and prospective jurors in their damage awards in a civil case (Bothwell, Pigott, Foley, & McFatter, 2006). Higgins, Heath, and Grannemann (2007) compared decisions by older and younger mock jurors and found no main-effect differences in the primary dependent measures of guilt and sentence (though older jurors were more confident). Tests of interactions between juror type and the manipulated variables (type of excuse offered by the defendant and defendant age) revealed no significant differences on guilt or sentence. Finally, a meta-analysis of 48 studies suggests that student and non-student jurors were not differentially sensitive to inadmissible evidence, which had a reliable effect on verdicts when jurors were told not to consider it. Overall, Bornstein's conclusion that juror-type interactions with substantive variables are the exception, rather than the rule, is not challenged by subsequent research.

OTHER ASPECTS OF JURY RESEARCH GENERALIZABILITY

What about the generalizability of results from studies that vary in other characteristics that have been the target of criticism? Space limitations make it impossible to consider other factors in the same detail that we have examined juror type, but we will discuss briefly some of the conclusions drawn in the previously mentioned reviews of methodological issues in jury decision-making studies (e.g., Bornstein, 1999; Nietzel et al., 1999) and in newer meta-analyses.

METHODS OF TRIAL PRESENTATION

Do methods of trial presentation produce main-effect differences or interact with (i.e., moderate) the effects of substantive variables examined in jury research? Bornstein (1999) reported that 3 of 11 studies comparing methods of trial presentation yielded significant main-effect differences in criminal conviction rates, but the differences did not display a consistent pattern (two went in one direction and the third in the other direction). Only one of the 11 studies yielded a trial-mode interaction with another variable: a manipulation of the number of character witnesses in a trial influenced verdicts when the trial was presented in video format but not when the trial transcript was read to jurors (Borgida, 1979).

Nietzel et al. (1999) also compared effect sizes across presentation methods and found some noteworthy differences. More realistic forms of presentation appear to weaken the relationship between death penalty attitudes and juror verdicts; the effect sizes for real trials and written transcripts ($r = .10$) were smaller than for videotaped presentations ($r = .16$), audiotaped presentations ($r = .34$), and questionnaires ($r = .16$). For studies of jury instruction, videotapes yielded larger effects than did transcripts in three of four instances. However, there was no consistent pattern for studies of expert testimony. Audiotaped and written presentations yielded larger effect sizes ($r = .21$) than did live simulations ($r = .17$) or videotapes ($r = .13$). Nietzel et al. concluded that more complex stimulus materials might reduce the relationship between death penalty attitudes and juror judgments.

JURY DELIBERATIONS

Does deliberation moderate the effects of substantive variables on jury verdicts? One might imagine that pretrial publicity could influence individual juror judgments but that as a result of careful consideration of trial evidence during deliberation, pretrial publicity effects are reduced or eliminated. Perhaps the bias engendered in some individuals is offset by different biases engendered in other jurors or, as a result of considering the trial evidence, the non-evidentiary issues raised in pretrial publicity fade in relevance and importance. Obviously one can generate other explanations for the possible moderating effects of deliberation on substantive variables (interactions between deliberating or not deliberating and substantive variables).

Although Bornstein (1999) did not consider deliberation effects in his paper, Nietzel et al. (1999) did. They report that the magnitude of the relationship between death penalty attitudes and verdicts was roughly comparable in studies that used deliberations ($r = .15$) and in those that did not ($r = .17$). Within studies that manipulated some aspect of jury instructions, there were slightly smaller effects (on jury decisions) for studies that did not include deliberations, with unweighted averages of $r = .11$ for studies without deliberation versus $r = .14$ for those with deliberation (Nietzel et al., 1999). The average effect of expert testimony did not differ as a function of deliberation ($r = .16$ without and $r = .15$ with deliberation). In studies examining the effects of joining (or not joining) multiple charges against a defendant into a single trial, deliberation increased the impact of joinder on verdicts ($r = .33$ with deliberation and $r = .25$ without deliberation). In short, the pattern of moderating effects for deliberation was not consistent.

These findings are consistent with the pattern of findings from studies assessing the attitude–verdict relationship among impaneled jurors (Moran & Comfort, 1982, 1986). These studies gathered pre-deliberation verdicts from individuals who had served on felony juries as well as the verdict reached by the jury. In the first study (Moran & Comfort, 1982), the correlation between the pre-deliberation verdict and attitude was $r = .11$. The correlation between the jury verdict and juror attitude was much lower—$r = .00$. This pattern was repeated in the second study with a pre-deliberation attitude–verdict correlation of .11 and a juror attitude–jury verdict correlation of -.05. These results suggest that deliberation (or the reliance on a group judgment that might be reached with little or no deliberation) weakens the predictive value of pre-deliberation attitudes.

ALTERNATIVE RESEARCH METHODS

Although our emphasis in this chapter has been on the generalizability of jury studies, which are predominantly laboratory experiments, it is important to note that there are alternative methods that carry research out of the laboratory and closer to (maybe even amidst) real jurors and real cases.

ARCHIVAL STUDIES

Archival studies involve the use of existing records to address research questions. Vidmar (2008) reviewed a number of archival studies, arguing that such studies reflect actual decision making by actual juries and can often yield a richness of detail about jury decision making across a range of cases that cannot be obtained in laboratory simulations of jury decision making. The method (and its weaknesses) can be illustrated with a few examples. Lempert (1993) examined reports of 12 complex trials including toxic torts involving injuries to large numbers of people, conspiracy and antitrust cases, stock fraud, sexual harassment claims, contracts, and improper disclosure of trade secrets. Lempert concluded in two cases—one a patent case with technical evidence and a second with epidemiological and geological evidence—that the cases were so complex that neither juries nor judges were likely to have understood them. Because of these complexities, Lempert thought it desirable to consider alternative ways to decide the cases. In the other cases, Lempert thought that the evidence was simple enough that jurors could decide the cases intelligently. Of course, 12 cases is hardly the universe of cases and these 12 may not represent a fair sampling (even of complex cases); thus, it is difficult to generalize to the universe of complex cases from this small sample.

Eisenberg and his colleagues (2005, 2006) have reported a number of studies in which they used archival data to compare criminal case verdicts and punitive damages awards made by juries versus those made by judges. The issue of whether judges and juries decide cases differently is a matter of longstanding debate. In the Kalven and Zeisel (1996) study mentioned at the outset of this chapter, the researchers compared judges' decisions with jury decisions by asking hundreds of judges to indicate whether they would have decided cases differently as compared with the decisions actually made by jurors. The Kalven and Zeisel method makes it possible to compare decisions in the same cases. However, when one relies on archival records, including some cases decided by juries and others decided by judges, the comparison may well be one of "apples and oranges." In actual cases where one of the parties can exercise some discretion about whether the case will be tried by a judge or a jury, it is possible the cases that go to judges and those that go to juries may differ, so these studies require substantial efforts to statistically control for those differences (called "selection effects"). After such controls are applied, these studies indicate that judges and juries produce fairly similar awards.

FIELD EXPERIMENTS

An alternative approach to the study of juries is the use of field experiments. As with laboratory experiments, there is an element of random assignment in field experiments—actual cases are randomly assigned to different experimental (or "treatment") conditions and the verdicts or other outcome variables of interest may be compared as a function of the treatment conditions. Of course, random assignment of real "cases" is quite a routine phenomenon in a discipline such as medicine, where researchers are interested in the effects of new versus old medicines or medical procedures. Although medicine is far ahead of the law in the use of sound experimental methods, in some instances courts have agreed to undertake random assignment of cases to experimental conditions. Heuer and Penrod (1989, 1994) persuaded judges in Wisconsin (1989) and nationally (1994) to undertake random assignment of cases to conditions in which jurors were permitted to ask questions of witnesses (or not, with "not" being the standard procedure) and were permitted to take notes during trial (or not, with "not" being the traditional practice). At the conclusion of these trials (67 cases in Wisconsin and 160 in the national study), jurors, judges, and attorneys completed questionnaires relating to many aspects of the trials, in particular about the manipulated variables. Despite many concerns raised by critics of juror questions and note taking, the procedures proved quite innocuous, and their use has been growing around the country (only partly as a result of the research findings).

Of course, there are many advantages to randomly assigning actual cases to treatment conditions. Because the cases are actual cases being decided by actual jurors, some of the concerns that have been the focal point of this chapter are reduced or eliminated; the cases are real, the jurors are real, the procedures are complete, there is deliberation, and the jurors' decisions have real consequences. In short, any issues of generalization are dramatically reduced (though not necessarily eliminated—do results from Wisconsin generalize to Texas?). The downside of attempting random assignment of cases to alternative treatments is a concern among judges, who fear that the treatments might affect outcomes (if that logic prevailed in medicine, we might still be subjected to bloodletting as a cure for many ills!). Arguably, whenever there is a serious choice to be make about alternative procedures or legal rules that may have an impact on trial outcomes, the best way to resolve the issue is with sound experimental study.

Returning for a moment to the Heuer and Penrod experiments, we would note that among the measures collected in the national study were judge and jury verdicts, which were in agreement at about the same rates as reported by others (Hannaford, Hans, & Munsterman, 2000; Kalven & Zeisel, 1966). This convergence of results from studies using different research methods heightens our confidence in the reliability of the findings. Heuer and Penrod also collected measures of case complexity, which permitted them to assess the impact that multiple aspects of complexity (evidence complexity, legal complexity, and quantity of information) had on juries in both criminal and civil cases. Among the advantages of the study were that data were available on a large number of cases that varied greatly in complexity, and both judge and jury perceptions of complexity (together with objective measures of complexity) were assessed.

Analyses showed that none of the complexity components was significantly related to judge–jury agreement rates. The different components had different effects on jurors' assessment of the trial, but none affected judge or juror satisfaction. Juror questions appeared to assist jurors in coping with legal and evidence complexity. Other researchers have examined juror note-taking in jury simulation studies (ForsterLee & Horowitz, 1997; ForsterLee, Horowitz, & Bourgeois, 1994; Rosenhan, Eisner, & Robinson,

1994). These studies have confirmed and significantly extended the findings from Heuer and Penrod's field experiments—in part, because it is possible to do things in mock jury experiments that prove very difficult in actual cases. These include tests of memory for case facts and legal instructions: There can be identical evidence and law to remember across juries in a simulation experiment, but the evidence and the law to be remembered will naturally vary across actual trials.

SOME FINAL NOTES

As we hope has become clear from our discussion of jury research methods and our review of research on the impact of methods on the generalizability of jury simulation experiments, we are strong advocates of those simulation methods. We prefer simulation methods because they give us much greater control over what our research participants experience, which means we can have much greater confidence that differences in verdicts or other aspects of jury performance actually flow from our experimental manipulations. As we have noted, simulation studies are much less expensive and cumbersome to run as compared with field experiments and, frankly, field experimentation is extremely difficult in an environment where the actors who control the system are much less hospitable to experimentation than in a discipline such as medicine.

Until the law becomes a truly experimental discipline, we are reassured by two major factors that our simulation methods are providing us with sound results. First, as we have seen in this chapter, our results appear to generalize well across research methods. Second, experience to date indicates that alternative methods such as archival research and field experiments yield findings that converge with those from simulation studies. Although we clearly prefer experimental methods to nonexperimental methods (partly because random assignment reduces or eliminates selection effects that plague methods such as archival research), we certainly acknowledge that alternative methods have an important place in jury research, and we encourage researchers to bring a wide range of methods to bear on the jury questions that interest all of us.

REFERENCES

Allen, M., Mabry, E., & McKelton, D. M. (1998). Impact of juror attitudes about the death penalty on juror evaluations of guilt and punishment: A meta-analysis. *Law and Human Behavior, 22,* 715–731. doi: 10.1023/A:1025763008533

Borgida, E. (1979). Character proof and the fireside induction. *Law and Human Behavior, 3,* 189–202. doi: 10.1007/BF01039790

Bornstein, B. H. (1999). The ecological validity of jury simulations: Is the jury still out? *Law and Human Behavior, 23,* 75–91. doi: 10.1023/A:1022326807441

Bornstein, B. H., & Rajki, M. (1994). Extralegal factors and product liability: The influence of mock jurors' demographic characteristics and intuitions about the cause of an injury. *Behavioral Sciences and* the Law, 12, 127–147. doi: 10.1002/bsl.2370120204

Bothwell, R. K., Pigott, M. A., Foley, L. A., & McFatter, R. M. (2006). Racial bias in juridic judgment at private and public levels. *Journal of Applied Social Psychology*, 36, 2134–2149. doi: 10.1111/j.0021-9029.2006.00098.x

Bray, R. M., & Kerr, N. L. (1979). Use of the simulation method in the study of jury behavior: Some methodological considerations. *Law and Human Behavior*, 3, 107–119. doi: 10.1007/BF01039151

Bray, R. M., & Kerr, N. L. (1982). Methodological considerations in the study of the psychology of the courtroom. In N. L. Kerr & R. M. Bray (Eds.), *The psychology of the courtroom* (pp. 287–323). New York, NY: Academic Press.

Brekke, N., & Borgida, E. (1988). Expert psychological testimony in rape trials: A social cognitive analysis. *Journal of Personality and Social Psychology*, 55, 372–386. doi: 10.1037/0022–3514.55.3.372

Brewer, M. (2000). Research design and issues of validity. In H. Reis & C. Judd (Eds.), *Handbook of research methods in social and personality psychology* (pp. 3–16). Cambridge, England: Cambridge University Press.

Broeder, D. W. (1958). The University of Chicago jury project. *Nebraska Law Review*, 88, 744–760.

Burtt, H. E., & Dobell, E. M. (1925). The curve of forgetting for advertising material. *Journal of Applied Psychology*, 9, 5–21.

Burtt, M. (1931). *Legal psychology*. Englewood Cliffs, NJ: Prentice-Hall.

Cowan, C. L., Thompson, W. C., & Ellsworth, P. C. (1984). The effects of death qualification on jurors' predisposition to convict and on the quality of deliberation. *Law and Human Behavior*, 8, 53–79. doi: 10.1007/BF01044351

Cutler, B. L., Penrod, S. D., & Dexter, H. R. (1990). Juror sensitivity to eyewitness identification evidence. *Law and Human Behavior*, 14, 185–191. doi: 10.1007/BF01062972

Eisenberg, T., Hannaford-Agor, P. L., Hans, V. P., Waters, N. L., Munsterman, G. T., Schwab, S. J., & Wells, M. T. (2005). Judge-jury agreement in criminal cases: A partial replication of Kalven and Zeisel's The American Jury. *Journal of Empirical Legal Studies*, 2, 171–207. DOI: 10.1111/j.1740-1461. 2005.00035.x

Eisenberg, T., Hannaford-Agor, P. L., Heise, M., LaFountain, N., Munsterman, G. T.,

Ostrom, B., & Wells, M. T. (2006). Juries, judges, and punitive damages: Empirical analyses using the civil justice survey of state courts, 1992, 1996, and 2001 data. *Journal of Empirical Legal Studies*, 3, 263–295. doi: 10.1111/j. 1740-1461.2006.00070.x

Elwork, A., Sales, B. D., & Alfini, J. (1977). Juridic decisions: In ignorance of the law or in light of it? *Law and Human Behavior*, 1, 163–189. doi: 10.1007/BF01053437

Finkel, N., & Duff, K. B. (1991). Felony-murder and community sentiment: Testing the Supreme Court's assertions. *Law and Human Behavior*, 15, 405–429. doi: 10.1007/BF02074079

Finkel, N. J., & Handel, S. F. (1989). How jurors construe "insanity." *Law and Human Behavior*, 13, 41–59. doi: 10.1007/BF01056162

Finkel, N. J., Hughes, K. C., Smith, S. F., & Hurabiell, M. L. (1994). Killing kids: The juvenile death penalty and community sentiment. *Behavioral Sciences and the Law*, 12, 5–20. doi: 10.1002/bsl.2370120103

Finkel, N. J., Hurabiell, M. L., & Hughes, K. C. (1993a). Compentency, and other constructs, in right to die cases. *Behavioral Sciences & the Law*, 11, 135–150. doi: 10.1002/bsl.2370110106

Finkel, N. J., Hurabiell, M. L., & Hughes, K. C. (1993b). Right to die, euthanasia, and community sentiment: Crossing the public/private boundary. *Law and Human Behavior*, 17, 487–506. doi: 10.1007/BF01045070

Finkel, N. J., Meister, K. H., & Lightfoot, D. M. (1991). The self-defense defense and community sentiment. *Law and Human Behavior*, 15, 585–602. doi: 10.1007/BF01065854

Finkel, N. J., Shaw, R., Bercaw, S., & Koch, J. (1985). Insanity defenses: From the jurors' perspective. *Law and Psychology Review*, 9, 77–92. doi: 1986-09032-001

ForsterLee, L., & Horowitz, I. A. (1997). Enhancing juror competence in a complex trial. *Applied Cognitive Psychology*, 11, 305–319. doi: 10.1002/(SICI)1099-0720(199708)11:4<305::AID-ACP457>3.0.CO;2-J

ForsterLee, L., Horowitz, I. A., & Bourgeois, M. (1994). Effects of notetaking on verdicts and evidence processing in a civil trial. *Law and Human Behavior*, 18, 567–578. doi: 10.1007/BF01499175

Fulero, S. M., & Finkel, N. J. (1991). Barring ultimate issue testimony: An "insane" rule? *Law and Human Behavior*, 15, 495–507. doi: 10.1007/BF01650291

Fulero, S. M., & Penrod, S. D. (1990). Attorney jury selection folklore: What do they think and how can psychologists help? *Forensic Reports*, *3*, 233–259.

Gerbasi, K. C., Zuckerman, M., & Reis, H. T. (1977). Justice needs a new blindfold: A review of mock jury research. *Psychological Bulletin*, *84*, 323–345. doi: 10.1037/0033-2909.84.2.323

Hannaford, P. L., Hans, V. P., & Munsterman, G. T. (2000). Permitting jury discussions during trial: Impact of the Arizona reform. *Law and Human Behavior*, *24*, 359–382. doi: 10.1023/A:1005540305832

Hastie, R., Penrod, S. D., & Pennington, N. (1983). *Inside the jury*. Cambridge, MA: Harvard University Press.

Hepburn, J. R. (1980). The objective reality of evidence and the utility of systematic jury selection. *Law and Human Behavior*, *4*, 89–101. doi: 10.1007/BF01040485

Heuer, L., & Penrod, S. D. (1989). Instructing jurors: A field experiment with written and preliminary instructions. *Law and Human Behavior*, *13*, 409–430. doi: 10.1007/BF01056412

Heuer, L., & Penrod, S. D. (1994). Juror note-taking and question asking during trials: A national field experiment. *Law and Human Behavior*, *18*, 121–150. doi: 10.1007/BF01499012

Higgins, P. L., Heath, W. P., & Grannemann, B. D. (2007). How type of excuse defense, mock juror age, and defendant age affect mock jurors' decisions. *The Journal of Social Psychology*, *147*, 371–392. doi: 10.3200/SOCP.147.4.371-392

Hutchins, R. M., & Slesinger, D. (1928). Some observations on the law of evidence: Memory. *Harvard Law Review*, *41*, 860–873.

Hutchins, R. M., & Slesinger, D. (1929a). Legal psychology. *Psychological Review*, *36*, 13–26. doi: 10.1037/h0069902

Hutchins, R. M., & Slesinger, D. (1929b). Some observations on the law of evidence: Consciousness of guilt. *University of Pennsylvania Law Review*, *77*, 1–16.

James, R. M. (1959). Status and competence of jurors. *American Journal of Sociology*, *64*, 563–570.

Kagehiro, D. K., & Stanton, W. C. (1985). Legal vs. quantified definitions of standards of proof. *Law and Human Behavior*, *9*, 159–178. doi: 10.1007/BF01067049

Kalven, H., Jr., & Zeisel, H. (1966). *The American jury*. Boston, MA: Little, Brown.

Kovera, M. B., Gresham, A. W., Borgida, E., Gray, E., & Regan, P. C. (1997). Does expert psychological testimony inform or influence juror decision making? A social cognitive analysis. *Journal of Applied Psychology*, *82*, 178–191. doi: 10.1037/0021-9010.82.1.178

Kovera, M. B., Levy, R. J., Borgida, E., & Penrod, S. D. (1994). Expert testimony in child sexual abuse cases: Effects of expert evidence type and cross-examination. *Law and Human Behavior*, *18*, 653–674. doi: 10.1007/BF01499330

Lempert, R. O. (1993). Civil juries and complex cases: Taking stock after twelve years. In R. E. Litan (Ed.), *Verdict* (pp. 181–247). Washington, DC: Brookings Institution.

MacCoun, R. J., & Kerr, N. L. (1988). Asymmetric influence in mock jury deliberation: Jurors' bias for leniency. *Journal of Personality and Social Psychology*, *54*, 21–33. doi: 10.1037/0022-3514.54.1.21

Mazzella, R., & Feingold, A. (1994). The effects of physical attractiveness, race, socioeconomic status, and gender of defendants and victims on judgments of mock jurors: A meta-analysis. *Journal of Applied Social Psychology*, *24*, 1315–1344. doi: 10.1111/j.1559-1816.1994.tb01552.x

Mills, C. J., & Bohannon, W. E. (1980). Juror characteristics: To what extent are they related to jury verdicts? *Judicature*, *64*, 22–31.

Mitchell, T. L., Haw, R. M., Pfeifer, J. E., & Meissner, C. A. (2005). Racial bias in mock juror decision-making: A meta-analytic review of defendant treatment. *Law and Human Behavior*, *29*, 621–637. doi: 10.1007/s10979-005-8122-9

Moran, G., & Comfort, J. C. (1982). Scientific juror selection: Sex as a moderator of demographic and personality predictors of impaneled felony jury behavior. *Journal of Personality and Social Psychology*, *41*, 1052–1063. doi: 10.1037/0022-3514.43.5.1052

Moran, G., & Comfort, J. C. (1986). Neither "tentative" nor "fragmentary": Verdict preference of impaneled felony jurors as a function of attitude toward capital punishment. *Journal of Applied Psychology*, *71*, 146–155. doi: 10.1037/0021-9010.71.1.146

Narby, D. J., Cutler, B. L., & Moran, G. (1993). A meta-analysis of the association between authoritarianism and jurors' perceptions of defendant culpability. *Journal of Applied Psychology*, *78*, 34–42. doi: 10.1037/0021-9010.78.1.34

Nietzel, M. T., McCarthy, D. M., & Kern, M. J. (1999). Juries: The current state of the empirical literature. In R. Roesch, S. D. Hart, & J. R. P. Ogloff, (Eds.), *Psychology and law: The state of the discipline* (pp. 23–52). Dordrecht, Netherlands: Kluwer.

O'Neil, K. M., Patry, M. W., & Penrod, S. D. (2004). Exploring the effects of attitudes toward the death penalty on capital sentencing verdicts. *Psychology, Public Policy and Law*, *10*, 443–470. doi: 10.1037/1076-8971.10.4.443

Padawer-Singer, A., & Barton, A. H. (1975). Free press, fair trial. In R. J. Simon (Ed.), *The jury system in America* (pp. 123–139). Beverly Hills, CA: Sage.

Paynter, R. H. (1919). A psychological investigation of the likelihood of confusion between the words "Coca-Cola" and "Chero Cola." *Journal of Applied Psychology*, *3*, 329–351. doi: 10.1037/h0073713

Penrod, S. D. (1979). *Study of attorney and scientific jury selection models* (Doctoral dissertation). Harvard University, Cambridge, MA.

Penrod, S. D., & Hastie, R. (1979). Models of jury decision making: A critical review. *Psychological Bulletin*, *86*, 462–492. doi: 10.1037/0033-2909.86.3.462

Penrod, S. D., & Hastie, R. (1980). A computer simulation of jury decision making. *Psychological Review*, *87*, 133–159. doi: 10.1037/0033-295X.87.2.133

Pyszczynksi, T. A., Greenberg, J., Mack, D., & Wrightsman, L. S. (1981). Opening statements in a jury trial: The effect of promising more than the evidence can show. *Journal of Applied Social Psychology*, *11*, 434–444. doi: 10.1111/j.1559-1816.1981.tb00834.x

Reed, J. P. (1965). Jury deliberation, voting and verdict trends. *Southwestern Social Science Quarterly*, *45*, 361–374.

Rosenhan, D. L., Eisner, S. L., & Robinson, R. J. (1994). Notetaking can aid juror recall. *Law and Human Behavior*, *18*, 53–61. doi: 10.1007/BF01499143

Saks, M. J. (1976). The limits of scientific jury selection: Ethical and empirical. *Jurimetrics*, *3*, 3–22.

Saks, M. J., & Marti, M. W. (1997). A meta-analysis of the effects of jury size. *Law and Human Behavior*, *21*, 451–467. doi: 10.1023/A:1024819605652

Sales, B. D., Elwork, A., & Alfini, J. (1977). Improving comprehension for jury instructions. In B. D. Sales (Ed.), *The criminal justice system* (pp. 23–90). New York, NY: Plenum Press.

Schutte, J. W., & Hosch, H. M. (1997). Gender differences in sexual assault verdicts: A meta-analysis. *Journal of Social Behavior and Personality*, *12*, 759–772.

Sears, D. O. (1986). College sophomores in the laboratory: Influences of a narrow data base on social psychology's view of human nature. *Journal of Personality and Social Psychology*, *51*, 515–530. doi: 10.1037/0022-3514.51.3.515

Sigall, H., & Landy, D. (1972). Effects of the defendant's character and suffering on juridic judgment: A replication and clarification. *The Journal of Social Psychology*, *88*, 149–150.

Simon, R. J. (1967). *The jury and the defense of insanity*. Boston, MA: Little, Brown.

Steblay, N. M., Besirevic, J., Fulero, S. M., & Jimenez-Lorente, B. (1999). The effects of pretrial publicity on juror verdicts: A meta-analytic review. *Law and Human Behavior*, *23*, 219–235. doi: 10.1023/A:1022325019080

Steblay, N., Hosch, H. M., Culhane, S. E., & McWethy, A. (2006). The impact on juror verdicts of judicial instruction to disregard inadmissible evidence: A meta-analysis. *Law and Human Behavior*, *30*, 469–492. doi: 10.1007/s10979-006-9039-7

Strodtbeck, F. L., James, R. M., & Hawkins, C. (1957). Social status in jury deliberations. *American Sociological Review*, *22*, 713–719. doi: 10.2307/2089202

Strodtbeck, F. L., & Mann, R. D. (1956). Sex role differentiation in jury deliberations. *Sociometry*, *19*, 3–11.

Sweeney, L. T., & Haney, C. (1992). The influence of race on sentencing: A meta-analytic review of experimental studies. *Behavioral Sciences and the Law*, *10*, 179–195.

Thompson, W. C., Cowan, C. L., Ellsworth, P. C., & Harrington, J. C. (1984). Death penalty attitudes and conviction proneness: The translation of attitudes into verdicts. *Law and Human Behavior*, *8*, 95–113. doi: 10.1007/BF01044353

Vidmar, N. (2008). Civil juries in ecological context: Methodological implications for research. In B. H. Bornstein, R. L. Wiener, R. Schopp, & S. L. Willborn (Eds.), *Civil juries and civil justice: Psychological and legal perspectives* (pp. 35–65). New York, NY: Springer Science+Business Media.

Weiten, W., & Diamond, S. S. (1979). A critical review of the jury simulation paradigm: The case of defendant characteristics. *Law and Human Behavior, 3,* 71–93. doi: 10.1007/BF01039149

Wells, G. L., & Leippe, M. R. (1981). How do triers of fact infer the accuracy of eyewitness identifications? Using memory for peripheral detail can be misleading. *Journal of Applied Psychology, 66,* 682–687. doi: 10.1037/0021-9010.66.6.682

CHAPTER 12

Trial Consulting in High-Publicity Cases

LISA SPANO, TARIKA DAFTARY-KAPUR, AND STEVEN D. PENROD

INTRODUCTION AND HISTORY OF THE TRIAL-CONSULTING INDUSTRY

The field of trial consulting has a relatively short history as compared with other areas of the legal field. Before jury selection commenced on September 24, 1994, in the O. J. Simpson criminal trial, very few people were familiar with this once obscure field. During the past 16 years, however, the trial-consulting industry has grown significantly, and it shows no signs of slowing down in the future. While the terms "trial consultant" and "jury consultant" were popular topics of discussion by the media during the O. J. Simpson criminal trial, more people became aware of the industry in 2003 following the release of the movie *Runaway Jury* (based on John Grisham's novel *The Runaway Jury*). In this film, trial consultant Rankin Fitch, played by Gene Hackman, was portrayed as a villain who worked with the defense team by manipulating the jury selection process and using illegal tactics to assist his corporate gun manufacturer client during the trial. Although the movie is unrealistic in terms of how trial consultants conduct jury research, work with attorneys on trial strategy, and assist the team during jury selection, statements made by Gene Hackman's character such as "I hate Baptists as much as I hate Democrats!" are not too far off the reality and demonstrate one key goal consultants have in common: to identify jurors who are likely to hold strongly biased opinions against their client.

The first documented instance of scientific jury selection used in the courts occurred in 1972 when the United States unsuccessfully prosecuted the Harrisburg Seven, a group of religious antiwar activists charged with a variety of crimes during the Vietnam War era, including allegedly blowing up tunnels in Washington, DC and conspiring with others to destroy draft records. During that highly publicized trial, a group of social scientists who advocated antiwar activities volunteered to assist the defense with jury selection. To identify those individuals who would potentially favor conviction, the research team conducted a survey of more than 1,000 people in the trial venue.

As part of the survey, the researchers asked participants about their beliefs related to key case-specific issues, including religion, education, war resistance, and the U.S. government. Once the researchers collected the data they conducted statistical analysis to develop profiles of jurors who were likely to be pro-prosecution (i.e., jurors who were religious, held college degrees, and read the *Reader's Digest*) and pro-defense (i.e., females and those who held liberal political beliefs) (Hutson, 2007). During jury selection, the research team used these profiles to assist in de-deselecting those jurors, via peremptory challenge, who would lean towards the government in favor of conviction. Given that pre-trial community surveys suggested that 8 out of 10 registered voters held views unfavorable to the defense, many were shocked upon learning that the trial resulted in a hung jury on most charges and one insignificant conviction (for smuggling letters out of prison) (N. J. Kressel & Kressel, 2002).

Following the Harrisburg Seven trial, other social scientists across the country assisted attorneys during various civil and criminal trials, and the birth of scientific jury selection was marked. In 1975 the legal team defending an African American woman named Joan Little, accused of murdering a white prison guard at Beaufort County Jail in North Carolina, hired a group of social scientists to assist them in conducting research to support a change of venue motion and to help during the jury-selection phase of the trial. Based on survey results, the consultants assisting the defense developed a profile of jurors likely to be unsympathetic to Little's self-defense claim. After nearly one hour of deliberations, Little was acquitted on all criminal charges (N. J. Kressel & Kressel, 2002).

Throughout the 1970s, attorneys working on several high-profile cases caught onto the emerging trend of hiring trial consultants, and many of these trials ended favorably for their clients (Frederick, 1984). Today, it is unusual for an attorney working on a high-stakes case to go to trial without hiring a trial consultant (or a team of trial consultants). This holds true for both civil and criminal cases. In 1999, trial consulting was estimated to be a $400 million industry, with over 400 firms nationwide and over 700 practicing consultants (Strier, 1999). It is likely that these numbers have significantly increased since this time.

HOW DOES ONE BECOME A TRIAL CONSULTANT?

Trial consultants across the country come from various backgrounds, from the social sciences to theater. While many consultants hold doctoral, or master's degrees, some have law degrees, and others enter the field with a bachelor's degree and work their way up to the consultant level. At many of the well-known and well-established law firms, consultants are likely to have advanced degrees in psychology, sociology, or communications. Even though these degrees are not prerequisites for becoming a trial consultant, individuals with a solid educational background in the social sciences enter the field with a more in-depth understanding of the empirical research techniques that are often used to help trial attorneys prepare for their cases, as compared with their counterparts who come from other backgrounds.

Although there are no standards or guidelines that regulate the field of trial consulting, the American Society of Trial Consultants (ASTC) is the professional organization for the industry. The members of ASTC have developed ethical standards along with a professional code; however, as noted on the ASTC Web site, these standards are currently "evolving."[1]

GOALS OF A TRIAL CONSULTANT

Attorneys hire trial consultants to assist their legal team in a variety of areas for civil and criminal matters in both federal and state courts. Those not familiar with the services a consultant provides may recall movies such as *Runaway Jury* or the consultants who worked on the O. J. Simpson criminal trial and incorrectly infer that the primary goal of a consultant is to help attorneys during the jury-selection phase of trial. Advice on jury selection is an important service consultants provide to attorneys, however, the range of services consultants offer is much more comprehensive and spans all phases of a trial, from the discovery phase through the post-trial phase. Trial consulting services can include witness preparation, pre-trial preparation and testing of evidence, demonstratives, arguments, and jury selection based on pre-trial surveys and nonverbal behavior of prospective jurors. Consultants not only provide expert assistance during jury trials but often assist attorneys with bench trials, mediations, and arbitrations.

There are several book-length treatments of the many aspects of trial consulting (N. J. Kressel & Kressel, 2002; Lieberman & Sales, 2007; Posey & Wrightsman, 2005), and space does not permit us to undertake a broad consideration of trial consulting. Rather, in the sections that follow we will draw on our own area of expertise and focus on some of the past and present techniques and research methods used to study the effects of pre-trial publicity (PTP) on jurors' decision making. Specifically, we focus on PTP research conducted in the laboratory and in real-world settings. We begin by considering leading cases from the 1960s and 1970s, which established the most important legal precedents governing legal responses to PTP along with more recent cases in which PTP has posed challenges to the courts. We then examine empirical research that demonstrates the nature and extent of PTP effects, drawing on experimental studies, community attitudes, change of

---

1. http://www.astcweb.org/public/article.cfm/astc-professional-code

venue surveys, and content analysis of PTP. Finally, we examine the combinations of research methods that make the most compelling case for the general biasing effects of PTP.

HOW DOES PTP INFLUENCE JURORS' DECISION MAKING?

Empirical research conducted during the past 50 years demonstrates that pretrial publicity (PTP) has the potential to negatively influence jurors' perceptions of parties in criminal and civil cases that have received substantial media coverage. Changes in the news media over the years have made news coverage more accessible to the public; consequently, the challenges surrounding PTP and a defendant's right to a fair trial have steadily increased. For example, up-to-date news coverage is readily accessible to the public; 24-hour news networks such as CNN and MSNBC as well as local 24-hour news stations are watched by large portions of the public. In addition, cable network channels such as Court TV are dedicated to coverage of the judicial system and high-profile trials. Similarly, national news magazines such as *Time* or *Newsweek* often report on highly publicized cases as do many radio talk shows aired across the country, and online news sources such as *Google* and *Yahoo* enable Internet users to locate up-to-date and detailed news reports on criminal and civil trials. Furthermore, growing numbers of people use online newspapers, which complement printed newspapers with more detailed and updated information. Finally, social networking Web sites such as Facebook, Twitter, and MySpace pose additional challenges, as do personal blog pages on the Internet.

HISTORY OF PTP AND THE AMERICAN JUDICIAL SYSTEM

The American judicial system has struggled with problems associated with PTP for nearly two centuries, and complications continue to exist. The first documented case involving PTP arose in 1807, when the former vice president of the United States, Aaron Burr, was arrested on charges of treason against his country. Just prior to his trial, Burr's attorneys argued that the public had been so influenced by prejudicial statements made against him that the likelihood of finding an impartial jury was highly improbable. Given the impact of the negative publicity surrounding Aaron Burr, Chief Justice Marshall disqualified any individual who had expressed a positive opinion on any "essential" element of the crime. However, he also ruled that a juror would not be disqualified for simply having been exposed to a substantial amount of information about the case, for simply reading a news article about Burr's trial, or for having opinions on issues other than those which were "essential" elements of the trial (Abramson, 2000).

In the 1960s and 1970s, a series of Supreme Court cases involving high levels of publicity were decided. These decisions paved the way to more stringent guidelines, which directly addressed the problems associated with

PTP. In *Irvin v. Dowd* (1961), the Court ruled that defendant's motion for a change of venue should be granted if a defendant's right to a fair trial by an impartial jury would be jeopardized by the negative impact of PTP, as demonstrated during the voir dire process. A few years later, in *Rideau v. Louisiana* (1963), the Court concluded that due process required a change of venue when highly prejudicial PTP—as determined by the substance, quantity, and distribution of that PTP to potential jury members—created an inherently prejudicial atmosphere. Similarly, the Court in *Murphy v. Florida* (1975) found that a defendant could challenge the court's denial of a change of venue when and if, during individual voir dire, potential jury members exhibited "actual" or "inherent prejudice" as a result of PTP. Today's criminal courts adhere to this "totality of circumstances" test by placing the burden on the defendant to prove that potential jurors hold preconceived opinions about the guilt of a defendant, which would preclude the possibility of a fair trial. Finally, in the case of *Sheppard v. Maxwell* (1966), the Court reversed the conviction of Dr. Sam Sheppard as a result of massive inflammatory media accounts of this case.

Of course, one can readily find a vast number of contemporary cases that illustrate PTP problems. In connection with the Enron scandal, the defense attorneys unsuccessfully tried several times to move the criminal trials from Houston to a less-biased venue due to extensive negative pretrial publicity about the defendants charged with fraud (Flood, 2004). Other defendants whose cases have dominated the U.S. media for many months include Scott Peterson, who was convicted for murdering his wife and their unborn son; Andrea Yates, who drowned her five young children in the bathtub in her house. Yates's 2002 conviction of capital murder and sentence to life in prison was later overturned on appeal, and in 2006, a Texas jury determined that Yates was not guilty by reason of insanity. Other examples include Mary Winkler, who was convicted of voluntary manslaughter for killing her minister husband in 2006; Phil Spector, who was convicted in a second trial for the second-degree murder of actress Lana Clarkson (the first trial resulted in a mistrial when the jury was deadlocked 10 for guilty and 2 for not guilty); and O.J Simpson for the 2008 Las Vegas robbery case.

EXPERIMENTAL STUDIES OF PTP EFFECTS IN CRIMINAL AND CIVIL CASES

Laboratory and experimental methods are commonly used by social scientists to assess the effects of PTP on juror perceptions of defendant guilt, corporate liability, and verdict outcome. Depending on budgetary constraints, participants are typically either college students or potential jurors from the community. In experimental studies, participants are randomly assigned to receive various levels and types of PTP before making decisions about the case and about the defendant. All other aspects of the trial are held constant, giving the researchers control over what is presented to the participants and allowing for causal interpretability. For example, researchers may present different types of PTP to mock jurors before presenting a trial simulation in the format of a written summary or in a video presentation. More complex research designs may incorporate attorney voir dire (pretrial questioning of prospective jurors), judicial instructions, and group deliberations. Researchers then perform statistical analyses to examine the effects of the manipulated PTP on such dependent measures as evidence evaluations, perceptions of witnesses, perceptions of the defendant, and final verdict decisions.

A number of social scientists have conducted experimental studies in the laboratory to assess whether PTP has the potential to influence the way jurors make decisions in both criminal and civil cases. Although a limited number of studies suggest that jurors are insensitive to PTP effects (Carroll et al., 1986), the majority of past research reveals that PTP biased against a defendant has the potential to influence juror perceptions of defendant likeability, sympathy towards the defendant, perceptions of defendant criminality, judgments of pre-trial guilt, and, most importantly, final verdicts (Studebaker & Penrod, 1997).

The first experimental study to investigate the effects of PTP on mock jurors' decision making in a criminal trial was conducted in 1966 by Tans and Chaffee. In their study, participants read fictitious newspaper articles about three diverse crimes. Each story contained different types of information, including positive or negative indication of a confession, information about the arrest or release of the suspect, and favorable or unfavorable statements made by the prosecuting attorney. After reading the fictitious stories, participants answered several dependent measures about the defendant, including a measure assessing defendant guilt. Participants were more likely to render guilty verdicts when they were presented with all three newspaper elements that were biased against the defendant. This suggested that jurors who are exposed to more negative information about a defendant prior to a trial are more likely to hold biased opinions against the defendant as compared to jurors who are exposed to less PTP.

Subsequent research on PTP effects has continued to produce analogous findings, particularly when participants are exposed to information about the defendant that may be inadmissible at trial, such as the defendant's character, prior criminal record, confession to the crime at issue, gang membership, and the results of a defendant's lie detector test. When participants learn about this inadmissible information, they are more likely to conclude the defendant was guilty as compared with participants who do not learn about this biasing information (DeLuca, 1979; Hvistendahl, 1979; Padawer-Singer & Barton, 1975; Otto, Penrod, & Dexter, 1994). Other research conducted on emotionally laden versus purely factual PTP indicates that emotionally laden PTP can produce a persistent bias against the defendant, over and above that produced by negative but non-emotional information (Kramer, Kerr, & Carroll, 1990).

The biasing effects of PTP are not limited to case-specific publicity: other research has suggested that even general PTP (prominent information found in the news but unrelated to a particular case) may significantly influence jurors' perceptions of a defendant and may bias decision-making processes. In a study conducted by Greene and Wade (1988), publicity about the wrongful conviction of a serial killer led to a decrease in guilty verdicts among participants who served as mock jurors in an ostensibly unrelated robbery and assault case. More recently, Kovera (2002) demonstrated that individuals exposed to a televised rape story biased towards the defense expected more incriminating evidence against the defendant before rendering a guilty verdict as compared with individuals who watched a pro-prosecution rape story.

Overall, there has been relatively little research published on PTP in civil cases. However, the research conducted in this area demonstrates that the PTP effects observed in criminal cases are likely to be present and robust in civil cases (Bornstein, Whisenhunt, & Nemeth, 2002; Kline & Jess, 1966; Otto, Penrod, & Hirt, 1991). In other words, exposure to negative information about a corporate defendant can bias the way a potential juror determines defendant liability.

Shortcomings Associated With Experimental Studies of PTP

Experimental studies are ideal insofar as they allow methodical variations in the amount and type of PTP presented to participants while controlling for extraneous variables. This control allows researchers to infer a cause and effect relationship, such as when the exposure to PTP caused more guilty verdicts. Experimental research also allows psychologists to investigate very specific phenomena of interest that might not be sufficiently isolated in the real world, such as whether the PTP is emotional or factual. However, one can argue that experimental conditions typically do not parallel what occurs before or during an actual trial; thus, there are various drawbacks to experimental research designs. Consequently, some have argued that the conclusions garnered from experimental studies are based on methodologies that do not accurately and completely reflect what occurs during a real trial (Horowitz & Willging, 1984; Van Dyke, 1971). The majority of past experimental research has relied on artificial PTP that has been rather abbreviated, the PTP exposure often having consisted of only one article.

Clearly, this type of exposure to PTP is unrealistic, especially given that in today's media reports concerning highly publicized trials, potential jurors are exposed to many articles and news reports about any given case. For example, in the case of Timothy McVeigh, within a few months there were approximately 1,000 articles about the Oklahoma bombing in Oklahoma City newspapers (Studebaker, Robbennolt, Pathak-Sharma, & Penrod, 2000). Other features of past research on PTP have prompted questions about the generalizability of experimental findings, including the use of unrealistic case presentations and the use of undergraduate mock jurors. Although past results do tap into the decision-making processes associated with PTP effects, the courts have sometimes been hesitant to rely on these data when handling PTP-related issues in their own cases. A clear example is found in language from Judge Richard Matsch, the district judge sitting by designation, in his venue-change opinion for the Timothy McVeigh trial when he expressed his concerns about psychological research "consisting largely of simulated trials" as opposed to his personal experiences as a trial lawyer and judge (*U.S. v. McVeigh*, 1996, p. 1473; http://www.lectlaw.com/files/cas72.htm).

COMMUNITY ATTITUDE SURVEYS

A second common method researchers use to assess PTP effects takes advantage of real-life cases. This type of study also has the benefit of using respondents who have been naturally (rather than experimentally) exposed to pre-trial media. Community attitude surveys are frequently used by trial consultants who are hired by legal teams to assist them with high-stakes cases. These surveys examine the link between case-specific attitudes and socio-demographic information and are especially helpful to a consultant when constructing profiles of potential jurors who are likely to favor one side over the other and to determine what types of individuals as jurors favor high versus low damages in civil litigation. Moreover, in extremely hostile venues it is likely the defense will propose to move the trial to a friendlier venue in which potential venirepersons are less likely to have biased opinions about a defendant as compared with potential jurors in the actual trial venue. A change of venue survey can be a particularly persuasive tool in these situations. Finally, survey research is valuable in helping trial consultants develop juror questionnaires and draft voir dire questions for their clients to use during jury selection.

Data from survey research parallel the findings provided from experimental PTP methods. Specifically, this type of research demonstrates that jury-eligible respondents who have been exposed to biasing information provided by the media about a trial are more likely to hold pro-prosecution attitudes and to pre-judge the defendant as guilty as compared with respondents who have not been exposed to the same types of negative PTP. (For a review of past survey research, see Arbuthnot, Myers, & Leach, 2002; Costantini & King, 1980-1981; Moran & Cutler, 1991; Nietzel & Dillehay, 1983; Simon & Eimermann, 1971; Vidmar, 2003.)

HOW DO TRIAL CONSULTANTS CONDUCT COMMUNITY ATTITUDE SURVEYS?

LENGTH OF THE INTERVIEW

Community attitude surveys are generally short interviews conducted by telephone, which last no longer than 10 to 15 minutes (Nietzel et al., 1999). With a survey that lasts longer than 15 minutes the likelihood of attrition

during the interview increases. Furthermore, it is difficult to sustain participant attention via telephone if the survey runs longer than 15 minutes.

Designing the Survey Instrument

When developing any survey it is important for a trial consultant to work
closely with the legal team and to understand the key arguments from both
sides' perspective. An understanding of the key claims is essential when
writing the survey questions, particularly if the survey's purpose is to
support a change of venue motion. Before the interviewer asks participants
key survey questions, they read a brief script to potential respondents. In this
script, the interviewer asks individuals whether they are willing to participate
in a public-opinion survey about the justice system. They also tell potential
respondents that their responses are confidential. The interviewer does not
give participants any information about which party is conducting the
survey, nor do they talk about the case at the beginning of the interview.
Since the goal of the survey is to gather data that accurately reflect the
opinions of the population from which the sample is drawn, it is important
that the questions not be leading or suggestive. After some initial screening
questions, the interviewer asks a series of case-specific attitudinal questions.
For example, in a rape case a consultant may want to know about community
beliefs about rape laws. In a personal injury case, a consultant may want to
assess opinions about lawsuits or about damage awards in recent civil cases.
Responses to these questions are helpful in developing juror profiles, in
designing juror questionnaires, and in writing voir dire questions for attorneys to use during jury selection.

If the goal of the survey is to support a motion to change the trial venue, it is
crucial to ascertain whether respondents have been exposed to any PTP about
the target case, what they recall about the PTP, whether they have been
influenced by the publicity, and whether individuals believe they could fairly
decide the case (Pollock, 1977). When writing questions that are meant to
measure PTP exposure, it is crucial that the key questions aid a consultant in
determining whether jurors' initial opinions are directly reflected by the
amount and type of publicity they recall about the case. The following
questions are examples of how one can measure the relationship of PTP to
an individual's initial opinions about the case: (a) "Do you know, or have you
read, seen, or heard anything about this case?" (b) "What have you read, seen,
or heard about this case?" (c) "In your opinion, is the defendant, John Doe,
guilty?" (d) "Do you think you could be a fair and impartial juror to both
sides in the criminal case against John Doe?" Additionally, it is common for
consultants to ask community members open-ended questions about the
defendant or about the parties in the target case (Penrod, Groscup, & O'Neil,
2004). This is known as a free-association task. As an example, a respondent
may be asked the following question: "What words come to mind when you
hear the name John Doe?"

Consultants may also choose to develop a short script about the allegations in the target case for the interviewer to read to participants. When an interviewer presents participants with a brief scenario of the case, they are able to answer questions that enable a consultant to assess defendant guilt in a criminal case or defendant liability in a civil case. Finally, standard demographic questions such as marital status, education, occupation, political affiliation, union membership, and the like are presented to participants since this information is especially important to a consultant when developing juror profiles.

ORDER OF QUESTIONS

The order in which interviewers ask participants questions has been shown to influence responses to other questions in the survey (Schuman, Presser, & Ludwig, 1981). For example, when an interviewer asks participants for their opinions about case-specific issues, responses to one question can be a determinant of subsequent responses. Consequently, interviewers often rotate the order of case-specific questions.

SAMPLE SIZE

There are no set standards for determining sample size; however, the sample should be large enough to guarantee that the survey results are generalizable to the target population. Nietzel & Dillehay (1986) have suggested that a sample size of 400 is adequate, while others agree that the homogeneity of the target population should serve as an initial guideline since smaller samples are acceptable when they are selected from areas in which residents have similar demographic characteristics (Schutt, 2004). From our past experiences, we recommend a sample size of at least 300—and more if a key goal is to develop juror profiles.

VENUE SELECTION

In a change of venue survey, a consultant should aim to interview a minimum of 300 respondents in at least two or three jurisdictions. The first jurisdiction is the scheduled trial venue, while the other two venues are comparison trial venues (i.e., communities that have demographics similar to the scheduled trial venue and are legally viable alternative venues for the trial). Alternative venues are often adjacent counties that have not been subjected to as much publicity as the scheduled trial venue; they are typically preferred by judges. However, in cases that have had a great deal of PTP, it may be necessary to survey individuals in counties that are not adjacent to the scheduled trial venue.

RECRUITING PARTICIPANTS

Community attitude research typically requires a consultant to hire professionals from market research companies to recruit and interview participants, because they have the technology and the professional staff available to conduct these types of surveys. Moreover, market research firms are typically able to survey 300 to 400 participants in three to five days, whereas this would prove difficult if not impossible for a consulting company to accomplish. Prior to the recruiting phase, it is important for a consultant to check the local court statutes to determine juror eligibility, since it is critical that the sample be drawn from a subset of individuals who could potentially be called for jury duty in the target venue. For example, most venues require jurors to be over 18 years of age and U.S. citizens. Some jurisdictions require jurors to be either registered voters or licensed drivers.

The most common method used for contacting potential participants for a telephone survey is via random digit dialing (RDD). The major marketing companies across the United States have access to lists that allow inter-viewers to contact individuals with both listed and unlisted phone numbers. This methodology allows a researcher to recruit a larger number of indi-viduals than if only a phone directory were used to identify participants. In addition to RDD, stratified sampling may also be used, since it is important that the demographics of the survey respondents parallel those of potential jurors who will be called for the target trial. In stratified sampling, the consultant identifies relevant subgroups by categories such as gender, ethnicity, age, and education levels so that the target population is matched. If a database that contains information about the demographics of recent jury pools in the target venue is not readily available, similar information is easily obtained from the published census data. After demographic infor-mation has been identified, individuals from the target population are randomly sampled until they match the appropriate demographics for the target venue(s). For example, if a target venue is 50% Caucasian, 25% Hispanic, 20% African American, and 5% Asian, one would want 150 Caucasians, 75 Hispanics, 60 African Americans, and 15 Asians, if the total number of survey respondents is 300.

Assessing PTP Effects

First, it is important to compare data between respondents who have been exposed to PTP with those who are unfamiliar with the target case to assess whether PTP exposure has had an impact on juror biases. If PTP exposure has impacted respondents' judgments about the parties, a consultant will analyze PTP exposure rates across communities. If PTP exposure rates are higher in the trial venue, it is important to determine whether jurors in the scheduled trial venue are more likely to prejudge the defendant than individuals in communities that have had less PTP exposure. If the data confirm that members in the trial venue have biases that would prevent them from being fair jurors compared with jurors in alternative venues, the trial team will likely ask a consultant to present this information in an affidavit to support a motion for a venue change.

DEVELOPING JUROR PROFILES

Complex data analysis is seldom necessary to develop juror profiles. In most instances, simple cross-tabulations are performed to determine which demographic and experiential characteristics are indicative of pro-prosecution/pro-plaintiff versus pro-defense jurors. In cross-tabulation calculations, data on a categorical variable (such as judgment of defendant guilt) are cross-tabulated with other categorical variables such as sex, race, age, and so forth. The resulting data allow consultants to determine which juror characteristics would be the most damaging for their case. For example, in a rape case a consultant hired by the defense may want to know whether males or females would be more conviction-prone. Cross-tabulations allow one to determine whether gender is indicative of prosecution-oriented versus defense-oriented jurors.

Not surprisingly, it is usually a combination of factors that allows a consultant to determine characteristics that are likely to be predictors of verdict outcome. To determine the combination of demographic, experiential, and attitudinal characteristics that best predict a juror's preference for one party, a consultant may choose to perform multiple regression analysis. An analysis of this type allows one to examine the strength of several independent variables on verdict outcome. For example, in a rape case, while initial analysis may reveal that a female juror may be more conviction-prone than her male counterpart, it is possible that female jurors with conservative opinions about rape laws and those employed in mental health occupations will be more likely to favor the prosecution than a female with liberal opinions about rape laws.

SHORTCOMINGS ASSOCIATED WITH SURVEY RESEARCH

Survey methods are particularly valuable because they make use of large sample sizes that are representative of potential venirepersons. This type of research also takes advantage of naturally occurring publicity about real criminal and civil cases and allows trial consultants to identify potential jurors who are likely to view their client's case unfavorably. Nonetheless, as with every research design, there are limitations to using survey methods. First, survey research today has numerous problems associated with the recruiting phase. According to a commentary released by the Pew Research Center in 2009, response rates in surveys across the nation are declining for a number of reasons, including hectic lifestyles, concerns about privacy, and the growing number of cellular phone users who do not have landline phones. As demonstrated by the Consumer Confidence Index produced by the University of Michigan's Survey of Consumer Attitudes, survey response rates were 72% in 1979. However, the response rate decreased to 60% in 1996 and to 48% in 2003. Moreover, recent surveys conducted by major media polling institutes, including the Pew Research Center, reveal that today's response rates are only between 15% and 25%.

A second key concern for survey researchers is the lack of young individuals sampled. A shortage of respondents under the age of 30 may occur when RDD is used for recruiting purposes. Given that many young adults rely only on cellular phones as their primary means of communication, this population has become increasingly difficult to reach during telephone surveys. While the Pew Research Center indicates that recent survey estimates have not resulted in significant biases when samples are taken only from landlines, it is possible that the size of this bias is increasing as the cell-only population grows. Although it is possible to include cell-phone users in survey samples, one significant drawback to this method is that it is extremely expensive; according to the Pew Research Center, a cell-phone interview costs 2 to 2.5 times as much as a landline interview.

Third, because the results of community surveys do not use experimental designs, it is impossible to determine a causal relationship between media exposure and pre-trial bias. For example, is it the exposure to PTP that leads to negative perceptions about the defendant, or do those individuals with a pro-prosecution/pro-plaintiff leaning voluntarily expose themselves to publicity surrounding any given case (Moran & Cutler, 1991)? Additionally, survey research does not allow for an examination of the impact of PTP following the presentation of trial evidence or deliberations. Therefore, it is impossible to determine whether trial evidence and/or jury deliberation reduces the impact of PTP and by how much. Finally, it is very expensive to conduct community attitude surveys and change of venue studies, regardless of how the sample is obtained; without substantial resources, it is nearly impossible to conduct a reliable survey. However, when the stakes are high, attorneys may benefit greatly by hiring a trial consultant to conduct a community attitude survey or a change of venue study.

MEDIA CONTENT ANALYSIS

Although traditional research in support of change of venue motions has generally involved community surveys, PTP research has been successfully complemented with the addition of media content analyses in highly publicized cases, including the John Walker Lindh trial (Studebaker et al., 2000; Vidmar, 2003), the Timothy McVeigh trial (Studebaker et al., 2000), and the Elizabeth Grubman litigation (Studebaker & Penrod, 2005). With the addition of a newspaper (and/or television and radio) content analysis, researchers and consultants are able to measure the extent and nature of PTP in the trial venue, and they can compare that information with PTP in different venues. An analysis of this type permits a party—either the prosecution/plaintiff or the defense—to present this information to the court in a motion for a change of venue. This information, in addition to data collected from a community attitude survey, has the potential to be more persuasive to a judge, who has the power to either grant or deny these motions by providing an overall picture of the type and amount of information about the case to which the public has been exposed.

HOW DO TRIAL CONSULTANTS CONDUCT
MEDIA CONTENT ANALYSES?

The goal of a media content analysis is to obtain information about the type and amount of information that has been printed in the media about a target case. If the goal of the research is to support a motion for a change of venue, a consultant will conduct additional analyses across different newspapers in the various locations that have been identified as potential trial venues.

IDENTIFYING AND ACCESSING NEWSPAPER ARTICLES

The first step when analyzing newspaper articles for content is to identify the newspapers that have published information about the target case. Depending on the trial venue or venues of interest, this task is relatively straightforward. Online databases such as LexisNexis provide information about the major newspapers in any given location across the country. To determine which newspapers potential jurors most frequently read, it is important to obtain the daily as well as Sunday circulation rates and to learn about any daily regional editions that may be published.

The easiest way to obtain newspaper articles is to access them via the LexisNexis database and by selecting a search term that will yield as many articles as possible about the target case. Typically, searching an article by a defendant name will generate the most hits for your search. It is also possible to search for articles in the archived database of any given newspaper; more often than not, however, there are fees associated with this type of search. All articles containing information about the target case should be selected for coding, even if an article dates back several years prior to the trial date. Although the most comprehensive assessment of PTP for a target case could be obtained by analyzing all newspapers in any given area along with TV news reports and local radio reports, this method is quite expensive if not impossible. Further, it has been reported that recall for news events presented in newspaper format is higher than recall of news reports presented via television or radio (DeFleur, Davenport, Cronin, & DeFleur, 1992; Facorro & DeFleur, 1993); thus, we believe the methods previously described will prove to offer an adequate assessment of publicity surrounding the target.

MEASURES

First, one should record the month, the date, and the year each article was published. This information is important in assessing when the target case received the highest and lowest levels of publicity. Many judges incorrectly assume that jurors will be less influenced by PTP if publicity about a target case is at its highest following the incident at issue for trial and sharply declines a few months preceding a trial (Campbell, 1994). Therefore, the date and year each article was published could be particularly helpful for a change of venue motion, particularly if the PTP tapered off after the incident but analyses reveal that potential jurors nonetheless hold biases against a party. Next, one should identify and code the article type. For example, was the article a news story written by a local staff writer, a story from a national news service, a letter to the editor, an editorial, or in some other form? It is likely that stories written by a local staff writer or stories from a national news service are more influential than letters to the editor because of credibility/ bias considerations. Third, the article's location as well as the page number in that section should be coded. Common sense indicates that articles appearing on the front page of any given section have a greater potential of receiving more attention from newspaper readers as opposed to articles buried within any section.

A key factor likely to influence a juror's potential to have biased pretrial assessments of defendant guilt is the total amount of publicity to which the public has been exposed. Therefore, it is important to measure the volume of publicity written about a target case. The most obvious method for assessing the volume of publicity is to simply count the number of articles written in each newspaper one is analyzing. In addition, one should document the total amount of text allotted to each article by counting the number of words in each news story. Finally, if pictures accompany the articles, the number of pictures shown in each article should be recorded.

The bulk of a media content analysis will be dedicated to teasing apart the content of each news article. Based on past PTP research, we have learned that information such as negative characterizations of the defendant (Otto et al., 1994; Tanford & Cox, 1988), defendant confessions (DeLuca, 1979; Padawer-Singer & Barton, 1975; Tans & Chaffee, 1996), and emotional publicity (Kramer et al., 1990) are likely to influence the way potential jurors perceive a defendant. Consequently, it is paramount to ascertain whether this type of information has been publicized in any of the news articles. Past PTP research has honed in on biases created through pro-prosecution–oriented media. However, it is also possible for PTP to be skewed in favor of the defendant, particularly in rape cases.

Consider, for example, the highly publicized Kobe Bryant rape trial. The media reports on the Bryant case contained a plethora of negative information pertaining to the complainant; of particular importance was the promiscuous sexual history of the woman involved. Therefore, depending on the target case it may be important to identify information that has placed the complainant in a negative light. In cases for which the media has published both pro-prosecution/pro-plaintiff and pro-defense information, it is possible that final verdict preferences will be the result of what type of information—pro-prosecution/plaintiff or pro-defense—jurors recall from the PTP. Given that the type of information likely to be important to jurors in evaluating a case depends largely on the issues in the target case, we recommend that the content analysis be exploratory in nature as opposed to creating categories a priori.

When coding statements in the news articles, it is important to assess the nature of the issue frame (i.e., pro-prosecution/plaintiff, pro-defense, or neutral). This method has been used successfully in past media content analyses (Chrzanowski et al., 2006; Golan & Wanta, 2001; Studebaker et al., 2000). For example, a pro-prosecution/pro-plaintiff coded statement is one that has been written from the vantage point of the prosecution/plaintiff (e.g., complainant's/plaintiff's attorney, family members, friends, etc.), while a pro-defense code should be given to statements made by a defense attorney, a family member of the defendant, friends of the defendant, and so forth. A neutral statement is neither pro-prosecution/pro-plaintiff nor pro-defense. These statements are typically written by a neutral party, such as a staff writer or an editor. Thus, statements should be coded to indicate the nature of the statement and the type of statement. Any given statement can be operationalized as an allegation, an idea, or an impression and can be represented by a portion of a sentence, a complete sentence, or more than one sentence. No statement should be coded in more than one category.

CODERS

For reliability purposes, all coders should be trained properly before they begin the content analysis. The number of coders employed will depend on the number of newspaper articles published about the target case as well as the number of venues chosen. Inter-rater reliability should be at least 90%.

SHORTCOMINGS ASSOCIATED WITH CONTENT ANALYSES

The results taken from a content analysis of the media coverage of a case are particularly useful when studying the effects of PTP. Some evidence indicates that judges may be more persuaded to grant a change of venue motion if content analysis results are provided along with a change of venue survey. As discussed previously, a content analysis can help attorneys demonstrate the types of information to which potential venirepersons were exposed and the nature and extent of that exposure. The downside to conducting a media content analysis is that it is time-consuming and labor-intensive. For reliability purposes, it is necessary to spend several hours training several coders. Another shortcoming is the cost factor. Although some print news articles are available free of charge, many cost money. Finally, it is especially difficult to access the content of TV news reports, radio shows, and Internet sources.

In the real world, it would be extremely difficult to determine the differences in the magnitude of effects produced by the different forms of media to which potential jurors may be exposed. For example, in a nationwide poll of 3,000 adults, conducted from April 19 through May 12, 2004, the Pew Research Center reported that the total number of Americans who rely on newspapers as their primary source of news has fallen from 58% in 1994 to

42% in 2004, and newspaper readership among individuals under the age of 30 is only 23%. Their report also reveals that 41% of Americans listen to the radio as a means of obtaining news, and the number of people accessing the Internet for the purposes of accessing news reports has grown steadily during the past four years. Of those surveyed, 66% reported accessing the Internet for general purposes, and 29% reported logging on to the Internet at least three times per week to obtain the news. In a more recent analysis (December, 2008), the Pew Research Center determined that more individuals relied on Internet news than on newspapers, and this shift in consumption patterns should be considered when undertaking a media analysis.

USING MULTI-METHOD RESEARCH PROCEDURES

A more comprehensive understanding of PTP effects has been established in at least two research studies by taking advantage of multiple methods in the experimental context. In the first study, Chrzanowski (2006) examined the effects of PTP in a real case (while it was being tried), using a method that combines media analysis, natural and experimental exposure to PTP, and survey and experimental methods. The methods of their study are a substantial elaboration of previous PTP research; particularly important is the addition of an experimental component such that participants who were unfamiliar with a highly publicized case received experimental manipulations of PTP. The case studied involved an allegation that three teenage defendants sexually assaulted a 16-year-old girl while she was intoxicated. The defendants videotaped the incident, and that videotape was shown to the real jurors. The complainant admitted that she had had consensual sex with two of the defendants the night before the alleged crime.[2]

The research method involved five primary components:

1. A detailed media content analysis of over 120 articles taken from the *Los Angeles Times* to determine the amount and type of PTP about the case
2. A community attitude survey (administered by the prosecution) to 204 jury-eligible adults in Orange County to determine the level of publicity potential jurors had been exposed to before the start of the trial and to determine jurors' prejudgments about the defendants' guilt
3. The trial court's pre–voir dire survey of 246 jurors summoned for possible service in the trial
4. Three hundred forty-seven participants, who were experimentally exposed to PTP from the case and who read shortened versions of

---

2. It is noteworthy that the target case involved a retrial of the three defendants. In the initial trial, the jury was hung 11 to 1 towards acquittal on the most serious charge, rape by intoxication.

the real trial transcripts during the actual trial (experimental participants)[3]

5. One hundred forty-six participants from California who were naturally exposed to the PTP but who also read the same trial transcripts as the experimental participants during the actual trial (natural exposure participants). (Sixty-one of these participants reported being aware of the case; the others reported not being familiar with it.)

RESULTS

There were a number of notable differences in the information that appeared in print media (based on the content analysis) and what prospective jurors recalled about the case (court survey). Jurors were particularly likely to recall that the main defendant had prior involvement in a statutory rape case, had drunk driving and trespass arrests, and that the alleged assault was video-taped. It is noteworthy that none of the prospective jurors recalled information about the complainants' prior drug use and arrests (even though that information appeared nearly as often as the information about the defendants' record).

The nature and extent of PTP and case information recalled and reported by jurors was generally consistent across the community survey and summoned juror groups (and correlated significantly with pretrial judgments); about three-fourths of community survey respondents and venire members were familiar with the case. However, three-fourths of the community respondents, but less than 30% of venire members, believed the defendants were definitely or probably guilty. Impartiality and guilt beliefs were not correlated in either sample. Among community members, 55% reported an ability to be fair jurors versus 81% in the jury sample. The researchers attributed the marked differences in guilt prejudgments and impartiality judgments to social desirability effects, similar to Vidmar (2003).

Analyses concerning verdict preferences revealed that both natural and experimental PTP exposure systematically biased mock jurors' verdict preferences. High and moderate natural exposure (measured by PTP recall) produced verdict effects that were stronger than the effects observed in the experimental group exposed to high levels of prosecution PTP. In the remote locations, the biasing effect of manipulated PTP on pre-trial verdict preferences was $r = .58$. This effect size diminished to .18 post-trial, indicating that trial evidence attenuated PTP effects among those experimentally exposed to PTP. On the other hand, both the pre-trial and post-trial effects for jurors in the natural exposure sample

---

3. Comprehensive searches using LexisNexis did not show news coverage outside of the trial area. It is also worth noting there were no significant differences in remote jurors' prejudgments of defendant guilt between those reporting to have heard about the case and those reporting not to know about the case.

were .32; there was no evidence of attenuation. These results resonate with results from the Steblay et al. (1999) meta-analysis. They yielded greater effect sizes pre-trial for community members ($r = .30$) as compared with students ($r = .08$)—results that suggest that experimental studies (with student participants) may underestimate actual PTP effects among non-student samples.

Using a similar study design, Daftary-Kapur (2009) also examined the influence of PTP on juror decision making in an actual trial as it occurred. In addition to combining survey and experimental methodologies, making use of naturally occurring and manipulated PTP, she was able to use community members as participants. The case was tried in New York City and will be referred to as the Bell case. Briefly, the target case became a focal point of New York media and involved allegations that three police officers had used excessive and unjustified force leading to the death of a young man on the morning of his wedding. There was a vast amount of controversy surrounding the actions of the defendants and the victim the morning of the shooting. Additionally, the case led to much emotion surrounding African American victims and their treatment by the police. This case involved three defendants who are detectives with the New York Police Department. The defendants were on trial for manslaughter and were accused in the killing of Sean Bell, a young man who was celebrating his bachelor party at a nightclub in Queens. In a bench trial, the defendants were acquitted on all counts of the indictments against them.

The study involved

1. A selection of articles printed in local news sources to serve as PTP
2. Two hundred seventeen participants in Boston[4] who had no exposure to the facts of the case before participating in the study and were experimentally exposed to PTP (remote participants)
3. One hundred fifteen participants from New York who had differing levels of exposure to case information via the media and were not exposed to any experimentally manipulated PTP (natural exposure)

This study examined a number of variables, including the slant of the PTP (pro-prosecution, pro-defense), amount of PTP exposure (high, low, none), and medium of exposure (television, print).

RESULTS

Case familiarity was high in New York, with 85% of the participants indicating that they were familiar with the Bell case. Case familiarity was

---

4. An initial attempt was made to recruit participants from Albany, NY, which would have been the natural change of venue location for this case. Unfortunately, we were unable to recruit the required number of participants (we recruited only 10 participants) and therefore switched our focus to a larger metropolitan city, Boston.

almost nonexistent in Boston, with only 5% of the participants indicating that they were familiar with the Bell case. Participants were asked to rate how much they had read about the Bell case and had an average score of .85; ratings of guilt were at .83.

Multi-group analyses[5] were conducted to determine the influence of PTP bias and the amount of exposure on verdict preferences. Analyses revealed that participants' verdicts were systematically influenced by the nature of the PTP exposure. The effect of PTP on pretrial judgments of guilt in the natural condition was fully mediated by level of familiarity with the case such that participants who had, via natural exposure, read more pro-prosecution articles, were more likely to be familiar with the case and to rate the defendants guilty pre-trial, $\beta = .16$. The total effect of PTP on final verdict was $\beta = .17$, indicating that those who were exposed to pro-prosecution PTP were more likely to find the defendants guilty than those who were exposed to pro-defense PTP. This effect is indicative of the durability of PTP effects. PTP exposure occurred eight weeks prior to final verdicts in this study. Results indicate that the effect of PTP was not attenuated by the presentation of trial evidence and continued to have a significant influence on judgments of guilt.

Studies along the lines of those described here have several advantages. First, they provide evidence regarding the durability of PTP effects. In both studies PTP exposure took place weeks before verdicts were rendered and continued to have an influence on final verdicts. This addresses a common question raised in the courts, where skepticism exists vis-à-vis the durability of such effects. Second, no differences were found between the remote and natural exposure groups in Daftary-Kapur et al. (in preparation), providing support to the external validity of laboratory studies where participants are exposed to manipulated PTP.

In conclusion, the field of trial consulting is quickly evolving, and constantly growing. PTP is an important concern not only for the courts but for those who work with actors in the legal system, especially trial consultants. Research on PTP effects is extremely helpful to trial consultants in identifying aspects of real-world cases that may be problematic and determining how these potential problems may be addressed. More-over, research studies provide trial consultants with a sound research methodology that they can employ in their day-to-day practices. Overall, it would be prudent for trial consultants to use multi-method research processes to capitalize on the strengths of the various methodologies presented here. Through this process of triangulation, trial consultants can provide adequate support to their clients, all the while employing sound research methodology.

---

5. Multi-group analyses revealed no significant differences between the natural and experimental exposure groups. Thus the groups were collapsed for subsequent analyses.

REFERENCES

Abramson, J. (2000). *We the jury.* Cambridge, MA: Harvard University Press.

Arbuthnot, J., Myers, B., & Leach, J. (2002). Linking juror prejudgment and pretrial publicity knowledge: Some methodological considerations. *American Journal of Forensic Psychology, 20*(3), 53–71.

Bornstein, B. H., Whisenhunt, B. L., & Nemeth, R. J. (2002). Pretrial publicity and civil cases: A two-way street? *Law & Human Behavior, 21,* 3–17.

Campbell, D. S. (1994). *Free press v. fair trial: Supreme Court decisions since 1807.* Westport, CT: Praeger.

Carroll, J. S., Kerr, N. L., Alfini, J. J., Weaver, F. M., MacCoun, R. J., & Feldman, V. (1986). Free press and fair trial: The role of behavioral research. *Law and Human Behavior, 100,* 187–201.

Chrzanowski, L. M. (2006). *Rape? Truth? and the media: Laboratory and field assessments of pretrial publicity in a real case* (Doctoral dissertation). Available from proquest dissertations and theses database. (UMI No. AAI3204976.)

Chrzanowski, L., Solomonson, J., McAuliff, B. D., & Penrod, S. (2006, March). *Pretrial judgments of defendant guilt: Integrating content analysis with case survey methodologies.* AP-LS, St. Petersburg, FL.

Costantini, E., & King, J. (1980-1981). The partial juror: Correlates and causes of prejudgment. *Law and Society Review, 15,* 9–40.

Daftary-Kapur, T. (2009). *The influence of pre- and post-venire publicity on juror decision making* (Doctoral dissertation). Available from proquest dissertations and theses database (UMI No. AAT3378557.)

DeFleur, M. L., Davenport, L., Cronin, M., & DeFleur, M. (1992). Audience recall of news stories presented by newspaper, computer, television, and radio. *Journalism Quarterly, 69,* 1010–1022.

DeLuca, A. J. (1979). *Tipping the scales of justice: The effects of pretrial publicity* (Unpublished Master's thesis). Iowa State University, Ames, IA.

Facorro, L. B., & DeFleur, M. L. (1993). A cross-cultural experiment on how well audiences remember news stories from newspaper, computer, television, and radio. *Journalism Quarterly, 70,* 585–601.

Flood, M. (2004, November 9). Skilling seeks escape from Houston heat: Ex-Enron chief files for a change of venue after poll finds unflattering perceptions here. *Houston Chronicle,* 9.

Frederick, J. T. (1984). Social science involvement in voir dire: Preliminary data on the effectiveness of "scientific jury selection." *Behavioral Sciences and the Law, 2*(4), 375–394.

Golan, G., & Wanta, W. (2001). Second-level agenda setting in the New Hampshire primary: A comparison of coverage in three newspapers and public perceptions of candidates. *Journalism & Mass Communication Quarterly, 78,* 247–259.

Greene, E., & Wade, R. (1988). Of private talk and public print: General pre-trial publicity and juror decision-making. *Applied Cognitive Psychology, 2*(2), 123–135.

Horowitz, I. A., & Willging, T. E. (1984). *The psychology of law: Integrations and applications.* Boston, MA: Little, Brown.

Hvistendahl, J. K. (1979). The effect of placement on biasing information. *Journalism Quarterly, 56,* 863.

Hutson, M. (2007, March). Unnatural selection. *Psychology Today.*

Irvin v. Dowd, 366 U. S. 717 (1961).

Kline, F. G., & Jess, P. H. (1966). Prejudicial publicity: Its effects on law school mock juries. *Journalism Quarterly, 43,* 113–116.

Kovera, M. B. (2002). The effects of general pretrial publicity on juror decisions: An examination of moderators and mediating mechanisms. *Law and Human Behavior, 26* (1), 43–72.

Kramer, G. P., Kerr, N. L., & Carroll, J. S. (1990). Pretrial publicity, judicial remedies, and jury bias. *Law and Human Behavior, 14*(5), 409–438.

Kressel, N. J., & Kressel, D. F. (2002). *Stack and sway: The new science of jury consulting.* Boulder, CO: Westview Press.

Lieberman, J. D., & Sales, B. D. (2007). *Scientific jury selection.* Washington, DC: American Psychological Association.

Murphy v. Florida, 421 U.S. 794, 799–802 (1975).

Nietzel, M. T., & Dillehay, R. C. (1983). Psychologists as consultants for changes of venue: The use of public opinion surveys. *Law and Human Behavior, 7*(4), 309–335.

Otto, A. L., Penrod, S. D., & Dexter, H. R. (1994). The biasing impact of pretrial publicity on juror judgments. *Law and Human Behavior, 18*(4), 453–469.

Otto, A. L., Penrod, S. D., & Hirt, E. R. (1991). *The influence of pretrial publicity on juror judgments in civil cases.* Unpublished manuscript.

Padawer-Singer, A., & Barton, A. H. (1975). Free press, fair trial. In R. J. Simon (Ed.), *The jury system: A critical analysis.* Beverly Hills, CA: Sage.

Penrod, S., Groscup, J., & O'Neil, K. (2004). *Consulting issues in cases involving pretrial publicity.* Paper presented at the American Psychology-Law Society Conference, Scottsdale, AZ.

Pollock, A. (1977). The use of public opinion polls to obtain changes of venue and continuances in criminal trials. *Criminal Justice Journal, 1,* 269–288.

Posey, A. J., & Wrightsman, L. S. (2005). *Trial consulting.* New York, NY: Oxford University Press.

Rideau v. Louisiana, 373 U.S. 723 (1953).

Schuman, H., Presser, S., & Ludwig, J. (1981). Context effects on survey responses to questions about abortion. *Public Opinion Quarterly, 45,* 216–223.

Schutt, R. (2004). *Investigating the social world.* 4th edition. Thousand Oaks, CA: Pine Forge Press.

Sheppard v. Maxwell, 384 U.S. 333, 362 (1966).

Simon, R. J., & Eimermann, T. (1971). The jury finds not guilty: Another look at media influence on the jury. *Journalism Quarterly, 48,* 343–344.

Steblay, N. M., Besirevic, J., Fulero, S. M., & Jimenez-Lorente, B. (1999). The effects of pretrial publicity on juror verdicts: A meta-analytic review. *Law and Human Behavior, 23*(2), 219–235.

Strier, F. (1999). Whither trial consulting? Issues and projections. *Law and Human Behavior, 23,* 93–115.

Studebaker, C. A., & Penrod, S. D. (1997). Pretrial publicity: The media, the law, and common sense. *Psychology, Public Policy, and Law, 3*(2), 428–460.

Studebaker, C. A., & Penrod, S. D. (2005). Pretrial publicity and its influence on juror decision making. In N. Brewer & K. D. Williams, *Psychology and law: An empirical perspective.* New York, NY: Guilford Press.

Studebaker, C. A., Robbennolt, J. K., Pathak-Sharma, M. K., & Penrod, S. D. (2000). Assessing pretrial publicity effects: Integrating content analytic results. *Law and Human Behavior, 24*(3), 317–337.

Tanford, S., & Cox, M. (1988). The effects of impeachment evidence and limiting instructions on individual and group decision making. *Law and Human Behavior, 12*(4), 477–497.

Tans, M., & Chaffee, S. (1966). Pretrial publicity and juror prejudice. *Journalism Quarterly, 43,* 647–654.

United States v. McVeigh, 918 F. Supp. 1467 (1996).

Van Dyke, J. M. (1977). *Jury selection procedures: Our uncertain commitment to representative juries.* Cambridge, MA: Ballinger Publishing.

Vidmar, N. (2003). Symposium: III. The jury in practice: When all of us are victims: Juror prejudice and "terrorist" trials. *Chicago-Kent Law Review, 1143,* 1–42.

CHAPTER 13

Eyewitness Identification Research: Strengths and Weaknesses of Alternative Methods

GARY L. WELLS AND STEVEN D. PENROD

EYEWITNESS IDENTIFICATION RESEARCH has become an increasingly popular specialty among those interested in psychology and law. We have tried to write this chapter in a way that would be useful for new or "would be" eyewitness researchers, and we also think that there might be some points here that seasoned eyewitness researchers might find useful. The reader should keep in mind, however, that that there can be different views about what is the best methodology for eyewitness research. We offer our best advice, but that is no guarantee that following our advice will automatically disarm critics of any researcher's study. Furthermore, researchers should always consider any particular recommendation that we make in the context of the hypotheses, purposes, and goals of their own study.

For example, one of the authors of this chapter favors a methodology in which fillers are counterbalanced in and out of the position of the innocent suspect rather than having one person always serve as the innocent replacement for the culprit (a general preference of the second author). Both authors agree, however, that if the purpose of the study is to test ideas about lineup bias emanating from poor fillers, the counterbalancing methodology would not make sense. We cannot anticipate every hypothesis that researchers would want to pursue, so researchers will always have to think through every methodological decision within the context of the questions they are trying to answer.

Readers should also note that considerations of ecological validity, although often dominant in eyewitness research, can sometimes take a back seat to theoretical considerations. Consider, for example, the removal-without-replacement procedure for lineups in which the culprit-absent lineup is created by removing the culprit and replacing him/her with no one (Wells, 1993).

From the perspective of ecological validity, this is a peculiar methodology without much of a real-world counterpart. On the other hand, this methodology is powerful for testing certain types of theoretical questions and is, in some ways, a "cleaner" manipulation of the culprit-present lineup versus culprit-absent lineup variable. This is because the traditional method (replace the culprit with someone else) changes two variables at once (the culprit is removed, and a new face is introduced), whereas the removal-without-replacement procedure removes only the culprit. Depending on the purposes of the study, ecological validity does not always trump other concerns. In fact, the relative paucity of theory development in the eyewitness area is something that many researchers now believe needs to be rectified, which could lead to the use of methodologies that are less ecologically valid but more revealing of psychological processes (see *Applied Cognitive Psychology*, 2008, Volume 22(6), devoted to such discussions).

Readers should also keep in mind that methodological soundness is only one factor that determines whether an eyewitness study is likely to survive the rigorous review process and be accepted for publication. Many manuscripts are rejected from top journals despite their methodological soundness because the study does not significantly advance our knowledge. One of the poorest reasons to conduct a study is merely that "no one has done it:" All studies have to be justified at much deeper levels than that. Why is it important? How does it relate to the current literature? How does it advance our theoretical understanding? What are the applied implications? Novice eyewitness researchers would do well to examine carefully the introduction and discussion sections of well-cited eyewitness articles to develop a feel for how these articles were "packaged."

EYEWITNESS IDENTIFICATION LABORATORY EXPERIMENTAL METHODS

Designing, conducting, and analyzing an eyewitness identification experiment involves a series of decisions that can have considerable consequences for the results and their interpretations. Although we cannot exhaust all the possible decision junctures that confront eyewitness identification researchers, many of which depend on specifics of the hypothesis being tested, there are several that confront researchers in the design of almost all eyewitness identification experiments.

The basic idea of an eyewitness identification experiment is to expose participant witnesses to an event in which they view one or more actors engaged in some critical behavior. Later, the participant witnesses are given some type of eyewitness identification test, usually a photo array, in which they are asked to attempt to identify the individual(s). In most eyewitness identification experiments, the participant witnesses are also asked to indicate the confidence or certainty they have in their identification decisions. Depending on the focus of the experiment, other measures might be taken, such as decision latency, willingness of participant witnesses to testify about their identification decision, statements about how they made their decisions, and so on. In many respects, such an experiment seems rather straightforward. But the apparent simplicity of preparing such an experiment is somewhat deceptive.

THE EVENT

One of the initial decisions to be made is what kind of event to create. There are many examples in the eyewitness identification literature of live staged events, such as thefts, in which unsuspecting people become eyewitnesses (see Wells, Rydell, & Seelau, 1993, for an example). Increasingly, however, eyewitness identification researchers have come to rely on video events that the researchers create, often depicting some type of crime. Using video events is certainly easier than using live events, because video does not require continuing reenactments with actors, there are no concerns about participant witnesses intervening to stop the crime, the event is perfectly consistent in its presentation from one participant to the next, and institutional review boards typically have fewer concerns about video events than about live events. On the other hand, it is possible to raise concerns about ecological validity with video events due to the obvious fact that eyewitnesses in real cases witness events live, in three dimensions, and so on. But, at this point, it seems that eyewitness scientists have largely accepted the video-event method, leaving little incentive for researchers to use the more difficult and costly live-event method.

Regardless of the medium chosen for the witnessed event, we caution researchers to avoid designs in which large groups are nested within conditions of the study. At the extreme, imagine that a researcher was testing the weapon-focus effect by having a classroom disruptor flash a knife in Class A and the same disruptor have no weapon when disrupting Class B. In this case, groups (Classes A and B) are nested within conditions. Any differences between the classes are therefore confounded with the manipulated variable (weapon vs. no weapon). Surprisingly enough, the problem of nesting is not solved even if there were 400 students and they had been randomly assigned to Class A or Class B. The reason that this does not solve the problem is that it takes only one small glitch (which could easily be undetected) to affect an entire class (or a large portion of the class); if something affects the class, it affects the entire condition.

For example, maybe a student was suspicious, and a whispering rumor spread quickly in only one class. Contrast this with a fully randomized design in which the event was staged 400 times, once for each witness, and each was randomly assigned to the weapon versus no weapon condition. That one suspicious student could affect only one data point, which would have no appreciable effect on the condition in which that student fell. Consider also the possibility that the actor who plays the role of the disruptor is unable to enact the event in exactly the same way each time (which is likely). Sometimes the actor faces away from the group more than other times, or sometimes the actor moves a little faster. Any minor difference for Class A versus Class B could impact results for the entire condition (because each class is a full condition).

At the other extreme, where each enactment is done for each individual witness, these minor variations "wash out," because they will occur as often in one condition as they do in the other condition (the law of large numbers). Based on strict interpretations of a random design and the assumptions behind statistical analyses, the situation in which groups (Class A and Class B) are nested in conditions (weapon and no weapon) is the same as an experiment with a total sample size of two (one per condition), not 400 (200 per condition). These are extremes, of course, where in the nested case there is only one group per condition and in the other case there are no nestings of groups within conditions. Most reviewers and editors will permit some level of nesting within conditions. For example, groups of two or three witnesses at a time are usually not flagged as problematic nestings if the overall sample size is large enough. Still, researchers need to be prepared for the possibility that editors or reviewers will require some complicated higher-order statistical analyses that are harmful to statistical power when there are nestings. And, at the extreme where there is only one group per condition, there is no statistical solution. Such designs will be (and should be) rejected for publication in reputable journals.

Once a medium has been chosen for the event, questions arise, such as what participant witnesses are told prior to the event, how long the participant witnesses will be exposed to the culprit(s), and whether to use multiple culprits reenacting the same event. Most eyewitness identification researchers use mild deception to avoid cueing the witnesses prior to the event that they will witness. For example, in a video-event study, participant witnesses might be told that the study involves impressions of people or impressions of events. In live-event experiments, participants might be seated in a waiting room believing that the study has not yet started. The rationale for not alerting participant witnesses that they will be witnesses is simply that actual witnesses are generally taken by surprise.

The issue of exposure duration is a more difficult one, because the relation between exposure duration and eyewitness identification performance is not precise. The general idea is to find an exposure duration that avoids ceiling and basement effects. An extremely long exposure might result in eyewitness identification performance being virtually perfect, which might then prevent the researcher from showing that certain other variables (e.g., a better lineup procedure) can improve eyewitness identification perform-ance. Conversely, an exposure duration that is too brief might result in such a weak memory trace that there would be no chance to show how other variables (e.g., passage of time before the lineup) can harm eyewitness identification performance.

The appropriate exposure time can vary dramatically as a function of other aspects of the research design. Thus, for example, a study of identification accuracy by military personnel being trained in a military survival school found that under some high-stress circumstances, trainees could identify just over one in four interrogators involved in 40-minute interrogations (Morgan et al., 2004). In contrast, Memon, Hope, and Bull (2003) obtained slightly better performances from witnesses who viewed a target person in a video for just 12 seconds. Hence, pilot testing is highly recommended, which can often be done using just the control condition to make sure that there is room for performance to go up and down as a function of other manipulations. (Later, we discuss how lineup performance is assessed.)

The question of whether to use multiple culprits, each reenacting the same crime, is generally construed as an issue of "stimulus sampling." The idea of stimulus sampling is to ensure that the results are not due to the particular characteristics of the individual who was selected to serve as the culprit in the study. For example, we know that some people are more recognizable than others, in large part because some people have a more distinctive (unusual) appearance than other people. However, the need for stimulus sampling is more important for some studies than it is for others. In general, the issue of stimulus sampling is extremely important when the manipulated (or predictor) variable is an exemplar from a category.

For example, if the experiment is examining how eyewitnesses perform when the culprit is Black versus White or male versus female, stimulus sampling is essential. Clearly, one must compare many different Black culprit-actors with many different White culprit-actors or many male culprit-actors with many female culprit-actors to reach any proper conclusions. Using only one or two such actors threatens construct validity (a very serious threat) in this case, because the category variable (e.g. male versus female) is confounded with characteristics of the exemplars.

However, if the critical manipulated variable is not a characteristic of the stimuli themselves (e.g., a pre-lineup instruction), then the use of only one or two culprit-actors is a less serious threat, because the characteristics of the culprit-actor are the same in each condition. In the latter case, there can be issues of generalization (i.e., would other exemplars yield the same effects from the manipulated variables?) but not issues of construct validity. We encourage readers to examine an article by Wells and Windschitl (1999) on these points; it also includes discussions of how statistical interactions can lessen the need for stimulus sampling and how to analyze the data when stimulus sampling is used.

BUILDING THE LINEUP

Great care must be taken in making various decisions about building a lineup. The need for some decisions is obvious, such as how many people to use in the lineup, whether to present the lineup live or in photos, and so on. But some decisions are even more complex and require considerable forethought at a level often not exercised in the eyewitness identification literature. One of the first decisions to be made is whether to use both culprit-present and culprit-absent lineups. There are circumstances in which using only present— or only absent lineups—is perfectly legitimate, depending on the nature of the question being asked. Much of the research on the post-identification feed-back effect, for example, uses only culprit-absent lineups because the focus is on the development of false certainty after a mistaken identification has been made (e.g., Wells & Bradfield, 1998). Using a different rationale (a question that focused on witness performance in culprit-present arrays), Memon and Gabbert (2003) used only culprit-present lineups to examine simultaneous versus sequential lineups. Generally, however, if the hypothesis concerns eyewitness identification accuracy, it is critical to use both culprit-present and culprit-absent lineups.

The typical method for creating a culprit-absent lineup is to use the same fillers but replace the culprit with an innocent suspect. Theoretically, this simulates the situation in which police investigators have unknowingly focused the lineup on an innocent suspect. But the issue too often glossed over (or ignored altogether) by eyewitness identification researchers is how to select the person who will replace the culprit (i.e., how to select the innocent suspect). In some published experiments, researchers state that they selected a person who closely resembled the culprit. For example, the researchers might sort through a large number of photos, have them rated for similarity to the culprit, and then pick the most similar one to be the replacement for the culprit.

We believe, however, that the choice of strategy should depend on the questions being addressed by the researcher and what one assumes (if anything) about the ways in which innocent people become suspects. Most often, people do not become innocent suspects in actual cases because of their high similarity to the actual culprit. After all, the police investigators do not know who the actual culprit is (otherwise they would arrest the actual culprit instead). Instead, an innocent suspect may be someone who merely fits the general verbal description of the culprit that was given by the eyewitness. But if the innocent suspect in an experiment is selected a priori to look more like the culprit than do any of the fillers, this can serve to greatly overestimate the rate at which the innocent suspects would be identified in actual cases where the innocent person merely fits a general description.

Furthermore, selecting as the innocent replacement someone who looks a great deal like the culprit could serve to underestimate the confidence-accuracy relationship. At the extreme, replacing the culprit with a clone of the culprit would yield a result in which it is guaranteed that there can be no confidence-accuracy relation. In the general case of an experiment, we recommend a different method than one that selects a person who looks most like the culprit as the innocent replacement for the culprit. In particular, we recommend that the innocent replacement for the culprit be selected the same way that the fillers were selected (often, because they fit the general verbal description of the culprit). Using this method, there is no reason to specify any single one of the lineup members as the innocent replacement. Instead, each of the fillers can be rotated into the replacement position in the culprit-absent lineup. This type of counterbalancing can help stabilize the data and make the results more replicable, because the results do not depend on peculiarities associated with the selection of any single member of the culprit-absent lineup.

There are other circumstances in actual cases in which an innocent suspect might closely resemble the actual culprit. Mere chance is one of these circumstances; for example, a witness may be presented a set of photographs selected by a police officer—using the witness's description—from a database of photographs. By chance alone, one of the individuals in this "all-suspect" array may bear a strong resemblance to the perpetrator. But other circumstances may apply. Suppose, for example, the culprit's image was caught on surveillance video. As a result, the police might receive a tip that the person on the surveillance video closely resembles Person X and they might decide to conduct a lineup with Person X as their suspect.

Similarly, a person could become a suspect because he or she closely resembled a drawing or "composite" of the perpetrator prepared by one or more witnesses and published in the media. In this case, the police are selecting their suspect based on some knowledge of what the actual culprit looks like. This situation is what many eyewitness identification experiments are simulating when the eyewitnesses use their knowledge of what the confederate-culprit looks like in selecting an innocent suspect. Unless researchers specifically intend to simulate this circumstance or something like it, we recommend the counterbalancing method described in the preceding paragraph. This method can be coupled with a reporting of the rate at which the most-chosen innocent person was selected by witnesses. The most-chosen rate can give some indication of the risk of misidentification associated with the most-similar foil.

The issue of how to select fillers confronts virtually every eyewitness identification experiment. Obviously, if the experiment itself is testing hypotheses about the best way to select fillers, the hypotheses themselves dictate the selection method. But if the experiment is testing some other question (e.g., the effects of pre-lineup instructions or the effects of exposure duration), it is important to remember that the method of selecting fillers is still important. In general, researchers have focused on two methods for selecting fillers. One is to select fillers who fit the general verbal description of the culprit (as given by people who are shown the culprit and then asked to give a description from memory), which is called the match-to-description method. Another is to select fillers who show some level of similarity to the culprit (called the resemblance-to-culprit method) as rated by pilot study participants. (Note that how this plays out in any given experiment must be determined in part by how the innocent suspect is selected.)

In actual police practices there is jurisdictional variation. Some jurisdictions select their fillers based on the verbal description of the culprit that was given by the eyewitness(es). Other jurisdictions select the fillers based on their similarity to the suspect. The latter practice (similarity-to-suspect method) is actually different from the way fillers are selected in almost any experiment, because the fillers that are selected are more likely to be different if the suspect is innocent than if the suspect is guilty. In other words, the similarity-to-culprit method is not the same as the similarity-to-suspect method. Regardless of how an experimenter decides to select the fillers to be used in the study, it is essential that the method be fully described in any write-up of the study. Furthermore, researchers should usually report some measure of the final lineup product. Often, this measure is functional size (Wells, Leippe, & Ostrom, 1979) or effective size and defendant bias (Malpass, 1981), both of which involve the collection of additional data from "mock witnesses." However, it should be noted that these measures are totally insensitive to a bias that occurs when the innocent suspect is selected to resemble the culprit, whereas the fillers are selected to fit the description (Wells & Bradfield, 1999). In such a situation, the functional-size, effective-size, and defendant-bias measures will show no lineup bias, and the innocent suspect will actually stand out.

REPORTING AND ANALYZING THE DATA

IDENTIFICATION DATA

Clearly, there are many different approaches to reporting and analyzing data from an eyewitness identification experiment, and researchers must always consider the unique aspects of their experiments in deciding how to approach the data. Nevertheless, there are problems that reoccur frequently. The most common problem is one of underreporting the data. Too often, for example, researchers will collapse across types of accuracy (e.g., identifications of the culprit in a culprit-present lineup and correct rejections from a culprit-absent lineup) and types of inaccuracy (e.g., identifications of the innocent suspect, incorrect rejections when the lineup included the culprit, and filler identifications in both culprit-present and culprit-absent lineups).

Unfortunately, collapsing across both types of accuracy and both types of inaccuracy masks a lot of interesting and important information. We believe that any eyewitness identification experiment that includes culprit-present and culprit-absent lineups should minimally report the descriptive statistics that are characterized by Table 13.1. This kind of table is useful because it exhausts the possible responses that witnesses can make in response to each lineup type. Of course, this should be done for each condition of the experiment and here we have displayed two conditions—X and Y. Note that reporting both the percentages and the frequencies is important, especially if the conditions do not have equal sample sizes. In some cases, it can also be

Table 13.1
Distributions of Identification Decisions as a Function of Culprit-Present
and Culprit-Absent Conditions and the *XY* Manipulation

Lineup condition	Witness ID Decision			
	ID of Culprit	ID of Innocent Suspect	ID of Filler	No ID
Condition *X*				
Culprit-Present	65% (52)	Cannot occur	15% (12)	20% (16)
Culprit-Absent	Cannot occur	10% (8)	50% (40)	40% (32)
Condition *Y*				
Culprit-Present	75% (60)	Cannot occur	5% (4)	20% (16)
Culprit-Absent	Cannot occur	30% (24)	20% (16)	50% (40)

Note: Numbers in parentheses are frequencies.

useful to report the rate at which each individual filler in the lineup is identified rather than collapsing all fillers into one total.

The format of data presentation in Table 13.1 is based on a presumption that the design of the experiment used a single a priori innocent suspect rather than using the method of rotating the innocent suspect across all lineup members (the counterbalancing procedure discussed in the previous section). This is apparent from the fact that the innocent suspect in Condition *Y* received 30% of the choices whereas the five fillers in total received only 20% (an average rate of 4%). If the rotation method had been used, the innocent suspect rate of identification would be exactly the same as the filler rate divided by the number of fillers.

The format of Table 13.1 also permits a quick assessment of whether eyewitness performance is running above levels expected by chance. One way to define chance is to compare the rate of correct rejections (no identification in culprit-absent conditions) to incorrect rejections (no identifications in culprit-present conditions). Because the frequencies are reported in Table 13.1, anyone can quickly calculate a chi-square value to determine whether the rates are significantly different. The format of Table 13.1 also permits a quick assessment of diagnosticity.

Although space does not permit us to give a full treatment of the diagnosticity statistic, the diagnosticity of a suspect identification is the ratio of hits (identifications of the culprit) to false identifications (identifications of the innocent suspect). In the case of Condition *X* in Table 13.1, the diagnosticity ratio is 6.5, and in the case of Condition *Y*, the diagnosticity ratio is 2.5. In effect, the diagnosticity ratio for identifications of the suspect can be interpreted as how much more likely an eyewitness is to identify the guilty party from a culprit-present lineup than to identify an innocent suspect from a culprit-absent lineup. A diagnosticity ratio of 1.0 indicates no diagnosticity, and higher numbers indicate increasing levels of diagnosticity.

The diagnosticity ratio can be also computed for fillers and for no-identification decisions. Diagnosticity ratios are quite important for any analyses that attempt to use Bayesian statistics to calculate probabilities of error under different possible base rates for whether the lineup includes the culprit. Detailed treatments of eyewitness identification diagnosticity and Bayesian probabilities can be found in the eyewitness identification literature (Wells & Lindsay, 1980; Wells & Olson, 2002; Wells & Turtle, 1986). The article by Wells and Olson also describes how to test whether a diagnosticity ratio is significantly different from 1.0 or whether one diagnosticity ratio is significantly greater than another diagnosticity ratio.

Commonly, researchers first want to know whether the manipulation (e.g., conditions X vs. Y in Table 13.1) had any significant effect on eyewitness identification performance. Analyses of variance are generally not appropriate for data of this form (i.e., categorical data of a dichotomous form). An omnibus (overall) test of statistical significance is readily available, however, using a hierarchical log-linear analysis, which is contained in SPSS and other statistical packages. Individual contrasts (e.g., is the 10% rate of innocent suspect identifications in condition X statistically different from the 30% rate of innocent suspect identifications in condition Y?) are also easily conducted using the chi-square statistic.

CONFIDENCE DATA

Commonly, researchers are interested in using confidence measures to assess the relation between confidence and accuracy. The point-biserial correlation has been the most common method for doing this in the eyewitness identification literature, but numerous researchers have questioned the appropriateness of the point-biserial correlation and have instead argued for measures of calibration and resolution (e.g., Brewer, Keast, & Rishworth, 2002; Brewer & Wells, 2006; Juslin, Olson, & Winman, 1996). One problem is that calibration and resolution statistics require either extremely large sample sizes or a large number of repeated measures per participant. Note, however, that calibration can be calculated properly only if the confidence scale is categorical from 0% to 100% (i.e., the commonly used 7-point scale cannot be used)[1]. Further complicating the traditional practice of reporting the point-biserial correlation between confidence and accuracy is the fact that the point-biserial

---

1. The fact that confidence calibration calculations require 0–100% scales rather than other common scales (e.g., 1–7) might itself be a good reason to use 0–100% confidence scales in eyewitness identification studies. In general, the authors recommend percentage scales for confidence questions, because percentage scales have some degree of lay comprehension and meaning. Hence, percentages might be more natural and readily grasped by participant witnesses. Furthermore, text, figures, and tables in articles that refer to mean confidence levels, such as 3.9, require the reader to go back to the methods section and look again at what kind of scale was used (5 point? 7 point? 9 point?) to get a sense of where participant-witnesses were on the scale. Percentage confidence, on the other hand, does not impose this ambiguity or extra burden on the reader.

Table 13.2

Frequency Array for Confidence Level by Accuracy

Accuracy	0%	10%	20%	30%	40%	50%	60%	70%	80%	90%	100%
Accurate	0	0	0	2	3	5	10	34	21	17	8
Inaccurate	0	0	1	4	12	15	15	33	17	2	1

correlation is sensitive to base rates (McGrath & Meyer, 2006). In the current context, that means that the base rate for accuracy affects the point-biserial correlation.

Regardless of the summary statistic used to express the relation between eyewitness identification confidence and accuracy, we recommend that researchers also consider reporting confidence level using accuracy/ frequency arrays. Table 13.2 gives an example of such an array. This array is extremely useful because it permits readers to calculate the point-biserial correlation, or d, or any other statistic. Importantly, it also permits those who are doing meta-analyses to easily collapse across studies. And, it allows researchers to explore the idea that extreme confidence (e.g., 90% or more confident) might be populated almost exclusively by accurate witnesses (in this case 89% of witnesses with confidence of 90% or better are accurate) even when the overall distribution shows a modest or weak relation.

It is now well documented that the relation between eyewitness identification accuracy and confidence is consistently moderated by whether the witnesses are choosers (i.e., made an identification) or non-choosers (e.g., see Sporer, Penrod, Read, & Cutler, 1995). Hence, it is not recommended that researchers collapse over both types of accuracy (accurate identifications and correct rejections) and both types of inaccuracy (mistaken identifications and incorrect rejections) when reporting confidence-accuracy relations, because this can hide the fact that the relation is stronger among choosers (accurate vs. inaccurate identifiers) than it is among non-choosers (correct rejecters vs. incorrect rejecters).

Finally, we note that researchers should consider the fact that the confidence-accuracy relation in eyewitness identification might also vary as a function of whether the identification of fillers in the culprit-present lineup are included among the choosers in calculating this relation. From a perspective of the ecology of the forensic situation, in actual cases we would not normally be interested in the question of whether eyewitness identification confidence helps to discriminate between identifications of a guilty suspect and identifications of fillers. Using the assumption of the single-suspect model for lineups (one person is the suspect and the remainder are known to be innocent fillers), it is already known in an actual case whether the identification of a filler was mistaken—clearly it was. Instead, eyewitness identification confidence is useful to the extent that it helps discriminate between accurate identifications (i.e., when the culprit is present) and mistaken identifications of an innocent suspect (i.e., when the culprit is absent).

In some cases, it might be informative to report the average confidence with which every lineup member was chosen; the suspect in the target-present lineup, each individual filler in the target-present lineup, and each individual member of the target-absent lineup. If standard deviations are also reported with each of these 12 means, it would be easy for the interested reader to calculate the confidence-accuracy correlation under any number of assumptions (e.g., if the most-selected filler was the innocent suspect versus the average filler).

Readers should note that many of the points we have made here about confidence apply as well to other continuous-variable "postdictors" of eyewitness identification accuracy, such as identification decision latencies. Again, however, the approach that a researcher takes can vary depending on the nature of the questions being asked. In the case of decision latencies, for example, Dunning and Perretta (2002) were interested in finding the number of seconds that represented the optimum separation of accurate and inaccurate witnesses. Hence, for their purposes it was useful to find the point along the decision latency time line that yielded the maximum chi-square value separating the accurate from the inaccurate witnesses.

ARCHIVAL RESEARCH AND FIELD EXPERIMENTS

Although our focus in this chapter has been on the design of experimental studies, it is important to note that other methods have been used to examine eyewitness performance. Here we consider two forms of research involving actual cases: (1) archival studies, which use police or prosecutor files to examine past cases or collect new data in police settings but do not involve any experimental methods, and (2) field experiments, which use experimental methods in connection with actual cases. A handful of studies of eyewitness identification performance in actual cases have made use of archival records. The largest and best of these studies have been conducted in the United Kingdom (e.g., Pike, Brace, & Kynan, 2002; Slater, 1994; Valentine, Pickering, & Darling, 2003; Wright & McDaid, 1996) and have involved nearly 15,000 eyewitnesses. Archival studies in North America have been much smaller in scale (e.g., Behrman & Davey, 2001; Behrman & Richards, 2005; Tollestrup, Turtle, & Yuille, 1994).

By *field experiments*, we mean experiments using eyewitnesses to actual crimes, usually conducted in conjunction with a police department. We are not using the term *field experiment* to refer to an experiment involving a simulated crime that happens to be conducted in the "field" (e.g., on the street or in a convenience store). (In the latter case, we consider these to be lab experiments that happen to step outside of the traditional lab and set up a lab in some other setting.) A superb example of a field experiment is one conducted by Wright and Skagerberg (2007), in which actual eyewitnesses to serious crimes were asked critical questions about their lineup identification either before or after being told whether the person they identified was the suspect in the case or merely a filler. In the case of this field experiment, it did not matter whether the suspect was the actual perpetrator or an innocent suspect, because the question concerned the effects of receiving feedback.

If the issue is one of accuracy of identification decisions, archival studies and field experiments present special challenges. This is readily apparent in the highly controversial field experiment conducted by an employee of the Chicago Police Department (Mecklenburg, 2006). The methodological problems with this study are well documented (e.g., see Schacter et al., 2007; Steblay, in press). For current purposes, however, we are more concerned with the factors that lead to ambiguity regarding whether an identification was or was not accurate. In a lab experiment on eyewitness identification, it is definitively known whether a suspect in a lineup is in fact the culprit. Hence, there is no ambiguity in a lab experiment as to whether a given identification was accurate or inaccurate. In an archival study or field experiment, however, the identification of a suspect might or might not be an accurate identification. In all of the DNA exoneration cases involving mistaken identification, for example, the identification that was made was the identification of a suspect, albeit an innocent one.

One way to partially get around this problem in archival studies and field experiments is to note that the identification of a filler is always an error whereas the identification of a suspect would sometimes be an error and sometimes not. In the UK studies, approximately one in three positive identifications made by witnesses was a foil identification. However, even this strategy for determining errors can be problematic in archival studies and field experiments due to poor record keeping. For example, Tollestrup et al. (1994) observed that the Royal Canadian Mounted Police did not distinguish between misidentifications of foils and rejections of lineups—both were recorded as a failure to identify anyone. Behrman and Davey (2001) reported the same problem in their study, and it is clear from footnote 3 in an appendix to the Chicago experiment that foil identifications were not recorded because they were considered "tentative," at least in conditions where the administrator knew the identity of the suspect.

Of course, even without knowing whether the identification of the suspect is accurate, one can assume that such an identification is more likely to be accurate than is the identification of a filler. In this sense, it could be argued that variables that increase identifications of suspects or decrease identifications of fillers are promoting accuracy, whereas variables that decrease identifications of suspects or increase identifications of fillers are promoting inaccuracy. Still, great caution must be exercised in using this logic. Consider, for instance, the myriad ways that one might increase identifications of suspects and decrease identifications of fillers in a field experiment. For example, comparing a condition in which witnesses are kept blind as to which person is the suspect with a condition in which witnesses are told prior to their identification decision which person is the suspect and which ones are merely fillers. The latter would serve to depress the identification of fillers and increase identifications of the suspect. Surely we would not accept this as evidence that witnesses should be told which person is the suspect and which are fillers.

Alternatively, consider what happens if the fillers in the lineup are selected specifically to be implausible lineup members (e.g., do not fit the witness's description of the culprit). That would also serve to depress filler identifications and increase identifications of the suspect. But does that promote accuracy? As a final example, if the depression of filler identifications is a good outcome, then why use fillers at all? Why not make every lineup a show-up instead? The point here is that it is not automatically true that variables that decrease filler identifications or increase suspect identifications in field experiments necessarily promote accuracy (Wells, 2008).

Similar problems can emerge when examining the confidence-accuracy relation in archival and field experiments. Again, the idea is that filler identifications are definitely inaccurate whereas identifications of suspects have at least some (perhaps the most) accurate identifications in the mix. Hence, the relation between eyewitness identification confidence and the filler versus suspect identification decisions can be a proxy for the confidence-accuracy relation in field experiments. Caution must be exercised here as well, because there is compelling lab-based evidence that non-blind lineup administrators (who are the ones soliciting the confidence statement) influence the confidence of the witness based on the lineup administrators' knowledge of whether the witness identified a filler or the suspect (e.g., see Garrioch & Brimacombe, 2001). Hence, in any jurisdiction in which the lineup administrator is the case detective or someone who knows which person is the suspect and which ones are fillers (which is the case in most jurisdictions in the United States), the relation between witness confidence and whether the witness picked a filler instead of the suspect is likely to be artificially inflated by the lineup administrators' influence on the witness.

In general, field experiments that are designed to examine the accuracy or confidence of witnesses should routinely use double-blind procedures (Wells, 2008). This means that neither the case detective nor any other individual who knows which members are fillers and which is the suspect should be the one who administers the lineup.

Finally, we note that field experiments also differ from lab experiments in numerous ways that increase the need for quite large sample sizes. In lab experiments, for example, it is possible to give all witnesses the same type and quality of view, the same duration of exposure, the same delay between witnessing and testing, the same fillers, and approximately the same levels of anxiety, fear, arousal, and so on. In a field experiment, in contrast, these and numerous other variables float freely and vary widely from one witness to the next. Careful measures of these free-floating variables can help at the level of data analysis if they are statistically controlled, but in general, they contribute noise to the data that results in the need for larger sample sizes than are needed in the typical lab experiment.

GENERALIZING RESEARCH FINDINGS

Our emphasis in this chapter has been on experimental methods. We have noted a number of the strengths of experimental methods and some of the advantages of laboratory and staged-event experiments over archival studies and field experiments involving actual cases. Our emphasis naturally raises the question of whether the results from laboratory and staged-event experiments generalize to real-world witnesses and what evidence we might use to address that question. Although space does not permit us to undertake a full review of relevant research findings, we do wish to highlight some of the ways in which the question can be addressed and note a few example findings.

Do Experimental Studies and Studies With Actual Witnesses Yield Convergent Findings?

A number of archival researchers have endeavored to test whether findings revealed in experimental studies are replicated with actual witnesses. For example, laboratory studies indicate that the probability of identifying a perpetrator is reduced by the presence of a weapon (e.g., E. F. Loftus, Loftus, & Messo, 1987; Maass & Köhnken, 1989), and Steblay (1992) reported a reliable impairment from the presence of a weapon in a meta-analysis of 19 studies. In their archival study, Tollestrup et al. (1994) found that the presence of a weapon reduces the likelihood of the suspect's being identified: 41% of robbery suspects in cases involving a weapon were identified, as compared with 71% of suspects in robberies without a weapon. In contrast, Behrman and Davey (2001) found similar rates of identification of police suspects when they compared 240 witnesses to crimes in which a weapon was used with 49 witnesses in crimes without weapons. In their study of 640 witnesses, Valentine, Pickering, and Darling (2003) found that the presence of a weapon had no effect on the likelihood of identifying a suspect, but witnesses were more likely to identify a foil if a weapon was not present. Similar comparisons of experimental and archival findings involving other variables have been made by Valentine et al. along with others, and it is not uncommon to see that the findings do not converge. Does this mean the experimental findings are wrong?

We believe it is entirely too early to reach any conclusions from comparisons of this kind. Certainly there is little doubt that a great many variables have been shown to reliably affect witness performance using laboratory and staged-event experimental methods (see, e.g., the review by Wells, Memon, & Penrod, 2006). However, archival and field-experiment data suffer from a number of deficiencies. As we have noted previously, archival studies and field experiments generally cannot authoritatively establish whether witnesses have made correct identifications. They rely on suspect choices as a primary variable, and because suspect choices can involve a mixture of correct and incorrect identifications, researchers should not be too surprised to observe a different pattern of results when they compare such studies with results from experiments in which accuracy is known.

Another important difference between experimental studies and field or archival studies is that field and archival studies cannot easily isolate variables, because those variables are correlated with other variables, many of which might not have even been measured. Consider, for example, a field study that involved numerous witnesses to a shooting in which it was found that those who were most stressed by the shooting were the most accurate in reporting details of the event (Tollestrup et al., 1994). This finding seemingly goes against the general consensus of the experimental literature on stress and accuracy. However, a closer examination of the data also shows that witnesses who were physically closest to the shooting were the most stressed (which makes sense), and those closest to the event had the better view and were more accurate. These are called multi-collinearity problems, and they are rampant in field and archival studies, which makes it difficult to reach conclusions about the role of individual variables.

There are certainly other features of field data that can muddy the results from such studies. Consider, for example, that in field studies it may be difficult to determine whether a weapon was actually visible to a witness or for how long. In addition, not all witnesses are necessarily tested when the police have a suspect. Witnesses who report a poor memory (those who saw a weapon?) may indicate that they do not really remember what the perpetrator looked like and might, therefore, not be shown a suspect. Furthermore, one might ask about case "selection" effects. Are the police differentially selecting weapon versus non-weapon cases for more intensive investigation (we hope so)? Does more intensive investigation of weapons cases yield a higher proportion of guilty suspects (and a higher proportion of suspect choices) as compared with non-weapons cases? We do not know the answer to those questions, though they are subject to research.

Do Different Research Methods Produce Different Results?

As we highlighted earlier in this chapter, researchers are confronted with a variety of methodological choices when they construct their research studies, giving rise to the following questions:

- Should a long or short video be used rather than a staged event containing one or several culprits?
- Should the culprit be replaced with a look-alike when making culprit-absent arrays?
- How many fillers should be selected and in what manner?
- Do these choices yield differences in results that might prompt us to be concerned about the generalizability of our findings?

We would point to two types of analysis that address the question.

Shapiro and Penrod (1986) published a meta-analysis of factors influencing facial identification. They drew on results from over 190 individual studies reported in 128 articles on face recognition and eyewitness memory. Overall, the studies contained 960 experimental conditions under which identifications were made and included more than 16,950 participants. Most (80%) of the studies analyzed by Shapiro and Penrod (1986) were laboratory-based studies of facial recognition rather than of more realistic eyewitness simulations, such as videotaped or staged events. They noted that type of study (face recognition vs. eyewitness) accounted for 35% of the variance in performance across experimental conditions. Performance levels were higher in the laboratory studies, which raises the question of whether the results are generalizable across research methods.

Similarly, Lindsay and Harvie (1988) conducted a meta-analysis that compared a sample of face recognition and staged-crime studies. They found that the overall correct identification rate (.64) in 113 face-recognition studies was significantly higher than the rate (.58) in 47 staged-crime studies and that the false alarm rate (.18) in 64 face-recognition studies was significantly lower than two types of mistaken identifications in staged-crime studies—those made from 47 target-present arrays (.29) and 12 target-absent arrays (.41).

Although these comparisons of laboratory-based face recognition and more realistic eyewitness studies initially may seem to raise concerns about external validity, the difference in performance between the two types of studies would not raise such concerns if explained by variables (e.g., retention interval) that generally differ in face-recognition versus eyewitness studies. Shapiro and Penrod (1986) tested whether "study characteristics" might explain the differences in identification accuracy rates. They found that variables associated with *attention* variables (including knowledge about an upcoming test and mode of presentation) made significant individual contributions. The *duration of exposure* per face, *pose, memory load at study* (number of faces studied), and *retention interval* accounted for differences in performance. Once all those variables were accounted for, the type of study (facial recognition vs. eyewitness) accounted for just 3% of performance variance (rather than 35%).

A second way to address the generalizability issue was addressed in detail by Penrod & Bornstein (2007), who examined meta-analyses that have appeared since Shapiro and Penrod's (1986) study. These later meta-analyses permit comparisons of performance across research methodologies that vary over studies; these meta-analyses often ask whether methodological variables interact with substantive variables. Penrod and Bornstein show that these meta-analyses consistently demonstrate that whenever the effects of substantive variables vary across research methodologies, they are larger for more realistic procedures. Factors such as lineup presentation (simultaneous vs. sequential), weapon focus, stress, live versus video testing, instructions to witnesses, cross-race identifications, and the like exert larger effects on eyewitness performance when testing conditions more closely match real witnessing conditions (e.g., staged crime or other eyewitness event and live or video stimuli) than when the situation is relatively contrived and controlled. This pattern of results suggests that if there is a generalizability issue, it is that much eyewitness research underestimates the magnitude of effects being studied. Based on research to date, researchers and practitioners can be reasonably confident that experimental findings generalize to real eyewitness situations.

CONCLUDING REMARKS

In this chapter, we have described a number of methodological issues that confront every researcher who designs and conducts an eyewitness identification study. In many cases, researchers fail to think these issues through fully and end up learning the hard way by having their manuscripts rejected on methodological grounds or discovering the problem later and having to redo the study.

We think this chapter might be especially useful for novice eyewitness researchers. Sometimes we are surprised, however, to find even experienced eyewitness researchers failing to consider some of these issues, and neither of the authors of this chapter can claim to be fully exempt from having made a bad call on one of these methodological issues. No study is perfect, and research involves a constant process of improvement.

We also want to emphasize that with only a few exceptions, our recommendations in this chapter are not universal rules applicable to all studies. Researchers need to consider the issues we have raised in the context of their hypotheses and goals. We gave examples of some instances of this sort, such as when it is acceptable to use only target-present or only target-absent lineups. However, when the question being tested is purely theoretical, some of the ecological validity considerations can become moot.

Finally, we encourage would-be eyewitness identification researchers to read the eyewitness identification literature carefully to gain a sense of other methodological issues that are often unique to a given study. But, we caution researchers not to assume that a study is devoid of all possible methodological problems merely because it was published. The standards for methodological soundness in eyewitness identification research and completeness of reporting are higher today than they were only a few years ago, and this trend will undoubtedly continue.

REFERENCES

Behrman, B. W., & Davey, S. L. (2001). Eyewitness identification in actual criminal cases: An archival analysis. *Law and Human Behavior, 25*, 475–491.

Behrman, B. W., & Richards, R. E. (2005). Suspect/foil identification in actual crimes and in the laboratory: A reality monitoring analysis. *Law and Human Behavior, 29*, 279–301.

Brewer, N., Keast, A., & Rishworth, A. (2002). The confidence-accuracy relationship in eyewitness identification: The effects of reflection and disconfirmation on correlation and calibration. *Journal of Experimental Psychology: Applied, 8,* 44–56.

Brewer, N., & Wells, G. L. (2006). The confidence-accuracy relationship in eyewitness identification: Effects of lineup instructions, foil similarity and target-absent base rates. *Journal of Experimental Psychology: Applied, 12,* 11–30.

Dunning, D., & Perretta, S. (2002). Automaticity and eyewitness accuracy: A 10- to 12-second rule for distinguishing accurate from inaccurate positive identifications. *Journal of Applied Psychology, 87,* 951–962.

Garrioch, L., & Brimacombe, C. A. E. (2001). Lineup administrators' expectations: Their impact on eyewitness confidence. *Law & Human Behavior, 25,* 299–314.

Juslin, P., Olson, N., & Winman, A. (1996). Calibration and diagnosticity of confidence in eyewitness identification: Comments on what can and cannot be inferred from a low confidence-accuracy correlation. *Journal of Experimental Psychology: Learning, Memory, and Cognition, 5,* 1304–1316.

Lindsay, R. C. L., & Harvie, V. L. (1988). Hits, false alarms, correct and mistaken identifications: The effect of method of data collection on facial memory. In M. Gruneberg, P. Morris, & R. Sykes (Eds.), *Practical aspects of memory: Current research and issues* (pp. 47–52). Chichester, England: Wiley.

Loftus, E. F., Loftus, G. R., & Messo, J. (1987). Some facts about "weapon focus." *Law and Human Behavior, 11,* 55–62.

Maass, A., & Köhnken, G. (1989). Eyewitness identification: Simulating the "weapon effect." *Law and Human Behavior, 13,* 397–408.

McGrath, R. E., & Meyer, G. J. (2006). When effect sizes disagree: The case of *r* and *d*. *Psychological Methods, 11,* 386–401.

Mecklenburg, S. (2006). *Report to the legislature of the state of Illinois: The Illinois Pilot Program on sequential double-blind identification procedures.* Retrieved November 15, 2010, from http://www.chicago police.org/IL%20Pilot%20on%20 Eyewitness%20ID.pdf

Malpass, R. S. (1981). Effective size and defendant bias in eyewitness identification lineups. *Law and Human Behavior, 5,* 299–309.

Memon, A., & Gabbert, F. (2003). Unraveling the effects of sequential presentation in culprit-present lineups. *Applied Cognitive Psychology, 17,* 703–714.

Memon, A., Hope, L., & Bull, R. H. C. (2003). Exposure duration: Effects on eyewitness accuracy and confidence. *British Journal of Psychology, 94,* 339–354.

Morgan, C. A., Hazlett, G., Doran, A., Garrett, S., Hoyt, G., Thomas, P., Southwick, S. M. (2004). Accuracy of eyewitness memory for persons encountered during exposure to highly intense stress. *International Journal of Law and Psychiatry, 27,* 265–279.

Penrod, S. D., & Bornstein, B. H. (2007). Generalizing eyewitness reliability research. In R. C. L. Lindsay, D. Ross, D. Read, & M. Toglia (Eds.), *Handbook of eyewitness psychology (Vol. II): Memory for people.* Mahwah, NJ: Lawrence Erlbaum.

Pike, G., Brace, N., & Kynan, S. (2002, March). The visual identification of suspects: Procedures and practice (Briefing Note No. 2/02). London, England: Home Office Research Development and Statistics Directorate.

Schacter, D., Dawes, R., Jacoby, L. L., Kahneman, D., Lempert, R., Roediger, H. L., & Rosenthal, R. (2007). Studying eyewitness investigations in the field. *Law and Human Behavior, 31,* 3–5.

Shapiro, P., & Penrod, S. (1986). A meta-analysis of facial identification studies. *Psychological Bulletin, 100,* 139–156.

Slater, A. (1994). Identification parades: A scientific evaluation. Police Research Award Scheme. London, England: Police Research Group, Home Office.

Sporer, S., Penrod, S., Read, D., & Cutler, B. L. (1995). Choosing, confidence, and accuracy: A meta-analysis of the confidence-accuracy relation in eyewitness identification studies. *Psychological Bulletin, 118,* 315–327.

Steblay, N. M. (1992). A meta-analytic review of the weapon focus effect. *Law and Human Behavior, 16,* 413–424.

Steblay, N. M. (In press). What we know now: The Evanston Illinois field lineups. *Law and Human Behavior.* doi: 10.1007/s10979-009-9207-7

Tollestrup, P., Turtle, J., & Yuille, J. (1994). Actual victims and witnesses to robbery and fraud: An archival analysis. In D. F. Ross, J. D. Read, & M. P. Toglia (Eds.), *Adult eyewitness testimony: Current trends and developments* (pp. 44–160). New York, NY: Cambridge University Press.

Valentine, T., Pickering, A., & Darling, S. (2003). Characteristics of eyewitness identification that predict the outcome of real lineups. *Applied Cognitive Psychology, 17*, 969–993.

Wells, G. L. (1993). What do we know about eyewitness identification? *American Psychologist, 48*, 553–571.

Wells, G. L. (2008). Field experiments on eyewitness identification: Towards a better understanding of pitfalls and prospects. *Law and Human Behavior, 32*, 6–10.

Wells, G. L., & Bradfield, A. L. (1998). "Good, you identified the suspect:" Feedback to eyewitnesses distorts their reports of the witnessing experience. *Journal of Applied Psychology, 83*, 360–376.

Wells, G. L., & Bradfield, A. L. (1999). Measuring the goodness of lineups: Parameter estimation, question effects, and limits to the mock witness paradigm. *Applied Cognitive Psychology, 13S*, 27–40.

Wells, G. L., Leippe, M. R., & Ostrom, T. M. (1979). Guidelines for empirically assessing the fairness of a lineup. *Law and Human Behavior, 3*, 285–293.

Wells, G. L., & Lindsay, R. C. L. (1980). On estimating the diagnosticity of eyewitness nonidentifications. *Psychological Bulletin, 88*, 776–784.

Wells, G. L., Memon, A. & Penrod, S. D. (2006). Eyewitness evidence: Improving its probative value. *Psychological Science in the Public Interest, 7*, 45–75.

Wells, G. L., & Olson, E. (2002). Eyewitness identification: Information gain from incriminating and exonerating behaviors. *Journal of Experimental Psychology: Applied, 8*, 155–167.

Wells, G. L., Rydell, S. M., & Seelau, E. P. (1993). On the selection of distractors for eyewitness lineups. *Journal of Applied Psychology, 78*, 835–844.

Wells, G. L., & Turtle, J. W. (1986). Eyewitness identification: The importance of lineup models. *Psychological Bulletin, 99*, 320–329.

Wells, G. L., & Windschitl, P. D. (1999). Stimulus sampling in social psychological experimentation. *Personality and Social Psychology Bulletin, 25*, 1115–1125.

Wright, D. B., & McDaid, A. T. (1996). Comparing system and estimator variables using data from real lineups. *Applied Cognitive Psychology, 10*, 75–84.

Wright, D. B., & Skagerberg, E. M. (2007). Post-identification feedback affects real eyewitnesses. *Psychological Science, 18*, 172–178.

CHAPTER 14

Children's Eyewitness Memory: Methodological Issues

GAIL S. GOODMAN, MARGARET-ELLEN PIPE, AND KELLY McWILLIAMS

An 8-year-old girl whose mother was murdered last November yesterday testified for the prosecution in the inquiry in which two relatives, a mother and a son, are charged with the killing. Felicia was called as a witness for the State in the ongoing preliminary inquiry . . . of the murder of Felicia's mother, La Toya King, 24 . . . during a family argument. King was stabbed and later died . . . . Felicia . . . was barely visible in the witness-box which is about four feet high. The microphone in the witness box was bent low to reach her. McNicolls [the judge] . . . questioned her briefly to ensure that she understood the idea of a duty to tell the truth. "Do you know you must speak the truth every day?" he asked. "Yes," she replied in a soft voice, nodding her head. "What will happen if you don't speak the truth?" McNicolls probed. "You will get in trouble," the girl said.

(Bagoo, 2008)

Andre R. Williams, 29, carried on a six-year sexual relationship with a now 13 year-old girl. She recounted the nature of their relationship to a neighbor who promptly contacted the authorities. Andre R. Williams pled guilty to one-count of first degree criminal sexual act.

(McGuire, 2009)

In a highly charged atmosphere, a 10-year-old witness, the youngest to testify so far in the Mumbai [India] terror attack case, identified Ajmal Kasab, the lone captured terrorist, as the man who sprayed bullets on innocent people on the fateful night of November 26, 2008. The witness, who was shot on her leg during the attack inside the Chhatrapati Shivaji Terminal (CST) in Mumbai, and her father Natwarlal deposed before the special court in the CST attack case in which Kasab is charged with killing over 50 people.

(Shetty, 2009)

THESE DRAMATIC EXAMPLES illustrate some of the many legal cases that motivate researchers to study children's eyewitness memory. In such highly charged prosecutions, the accuracy of children's reports becomes crucial for justice. Protecting children from trauma and crime, the innocent from false report, and children from false memories are important goals of the legal system. Given that the legal system was not devised with child witnesses in mind, it often looks to psychologists for information on how best to interview children and how much to rely on their reports. Thus, from an applied perspective, research on children's eyewitness memory has much to offer. However, in addition to these applied issues, there are many fascinating theoretical questions that arise about children's eyewitness memory, including: How does trauma affect children's eyewitness reports? How malleable is children's memory? What are the best ways to interview children to obtain accurate and complete statements? Many of the applied and theoretical issues are best answered through rigorous scientific research, but the study of children's eyewitness memory poses a variety of methodological challenges, many of which we discuss here.

In this chapter, we first describe a modicum of case law that concerns child witnesses. We then turn to a brief history of scientific research on child eyewitness memory. Internal and external validity issues and ethical concerns are also reviewed. We then discuss methodological issues regarding trauma and child memory, child maltreatment and memory, children's suggestibility and false memory, forensic protocols, and children's testimony in court.

CASE LAW

In the United States, there is no lower limit to the age at which children can potentially testify in court. However, in reality, children younger than 4 or 5 years rarely take the stand. This is because, in part, young preschoolers are likely to have their competence successfully challenged by the opposing attorney. In this case, a competence hearing will be held, during which the child will be questioned by the attorneys and the judge. At issue will be such matters as whether the child knows the difference between the truth and a lie and that one gets in trouble for lying (as in the example at the start of this chapter), and whether the child has an uncoached memory of what occurred. The judge will then decide whether the child is "competent" to serve as a witness in the trial.

If the child is deemed competent to testify or if the child's competence is not challenged, the child might be called to testify at trial. In such cases, the child will likely be subjected to direct and cross-examination in open court facing the defendant. Such face-to-face confrontation is considered a fundamental constitutional right of the defendant, as stated in the Sixth

Amendment of the U.S. Constitution. However, that right is not absolute. If the child would be so traumatized as not to be able to reasonably communicate, at least in child sexual abuse trials, the child can in principle be permitted to testify via closed-circuit TV (Goodman et al., 1998). Nevertheless, U.S. prosecutors are hesitant to have children testify in this way for fear the children's testimony will have less impact on jurors, a fear that may well be justified (Goodman, Quas, Bulkley, & Shapiro, 1999). In many other countries, children rarely if ever actually testify in court. Instead, their statements during forensic interviews are recorded on videotape, and the videotape is entered as evidence at trial (Cordon, Goodman, & Anderson, 2003).

However, even in the United States, taking the stand is not the only way that children's voices are heard in court. Although the U.S. legal system generally has distaste for hearsay, there are several hearsay exceptions that apply to cases involving child witnesses (Myers, Cordon, Ghetti, & Goodman, 2002). For example, special hearsay exceptions can permit a mother, teacher, or doctor to testify at trial about what the child said out of court, such as when the child first disclosed the crime. Even if the child is deemed "unavailable" as a witness, such hearsay can be entered into evidence.

Although the U.S. Supreme Court has started restricting such hearsay, if the child's out-of-court statements were made in the context of a legal investigation—that is, if the context was "testimonial" (*Crawford v. Washington*, 2004)—and the child is available for cross-examination, the child's statements are admissible. Thus, if a child had disclosed to a social worker or police officer, that official could still recount to the jury what the child said during the forensic interview, but only if the child also takes the stand and is subjected to cross-examination. A videotaped forensic interview is also considered hearsay in the U.S. legal system. Thus, according to the *Crawford* decision, it likely would be shown to the jury only if the child also testifies in court. Because the U.S. Supreme Court did not define what it meant by "testimonial," courts vary in how they have defined the word, leaving much still to the judge's discretion.

This sampling of case law provides a sense of some of the complexities of the legal system in regard to child witnesses, but it is just a small taste. More thorough, in-depth coverage of relevant legal issues can be found in Lyon and LaMagna (2007) and Myers (1998).

THE BEGINNINGS OF THE SCIENTIFIC STUDY OF CHILD WITNESSES

The scientific study of children's testimony began around the turn of the twentieth century and blossomed for a little over two decades before coming to a virtual halt and entering a hiatus that lasted more than 50 years (Goodman, 1984, 2006). This first phase of research was summarized in

Goodman's (1984) review, in which the dearth of current research at that time was lamented, although the situation was to change drastically in the following years (Goodman, 2006).

Although short-lived, the early phase of research on children's testimony had a profound and enduring influence on beliefs about children's abilities as witnesses and set the stage in terms of focus and methodology for many contemporary studies. From the outset, the focus of research on children's testimony was the fallibility of children's memory and children's susceptibility to suggestion. Researchers found that in response to what was often highly suggestive questioning, children were more likely to make errors than adults, with age differences in childhood also sometimes reported (e.g., Binet, 1900; Goodman, 1984; Pear & Wyatt, 1914; Stern, 1910, 1939; Varendonck, 1911).

The basic paradigm used in these early studies was for researchers to present children with a visual stimulus, such as a card with items attached or a picture of a scene, and then to question children about the contents of the card or picture (Binet, 1900; Stern, 1910, 1939). In one study, for example, Binet (1900) asked different groups of children and young adults neutral, moderately suggestive, and strongly suggestive questions about items on a card they had been shown and found that children were more likely to acquiesce to the suggestive questions than were young adults (Binet 1900; see also, e.g., Stern, 1910, 1939).

Also from the outset was a concern about the relevance of research to the legal context—the issue of external validity that continues to challenge contemporary researchers studying children's testimony. Questions about the relevance of the "picture tests" led to the more realistic "event tests" of memory, as illustrated in a series of studies conducted by Varendonck (1911). In the context of a highly publicized child murder trial in which he was called upon as an expert, Varendonck questioned children about the physical features of a familiar person (e.g., children were asked about the color of a teacher's beard when, in fact, the teacher did not sport a beard) or what had taken place in a staged classroom interaction (e.g., children were asked whether a man entering had held his hat in his left or right hand, when in fact and contrary to custom of the time, he had not taken it off at all).

Even under these more realistic conditions, with questions more closely approximating those that a child witness might be asked, the conclusions remained essentially the same: Children tended to be less reliable witnesses when faced with misleading and suggestive questions than adults (Varendonck, 1911; Pear & Wyatt, 1914). When Varendonck asked rhetorically, "When are we going to give up, in all civilized nations, listening to children in courts of law?" he summed up the implications that were drawn from the research of the time in no uncertain terms: children were unreliable witnesses, and their testimony should not be trusted.

It was clear, however, even from these early studies, that it was suggestive questioning that produced inaccuracies in children's accounts rather than defective memories per se. Pear and Wyatt (1914), for example, had noted that children's free recall narratives of a staged interaction were quite accurate, in contrast to their responses to misleading and suggestive questioning. Yet it was not until the 1980s, largely in response to the growing awareness of the prevalence of child sexual abuse and recognition that in the vast majority of cases the only evidence of sexual abuse was the child's testimony, that researchers began to explore with any vigor conditions under which, as it turned out, children could provide highly reliable testimony (see also Dent & Stephenson, 1979).

The first studies specifically focusing on the conditions under which children were found to be reliable—not only providing narrative accounts of their experiences but resisting misleading questioning—were those of Goodman and her students (e.g., Rudy & Goodman, 1991; see Goodman, 2006, for review). These studies examined children's memory and suggestibility in relation to events in which children had been participants (rather than simply bystander witnesses). They also incorporated features mimicking aspects of sexually abusive experiences insofar as ethical considerations allowed, such as interacting with an unfamiliar adult, removing items of clothing, touching each other, and so on (see Goodman, 2006, for review).

Although these researchers expected that young children would still be highly suggestible about such abuse-related acts, in fact, the children were surprisingly accurate. The question of whether children could after all provide reliable testimony about child sexual abuse raised a host of other questions, such as whether and how trauma affects children's memory. Studies of children's memory for mildly stressful medical procedures as analogs to memory for child abuse were first published in the early 1990s (Goodman, Hirschman, Hepps, & Rudy, 1991). Subsequent studies, which quickly followed, were based on much more distressing medical experiences, such as injuries seen in the emergency room and radiological techniques involving genital catheterization (Goodman, Quas, Batterman-Faunce, Riddlesberger, & Kuhn, 1997; Merritt, Ornstein, & Spiker, 1994; Peterson & Bell, 1996).

At around the same time in the 1990s, researchers began to evaluate techniques that could be incorporated into interviews conducted with suspected victims of abuse to facilitate disclosure and accurate reporting of abuse, such as training and preparation procedures, the effects of dolls and other props, as well as protocols for interviewing suspected victims (e.g., Dent & Flin, 1992; Goodman & Bottoms, 1993; Saywitz & Snyder, 1996). They also turned to other questions, such as the effects of testifying on children in both the short and the long term, methods for assessing children's competence to testify, and children's understanding of relevant concepts that might help explain why children failed to disclose abuse for long periods of time, if they disclosed it at all (e.g., Bussey & Grimbeek, 1995; Cashmore & de Haas, 1995; Goodman et al., 1992; Saywitz, Jaenicke, & Camparo, 1990). Despite these wide-ranging research topics relating to children's testimony, the concern about the risks of children making memory errors and false reports that had characterized the studies of 50 years earlier continued to dominate the field, as they do to this day. The highly publicized, sensational preschool and custody cases of the 1980s highlighted the contemporary relevance of these concerns in the new context of suspected sexual abuse, and researchers have continued to explore these questions, as discussed subsequently in this chapter.

INTERNAL AND EXTERNAL VALIDITY AND ETHICAL ISSUES

In the following sections, we have selected several topic areas to illustrate the range of contemporary approaches to the study of children's testimony, the strengths and weaknesses of the approaches, the particular issues they raise, and how these are typically dealt with. All researchers addressing questions related to children's testimony are likely to find themselves challenged by the oftentimes conflicting demands relating to the external and internal validity of the research. On the one hand, researchers attempt to maximize the external validity of the research, so that they can be confident that their findings are relevant and applicable to questions that arise in actual cases when children give testimony in court or other forensic contexts. On the other hand, they strive to maintain good internal validity, so that they can be confident that their findings reflect the variables they identify as important, not other variables that they have been unable to control. There are no easy solutions to these dilemmas.

Laboratory style research is typically high on internal validity, because the researcher has control over all aspects of the research likely to be of interest. These relate to the selection of participants by characteristics of interest (e.g., age and gender) and their random assignment to groups; the to-be-remembered event or information (e.g., whether in the form of an experienced or witnessed event, word lists, or a video or story); the delay between the event and when the child is interviewed (whether minutes, days, weeks, months, or years); and the way in which the child's account is elicited (e.g., a structured or scripted interview, free recall questions, leading and/or suggestive questions). However, such a highly controlled laboratory approach is not well suited to many of the questions of interest to those concerned with the accuracy of children's testimony, at least not without sacrificing external validity.

To take an example, ethically it is difficult to conduct studies involving the elicitation of false reports of child abuse, so researchers turn to studies of false reports of non-abusive events (Goodman, 2006). But the question that inevitably arises is whether children are equally vulnerable (or resistant) to attempts to elicit false reports in connection with abusive events as they are with non-abusive events (Goodman, 2006). In attempts to circumvent such problems, researchers have continued to expand the kinds of experiences about which false memories are likely to be created, in an attempt to maximize external validity. Conversely, although field studies of children's accounts of abusive experiences are undeniably high on external validity, these studies encounter many threats to internal validity—for example, because researchers seldom have independent information verifying what actually happened. The challenges may also lead to innovative solutions, however, and some researchers have taken advantage of unique opportunities, albeit rare, to verify children's abuse reports, such as when the abuse has been recorded by the perpetrator. Such studies provide important "checks" on the generalizability of findings from more controlled laboratory-style research.

The dilemma of how best to balance internal and external validity is, at least in part, tied to ethical issues. Ethically, researchers cannot, for example, expose children to actual crimes to study the accuracy of the children's later statements so as to simultaneously enhance both the internal and external validity of the experiment. Ethical issues clearly place limitations on the child witness topics scientists can rigorously study.

There are many ethical issues to consider in conducting research on children's eyewitness memory. These issues are of paramount importance for the participants' protection. Researchers must also keep in mind that some of the issues are also crucial for protection of researchers themselves as well as universities (e.g., from civil suit). We review a few of the key ethical issues here.

In the United States and many other countries, research must be approved by institutional review boards (IRBs). Federal guidelines govern the rules used by IRBs (e.g., see http://www.hhs.gov/ohrp/humansubjects/guidance/45cfr46 .htm), although each IRB has a certain degree of freedom to develop its own guidelines. Research with children, prisoners, victims, and other vulnerable populations tends to receive particular scrutiny from IRBs. Nevertheless, researchers have found ethical ways to study quite sensitive topics (see Chae, Bederian-Gardner, Lindsay, & Goodman, in press).

The federal regulations stipulate that "[N]o investigator may involve a human being as a subject in research . . . unless the investigator has obtained the legally effective informed consent of the subject or the subject's legally authorized representative." Children are not permitted to provide informed consent; typically, one or both of their parents must do so as their "legally authorized representative." In much of the research on children's eyewitness memory, obtaining parental consent has been fairly easy, because the children were from non-abusive, middle-class families. However, when studying eyewitness memory in child abuse victims, the children may have been removed from home and placed in foster care. Foster parents typically cannot serve as "legally authorized representatives" in regard to children's research participation. Instead, it may be necessary to obtain consent from the juvenile court judge, the children's juvenile court attorneys, or child protective services, and this is often not easy. When maltreated children are still living at home or have returned home, parental consent is again a viable alternative.

Another tricky issue regarding informed consent is that typically in child eyewitness memory research, children should not know that their memory will be tested. The researcher's goal is to make the situation analogous to a criminal event; prior to a real crime, it is unlikely children would have forewarning that a memory test would follow. Such knowledge could bias the memory strategies used. Even informing the parents of the memory test can be risky, because the parents may then coach the child between laboratory sessions, also affecting the child's memory. Thus, researchers have to work with their local IRBs to help them understand this consideration.

Fortunately, informed consent and children's assent (often IRBs require assent from children 12 to 17 years old) can be relatively vague on this minor form of deception by mentioning in consent forms that children will experience an event and later the children will be given several assessments and interviewed. Immediately before the memory test, parents can be informed of the true intent of the research, review the questions to be asked, and sign a form stating they have approved all questions or that they have crossed any out that they do not want asked. It is especially important for the parents to review the memory questionnaire if misleading questions or suggestive techniques are to be included, and it is also particularly important for the children to be debriefed to reinstate accurate memory and explain that the interviewers made mistakes in what they suggested. This can be used as a type of moral lesson about not necessarily agreeing with false information interviewers or others might suggest.

Another ethical issue, no less thorny, concerns the possibility of having to report child abuse to authorities. In child eyewitness memory research, it is often of interest to assess children's trauma histories. In some cases, a non-abused control group is to be included. In such cases, questions about former child abuse may need to be asked in an attempt to screen child victims from the control condition. There are several standardized measures of trauma histories for children (e.g., see Bernstein & Fink, 1998; Assessment-National Center for PTSD, 2009). However, if researchers ask about children's trauma histories, they may well obtain disclosures of possible abuse. Depending on state law, researchers may be mandated reporters, required by law to report suspicions of abuse to authorities (child protective services or the police). Even if researchers are not mandated reporters, they may feel ethically and morally obligated to report suspicions of abuse (Steinberg, Pynoos, Goenjian, Sossanabadi, & Sherr, 1999; Urquiza, 1991). Yet, many IRBs require researchers to state in consent forms that the information obtained in a research project will be kept confidential unless subpoenaed. Fortunately, researchers can apply to the federal government for a Certificate of Confidentiality, which both protects the research data from being subpoenaed and provides researchers with the option to report suspicions of abuse to authorities.

CHILD EYEWITNESS MEMORY RESEARCH

The research described in the following sections illustrates a range of approaches to the study of children's testimony, including tightly controlled experimental studies designed to advance theoretical understanding, such as laboratory-style studies, in which researchers stage experiences for children and then interview them about the experiences; analog studies that capitalize on naturally occurring events such as medical procedures and injuries characterized by some of the variables of particular interest in the context of children's testimony; false memories in which researchers determine whether they can "implant" memory for entire events that did not occur; and field studies in which researchers examine children's accounts of abuse elicited in the context of an actual investigation. We discuss the advantages and disadvantages of these methodological approaches and special issues and considerations in relation to the topics they address.

TRAUMA AND MEMORY

Cases involving child witnesses are often dramatic if not heart wrenching. When a child is victimized and then needs to recount what happened so that the criminal can be apprehended before hurting others, the issue of the accuracy of the children's memory for trauma becomes critical. Fortunately, researchers have found ways to study the accuracy of children's testimony regarding traumatic events.

For many years, psychiatrists and others wrote case histories about children's memory for trauma, but typically they had no way to code the children's reports for accuracy (but see Terr, 1988). To know how accurate memory is, objective documentation (e.g., a videotape) of the event is required against which to evaluate the child's report. In recent years, scientists have been able to conduct "scientific case studies," because more and more it seems, perpetrators are actually recording their crimes against children, either through videotapes, photographs, audio recordings, or computer files. This documentation, when discovered by the police and turned over to researchers, permits scientists to compare the child victims' statements in forensic interviews or in court with the actual objective record of the crime (see Paz-Alonso, Ogle, & Goodman, 2009, for review).

For example, Bidrose and Goodman (2000) were permitted to evaluate the statements of four girls, ranging in age from 8 to 15 years, who were involved in a "sex ring" (a group of adult males who sexually abused and prostituted the girls). The main perpetrator recorded many of the assaults on the girls via audiotape and photographs. In fact, when the case broke and the police invaded the man's apartment, sexual acts had been occurring at that very time, all of which were being recorded by the main perpetrator. Bidrose and Goodman found that the girls later, in their statements to the police and in court, left out considerable information about the sexual acts and also downplayed their own role in the abuse. More recently, Leander and her colleagues (Leander, Christianson, & Granhag, 2007, Leander, Granhag, & Christianson, 2005) have conducted several scientific case studies, with the crimes studied ranging from young children being kidnapped and sexually assaulted to older children being lured into sexual acts through the Internet, finding that the children's reports tend to be quite accurate but that the children often try to avoid discussion of the sexual acts.

Such research has the great advantage of external validity (real crimes and real eyewitness testimony is involved). However, from a scientific perspective, such research is limited. For example, one disadvantage is that it is difficult to study false reports using this research paradigm. It is also difficult to examine cause–effect relations, which is a fundamental scientific goal. Thus, researchers also conduct analog and laboratory research on children's memory for traumatic and stressful events.

Although researchers cannot traumatize children for purposes of studying children's memory for criminal-type events, researchers can take advantage, in analog research, of traumatic events children will experience in the course of their lives. For research on child eyewitness memory, the most commonly used traumatic events are stressful medical procedures. Such procedures are ordered by doctors for medical purposes and are thus not imposed by researchers; with permission, however, researchers can document what happened and then test the children's memory later as though a forensic investigation were underway. Such analog research on trauma and memory has included medical procedures such as inoculations, facial surgery, and invasive radiology procedures.

As an example of such methodology, Goodman, Quas, Batterman-Faunce, Kuhn, and Riddlesburger (1994) examined 3- to 10-year-olds' memory for voiding cystourethrogram fluoroscopy (VCUG). This is a medical procedure used to detect urinary tract problems. It involves children being restrained while they are catheterized through their urethras. It can be painful and embarrassing for children, and because it involves penetration of the genitals, it can serve as an analog to child rape. For the study, researchers were permitted (with parental consent) to observe and document children undergoing the procedure. A week to a month later, the children's memory was tested for what happened. The children were first asked general free recall questions and then invited to use anatomical dolls and props to tell and show what happened. Finally, the children were asked a mix of specific (leading) and misleading questions. Parents completed several questionnaires about their child and themselves, including a questionnaire on adult attachment (Bowlby, 1980; Mikulincer & Shaver, 2007) and a questionnaire on how they helped prepare the child for the medical test and how they treated the child afterwards.

The results indicated typical age differences, with younger (as compared with older) children providing less information in free recall and making more errors in answering specific and misleading questions. However, in addition to age, the parents' attachment orientation was a robust predictor of the children's accuracy. Parents who were more avoidant of intimacy were less likely to prepare the children for the medical test and were less sympathetic to the children afterwards, which seemed to affect the children's memory (see also Chae, Ogle, & Goodman, 2009; Quas et al., 1999).

A great advantage of such analog studies is that they permit researchers to examine the accuracy of children's memory for traumatic events with great precision. However, there are several disadvantages as well. One is that the analog situations invariably differ from real crime situations in potentially important ways. For example, medical procedures are socially sanctioned and are typically not subject to the same degree of secrecy and shame as are real crimes such as child sexual abuse. Another disadvantage is that the medical procedures may differ somewhat across children, resulting in less standardization of the to-be-remembered information than one can expect in the laboratory. Researchers thus often turn to the laboratory to study children's memory.

In principle, laboratory research is preferable because it permits true experimentation. It is also particularly useful for testing theory. However, for ethical reasons, laboratory research on children's eyewitness memory has dealt with somewhat stressful but not highly traumatic events. For example, a videoclip of an accident might be shown to children (Paz-Alonso, 2004) or a fake fire alarm set off in the lab (Quas, Bauer, & Boyce, 2004; Stein & Boyce, 1995), and children's eyewitness memory subsequently tested for the event. Paz-Alonso (2004), for example, first questioned a large group of children about events they considered highly stressful. Being hurt during an accident was mentioned prominently. He then constructed two nearly identical videotapes of a family going out to the country for a day of relaxation. However, in one version of the videotape, the children are shown being hurt during a bicycle accident, whereas in the other version, the children are not hurt while riding their bicycles. A new group of children were then randomly assigned to watch one or the other version of the videotape, and then their memory and suggestibility were tested.

The great advantage for scientists of such research is its relatively high internal validity. The experimental stimuli can be precisely controlled, children can be randomly assigned to groups, and independent variables such as the duration of the stimulus, the delay before testing, the age of the children, and so forth can be manipulated. True experiments can be performed. Nevertheless, even in terms of internal validity, such research is not always as scientifically pure as one might hope. The problem is that it is difficult from such studies to make solid causal inferences about the effects of stress on memory, because two factors typically vary at the same time: the stressfulness of the information and the content of the videoclip. Thus, even in the laboratory, it can be difficult to pinpoint the effects of distress on children's eyewitness memory. Moreover, such research suffers from relatively low external validity. For example, watching a video is likely not as stressful as experiencing a violent crime. Nevertheless, much can be learned about the accuracy of children's eyewitness memory from laboratory research.

MALTREATMENT AND MEMORY

The studies described so far concern memory of stressful or traumatic events in children without known histories of trauma. However, many children who come into contact with the legal system have trauma histories—for example, histories of child maltreatment. It can be difficult to gain research access to children with such histories. However, collaboration with clinics that serve maltreated children can facilitate such research. In one such collaboration, Eisen et al. (2002, 2007) were able to take methodology developed by Saywitz, Goodman, Nicholas, and Moan (1991) and apply it to maltreated children. Saywitz et al. had examined children's memory for an anogenital examination, performed by a pediatrician, to explore the accuracy of children's reports of genital touch. Eisen et al. incorporated that methodology into a study that took advantage of the fact that maltreated children experience anogenital examinations by pediatricians during forensic evaluations of abuse. Such examinations are performed for forensic and medical purposes to look for evidence of sexual violation, specifically penetration, as well as the possibility of a sexually transmitted disease.

In two studies, Eisen and colleagues tested several hundred maltreated children ranging in age from 3 to 17 years in regard to their memory and suggestibility for an anogenital examination. These children had been removed from home because of suspicions of child maltreatment (e.g., neglect, sexual abuse, and/or physical abuse). They came from some of the most crime-ridden and traumatizing neighborhoods in Chicago. Measures of trauma-related psychopathology (e.g., PTSD, dissociation), intelligence, and type of maltreatment were also included. Among the findings were that, at least under the conditions of the memory testing, typical age trends in memory and suggestibility existed in this population, the maltreated children were not highly suggestible about abuse, sexually abused children were less error-prone than the other children regarding the anogenital examination, and neglected children tended to make the most errors.

An advantage of such research is that actual child victims can be studied. Also, in some circumstances, children can be tested in the throes of actual legal investigations, as accomplished by Eisen et al. (2002, 2007), adding considerably to the external validity of the research. Disadvantages include that such research is quite difficult and expensive to perform and typically requires extensive ethical review, approvals from child protective services, and considerable grant support. Yet such research is vital for understanding memory and suggestibility in children who are likely to serve as witnesses in court.

SUGGESTIBILITY

Clyde Ray Spencer has spent the past 20 years in prison for molesting his children Matthew and Katherine (now 33 and 30, respectively). The children now say that the abuse never took place. Matthew, who was

9 at the time of the allegation, says that he only made the report after incessant questioning by the sheriff . . . . He claims he only made the allegation so that the sheriff would leave him alone and stop asking questions. Katherine, also claims that she made the report after the sheriff bought her ice cream. She says now that the abuse never took place.

("Kids Recant Abuse," 2009)

In 1991, when she was 3 years old, Desiree Andaverde told police she saw "daddy put mommy in the trunk." A few days later, Desiree's mother was found frozen, in a car outside her favorite bar. Despite the statements made by 3-year-old Desiree, police did not bring charges against the girl's step-father, Thomas Zich. Now, 17 years later, Desiree (20) will testify against her step-father. The defense contends that the girl's memories are too old and have been tainted by family members.

(Seewer, 2009)

Concern about children's susceptibility to false reports due to mis-information presented, for example, by family members or during forensic interviews has fueled much of the research on children's eyewitness memory. In this section, we discuss methodology for studying suggestibility about details of experienced events, and in the next section we discuss "false memory."

To study child suggestibility regarding details of an event, two main paradigms have been employed: the post-event misinformation paradigm (Loftus, 1979) and the leading/misleading questions paradigm. In the post-event misinformation paradigm, children (as well as adults) are typically presented with a slide show or videotape (e.g., of a car-pedestrian accident), and then after a delay, questions are asked or statements are made in which misinformation about details of the events is embedded. This introduction of misinformation is typically fairly subtle, with researchers using presuppo-sitions, such as "How fast was the car going when it passed the country barn?" when in fact the slide show did not depict a country barn. The delay permits memory to fade, making it more likely that the misinformation will be unnoticed.

Note that the misinformation is not first introduced during the main memory test itself but rather during the delay interval. After a second delay, a recognition test is presented in which participants have to indicate whether or not the misinformation was actually viewed in the original presentation. (Recall tests can also be employed: Zaragoza, McCloskey, & Jamis, 1987.) Using this basic paradigm, researchers have discovered that young child-ren are more likely than adults to incorporate the misinformation into their memory reports (Ceci, Ross, & Toglia, 1987; see Schwartz-Kenney & Goodman, 1999, for use of this same basic paradigm to study children's memory malleability regarding a real-life event). There have been several takeoffs on this basic methodology, including those that investigate whether the results indicate actual memory change, source-monitoring errors, or simply social compliance (e.g., Lindsay & Johnson, 1989; McCloskey & Zaragoza, 1985; Paz-Alonso & Goodman, 2008; Schaaf, 2001), all of which seem to be involved. More recently, researchers have added manipulations showing that parents' introduction of misinformation can contaminate children's reports (Poole & Lindsay, 2002), and that the adverse effects of misinformation on children's reports can last a year's time (London, Bruck, & Melnyk, 2009; but see Huffman, Crossman, & Ceci, 1997).

In contrast, in the leading/misleading questions paradigm, children experience an event and are later interviewed about it. Leading statements and misinformation are presented within the questions that constitute the memory test—that is, during the memory interview. The applied reason to examine the accuracy of children's eyewitness reports using this paradigm is that parents or forensic interviewers might inadvertently introduce misinformation in their questions because, for example, children might believe something occurred, even though it had not happened. For example, a divorced parent could have suspicions of sexual abuse in the context of a custody battle and be highly motivated to question the child, or a forensic interviewer could become overzealous in trying to identify a possible perpetrator.

Specific questions such as "Was his shirt blue?" suggest information, and in that sense are leading (unless the witness has already indicated the information). If specific questions contain *false* information, they increase children's errors (compared with free recall questions). Misleading tag questions, such as "His shirt was blue, wasn't it?" (when the person's shirt was not blue) not only introduce false information but put pressure on the child to agree. Other types of misleading questions presuppose false information (e.g., "How many times did he hit you?" when the child had not been hit). Using this paradigm, Rudy and Goodman (1991), for example, had pairs of 4-year-old children or pairs of 7-year-old children play games with a man in a trailer. One child actively played the games with the man, whereas the other child was encouraged to watch. About 11 days later, each child was individually interviewed with a mix of leading and misleading questions. Children who merely observed tended to make more errors than children who participated in the games in the trailer.

Although it is clear that misinformation can distort children's and adults' reports, it should be noted that memory taint is not inevitable. For example, if blatant misinformation is presented while memory is strong—even if it is presented repeatedly—the misinformation might actually help consolidate accurate memory rather than impair it (e.g., Quas et al., 2007).

Moreover, because interviewers in the field (and attorneys in the courtroom) do not follow a scripted interview, as used in many suggestibility studies, but base their questions on children's prior responses, researchers may need to keep in mind not only that children respond to interviewers' questions but that interviewers respond to children's responses in formulating their questions, a point highlighted by the work of Gilstrap (e.g., Gilstrap & Ceci, 2005; Gilstrap & Papierno, 2004). In Gilstrap's studies, investigative interviewers who conduct real forensic interviews with children suspected of having been abused are asked to interview children about an event contrived for the purposes of the study (see also Melinder et al., 2010).

The advantage of this strategy is, of course, that the accuracy of the information the interviewers elicit can be assessed. At the same time, the interviews are conducted as they would be in the field. Gilstrap and Ceci (2005), for example, used sequential analyses to examine the stream of conversation between child and interviewer, to identify relationships between the interviewer's and a child's verbal behaviors. Perhaps surprisingly, this analysis revealed that in these unscripted interviews children's prior responses predicted their responses to subsequent leading questions and that in general, leading questions were not driving children's acquiescence. As the authors conclude, "[S]equential analysis of temporal data in unstructured interviews is capable of providing insights and generating hypotheses that would not be generated with traditional nonsequential approaches" (p. 52). This is a potentially fruitful direction for future studies of children's suggestibility.

Overall, research on children's suggestibility has tended to have high internal validity, being laboratory based. This represents a considerable advantage over other methodologies, such as field studies. Because children's propensity to make false reports is usually the main issue in suggestibility research, it is not necessary that the children experience crime events. Rather, the interest is in conditions that produce memory errors, thus contributing to false reports, and the underlying psychological mechanisms involved. The limits on external validity typically come from such factors as the type of misinformation researchers can suggest. Ethically, for example, it is difficult to suggest to children that they have been sexually molested. Yet when researchers have been able to ask abuse-related questions, children at least by around 4 or 5 years of age are often (although not always) more resistant to suggestion than previously believed (e.g., Rudy & Goodman, 1991; but see Ceci, Kulkofsky, Klemfuss, Sweeney, & Bruck, 2007; Poole & Lindsay, 2002), highlighting the importance of external validity.

FALSE MEMORY

Beth Rutherford began therapy in Springfield, Missouri at the age of 19. At the time, she felt she had a good family and healthy past, she just needed someone to talk to about stress at work. While undergoing two and a half years of therapy, she began to recover memories of sexual abuse at the hands of her father. She recounted memories of sexual abuse from the ages of 7 to 14, and even remembered being impregnated twice. Beth went as far as to claim her father had performed coat hanger abortions to terminate her pregnancy. Before her father could be prosecuted, medical examinations revealed that not only had no coat hanger abortions been performed, but Ms. Rutherford was in fact a virgin. Beth would later recant her statements and rejoin her family. Beth now speaks out about her experience, and hopes to inform others about the nature of false memories.

(Rutherford, 1998)

This is just one case of false memories; fortunately, the false memories did not lead to false arrest and prosecution. It is unknown how many false memory cases exist; however, the often serious nature of the claims makes false memories important to understand. Psychologists have tried to examine how false memories come about. Researchers use several techniques to investigate this phenomenon (Brainerd & Reyna, 2005). To understand the techniques used by researchers, we describe two of the most widely employed methodologies.

One of the most accepted techniques is the "implantation technique." In these studies, researchers attempt to create coherent and detailed false memories for events that never actually occurred. In the first implantation technique study, Loftus and Pickrell (1995) interviewed 24 adults (ages 18–53) about four events—three true events and one false event. The false event entailed getting lost in a shopping mall at the age of 5. The researchers asked participants to recall the memories over three separate sessions, and by the final session they found that 25% of the participants had developed a full or partial false memory about being lost in the shopping mall (see also Qin, Ogle, & Goodman, 2008).

Similar methodology was later employed by Ceci, Hoffman, Smith, and Loftus (1994) to study false memory in preschoolers (3 to 4 and 5 to 6 years old). The researchers confronted the children with four events, two of which had actually happened to the child during the past year, and two false events. The false events included, for example, getting one's hand caught in a mousetrap requiring a trip to the hospital, and a hot air balloon ride with one's classmates. The children were asked which of the four events had really happened and were asked to recall the event. Children were asked about the event on 7 to 10 separate occasions. The researchers found that younger children were more likely to claim that a false event had happened to them; however, the number of false memories did not increase over time. In a second study, when even more suggestive techniques were employed (e.g., telling children that their mothers said the events occurred), repeated questioning about the events increased the rate of false affirmations (Ceci, Loftus, Leichtman, & Bruck, 1994). However, one really cannot know for sure whether false memories are being formed or the children are simply acquiescing to interviewer suggestions. Furthermore, in such studies, false memories are generally easier to create for positive and neutral events than for negative events, and the latter are more comparable to crimes.

Schaaf, Alexander, and Goodman (2008) examined how valence, interview style, and individual differences affected true and false memories in an implantation study. They interviewed 82 children, ages 3 and 5 years, about eight events—four true events and four false events. Children were asked about positive (e.g., taking a trip or receiving a gift) and negative (e.g., being embarrassed or punished) true and false events. Within a single interview, children were repeatedly asked about each event. The researchers also measured the children's attachment, inhibitory control, and behavioral adjustment, as well as the parent's attachment. For true events, 3-year-olds and 5-year-olds quickly confirmed that the events occurred. However, for false events, the younger children were more likely than older children to report a false memory early in the questioning. The study also found that behavioral problems, attachment, and inhibitory control were related to children's reports of false memories. The implantation method has provided fascinating data indicating that conditions exist under which coherent and vivid memories for events that never happened can be created.

False memory research continues to grow as a field, and new techniques are being developed. The literature has expanded, for example, to include studies using the Deese-Roediger-McDermott (DRM) paradigm. The DRM paradigm involves presenting a list of words that all are semantically or phonologically related. Participants are then asked to recall or recognize words that appeared in the list. Adults and children recall and recognize words that are related to the list words, yet were not actually present on the list (e.g., Howe, Wimmer, & Blease, 2009). The DRM task is widely used in research classified as addressing false memory; however, there is an ongoing debate as to how well the results generalize to actual cases of false memories of abuse (Pezdek & Lam, 2007; Wade et al., 2007). Clearly the external validity of research on word lists can be legitimately questioned when applied to memory for real crimes. However, it is also possible that people who have a lax criterion for what they are willing to call a memory on the DRM task also have a lax criterion about memory generally (Qin et al., 2008). Researchers will likely continue to develop new and innovative methods to probe further into the phenomenon of false memory.

FORENSIC PROTOCOLS

Studies based on actual investigative interviews of suspected abuse victims are an essential complement to laboratory style and analog studies. Even when a recording of the abusive events is not available, through field studies researchers can document existing practices, assess how recommendations based on laboratory style and analog studies translate into practice, evaluate the implementation of new techniques and protocols, and address theoretically interesting subjects (e.g., the social and emotional factors that affect the testimony children provide) that are difficult if not impossible to address in other studies. Because field studies are conducted with the population of interest (children suspected of having been abused or who have witnessed a crime and who are likely to testify in court) and because their accounts concern actual (or suspected) crimes, the strength of field studies is their external validity. In contrast to laboratory and analog studies, however, field studies often face threats to internal validity; many variables that may influence children's testimony cannot be controlled directly in field studies, and alternative strategies for taking them into account, through selection of cases or statistical procedures, must be adopted.

In addition, in field studies opportunities to assess the accuracy of children's accounts—the ground truth of what actually happened—are rare, and for the most part, researchers must turn back to the laboratory or analog research to infer accuracy based on the means by which the information was elicited. Studies in which researchers have recognized and taken advantage of unique opportunities to assess the accuracy of children's accounts, as described previously, are particularly important in this regard. With recording technologies becoming increasingly accessible to perpetrators of abuse, such studies are likely to become more common (cf. Goodman, 2006).

Recently, important field studies have been published evaluating the use of forensic interview protocols. Such field studies are typically based on transcripts of interviews, although they may also involve videotaped interviews to capture nonverbal information—for example, pointing to a body diagram or demonstrating on a doll. Several descriptive field studies have examined audio or videotaped interviews regarding the numbers and/or proportions of desirable interviewer prompts used (e.g., free recall "invitations" for the child to tell what happened in his or her own words) as well as less desirable prompts and questioning techniques (such as yes/no questions or leading and suggestive questions), together with their relative effectiveness in eliciting detailed accounts from children.

Because in actual investigations researchers have no control over the types and frequencies of prompts used (indeed, this is often a dependent measure), relative measures of their effectiveness in eliciting information from children are often analyzed—for example, the numbers of details elicited per prompt, if the focus is on the effectiveness of different kinds of prompts. A general finding has been that in the absence of extensive training and feedback on desirable interviewing techniques, interviewers often resort to the kinds of specific yes/no and option-posing (i.e., multiple choice) questions demonstrated in laboratory studies to lead to inaccurate reporting, and that not enough opportunities are given to children to provide narratives in response to free recall prompts (see Lamb et al., 2008; Orbach et al., 2000, for review).

Based on such findings and those of laboratory as well as analog studies of children's eyewitness memory, researchers from the National Institute of Child Health and Human Development (NICHD) developed an interview protocol that relies primarily on free recall and open-ended questions. They then wanted to evaluate the effects of having training interviewers use the NICHD Protocol they had developed on both the kinds of questions and prompts interviewers used and on the amount and "quality" of information children provided (Orbach et al., 2000; see Lamb et al., 2008, for review). Whereas in a laboratory or analog study one might randomly assign children to interviewers trained to use various approaches to interviewing, random assignment to treatment conditions is seldom feasible in the context of interviews conducted in the field.

As an alternative to random assignment, the NICHD researchers compared interviewer prompts and children's responses in interviews conducted by the same interviewers before and after they were trained to use the NICHD Investigative Interview Protocol. Because the same interviewers conducted protocol and pre-protocol interviews, the effects of individual differences in interviewer style and effectiveness were controlled across the intervention. To control for other variables likely to affect children's responsiveness, the researchers selected cases from the pre- and post-training periods that were matched on the potentially influential variables of age and gender of the child victim and of the suspect, the familiarity of the suspect to the child, the type of abuse, and whether it occurred a single time or was recurrent.

Training interviewers on the NICHD Protocol significantly improved the quality of the interviews in terms of the use of recommended strategies for eliciting free-recall narratives from children and decreased interviewers' reliance on the riskier types of questions and prompts (see Lamb, Hershkowitz, Orbach, & Esplin, 2008, for review). Although the accuracy of children's reports could not be assessed directly, these findings are important in view of experimental research demonstrating that the way memories are accessed and accounts are elicited are crucial determinants of the accuracy of the information children report.

For such research, transcripts are typically "sanitized" before they are released to researchers to remove any information that might identify the child or the suspected perpetrator. The interviewer's prompts and children's narrative accounts and responses to questions are then coded from the transcripts. The researcher may adopt (or adapt) an existing system for categorizing the interviewers' prompts and questions, as well as children's responses, to quantify the (relative) frequency with which interviewers use different strategies and their effectiveness in eliciting information from children. The development of a reliable coding system is often a major component of this type of field research study, and it can be a time-consuming process.

Although there is general consensus on some categories of interviewer prompts, such as what constitutes an open-ended free-recall prompt (e.g., "Tell me what happened") or a strongly suggestive prompt or question (e.g., "Uncle Jimmy was in the room also at that time, wasn't he?"), the researcher should be aware that definitions of some question types differ across studies. For example, the question "Who else was in the room?" is coded by some researchers as suggestive if the child has not already mentioned others in the room (e.g., Orbach et al., 2000), and by others as a neutral question (e.g., see Gilstrap, 2004). The coding system developed by researchers at NICHD has been used in several studies by that group (see Lamb et al., 2008; Orbach & Lamb, 2000) and modified in others (e.g., Melinder et al., 2010: Paterson & Pipe, in press), but other systems have been used to code the questions and prompts of field interviewers (e.g., Gilstrap, 2004).

The approach described here relies on matching. An alternative strategy is to control for the effects of potentially confounding variables statistically, using regression analyses to identify the influence variables in addition to those of interest, and to control for them when evaluating the effects of the variable of interest. This approach is illustrated in a second example evaluating the NICHD Protocol. In this study, the researchers wanted to evaluate whether improvements in the quality of interviewing, described previously, affected the *outcomes* of cases as they proceeded through the investigation process and the legal system (Pipe, Orbach, Lamb, Abbott, & Stewart, 2008). Using a before-and-after design, as described, the researchers shifted the unit of analysis from the interview to the outcomes of cases. The outcome of a case was defined by the decisions made by police detectives and district attorneys, for example, whether to forward the case and file criminal charges.

Multiple regression analyses were used to examine the effects of the investigative interview (NICHD Protocol vs. pre-protocol interview) while controlling for variables likely to influence case outcomes. Potentially significant predictors (type of interview, type of abuse, victim's age, gender of suspect, age of suspect, and victim/suspect familiarity) were entered concurrently. The analyses confirmed that each of the potential predictors *independently* contributed to the outcomes of the cases as they proceeded through the system.

This research showed that the implementation of the NICHD Protocol for conducting interviews increased the probability that charges would be filed (from 45% to 54% of cases), following which the most likely outcome was a guilty plea to one or more charges (80%). Of the small number of cases that proceeded to trial, only 1 (6%) of the 17 protocol cases did not result in a conviction of the suspect, in contrast to 6 (46%) of the 13 pre-protocol cases. Clearly, researchers must conduct field research to examine such outcomes; it is not possible to perform this type of research in the laboratory.

Overall, in terms of advantages and disadvantages, field research can be challenging and time-consuming, but it can also be quite productive. Advantages include that such research potentially validates the generalization of findings from more tightly controlled studies and can also generate questions to take back into the lab. At the end of the day, however, the issue of internal validity remains; for example, relevant to the NICHD Protocol studies just described, prospective research replicating the effects would certainly provide further validation of the value "downstream" of improving the quality of investigative interviews. Replication studies generally increase confidence in one's findings; unfortunately, however, they are undervalued by journal editors and grant-funding agencies; given the time and effort involved, they are all too infrequently conducted. Ultimately, the convergence of findings from various approaches validates and increases our confidence in the contribution and value of each.

CHILDREN'S TESTIMONY IN THE COURTROOM

The studies discussed so far focus on children's eyewitness testimony in forensic interviews. However, if a legal case proceeds to trial, children may have to take the stand, at which time the accuracy of their statements in the courtroom becomes paramount. Although field research has examined children's experiences in court, such studies do not address the accuracy of children's testimony (e.g., Brennan & Brennan, 1990; Goodman et al., 1992). Fortunately, researchers have devised laboratory methodology to study the accuracy of children's testimony in the courtroom or courtroom-like situations. To take just a few examples, Zajac first analyzed questions posed to children during actual cross-examinations conducted in the courtroom and the changes in children's responses that result (Zajac, Gross, & Hayne, 2003). She and her colleagues then followed these field studies with analog studies to better understand the phenomena observed in the courtroom (e.g., Zajac & Hayne, 2003, 2006).

In one of the analog studies, Zajac and Hayne (2003) examined the effects of cross-examination on the accuracy of 5- and 6-year-old children's reports of a documented laboratory event. During cross-examination, children changed their original responses irrespective of their original accuracy. Moreover, prior exposure to misleading information did not decrease the accuracy of children's responses during cross-examination, because even children with no prior exposure to misinformation altered their original responses, decreasing their ultimate levels of accuracy. The authors concluded that in search for the truth, cross-examination is inappropriate for young children. Such investigations illustrate the productive "dialog" between research conducted in the field and in more tightly controlled analog studies.

As another example, Goodman et al. (1998) were interested in the effects of testifying in open court versus via closed-circuit TV on the accuracy of children's eyewitness memory and jurors' abilities to reach the truth. Five- to 6-year-olds and 8- to 9-year-olds individually participated in a play session with an unfamiliar male. Approximately two weeks later, the children testified about the event in a real city courtroom. Mock jurors from the community—more than a thousand of them—viewed the trials, with the child's testimony being presented either live in open court or over closed-circuit TV. Testifying in open court was also associated with children's experiencing greater pre-trial anxiety. The use of closed-circuit TV led to decreased suggestibility for younger children, did not decrease factfinders' abilities to discriminate accurate from inaccurate child testimony, and did not directly bias jurors against the defendant. However, closed-circuit testimony biased jurors against child witnesses; the children were rated as less intelligent, less cute, and less credible if they testified via closed-circuit TV than in open court.

As can likely be inferred, when studying children's eyewitness testimony in court, there are advantages and disadvantages to various approaches. In actual field studies, children's experiences can be documented (e.g., types of questions asked, length of testimony), but typically, accuracy cannot be assessed. In mock trial studies, researchers can have children participate in an event that is documented and can later have the children testify in court-like situations to examine how various factors (e.g., cross-examination, use of closed-circuit TV) affects the children's accuracy. The internal validity of the latter type of study can be quite high, but its external validity suffers in that the children do not testify about real crimes and the stakes are not nearly as high as those in a real trial, where a defendant may risk imprisonment for years if not life, and the child may fear severe reprisals, including death.

CONCLUSIONS

The study of children's eyewitness memory has led to important insights for legal application and psychological theory. The accuracy of children's statements within the legal context is often hotly debated given the potentially life-altering consequences at stake—for example, that a child will continue to be abused or even murdered, or that an innocent adult will go to prison. This is an area of study where the research findings often quickly affect actual forensic practice and courtroom procedures. Even the U.S. Supreme Court has relied on studies of children's eyewitness memory in reaching decisions that become "law of the land" (e.g., *Kennedy v. Louisiana*, 2008). It is therefore crucial that researchers employ the best scientific methodology possible and are measured in the conclusions they reach, while optimizing internal and external validity in their studies. We hope this chapter provides readers with a sense of key methodological issues involved in this exciting and important area of research.

REFERENCES

Assessment—National Center for PTSD. (2009). Retrieved July, 30, 2009, from the U.S. Department of Veterans Affairs Web site: http://www.ptsd.va.gov/professional/pages/assessments/assessment.asp

Bagoo, A. (2008, March 18). Child witness. *Trinidad & Tobago's Newsday*. Retrieved on July 16, 2009, from http://www.newsday.co.tt/news/0,75197.html

Bernstein, D., & Fink, L. (1998). *Childhood Trauma Questionnaire: A retrospective self-report*. San Antonio, TX: The Psychological Corporation.

Bidrose, S., & Goodman, G. S. (2000). Testimony and evidence: A scientific case study of memory for child sexual abuse. *Applied Cognitive Psychology, 14*, 197–213.

Binet, A. (1900). La suggestibilité [On suggestibility]. Paris, France: Schleicher.

Bowlby, J. (1980). *Attachment and loss: Vol. 3. Loss: Sadness and depression*. New York, NY: Basic Books.

Brainerd, C., & Reyna, V. (2005). *The science of false memory.* New York, NY: Oxford University Press.

Brennan, M., & Brennan, R. (1990). *Strange language. Child victims under cross examination.* Centre for Teaching and Research in Literacy, CSU-R, P.O. Box 588, Wagga Wagga, New South Wales.

Bussey, K., & Grimbeek, E. J. (1995). Disclosure processes: Issues for child sexual abuse victims. In K. J. Rotenberg (Ed.), *Disclosure processes in children and adolescents* (pp. 166–203). Cambridge, England: Cambridge University Press.

Cashmore, J., & de Haas, N. (1992). *The use of closed circuit television for child witnesses in the ACT.* Sydney: Australian Law Reform Commission.

Ceci, S. J., Hoffman, M. L. C., Smith, E., & Loftus, E. F. (1994). Repeatedly thinking about a non-event: Source misattributions among preschoolers. *Consciousness & Cognition, 3,* 388–407.

Ceci, S. J., Kulkofsky, S., Klemfuss, J. Z., Sweeney, C. D., & Bruck, M. (2007). Unwarranted assumptions about children's testimonial accuracy. *Annual Review of Clinical Psychology, 3,* 331–328.

Ceci, S. J., Loftus, E. F., Leichtman, M. D., & Bruck, M. (1994). The possible role of source misattributions in the creation of false beliefs among preschoolers. *International Journal of Clinical and Experimental Hypnosis, 42,* 304–320.

Ceci, S. J., Ross, D. F., & Toglia, M. P. (1987). Suggestibility of children's memory: Psycholegal implications. *Journal of Experimental Psychology: General, 116,* 38–49.

Chae, Y., Bederian-Gardner, D., Lindsay, A., & Goodman, G. S. (in press). Methodological issues and strategies in child maltreatment research. *Child Abuse and Neglect.*

Chae, Y., Ogle, C. M., & Goodman, G. S. (2009). Remembering negative childhood experiences: An attachment theory perspective. In J. A. Quas & R. Fivush (Eds.), *Emotion and memory in development: Biological, cognitive, and social considerations* (pp. 3–27). New York, NY: Oxford University Press.

Cordon, I., Goodman, G. S., & Anderson, S. (2003). Children in court. In P. Van Koppen & S. Penrod (Eds.), *Adversarial versus inquisitorial legal systems* (pp. 167–189). New York, NY: Kluwer Academic.

Crawford v. Washington, 541 U.S. 36. (2004).

Dent, H., & Flin, R. H. (1992). *Children as witnesses.* Chichester, England: Wiley.

Dent, H. R., & Stephenson, G. M. (1979). An experimental study of the effectiveness of different techniques of questioning child witnesses. *British Journal of Social and Clinical Psychology, 18,* 41–51.

Eisen, M. L., Goodman, G. S., Qin, J., Davis, S., & Crayton, J. (2007). Maltreated children's memory: Accuracy, suggestibility, and psychopathology. *Developmental Psychology, 43,* 1275–1294.

Eisen, M. L., Qin, J., Goodman, G. S., & Davis, S. (2002). Memory and suggestibility in maltreated children: Age, stress, arousal, dissociation, and psychopathology. *Journal of Experimental Child Psychology, 83,* 167–212.

Gilstrap, L. L. (2004). A missing link in suggestibility research: What is known about the behavior of field interviewers in unstructured interviews with young children? *Journal of Experimental Psychology: Applied, 10,* 13–24.

Gilstrap, L. L., & Ceci, S. J. (2005). Reconceptualizing children's suggestibility: Bidirectional and temporal properties. *Child Development, 76,* 40–53.

Gilstrap, L. L., & Papierno, P. B. (2004). Is the cart pushing the horse? The effects of child characteristics on children's and adults' interview behaviors. *Applied Cognitive Psychology, 18,* 1059–1078.

Goodman, G. S. (1984). Children's testimony in historical perspective. *Journal of Social Issues, 40,* 9–32.

Goodman, G. S. (2006). Children's eyewitness memory: A modern history and contemporary commentary. *Journal of Social Issues, 62,* 811–832.

Goodman, G. S., & Bottoms, B. (1993). *Child victims, child witnesses: Understanding and improving testimony.* New York, NY: Guilford Press.

Goodman, G. S., Hirschman, J. E., Hepps, D., & Rudy, L. (1991). Children's memory for stressful events. *Merrill-Palmer Quarterly, 37,* 109–157.

Goodman, G. S., Pyle-Taub, E., Jones, D. P. H., England, P., Port, L., Rudy, L., & Prado, L. (1992). Testifying in criminal court: Emotional effects on child sexual assault victims. *Monographs of the Society for Research in Child Development, 57,* Serial No. 229.

Goodman, G., Quas, J., Batterman-Faunce, J., Riddlesberger, M., & Kuhn, J. (1994). Predictors of accurate and inaccurate memories of traumatic events experienced in childhood. *Consciousness & Cognition, 3,* 269–294.

Goodman, G. S., Quas, J., Batterman-Faunce, J., Riddlesberger, M., & Kuhn, J. (1997). Children's reaction to and memory of a stressful event: Influences of age, anatomical dolls, knowledge, and parental attachment. *Applied Developmental Sciences, 1,* 54–75.

Goodman, G. S., Quas, J., Bulkley, J., & Shapiro, C. (1999). Innovations for child witnesses: A national survey. *Psychology, Public Policy, and Law, 5,* 255–281.

Goodman, G. S., Tobey, A., Batterman-Faunce, J., Orcutt, H., Thomas, S., Shapiro, C., & Sachsenmaier, T. (1998). Face-to-face confrontation: Effects of closed-circuit technology on children's eyewitness testimony and jurors' decisions. *Law and Human Behavior, 22,* 165–203.

Howe, M., L., Wimmer, M. C., & Blease, K. (2009). The role of associative strength in children's false memory illusions. *Memory, 17,* 8–16.

Huffman, M. L., Crossman, A. M., & Ceci, S. J. (1997). "Are false memories permanent?": An investigation on the long-term effects of source misattribution. *Consciousness and Cognition, 6,* 482–490.

Kennedy v. Louisiana, 128 S.Ct. 2641 (2008).

Lamb, M. E., Hershkowitz, I., Orbach, Y., & Esplin, P. (2008). *Tell me what happened: Structured investigative interviews of child victims and witnesses.* Hoboken, NJ: Wiley.

Leander, L., Christianson, S. Å., & Granhag, P. A. (2007). Children's memories and reports: A sexual abuse case study. *Psychiatry, Psychology and Law, 14,* 120–129.

Leander, L., Christianson, S. Å., & Granhag, P. A. (in press). Internet-initiated sexual abuse: Adolescent victims' reports about on- and off-line sexual activities. *Applied Cognitive Psychology.*

Leander, L., Granhag, P. A., & Christianson, S. Å. (2005). Children exposed to obscene phone calls: What they remember and tell. *Child Abuse & Neglect, 29,* 871–888.

Lindsay, D. S., & Johnson, M. K. (1989). The reversed eyewitness suggestibility effect. *Bulletin of the Psychonomic Society, 27,* 111–113.

Loftus, E. F. (1979). *Eyewitness testimony.* Cambridge, MA: Harvard University Press.

Loftus, E. F., & Pickrell, J. E. (1995). The formation of false memories. *Psychiatric Annals, 25,* 720–725.

London, K., Bruck, M., & Melnyk, L. (2009). Post-event information affects children's autobiographical memory after one year. *Law & Human Behavior, 33,* 344–355.

Lyon, T. D., & LaMagna, R. (2007). The history of children's hearsay: From Old Bailey to post-Davis. *Indiana Law Journal, 82,* 1029–1058.

McCloskey, M., & Zaragoza, M. (1985). Misleading postevent information and memory for events: Arguments and evidence against memory impairment hypotheses. *Journal of Experimental Psychology: General, 114,* 1–16.

McGuire, J. (2009, July 21). Gloversville man gets 8 years in prison for child sexual abuse. *Daily gazette.com.* Retrieved July 27, 2009, from http://www.dailygazette.com/news/2009/jul/21/72109_glovesex/.

Melinder, A., Alexander, K., Cho, Y., Goodman, G. S., Thoresen, C., Lonnum, K., & Magnussen, S. (2010). Children's eyewitness memory: A comparison of two interviewing strategies as realized by forensic professionals. *Journal of Experimental Child Psychology, 105,* 156–177.

Merritt, K. A., Ornstein, P. A., & Spiker, B. (1994). Children's memory for a salient medical procedure: Implications for testimony. *Pediatrics, 94,* 17–23.

Mikulincer, M., & Shaver, P. R. (2007). An attachment and behavioral systems perspective on social support. *Journal of Social and Personal Relationships, 26,* 7–19.

Myers, J. B. (1998). *Legal issues in child abuse and neglect practice,* Volume 1. Thousand Oaks, CA: Sage.

Myers, J., Cordon, I., Ghetti, S., & Goodman, G. S. (2002). Hearsay exceptions: Adjusting the ratio of intuition to psychological science. *Law and Contemporary Problems, 65,* 3–46.

Orbach, Y., Hershkowitz, I., Lamb, M. E., Sternberg, K. J., Esplin, P. W., & Horowitz, D. (2000). Assessing the value of structured protocols for forensic interview of alleged child abuse victims. *Child Abuse & Neglect, 24,* 733–752.

Orbach, Y., & Lamb, M. E. (2000). Enhancing children's narratives in investigative interviews. *Child Abuse & Neglect, 24,* 1631–1648.

Paterson, T., & Pipe, M-E (in press). Exploratory assessments of child abuse across multiple interview sessions: Children's responses to interviewer's questions. *Child Abuse & Neglect.*

Paz-Alonso, P. M. (2004). *Misinformation effects on children and adults' eyewitness memory and suggestibility* (Doctoral dissertation). University of the Basque Country, Bilbao, Spain.

Paz-Alonso, P. M., & Goodman, G. S. (2008). Trauma and memory: Effects of post-event misinformation retrieval order, and retention interval. *Memory, 16*, 58–75.

Paz-Alonso, P. M., Ogle, C. M., & Goodman, G. S. (2009). Memory for abuse: Case studies. In M. Ternes, D. Griesel, & B. Cooper (Eds.), *Applied issues in investigative interviewing, eyewitness memory, and credibility assessment*. New York, NY: Springer.

Pear, T. H., & Wyatt, S. (1914). The testimony of normal and mentally defective children. *British Journal of Psychology, 6*, 387–419.

Peterson, C., & Bell, M. (1996). Children's memory for traumatic injury. *Child Development, 67*, 3045–3070.

Pezdek, K., & Lam, S. (2007). What research paradigms have cognitive psychologists used to study "false memory," and what are the implications of these choices? *Consciousness & Cognition, 16*, 2–17.

Pipe, M. E., Orbach, Y., Lamb, M. E., Abbott, C. B., & Stewart, H. L. (2008). *Do best practice interviews with child abuse victims influence cast outcomes?* Final Report to National Institute of Justice (Grant Number: 2006-IJ-CX-0019). Washington, DC: Department of Justice.

Poole, D. A., & Lindsay, D. S. (2002). Reducing child witnesses' false reports of misinformation from parents. *Journal of Experimental Child Psychology, 81*, 117–140.

Qin, J., Ogle, C., & Goodman, G. S. (2008). True and false memory: Accuracy and discernment. *Journal of Experimental Psychology: Applied, 14*, 373–391.

Quas, J. A., Bauer, A. B., & Boyce, W. T. B. (2004). Emotion, reactivity, and memory in early childhood. *Child Development, 75*, 797–814.

Quas, J. A., Goodman, G. S., Bidrose, B. L., Pipe, M. E., Craw, S., & Ablin, D. (1999). Emotion and memory: Children's long-term remembering, forgetting, and suggestibility. *Journal of Experimental Child Psychology, 72*, 235–270.

Quas, J. A., Malloy, L., Melinder, A. M., D'Mello, M., Goodman, G. S., & Schaaf, J. (2007.) Developmental differences in the effects of repeated interviews and interviewer bias on young children's

event memory and false reports. *Developmental Psychology, 43*, 823–837.

Rudy, L., & Goodman, G. (1991). Effects of participation on children's reports: Implications for children's testimony. *Developmental Psychology, 27*, 527–538.

Rutherford, B. (1998, January/February). A retractor speaks. *FMS Foundation Newsletter, 7*. Retrieved on July 10, 2009, from http://www.fmsfonline.org/fmsf98.128.html.

Saywitz, K., Goodman, G., Nicholas, E., & Moan, S. (1991). Children's memory for a genital examination: Implications for child sexual abuse cases. *Journal of Consulting and Clinical Psychology, 59*, 682–691.

Saywitz, K., Jaenicke, C., & Camparo, L. (1990). *Children's knowledge of legal terminology. Law and Human Behavior, 14*, 523–535.

Saywitz, K., & Snyder, L. (1996). Narrative elaboration: Test of a new procedure for interviewing children. *Journal of Consulting and Clinical Psychology, 664*, 1347–1357.

Schaaf, J. M. (2001). *Developmental changes in false memory formation: Errors as by-products of a functional system*. Presented at the Society for Research in Child Development, Minneapolis, MN.

Schaaf, J. M., Alexander, K. W., & Goodman, G. S. (2008). Children's false memory and true disclosure in the face of repeated questions. *Journal of Experimental Child Psychology, 100*, 157–185.

Schwartz-Kenney, B., & Goodman, G. S. (1999). Children's memory of a naturalistic event following misinformation. *Applied Developmental Sciences, 3*, 34–46.

Seewer, J. (2009, June 15). Ohio murder trial focuses on woman's old memories. *Mercurynews.com*. Retrieved on July 16, 2009, from http://www.mercurynews.com/ci_12594572?nclick_check=1

Shetty, R. (2009, June 10). Child witness recounts Kasab's murder spree. *IBNLive*. Retrieved July 16, 2009, from http://ibnlive.in.com/news/child-witness-recounts-kasabs-murder-spree/94588-3.html

Stein, N., & Boyce, T. (1995). *The role of physiological reactivity in attending to, remembering, and responding to an emotional event*. Paper presented at the biennial meeting of the Society for Research in Child Development, Indianapolis, IN.

Steinberg, A. M., Pynoos, R. S., Goenjian, A. K., Sossanabadi, H., & Sherr, L. (1999). Are researchers bound by child abuse reporting laws? *Child Abuse & Neglect, 23*, 771–777.

Stern, W. (1910). Abstracts of lectures on the psychology of testimony and on the study of individuality. *American Journal of Psychology, 21*, 270–282.

Stern, W. (1939). The psychology of testimony. *Journal of Abnormal and Social Psychology, 34*, 3–30.

Terr, L. (1988). What happens to early memories of trauma? A study of twenty children under the age five at the time of documented traumatic events. *Journal of the American Academy of Child and Adolescent Psychiatry, 27*, 96–104.

Urquiza, A. J. (1991). Retrospective methodology in family violence research: Our duty to report past abuse. *Journal of Interpersonal Violence, 6*, 119–126.

Varendonck, J. (1911). Les temoignages d'enfants dans un process retentissant. *Archives de Psychologie, 11*, 129–171.

Wade, K. A., Sherman, S. J., Garry, M., Memon, A., Mazzoni, G., Merckelbach, H., & Loftus, E. F. (2007). False claims about false memory research. *Consciousness & Cognition, 16*, 18–28.

Zajac, R., Gross, J., & Hayne, H. (2003). Asked and answered: Questioning children in the courtroom. *Psychiatry, Psychology & Law, 10*, 199–209.

Zajac, R. & Hayne, H. (2003). I don't think that's what really happened: The effect of cross-examination on the accuracy of children's reports. *Journal of Experimental Psychology: Applied, 9*, 187–195.

Zajac, R., & Hayne, H. (2006). The negative effect of cross-examination style questioning on children's accuracy: Older children are not immune. *Applied Cognitive Psychology, 20*, 3–16.

Zaragoza, M. S., McCloskey, M., & Jamis, M. (1987). Misleading postevent information and recall of the original event: Further evidence against the memory impairment hypothesis. *Journal of Experimental Psychology: Learning, Memory, and Cognition, 13*, 36–44.

CHAPTER 15

Procedural Justice: Theory and Method

LARRY HEUER AND DIANE SIVASUBRAMANIAM

I N THE FIRST of four volumes of *The American Soldier*, Stouffer and colleagues (Stouffer, Suchman, DeVinney, Star, & Williams, 1949) summarized the findings of their survey work conducted on behalf of a research branch of the U.S. War Department (as the U.S. Department of Defense was then known)—work undertaken in part to assist with the management of military personnel (Clausen, 1984). One important aspect of this inquiry concerned the bases of soldiers' satisfaction with their military service. Among the non-intuitive findings to emerge from this research was one showing satisfaction to be lower among personnel in units with relatively rapid rates of promotion (the Army Air Corps) than among personnel in units being promoted more slowly (the Military Police). This finding led Stouffer et al. to invoke the construct of relative deprivation: the experience of deprivation relative to someone—including oneself in the past—who is better off (Crosby, 1976). While Stouffer and colleagues did not clearly define the construct or propose a theory about it, several variations of relative deprivation theory (e.g., Crosby, 1976; Davis, 1959; Merton & Kitt, 1950; Runciman, 1972) developed out of this early work.

Relative deprivation theory addressed social justice questions, but it was not a theory of fairness. The original psychological theorizing about fairness as the key to satisfaction was put forward by Homans (1950, 1961), who theorized about the importance of distributive fairness for satisfaction, and Adams (1965), whose equity theory postulated that the dissatisfaction that results from relative deprivation stems from the perceived injustice of inequitable distributions. Critically, both Homans and Adams conducted research devised to test their theories. Homans (1953), for example, interviewed clerical workers at a utilities company. Of the cash posters and ledger clerks who worked in the same room for equal wages, the ledger clerks viewed their positions as having greater responsibility, held by individuals with greater seniority and experience. In concluding observations that fore-shadowed equity theory as well as contemporary theorizing about deserv-ingness (Boeckmann & Feather, 2007; Feather, 2002), Homans speculated that the ledger clerks would have been more satisfied if a pay differential were in place to reflect the perceived status differential.

In an early experimental test of equity theory, Adams (Adams & Rosenbaum, 1962) led undergraduates at New York University to believe they had been hired for part-time temporary work as interviewers. On their arrival for their first day of work, the workers were randomly assigned to believe that they were appropriately qualified ("You meet all of the qualifi-cations required for the job") or underqualified ("You don't have nearly enough experience") for their $3.50 hourly wage. Based on equity theory, it was predicted that participants who believed they were underqualified would increase their productivity to reduce the discomfort that would otherwise result from their inequitable rate of pay. This hypothesis was supported: the underqualified workers produced .27 interviews per minute compared with the .19 interviews per minute completed by the control (appropriately qualified) participants. Similar experimental results were reported by Adams and Jacobsen (1964) in a study that also employed deception to create the impression of high or low inequity among student workers performing a proofreading task.

By 1976, in an issue of *Advances in Experimental Social Psychology* devoted entirely to equity theory and research, E. Walster, Berscheid, and Walster (1976) pointed to support for equity theory predictions in work settings (predictions concerning pay satisfaction, and attitudes about employers, productivity, and work quality); in exploitive relationships (predictions concerning victim derogation, victim compensation, denial of victim suffer-ing, victim distress, and victim retaliation); in helping relationships (predic-tions concerning benefactor and recipient discomfort with inequitable exchanges); and even in interpersonal relationships (predictions concerning partner preferences).

Although E. Walster, Berscheid, and Walster did not reference research in legal settings, another chapter in the same *Advances* volume did; Austin, Walster, and Utne (1976) reviewed early research concerning how equity concerns influence reactions to the legal system among harm doers, victims, and impartial observers. Utne (1974), for example, posed a test of equity theory by having undergraduates read an account of an embezzlement case with the belief that their judgments on this case could influence the defendant's punishment. Overall, the authors interpreted these studies as supportive of equity theory predictions regarding such legal questions as sympathy for the defendant and sentencing preferences. Around the same time, other psychologists (Brickman, 1977; Lerner, 1977) were also theorizing about the psychology of justice and hypothesizing about its implications for legal attitudes and legal behaviors. Lerner and colleagues, for example, were testing the just-world theory prediction that people are motivated to believe the world is a fair place, even to the point of protecting that belief by derogating victims whose suffering they are unable to relieve (Lerner & Matthews, 1967; Lerner, Miller, & Holmes, 1976; Lerner & Simmons, 1966).

THEORY AS METHOD

Shortly after its emergence from a purely applied context (Stouffer et al., 1949 set out to study ways to maintain the satisfaction and morale of U.S. soldiers), the relative deprivation hypothesis generated considerable enthusiasm among psychologists interested in the processes affecting satisfaction in situations of social conflict or exchange—enough that within a decade after Adams proposed equity theory, Austin et al. (1976) were able to devote an entire chapter to an early version of the same question that continues to generate research by justice scholars today: What is the effect of justice reasoning on legal processes and outcomes? However, the research reviewed in their chapter was conducted overwhelmingly in laboratory settings, including some involving studies of children asked to think about justice problems, and undergraduates misled to believe they were conducting interviews on the first day of a new summer job, or asked to imagine themselves as participants in a fictitious dispute—legal or otherwise. Despite the absence of systematic research conducted on legal actors in actual legal settings, these early justice scholars generalized from their findings to assertions about the consequences of fairness in actual legal contexts.

At about the same time, a similar phenomenon was occurring among justice scholars who were exploring a related question—one about the role of *procedural* justice in legal contexts. In 1975, Thibaut and Walker's seminal book initiated a profound shift from the exclusive focus on distributive justice in psychological theorizing and research. Their book focused on the institutional procedures employed for resolving conflicts that result in litigation, and it began by posing the question "What procedures are just?" (Thibaut & Walker, 1975, p. 1). The authors noted that despite a long history of attention to fair legal procedures by policy makers throughout U.S. history (such as that in the U.S. Constitution and the Fourteenth Amendment's guarantee of due process) and attention to it in the social sciences (including Kalven and Zeisel's 1966 seminal study of jury procedures), there had been little progress toward the development of a conceptual framework for classifying or comparing various conflict resolution procedures. Drawing a distinction between distributive and procedural fairness, the authors proposed that procedures could be classified according to the manner in which they allocated control between the disputants and the third parties who officiate over them.

The studies described in this classic book were strongly supportive of Thibaut and Walker's original claims. Participants reported that adversarial procedures (such as those employed in U.S. courtrooms in which the disputants control the presentation of evidence and third parties control the final decision) were fairer and more satisfying than inquisitorial ones (such as those employed in many European courts). Furthermore, this preference for adversarial procedures was unqualified by whether the disputants in these simulation studies were found guilty or innocent of the charged offenses. Importantly, research with participants from Germany and France—countries whose legal systems are based on inquisitorial procedures—replicated the finding of a preference for adversarial procedures, suggesting that these preferences are not merely a reflection of cultural biases for procedures similar to those employed in the participants' native countries.

In 1978, Thibaut and Walker proposed what is arguably the first psychological theory of procedural justice, though earlier work by Lewin, Lippitt, & White (1939) on leadership style and by Hollander and Julian (1970) on the legitimacy of leaders were clear precursors. The theory included a system for classifying procedures, it implied testable hypotheses about the consequences of procedures for obtaining the goals of truth and justice, and it postulated about the psychological bases of procedural preferences. Furthermore, like the distributive justice theories that preceded it, the theory was pitched broadly as "a general framework for analyzing and classifying *all conflict resolution procedures*, including, of course, all procedures employed in the legal process" (p. 541, italics added). Thus, it was expressly not bound by such situational variables as whether the procedures under consideration were employed in civil or criminal or administrative hearings, nor by whether the disputes involved legal or other (e.g., organizational, political, educational, medical) issues; rather, Thibaut and Walker claimed that their theory permitted generalization about justice processes and consequences across contexts, populations, and operationalizations.

Our primary concern in the remainder of this chapter is the validity of the sort of generalizations employed by these early distributive justice and procedural justice scholars. Our fundamental argument in this chapter is that the breadth of the claims advanced by Thibaut and Walker, and the distributive justice researchers who preceded them, despite the rather narrow range of contexts in which these theories had been tested (to our knowledge, all of the studies conducted by Thibaut and Walker and their students between 1974 and 1978 were simulation studies conducted in contrived and carefully controlled settings, using mostly undergraduate and some law school students as participants), was justified by a particular aspect of this early work: a reliance on basic psychological theory. This continues to play a central role in shaping the procedural justice research questions, research methods, and the interpretation of this research—particularly those interpretations that have targeted applied concerns such as legal attitudes and legal behavior. We develop this argument further after a brief summary of a few of the important advances in the theory and research since Thibaut and Walker's seminal work.

PROCEDURAL JUSTICE THEORY AND RESEARCH:
THE FAIR PROCESS EFFECT

Thibaut and Walker's (1975, 1978) theory postulated that process control, or voice, increased disputants' perceptions that procedures are fair, and their research was the first to demonstrate the fair process effect—that is, when disputants consider procedures to be fair, they are more satisfied with the outcomes they receive. This finding is now sufficiently well established that Brockner and colleagues (Brockner et al., 2001) have referred to it as one of the most robust findings in the justice literature. Furthermore, additional research has established that fair treatment enhances satisfaction with and the perception of the legitimacy of legal authorities and legal institutions. This is an effect that has been observed in studies of civilian–police encounters (Sunshine & Tyler, 2003; Tyler, 1989, 1990); in studies of alternative dispute resolution (ADR) procedures such as mediation (Pruitt, Peirce, McGillicuddy, Welton, & Castrianno, 1993) and restorative justice (Latimer, Dowden, & Muise, 2001; Sherman, Strang, & Woods, 2003); as well as in compliance settings, such as studies of people's encounters with tax officials (Wenzel, 2004, 2005, 2006).

Thibaut and Walker's (1975, 1978) control model of procedural justice proposed that process control enhanced fairness because it allowed disputants to influence their outcomes, and much early research was supportive of this claim. However, subsequent research revealed a considerable challenge to this view. For example, Lind, Kanfer, and Earley (1990) demonstrated that voice enhanced fairness perceptions in decision-making procedures even when the disputants were aware that their outcomes had been decided before they communicated their preferences. Such findings led Lind and Tyler (1988) to propose a group value model of procedural justice, which has been highly influential in shaping subsequent procedural justice research.

The group value model is based on people's concern with their social relationships. It posits that when people interact with authorities that represent valued groups (such as legal institutions), they look for information concerning their standing in the social group: When procedures make people feel like valued and respected members of their social groups, they judge those procedures to be fair. According to the group value model, voice enhances fairness because of the symbolic message it conveys about one's within-group standing. Subsequent theorizing and research (Tyler, 1989) suggests that three procedural criteria—neutrality, trustworthiness of authorities, and respectful treatment—are particularly important for judgments of procedural fairness.

Since the group value theory was proposed, numerous alternative views have been offered. For example, Tyler and Lind (1992) proposed a relational model of procedural justice, which extended the predictions about the consequences of procedural justice to include judgments about satisfaction with authorities and beliefs about their legitimacy. Subsequently, van den Bos, Wilke, and Lind (1998) proposed their fairness heuristic theory (FHT), which offered an alternative explanation for people's concern with procedures such as voice and process control. Noting that social interdependence creates an inequality of power between individuals and group authorities, FHT asserts a social dilemma: Membership in a group provides benefits but, at the same time, authorities can impose severe negative outcomes (Lind, Kulik, Ambrose, & de Vera Park, 1993). According to FHT, the most common psychological response to the fundamental social dilemma is to employ fairness judgments as a cognitive heuristic to guide behavior toward compliance with or defiance of the decisions of an authority figure. In another variant, van den Bos, Lind, and Wilke (2001) proposed an uncertainty management model of procedural fairness, which asserted that fairness concerns arise from uncertainty, and uncertainty is managed by procedural fairness.

METHODOLOGICAL CONSIDERATIONS

Rather than survey the research methods being employed by procedural justice researchers (methods that we judge to be generally indistinguishable from those employed by social psychologists throughout our discipline), our methodological considerations focus on the validity of the claims advanced by procedural justice researchers about the role of procedural justice in legal contexts. We draw heavily from two perspectives on this matter. First, we discuss validity criteria proposed by Campbell and Stanley (1966), developed further by Cook and Campbell (1976, 1979), and widely adopted by researchers throughout the social science disciplines. These include statistical conclusion validity (is the inference of covariation of the independent and dependent variable justified?); internal validity (is the covariation between the independent and dependent variable indicative of a causal relationship?); construct validity (are the operations of the variables representative of the relevant theoretical constructs?); and external validity (can the relationships observed in a particular study be generalized across measures, persons, settings, and times?).

Second, we observe that while these validity criteria are well known to researchers in our discipline, they are not universally endorsed. Kruglanski and Kroy (1976), for example, are critical of Campbell and Stanley's construct of internal validity, as are others[1] (e.g., Cronbach, 1982). For example, whereas Campbell and Stanley characterized internal validity as addressing whether a causal relationship exists between the independent and dependent

---

1. An additional informative critique of the construct of internal validity is provided by Pawson and Tilley (1994, 1997). For overviews of validity criteria, see Cook and Shadish (1994) and Shadish, Cook, and Campbell (2002).

variables in the specific context and the specific instance in which they had been tested, Kruglanski and Kroy (1976) say this establishes an impossibly narrow standard. Rather, they assert that experiments are meaningful only as tests of hypotheses considered in general terms—hypotheses about general relationships among variables as general conceptual categories based on a theory concerning the relationships among those variables.

Kruglanski and Kroy are also critical of the distinction between internal validity as a concern with the treatment and the observations, and external validity as a concern with settings, operations, and subjects. Instead, they argue that validity, both internal and external, concerns a hypothesis being tested about the relationship between treatments and measures—whether a particular treatment and measure (internal) or categories of treatments and measures (external). Like Cook and Campbell (1976, 1979), Kruglanski and Kroy (1976) also argue for the operations of the variables to be representative of the relevant theoretical constructs, and specify a standard of construct validity that is sensitive to the validity referents of the *independent variable* (is the treatment appropriately representative of the conceptual variable under consideration?) and the *dependent variable* (are the measures appropriately representative of the conceptual variables under consideration?).

We offer an assessment of the validity of the claims advanced about procedural justice in legal contexts from the perspective advanced by Kruglanski and Kroy, that the fundamental validity concern is the question of whether the results of the experiments are relevant to the research hypothesis (broadly, that procedural justice matters in legal settings). Our assessment relies most on three of the four threats to validity they proposed: the universe of application, the validity of the independent variable, and the validity of the dependent variable (we do not discuss the fourth threat, analogous to what Cook and Campbell characterized as statistical conclusion validity, primarily because we think it reveals rather few insights that are particular to the procedural justice research compared with the other areas of research discussed throughout this volume).

Our assessment begins with a consideration of claims regarding the universe of application: the generalizability of the findings of the procedural justice research to legal contexts. Overall, we assert that on this criterion, the research fares well, in large part due to its consistent reliance on basic theory, and because of the considerable accumulation of diverse studies converging on similar conclusions and the increasing reliance on meta-analyses that have greatly assisted with this effort. Finally, we turn to a discussion of construct validity and the validity referents that Kruglanski and Kroy (1976) refer to as *independent variable validity* (is the treatment appropriately representative of the conceptual variable under consideration?) and *dependent variable validity*. Our assessment of these validity referents is somewhat more critical, as we draw on criticisms of the procedural justice literature that we think are representative of challenges to the theoretical and operational validity of the independent and dependent variables.

GENERALIZABILITY (THE UNIVERSE OF APPLICATION)

Theory and Generalizability In one early empirical test of procedural justice theory, Houlden (1980–1981a) randomly assigned research participants to one of four conditions in a study that examined defendant preferences for various plea-bargaining procedures. The participants rated six plea-bargaining proce- dures (varying according to the extent to which they permitted litigants to participate in the plea negotiation concerning the charge) from the perspective of defendants who were either innocent or guilty of first-degree murder, and who were facing evidence against them that was either weak or strong. Participants in this study included actual defendants and undergraduate participants who reported their procedural preferences on Likert-type scales. Overall, the participants expressed a preference for a plea-bargaining proce- dure that included their participation. In her discussion of these results, Houlden stated, "The major implication of this research is that defendants' acceptance of plea bargaining might be greatly increased by allowing them to attend the plea negotiation session and participate whenever they felt their case would benefit by such intervention." Furthermore, she noted that in light of some differences between the undergraduate and prisoner samples, appro- priate caution was advised in advancing plea-bargaining policy recommen- dations exclusively on the basis of research with undergraduates.

Anderson and Hayden (1980–1981) were critical of Houlden's claims regarding the legal policy implications of this research, asserting that they might be seriously misleading absent greater sociological verisimilitude (how well does the simulation capture the role of the institution "as a component of a complex social system"?; p. 295), conceptual verisimilitude (how well does the simulation "correspond to a problem as it would be identified from a knowledgeable legal perspective"?; p. 296), and structural verisimilitude ("how well does the simulation correspond to the actual form of the institu- tion being investigated?"; p. 295). Specifically, they asserted that (a) structural similitude was threatened because plea negotiations vary on a continuum from explicit to implicit, and in jurisdictions where negotiations are implicit, defendants' unfamiliarity with the nuances of implicit bargaining would undermine any benefits of their participation; and (b) sociological similitude was threatened by virtue of the likely variability in defendants' competence and knowledge to make use of their appearance in a bargaining session.

Houlden's (1980–1981b) reply, a defense of the external validity of this research (see also Berkowitz & Donnerstein, 1982, 1984; Kruglanski, 1975; Lind & Walker, 1979), is highly persuasive, and we cannot do justice to it here. However, we wish to underscore a critical aspect of her argument. Anderson and Hayden's critique mistakenly assumes that the finding of the single simulation study capturing a particular situation was treated as the basis for asserting policy implications in other settings. Rather, the experiment posed a test of a theory about participation, and its results were consistent with the predictions of that theory; inasmuch as the theory was not falsified, it remains rich in implications for settings beyond the specific one tested in this study.

Anderson and Hayden's skepticism about generalizing beyond the simulation created in the laboratory leads them to suggest that if a study simulates a tort dispute, its sociological validity is threatened by generalizing to all disputes, or even just to contract disputes, until those types of disputes have been studied. Furthermore, they argue that either of these generalizations is contingent on the absence of other moderator variables, such as the extent to which the participant is familiar with the other parties in the dispute, the participant's knowledge of the legal system, the participant's actual versus potential involvement in the negotiation, and whether the procedure under consideration entails an adjudicatory or a negotiation process.

We think two observations are relevant to these concerns, both of which complement Houlden's defense of her generalizations. First, Anderson and Hayden appear to employ precisely the validity standard that Kruglanski and Kroy describe as impossibly narrow; no other instance of these variables (participation and satisfaction in Houlden's research) will ever reproduce precisely the same relationship as captured in this particular instance. Furthermore, no two study participants received precisely the same treatment. Therefore, to challenge a theory with any prospect of claiming knowledge about the predicted relationships among the constituent variables, researchers must recognize that they are testing relationships among conceptual-level variables. To cast these observations more broadly, Anderson and Hayden's critique could be applied more aggressively to challenge the validity of assertions about causality among variables beyond their realization in virtually any experimental test, so that generalizations cannot be justified beyond a virtual match between the experimental setting and the applied setting of interest. On this point, numerous psychologists as well as philosophers of science (Berkowitz & Donnerstein, 1982; Cook & Shadish, 1994; Kruglanski & Kroy, 1976; see also Lucas, 2003; Popper, 1959) converge on the view that the theoretical concepts being examined must be recognized as general, and conclusions about the relationships among these concepts are based on theory about the resemblances between various concrete instances.

Second, Kruglanski and Kroy describe two types of research propositions, those that are asserted to apply generally or universally, and those that apply only to designated aggregates. While there are propositions advanced in psychology and law that are of the aggregate type (e.g., clinical theories about predicting violent reoffending), most theories in social psychology are asserted generally. Lind and Walker (1979) point out that the simulation methods employed by Thibaut and Walker and their students were designed to test a legal theory that "eschews restrictions, phrasing its assumptions and predictions in terms of general human propensities in dispute resolution contexts" (p. 8). Thibaut and Walker (1978) theorized about the conflict resolution procedures best suited to obtaining the goals of truth and justice, and about the influence of the manner in which control is distributed between decision makers and decision recipients. They explicitly asserted that theirs was a theory "intended to apply to all instances of interpersonal conflict" (p. 542); it was explicitly not limited to particular settings (e.g., criminal conflicts, or even legal conflicts) or to particular populations (e.g., to more or less sophisticated disputants, to decision recipients or decision makers, or to particular nationalities). While not often stated explicitly, we believe that virtually all of the procedural justice theories to emerge since Thibaut and Walker's make similarly universal propositions.

A final point on the desirability of similitude or proximal similarity (Campbell, 1986) in experimental designs (as called for by Anderson and Hayden) concerns the inherent trade-off between increasing the heterogeneity of the research populations and settings (in an effort to drive up structural, sociological, and conceptual similitude) and the power of hypothesis tests. Lucas (2003) points out that reliance on homogeneous samples, such as those drawn entirely from undergraduate populations, reduces error variance, thus increasing the likelihood of rejecting a false null hypothesis—an argument that would seem to apply equally well to strict control (i.e., homogeneity) of the settings in which the research is conducted. Therefore, if one accepts the claims about research as a tool for assessing general relationships among variables as general conceptual categories based on a theory concerning those relationships, Lucas's arguments imply benefits, both theoretical and applied, of a reliance on homogeneous samples.

By the standards we have emphasized—general theories testing predicted relationships among general concepts—the claims advanced by Houlden (1980–1981b) and Lind and Walker (1979) constitute a strong argument for the external validity of theory-based procedural justice research to actual legal settings: When studies (including laboratory simulations) pose internally valid tests of treatments and outcomes that are representative of the concepts articulated by the theory, they facilitate the application of theory to practical legal questions. Accordingly, the application of research to practical legal questions should not be judged by the degree to which its methods simulate the context where the application might apply, but rather be judged by the fit between the theory tested by the research and the applicability of that theory to the context of interest. Ultimately, our arguments in this section culminate in a claim for the research on procedural justice in legal settings that was advanced more generally by Lewin (1951) before either of us was born: "There is nothing so practical as a good theory" (p. 169).

Data (Replication) and Generalizability A second argument for the generalizability, or external validity, of the basic claims of procedural justice research can be advanced more forcefully now than when Houlden (1980–1981b) and Lind and Walker (1979) wrote about the role of theory for external validity. In the three decades since these papers were written, hundreds of procedural justice studies have been published, considerably strengthening the claim to external validity by virtue of the collective diversity in the research: These studies have varied greatly in the populations sampled (e.g., undergraduate students, nonstudent adults, volunteers, paid participants, as well as participants from varying countries, cultures, and socioeconomic and age groups); the research settings (e.g., psychology laboratories, as well as organizational, legal, educational, political, medical, family, and interpersonal contexts); and the research methods (e.g., laboratory experiments employing deception versus ones employing fictitious imaginary vignettes, field experiments, or field surveys). Furthermore, these studies have varied in their operationalizations of procedural fairness (e.g., manipulations of fair procedures such as voice, neutrality, respect, or accuracy; fair process measures that ask about fair process generally, or specific procedural fairness criteria such as voice, respect, accuracy, and correctability); their dependent variables (e.g., fairness, satisfaction, positive behaviors such as compliance with the law or more voluntary organizational citizenship behaviors, negative behaviors such as stealing, and affect); and their measures of these dependent variables. Despite this considerable variability, the findings have been consistently supportive of the predictions of the procedural fairness theories—a strong argument that the support is not limited to a narrow range of subjects, settings, times, operationalizations, or measures.

While such replication, along with narrative reviews of the accumulated research, is widely recognized as enhancing claims to external validity, this approach to synthesis has numerous shortcomings (Johnson & Eagly, 2000; Lipsey & Wilson, 1996). Fortunately, quantitative syntheses in the form of meta-analyses of procedural justice studies have also begun to emerge. These systematic analyses of large numbers of justice studies have numerous advantages over the simple observation or tallying of replications, including pooling the estimates of the magnitudes of various justice effects to gain more stable estimates, and particularly to permit comparisons of the magnitude of different justice effects (e.g., what are the effects of different procedural criteria, such as voice, or respect, or explanations, on outcome satisfaction? What are the effects of procedural fairness versus distributive fairness, or outcome favorability on outcome satisfaction?). In addition, meta-analyses permit a more rigorous test of the role of potential moderators of justice effects than can easily be estimated within any single study. So, for example, a meta-analysis across a body of studies permits a test of whether justice effects vary according to whether they are tested in more or less realistic settings— a concern raised by Anderson and Hayden.

Several recently published meta-analyses have made important contributions to establishing the reliability of some critical claims of procedural justice theories. For example, two meta-analyses of procedural justice research in organizational contexts—one that synthesized the data from 148 studies (Cohen-Charash & Spector, 2002) and another that included 183 studies (Colquitt, Conlon, Wesson, Porter, & Ng, 2001)—provided strong convergent evidence for the claims that procedural justice has a positive influence on people's behavioral, attitudinal, and affective reactions to encounters in organizational settings. While these reviews did not examine justice reactions in legal settings, the behaviors (such as work performance or organizational citizenship behaviors), attitudes (such as support for the organization or for organizational authorities), and affective reactions (such as to outcomes) examined are similar to ones that have been reported in response to fair procedures in a variety of legal encounters. These include a perceived obligation to comply with the law as well as actual legal compliance (Pruitt et al., 1993; Tyler, 1989; Wenzel, 2006); support for legal institutions and legal authorities (Tyler, 1984, 1989); and satisfaction with the outcomes of legal encounters (Tyler, 1984). Consistent with our previously stated claims concerning the role of theory and generalizability, we view the convergent findings in these meta-analyses and the converging findings obtained in legal settings to be a particularly compelling accumulation of evidence for the generality of these procedural justice effects.

Two of the meta-analyses also exploit the procedure's ability to examine the effect of study characteristics on procedural justice effects, and we summarize these findings briefly to illustrate the potential of this research method to test for potential moderators of effects (recall that much of Anderson and Hayden's critique of early procedural justice research concerned the potential of numerous variables confounded with laboratory versus field settings to moderate procedural justice effects) across studies rather than within any single study.

Cohen-Charash and Spector (2001, 2002) reported that laboratory and field studies produce comparable results concerning the effect of procedural justice on work performance and satisfaction with authority, a finding that bodes favorably for generalization from laboratory settings to field settings. Furthermore, Skitka, Winquist, and Hutchinson's (2003) meta-analysis of 89 studies examined study characteristics to test a question concerning a validity criterion that we consider in greater detail subsequently—independent variable validity. Their analysis coded study characteristics to test two questions concerning the magnitude of the fair process effect as a function of the manner in which critical theoretical variables are operationalized. First, they compared procedural justice effects across studies that operationalized fairness (in experiments or surveys) as voice versus what they referred to as "non-voice" operationalizations (e.g., trust, neutrality, standing, accuracy, or combinations of such procedural variables).

Overall, while they found consistent support for the fair process effect, they also found greater effects of procedural justice on outcome satisfaction and outcome fairness in those studies that employed the nonvoice operationalizations. While additional research (meta-analyses and individual studies) is necessary to tease apart the particular constructs that are responsible for this effect, this finding is consistent with the group value theory's (Tyler, 1989) claim that symbolic (noninstrumental) variables such as trust, neutrality, and respect have greater effects than the instrumental variables of process control (typically operationalized as voice) and decision control highlighted by Thibaut and Walker's (1975, 1978) procedural justice theory.

Skitka and colleagues also asked whether the fair process effect is moderated by whether respondents are judging outcomes operationalized as outcome *favorability* or outcome *fairness*—constructs that they point out are often not clearly distinguished. This distinction turns out to be an important one in several regards. First, while they found evidence for procedure by outcome interactions consistent with numerous studies by Brockner and colleagues showing that fair process effects are particularly pronounced when outcomes are negative (Brockner & Wiesenfeld, 1996, 2005), they also found that this interaction was present when outcomes were operationalized to include outcome favorability, but not when operationalized exclusively as outcome fairness. The outcome fairness/outcome favorability distinction also permitted a comparison of the effects of outcome favorability, outcome fairness, and procedural fairness on variables such as behaviors (e.g., compliance), decision acceptance, evaluations of authority, and satisfaction. This analysis revealed that outcome fairness exerted greater effects than did procedural fairness, which exerted greater effects than did outcome favorability—a finding that challenges the claim that people are more concerned with procedures than with outcomes (e.g., Lind & Tyler, 1988).

Summary: Generalizability, Theory, and Replication   We began this section with a focus on the generalizability of individual studies of procedural justice, and we emphasized the importance of construing variables generally, focusing on the concepts that the operations and measures are intended to test rather than adopting too narrow a view of the precise operations and how they might limit the validity of generalization. Then we moved from a consideration of individual studies to the consideration of a body of research, and we suggested that a strength of meta-analyses is that they exploit the *heterogeneity* that occurs across studies to address questions about moderation, at the same time that they exploit the power that results from combining multiple studies. This approach permits the possibility of identifying propositions that are more appropriately cast aggregately than universally, or inviting theory revision that integrates moderators into revised universal theory.

Overall, our claim in this section is that questions concerning the external validity of theory-based research, including the procedural justice research examining legal attitudes and behaviors, should be considered from the perspective of the appropriate psychological theory rather than from an overly restrictive view about precise operationalizations, measures, settings, or populations. So, rather than broad, limiting statements stemming from concerns about verisimilitude, critiques about external validity should be driven first by the fit between the theoretical concepts tested in each experiment and the concepts they are proposed to address in an actual legal context, and second by the extent of convergent evidence that emerges from

additional studies (varying in methods, populations, settings, operationalizations, and measures) and the meta-analyses of those studies.

CONSTRUCT VALIDITY (OF THE INDEPENDENT AND DEPENDENT VARIABLES)

In this section, we attempt to incorporate the suggestion that validity, both
internal and external, concerns a hypothesis being tested about the relationship between treatments and measures—whether a particular treatment and
measure (internal) or categories of treatments and measures (external). We do
so by employing a standard of construct validity that is sensitive to the
validity referents of the *independent variable* (is the treatment appropriately
representative of the conceptual variable under consideration?) and the
dependent variable (are the measures appropriately representative of the
conceptual variables under consideration?), and we consider these validity
questions as they apply to the procedural justice research operations and
theories.

CONSTRUCT VALIDITY AT THE OPERATIONAL LEVEL

Previously, we described several critical predictions of various procedural
justice theories—among them, that procedural fairness is an important
determinant of satisfaction with the resolution of social conflicts. One of
the earliest and most influential theories to assert a concern with justice in
social interactions was the justice motive theory (Lerner, 1977, 1980), which
postulated a concern for justice as a distinct motive. For example, Lerner
(e.g., Lerner, 1971; Lerner & Simmons, 1966) showed that participants
confronted with a vivid depiction of the suffering of a fellow research
participant responded in various ways, depending on their ability to relieve
the victim's suffering. Participants permitted the opportunity to assist
the victim did so, and provided the victim with compensation. However,
participants not permitted to alter the victim's fate responded to the
suffering by derogating the victim's character. Based on justice motive
theory, Lerner interpreted these findings as follows: By assisting the victim,
the observers were able to put a stop to the victim's unjust suffering and
retain their belief in a just world. Alternatively, those observers who were
helpless to relieve the victim of suffering were confronted with the victim's
unjust fate, and therefore altered their judgments of the victim so as to
protect their belief in a just world.

More recently Lerner (2003) has been critical of justice theorizing and
research that points to a self-interest motive as one that shapes justice
judgments. Lerner's critique poses questions that we believe reflect a concern
with the operational level of the validity of both the independent and the
dependent variables in this research: whether the treatment or measures
as operationalized in a particular experiment are representative of the

theoretically conceptualized categories. Lerner notes that recent justice theorizing suggests that rather than being driven by the justice motive, justice is
employed as a social device for obtaining desired outcomes. A primary
example of this type of theorizing occurs in Walster, Walster, and Berscheid's
(1978) equity theory, which leads them to assert, "So long as individuals
perceive that they can maximize their outcomes by behaving equitably, they
will do so. Should they perceive that they can maximize their outcomes by
behaving inequitably, they will do so" (p. 5).

According to Lerner, such views of the justice motive are an artifact of a
methodological shortcoming. Early justice studies (those that supported the
claim of a distinct justice motive) employed manipulations of justice that were
vivid and engaging (the participants in Lerner's studies actually believed they
were watching a victim suffer), and they operationalized the independent
variable in a manner that produced automatic or emotional responses, which
produced justice reactions. However, later studies (those supporting the view
of justice as a social device for maximizing self-interest) are less engaging,
such as surveys asking respondents to report about past encounters, and they
permit greater opportunities for systematic cognitive processing, leading the
participants to report normatively appropriate, self-interested responses
(Miller & Ratner, 1996, 1998; Ratner & Miller, 2001). Lerner's claim—that
the manipulations in the early studies presented participants with varying
justice demands and those in the later studies presented participants
with varying normative demands—exemplifies a critique of the operational
validity (Kruglanski & Kroy, 1976) of the independent variable in the survey
research, much of which is used to test procedural justice predictions in
legal settings.

In the same critique, Lerner advances a related point that poses a challenge
to the validity of the *dependent* variable in the same survey studies. Pointing to
a study by Tyler (1994), Lerner suggests that starting the surveys by asking the
participants about their attitudes toward authorities alerted them to their
attitudes prior to administering the subsequent dependent measures. Consequently, the validity of the subsequent measures was threatened by the
likelihood that they were driven by the respondents' effort to respond
consistently with those attitudes, rendering the dependent measures a unitary attitudinal construct of the respondents' *normatively driven* reactions to
the authorities, rather than a more nuanced set of measures capable of
distinguishing among emotions, satisfaction, and fairness.

CONSTRUCT VALIDITY AT THE THEORETICAL LEVEL

In addition to operational-level threats, Kruglanski and Kroy (1976) also
described theoretical-level threats to variable validity, such as "whether the
experimental treatment employed in a given study, in fact, represents the
relevant theoretical construct" (p. 173). By this validity criterion, we think
the theoretical and empirical justice literature (and we focus in particular

on the literature concerning the group value theory) is revealed to be in the greatest need of closer attention. Recall that the criteria by which the group value theory asserts procedural fairness is determined (trust, neutrality, and standing) are variables theorized to be informative about whether people are valued and respected members of their valued groups. These criteria are hypothesized to influence justice judgments because of their implications for group status and group membership.

While numerous examples of validity threats concerning the match of experimental treatments and the target theoretical construct are available, in the interest of brevity we draw on one procedural justice study (van Prooijen, van den Bos, & Wilke, 2002) that we suspect poses such a theoretical-level threat to the validity of both the independent and the dependent variables. In the first study of this dual-study paper, the authors propose to test the hypothesis that status salience moderates people's reactions to fair and unfair procedures, such that procedural fairness effects will be greater when status salience is high. In a 2 (status salience) × 2 (procedure) factorial design, status salience was manipulated by asking respondents to respond to two open-ended questions concerning their thoughts about the concept of status. The procedure manipulation was operationalized as permitting or not permitting participants to voice their opinions concerning the preferred distribution of lottery tickets between themselves and other participants. The dependent measure was a three-item "relational treatment scale" that included questions asking the participants whether the experimenter respected them, trusted them, and treated them politely.

Manipulation checks revealed that participants in the high-status-salience condition reported thinking more about status than participants in the low-status-salience condition, and that participants in the high-voice condition indicated a greater opportunity to voice their opinions. A main effect of the voice manipulation influenced participants' report that the procedure used to divide lottery tickets was fair: High-voice participants reported greater fairness. Additionally, there was a status salience × voice interaction on the relational treatment scale, such that the effect of voice was greater among the high-status participants. The study's authors claim that this interaction supports their hypothesis that procedural fairness effects are greater when status salience is high. We propose that this study raises questions about the validity of both the independent and dependent variables. In both instances the problem concerns the ambiguity of the fit between the variables' operationalizations and the theoretical constructs they are intended to represent.

In part, the threat to the validity of the independent variable in this study stems from some tension in the theoretical literature concerning the precise meaning of group standing—a point the authors raise in their introduction. In one view (Tyler, 1989, 1994), group standing seems to refer most clearly to one's status or rank within the group, a construct that Tyler and Blader (2002) have referred to as comparative status. Alternatively, group standing has also been characterized as autonomous status, a construct regarding one's inclusion in a valued group (Lind, 2001) or one's fit with the group's values and norms (Tyler & Blader, 2002). However, van Prooijen et al. suggest that these constructs boil down to a single construct of "people's perceptions of the regard and approval they receive from others" (p. 1354). To complicate matters somewhat further, while the group value theory is clear about the role of trust, neutrality, and respect as indicators of one's group standing, there is also some ambiguity concerning the precise nature of these three constructs. For example, Tyler (1989, 1994) characterizes respect as involving both politeness and respect for one's rights.

Consider the concept invoked by van Prooijen et al.'s manipulation of voice in order to test their prediction that procedural fairness matters more when status salience is high. For about a decade after Thibaut and Walker proposed their control theory of procedural fairness in 1975, manipulations of voice were often employed to test the hypothesis that process control was a determinant of procedural fairness. However, van Prooijen and colleagues employed a voice manipulation as a test of a relational (noncontrol) procedural justice variable. In essence, even though these authors report that the manipulation check was successful in manipulating people's reports of how much of a voice they had in this allocation procedure, it is unclear to what extent this manipulation of the independent variable was effective because of its effect on the concept of control, politeness, respect for rights, comparative status, or autonomous status.

Furthermore, consider the dependent measure in this study, a three-item relational treatment scale that asked participants whether the authority trusted them, respected them, and treated them politely. The authors introduce this study as one that tests whether fairness effects are moderated by status salience; based on their finding that status salience moderates the influence of voice on people's reporting that they were treated respectfully, they conclude that fairness effects are enhanced when status salience is high. The relational treatment measure employed in this study asked about perceptions of politeness and respect—a measure we think is more appropriately characterized as a manipulation check than a measure of the dependent variable, fairness. Herein lies what we think is a second validity threat that occurs with some regularity in the procedural justice literature: Researchers frequently characterize forms of treatment, such as respect, voice, trust, bias, or accuracy, as though they were operationalizations of procedural fairness.

We suggest that these various forms of treatment are not operationalizations of procedural fairness, any more than process control is an operationalization of procedural fairness, or equity is an operationalization of distributive fairness or, in another domain, any more than physical attractiveness is an operationalization of interpersonal attraction. Rather, in our interpretation of procedural justice theories, politeness, neutrality, and trustworthiness, as well as voice, process control, decision control, and accuracy, to name some of the other procedural criteria, are the types of treatment that are theorized to enhance procedural fairness. In this view, the measure of procedural fairness would have greater face validity if it asked the participants whether they were treated fairly. In fact, van Prooijen et al. did include a measure of procedural fairness, and it was affected only by the voice manipulation in this study, not by a voice × status salience interaction, a finding that seems a threat to the claim that fairness effects are enhanced when status salience is high.

Several other researchers have advanced similar though not identical claims concerning the fit between the manipulations (in experimental work) or the measures (in survey research) and the constructs they are asserted to represent. For example, in an important paper Skitka et al. (2003) note that researchers often combine measures of outcome fairness and outcome favorability when testing the claim that procedures are more important determinants of fairness reasoning than are outcomes (e.g., Lind & Tyler, 1988). However, they also point out that such claims are difficult to assess in light of a tendency in much of the justice research to conflate distributive fairness with outcome favorability or outcome satisfaction—constructs that are clearly distinguished by any justice theory claiming that justice effects make contributions to satisfaction independent of outcome favorability. We referred previously to Skitka and colleagues' meta-analysis that disentangled the effects of procedural fairness, distributive fairness, and outcome favorability and revealed that the procedure by outcome interaction (in which procedures matter most when outcomes are negative—Brockner & Wiesenfeld, 1996, 2005) are observed primarily when outcomes are measured as outcome favorability but not when measured as outcome fairness. This study also revealed that outcome fairness explains more variance in perceived fairness (a composite measure that combined procedural fairness and distributive fairness) than both outcome favorability and procedural fairness, and that outcome fairness has greater effects on procedural fairness than procedural fairness has on outcome fairness.

More recently, Reisig, Bratton, and Gertz (2007) noted that the research testing the effect of procedural justice on legitimacy and compliance with the police has operationalized key constructs inconsistently and that little work has examined the construct validity of the scales used as indicators of these constructs—a critique that concerns the theoretical validity of both the independent and dependent variables. As one example, they point to the inconsistent operationalizations of legitimacy in two studies of police officers' treatment of civilians (Sunshine & Tyler, 2003). One of these studies operationalized legitimacy as a perceived obligation to obey legal authority, trust in the police officers, and affect toward the police, whereas the other study excluded the affective component. This concern with inconsistent measures across studies of justice effects in police encounters echoes one that emerged from a meta-analysis of nearly 200 procedural justice studies in organizations (Colquitt et al., 2001).

Overall, these examples converge on a concern about a pervasive inconsistency in the measures of independent and dependent variables in the justice literature, as well as instances of a questionable fit between operationalizations and theoretical constructs, problems that stem in part from ambiguity in justice theorizing, as well as from a paucity of measurement research devoted to developing construct-valid justice measures.

SUMMARY: CONSTRUCT VALIDITY OF OPERATIONS AND THEORY

In this section, we addressed the issue of construct validity as it applies to the operational and theoretical levels of the independent and dependent variables. Contrary to our discussion of external validity, which was largely a defense of the body of justice work as it has been applied to legal attitudes and behavior, here we pointed to some examples of research that we believe posed challenges to the construct validity of this research. As an example of a threat to the validity of the operations of justice-related constructs (at the levels of both the independent and dependent variables), we pointed to a critique by Lerner (2003) in which he argues that recent survey or role-play operationalizations of fairness engage thoughtful, cognitive processes rather than the automatic affective ones that were engaged by more emotionally involving manipulations in some earlier research. According to Lerner, the consequence of this is that the researchers' operationalizations produce normative effects (such as impression management) that reflect self-interest rather than the automatic effects that reflect the justice motive when emotional motives were engaged.

Second, we discussed a threat to the construct validity of justice variables at the theoretical level. Here we offered a critique of two studies that we think exemplify a broader challenge to the claim that the operationalizations of the independent and the dependent variables in the recent justice research represent the relevant theoretical constructs. We argued that the examples we selected reveal ambiguity concerning which constructs are being engaged in the research, as well as some ambiguities in the theorizing concerning a variety of overlapping constructs that might be expected to influence justice judgments.

CONCLUDING REMARKS

Since shortly after its start in the 1940s, the psychological research on social conflict and social justice has been heavily theory-driven. Our overarching assumption throughout this chapter has been that this theory-driven approach importantly conditions the assessment of the research methods employed by the community of justice researchers focused on psychology and the law. We have mostly limited our attention to two desiderata for applied legal research: external validity and construct validity. As to the concern with external validity, we have argued that justice theories have played a critical role in the process of generalizing from the specific instances captured in the justice research to the widely varied contexts where justice processes are engaged in everyday legal encounters. As to the concern with construct validity, we have pointed to some areas in which we think more attention to the link between the theoretical constructs and the operations of those constructs is warranted.

REFERENCES

Adams, J. S. (1965). Inequity in social exchange. In L. Berkowitz (Ed.), *Advances in experimental social psychology* (Vol. 2, pp. 267–299). New York, NY: Academic Press.

Adams, J. S., & Jacobsen, P. R. (1964). Effects of wage inequities on work quality. *Journal of Abnormal & Social Psychology, 69*, 19–25.

Adams, J. S., & Rosenbaum, W. E. (1962). The relationship of worker productivity to cognitive dissonance about wage inequity. *Journal of Applied Psychology, 46*, 161–164.

Anderson, J. K., & Hayden, R. M. (1980–1981). Questions of validity and drawing conclusions from simulation studies in procedural justice: A comment. *Law & Human Behavior, 15*(2), 293–303.

Austin, W., Walster, E., & Utne, M. K. (1976). Equity and the law: The effect of a harmdoer's "suffering in the act" on liking and assigned punishment. In L. Berkowitz & E. Walster (Eds.), *Advances in experimental social psychology* (Vol. 9, pp. 163–190). New York, NY: Academic Press.

Berkowitz, L., & Donnerstein, E. (1982). External validity is more than skin deep: Some answers to criticisms of laboratory experiments. *American Psychologist, 37*(3), 245–257.

Berkowitz, L., & Donnerstein, E. (1984). On the possibility of generalizing laboratory results in psychology. *Bollettino di Psicologia Applicata, 172*, 3–19.

Boeckmann, R. J., & Feather, N. (2007). Gender, discrimination beliefs, group-based guilt, and response to affirmative action for Australian women. *Psychology of Women Quarterly, 31*(3), 290–304.

Brickman, P. (1977). Crime and punishment in sports and society. *Journal of Social Issues, 33*(1), 140–164.

Brockner, J., Ackerman, G., Greenberg, J., Gelfand, M. J., Francesco, A. M., Chen, Z. X., . . . Shapiro, D. (2001). Culture and procedural justice: The influence of power distance on reactions to voice. *Journal of Experimental Social Psychology, 37*(4), 300–315.

Brockner, J., & Wiesenfeld, B. M. (1996). An integrative framework for explaining reactions to decisions: Interactive effects of outcomes and procedures. *Psychological Bulletin, 120*(2), 189–208.

Brockner, J., & Wiesenfeld, B. M. (2005). How, when, and why does outcome favorability interact with procedural fairness? In J. Greenberg & J. A. Colquitt (Eds.), *Handbook of organizational justice* (pp. 525–553). Mahwah, NJ: Erlbaum Associates.

Campbell, D. T. (1986). Relabeling internal and external validity for applied social scientists. *New Directions for Program Evaluation, 31*, 67–77.

Campbell, D. T., & Stanley, J. C. (1966). *Experimental and quasi-experimental designs for research.* Chicago, IL: Rand McNally.

Clausen, J. A. (1984). *The American Soldier* and social psychology: Introduction. *Social Psychology Quarterly, 47*(2), 184–185.

Cohen-Charash, Y., & Spector, P. E. (2001). The role of justice in organizations: A meta-analysis. *Organizational Behavior & Human Decision Processes, 86*(2), 278–321.

Cohen-Charash, Y., & Spector, P. E. (2002). The role of justice in organizations: A meta-analysis: Erratum. *Organizational Behavior & Human Decision Processes, 89*(2), 1215.

Colquitt, J. A., Conlon, D. E., Wesson, M. J., Porter, C. O., & Ng, K. (2001). Justice at the millennium: A meta-analytic review of 25 years of organizational justice research. *Journal of Applied Psychology, 86*(3), 425–445.

Cook, T. D., & Campbell, D. T. (1976). The design and conduct of quasi-experiments and true experiments in field settings. In M. Dunnete (Ed.), *Handbook of industrial and organizational psychology.* Skokie, IL: Rand McNally.

Cook, T. D., & Campbell, D. T. (1979). *Quasi-experimentation: Design and analysis for field settings.* Chicago, IL: Rand McNally.

Cook, T. D., & Shadish, W. R. (1994). Social experiments: Some developments over the past fifteen years. *Annual Review of Psychology, 45*, 545–580.

Cronbach, L. (1982). *Designing evaluations of educational and social programs.* San Francisco, CA: Jossey-Bass.

Crosby, F. (1976). A model of egoistical relative deprivation. *Psychological Review, 83* (2), 85–113.

Davis, J. A. (1959). A formal interpretation of the theory of relative deprivation. *Sociometry, 22,* 280–296.

Feather, N. (2002). Deservingness, entitlement, and reactions to outcomes. In M. Ross & D. T. Miller (Eds.), *The justice motive in everyday life* (pp. 334–349). New York, NY: Cambridge University Press.

Hollander, E. P., & Julian, J. W. (1970). Studies in leader legitimacy, influence, and innovation. *Advances in Experimental Social Psychology, 5,* 33–69.

Homans, G. (1950). *The human group.* New York, NY: Harcourt Brace.

Homans, G. (1953). Status among clerical workers. *Human Organization, 12,* 10–15.

Homans, G. (1961). *Social behavior: Its elementary forms.* New York, NY: Harcourt Brace.

Houlden, P. (1980–1981a). Impact of procedural modifications on evaluations of plea bargaining. *Law & Society Review, 15*(2), 267–291.

Houlden, P. (1980–1981b). A philosophy of science perspective on the validity of research conclusions: Response to Anderson and Hayden. *Law & Society Review, 15*(2), 305–316.

Johnson, B. T., & Eagly, A. H. (2000). Quantitative synthesis of social psychological research. In H. T. Reis & C. M. Judd (Eds.), *Handbook of research methods in social and personality psychology* (pp. 496–528). London, England: Cambridge University Press.

Kalven, J. J., & Zeisel, H. (1966). *The American jury.* Boston, MA: Little, Brown.

Kruglanski, A. (1975). Context, meaning, and the validity of results in psychological research. *British Journal of Psychology, 66*(3), 373–382.

Kruglanski, A., & Kroy, M. (1976). Outcome validity in experimental research: A reconceptualization. *Representative Research in Social Psychology, 7,* 166–178.

Latimer, J., Dowden, C., & Muise, D. (2001). *The effectiveness of restorative practices: A meta-analysis.* Ottawa, Canada: Department of Justice.

Lerner, M. J. (1971). Observers' evaluation of a victim: Justice, guilt, and veridical perception. *Journal of Personality and Social Psychology, 20,* 17–35.

Lerner, M. J. (1977). The justice motive: Some hypotheses as to its origins and forms. *Journal of Personality, 45,* 1–52.

Lerner, M. J. (1980). *The belief in a just world: A fundamental delusion.* New York, NY: Plenum Press.

Lerner, M. J. (2003). The justice motive: Where psychologists found it, how they lost it, and why they may not find it again. *Personality and Social Psychology Review, 7,* 388–399.

Lerner, M. J., & Matthews, G. (1967). Reactions to suffering of others under conditions of indirect responsibility. *Journal of Personality and Social Psychology, 5*(3), 319–325.

Lerner, M. J., Miller, D. T., & Holmes, J. G. (1976). Deserving and the emergence of forms of justice. In L. Berkowitz & E. Walster (Eds.), *Advances in experimental social psychology* (Vol. 9, pp. 133–162). New York, NY: Academic Press.

Lerner, M. J., & Simmons, C. H. (1966). Observer's reaction to the "innocent victim": Compassion or rejection? *Journal of Personality and Social Psychology, 4,* 203–210.

Lewin, K. (1951). Problems of research in social psychology. In D. Cartwright (Ed.), *Field theory in social science* (pp. 155–169). New York, NY: Harper & Row.

Lewin, K., Lippitt, R., & White, R. (1939). Patterns of aggressive behavior in experimentally created "social climates." *Journal of Social Psychology, 10,* 271–299.

Lind, E. A. (2001). Thinking critically about justice judgments. *Journal of Vocational Behavior, 58*(2), 220–226.

Lind, E. A., Kanfer, R., & Earley, P. (1990). Voice, control, and procedural justice: Instrumental and noninstrumental concerns in fairness judgments. *Journal of Personality and Social Psychology, 59*(5), 952–959.

Lind, E. A., Kulik, C. T., Ambrose, M., & de Vera Park, M. V. (1993). Individual and corporate dispute resolution: Using procedural fairness as a decision heuristic. *Administrative Science Quarterly, 38*(2), 224–251.

Lind, E. A., & Tyler, T. R. (1988). *The social psychology of procedural justice.* New York, NY: Plenum Press.

Lind, E. A., & Walker, E. (1979). Theory testing, theory development, and laboratory research on legal issues. *Law & Human Behavior, 3*(1/2), 5–19.

Lipsey, M. W., & Wilson, D. B. (1996). *Toolkit for practical meta-analysis*. Cambridge, MA: Human Services Research Institute.

Lucas, J. W. (2003). Theory-testing, generalization, and the problem of external validity. *Sociological Theory, 21*(3), 236–253.

Merton, R. K., & Kitt, A. S. (1950). Contributions to the theory of reference group behavior. In R. K. Merton & P. F. Lazarsfeld (Eds.), *Continuities in social research: Studies in the scope and method of* The American Soldier (pp. 40–105). Glencoe, IL: Free Press.

Miller, D. T., & Ratner, R. K. (1996). The power of the myth of self-interest. In L. Montada and M. J. Lerner (Eds.), *Current societal concerns about justice: Critical issues in social justice* (pp. 25–48). New York, NY: Plenium.

Miller, D. T., & Ratner, R. K. (1998). The disparity between the actual and assumed power of self-interest. *Journal of Personality & Social Psychology, 74*(1), 53–62.

Pawson, R., & Tilley, N. (1994). What works in evaluation research? *British Journal of Criminology, 34*, 291–306.

Pawson, R., & Tilley, N. (1997). *Realistic evaluation*. London, England: Sage.

Popper, K. R. (1959). *The logic of scientific discovery*. New York, NY: Harper.

Pruitt, D. G., Peirce, R. S., McGillicuddy, N. B., Welton, G. L., & Castrianno, L. M. (1993). Long-term success in mediation. *Law & Human Behavior, 17*(3), 313–330.

Ratner, R. K., & Miller, D. T. (2001). The norm of self-interest and its effects on social action. *Journal of Personality & Social Psychology, 81*(1), 5–16.

Reisig, M. D., Bratton, J., & Gertz, M. G. (2007). The construct validity and refinement of process-based policing measures. *Criminal Justice and Behavior, 34*(8), 1005–1028.

Runciman, W. G. (1972). Postscript to the 1972 edition of *Relative deprivation and social justice*: Some lessons of hindsight. *Relative deprivation and social justice*. Harmondsworth, Middlesex, England: Penguin Books.

Shadish, W. R., Cook, T. D., & Campbell, D. T. (2002). *Experimental and quasi-experimental designs for generalized causal inference*. Boston, MA: Houghton Mifflin.

Sherman, L. W., Strang, H., & Woods, D. J. (2003). Captains of restorative justice: Experience, legitimacy and recidivism by type of offence. In E. G. M. Weitekamp

& H. J. Kerner (Eds.), *Restorative justice in context: International practices and directions*. Collompton, England: Willan Publishing.

Skitka, L., Winquist, J., & Hutchinson, S. (2003). Are outcome fairness and outcome favorability distinguishable constructs? A meta-analytic review. *Social Justice Research, 16*(4), 309–341.

Stouffer, S. A., Suchman, E. A., DeVinney, L. C., Star, S. A., & Williams, R. M., Jr. (1949). *The American soldier: Adjustment during army life* (Vol. 1). Princeton, NJ: Princeton University Press.

Sunshine, J., & Tyler, T. R. (2003). The role of procedural justice and legitimacy in shaping public support for policing. *Law & Society Review, 37*(3), 513–548.

Thibaut, J., & Walker, L. (1975). *Procedural justice: A psychological analysis*. Hillsdale, NJ: Erlbaum Associates.

Thibaut, J., & Walker, L. (1978). A theory of procedure. *California Law Review, 66*, 541–566.

Tyler, T. R. (1984). The role of perceived injustice in defendants' evaluations of their courtroom experience. *Law & Society Review, 18*(1), 51–74.

Tyler, T. R. (1989). The psychology of procedural justice: A test of the group-value model. *Journal of Personality & Social Psychology, 25*(3), 1–35.

Tyler, T. R. (1990). *Why people obey the law*. New Haven, CT: Yale University Press.

Tyler, T. R. (1994). Psychological models of the justice motive: Antecedents of distributive and procedural justice. *Journal of Personality & Social Psychology, 67*(5), 850–863.

Tyler, T. R., & Blader, S. L. (2002). Autonomous vs. comparative status: Must we be better than others to feel good about ourselves? *Organizational Behavior & Human Decision Processes, 89*(1), 813–838.

Tyler, T. R., & Lind, E. A. (1992). A relational model of authority in groups. In M. P. Zanna (Ed.), *Advances in experimental social psychology* (Vol. 25, pp. 115–192). New York, NY: Academic Press.

Utne, M. K. (1974). *Functions of expressions of liking in response to inequity* (Master's thesis). University of Wisconsin–Madison, Madison, WI.

van den Bos, K., Lind, E. A., & Wilke, H. A. M. (2001). The psychology of procedural and distributive justice viewed from the perspective of fairness heuristic theory. In R. Cropanzano (Ed.), *Justice in the workplace: From theory to practice. Series in Applied Psychology* (Vol. 2, pp. 49–66). Mahwah, NJ: Erlbaum Associates.

van den Bos, K., Wilke, H. A., & Lind, E. A. (1998). When do we need procedural fairness? The role of trust in authority. *Journal of Personality and Social Psychology, 75*(6), 1449–1458.

van Prooijen, J. W., van den Bos, K., & Wilke, H. A. (2002). Procedural justice and status: Status salience as antecedent of procedural fairness effects. *Journal of Personality & Social Psychology, 83*(6), 1353–1361.

Walster, E., Berscheid, E., & Walster, G. W. (1976). New directions in equity research. In L. Berkowitz (Ed.), *Advances in experimental social psychology* (Vol. 9, pp. 1–42). New York, NY: Academic Press.

Walster, E., Walster, G. W., & Berscheid, E. (1978). *Equity: Theory and research.* Boston, MA: Allyn & Bacon.

Wenzel, M. (2004). An analysis of norm processes in tax compliance. *Journal of Economic Psychology, 25*(2), 213–228.

Wenzel, M. (2005). Motivation or rationalisation? Causal relations between ethics, norms and tax compliance. *Journal of Economic Psychology, 26*(4), 491–508.

Wenzel, M. (2006). A letter from the tax office: Compliance effects of informational and interpersonal justice. *Social Justice Research, 19*(3), 345–364.

PART IV

CRIMINAL LAW— POST-TRIAL ISSUES AND SPECIAL POPULATIONS

CHAPTER 16

Conducting Psychotherapy Outcome Research in Forensic Settings

BARRY ROSENFELD, KATHRYN BYARS, AND MICHELE GALIETTA

THE IMPORTANCE OF demonstrating that mental health treatments are effective is unequivocal. However, attention to the empirical basis of interventions is arguably even more important in forensic settings, where an individual's liberty may depend on a determination that treatment has been effective. Civil commitment of dangerous sex offenders often hinges on whether an individual has completed a required treatment program and, correspondingly, has demonstrated sufficient improvement. Similarly, individuals found not guilty by reason of insanity or incompetent to stand trial may be detained for extended periods of time while awaiting a clinician's determination that their functioning has improved. Even in "minor" criminal cases, such as domestic violence or drug arrests, treatment is routinely ordered in lieu of prosecution or incarceration. Indeed, the range of forensic settings in which offender treatment constitutes a central focus is extensive, including substance abuse, child abuse, sexual deviance, personality-disordered offenders, and adolescents who exhibit severe behavioral problems. Thus, clinicians working in offender treatment settings bear the responsibility of using the best treatment technologies available. Unfortunately, the empirical basis for most interventions used with forensic populations lags far behind the data available for traditional clinical settings.

During the past two decades, there has been much debate in the psychological literature about the degree of empirical support for various interventions (Chambless & Ollendick, 2001). The standard of care in community settings has shifted towards provision of services with demonstrated efficacy, and in the absence of such data, to the use of "best practices." In the United States, a number of civil lawsuits have been filed on behalf of incarcerated individuals, focusing on the right to adequate treatment (Metzner, 2002). Increasingly, the result of these lawsuits is a demand to provide the standard of care available in the community to those in forensic and correctional settings. The population of individuals who are forensically involved presents unique, often complex, challenges with regard to provision of mental health treatment. Moreover, in the settings in which such individuals are embedded, treatment is often not a primary concern. The task of conducting applied research in forensic settings is formidable yet sorely needed. This chapter focuses on considerations relative to the conduct of treatment outcome research in forensic settings—when possible, highlighting strategies to overcome obstacles inherent in this type of research.

Among the many challenges to conducting mental health treatment research in forensic settings are those that may be considered "typical" challenges common to all treatment research (e.g., maintaining and measuring treatment integrity, difficulty in operationalizing outcome variables, the confounding influence of concurrent interventions, problems with attrition and follow-up) as well as challenges unique to forensic settings (e.g., motivation to distort treatment progress or outcome, limitations on random assignment to conditions, issues of confidentiality). Although this chapter cannot provide an exhaustive review of all aspects of forensic treatment research, we address a number of critical issues that complicate this important endeavor. The chapter is divided into several broad subsections addressing, respectively, treatment development and adherence; operationalization and measurement of relevant variables; design and analytic issues; and ethical and legal issues related to consent, confidentiality, and professional responsibility.

TREATMENT DEVELOPMENT AND ADHERENCE

A concern central to all treatment outcome research pertains to careful delineation of the treatment being provided. Although infrequently applied in clinical practice, manualized treatments are a virtual prerequisite to conducting rigorous treatment outcome research. The reasons for this are perhaps obvious, but they include the improved ability to maintain consistency across different clinicians and to disseminate effective treatments (i.e., treatment adherence). Typically, the debate around manualized approaches to psychotherapy centers on issues of internal versus external validity. Without question, manualized approaches enhance internal validity, ensuring that it was the treatment (rather than aspects of treatment application) that produced an effect in the given problem or sample. In practice, however, most clinicians deviate from established treatment manuals, even when they are highly skilled in their use (Addis, Wade, & Hatgis, 1999).

Although manualized treatments are not necessarily a requirement of rigorous treatment outcome research, there are a number of disadvantages to studying unstructured treatments, particularly when equivocal results emerge (as is often the case). Without rigorous control over the intervention itself, researchers cannot determine whether the failure to demonstrate treatment effects is due to shortcomings in the treatment or its application. However, even referring to treatments as "manualized" may oversimplify a complex set of issues. For example, some interventions follow a highly scripted model in which participants progress through a predetermined set of stages or tasks. On the other hand, many manualized interventions utilize a principle-driven approach, in which the general elements and techniques of an intervention are established but the specific applications of these techniques are not highly scripted.

All manualized psychotherapy interventions must contain both of these elements, but the highly scripted approach typically places more emphasis on specific techniques whereas a principle-driven model places greater emphasis on the general approach (Dobson & Shaw, 1988). Because of these requirements, most manualized interventions are behavioral or cognitive-behavioral in nature, but many also integrate psychodynamic, humanistic, or existential elements into the treatment approach (e.g., Interpersonal Psychotherapy, Weissman, Markowitz, & Klerman, 2000; Meaning-Centered Psychotherapy, Breitbart, 2002). Without question, an entire chapter, if not an entire volume, could be devoted to the process for developing manualized psychotherapy interventions, but this topic is clearly beyond the scope of the present chapter and probably only appropriate for highly skilled clinical researchers. Given the challenges involved in treatment development, most psychotherapy researchers instead focus their efforts on the use or adaptation of existing interventions that have potential utility for forensic settings. Of course, any adaptations that are made must be clearly documented to enable the replication of seemingly successful treatment approaches.

Once a treatment approach has been identified, whether developed, adapted for forensic settings, or simply adopted, researchers must consider issues of treatment integrity. Treatment integrity refers to the demonstration that treatment was delivered as intended and typically encompasses three distinct issues: therapist training, treatment adherence, and treatment differentiation. These three elements are described in brief here, but are reviewed in more detail elsewhere (e.g., Nezu & Nezu, 2008; Perepletchikova & Kazdin, 2005). Therapist training is perhaps the most straightforward of these issues, although the extent to which the goal of adequate training can be achieved inevitably depends on the complexity of the intervention and the resources available to the investigators. Many popular interventions are highly complex and may be difficult for novice clinicians to learn, even when they are motivated and provided intensive training (e.g., Dialectical Behavior Therapy [DBT], Linehan, 1993; Schema-Focused Therapy, Young, 1990).

There are no simple answers to questions such as how much training is necessary or even what approach should be used for training, but formal skill development and supervision of practice cases are often critical in helping clinicians develop the requisite level of skill. Of course, pragmatic considerations are also pronounced—particularly in forensic settings—where staff selection may be as limited as the volume of time and monetary resources that can be devoted to training and supervision. Similarly, the time and financial resources available to the investigators will no doubt vary substantially, which will impact multiple aspects of the intervention, beginning with staff training. Regardless of how training is conducted, study clinicians will ideally be trained to a minimum level of competence *prior to* treating study participants.

The determination that a therapist is indeed applying the intervention as directed constitutes the issue of *adherence*. Most manualized interventions also include formal procedures for evaluating therapist adherence, typically in the form of checklists or observational rating scales. When such tools are not present or are not adequate for the purposes of a particular study (e.g., because of adaptations to existing interventions), researchers may need to develop their own measures. In most rigorous treatment outcome studies, adherence procedures are used at the point of therapist training to ensure that clinicians have reached a sufficient level of adequacy, as well as periodically during the course of treatment, to prevent therapist drift. For treatment settings where audiotaping or videotaping sessions is feasible, researchers often select a random subset of sessions to monitor and code for adherence.

Though random session selection and blind adherence rating is optimal, certain structured treatments may preclude one or both of these rating methods (e.g., if session content is specific to each session, raters may need to know which session is being monitored). Adherence ratings are often particularly challenging in forensic settings, where audiotaping or videotaping treatment sessions may pose logistical and legal concerns. Participants may also have understandable concerns about recording treatment sessions, as do many institutional review boards (although these concerns are often tempered when recordings are destroyed after adherence ratings have been completed). Our research conducting DBT with offenders has relied on direct observation (usually via a nonrecording video monitor, to minimize intrusion into the session) in an effort to minimize the potential problems associated with recordings.

A more variable issue with regard to treatment adherence pertains to the determination of "adequate" adherence. No gold standard or bright line exists against which to compare clinician performance, and arbitrary thresholds (e.g., 80% adherence) are largely fictitious, given the lack of clear guidelines as to what should be measured. There are, however, unequivocal benefits of adherence ratings, including (a) using the ratings to improve adherence and identify areas that require further training and (b) differentiating between more and less adherent clinicians. Large-scale studies might assess whether an association exists between adherence and clinical outcome or compare novice versus experienced or expert clinicians. Such an approach can also help illuminate the active ingredients of a treatment approach.

The content of adherence ratings should also address the issue of treatment differentiation. Particularly in studies that compare two alternative treatments, demonstrating that the interventions are distinct from one another, and particularly when one intervention that is conceptualized as "t[...] as usual," may be as critical as demonstrating adequate adherence t[...] treatment arm. Ensuring that adherence rating forms contain elements tha[...] are unique to each treatment, and therefore, can allow raters to distinguish between the two treatment arms is a crucial step towards establishing treatment integrity. A related concern, particularly when one research team conducts both arms of an intervention, pertains to the issue of treatment "bleed" (when procedures and techniques from one treatment infiltrate the other treatment arm). Ideally, study clinicians would be trained in only one of the treatment approaches in order to minimize the possibility that interventions will become blurred and would use adherence ratings to ensure that they do not inadvertently adopt elements of the comparison intervention. Given these multiple needs, it is not surprising that few researchers attempt large-scale treatment outcome studies without substantial institutional or external support.

OPERATIONALIZING AND MEASURING RELEVANT VARIABLES

A critical element of all treatment outcome research is the reliable and valid measurement of outcome variables and potential mediating or moderating variables. These concerns are heightened in offender treatment research, where the reliability of self-report data is often questionable or nonexistent. The primary issues involved in measurement are detailed in the following paragraphs, beginning with perhaps the most critical issue of all, operationalizing and measuring the relevant outcome variables.

In many psychotherapy treatment studies, researchers use self-report measures and clinician observation to determine whether depression has improved or anxiety has diminished. But in offender treatment settings, the most relevant outcome variables are often those related to criminal behavior, such as re-arrest or re-conviction. Yet even the question of which of these two criminal justice outcome variables (re-arrest or re-conviction) is preferable could fill an entire chapter, as there are obvious strengths and limitations to each. There is little doubt that re-conviction underestimates recidivism, as many offenses are undetected and many detected offenses do not result in a criminal conviction. Re-arrest, on the other hand, is somewhat more sensitive than reconviction but has a greater potential for false positives (wrongful arrests). Moreover, because of the variable time between arrest and conviction, studies that use brief follow-up periods may actually be more vulnerable to false negatives (failure to identify cases in which re-offense has indeed occurred). Given the low likelihood that false positives will exert a disproportionate impact on treatment outcome (i.e., it is likely to be comparably low across all treatment arms), re-arrest may be a more relevant, albeit less conservative outcome measure.

Another alternative to the exclusive reliance on official records of arrests or convictions is to use self- or informant reports of the participant's behavior.

...acArthur Risk Assessment study used a combination of
...oth criminal justice and psychiatric hospital records), self-
behavior, and the reports of friends or family members.
...ajority of violent incidents were documented in the official
...ne participants themselves and the collateral informants
...onal undocumented incidents that would not have otherwise

...on of when and how to rely on self-report data is another challenge faced by clinical researchers working in offender treatment settings. Many relevant psychological constructs are measured through self-report questionnaires, and a number of relevant scales exist (e.g., the Aggression Questionnaire, Buss & Perry, 1992; the Barratt Impulsivity Scale, Patton, Stanford, & Barratt, 1995; the State-Trait Anger Expression Inventory; Spielberger, Jacobs, Russell, & Crane, 1983). However, these measures present obvious challenges when participants are motivated to minimize the extent of their psychological problems. Indeed, in our own research (Rosenfeld et al., 2007), we have frequently observed deliberate minimization during pre-treatment assessments, whereas offenders who successfully complete treatment are often more honest. This pattern can present particular challenges to data analysis, as it gives the appearance of a worsening in psychological functioning after treatment when, in fact, this outcome is an artifact of distorted responding. Although measures of defensiveness or social desirability exist and can help quantify the extent of a participant's defensiveness (e.g., the Paulhaus Deception Scales; Paulhaus, 1998), such measures do not adequately resolve the dilemma of how to interpret self-report questionnaires in offender treatment but rather offer a mechanism for identifying one type of distorted responding.

When treatment outcomes are not defined simply as re-offense or re-newed violence (as opposed to their absence), researchers must determine when clinically significant improvement has occurred. This issue is central to the use of intent-to-treat analyses, in which the researcher classifies treatment dropouts as treatment failures and analyzes the rate of treatment success among those randomized to different treatment arms. Again, the contrast with "typical" psychotherapy research studies may be informative. For example, depression research typically uses a combination of decreased symptom severity (e.g., a 25% or greater reduction in depressive symptoms) and a reduction in symptoms below the threshold required for a clinical diagnosis (i.e., no longer meeting criteria for a Major Depressive Episode). By using an intent-to-treat analysis, the researcher does not capitalize on the fact that many treatment refractory individuals withdraw from treatment prematurely, leaving a far more motivated and often successful group remaining in the subsample of treatment program completers (and hence inflating treatment effects within that group). In offender treatment, how-ever, determining when clinically significant improvement has occurred is far more challenging.

This challenge is due in part to the unreliability of self-report data, as well as the fact that the targets of mental health intervention often occur sporadically (e.g., criminal offending, violent behavior). With more objective markers of treatment outcome, forensic researchers need lengthy follow-up periods before concluding that treatment has been successful (i.e., demonstrating that an offender has not been rearrested during the 90 days following treatment is usually insufficient to determine that treatment has successfully reduced the likelihood of recidivism). No offender treatment setting better exemplifies this problem than the treatment of sex offenders, since renewed offending can be detected decades after treatment has concluded. The premature determination that treatment has been successful can lead to incorrect conclusions about effectiveness and hinder the ability to detect real differences between those individuals who benefit from treatment and those who do not.

A related issue that has particular relevance for research in which changes in psychological characteristics are the primary focus involves the determination of what constitutes the "baseline" assessment point. Offenders may enter treatment at varying points along their offending career, and exposure to prior or even concurrent treatments is common. Although researchers often simplify this question by considering the time of treatment initiation to be the baseline for examining changes, the extension of this logic to untreated control groups is far less clear. Similarly, determining the appropriate number of assessment points to be used is no less critical, particularly in light of response characteristics involving defensiveness described previously. Researchers may use one or more mid-treatment assessment points as an alternative or supplement to the pre-treatment assessment, particularly if these data provide a more reliable indicator of pre-treatment attitudes or behavior. As a general rule, few researchers would argue that more assessment points are better than fewer, but the burden imposed on staff resources and participant motivation places external limits on the desire to collect data that may in fact be excessive.

A final issue in the measurement of treatment effects pertains to the measurement of treatment dose and determinations of treatment program completion. These two variables are obviously intertwined, as many researchers conceptualize treatment completion as an either/or phenomenon (either treatment was completed or it was not). However, in many instances, treatment may be open-ended, and hence, completion does not truly occur. Although the former issue may appear straightforward, quantifying treatment dose can present a number of challenges, some of which are unique to offender treatment and others that are not. In most clinical settings, where participants are motivated to attend all or nearly all of the scheduled treatment sessions, there may be relatively little variability in treatment dose. However, in offender treatment, missed sessions or partial attendance (e.g., arriving late for a scheduled session) are common occurrences, and might lead an individual to receive less treatment than is expected or require a longer period of time to complete the intervention. Clinicians must determine whether treatment dose is best conceptualized as a continuous variable (amount of treatment received), a dichotomous variable (completed or not completed), or some other variation (e.g., proportion of sessions attended).

Of course, the problem of concomitant treatments exists in all psychotherapy outcome research, given that many individuals will receive pharmacotherapy that might confound their response to psychotherapy or behavioral interventions (or give the appearance of a successful response to a no-treatment control condition), or they may engage in other, non-pharmacological interventions that can influence outcome (e.g., substance abuse treatment). Such concomitant interventions are no less common in offender treatment settings, and they may be compounded by the fact that many treatments are intentionally open-ended. For example, determining when an offender has "completed" substance-abuse or sex-offender treatment may be impossible, as these interventions are often intended to continue for the duration of an individual's incarceration or hospitalization. Thus, clinicians may need to rely on comparisons to usual care in examining the unique effects of a particular intervention. The issue of control and comparison groups is discussed in more detail in the section that follows.

EXPERIMENTAL DESIGN AND DATA ANALYSIS

The randomized clinical trial (RCT) design is undoubtedly familiar to any psychologist as the standard by which controlled experimental research is done. By including some type of control group and randomly assigning individuals to the different treatment arms, the researcher maintains a great deal of experimental control and is poised to make strong statements about the effects of an intervention. Unfortunately, the ideals of RCT are often difficult to fulfill in most clinical settings; they are even more challenging in offender treatment settings where ethical and logistical constraints often limit the extent to which true RCT designs can be used. Less rigorously controlled designs often require multiple replications over time to discern the unique versus combined effects of multiple treatments or subject by treatment interaction effects (Kazdin, 1982).

One obvious challenge to an RCT is the need to obtain sufficiently large samples such that threats to internal validity (e.g., group differences in critical variables) can be eliminated. Perhaps more importantly, the use of a true control group is often challenged on ethical grounds, particularly if one seeks to study an intervention that, while perhaps insufficiently tested or validated in other settings, has been used with some degree of frequency. Offender treatment settings are perhaps the most challenging clinical setting in this regard, as many institutions would permit the application of a novel treatment but not the random assignment of individuals to conditions. Particularly in the treatment of high-risk offenders, the suggestion that a potentially violent or suicidal individual might be randomized to a "no treatment" group is troubling for many administrators and review boards.

One alternative that has been increasingly used is the comparison with "usual care," whereby a treatment group is compared with an untreated group whose members continue to receive whatever services are normally provided. Even when a novel treatment hasn't been established as useful, it is likely that settings will wish to populate that condition with the most problematic subset of offenders. One partial solution to this dilemma is to use an "enhanced usual care" comparison group (e.g., a referral for a mental health evaluation or case management without mental health treatment) as a way to supplement the typical services that may be grossly inadequate once a problem has been identified, but without providing the actual intervention under investigation. Of course, the greater the likely impact of a comparison or control condition, the smaller any differences in treatment effects, and by extension, the more participants that will be needed to detect group differences.

A common alternative to the true randomized design is the use of quasi-experimental designs (Campbell & Stanley, 1963). The primary distinction between RCTs and quasi-experimental designs is the use of a nonequivalent comparison group. This alternative is common in offender treatment settings, where ethical or logistical problems may preclude the use of randomization or a true control group. This approach may be particularly appealing where one unit or facility adopts an innovative treatment and the researchers seek to compare their sample of offenders to those in another facility or on a different unit. While the equivalence of these sites might be (and should be) tested, particularly if the researchers identify the comparison setting in advance of initiating the intervention, it is likely that some differences between sites or units will be identified.

Moreover, even when an intervention has been adopted by an entire facility, it is highly unlikely that all the offenders referred for treatment will actually agree to participate. More often, researchers will compare a sample of offenders who sought or agreed to treatment against a sample who were either not referred for treatment or refused to participate. This may result in a treatment group composed of more severely impaired individuals or a comparison group that is more refractory (e.g., less motivated); hence, observed treatment effects might simply represent spontaneous remission or regression to the mean on clinical measures (Campbell & Stanley, 1963). One mechanism for handling these deviations from true RCT designs is through the use of an intent-to-treat analysis (described previously), but other approaches exist as well. For example, treatment outcome researchers have increasingly relied on propensity scores to statistically control for the likelihood of treatment assignment completion (Rosenbaum & Rubin, 1984). Propensity scores do not necessarily overcome the problems caused by imbalanced groups, and their effectiveness varies across studies (e.g., depending on the extent to which covariates can predict group membership), but are one tool in the researcher's arsenal when faced with non-random assignment or non-equivalent treatment groups.

In addition to the intent-to-treat analysis, which often relies on a simple frequency analysis contrasting the proportion of treatment "success" within treatment and comparison samples, there is an increasing array of data analytic approaches for treatment outcome research (e.g., survival analysis, hierarchical linear models, generalized estimating equations), each of which has advantages and disadvantages. Many of these approaches require repeated measurements of the dependent (and often independent) variables, which increases statistical power as well as subject burden (and study expenses). Entire textbooks exist for each of these analytic approaches, and thus only a cursory review is possible in this chapter. The interested reader is directed to these sources for a more thorough discussion of the analytic approaches that can only be outlined in brief here.

One common approach to outcome research, drawn from the health service literature, is survival analysis (Allison, 1995). Survival analysis is particularly useful when the goal of treatment is to reduce the occurrence of specific outcomes, such as violent behavior or criminal recidivism, in that survival curves model the time to occurrence rather than simply whether an event occurred or not. Group differences, along with other potentially relevant covariates, can be incorporated into survival analysis (e.g., using Cox Proportional Hazard models), although the sample size demands increase markedly as multiple predictors are added to a model.

When the focus of an intervention involves changes in one or more variables (e.g., anger or empathy), rather than reducing the occurrence of adverse outcomes, hierarchical linear models (HLM; Raudenbush & Burk, 2002) may be far more useful than the standard ANOVA or ANCOVA techniques that are frequently used in treatment research. HLM was initially developed for educational settings, as a way to compare change in nested groups, but has increasingly been applied to intervention studies more broadly. When applied to treatment outcome research, the researcher expects that the trajectory of improvement (which can be thought of as a regression slope for the dependent variable) will be steeper for the experimental condition than for the control or comparison sample (i.e., the average individual's regression slope will be steeper in the experimental group than the comparison or control group). A minimum of three time points is needed for HLM, but as noted above, more assessment points are better since additional data points increases the reliability of the regression slopes.

One of the most important advantages of HLM for treatment outcome research is that individuals who fail to complete treatment can often be included in the analysis, since treatment dropouts may have provided sufficient data to calculate a regression slope. Many researchers use interim data collection points for this purpose (e.g., at one or more predetermined points during the intervention) rather than relying exclusively on baseline, post-treatment, and follow-up data collection, enhancing the ability to include subjects who may withdraw or refuse to participate in follow-up assessments. Another important advantage of HLM is that covariates can be incorporated into the models, allowing for an examination of potentially confounding variables such as therapist differences in treatment effects or site differences within treatment arm. Of course, as the complexity of the design increases, so do the demands on the resources of the research team, which are often quite limited in offender treatment settings.

Another approach to treatment outcome research that can be used in settings where RCT's or quasi-experimental designs are impractical is the single-subject design (also known as small-N, N-of-one, or single-case designs). The single-subject design typically involves the repeated assessment of a dependent variable at baseline and at standardized points throughout (and perhaps after) the implementation of an intervention. Using this methodology, treatment effects would be considered present when the introduction of the intervention coincides with a change in the dependent variable (Freeman, 2003, Kazdin, 1982). The more rigorous variations on single-subject designs allow further causal inference when the introduction of the intervention repeatedly and consistently influences the dependent variable within (a time-series design) or across (multiple baseline designs) participants (Freeman, 2003). It should be noted that the single-subject design is not the same as a "case study," in that the latter often does not impose any degree of experimental rigor on the implementation or measurement of change.

Although the disadvantages of single-subject designs are probably obvious (e.g., questionable internal validity and generalizability), there are also a number of advantages to this approach. For example, alterations in the study design can be easily accommodated without jeopardizing a standardized protocol or data already collected on other subjects. Indeed, alterations in the administration of a treatment can allow for greater confidence in observed results, if the changes follow expected patterns or conform to study hypotheses (Freeman, 2003).

Moreover, threats to internal validity (e.g., maturation effects, confounding variables) can be minimized by implementing repeated measurements of the dependent variable over time and comparing assessments conducted across these multiple time points (Freeman, 2003). Differences in the generalizability of single-case designs and RCTs may also be exaggerated, since large sample sizes do not guarantee the representativeness of the sample, particularly when researchers exclude individuals based on the presence of confounding variables such as substance abuse or comorbid psychiatric symptoms. Indeed, some researchers argue that single-subject designs are actually more generalizable than RCTs or quasi-experimental designs due to their focus on individual effects that are then replicated, rather than group differences that can mask variable treatment effects (Wilson, 2006).

It should be noted that there are many variations on the single-subject design that vary in the degree to which they demonstrate experimental control. Although a thorough review of this design is beyond the scope of this chapter, the topic is reviewed in brief here because of the obvious appeal that single-subject designs hold for offender treatment research. A number of these designs fall under the general heading of time-series designs (often called A-B or A-B-A designs), in which the researcher assesses the dependent variable at baseline (A) and again during intervention (B). Often, a third assessment point (or more) occurs after treatment has been discontinued (hence, the second A in the A-B-A design), to determine whether treatment effects have remained present or have dissipated (Freeman, 2003). Because this design does not control for any non-treatment factors that may account for observed changes, confounding variables (e.g., maturation or history) limit the internal validity of this design.

In traditional A-B-A designs, the researcher expects that the behavior under investigation will return to baseline after an intervention has been discontinued, thus minimizing the possibility that maturation or confounding variables will give the appearance of treatment effects. However, in many clinical settings this expectation is either unwarranted or unwanted (e.g., if one seeks to demonstrate lasting change in response to an intervention), and hence the design is less useful. Withdrawal of a seemingly effective treatment may also be unethical, further limiting the use of a post-treatment assessment for evaluating treatment effects. Of note, there are a number of extensions of the time-series design, such as the analysis of treatment withdrawal (A-B-A-B), the comparison with a second intervention (A-B-A-C or A-B-A-C-A design), and the use of a multiple baseline design. The latter, which involve implementing an intervention sequentially across a series of subjects to analyze the onset of treatment-related changes across multiple individuals, can be used in settings where a greater degree of control over the implementation of an intervention is possible but randomization, withholding of treatment, or even quasi-experimental designs cannot be used. The interested reader is directed to a more extensive description of these designs, as they are infrequently used in offender treatment research.

ETHICAL AND LEGAL ISSUES

Perhaps the most challenging aspect of conducting psychotherapy outcome research with offender samples is the many ethical and legal issues that arise. Although the general principles described below are common to all psychotherapy research studies, they are far more common and pronounced in forensic clinical settings, where concerns regarding potential violence towards treatment staff and towards others arise with considerable frequency. Among the foremost issues that complicate offender treatment are the need to address confidentiality and the duty to warn.

When therapists initiate treatment with criminal offenders, negotiating the limits and boundaries of confidentiality is a crucial first step. The extent to which confidentiality issues will arise depends, to some extent, on the nature of the treatment that is being provided and the setting in which treatment occurs. In any court-ordered treatment, researchers are likely to maintain collaborative relationships with criminal justice system personnel (e.g., probation or parole offices, mental health courts, diversion program staff). Thus, the limits of confidentiality must be explicit from the outset of treatment, including outlining the nature and types of information that will be disclosed to the justice system (e.g., only attendance/nonattendance or progress in treatment or the specific topics discussed in treatment). Moreover, procedures for dealing with perceived violence risk, continued criminal behavior, or other potential violations (e.g., alcohol or drug use), require explicit acknowledgment by the treatment provider and agreement from the client in advance of any disclosures occurring. Most importantly, participants should be informed about the duty to warn and/or protect identified victims. These precautions are not only ethically mandated, but can be therapeutic, in that they limit the participant's surprise and feelings of betrayal that might arise when a reportable event emerges and reduces or avoids subsequent conflicts when such disclosures are warranted.

Although open acknowledgment of the limits of confidentiality may be perceived by clinicians as hindering the development of a trusting therapeutic alliance, this perception is usually ill-founded (Binder & McNeil, 1986). Particularly when offenders are court ordered to attend treatment, an open discussion of confidentiality issues can actually foster trust by reassuring the client that the clinician is aware of and concerned about these issues. If breaches of confidentiality do become necessary, informing the patient what information will be disclosed and the reasons for the disclosure can also reduce adverse reactions. This therapist behavior also demonstrates to the client that even difficult topics can be discussed in an open and forthright manner.

Of course, concerns about confidentiality are often contingent on a recognition that violence has either occurred or is likely to occur. In some treatment settings, identifying potentially violent patients may simply be an aspect of the referral process, such as when the treatment is focused specifically on treating violent or dangerous offenders. However, in other settings, the risk of violence may be sufficiently variable as to require more careful monitoring. A review of violence risk assessment techniques is beyond the scope of this chapter, but regardless of how violence risk is assessed and monitored, treatment settings must provide a safe environment for both clients and staff. Ideally, the physical space itself will be structured to maximize safety, including sufficient security personnel and clearly identified policies for managing aggressive or threatening behavior.

Treatment providers must also be cognizant of their responsibility to individuals outside of the treatment setting. Ever since the seminal case of *Tarasoff v. Regents of University of California* (1976), in which the California

Supreme Court ruled that a mental health professional can be held liable for failure to protect a potential victim from a client who presents a serious risk of harm, clinicians have been forced to recognize the limits of confidentiality and their responsibilities when violence risk has been identified. The specific requirements that fall under the heading "duty to protect" vary across jurisdictions, but in most settings clinicians are obligated to inform potential victims and/or to take steps to minimize the risk of violence (e.g., by notifying the police or initiating psychiatric hospitalization). Of course, clinical researchers must be familiar with the statutes and case law that apply in their jurisdiction, since the legal requirements will inevitably differ. For example, in some jurisdictions the clinician is merely required to warn the identified victim, whereas other jurisdictions require the clinician to intervene to prevent violence from occurring; some jurisdictions have no *Tarasoff* requirements at all.

A final issue that warrants note in offender treatment research pertains to the release of study information. Beyond those disclosures that are mandated by law or ethical standards (see, for example, Standard 4.05[b] of the American Psychological Association's Ethics Code, 2002), researchers are often confronted with requests to release treatment records. In offender treatment settings, these requests can be particularly contentious, since study data may contain information that is potentially damaging to the participant (e.g., score on a psychopathy rating scale, clinical diagnosis, history of violence, or even rule violations disclosed during treatment). Researchers should anticipate such requests and should develop study protocols that will best protect their participants. One commonly used tool for navigating this issue is to seek a Certificate of Confidentiality from the National Institutes of Health. This certificate, which is not limited to federally funded research but can be sought for any research study, allows the researcher to withhold any study information. It does not, however, preclude the researcher from responding to a participant's request to release his or her medical records.

Given the nature of clinical research, where the boundaries between medical records and research data can become blurred, some researchers make a bright-line distinction between these two types of data, even maintaining separate files for research data (e.g., study measures, screening procedures) and clinical data (e.g., treatment notes). In some treatment settings, disclosures of protected health information will be guided by the Health Insurance Protection and Portability Act (HIPPA), but the applicability of this legislation depends on the setting (i.e., it applies to covered entities, which are typically health insurers or medical facilities that transmit information electronically); in some settings, the clinical treatment research may be exempt from HIPPA regulations. In all settings, however, psychologists are governed by the relevant ethical and legal guidelines, such as the APA Ethics Code, which stipulates that psychologists *may* disclose information, but are not required to do so. Researchers are urged to consider these issues before they begin data collection, because the nature of the information that may be released or withheld should likely be addressed during the process of informed consent and/or seeking IRB approval.

CONCLUSION

Few areas of forensic clinical research are as challenging or as potentially important as treatment outcome research. The need to develop effective interventions for some of the most challenging clinical populations is undisputed. However, protecting participants and treatment staff while maintaining a level of scientific rigor sufficient to successfully test the interventions under investigation, requires careful attention to a wide range of potential pitfalls. This chapter provides a broad overview of many of the issues that arise in offender treatment outcome research, but the interested researcher should seek guidance from as many sources as possible to maximize the likelihood that their research efforts will be fruitful, regardless of whether the investigation being studied is ultimately found to effective.

REFERENCES

Addis, M. E., Wade, W. A., & Hatgis, C. (1999). Barriers to dissemination of evidence-based practices: Addressing practitioners' concerns about manual-based psychotherapies. *Clinical Psychology: Science and Practice, 6*, 431–441.

Allison, P. D. (1995). *Survival analysis using the SAS system*. Cary, NC: SAS Institute, Inc.

American Psychological Association. (2002). Ethical principles of psychologists and code of conduct. *American Psychologist, 57*, 1060–1073.

Binder, R. L., & McNeil, D. E. (1986). Victims and families of violent psychiatric patients. *Bulletin of the American Academy of Psychiatry and Law, 14*(2), 131–139.

Breitbart, W. (2002). Spirituality and meaning in supportive care: Spirituality- and meaning-centered group psychotherapy interventions in advanced cancer. *Supportive Care in Cancer, 10*, 272–280.

Buss, A. H., & Perry, M. (1992). The aggression questionnaire. *Journal of Personality and Social Psychology, 63*, 452–459.

Campbell, B., & Stanley, J. C. (1963). *Experimental and quasi-experimental designs for research*. Boston, MA: Houghton Mifflin.

Chambless, D. L., & Ollendick, T. H. (2001). Empirically supported psychological interventions: Controversies and evidence. *Annual Review of Psychology, 52*, 685–716.

Dobson, K. S., & Shaw, B. F. (1988). The use of treatment manuals in cognitive therapy: Experience and issues. *Journal of Consulting and Clinical Psychology, 56*(5), 673–680.

Freeman, K. A. (2003). Single subject designs. In J. C. Thomas & M. Hersen (Eds.), *Understanding research in clinical and counseling psychology*. Mahwah, NJ: Lawrence Erlbaum.

Kazdin, A. E. (1982). Single-case experimental designs in clinical research and practice. In A. E. Kazdin & A. H. Tuma (Eds.). *New directions for methodology of social and behavioral sciences: Single-case research designs*. San Francisco, CA: Jossey-Bass.

Linehan, M. M. (1993). *Cognitive behavioral treatment of borderline personality disorder*. New York, NY: Guilford Press.

Metzner, J. L. (2002). Class action litigation in correctional psychiatry. *Journal of the American Academy of Psychiatry and Law, 30*, 19–29.

Nezu, A. M., & Nezu, C. M. (Eds.) (2008). *Evidence-based outcome research: A practical guide to conducting randomized clinical trials for psychosocial interventions*. New York, NY: Oxford University Press.

Patton, J. H., Stanford, M. S., and Barratt, E. S. (1995). Factor structure of the Barratt impulsiveness scale. *Journal of Clinical Psychology, 51*, 766–774.

Paulhaus, D. L. (1998). *Paulhaus deception scales*. Toronto, Canada: Multi-Health Systems, Inc.

Perepletchikova, F., & Kazdin, A. E. (2005). Treatment integrity and therapeutic change: Issues and research recommendations. *Clinical Psychology: Science and Practice, 12*(4), 35–383.

Raudenbush, S. W., & Burk, A. S. (2002). *Hierarchical linear models* (2nd ed.). Newbury Park, CA: Sage.

Rosenbaum, P. R., & Rubin, D. B. (1984). Reducing bias in observational studies using subclassification on the propensity score. *Journal of the American Statistical Association, 79*, 516–524.

Rosenfeld, B., Galietta, M., Ivanoff, A., Garcia-Mansilla, A., Martinez, R., Fava, J., Fineran, V., & Green, D. (2007). Dialectical behavior therapy for the treatment of stalking offenders. *International Journal of Forensic Mental Health, 6*, 95–103.

Spielberger, C. D., Jacobs, G. A., Russell, S. F., & Crane, R. S. (1983). Assessment of anger: the State-Trait Anger scale. In J. N. Butcher & C. D. Spielberger (Eds.), *Advances in personality assessment* (Vol. 2, pp. 161–189). Hillsdale, NJ: Lawrence Erlbaum.

Tarasoff v. Regents of University of California, 131 Cal. Rptr. 14, 551 P.2d 334 (1976).

Weissman, M. M., Markowitz, J. C., & Klerman, G. L. (2000). *Comprehensive guide to interpersonal psychotherapy*. New York, NY: Basic Books.

Wilson, B. A. (2006). Single-case experimental designs. In M. Slade & C.E. Priebe (Eds.), *Choosing methods in mental health research: Mental health research from theory to practice* (pp. 9–23). New York, NY: Routledge/Taylor & Francis Group.

Young, J. E. (1990). *Cognitive therapy for personality disorders: A schema-focused approach*. Sarasota, FL: Professional Resource Press.

CHAPTER 17

Research Methods in Violence Risk Assessment

KEVIN S. DOUGLAS, JENNIFER L. SKEEM, AND ELIZABETH NICHOLSON

MAKING ACCURATE STATEMENTS about a person's future behavior is a task rife with challenges and pitfalls. Yet, this is precisely what is required in numerous legal and clinical settings in the form of violence risk–assessment. Although legal parameters vary across contexts and settings, the common task is to help decision makers determine whether those under their authority pose an undue risk of future violent behavior. Consequences of inaccurate decisions include inappropriately depriving persons of liberty (e.g., custodial vs. community sentences; denial of institutional release) or placing third parties in harm's way. Because stakes are high for all involved, it is vital to build and maintain a sound base of research that can inform assessments of violence risk. In this chapter, we provide a roadmap for doing so, focusing on common methodological tasks that face risk-assessment researchers.

LEGAL CONTEXT

The difficult nature of conducting accurate violence risk assessments was not brought fully to light until the 1960s and 1970s. The presumption prior to that time was that violence prediction was just part of the routine duties of mental health professionals, who were fully qualified to carry it out effectively (Douglas & Webster, 1999). However, several landmark legal cases and subsequent empirical studies of persons affected by those legal cases have changed everything.

The legal case with the greatest influence on the field of risk assessment was *Baxstrom v. Herold* (1966), a decision of the U.S. Supreme Court. This decision forced the release or reduction in security of more than 900 offenders with mental illness from the Dannemora State Hospital for the Criminally Insane

(Dannemora, NY) on the basis of their unconstitutional post-sentence detention. Steadman and Cocozza (1974) followed these offenders over time and reported that while young age and prior criminality predicted future arrests, for every correct prediction made from these variables, there were two predictions of future violence that were not borne out. Further, all of these patients were considered (predicted to be) "dangerous," yet of 98 ostensibly dangerous offenders released to the community, only 20 were arrested over a four year period, and of these, only 7 committed violent offenses. Similar findings were reported by Thornberry and Jacoby (1979) about a cohort of offenders with mental illness who were released or transferred from a prison hospital in Pennsylvania as a result of *Dixon v. Attorney General of the Commonwealth of Pennsylvania* (1971).

These cases, along with the initial series of studies surrounding them, surprised mental health and legal professionals and essentially kicked off the field of risk assessment. Researchers started to study what, if anything, predicted violence and whether clinicians could in fact predict it accurately. Based on this early research suggesting that clinicians could not predict violence with any reasonable degree of accuracy, more legal challenges came. In the criminal justice arena, a judge defending the constitutionality of the *Bail Reform Act* (1984) and the risk assessments it entailed, stated that "there is nothing inherently unattainable about a prediction of future criminal conduct" (*U.S. v. Salerno*, 1987, p. 751). The constitutionality of violence predictions was again considered in *Barefoot v. Estelle* (1983) in the context of jurors making decisions about future violent behavior of defendants and whether such decisions could be used to inform decisions about who should be executed.

The U.S. Supreme Court did acknowledge the argument that psychiatrists were unable to predict future violence accurately, but upheld its constitutionality, claiming that while "psychiatric predictions of violence are wrong in at least two out of every three cases . . . it makes little sense, if any, that psychiatrists, out of the entire universe of persons who might have an opinion on this issue, would know so little about the subject that they should not be permitted to testify" (pp. 896–897). The U.S. Supreme Court again supported the validity of violence predictions in *Schall v. Martin* (1984), this time in the context of pretrial detainment of young offenders judged to be dangerous. Other landmark cases (i.e., *Tarasoff v. Regents of the University of California*, 1976 and progeny) in fact held that in some circumstances, mental health professionals had a positive duty to protect potential victims against clients or patients who they knew, or ought to have known, would be violent (for a recent update on the various forms that this "duty to protect" now takes, see Monahan, 2006).

In essence, the law secured or at the very least did not thwart the role of violence predictions in correctional, mental health, and other settings. As a result of these early legal and research developments, studies on violence risk factors proliferated throughout the 1980s and 1990s. More recently, during the past 15 years or so, a large focus of risk-assessment research has been the development and evaluation of violence risk–assessment instruments. Such instruments compile, in one manner or another, a set of putative violence risk factors, and produce estimates of the likelihood of a person's future risk of violence. Since Monahan's (1981) influential monograph, there have been literally hundreds of empirical studies that focus on risk-assessment instruments alone; it is clear that a good deal more is known today than in the past about how best to assess and study violence risk. In this chapter, we outline key methodological issues in risk assessment that, if followed, will promote sound research and practice regarding this important topic.

THE ROLE OF TEST STANDARDS

According to current test standards derived and adopted in 1999 by the American Psychological Association (APA) and other organizations (hereinafter "the *Standards*"), a test "is an evaluative device or procedure in which a sample of an examinee's behavior in a specified domain is obtained and subsequently evaluated and scored using a standardized process" (p. 3). In our view, risk-assessment instruments are tests subject to the *Standards,* given that all have some degree of standardization, involve scoring "samples of behavior," and purport to provide an estimate of future behavior.

In keeping with the *Standards*, risk-assessment measures should be tested and evaluated in accord with their intended clinical use(s). The type of reliability that is of prime interest (e.g., internal consistency; inter-rater reliability) depends on the characterization and intended use of the instrument. If a violence risk–assessment measure is intended to guide clinical practice through consideration of total scores or risk classifications, these total scores or classifications should serve as the level of analysis. We have used this basic principle of "application-evaluation symmetry" in selecting the types of reliability and validity that are most important in violence risk–assessment research.

DEVELOPING RISK-ASSESSMENT INSTRUMENTS

If investigators choose to develop a new risk-assessment instrument, they will face two classic choice points: (1) how to select items and (2) how to integrate them to arrive at a risk estimate. These choice points and the divergences between them underpin the actuarial versus clinical debate in risk assessment. Both approaches have clear strengths and weaknesses, which may explain why one of the most successful approaches to risk assessment was developed using both approaches (Andrews, Bonta, & Wormith, 2010). These strengths and weaknesses are outlined here, along with recommendations for the use of each type of item selection.

ITEM SELECTION

In terms of item selection, the two principle methods are *empirical item selection* and *rational item selection*. Empirical item selection chooses items based on demonstrated statistical associations between risk factors and outcome. This approach has both strengths and weaknesses. Its strengths are that (a) it selects only those risk factors that in fact predict violence in a given sample; (b) it optimizes predictive strength, at least in the sample(s) initially used to select the risk factors (called the derivation, development, or calibration sample); and (c) it can be used to weight risk factors according to their predictive strength in the initial sample. The drawbacks of this approach sometimes overlap with its apparent strengths. First, any statistical procedure is susceptible to the quality and unique features of the sample(s) in which it is used. It capitalizes on chance, is partially dependent on the reliability of measures used in the sample; and, by definition, it optimizes predictive strength for that sample. Second, most risk-assessment instruments that have used this technique have relied on single samples. This increases the odds that the resulting predictive equation will be tied very closely to that sample and may not generalize to other samples. Third, reliance on single samples, or even a small number of samples, risks omitting potentially important var-iables that did not enter the predictive model in those samples but have been shown to predict violence in other samples. Finally, empirical item selection may omit certain potentially important risk factors if they occur with low frequency within that sample.

For these reasons, if researchers choose to apply empirical item selection, we recommend that they (a) use only highly reliable measures; (b) specify a priori the most potentially important risk factors that should be tested and attend to the domain coverage to ensure that important risk factors are not omitted; (c) use multiple samples; (d) cross-validate the resulting set of risk factors prior to recommending the instrument for use; and (e) consider using unweighted (unit-weighted) items, given that they can perform as well as weighted items (Dawes, 1979; Grann & Långström, 2007). The development of the Classification of Violence Risk, or COVR (Monahan et al., 2005a) serves as a partial illustration of these points. The COVR development process relied on a carefully defined and well-measured set of promising risk factors, involved multiple psychiatric sites, applied an iterative classification tree approach that with bootstrapping was designed to reduce overfitting, and included a cross-validation study.

An alternative to empirical item selection is *rational item selection*, which involves the use of human judgment to select items, based on a review of the scientific literature as a whole. Typically, instruments that use this approach (Borum, Bartel, & Forth, 2006; Kropp, Hart, Webster, & Eaves, 1999; Webster, Douglas, Eaves, & Hart, 1997) do not weight items (i.e., use unit-weighting). The strength of this approach is its ability to facilitate generalizability across settings because the risk factors are not tied to sample peculiarities. The potential downside is the converse—because it is not optimized, it risks being less than maximally predictive in any given application. Similarly, there are no uniform articulated criteria for item selection; because item selection ultimately relies on human judgment, items selected by one group of judges may well differ from those selected by another, even if the evidence base that the group consults is held constant.

Although a similar critique could be levied against the actuarial approach for the "upstream" process of composing the *pool* of candidate items, the "downstream" process of item selection references algorithms that can be clearly articulated and data sets that must be clearly described. For the rational approach, the "lack of uniform criteria" critique applies at both the "upstream" and "downstream" levels. Further, given the use of unit weighting, users have little guidance about which risk factors, on average, are most important at the nomothetic level. Researchers who use rational item selection should pay attention to whether the risk factors they have chosen ultimately show validity across settings. They also should clearly articulate what sources of information were considered in developing the instrument (e.g., primary studies, reviews, theories), and what reasoning underpins their selection of the risk factors included in it.

ITEM INTEGRATION

Once a set of risk factors has been selected, some mechanism is required to combine such factors into risk estimates. There are two primary choices here: actuarial and non-actuarial. Actuarial or "mechanical" combination refers to the application of a set of replicable rules to the combination of data, be it a formula, algorithm, or actuarial table (Grove & Meehl, 1996; Meehl, 1954). Although this need not be the case, actuarial combination of items often has been yoked with empirical item selection in the creation of violence risk–assessment tools. That is, through empirical item selection, one or more formulae are identified on the basis of optimal prediction in a given sample or samples. This process can yield a numeric estimate of the probability of violence, based on the base rate of violence observed for an identically classified subgroup in the sample(s) from which the formula(s) was derived (e.g., Monahan et al., 2005a, 2005b; Quinsey, Harris, Rice, & Cormier, 1998, 2006).

Non-actuarial approaches to item combination do not use prespecified rules or formulas for item combination. This method is exemplified by the structured professional judgment (SPJ) approach to risk assessment (for reviews, see Heilbrun, Douglas, & Yasuhara, 2009; Heilbrun, Yasuhara, & Shah, 2010). The tests developed under this approach offer risk-assessment guidelines that include (a) a standard set of operationally defined risk factors that are unit weighted and that must be considered in the assessment process; (b) procedures for evaluating whether risk factors are both present and relevant to a person's risk for violence; and (c) recommendations for determining whether a person is low, moderate, or high risk for violence or crime, based on the number and relevance of risk factors that are present and the degree of intervention that would be required to mitigate risk. At present, SPJ approaches generally focus more on dynamic risk factors relevant to risk management than most actuarial tools. Nevertheless, dynamic risk factors are included in some actuarial tools (Skeem & Monahan, in press) and may become the primary focus of others (Mills, 2009).

The debate about the superiority of actuarial (mechanical) vs. clinical (nonmechanical) item integration has a long history, first detailed by Meehl (1954). Grove et al.'s (2000) meta-analysis of 136 prediction studies in the medical, behavioral, and social sciences provides a seemingly sound estimate of the relative accuracy of actuarial and clinical prediction. On average, actuarial prediction outperformed clinical prediction about half the time, with an 11% increase in the "hit rate" of predictions. Proponents of actuarial violence risk–assessment tools refer to such findings for support (Quinsey et al., 1998, 2006). They also note that the actuarial approach is highly reliable; if applied consistently, formulae or actuarial tables will yield the same results across raters or short time intervals.

On the other hand, critics of the actuarial approach have noted that (a) empirical item selection and mechanical integration may be over-optimized and may not apply well in new samples (for evidence, see Blair, Marcus, & Boccaccini, 2008); (b) empirical item selection may exclude important risk factors that were not significant in a given study, but have been shown to be important in other studies; (c) some actuarial instruments exclude dynamic risk factors that are of most relevance for risk management (for exceptions, see the Level of Service/Case Management Inventory, or LS/CMI, COVR, and Skeem and Monahan's [in press] explanation of the compatibility between actuarial approaches and dynamic risk assessment); and (d) offering ostensibly precise numeric estimates of recidivism is misleading because the application of prescribed formulas or cut-off scores often yields different numeric estimates in different samples (for evidence, see Mills, Jones, & Kroner, 2005; for reviews, see Douglas & Reeves, 2010; Hart, 1998). At present, research that compares these approaches typically shows that they perform about equally well in predicting violence (Heilbrun et al., 2009, 2010).

RESEARCH DESIGNS

Two basic research designs can be used in risk-assessment research: (a) retrospective or (b) prospective. *Retrospective* designs look backward in time, often using file data, to determine whether a variable of interest (e.g., a risk factor) is associated with the criterion of interest (e.g., violence). In the poorest version of this design, sometimes called "postdictive," the investigator completes a risk-assessment measure today (e.g., the Psychopathy Checklist-Revised, or PCL-R) and correlates this with whether violence has occurred in the past. A chief threat to the validity of this approach is criterion contamination, which occurs when (a) raters who complete risk-assessment measures are influenced by knowing that a person has or has not been violent (e.g., past violence is featured in multiple item ratings on the PCL-R); and (b) there is overlap between the "outcome" of interest—violence—and the risk-assessment variable or measure (e.g., ratings of PCL-R "callousness" refer to treatment of a victim during a violent incident that also served as the criterion).

In a better version of this design, sometimes called "retrospective follow-up" or "pseudo-prospective," the investigator attempts to mimic a prospective design by basing ratings of risk variables on information available for one interval of time (e.g., based on all information about a person prior to discharge from prison), and assessing violence based on information available for a later interval in time (e.g., after the person was discharged from prison). The investigator attempts to address the issue of criterion contamination by having different raters code the risk data versus the outcome data. Still, even the "better" version of this design is subject to two key problems with retrospective research. First, this approach relies on file data, and files may not have complete information on the variables of interest for the time periods in question. Second, this design cannot be used to draw any firm conclusions about what *predicts future violence*. However, it is stronger than a postdictive design and is a reasonable option early in the evaluation process if there are insufficient resources for a prospective design.

Prospective designs are most appropriate for violence risk–assessment research. Prospective designs allow the most flexibility in terms of specifying a priori what will be measured and how. This is particularly so if multiple methods of gathering data are used (a topic covered subsequently). Researchers are not forced to rely on preexisting ratings of risk factors or to limit themselves only to what appears in past files in order to measure risk factors of interest. This approach also facilitates multiple methods of data collection (i.e., contacting and interviewing participants and third parties as well as accessing official file information).

Several basic options can be used in prospective designs. The first is a simple baseline with single follow-up. This permits tests of predictive validity but does not permit testing of changes over time in risk factors, should that be an important consideration. To test change over time, multiple follow-up periods are required so that changes can be tracked over time. Although change over time technically could be measured retrospectively, such an approach is highly dependent on participant recall or file information, both of which have been shown to be limited (Monahan et al., 2001; Roberts, Mulvey, Horney, Lewis, & Arter, 2005).

Prospective designs also are best suited to incorporate additional methodological features that can enhance or extend a risk-assessment study. First, a matched comparison or control group could be added to a study to test whether the increased contact with and observation of participants in a follow-up period decreases the frequency of violence. Second, prospective designs with multiple repeated observations are best suited to testing theory-based predictions about influences on violence in which the order of occurrence of events is critical (i.e., does stress lead to violence, or does violence lead to stress?). If such a design is used, investigators are faced with additional challenges of locating participants in the community and retaining them in the study (see Schubert, Mulvey, Lidz, Gardner, & Skeem, 2005, for excellent recommendations for dealing with such challenges). Third, risk-assessment approaches that include a risk-management element would be best tested in a prospective design that randomly assigns participants to either the risk-management or a control condition. This would allow the testing of approaches that purport to include risk *reduction* as part of their mission. We refer researchers interested in such questions to key sources on evaluating services and interventions (see, for example, Ashford, Sales, & Reid, 2000; Kleespies, 2009; Roth & Fonagy, 2004).

There are two primary drawbacks to prospective designs. First, they are more resource intensive than retrospective designs. In our view, this usually is offset by the ability that prospective designs afford to draw the chief conclusion of interest—that a given variable is a risk factor in that it precedes and increases the risk of violence. Second, some prospective designs can risk influencing the likelihood of violence itself. For example, if persons who are responsible for the management, supervision, or custody of research participants (i.e., clinicians; criminal justice personnel) have access to information about a participant's score on a risk-assessment tool, they may decide to intervene in high-risk cases (i.e., increase supervision or revoke conditional discharges or parole). In this case, an "intervention success" looks like a predictive failure (high risk coupled with lack of violence). One way to circumvent this potential problem is to design the study so that no persons who make decisions about participants' actual supervision or custodial standing collect data or are allowed to know participants' scores on any study measures. In fact, this is fairly standard practice for ensuring the validity of what is fundamentally observational research (where the goal is to avoid influencing the process being studied). In the United States, the investigator may, in fact, apply for a Federal Certificate of Confidentiality to protect against disclosure of participants' data, perhaps even in the face of a court subpoena.

The downside to conducting a study in which the results of risk assessments are not known to agency staff is a lack of realism. That is, in practice agency staff conduct risk assessments to inform decisions about individuals. In studies of applied risk assessment, we recommend that in addition to collecting outcome data on violence, researchers collect data on a broader array of events that might occur in the outcome period (i.e., revocations or changes in supervision level). Although these actions can inform researchers whether higher-risk persons were more likely to be revoked and hence no longer presented a risk in the community, they do not solve the fundamental problem that risk assessments conducted by agency staff can influence the evaluation of an instrument's predictive validity. For this reason, as with treatment research (Seligman, 1995), we recommend that studies be conducted of how well instruments can predict violence in principle (akin to efficacy research in the psychotherapy literature) and how well they predict violence in practice (akin to effectiveness research). An excellent example of this distinction is reported in a line of research showing that despite excellent inter-rater reliability (i.e., ICC = .85+) of the PCL-R in research studies (see Hare, 2003), agreement between raters in actual (adversarial) practice (i.e., in sexually violent predator adjudications) is substantially lower, with ICC values below .50 (Boccaccini, Murrie, & Turner, 2008; Murrie, Boccaccini, Johnson, & Janke, 2008; Murrie, Boccaccini, Turner, Meeks, & Woods, 2009). Similar studies of the predictive validity of risk-assessment instruments are uncommon (see Manchak, Skeem, & Douglas, 2008) but valuable.

ISSUES OF RELIABILITY

Reliability, or low measurement error, is the most basic requirement for a risk-assessment instrument or a measure of a single risk factor. A tool must be reliable to be valid; but the reverse is not true. One can reliably measure something that does not predict future violence. Three forms of reliability are particularly relevant in the violence risk–assessment field: (1) inter-rater, (2) test-retest, and (3) internal consistency.

Inter-rater reliability is important whenever a rater uses his or her judgment to assess a risk variable of interest. Inter-rater reliability is not relevant to measures that are completed solely by the examinee (i.e., self-report measures of risk factors). It indicates that one rater will score an examinee similarly to another rater. It is important to ensure that an examinee's score is a function of his or her "true" scores on a given measure, rather than the particular rater selected. Inter-rater reliability is assessed by having the same examinee rated by different raters and then assessing their agreement on offenders' scores.

There are several important issues that researchers must decide on with respect to inter-rater reliability, including the number of cases that will be used for inter-rater reliability analyses, how those cases are selected, and how many raters are used. Generally, we would recommend that at least 20 to 30 cases form the basis of inter-rater reliability analyses to ensure stable estimates—more if possible. This is a rough estimate that typically will be sufficient, particularly if three rather than two ratings of each participant are made (Walter, Eliasziw, & Donner, 1998). Resources permitting, *all* cases can be rated by more than one rater, and either averaged or consensus scores can be used for validity analyses (both of which are more reliable than individual scores). Ideally, cases for inter-rater reliability should be selected to span the data collection period, as ratings may be less reliable at the beginning (because raters are still learning the process and becoming "calibrated" with one another) and at the end (due to rater drift). Every Nth case can be designated a reliability case, depending on the total anticipated sample size.

Ideally, each rater should be involved in evaluating inter-rater reliability. If there are five raters on a project, for instance, they can take turns providing reliability ratings for one another according to some schedule (random or otherwise) that will ensure that each rater is involved as both primary and secondary rater. Alternatively, each rater could be paired with a well-trained rater who is responsible only for providing secondary ratings. Other options can be chosen, such as taping interviews and providing copies of case materials from a single case to all raters on a project, who then provide independent ratings.

We also recommend that prior to commencing a research project, the reliability of raters who will code measures be established. This can be done by having all raters on a project independently rate the same practice cases (either live, recorded, or reduced to paper vignettes), and calculating their individual reliability vis-à-vis criterion scores for the practice cases. Booster training sessions can help to reduce rater drift, as can periodic review and discussion of case ratings.

Test-retest reliability indicates that an examinee obtains similar scores on an instrument when tested at two different time points. Reliability estimates should be expected to be high only if scores on instruments are not expected to change (i.e., ratings of severity of past child abuse). Ratings of risk factors that may change acutely (i.e., current anger intensity) are not expected to be the same over time; hence, low "reliability" scores may just index this change.

Internal consistency reliability indicates that the items on a given instrument are homogeneous. The coefficient *alpha* often is used to assess internal consistency on scales. Alpha ranges from 0 to 1.0. Generally, values of .70 and greater may be considered appropriate for measures that will be applied to make important decisions about people (see Pedhazur & Schmelkin, 1991). Internal consistency is relevant only when a test purports to measure an underlying construct, such as anger, stress, or psychopathy. The internal consistency of multi-item measures of individual risk factors (e.g., the Novaco Anger Scale and Provocation Inventory, Novaco, 2003) should be tested. Similarly, for risk-assessment instruments that were designed to measure constructs, which in turn are expected to influence a person's risk for violence, internal consistency is relevant. Such is the case for the level of service (LS) family of instruments (Andrews et al., 2010; Hoge, 2010). However, for many risk-assessment instruments, internal consistency is irrelevant because the instrument was not intended to measure an underlying construct. Examples of risk-assessment instruments for which internal consistency is irrelevant include the VRAG, HCR-20, and Static-99.

ISSUES OF VALIDITY

PREDICTIVE VALIDITY

Predictive validity is the most important type of validity to demonstrate for a risk-assessment instrument. Simply put, something that purports to identify who is at more or less at risk for future violence must be shown to be able to do so. In evaluating the predictive utility of an instrument, two elements are particularly important. First, it should generate a standard score that can be evaluated across studies as the "predictor," be it an algorithm, a total score, a cut-off score, or a risk-category system. Second, because a risk-assessment tool is only as good as the criterion against which it is validated (Thorndike, 1949), the outcome variable (violence, recidivism, etc.) must be measured later in time than the predictor.

We have several recommendations for evaluating the predictive validity of risk-assessment instruments. First, risk-assessment instruments should be evaluated according to the manner in which they are intended to be used. Unfortunately, this is the exception rather than the rule in risk-assessment research. Because most studies simply report general indices of predictive strength (i.e., correlation coefficients, AUCs) that are secondary to the intended use of the instruments, we provide some concrete suggestions here for evaluating both SPJ and actuarial tools.

SPJ instruments presume that judgments of low, moderate, or high risk will (a) provide meaningful differentiation of evaluatees in terms of future violence risk and (b) predict as well as or better than numeric use of the instruments. To test the first presumption, investigators could report the observed rates of violence across an SPJ instrument's risk classifications (low, medium, high), which should follow an increasing monotonic pattern and could test how well the instrument has dispersed cases into subgroups whose observed base rates of violence are distant from the total sample base rate (see Silver, Smith, & Banks, 2000). Investigators could also report relative risk ratios (for simple cross-tabulations) or odds or hazard ratios (for survival or other analyses) that describe the increase in the probability of observing violence as a function of risk classification. To test the second assumption, researchers should test whether—and how much—judgments of low, moderate, and high risk add incrementally to numeric use of the instruments on which they are based using multivariate procedures (for examples, see de Vogel & de Ruiter, 2006; Douglas & Reeves, 2010; Douglas, Yeomans, & Boer, 2005; Kropp & Hart, 2000).

Most actuarial instruments presume to identify groups of persons with $X\%$ risk of violence. To test this presumption, investigators could follow the previously stated recommendations for reporting and testing differences among risk classifications. In addition, investigators should report how closely rates of violence observed among persons classified in various groups map onto the estimated frequencies provided in test manuals or development research (for examples, see Harris, Rice, & Cormier, 2002; Manchak, Skeem, & Douglas, 2008; Mills et al., 2005; Monahan et al., 2005a, 2005b).

Second, general effect sizes, even though they are of secondary importance, should still be reported so that the general predictive strength of a risk factor or instrument can be compared with other instruments. Most effect sizes can be classified as indicating small, moderate, or large associations between a predictor and an outcome. Common examples include difference scores (d), beta-coefficients, correlation coefficients, and odds ratios. Interpretations of many effect sizes can be found in Cohen (1988). We emphasize that these outcomes cannot substitute for the reporting of analyses of instruments according to their intended uses, as described previously.

Third, statistical procedures used should both match the nature of the data and the research question and account for data irregularities. For example, if recidivism is known only to have occurred or not, a procedure that can handle dichotomous outcome data is appropriate (i.e., logistic regression). If count data are used, a Poisson regression may be appropriate. If time to event is of interest, survival analysis is appropriate. If the proportion correctly classified is of interest, classification indices such as hit rates, positive/negative predictive power, and true/false positive rates are relevant. In terms of data irregularities, if outcomes have very low (or high) base rates, statistical procedures that are less susceptible to base rates (i.e., receiver operating characteristics, reviewed subsequently) should be relied on more so than those that are more susceptible (i.e., correlation coefficients).

Finally, as much as possible, the follow-up period should be comparable for all participants. If possible, having a uniform follow-up period (i.e., one year) is ideal. Variations in time at risk can partially be accounted for by statistical techniques that incorporate time (e.g., survival analysis) and by controlling for the amount of time a person spent re-incarcerated, re-hospitalized, or otherwise "not at risk" for community violence during the follow-up period (see Douglas, Ogloff, Nicholls, & Grant, 1999, for an example). However, in many instances, simply knowing which participants were and were not violent over some policy-relevant time frame is important.

INCREMENTAL VALIDITY

Incremental validity refers to the extent to which one variable (be it a risk-assessment measure or a measure of a single construct) improves the predictive validity of a second variable or even a set of variables (Hunsley, 2003). This form of validity is important if a researcher wants to test whether a measure offers unique predictive validity beyond another measure. It can also be used to evaluate which of two (or more) measures is more strongly related to an outcome.

There are three primary uses of incremental validity within the field of violence risk assessment: (1) testing the incremental validity of risk-assessment measures vis-à-vis other risk-assessment measures, (2) testing the incremental validity of risk-assessment measures vis-à-vis important covariates, and (3) testing the incremental validity of violence risk factors vis-à-vis other putative risk factors. Although incremental validity is an important concept, it has unfortunately been used infrequently in the risk-assessment field.

First, researchers may want to know whether risk-assessment measure "A" predicts above and beyond risk-assessment measure "B." This could be important in determining, for example, whether a correctional agency should adopt one measure or another (see Doyle & Dolan, 2006). Second, it is important to determine whether risk-assessment measures, which often are time- and resource-intensive and may require highly trained professionals, add incrementally to easy-to-collect risk factors or covariates, such as young age and a history of violence (see Douglas, Epstein, & Poythress, 2008). If not, they may not be worth the added resources. Third, to disentangle the predictive effects of individual risk factors, which often are correlated, the incremental validity of risk factors can be tested against one another (see Skeem et al., 2006). This can be important if researchers want to compile a set of risk factors with minimal redundancy.

Although there are numerous ways in which to carry out incremental validity analyses (Hunsley, 2003), we highlight two. First, researchers can test incremental validity within any multivariate predictive statistical procedure, such as linear, logistic, or Cox regression (depending on the nature of the coding of the outcome and whether factors such as time to event are relevant to the research question). In such analyses, typically the "comparison" measure—or covariate(s), as the case may be—are entered as the first block of predictors. The "target" measure is then entered as the second block. The researcher is interested in whether entering the target measure (a) improves model fit significantly and (b) achieves statistical significance within the model, and wants to know the relative size of effect between the target and comparison measures.

Another approach, illustrated by Edens, Skeem, and Douglas (2006), involves testing the predictive strength of target and comparison measures once the variance in each attributable to the other is removed. Edens et al. used this approach to compare the incremental validity of the Psychopathy Checklist: Screening Version (PCL:SV; Hart, Cox, & Hare, 1995) and a modified Violence Risk Appraisal Guide (VRAG; Quinsey et al., 1998, 2006). They reported that the bivariate association between the PCL:SV and later violence was reduced from an area under the curve (AUC; see the following section) of .78 to .75, whereas the AUC for the modified VRAG was reduced from .73 to .58, indicating that the predictive strength of the modified VRAG is attributable primarily to its shared variance with the PCL:SV, but the converse is not true. This approach is closely related to *partial correlations.*

CONSTRUCT VALIDITY

Construct validity refers to evidence that an outcome measures the theoretical construct it purports to measure. Like internal consistency, construct validity is relevant only to risk-assessment instruments that purport to measure constructs (such as the LS instruments) and not to those that do not. It can be inferred through logical analysis, internal structure analysis, and cross-structure analysis (Pedhazer & Schmelkin, 1991), each of which is defined below.

Logical analysis involves the selection of items on an instrument and the manner in which they are scored and combined. One may analyze the content to determine how well its item content comports with the abstract concepts or constructs that are proposed to underlie them. For example, on the Level of Service/Case Management Inventory, it would be important to know whether the items on the "procriminal attitudes" scale comport with the literature on that particular criminogenic need.

Internal structure analysis involves determining whether there is correspondence between the structure of a set of items and the constructs they are said to reflect. One can use confirmatory factor analytic techniques to test (a) whether the relationships among items selected for the measure can be explained by the scales they are supposed to reflect and (b) whether the items on each of those scales measure the same construct. The latter point pertains to whether the scales actually "hang together," or are homogeneous, which reflects factorial validity or unidimensionality. It makes little sense to combine a set of heterogeneous items into a scale for the purpose of measuring a purported homogeneous underlying construct if they are not measuring the same thing.

Cross-structure analysis is a necessary and relatively demanding condition for construct validity. Finding that the items on a scale are homogeneous does not preclude the possibility that the single construct being measured is different from the one the investigator meant to tap. Cross-structure analysis involves examining the relationship between the measure of interest and external measures of theoretically related constructs. First, there must be evidence of convergent validity—measures of the same construct obtained through different methods or measures should correlate with one another. For example the antisocial (ANT) scale of the Personality Assessment Inventory (PAI) should converge with clinicians' independent diagnoses of antisocial personality disorder. Second, there must be evidence of discriminant validity; there should be divergence in measures or methods designed to measure different constructs. For example, the ANT and AGG (aggression) scales of the PAI should not be so highly correlated with one another as to raise doubt as to whether distinct constructs are being assessed.

CONSTRUCT VALIDITY OF DYNAMIC RISK FACTORS

Some risk-assessment measures and approaches emphasize the importance of capturing changes in risk factors over time. This is the case for the LS (Andrews et al., 2010) and SPJ (Douglas & Reeves, 2008, 2010) instruments. In principle, actuarial approaches to risk assessment could also include such an emphasis. The basic argument is that if a risk factor becomes worse (i.e., someone becomes more angry), risk for violence increases, and if it becomes better, risk decreases. Also, if risk factors are changeable, they might represent particularly promising avenues for intervention because mental health or correctional personnel can deliberately attempt to change them for the better (Douglas & Skeem, 2005).

If a risk-assessment measure includes purportedly changeable or dynamic risk factors, part of its evaluation should include analysis of whether its risk factors are capable of indexing change over time and whether such changes are associated with violence. There have been very few studies of this issue. There are many studies that show that certain measures of *individual* risk factors (i.e., anger, stress, substance use problems) can capture change (for a review, see Douglas & Skeem, 2005). There are fewer studies of whether risk-assessment instruments index change over time and fewer still of whether such changes are predictive of violence (for a review of a handful of such studies that use the LS system, see Andrews & Bonta, 2010).

GENERALIZABILITY

Researchers should explore whether the risk factors or measures of interest generalize to the population of interest (i.e., offenders with mental illness, general criminal offenders, psychiatric patients, or some mixture thereof). For actuarial tools, the formula developed in one sample must be shown to generalize to and "work" in another sample from the same population and for any new populations of interest. For SPJ instruments, there is less risk of statistical optimization, but the tools must be shown to "work" not only for a sample from the population initially considered by developers, but for any new populations of interest.

There are two particularly important features of evaluating generalizability of risk-assessment measures. First, as detailed previously, researchers should evaluate the element of an instrument that is intended to be used in practice (e.g., ordinal or more ostensibly precise risk classifications). Second, researchers should attempt to replicate, as closely as possible, the methodological features that were used in derivation samples. This is particularly important in early cross-validation studies in which the basic issue of "whether the instrument holds up" is being tested. If findings are positive, tests of generalizability under different conditions (i.e., with different samples, over different time frames) should be carried out. If an initial cross-validation study uses methods that differ considerably from those used in the derivation sample and different results are obtained, researchers would be unable to make conclusions about the cross-validated adequacy of the instrument, because they have essentially recalibrated it under different conditions. This, ironically, would call for yet further cross-validation to test whether the recalibration is robust.

CRITERION-RELATED ISSUES

To predict violence, one must first define and assess it. Given that studies vary in their definitions of violence, we recommend adopting a crystal-clear definition that is easily understood and promotes comparison with the results of past key studies. First, one might start with a broad definition of violence-relevant behavior and then clearly define subcategories so that researchers can evaluate the validity of instruments and predictors across a range of potentially relevant violent outcomes. This could maximize the relevance of the research to different settings. For example, in some contexts (i.e., parole release), it may be most important to assess risk for physical violence. In other contexts (i.e., community supervision of persons on conditional release), knowing whether a person attempted physical violence (i.e., a "swing and a miss" with her fist) is relevant. One broad definition of such behavior can be found in the HCR-20 (Webster et al., 1997), where the authors define violence as "actual, attempted, or threatened harm to a person or persons" (p. 24). This definition incorporates unambiguous threats and fear-inducing behavior (e.g., stalking), which do not constitute physical acts of violence.

Second, beyond such a broad definition, one might adopt a specific definition of physical violence. One way to do so that would facilitate comparison with other research is to use the definitions ultimately adopted by the MacArthur Violence Risk Assessment Study (Monahan et al., 2001). Here, "violence" is defined as acts of battery resulting in injury (from minor bruises or cuts to serious injury), assaultive acts involving weapon use, sexual assault, and threats made with a weapon in hand, whereas "other aggressive acts" are defined as battery that did not result in any injury.

In addition to settling on a general definition of violence, physical or otherwise, researchers may wish to code for certain elements of violence if they have research questions pertaining to them, such as targets, location, victim characteristics (e.g. spousal violence, sexual violence), or to motivation (i.e., instrumental, or predatory and goal directed, vs. hostile/reactive, or impulsive and emotionally driven). Additional data regarding the frequency and imminence of violent behavior may also be collected.

Given this broad umbrella for violence-relevant behavior and specific definitions of physical violence, how should one go about *assessing* the criterion of interest? Where possible, we recommend the use of standardized instruments, which facilitate comparison across studies. Examples of standardized instruments include the Overt Aggression Scale, which measures observable aggressive behaviors including verbal and physical aggression towards self and others, and the violence coding form used in the MacArthur study (Monahan et al., 2001), which was based on the Revised Conflict Tactics Scale (CTS-2). In some instances (i.e., if violence is coded from rap sheets), such instruments cannot be used.

STATISTICAL ANALYSIS

Literally dozens of statistical approaches can be used in the evaluation of risk-assessment measures and risk factors. We briefly review some of these here, referring readers to Chapter 3 in this volume for more detail. As general principles and as noted above, we recommend choosing analytic approaches that best match the research question and form of data.

Receiver operating characteristics (ROC) analysis is a bivariate procedure frequently used to test the simple predictive accuracy of a risk-assessment instrument. ROC is based on signal detection theory and creates a visual representation of the relationship of sensitivity (detection of a true positive) versus 1-specificity (detection of a false negative) for a continuous predictor and binary outcome. The numerical value produced is the area under the curve (AUC) which ranges from 0 (perfect negative prediction) to 0.5 (chance performance) to 1.0 (perfect positive prediction). Put another way, the AUC can describe the chance that a randomly selected individual who perpetrates violence will obtain a higher score on a risk-assessment instrument than a randomly selected individual who does not perpetrate violence.

One of the reasons for ROC's popularity is its lack of statistical dependence on base rates. Outcomes common in risk-assessment research sometimes have low base rates leading to attenuated effect sizes for analyses that are dependent on base rates, such as correlations. Moreover, using a single statistic to assess the predictive accuracy of risk-assessment tools facilitates ease in comparisons across tools. ROC analysis provides an average estimate of predictive strength across the entire range of a continuous predictor; it can be used to identify optimal cut-off scores and to identify how classification indices change at different scores. However, its primary index, the AUC, is of little utility when it comes to actually using an instrument in practice (how does an AUC of .75 inform actual decisions?).

Regression approaches can be useful both for developing and validating risk-assessment instruments. Simple bivariate regression is used to predict an outcome (e.g., violence) from another variable referred to as a predictor (e.g., impulsivity). Multiple regression can be used to assess the relationship between one continuous outcome and two or more continuous or categorical predictors that may or may not be correlated. Multivariate regression is used in any situation with one or more predictors and two or more outcomes. The particular form of regression chosen (i.e., linear, logistic, survival analysis) depends on the format of the data.

SOURCES OF DATA COLLECTION

We recommend where possible that researchers collect data from different sources and use different methods, both for predictors and outcomes. This is to avoid a "mono-method" bias, or overreliance on a single source of data that might systematically over- or underestimate the presence or severity of risk factors or of outcomes. Use of multiple methods reduces this risk. In terms of gathering information to rate risk-assessment instruments, therefore, we recommend that important file documents be reviewed for pertinent information, along with an interview. In some instances, observation or collateral report might be available as well. Note that this recommendation does not apply to instruments or measures that are intended to be rated based solely on one source or method, such as self-report measures of risk factors (i.e., anger) or some risk-assessment instruments (i.e., VRAG; Static-99).

On the outcome side of the equation, there are several telling demonstrations of the importance of using multiple methods of data collection. Mulvey, Shaw, and Lidz (1994), for instance, followed approximately 650 psychiatric patients for six months after release from a psychiatric hospital. When they calculated the base rate of violence based solely on official record data, it was 12%. When they included both self- and collateral reports of violence, the base rate rose to 47%. Sole reliance on official records in this study would have drastically underestimated the base rate of violence and detrimentally affected any attempts to validate risk factors or measures because many of the people classified as "nonviolent" in reality were violent. Similar findings were made by Steadman et al. (1998) for the aforementioned MacArthur study. In fact, they reported that the majority of incidents were obtained from patient reports, suggesting that collateral reports might not be necessary.

Even within a single domain or type of outcome information, reliance on single versus multiple sources of data can impact predictive estimates. Douglas and Ogloff (2003), influenced by Mulvey et al.'s paper, tested whether this effect held within a single domain of outcome information— reliance on single versus multiple sources of file-based outcome data (recidivism, psychiatric hospital, or general hospital records only, vs. all three). They reported that even within a single domain, the source of outcome data impacted the accuracy of violence predictions (here, using the HCR-20 and the PCL:SV) in a study of 279 psychiatric patients discharged from hospital. First, violence detected by these sources correlated only up to .21 with one another, indicating that each is capturing unique instances of violence. Second, accuracy of the HCR-20 and PCL:SV varied across single-source outcome sources, particularly for the PCL:SV. For example, using physical violence as the outcome, the AUC ranged from .60 (using psychiatric readmission records to measure outcome) to .78 (using criminal records to measure outcome), with an average of .73 across combined sources. Use of multiple versus single sources of outcome is most likely to result in stable— and likely the most unbiased—estimates of predictive accuracy.

CONCLUSION

In correctional, forensic, and psychiatric settings, violence risk assessment plays a crucial role in determining persons' fates, and may impact others' safety. These decisions must be made carefully and systematically, because often they influence who is deemed "safe enough" to live in the community and who must be locked up or otherwise institutionalized. Further, even careful and systematic decisions must be backed up by sufficient empirical research. Our chapter highlighted the many decisions that risk-assessment researchers must make to develop and evaluate risk-assessment factors, instruments, and models.

Our take-home points are as follows; researchers should

- Evaluate risk-assessment tests and models according to their prescribed applied uses; otherwise the evaluation is at best of secondary relevance.
- If possible, use a prospective design.
- Clearly define violence in a manner that is relevant to the legal and clinical context in which the risk-assessment instrument is intended to be used.
- Use multiple sources of information to measure predictor and criterion measures.
- Evaluate only the types of reliability and validity that are relevant to a particular risk factor, instrument, or model.
- Use statistical procedures that align optimally with the intended tests of reliability and validity, which in turn align with intended applied uses.

REFERENCES

Andrews, D. A., & Bonta, J. (2010). *The psychology of criminal conduct* (5th ed.). Newark, NJ: LexisNexis/Matthew Bender.

Andrews, D. A., Bonta, J., & Wormith, J. S. (2010). The Level of Service (LS) assessment of adults and older adolescents. In R. K. Otto & K. S. Douglas (Eds.), *Handbook of violence risk assessment* (pp. 199–225). New York, NY: Routledge: Taylor & Francis Group.

American Educational Research Association, American Psychological Association, and the National Council on Measurement in Education. (1999). *Standards for educational and psychological testing.* Washington, DC: American Educational Research Association.

Ashford, J. B., Sales, B. D., & Reid, W. H. (2000) (Eds.). *Treating adult and juvenile offenders with special needs.* Washington, DC: American Psychological Association.

Bail Reform Act (1984). *United States Statutes at Large.* Volume 98, Part 2, Title 18, USC 3141, § 202, p. 1976.

Barefoot v. Estelle, 463 U.S. 880 (1983).

Baxstrom v. Herold, 383 U.S. 107 (1966).

Blair, P. R., Marcus, D. K., & Boccaccini, M. T. (2008). Is there an allegiance effect for assessment instruments? Actuarial risk assessment as an exemplar. *Clinical Psychology: Research and Practice, 15,* 346–360.

Boccaccini, M. T., Turner, D. B., & Murrie, D. C. (2008). Do some evaluators report consistently higher or lower PCL-R scores than others? Findings from a statewide sample of sexually violent evaluations. *Psychology, Public Policy, and Law, 14,* 262–283.

Borum, R., Bartel, P., & Forth, A. (2006). *Manual for the structured assessment for violence risk in youth (SAVRY).* Odessa, FL: Psychological Assessment Resources.

Cohen, J. (1988). *Statistical power analysis for the behavioral sciences* (2nd ed.). Hillsdale, NJ: Lawrence Erlbaum.

Dawes, R. M. (1979). The robust beauty of improper linear models in decision making. *American Psychologist, 34,* 571–582.

de Vogel, V., & de Ruiter, C. (2006). Structured professional judgment of violence risk in forensic clinical practice: A prospective study into the predictive validity of the Dutch HCR-20. *Psychology, Crime & Law, 12,* 321–336.

Dixon v. Attorney General of the Commonwealth of Pennsylvania, 325 F. Supp. 966 (M. D. Pa. 1971).

Douglas, K. S., Epstein, M. E., & Poythress, N. G. (2008). Criminal recidivism among juvenile offenders: Evaluating the incremental and predictive validity of three measures of psychopathic features. *Law and Human Behavior, 32,* 423–438.

Douglas, K. S., & Ogloff, J. R. P. (2003). Violence by psychiatric patients: The impact of archival measurement source on violence prevalence and risk assessment accuracy. *Canadian Journal of Psychiatry, 48*, 734–740.

Douglas, K. S., Ogloff, J. R. P., Nicholls, T. L., & Grant, I. (1999). Assessing risk for violence among psychiatric patients: The HCR-20 violence risk assessment scheme and the Psychopathy Checklist: Screening Version. *Journal of Consulting and Clinical Psychology, 67*, 917–930.

Douglas, K. S., & Reeves, K. (2008). Violence risk assessment. In B. Cutler (Ed.), *Encyclopedia of psychology and law*. Thousand Oaks, CA: Sage.

Douglas, K. S., & Reeves, K. (2010). The HCR-20 violence risk assessment scheme: Overview and review of the research. In R. Otto & K. S. Douglas (Eds.), *Handbook of violence risk assessment* (pp. 147–185). New York, NY: Routledge: Taylor & Francis Group.

Douglas, K., S., & Skeem, J. L. (2005). Violence risk assessment: Getting specific about being dynamic. *Psychology, Public Policy, and Law, 11*, 347–383.

Douglas, K. S., & Webster, C. D. (1999). Predicting violence in mentally and personality disordered individuals. In R. Roesch, S. D. Hart, & J. R. P. Ogloff (Eds.), *Psychology and law: The state of the discipline* (pp. 175–239). New York, NY: Plenum.

Douglas, K. S., Yeomans, M., & Boer, D. P. (2005). Comparative validity analysis of multiple measures of violence risk in a general population sample of criminal offenders. *Criminal Justice and Behavior, 32*, 479–510.

Doyle, M., & Dolan, M. (2006). Predicting community violence from patients discharged from community mental health services. *British Journal of Psychiatry, 189*, 520–526.

Edens, J. F., Skeem, J. L., & Douglas, K. S. (2006). Generalizability of the VRAG or generalizability of the PCL:SV? Incremental validity analyses of the MacArthur violence risk assessment data. *Assessment, 13*, 368–374.

Grann, M., & Långström, N. (2007). Actuarial assessment of violence risk: To weigh or not to weigh? *Criminal Justice and Behavior, 34*, 22–36.

Grove, W. M., & Meehl, P. E. (1996). Comparative efficiency of informal (subjective, impressionistic) and formal (mechanical, algorithmic) prediction procedures: The clinical-statistical controversy. *Psychology, Public Policy, and Law, 2*, 293–323.

Grove, W. M., Zald, D. H., Lebow, B. S., Snitz, B. E., & Nelson, C. (2000). Clinical versus mechanical prediction: A meta-analysis. *Psychological Assessment, 12*, 19–30.

Hare, R. D. (2003). *The Hare Psychopathy Checklist—Revised manual* (2nd ed.). North Tonawanda, NY: Multi-Health Systems.

Hart, S. D. (1998). The role of psychopathy in assessing risk for violence: Conceptual and methodological issues. *Legal and Criminological Psychology, 3*, 121–137.

Hart, S. D., Cox, D. N., & Hare, R. D. (1995). *The Hare Psychopathy Checklist: Screening version* (PCL:SV). Toronto, Canada: Multi-Health Systems.

Harris, G. T., Rice, M. E., & Cormier, C. A. (2002). Prospective replication of the *Violence Risk Appraisal Guide* in predicting violent recidivism among forensic patients. *Law and Human Behavior, 26*, 377–394.

Heilbrun, K., Douglas, K. S., & Yasuhara, K. (2009). Controversies in violence risk assessment. In J. L. Skeem, K. S. Douglas, & S. O. Lilienfeld (Eds), *Psychological science in the courtroom: Controversies and consensus* (pp. 333–356). New York, NY: Guilford Press.

Heilbrun, K., Yasuhara, K., & Shah, S. (2010). Violence risk assessment tools: Overview and critical analysis. In R. K. Otto & K. S. Douglas (Eds.), *Handbook of violence risk assessment* (pp. 333–357). New York, NY: Routledge/Taylor & Francis.

Hoge, R. D. (2010). Youth level of service/case management inventory. In R. K. Otto & K. S. Douglas (Eds.), *Handbook of violence risk assessment* (pp. 81–95). New York, NY: Routledge: Taylor & Francis Group.

Hunsley, J. (2003). Introduction to the special section on incremental validity and utility in clinical assessment. *Psychological Assessment, 15*, 443–445.

Kleespies, P. M. (2009) (Ed.). *Behavioral emergencies: An evidence-based resource for evaluating and managing risk of suicide, violence, and victimization*. Washington, DC: American Psychological Association.

Kropp, P. R., & Hart, S. D. (2000). The Spousal Assault Risk Assessment (SARA) Guide: Reliability and validity in adult male offenders. *Law and Human Behavior, 24*, 101–118.

Kropp, P. R., Hart, S. D., Webster, C.W., & Eaves, D. (1999). *Spousal assault risk assessment: User's guide*. Toronto, Canada: Multi-Health Systems, Inc.

Manchak, S. M., Skeem, J. L., & Douglas, K. S. (2008). Utility of the Revised Level of Service Inventory (LSI-R) in predicting recidivism after long-term incarceration. *Law and Human Behavior, 32,* 477–488.

Meehl, P. E. (1954). *Clinical versus statistical prediction*. Minneapolis, MN: University of Minnesota Press.

Mills, J. (2009, March). The role of assessment in the Bi-Adaptive Model. In R. Morgan (Chair), *Treating the mentally disordered offender: A model and guide for empirically supported practice*. Symposium conducted at the annual meeting of the American Psychology-Law Society (San Antonio, TX).

Mills, J. F., Jones, M. N., & Kroner, D. G. (2005). An examination of the generalizability of the LSI-R and VRAG probability bins. *Criminal Justice and Behavior, 32,* 565–585.

Monahan, J. (1981). *Predicting violent behavior: An assessment of clinical techniques*. Beverly Hills, CA: Sage.

Monahan, J. (2006). *Tarasoff* at thirty: How developments in science and policy shape the common law. *University of Cincinnati Law Review, 75,* 497–521.

Monahan, J., Steadman, H., Appelbaum, P., Grisso, T., Mulvey, E., Roth, L., . . . Silver, E. (2005a). *The classification of violence risk*. Lutz, FL: Psychological Assessment Resources.

Monahan, J, Steadman, H., Robbins, P., Appelbaum, P., Banks, S., Grisso, T., . . . Silver, E. (2005b). An actuarial model of violence risk assessment for persons with mental disorders. *Psychiatric Services, 56,* 810–815.

Monahan, J., Steadman, H. J., Silver, E., Appelbaum, P. S., Robbins, P. C., Mulvey, E. P., . . . Banks, S. (2001). *Rethinking risk assessment: The MacArthur Study of mental disorder and violence*. New York, NY: Oxford University Press.

Mulvey, E. P., Shaw, E., & Lidz, C. W. (1994). Why use multiple sources in research on patient violence in the community? *Criminal Behavior and Mental Health, 4,* 253–258.

Murrie, D. C., Boccaccini, M. T., Johnson, J. T., & Janke, C. (2008). Does interrater (dis) agreement on Psychopathy Checklist scores in sexually violent predator trials suggest partisan allegiance in forensic evaluations? *Law and Human Behavior, 32,* 352–362.

Murrie, D. C., Boccaccini, M. T., Turner, D. B., Meeks, M., & Woods, C. (2009). Rater (dis) agreement on risk assessment measures in sexually violent predator proceedings: Evidence of adversarial allegiance in forensic evaluation? *Psychology, Public Policy, and Law, 15,* 19–53.

Novaco, R. W. (2003). *The Novaco Anger Scale and Provocation Inventory*. Los Angeles, CA: Western Psychological Services.

Pedhazur, E. J., & Schmelkin, P. (1991). *Measurement, design, and analysis: An integrated approach*. Hillsdale, NJ: Lawrence Erlbaum.

Quinsey, V. L., Harris, G. T., Rice, M. E., & Cormier, C. A. (1998). *Violent offenders: Appraising and managing risk*. Washington, DC: American Psychological Association.

Quinsey, V. L., Harris, G. T., Rice, M. E., & Cormier, C. A. (2006). *Violent offenders: Appraising and managing risk* (2nd ed.). Washington, DC: American Psychological Association.

Roberts, J., Mulvey, E. P., Horney, J., Lewis, J., & Arter, M. L. (2005). A test of two methods of recall for violent events. *Journal of Quantitative Criminology, 21,* 175–193.

Roth, A., & Fonagy, P. (2004). *What works for whom?* (2nd ed.). New York, NY: Guilford Press.

Schall v. Martin, 104 S. Ct. 2403 (1984).

Schubert, C. A., Mulvey, E. P., Lidz, C. W., Gardner, W. P., & Skeem, J. L. (2005). Weekly community interviews with high-risk participants: Operational issues. *Journal of Interpersonal Violence, 20,* 632–646.

Seligman, M. E. P. (1995). The effectiveness of psychotherapy: The *Consumer Reports* study. *American Psychologist, 50,* 965–974.

Silver, E., Smith, W., & Banks, S. (2000). Constructing actuarial devices for predicting recidivism: A comparison of methods. *Criminal Justice and Behavior, 27,* 733–764.

Skeem, J. L., Schubert, C., Odgers, C., Mulvey, E. P., Gardner, W., & Lidz, C. (2006). Psychiatric symptoms and community violence among high-risk patients: A test of the relationship at the weekly level. *Journal of Consulting and Clinical Psychology, 74,* 967–979.

Skeem, J., & Monahan, J. (in press). Current directions in violence risk assessment. *Current Directions in Psychological Science*.

Steadman, H. J., & Cocozza, J. (1974). *Careers of the criminally insane*. Lexington, MA: Lexington Books.

Steadman, H. J., Mulvey, E., Monahan, J., Robbins, P. C., Appelbaum, P. S., Grisso, T., . . . Silver, E. (1998). Violence by people discharged from acute psychiatric inpatient facilities and by others in the same neighborhoods. *Archives of General Psychiatry, 55,* 393–401.

Tarasoff v. Regents of the University of California, 551 P2d. 334 (1976).

Thornberry, T. P., & Jacoby, J. E. (1979). *The criminally insane: A community follow-up of mentally ill offenders.* Chicago, IL.: University of Chicago Press.

Thorndike, R. L. (1949). *Personnel selection.* New York, NY: Wiley.

U.S. v. Salerno, 481 U.S. 739 (1987).

Walter, S. D., Eliasziw, M., & Donner, A. (1998). Sample size and optimal designs for reliability studies. *Statistics in Medicine, 17,* 101–110.

Webster, C. D., Douglas, K. S., Eaves, D., & Hart, S. D. (1997). *HCR-20: Assessing risk for violence* (Version 2). Burnaby, Canada: Mental Health, Law, and Policy Institute, Simon Fraser University.

CHAPTER 18

Psychopathy in Forensic Psychology: Assessment and Methodology

ROSS D. GRIMES, ZINA LEE, AND RANDALL T. SALEKIN

CLECKLEY (1955) WROTE of the psychopath "these people called psychopaths present a problem which must be better understood by lawyers, social workers, school teachers, and by the general public, if any satisfactory way of dealing with them is to be worked out" (p. 233). Half a century later, we write with perhaps more knowledge but with similar concerns that include the specific goal of better understanding and reducing the potential harm exacted by the psychopath. In addition, there is a need to potentially facilitate the psychopathic individual's adaptation into his or her environment in a manner that allows for prosocial participation in society. In the clinical and developmental literatures the focus is on charting the developmental course of psychopathy and alleviating its symptoms; the study and application of psychopathy in legal settings represents a departure from psychology's typical overarching goal to reduce disorder and promote psychological health. While mental health professionals often provide knowledge to the courts about how to understand psychological phenomena—e.g., perhaps even psychopathy—they more frequently provide assessments intended to address a legal question, such as the degree to which an offender is dangerous or amenable to treatment. Such assessments are intended to help legal decision makers balance individual liberty and public safety. As such, assessments of psychopathy in this realm may be used to support the punitive rather than the rehabilitative goals of the legal system.

Given that psychopathy has potentially wide ranging implications on individuals being assessed in forensic settings, we recommend that researchers in this area make sure that the science they produce has a high degree of internal and external validity and that their research findings are used to help those within and outside of forensic settings better understand psychological phenomena such as psychopathy. Researchers can do so by designing studies with sound methodology, providing proper interpretation of their results, and educating their consumers with respect to their findings. Poor research methodology in this arena has implications beyond passive harm and may actively contribute to unnecessary or ineffectual reductions in individual freedom.

This chapter explores the methodological issues for the study of psychopathy. We divide the chapter into four main sections. The first section provides a definition of psychopathy. Here we elaborate on some of the conceptual differences found in views of psychopathy. The lack of a clear consensus on both the symptoms of psychopathy and the measurement of those symptoms, when coupled with the significant implications of such a label, requires the forensic researcher to understand both the rationale for and the scientific merit of different conceptualizations of psychopathy. The second section discusses the various commonly used measures of psychopathy and their psychometric properties to further illustrate the importance of the conceptualization of psychopathy and its influence on scale development.

The third section discusses the rationale for incorporating information about psychopathy into forensic psychology and addresses psychopathy's particular relevance to legal decision making in the context of criminal law including its relevance to pertinent topics such as risk and treatment amenability. The final section provides some suggestions for conducting research in psychopathy and the important next steps for psychopathy research in the forensic arena if it is to further advance the field's knowledge. In this section, we aim to provide researchers with an integrative framework for the scientific investigation of psychopathy that will further our understanding of the construct as well as provide forensic researchers, clinicians, and legal professionals with information about the utility of the construct. The key components of this framework are a sound methodological foundation and a strong grasp of the overlap and separation between the psychological construct of psychopathy and the relevant legal questions the construct informs.

PSYCHOPATHY: DIFFERING CONCEPTUALIZATIONS

Psychopathy is a personality disorder encompassing interpersonal, affective, behavioral, and antisocial lifestyle characteristics. Early definitions of the disorder discussed how psychopaths were superficially charming, egocentric, and engaged in aggressive and antisocial behavior. Historically, there have been disagreements about the core defining features of psychopathy. Although the field has had a number of major contributors, three key scholars stand out as having influenced our understanding of psychopathy. One of the field's pioneers, Hervey Cleckley (1955), suggested that psychopathy was made up of 16 characteristics, the majority of which were personality-based. Lee Robins (1966), a major pioneer in the field of antisocial behavior, emphasized that sociopathy—the diagnostic precursor to what is now termed psychopathy—was probably better indexed by behavioral characteristics, because these were more informative of personality traits such as a lack of remorse or empathy. In this view, features such as a lack of empathy can be inferred from a pattern of unprovoked aggression and violence. Later, Hare's framework for assessing psychopathy incorporated features from both Cleckley and Robins but also offered some conceptual differences from the early forerunners by dropping aspects that were thought to be unnecessary or difficult to assess and adding symptoms that were more easily measured and/or more discriminatory.

Using Cleckley and Robins's criteria as guides, Hare developed the Psychopathy Checklist-Revised (PCL-R; Hare, 1991, 2003) to assess psychopathy in criminal populations. Hare's model, to some extent, joins the theories of Cleckley and Robins by incorporating the interpersonal, affective, and behavioral components. Table 18.1 shows how items from Robins's Sociopathic Personality and Cleckley's Psychopathic Personality map onto the Hare criteria as measured by the PCL-R. Table 18.2 lists the items from each of the three conceptualizations that are distinct from one another. Although some items (e.g., impulsive behavior) are consistent across definitions, it is clear that Robins's criteria tend to include more quantifiable behaviors whereas Cleckley's criteria focus on the interpersonal and affective deficits. While Hare developed the PCL-R primarily as a measure of the Cleckley psychopath, examination of the items suggests a broader theoretical base: 30% of the Hare items map onto one of Cleckley's characteristic traits, 20% map onto one of Robins's characteristic traits, and 25% map onto both a Cleckley and Robins trait. The remaining 25% of items do not have a clearly identifiable historical ancestor. Clearly, Hare's construct is not simply a union of Cleckley's personality view and Robins's behavioral perspective. Furthermore, while Cleckley highlights the relevance of psychopathy outside criminality, Hare developed the PCL-R among inmates (Hare, 1991, 2003).

Work with the PCL-R has brought the field of psychology considerable information about the concept of psychopathy, primarily by providing a common metric for discussion. Although it is well known and widely used among researchers and clinicians, care must be taken not to equate the measure with the term psychopathy and its underlying factors. One reason is that there has been considerable debate during the past five years over two issues: (1) what defines the construct of psychopathy and (2) what factors or subcomponents underlie the construct. A large part of this debate centers on previously held conceptions and views of psychopathy that have now resurfaced, particularly the importance of behavior and the expression of underlying psychopathic characteristics in multiple contexts.

The development of the PCL-R led to the conceptualization and study of psychopathy as a multi-faceted construct rather than simply a unidimensional trait. Early factor studies of the PCL indicated two factors: factor 1 contained items assessing affective and interpersonal aspects of psychopathy, whereas factor 2 contained items assessing impulsive and antisocial

Table 18.1

Conceptions of Psychopathy: Hare, Cleckley, and Robins

	2-Factor	4-Factor	Hare[*]	Cleckley[**]	Robins[***]
1	1	1	Glibness/superficial charm	Superficial charm and good intelligence	
2	1	1	Grandiose sense of self-worth	Pathologic egocentricity and incapacity for love	
3	2	3	Need for stimulation/proneness to boredom	Poor judgment and failure to learn by experience	
4	1	1	Pathological lying	Untruthfulness and insincerity	Pathological lying
5	1	1	Conning/manipulative	Unreliability	
6	1	2	Lack of remorse or guilt	Lack of remorse or shame	Lack of guilt about sexual exploits and crimes
7	1	2	Shallow affect	General poverty in major affective reactions	
8	1	2	Callous/lack of empathy		
9	2	2	Parasitic lifestyle		Public financial care
10	2	4	Poor behavioral controls	Inadequately motivated antisocial behavior	Physical aggression
11			Promiscuous sexual behavior	Sex life impersonal, trivial, and poorly integrated	Sexual promiscuity or perversion
12	2	4	Early behavior problems		Reckless youth
13	2	3	Lack of realistic, long-term goals	Failure to follow any life plan	
14	2	3	Impulsivity	Fantastic and uninviting behavior, with drink and sometimes without	Impulsive behavior
15	2	3	Irresponsibility		
16	1	2	Failure to accept responsibility		
17			Many short-term marital relationships		Poor marital history
18	2	4	Juvenile delinquency		
19	2	4	Revocation of conditional release		
20	2	4	Criminal versatility		Repeated arrests

[*]Hare, R. D. (2003). *Hare Psychopathy Checklist-Revised (PCL-R): 2nd edition.* Toronto, ON: Multi-Health Systems.

[**]Cleckley, H. (1955). *The mask of sanity. Characteristic points of the psychopathic personality,* pp. 380–381.

[***]Robins, L. (1966). *Deviant children grown up.* Items from "Sociopathic Personality" as described in Appendix D, pp. 342–343.

Table 18.2
Distinct Items: Hare, Cleckley, and Robins

Hare	Robins	Cleckley
Callous/lack of empathy	Poor work history	Absence of delusions and other signs of irrational thinking
Irresponsibility	Excessive drugs	Absence of nervousness or psychoneurotic manifestations
Failure to accept responsibility	Heavy drinking	Specific loss of insight
Juvenile delinquency	Suicide (attempts)	Unresponsiveness in general interpersonal relations
Revocation of conditional release	School problems and truancy	Suicide rarely carried out
	Poor armed services record	
	Vagrancy	
	Many somatic symptoms	
	Lack of friends	
	Use of aliases	

lifestyle aspects (Harpur, Hare, & Hakstian, 1989). More recent studies have explored 3- and 4-factor solutions. Cooke and Michie (2001) found that a hierarchical 3-factor structure better defines psychopathy: arrogant and deceitful interpersonal style, deficient affective experience, and impulsive and irresponsible behavioral style. In addition to the 2- and 3-factor solutions, the revised PCL-R manual notes a 4-factor structure, which incorporates the three factors identified by Cooke and Michie (2001) and includes a fourth factor that represents the antisocial features of psychopathy. In sum, there is substantial research support for the conceptualization of psychopathy as a multidimensional construct containing between two and four factors that assess the personality, behavioral, and antisocial features of the disorder (Neumann, Kosson, & Salekin, 2007) (see Figure 18.1).

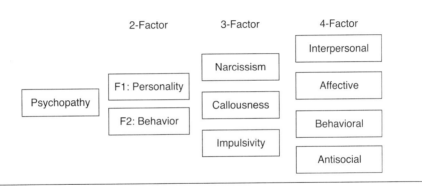

Figure 18.1 Factor structure of psychopathy

Debate regarding the factor structure of psychopathy is likely to continue, and it is important to note that these different conceptualizations have obvious implications for what the construct means in terms of behavioral expression (e.g., risk assessment). For these reasons, we refrain from statements about which conception of psychopathy is best or "correct." However, it is necessary to understand the origin of various theories, the theoretical underpinnings of various measures, and the extent to which current indices embody aspects of various theoretical views.

MEASUREMENT OF PSYCHOPATHY

We briefly review the major instruments used for assessing psychopathy across three categories: (1) clinician-rated measures, (2) self- and other-report measures, and (3) scales derived from general inventories. Table 18.3 lists some of the primary measures and their characteristics.

CLINICIAN-RATED MEASURES

Psychopathy Checklist-Revised The PCL-R (Hare, 1991, 2003) is a 20-item clinical rating scale that assesses psychopathy on the basis of a semistructured interview and file review. Each item is rated on a 3-point scale (0 = *item does not apply*, 1 = *item applies somewhat*, 2 = *item definitely applies*) and summed to yield a total score. The manual recommends that individuals who score 30 or higher be considered "psychopathic." The PCL-R is the most commonly used and validated measure of psychopathy. Full administration, including interview, file review, and scoring, can take between two to three hours, and the measure is used primarily in adult forensic and criminal populations. Extensive data on reliability and psychometric properties of the PCL-R is available (see Hare & Neumann, 2006). Across both correctional and forensic settings, total scores demonstrate excellent internal consistency and inter-rater reliability.

Despite the extensive history of the PCL-R, its use for the assessment of psychopathy in females is more limited. Only during the past decade or so have gender differences received significant attention. Although internal consistency and inter-rater reliability have been documented in females (see Vitale & Newman, 2001), there is evidence that the factor structure may differ in females (Salekin, Rogers, & Sewell, 1997). Furthermore, fewer females score in the psychopathic range as compared with males (Grann, 2000; Salekin et al., 1997). Psychopathy also shows similar associations with various personality traits and other forms of psychopathology in both males and females; however, it does not appear to be as robust a predictor of violence in some studies on females (Verona & Vitale, 2006) However, Leistico et al. (2008) provide a comparison across males and females showing some similarities. In general, the evidence suggests that although

Table 18.3

Psychopathy Measures

Name	Author	Items	Format	Factors	Target Group
Psychopathy Checklist-Revised (PCL-R)	Hare	20	File review, interview, clinician rating	2 (Personality, behavior) 3 (narcissism, callousness, impulsivity) 4 (interpersonal, affective, impulsive, antisocial)	Adult males in forensic and criminal settings
Interpersonal Measure of Psychopathy (IM-P)	Kosson	21	Interview/observation and rating	1 (Corresponds to PCL-R Factor 1)	Same as PCL-R but with interest specifically in interpersonal aspects
Psychopathic Personality Inventory (PPI)	Lilienfeld & Andrews	160	Self-report	8	Community samples
Psychopathy Checklist: Screening Version (PCL:SV)	Hart, Cox, & Hare	12	File review, interview, clinician rated	2, 3, 4 (Same as PCL-R)	Adult males in forensic and criminal settings
Psychopathy Checklist: Youth Version (PCL:YV)	Forth, Kosson, & Hare	20	Files review, interview, clinician rating	2, 3, 4 (Same as PCL-R)	Delinquent and forensic adolescents
Antisocial Process Screening Device (APSD)	Frick & Hare	20	Item ratings, parent, teacher, and self-report versions	2- and 3-factor versions corresponding to PCL-R	Children and adolescents

psychopathy can be assessed reliably in women, the construct may differ somewhat across gender.

Despite its success, some of the critiques leveled at the PCL-R bear mention (Campbell, 2007). In particular, there is concern that ratings can be consciously or unconsciously affected by the examiner. In other words, even with well-developed and specific scoring guidelines for each item, the nature of the instrument allows for subtle variations in scores that can be pulled by raters. Second, there remain concerns about the quality of the information obtained from a file review, particularly when that is the only method used to determine item scores. Finally, the training that psychologists receive in the use of the PCL-R may vary. Hare and others have stressed the importance of comprehensive training required to use the PCL-R, focusing on the need for diagnostic and inter-rater reliability and for balancing its potential prejudicial impact. The issues of training and competence are made more salient by reports of inappropriate use of the PCL-R, not just in drawing inferences regarding offenders but also in poor adherence to basic assessment standards (Edens, 2001; Murrie et al., 2009).

Psychopathy Checklist: Screening Version The PCL:SV (Hart, Cox, & Hare, 1995) was developed to screen for psychopathy in forensic and civil settings. The PCL:SV is a 12-item derivative of the PCL-R that possesses the traditional 2-factor structure of the PCL-R (Hart, Hare, & Forth, 1994). Recent work has also looked at the applicability of 3- and 4-factor models to the PCL:SV, with promising results (Hill, Neumann, & Rogers, 2004; Skeem, Mulvey, & Grisso, 2003). There is evidence for the validity of the PCL:SV in that it is associated with psychopathology (Douglas, Strand, Belfrage, Fransson, & Levander, 2005) and is predictive of violence and recidivism (Edens, Skeem, & Douglas, 2006; Guy & Douglas, 2006; Leistico, Salekin, DeCoster, & Rogers, 2008).

Psychopathy Checklist: Youth Version In order to assess psychopathic features at younger ages, researchers have modified the PCL-R for use in juvenile populations. This effort culminated in the Psychopathy Checklist: Youth Version (PCL:YV; Forth, Kosson, & Hare, 2003). The PCL:YV is a 20-item clinician rated scale, with items that largely map onto corresponding PCL-R items, with modifications to reflect age and developmental status. The PCL:YV demonstrates a similar factor structure to the PCL-R, with well-validated 2- (Brandt, Kennedy, Patrick, & Curtin, 1997), 3- (Kosson, Cyterski, Steuerwald, Neumann, & Walker-Matthews, 2002; Salekin, Brannen, Zalot, Leistico, & Neumann, 2006), and 4-factor models (Neumann, Kosson, Forth, & Hare, 2006) in both incarcerated and delinquent youth. With respect to validity, the PCL:YV shows correspondence with psychopathology (Salekin, Leistico, Neumann, DiCicco, & Duros, 2004), violence (Kosson et al., 2002), and recidivism (Corrado, Vincent, Hart, & Cohen, 2004; Leistico et al., 2008; Salekin, 2008; Salekin & Lynam, 2010).

INTERPERSONAL MEASURE OF PSYCHOPATHY

The Interpersonal Measure of Psychopathy (IM-P; Kosson, Steuerwald, Forth, & Kirkhart, 1997) was developed, in part, to capture the personality features of psychopathy. The IM-P identifies and rates specific aspects of the interaction between participants and interviewers. It is a 21-item measure, with each item assessed on a 4-point scale (1 = *not at all*, 4 = *perfectly*), to determine how well the individual or interaction fits each trait. Internal consistency is acceptable, ranging from .75 via videotape observation only to .91 when rated following a live interaction, and inter-rater agreement is also strong (Kosson et al., 1997; Zolondek, Lilienfeld, Patrick, & Fowler, 2006; Vitacco & Kosson, 2010).

SELF- AND OTHER-REPORT MEASURES OF PSYCHOPATHY

Clinical assessments of psychopathy, coupled with the need to assess other constructs of legal relevance, can be time-consuming (Lilienfeld & Fowler, 2006). As a result, a number of self- and informant-report measures have been developed. There remains substantial debate about the value of self-report measures of psychopathy, particularly regarding their validity and accuracy in assessing a disorder characterized by lying, manipulation, and egocentricity. These concerns are based on studies demonstrating typically low correlations between self-report measures and the clinical rating scales, which purport to measure the same latent construct (Edens, Hart, D. W. Johnson, Johnson, & Olver, 2000; Lee, Vincent, Hart, & Corrado, 2003; Lilienfeld & Fowler, 2006; Murrie & Cornell, 2002).

Psychopathic Personality Inventory The Psychopathic Personality Inventory (PPI; Lilienfeld & Andrews, 1996) was developed to assess the core personality features of psychopathy. It is a 160-item measure that consists of eight subscales, with each item rated on a 4-point scale (false, mostly false, mostly true, true). Initial studies using undergraduate samples found acceptable internal consistency for the total and subscale scores, as well as high test-retest reliability (Lilienfeld & Andrews, 1996). The PPI yields a 2-factor solution, with one factor representing emotional/interpersonal traits and a second factor representing social deviance traits (Benning, Patrick, Hicks, Blonigen, & Krueger, 2003). With respect to validity, the PPI has demonstrated differential relations to each of the big-5 personality features (Benning, Patrick, Salekin, & Leistico, 2005). Studies have also assessed its validity with females (Berardino, Meloy, Sherman, & Jacobs, 2005) and adolescent offenders (Poythress, Edens, & Lilienfeld, 1998), finding convergence with both PCL-R facets.

Antisocial Process Screening Device The antisocial process screening device (APSD; Frick & Hare, 2001) was designed to assess psychopathic traits in children between the ages of 6 and 13. The APSD is a 20-item measure to be completed by the child's parent and/or teacher. A self-report version is also available for use with adolescents (Caputo, Frick, & Brodsky, 1999). Factor analyses have yielded a 2-factor (Frick, O'Brien, Wootton, & McBurnett, 1994) and a 3-factor (Frick, Bodin, & Barry, 2000; Vitacco, Rogers, & Neumann, 2003) solution. Evidence indicates adequate to excellent internal consistency of the total and factor scores (Kotler & McMahon, 2005, 2010; Lynam & Gudonis, 2005). With respect to validity, the APSD shows correspondence with various psychosocial variables, such as fearlessness (Barry et al., 2000; Frick, Lilienfeld, Ellis, Loney, & Silverthorn, 1999), conduct problems (Poythress, Dembo, Wareham, & Greenbaum, 2006; Salekin et al., 2004), and recidivism (Falkenbach, Poythress, & Heide, 2003).

Childhood Psychopathy Scale The childhood psychopathy scale (CPS; Lynam, 1997) was constructed to assess psychopathic traits in children and adolescents. The CPS items are downward extensions of the PCL-R items, representing 13 of the 20, and were drawn from the Childhood Behavior Checklist and the Common Language California Child Q-Set. Both the caregiver and self-report versions of the measure demonstrate excellent internal consistency of the total scores (Lynam & Gudonis, 2005). Regarding validity, there is evidence that the CPS is associated with psychopathology, general personality traits, and delinquency (Kotler & McMahon, 2010; Lynam, 1997; Lynam et al., 2005; Salekin, Leistico, Trobst, Schrum, & Lochman, 2005).

PSYCHOPATHY SCALES FROM GENERAL OR MULTI-SCALE ASSESSMENT INVENTORIES

Although a number of broader personality inventories contain items or scales that purport to assess antisocial behavior or psychopathy, there is little support for the use of general inventories when psychopathy is indicated prior to the evaluation. Rather, there may be benefits to considering evidence for psychopathic traits based on these general inventories when such a broad-based assessment is the maximum utility method. We discuss three inventories that have received attention in the psychopathy literature.

Minnesota Multiphasic Personality Inventory The Minnesota Multiphasic Personality Inventory (MMPI-2l; Butcher et al., 2001) is one of the most widely used personality inventories. Two scales within the MMPI are relevant to the study of psychopathy, the psychopathic deviate (Pd) scale and the antisocial practices (ASP) content scale. There is some evidence for the validity of the ASP scale (e.g., Lilienfeld, 1996). The Pd scale is composed of a number of subscales (familial discord, authority problems, social imperturbability, social alienation, and self-alienation) and as such, measures a heterogeneous construct that limits interpretability (Lilienfeld, 1999). It appears the authority problems subscale is associated with psychopathy. However, the other subscales were found to provide potentially relevant information about different facets of psychopathy. For example, social imperturbability was associated with low anxiety and social alienation correlated with blame externalization. This difficulty in using the MMPI also extends to the adolescent version. Hume, Kennedy, Patrick, and Partyka (1996) found no practical differences between psychopathic and nonpsychopathic adolescent offenders on MMPI-A scores. The RF scales will likely undergo research with respect to psychopathy and may add to this literature base.

Personality Assessment Inventory The Personality Assessment Inventory (PAI; Morey, 1991) is a general inventory of clinical symptomatology consisting of 344 items rated on a 4-point scale based on how true the statement is for the individual. The antisocial features (ANT) scale of the PAI was designed to assess characteristics of antisocial personality disorder and psychopathy; it has three subscales measuring behavior (ANT-A), callous/unemotional traits (ANT-E), and stimulation-seeking (ANT-S). The PAI correlates with the PCL-R factors (Douglas, Guy, Edens, Boer, & Hamilton, 2007; Salekin et al., 1997). In addition, the measure shows predictive validity for dominance, drug problems, and treatment rejection (Douglas et al., 2007), as well as for recidivism (Walters & Duncan, 2005; Salekin, 2008).

Millon Adolescent Clinical Inventory The Millon Adolescent Clinical Inventory (MACI; Millon, 1993) is a self-report measure containing 160 true-false questions designed specifically for disordered and delinquent youth. Utilizing theoretical considerations and experienced raters, Murrie and Cornell (2000) developed a content scale for assessing adolescent psychopathic traits, composed of 20 MACI items. Although there is a strong association between this scale and the PCL-R (Murrie & Cornell, 2000), the measure shows small associations with general and violent recidivism (Salekin, Ziegler, Larrea, Anthony, & Bennett, 2003). Salekin et al. (2003) also developed a 16-item scale based on the work of Cooke and Michie (2003) and Frick et al. (2000), and found this scale to be strongly associated with both general and violent recidivism.

PSYCHOPATHY AND OUTCOMES RELEVANT TO THE LEGAL SYSTEM

For the forensic researcher, the proper identification of psychopathy is only the first step. Forensic researchers and clinicians must be mindful of the degree to which findings bear on legal constructs and take care not to overstate the relevance of nonlegal constructs in a legal context. Careful definition of variables and study parameters can ensure that researchers maximize the value of information provided to the legal system. Furthermore, it is important to be cautious about disseminating results obtained from groups rather than individuals. There are few, if any, psychological constructs with highly predictable and immutable outcomes for any specific individual, the level of analysis for legal decisions. Put another way, *statistical significance* is not synonymous with *beyond a reasonable doubt*. With this in mind, we briefly review the associations between psychopathy and outcomes relevant to the legal system, including recidivism and institutional misconduct.

RECIDIVISM

Decisions concerning conditional or early release and initial sentencing can be informed by information about the likelihood of future offending by an individual. There are several bases for this statement. First, in general, there is substantial evidence that psychopathy is able to predict criminal recidivism (Douglas, Vincent, & Edens, 2006; Leistico et al., 2008). Specifically, there are moderate effect sizes for both general and violent recidivism, with the behavioral/antisocial traits demonstrating a stronger association than the interpersonal/affective traits. Second, these moderate effect sizes emerge across correctional, forensic, and civil psychiatric settings. Third, psychopathy continues to be a predictor of recidivism after controlling for a number of other variables, such as prior history of violence and substance abuse. Fourth, the effect sizes are typically stronger across longer follow-up periods and in samples with a greater proportion of Caucasian participants. Finally, relative to general and violent recidivism, psychopathy is a less robust predictor of sexual recidivism.

Similar findings arise in adolescent populations, with moderate effect sizes between psychopathy and recidivism (Edens, Campbell, & Weir, 2007; Forth & Book, 2010), although there are also some differences. First, the evidence is not as strong for the greater predictive ability of the behavioral/antisocial traits relative to the interpersonal/affective traits. More importantly, the behavioral/antisocial traits demonstrate a weaker relationship with violent recidivism in more ethnically heterogeneous samples. Second, although the relationship between psychopathy and general recidivism is comparable in males and females, the literature is mixed as to whether psychopathy is a stronger predictor of violent recidivism in males. Finally, unlike with adults, there is a small, nonsignificant association between adolescent psychopathic traits and sexual recidivism.

INSTITUTIONAL CONDUCT

Evidence that psychopathy can inform decisions about future offending have led to the question of whether it may also assist in decisions about institutional placement and restrictions. The ability to predict institutional conduct allows a more accurate match between individuals and security level and at the same time reduces risk to the general population and staff. In general, meta-analyses have found similar results between recidivism and institutional misconduct (Edens & Campbell, 2007; Guy, Edens, Anthony, & Douglas, 2005; Leistico et al., 2008; Walters, 2003). There is a small-to-moderate association in both adults and adolescents. In addition, although the behavioral/antisocial traits demonstrate stronger effect sizes than the interpersonal/affective traits in adults, there is no significant difference in adolescents. More importantly, there is considerable heterogeneity across studies and also considerable variability when institutional misconduct is delineated into specific categories. Guy et al. (2005) found that adult psychopathy was more strongly associated with verbal aggression/destruction (.26) than with either nonaggressive misconduct (.21) or physical violence (.17). In contrast, Edens and Campbell (2007) found that adolescent psychopathic traits were more strongly associated with physically violent misconduct (.28) than with more general aggressive misconduct (.25). Also, see Leistico et al. (2008) for large-scale meta-analytic estimates.

In sum, there are small-to-moderate effect sizes between psychopathy and recidivism and institutional misconduct in both adults and adolescents. However, there is considerable heterogeneity across studies, which suggests that psychopathy is only one important risk factor for consideration. Less is known about the incremental predictive ability of psychopathy beyond other known risk factors and whether psychopathic traits interact with other variables. Furthermore, more research is needed to examine whether there are differential associations by gender and ethnicity (see Leistico et al., 2008). Finally, very little work has examined the 3- and 4-factor models of psychopathy, which would indicate specific symptom clusters that are stronger and weaker predictors. Although the general trend indicates that the behavioral/antisocial traits are stronger predictors, the personality aspects of the syndrome may still be useful. In particular, knowledge about whether individuals engage in impression management and deceitful strategies may assist personnel in evaluating the credibility of accounts when making decisions about conditional or early release and may assist staff in managing group dynamics within institutions.

TREATMENT AMENABILITY

Psychopathy has long had a reputation as an untreatable condition, which justifies enhanced punishment and minimal treatment effort. This view is supported by studies indicating that psychopathic individuals typically demonstrate lower motivation and higher dropout rates (e.g., Ogloff, Wong, & Greenwood, 1990). Furthermore, there is evidence that treatment can be detrimental, resulting in increased rates of recidivism among treated psychopaths (e.g., Rice, Harris, & Cormier, 1992). However, a meta-analysis by Salekin (2002) challenged this view, finding that various interventions demonstrated success with psychopathic individuals. Despite this, some have suggested that there is reason to be cautious in adopting an overly positive outlook. A review by Harris and Rice (2006) is critical of the previous meta-analysis and other recent studies, noting that the work uses many case studies, therapists' opinions, a wide variety of treatment outcome and a lack of random clinical trials, thereby making it difficult to place much weight on the findings. However, Salekin, Worley, and Grimes (2010) have argued that for a first generation of research the findings may provide important information. They also contend that therapists' opinions and heterogeneous outcomes are important to study contrasting Harris and Rice's (2006) view. Salekin and colleagues across studies (e.g., Salekin, 2002; Salekin et al., 2010) have acknowledged that more work is needed in terms of the psychopathy treatment relation and specifically the need for more clinical trials. There are some studies that have come close to approximating this. For instance, Skeem, Monahan, and Mulvey (2002) found that psychopathic civil psychiatric patients who received more outpatient services were approximately three times less likely to be violent at follow-up than psychopathic patients who received less treatment. Importantly, this finding held after controlling for a number of variables associated with treatment attendance.

Studies examining psychopathy and treatment responsivity in adolescents mirror the adult findings to some extent. There is evidence that psychopathic traits are associated with some treatment noncompliance, lower ratings of improvement, and higher rates of recidivism (Falkenbach et al., 2003; O'Neill, Lidz, & Heilbrun, 2003). However, there is also evidence to the contrary. Rogers, Jackson, Sewell, and Johansen (2004) found that self-reported psychopathy scores were not strongly associated with problematic hospital stays and were not associated with lengthier program completion or rate of improvement. In contrast, Spain, Douglas, Poythress, and Epstein (2004) found inconsistent results between psychopathic traits and treatment progress. The PCL:YV demonstrated negligible, nonsignificant associations, whereas the self-report APSD and CPS were moderately associated with slower progress in treatment. Importantly, there is also emerging evidence of a dose-response effect in adolescent offenders. Caldwell, Skeem, Salekin, and Van Rybroek (2006) found that psychopathic adolescents who participated in an intensive program targeted to reduce aggression were almost 3 times less likely to commit a violent offense across a two-year follow-up. Finally, Salekin et al. (2010) reviewed eight treatment studies for youth and found that six studies showed that youth improved.

Evidence supporting both pessimism and optimism are likely due to a number of factors, which are important considerations for future research. First, studies vary with respect to how psychopathic traits are defined. Many of the early studies did not use well-defined and reliable measures of psychopathy. Second, many studies do not include a comparison group—or more importantly, a control group. Consequently, firm conclusions about the (un)treatability of psychopathic individuals are difficult to make. Although randomized trials with a control group may not be possible, especially from an ethical standpoint, at the very least, an attempt should be made to create appropriate control or comparison groups. For example, individuals on a wait list may serve as a control group. Alternatively, comparison group participants should be matched on important factors that may affect treatment responsivity. Finally, it is unclear from many studies whether contamination between ratings of psychopathy and treatment improvement occurred. If the same raters assessed both psychopathic traits and various treatment indices, such as level of motivation and perceptions of improvement, there is the potential for biased ratings. In turn, these may affect the psychopathy-treatment amenability association. Double blind procedures would enhance study quality and the fidelity of study conclusions.

Beyond these methodological issues, more complex research designs would assist in providing a more comprehensive understanding of the psychopathy-treatment amenability relationship. Research designs with multiple outcomes across various domains of functioning may provide a more fine-grained analysis of the areas that demonstrate improvement and those that show little or no improvement. Furthermore, lengthy follow-up periods are particularly important to examine whether perceived gains in treatment are sustained in the long term and in noninstitutional settings. It may be that psychopathic individuals require periodic treatment akin to booster sessions to maintain improvements in their behavior in the community. Finally, future studies should examine whether specific symptom clusters are associated with more or fewer gains in treatment. These suggestions are not to imply that the existing body of research deserves little weight. The work conducted to date has led to great gains in understanding treatment amenability among psychopaths. However, at best the current state of the field is only cautiously optimistic, and much more work needs to be done to effectively manage psychopathic individuals and prevent the negative outcomes associated with the disorder.

PSYCHOPATHY AND THE LAW

It is important to bear in mind that psychopathy is not a legal concept; rather, it is a psychological construct with quantifiable relevance to legal concepts or questions. The role of psychopathy in the legal process is typically to address sentencing or other post-trial issues. Legal questions in this phase generally focus on the offender's risk of dangerousness or future violence, his or her likely adjustment to potential punitive environments, and the degree to which treatment is likely to reduce or improve the offender's behavior. The ability of psychopathy to inform these questions is supported by the body of research discussed in the previous sections on recidivism, institutional adjustment, and treatment amenability. For psychologists, each of these constructs must be considered through the lenses of multifinality and equifinality. That is, a determination of psychopathy does not guarantee that these outcomes will occur, and psychopathy is not the only variable relevant to or predictive of these variables. Most importantly, the assessment of psychopathy does not constitute a comprehensive risk assessment. Psychopathy is but one piece of the puzzle and must be considered in the context of other potentially relevant information.

Unlike many aspects of psychology, psychopathy is not seen as a justification for mitigating initial responsibility for criminal acts. Still, some have argued that the psychopath's lack of insight and inability to act in a morally congruent way with society's view of moral responsibility argues for mitigating criminal responsibility. However, psychopaths clearly display the planful and organized behavior to meet *mens rea* requirements that an individual have knowledge of and control over the actions that make up the elements of a crime, regardless of whether that individual has knowledge of or agreement with particular statutes or laws. Forensic psychologists should continue to be attuned to the way in which information about psychopathy may influence the legal construct of criminal responsibility.

The association between psychopathy and violence, criminality, and other legally deviant behaviors make it a prime candidate for consideration in legal decision making. A survey of forensic psychologists found that the PCL-R and PCL:SV were widely used and were the most commonly chosen risk assessment measures (Archer, Buffington-Vollum, Stredny, & Handel, 2006). Furthermore, an analysis of court records found that use of the PCL-R in court increased from 0 cases in 1991 to 30 cases in 2004 (DeMatteo & Edens, 2006) and is also frequently cited in the context of civil commitment under sexual predator statutes (Walsh & Walsh, 2006). Both studies highlight that the PCL-R is being increasingly relied upon and used in situations where it is likely to provide useful and relevant information.

However, there are several concerns regarding its applicability to specific contexts. For example, DeMatteo and Edens (2006) discuss one case whereby risk for violence was assessed with particular emphasis on a defendant's interpersonal psychopathy score. At the time, the state of the literature did not support a clear link between risk of violence and Factor 1 scores in particular. A second example concerned the PCL-R's ability to predict violence in institutional settings versus general violence in the community. Again, at the time, there was less evidence for the prediction of institutional maladjustment than general recidivism; thus, there was less support for the use of the PCL-R in such a context. DeMatteo and Edens (2006) suggest that the utility and appropriateness of the PCL-R should be specifically established in each particular case rather than assumed at the outset (i.e., the rationale for including psychopathy should be clearly outlined and justified). Above all, clinicians and researchers must carefully separate the psychological from the legal; psychology typically deals with groups and psychological terms, whereas the law deals with individual cases and legal terms (Ogloff, 1995). It is critical to approach research with sound methods and appropriate conclusions that respect the accumulated state of knowledge and provide useful information to legal decision makers.

Thus far, we have reviewed the applicability of psychopathy to forensic contexts, with particular emphasis on areas of overlap between the psychological construct of psychopathy and the psycholegal constructs relevant to legal decision makers. We examined the assessment of psychopathy, a critical step in any research methodology in this area, and we reviewed research investigating the ability of psychopathy to predict outcomes that have relevance to the legal process. The next section attempts to integrate these diffuse issues in order to develop a coherent, appropriate, and ethical set of guidelines regarding research in this area. We start with a process model for forensic psychopathy research, followed by suggestions for future research, focusing particularly on methodology.

IMPROVING RESEARCH ON PSYCHOPATHY

To provide valuable information to legal decision makers, researchers need not compromise their interests but should incorporate legal constructs into their design and methodology when possible. The first step of any research project is to identify the variables of interest. With regard to psychopathy, however, the next step should be to identify and, if appropriate, partial out the legally relevant aspects of those variable(s). Thus, to study offending patterns in psychopaths, the study design should operationalize those variables in a manner relevant to the legal process, incorporating aspects such as recidivism, reoffending, parole violations, and institutional violations. By acknowledging at the outset those aspects of a study that may be relevant to legal decision making, both psychology and the law will benefit. Attention should be paid to issues of sensitivity and specificity. Typically, this might include the use of multiple measures, related constructs, and potentially normative or community samples to address the key personality aspects of psychopathy in contrast to those aspects that are characteristic of offenders in general. Psychologists should also integrate their findings into the broader context of the literature, both psychological and, where appropriate, legal, by emphasizing areas of convergence and divergence. Finally, and perhaps most controversial, psychologists should explicitly clarify the legal relevance of their work, particularly when discussing the implications of their findings. Doing so can reduce the likelihood of misinterpreting findings and jeopardizing individual outcomes.

These suggestions require no commitment from researchers to assess psychopathy in clinical or legal contexts but rather to protect their work and findings, as well as that of the field, against inappropriate uses across contexts and disciplines. To the extent that the research area overlaps with relevant legal issues, psychologists would be well advised to design studies in a way that incorporates that overlap while continuing to address the original research question. The researcher may also wish to be explicit if the research does not overlap with a legal issue to avoid unintentional or inappropriate use by uninformed individuals.

In addition, just as any individual sample is an imperfect representation of a population, built upon assumptions and random variation, so too are studies assessing reliability and validity. Random error or spurious findings in individual studies are canceled out over time, leaving strong support for the measure as psychometrically valid. The weight of evidence for the PCL-R does not discount the utility of other measures; however, forensic researchers using an alternative assessment should consider evidence supporting its validity and appropriateness to the population of interest. Many of the traditional associations of interest between psychopathy and legally relevant constructs have been examined with the PCL-R, and thus stand the greatest chance of being accepted by a court under the Daubert standard, which governs the admissibility of scientific evidence in most legal contexts.

We end this chapter with some suggestions for future research in the field. These are based on the evidence to date as well as the needs of the field as a whole. In light of the gains made in understanding psychopathy during the past decade, there is significant forward momentum for the continued study of the topic.

SUGGESTIONS FOR FUTURE RESEARCH

CONSIDER THE DIMENSIONS OR FACTORS OF PSYCHOPATHY

Incorporating factor structures into a research design allows for more fine-grained analyses of the features of psychopathy that are relevant to the variable(s) of interest. This is particularly necessary because of the strong association between behavioral aspects of psychopathy and antisocial personality disorder, which may reduce the attention paid to personality factors. These considerations can also influence the choice of measures, with some topics perhaps suited to more interpersonal assessments and others to the more traditional Hare measures. It is not necessary that we as researchers in a field settle on one definition of psychopathy. That is, there might be different variants of psychopathy just as there are different variants of schizophrenia or depression. However, if we are discussing various types of psychopathy, we must know what being high in those traits or characteristics means in terms of potential future behavior. And, ultimately, the goal would be to move toward a more precise definition of the disorder and its subtypes.

CAREFULLY CONSIDER SAMPLE DEMOGRAPHICS

Too little attention is paid in studies of psychopathy to the nature of individual samples. Some attention has been paid in recent years to differentiating psychiatric facilities and level of security in other facilities, but there is room for further improvement. Prisons present the strong possibility for group effects due to similarities in offense type, age, mental status, or other variables, and the length of incarceration may impact the degree to which these effects manifest themselves. The sheer number of studies on psychopathy brings confidence to the results, but including multiple locations in a study and coding for location could assist in partialing out these potentially confounding variables such as location, security level, offense type, and age.

DIFFERENTIATE STATISTICAL SIGNIFICANCE FROM CLINICAL SIGNIFICANCE

A primary difficulty in the psychological arena as it is applied to legal settings is our use of the term *significant*. As demonstrated throughout this chapter, many of the findings regarding psychopathy are robust and significant across various demographics and settings. Despite this, they often lack the sensitivity or specificity necessary to be used heavily in individual decisions. The use of effect sizes may improve this, by relating significance to some objective yardstick, but it still allows for wide variability in interpretation. Researchers should clarify the relevance of their results in identifying or predicting specific outcomes for particular individuals, and acknowledge differences between statistical significance and clinical significance. Recent moves in psychology as a field have improved the situation substantially, such as discussions of effect size and incremental predictive validity and translation of these findings for the lay reader.

CONSIDER CONTEXT

Although a substantial body of evidence exists for the utility of the psychopathy construct, it is important to bear in mind that the bulk of evidence has been accumulated in a research context. Offenders, psychiatric patients, and others are advised that the assessments are conducted for the purposes of research. Similarly, clinicians and evaluators trained to make assessments are attuned to the importance of reliability. Importantly, the findings and conclusions reached in a research context have no implications for the placement, management, or disposition of participants. For example, there may be little agreement in psychopathy ratings between an evaluator hired by the prosecution and one retained by the defense or between different staff members within the same institution. This is not to suggest that less weight should be placed on these findings but to highlight the importance of examining whether context influences the reliability and validity of ratings.

The suggestions for future research presented here represent general aspects that should be considered when studying psychopathy. Also important are the specific areas that need further attention from researchers if psychopathy research is to continue providing information of value to the legal system. A few suggestions drawn from the topics discussed within this chapter are presented now with the hope that a future review can more confidently address the current state of knowledge within these areas.

ACCURACY OF SELF-REPORT VS. CLINICIAN OR INFORMANT RATINGS

The time and training required to administer the PCL-R and PCL:YV make the development of accurate self-report measures a tempting goal. With children, some evidence exists that measures such as the APSD correlate with clinician-rated scales, but the effect is small. Similarly, the scales derived from general self-report inventories such as the MMPI or PAI show some correlation with psychopathy but some researchers may regard them as inferior to psychopathy-specific measures. More research is needed regarding the usefulness of self-report measures, particularly with regard to correlations with the PCL-style measures and differences in factor score presentation.

TEMPORAL STABILITY OF PSYCHOPATHY

One very noticeable gap in knowledge in the psychopathy literature is that we know very little about how these individuals turn out in adulthood. We have a great deal of case study information and theory to suggest that the prognosis is not good, but we actually have very limited data on this topic. For instance, few studies have tested the temporal stability of the traits and concomitant outcomes. Therefore, we still do not know if youth who score high on psychopathy measures will be psychopathic in adulthood (although see Andershed, 2010). Nor do we have substantial data to suggest that high psychopathy scores at one point in time would result in high scores at another point in time. What is needed is a better understanding of the etiology of psychopathy and the role of its dimensions/factors in its presentation. In addition, the inclusion of potential theoretical moderators may provide a more comprehensive understanding of the expression and development of psychopathy.

PSYCHOPATHY ACROSS RACE AND GENDER

While progress is being made, more attention must be paid to the presentation of psychopathy across racial and gender lines. Findings on women, in particular, have shown great progress in recent years (e.g., Berardino et al., 2005; Schrum & Salekin, 2006), and more research is starting to emerge on ethnic differences in psychopathy (see Verona, Sadeh, & Javdani, 2010). Much of the early work has consisted primarily of validating the construct within these groups; future work should expand this to look at predictions about violence, recidivism, and other variables relevant to legal decision making.

CONCLUSIONS

The study of psychopathy has progressed substantially since its initial conceptualization. Researchers have made progress in identifying multiple facets within the disorder that encompass behavioral, affective, and interpersonal traits; they have validated its application to a variety of social and ethnic groups and have determined how traditional assessments can differ across these groups. The correlates of psychopathy to various psycholegal variables are now much more clearly delineated, while the assessment of psychopathy has been extended across the age range, using a variety of reporters and methods to obtain information. Most importantly, the information obtained has resulted in a renewed focus on the treatment and prevention of psychopathy, and the variables that influence treatment outcome and amenability. This breadth of knowledge makes psychopathy increasingly relevant to forensic contexts. Psychologists, and forensic psychologists in particular, have taken steps to increase the relevance of their work to other contexts. As the knowledge of psychopathy increases, it will become ever more important to use solid methodology and communicate the value and importance of that methodology for using information about psychopathy appropriately. Following the guidelines outlined in this chapter and using the information presented to improve empirical research is one step toward ensuring that the term psychopathy continues to have value to forensic psychologists and also to the "lawyers, social workers, school teachers, and . . . general public" that Cleckley emphasized some 50 years ago.

REFERENCES

Andershed, H. (2010). Stability and change of psychopathic traits: What do we know? In R. T. Salekin & D. R. Lynam (Eds.), *Handbook of child and adolescent psychopathy* (pp. 233–250). New York: Guilford Press.

Archer, R. P., Buffington-Vollum, J. K., Stredny, R. V., & Handel, R. W. (2006). A survey of psychological test use patterns among forensic psychologists. *Journal of Personality Assessment, 87,* 84–94.

Barry, C. T., Frick, P. J., DeShazo, T. M., McCoy, M. G., Ellis, M., & Loney, B. R. (2000). The importance of callous-unemotional traits for extending the concept of psychopathy to children. *Journal of Abnormal Psychology, 109,* 335–340.

Benning, S. D., Patrick, C. J., Hicks, B. M., Blonigen, D. M., & Krueger, R. F. (2003). Factor structure of the Psychopathic Personality Inventory: Validity and implications for clinical assessment. *Psychological Assessment, 15,* 340–350.

Benning, S. D., Patrick, C. J., Salekin, R. T., & Leistico, A. R. (2005). Convergent and discriminant validity of psychopathy factors assessed via self-report: A comparison of three instruments. *Assessment, 12,* 270–289.

Berardino, S. D., Meloy, J. R., Sherman, M., & Jacobs, D. (2005). Validation of the Psychopathic Personality Inventory on a female inmate sample. *Behavioral Sciences & the Law, 23,* 819–836.

Brandt, J. R., Kennedy, W. A., Patrick, C. J., & Curtin, J. J. (1997). Assessment of psychopathy in a population of incarcerated adolescent offenders. *Psychological Assessment, 9,* 429–435.

Butcher, J. N., Graham, J. R., Ben-Porath, Y. S., Tellegen, A., Dahlstrom, W. G., & Kaemmer, B. (2001). *Minnesota Multiphasic Personality Inventory-2: Manual for administration and scoring* (2nd ed.). Minneapolis, MN: University of Minnesota Press.

Caldwell, M., Skeem, J., Salekin, R., & Van Rybroek, G. (2006). Treatment response of adolescent offenders with psychopathy features: A 2-year follow-up. *Criminal Justice and Behavior, 33,* 571–596.

Campbell, T. W. (2007). The validity of the Psychopathy Checklist–Revised in adversarial proceedings. *Journal of Forensic Psychology Practice, 6,* 43–53.

Caputo, A. A., Frick, P. J., & Brodsky, S. L. (1999). Family violence and juvenile sex offending: The potential mediating role of psychopathic traits and negative attitudes towards women. *Criminal Justice and Behavior, 26,* 338–356.

Cleckley, H. (1955). *The mask of sanity: An attempt to clarify some issues about the so-called psychopathic personality.* St. Louis, MO: Mosby.

Cooke, D. J., & Michie, C. (2001). Refining the construct of psychopath: Towards a hierarchical model. *Psychological Assessment, 13,* 171–188.

Corrado, R. R., Vincent, G. M., Hart, S. D., & Cohen, I. M. (2004). Predictive validity of the Psychopathy Checklist: Youth Version for general and violent recidivism. *Behavioral Sciences and the Law, 22,* 5–22.

DeMatteo, D., & Edens, J. F. (2006). The role and relevance of the Psychopathy Checklist-Revised in court: A case law survey of U.S. courts (1991-2004). *Psychology, Public Policy, and Law, 12,* 214–241.

Douglas, K. S., Guy, L. S., Edens, J. F., Boer, D. P., & Hamilton, J. (2007). The Personality Assessment Inventory as a proxy for the Psychopathy Checklist-Revised: Testing the incremental validity and cross-sample robustness of the Antisocial Features Scale. *Assessment, 14,* 255–269.

Douglas, K. S., Strand, S., Belfrage, H., Fransson, G., & Levander, S. (2005). Reliability and validity evaluation of the Psychopathy Checklist: Screening Version (PCL:SV) in Swedish correctional and forensic psychiatric samples. *Assessment, 12,* 145–161.

Douglas, K. S., Vincent, G. M., & Edens, J. F. (2006). Risk for criminal recidivism: The role of psychopathy. In C. J. Patrick (Ed.), *Handbook of psychopathy* (pp. 533–554). New York, NY: Guilford Press.

Edens, J. F. (2001). Misuses of the Hare Psychopathy Checklist–Revised in court: Two case examples. *Journal of Interpersonal Violence, 16,* 1082–1093.

Edens, J. F., & Campbell, J. S. (2007). Identifying youths at risk for institutional misconduct: A meta-analytic investigation of the Psychopathy Checklist measures. *Psychological Services, 4,* 13–27.

Edens, J. F., Campbell, J. S., & Weir, J. M. (2007). Youth psychopathy and criminal recidivism: A meta-analysis of the Psychopathy Checklist measures. *Law and Human Behavior, 31,* 53–75.

Edens, J. F., Hart, S. D., Johnson, D. W., Johnson, J. K., & Olver, M. E. (2000). Use of the Personality Assessment Inventory to assess psychopathy in offender populations. *Psychological Assessment, 12,* 132–139.

Edens, J. F., Skeem, J. L., & Douglas, K. S. (2006). Incremental validity analyses of the Violence Risk Appraisal Guide and the Psychopathy Checklist: Screening Version in a civil psychiatric sample. *Assessment, 13,* 368–374.

Falkenbach, D. M., Poythress, N. G., & Heide, K. M. (2003). Psychopathic features in a juvenile diversion population: Reliability and predictive validity of two self-report measures. *Behavioral Sciences and the Law, 21,* 787–805.

Forth, A., & Book, A. S. (2010). Psychopathic traits in children and adolescents: The relationship with antisocial behaviors and aggression. In R. T. Salekin & D. R. Lynam (Eds.), *Handbook of child and adolescent psychopathy,* (pp. 251–283). New York, NY: Guilford Press.

Forth, A. E., Kosson, D. S., & Hare, R. D. (2003). *Hare Psychopathy Checklist: Youth Version (PCL:YV): Technical manual.* Toronto, Canada: Multi-Health Systems.

Frick, P. J., Bodin, S. D., & Barry, C. T. (2000). Psychopathic traits and conduct problems in community and clinic-referred samples of children: Further development of the Psychopathy Screening Device. *Psychological Assessment, 12,* 382–393.

Frick, P. J., & Hare, R. D. (2001). *The antisocial process screening device.* Toronto, Canada: Multi-Health Systems.

Frick, P. J., Lilienfeld, S. O., Ellis, M., Loney, B., & Silverthorn, P. (1999). The association between anxiety and psychopathy dimensions in children. *Journal of Abnormal Child Psychology, 27,* 383–392.

Frick, P. J., O'Brien, B. S., Wootton, J. S., & McBurnett, K. (1994). Psychopathy and conduct problems in children. *Journal of Abnormal Psychology, 103,* 700–707.

Grann, M. (2000). The PCL-R and gender. *European Journal of Psychological Assessment, 16,* 147–149.

Guy, L. S., & Douglas, K. S. (2006). Examining the utility of the PCL:SV as a screening measure using competing factor models of psychopathy. *Psychological Assessment, 18,* 225–230.

Guy, L. S., Edens, J. F., Anthony, C., & Douglas, K. S. (2005). Does psychopathy predict institutional misconduct among adults? A meta-analytic investigation. *Journal of Consulting and Clinical Psychology, 73,* 1056–1064.

Hare, R. D. (1991). *The Hare Psychopathy Checklist–Revised.* Toronto, Canada: Multi-Health Systems.

Hare, R. D. (2003). *Manual for the Revised Psychopathy Checklist* (2nd ed.). Toronto, Canada: Multi-Health Systems.

Hare, R. D., & Neumann, C. S. (2006). The PCL-R assessment of psychopathy: Development, structural properties, and new directions. In C. J. Patrick (Ed.), *Handbook of psychopathy* (pp. 58–88). New York, NY: Guilford Press.

Harpur, T. J., Hare, R. D., & Hakstian, A. R. (1989). Two-factor conceptualization of psychopathy: Construct validity and assessment implications. *Psychological Assessment, 1,* 6–17.

Harris, G. T., & Rice, M. E. (2006). Treatment of psychopathy: A review of empirical findings. In C. J. Patrick (Ed.), *Handbook of psychopathy* (pp. 555–572). New York, NY: Guilford Press.

Hart, S. D., Cox, D. N., & Hare, R. D. (1995). *Manual for the Hare Psychopathy Checklist–Revised: Screening Version (PCL:SV)*. Toronto, Canada: Multi-Health Systems.

Hart, S. D., Hare, R. D., & Forth, A. E. (1994). Psychopathy as a risk marker for violence: Development and validation of a screening version of the Revised Psychopathy Checklist. In J. Monahan & H. Steadman (Eds.), *Violence and mental disorder: Development in risk assessment* (pp. 81–98). Chicago, IL: University of Chicago Press.

Hill, C. D., Neumann, C. S., & Rogers, R. (2004). Confirmatory factor analysis of the Psychopathy Checklist: Screening Version in offenders with Axis I disorders. *Psychological Assessment, 16*, 90–95.

Hume, M. P., Kennedy, W. A., Patrick, C. J., & Partyka, D. J. (1996). Examination of the MMPI-A for the assessment of psychopathy in incarcerated adolescent male offenders. *International Journal of Offender Therapy and Comparative Criminology, 40*, 224–233.

Kosson, D. S., Cyterski, T. D., Steuerwald, B. L., Neumann, C. S., & Walker-Matthews, S. (2002). The reliability and validity of the Psychopathy Checklist: Youth Version (PCL:YV) in nonincarcerated adolescent males. *Psychological Assessment, 14*, 97–109.

Kosson, D. S., Steuerwald, B. L., Forth, A. E., & Kirkhart, K. J. (1997). A new method for assessing the interpersonal behavior of psychopathic individuals: Preliminary validation studies. *Psychological Assessment, 9*, 89–101.

Kotler, J. S., & McMahon, R. J. (2005). Child psychopathy: Theories, measurement, and relations with the development and persistence of conduct problems. *Clinical Child and Family Psychology Review, 8*, 291–325.

Kotler, J. S., & McMahon, R. J. (2010). Assessment of child and adolescent psychopathy. In R. T. Salekin & D. R. Lynam (Eds.), *Handbook of child and adolescent psychopathy* (pp. 79–109). New York, NY: Guilford Press.

Lee, Z., Vincent, G. M., Hart, S. D., & Corrado, R. R. (2003). The validity of the Antisocial Process Screening Device as a self-report measure of psychopathy in adolescent offenders. *Behavioral Sciences and the Law, 21*, 771–786.

Leistico, A. R., Salekin, R. T., DeCoster, J., & Rogers, R. (2008). A large-scale meta-analysis relating the Hare measures of psychopathy to antisocial conduct. *Law and Human Behavior, 32*, 28–45.

Lilienfeld, S. O. (1996). The MMPI-2 Antisocial Practices Content Scale: Construct validity and comparison with the Psychopathic Deviate Scale. *Psychological Assessment, 8*, 281–293.

Lilienfeld, S. O. (1999). The relation of the MMPI-2 Pd Harris-Lingoes subscales to psychopathy, psychopathy facets, and antisocial behavior: Implications for clinical practice. *Journal of Clinical Psychology, 55*, 241–255.

Lilienfeld, S. O., & Andrews, B. P. (1996). Development and preliminary validation of a self-report measure of psychopathic personality traits in noncriminal populations. *Journal of Personality Assessment, 66*, 488–524.

Lilienfeld, S. O., & Fowler, K. A. (2006). The self-report assessment of psychopathy: Problems, pitfalls, and promises. In C. J. Patrick (Ed.), *Handbook of psychopathy* (pp. 107–132). New York, NY: Guilford Press.

Lynam, D. R. (1997). Pursuing the psychopath: Capturing the fledgling psychopath in a nomological net. *Journal of Abnormal Psychology, 106*, 425–438.

Lynam, D. R., Caspi, A., Moffitt, T. E., Raine, A., Loeber, R., & Stouthamer-Loeber, M. (2005). Adolescent psychopathy and the big five: Results from two samples. *Journal of Abnormal Child Psychology, 33*, 431–443.

Lynam, D. R., & Gudonis, L. (2005). The development of psychopathy. *Annual Review of Clinical Psychology, 1*, 381–407.

Millon, T. (1993). *Millon Adolescent Clinical Inventory*. Minneapolis, MN: National Computer Systems.

Morey, L. C. (1991). *Personality Assessment Inventory professional manual*. Odessa, FL: Psychological Assessment Resources.

Murrie, D. C., Boccaccini, M. T., Turner, D. B., Meeks, M., Woods, C., & Tussey, C. (2009). Rater (dis)agreement on risk assessment measures in sexually violent predator proceedings: Evidence of adversarial allegiance in forensic evaluation? *Psychology, Public Policy, and Law, 15*, 19–53.

Murrie, D. C., & Cornell, D. G. (2000). *The Millon Adolescent Clinical Inventory and* psychopathy. *Journal of Personality Assessment, 75,* 110–125.

Murrie, D. C., & Cornell, D. G. (2002). Psychopathy screening of incarcerated juveniles: A comparison of measures. *Psychological Assessment, 14,* 390–396.

Neumann, C. S., Kosson, D. S., Forth, A. E., & Hare, R. D. (2006). Factor structure of the Hare Psychopathy Checklist: Youth Version (PCL:YV) in incarcerated adolescents. *Psychological Assessment, 18,* 142–154.

Neumann, C. S., Kosson, D. S., & Salekin, R. T. (2007). Exploratory and confirmatory factor analysis and its application to psychopathy: Conceptual and methodological issues. In H. Herve & J. Yuille (Eds.), *Psychopathy: Theory, research, and social implications.* Mahwah, NJ: Lawrence Erlbaum.

O'Neill, M. L., Lidz, V., & Heilbrun, K. (2003). Adolescents with psychopathic characteristics in a substance abusing cohort: Treatment process and outcomes. *Law and Human Behavior, 27,* 299–313.

Ogloff, J. R. P. (1995). Legal issues associated with the concept of psychopathy. *Issues in Criminological & Legal Psychology, 24,* 119–122.

Ogloff, J. R. P., Wong, S., & Greenwood, A. (1990). Treating criminal psychopaths in a therapeutic community program. *Behavioral Sciences & the Law, 8,* 181–190.

Poythress, N. G., Dembo, R., Wareham, J., & Greenbaum, P. E. (2006). Construct validity of the Youth Psychopathic Traits Inventory (YPI) and the Antisocial Process Screening Device (APSD) with justice-involved adolescents. *Criminal Justice and Behavior, 33,* 26–55.

Poythress, N. G., Edens, J. F., & Lilienfeld, S. O. (1998). Criterion-related validity of the Psychopathic Personality Inventory in a prison sample. *Psychological Assessment, 10,* 426–430.

Rice, M. E., Harris, G. T., & Cormier, C. A. (1992). An evaluation of a maximum security therapeutic community for psychopaths and other mentally disordered offenders. *Law and Human Behavior, 16,* 399–412.

Robins, L. N. (1966). *Deviant children grown up: A sociological and psychiatric study of sociopathic personality.* Baltimore, MD: Williams & Wilkins.

Rogers, R., Jackson, R. L., Sewell, K. W., & Johansen, J. (2004). Predictors of treatment outcome in dually-diagnosed antisocial

youth: An initial study of forensic inpatients. *Behavioral Sciences & the Law, 22,* 215–222.

Salekin, R. T. (2002). Psychopathy and therapeutic pessimism: Clinical lore or clinical reality? *Clinical Psychology Review, 22,* 79–112.

Salekin, R. T. (2008). Psychopathy and offending from mid-adolescence to young adulthood. *Journal of Abnormal Psychology, 117,* 386–395.

Salekin, R. T., Brannen, D. N., Zalot, A. A., Leistico, A. R., & Neumann, C. S. (2006). Factor structure of psychopathy in youth: Testing the applicability of the new four factor model. *Criminal Justice and Behavior, 33,* 135–157.

Salekin, R. T., Leistico, A. R., Neumann, C. S., DiCicco, T. M., & Duros, R. L. (2004). Psychopathy and comorbidity in a young offender sample: Taking a closer look at psychopathy's potential importance over disruptive behavior disorders. *Journal of Abnormal Psychology, 113,* 416–427.

Salekin, R. T., Leistico, A. R., Trobst, K. K., Schrum, C. L., & Lochman, J. E. (2005). Adolescent psychopathy and personality theory—the Interpersonal Circumplex: Expanding evidence of a nomological net. *Journal of Abnormal Child Psychology, 33,* 445–460.

Salekin, R. T., & Lynam, D. R. (2010). *Handbook of child and adolescent psychopathy.* New York, NY: Guilford Press.

Salekin, R. T., Rogers, R., & Sewell, K. W. (1996). A review and meta-analysis of the Psychopathy Checklist and Psychopathy Checklist-Revised: Predictive validity of dangerousness. *Clinical Psychology: Science and Practice, 3,* 203–215.

Salekin, R. T., Rogers, R., & Sewell, K. W. (1997). Construct validity of psychopathy in a female offender sample: A multitrait-multimethod evaluation. *Journal of Abnormal Psychology, 106,* 576–585.

Salekin, R. T., Worley, C. B., & Grimes, R. D. (2010). Treatment of psychopathy: A review and brief introduction to the mental models approach. *Behavioral Sciences and the Law, 28,* 235–266.

Salekin, R. T., Ziegler, T. A., Larrea, M. A., Anthony, V. L., & Bennett, A. D. (2003). Predicting dangerousness with two Millon Adolescent Clinical Inventory psychopathy scales: The importance of egocentric and callous traits. *Journal of Personality Assessment, 80,* 154–163.

Schrum, C. L., & Salekin, R. T. (2006). Psychopathy in adolescent female offenders: An item response theory analysis of the Psychopathy Checklist - Youth Version. *Behavioral Sciences and the Law, 24,* 39–63.

Skeem, J. L., Monahan, J., & Mulvey, E. P. (2002). Psychopathy, treatment involvement, and subsequent violence among civil psychiatric patients. *Law and Human Behavior, 26,* 577–603.

Skeem, J. L., Mulvey, E. P., & Grisso, T. (2003). Applicability of traditional and revised models of psychopathy to the Psychopathy Checklist: Screening Version. *Psychological Assessment, 15,* 41–55.

Spain, S. E., Douglas, K. S., Poythress, N. G., & Epstein, M. (2004). The relationship between psychopathic features, violence and treatment outcome: The comparison of three youth measures of psychopathic features. *Behavioral Sciences & the Law, 22,* 85–102.

Verona, E., Sadeh, N., & Javdani, S. (2010). The influences of gender and culture on child and adolescent psychopathy. In R. T. Salekin & D. R. Lynam (Eds.), *Handbook of child and adolescent psychopathy* (pp. 317–342). New York: Guilford Press.

Verona, E., & Vitale, J. (2006). Psychopathy in women: Assessment, manifestations, and etiology. In C. J. Patrick (Ed.), *Handbook of psychopathy* (pp. 415–436). New York, NY: Guilford.

Vitacco, M. J., & Kosson, D. S. (2010). Understanding psychopathy through an evaluation of interpersonal behavior: Testing the factor structure of the interpersonal measure of psychopathy in a large sample of jail detainees. *Psychological Assessment, 22,* 638–649.

Vitacco, M. J., Rogers, R., & Neumann, C. S. (2003). The Antisocial Process Screening Device: An examination of its construct and criterion-related validity. *Assessment, 10,* 143–150.

Vitale, J. E., & Newman, J. P. (2001). Using the Psychopathy Checklist-Revised with female samples: Reliability, validity, and implications for clinical utility. *Clinical Psychology: Science and Practice, 8,* 117–132.

Walsh, T., & Walsh, Z. (2006). The evidentiary introduction of Psychopathy Checklist-Revised assessed psychopathy in U.S. courts: Extent and appropriateness. *Law and Human Behavior, 30,* 493–507.

Walters, G. D. (2003). Predicting institutional adjustment and recidivism with the Psychopathy Checklist factor scores: A meta-analysis. *Law and Human Behavior, 27,* 541–558.

Walters, G. D., & Duncan, S. A. (2005). Use of the PCL-R and PAI to predict release outcome in inmates undergoing forensic evaluation. *Journal of Forensic Psychiatry & Psychology, 16,* 459–476.

Zolondek, S., Lilienfeld, S. O., Patrick, C. J., & Fowler, K. A. (2006). The Interpersonal Measure of Psychopathy: Construct and incremental validity in male prisoners. *Assessment, 13,* 470–482.

CHAPTER 19

Sex Offender Research in a Forensic Context

ROBERT A. PRENTKY, RAINA LAMADE, AND ANNA COWARD[1]

NLIKE MOST AREAS of clinical research, priorities in sex offender research are set primarily by statutory needs. The amount of legislation enacted over the past two decades directed at sex offender management is unprecedented. Federal legislation has included the Violence Against Women Act of 1994 (VAWA), the expanded VAWA legislation in 2000 (P. L.106-386, 18 U.S.C. 2261), the Wetterling Act, passed in 1994 as part of the Violent Crime Control and Law Enforcement Act (42 U.S.C. 14071), the amended Wetterling Act of 1996, known as "Megan's Law" (P. L. 104-145), the amended Federal Rules of Evidence in 1995 to include prior sex crimes, the Pam Lynchner Sexual Offender Tracking and Identification Act (42 U.S.C. 14072) in 1996, the Wetterling Improvements Act of 1997 (P.L. 105-119), the Victim's of Trafficking and Violence Prevention Act of 2000, and the Adam Walsh Child Protection and Safety Act of 2006 (P. L. No. 109-248, 42 U.S.C. 16901). Among other things, the Adam Walsh Act established a *comprehensive national system* for the registration of all sex offenders (Title I, §301).

At the state level, the most impactful legislation has taken the form of civil commitment laws targeting sex offenders. Beginning in 1990, with the passage of the first sexually violent predator (SVP) law in the state of Washington (WA Laws of 1990, ch. 3), 19 other states have now followed suit (cf. Gookin, 2007). In addition, as of 1997, every state has had some variant of a sexual offender public notification law pursuant to the Federal Wetterling Act of 1996, and some states are introducing residence restriction laws (Levenson & Cotter, 2005).

---

1. Acknowledgment: The authors wish to acknowledge the feedback to different parts of this chapter provided by Howard Barbaree, Steven Hart, Eric Janus, Austin Lee, Neil Malamuth, Todd Melnik, Joe Phelps, Nicole Pittman, Luis Rosell, and Rich Wollert. The authors assume full responsibility for the final product.

This new wave of SVP civil commitment laws all have the same three elements: (1) a predicate sexual offense, (2) a mental abnormality or personality disorder, and (3) the nexus between prior bad acts and mental abnormality, resulting in some presumptive risk of future sexually dangerous behavior. In addition, universal public notification typically assigns newly released sex offenders to one of three "tiers" based on some determination of risk. The net impact of this full court legal press has been to focus and reenergize research efforts in one target area critical to these laws: risk assessment. Between the civil commitment laws and universal community registration, we are confronted by the challenge of assessing risk of sexual dangerousness (i.e., likelihood of reoffending sexually). Although this challenge has assumed center stage for researchers, it by no means captures the full array of unanswered or partially answered empirical questions about sexually coercive behavior. This chapter attempts to set forth a comprehensive research agenda. Although the most demanding research questions inevitably involve risk assessment, stemming from the implementation of regulatory statutes, there are many other research issues that remain untouched or unresolved and that have practical import. We have organized these research issues into four major topical areas: classification and diagnosis, etiology, risk assessment, and remediation and management.

CLASSIFICATION AND DIAGNOSIS

The science of classification (taxonomy) is fundamental to all mature areas of science. The goal, simply stated, is to uncover the laws and principles that underlie the optimal differentiation, or "carving up," of a complex (heterogeneous) domain into subgroups that possess theoretically important similarities. The more complex and heterogeneous the domain, the more critical it is to improve the reliability and efficacy of decision making by isolating subgroups of greater homogeneity. An indisputable conclusion about sex offenders is that they constitute a markedly heterogeneous group (Knight, Rosenberg, & Schneider, 1985). This heterogeneity was fully appreciated in the 1960s and 1970s, with over a half-dozen clinically derived classification systems (cf. Knight et al., 1985), feeding the widely cited work of Cohen, Seghorn, and Groth (cf. Knight et al., 1985; Prentky & Burgess, 2000). All extant classification systems at that point were rationally derived. Empirically derived classification systems emerged in the mid-1980s as a programmatic continuation of Cohen and Seghorn's work (cf., Knight & Prentky, 1990). Development of classification systems during the 1980s was the direct result of the high priority status given such research by the National Institute of Justice. Although reasonable progress was made in the revision and validation of taxonomic systems for rapists and child molesters (Knight & Prentky, 1990), this research faded with a shift in priorities to the more pressing demand of risk assessment during the 1990s.

We are left today precisely where we were in the 1960s, recognizing the obvious heterogeneity of sex offenders while forging ahead without regard to it. Failure to develop valid models for sex offenders that reign in heterogeneity may undermine, indeed may severely undermine, progress in at least four major areas of research:

1. Developing etiologic models that point to different "paths" leading to different outcomes
2. Developing more sophisticated risk-assessment models that target optimal risk predictors for different subtypes of offenders
3. Informing treatment planning and clinical decision making
4. Informing discretionary and dispositional decisions within the criminal justice system

A fifth potential area is investigative profiling, wherein classification might improve bootstrapping in apprehending suspects (i.e., drawing valid inferences about the offender from victim statements and crime scene data).

The only system that is currently used for classifying sex offenders is the Diagnostic and Statistical Manual of the American Psychiatric Association (APA) (DSM-IV-TR, APA, 2000). Although the DSM-IV-TR is relied on in court, in practice it provides little help, since the DSM was never intended to classify subtypes of criminals, including sex offenders (Prentky, Coward, & Gabriel, 2008). The DSM includes a one-size-fits-all category (*pedophilia*) for all child molesters and no category specific to rapists. The category of *pedophilia*, used to classify all offenders that evidence some degree of sexual interest in children for a period of six months or longer, subsumes, under one taxonomic umbrella: (a) offenders with an exclusive sexual and social preference for children who profess to "love," or at the very least care for, their victims (i.e., "pedophiles" in the more technical use of the term); (b) offenders with a sexual and social preference for adolescents (i.e., "hebephiles"); (c) exclusive endogamous ("within family") offenders (i.e., "incest"); (d) offenders who appear to rely exclusively on Internet images of children for sexual gratification (i.e., not "travelers"); (e) antisocial offenders who seek out children because they are easy prey; and, at the extreme, (f) violent sadists.

Knight and Prentky proposed an empirically driven classification model for child molesters with two axes which, if crossed, would yield 24 separate subtypes (Knight, Carter, & Prentky, 1989; Knight & Prentky, 1990). Although clearly there aren't 24 subtypes (many of the cells resulting from a cross of both axes are functionally empty), it is evident that the number of discrete, theoretically and empirically defensible subtypes is considerable. The *Crime Classification Manual*, for example, lists no less than 12 separate categories of child molesters (Douglas, A. W. Burgess, Burgess, & Ressler, 1992).

From a methodological standpoint, models derived from sophisticated mathematical techniques applied to the rational, systematic ordering of clinical experience have been developed for, and tested on, criminal populations during the past 50 years. These techniques tend to fall into two categories: (1) simple univariate and bivariate methods, and (2) multivariate taxometric methods. Some of the vexing problems of classifying sexual offenders have been addressed (e.g., Are classification assignments stable over time? Can classification assignments be bootstrapped reliably using targeted information? Are classification assignments useful as indices of outcome in path models?) and predictive validity studies have provided encouraging results. Nevertheless, there is only a limited track record of predictive validity on diverse samples of sex offenders and only within two theoretically cohesive domains (extrafamilial child molesters and rapists).

Major methodological difficulties remain, including (a) weak or absent operational measurement, particularly the use of clinical and theoretical constructs that are abstract, unoperationalized, and essentially unmeasurable; (b) ambiguous, inadequate, or absent case-assignment rules; (c) inadequate power in predictive validity studies; and (d) predictive studies that are hampered by numerous methodological problems. Predictive validity studies raise a unique set of methodological problems associated with confinement conditions (e.g., presence of treatment, who participated, how to assess "benefit," etc.), release conditions (e.g., with or without supervision, nature of registration and community notification requirements), and parameters set for measuring re-offense (e.g., legal parameters, such as arrest or conviction, length of follow-up, and data sources used to assess re-offense).

As Brennan (1987) pointed out, the challenge of translating complex methods into user-friendly procedures that will be accepted and implemented faithfully by administrators and practitioners in the criminal justice system remains a critical issue. As noted previously, historically most classification systems derive from clinical, subjective, or "rational" pattern-recognition in which groups are based on personal or collective observation and inferential reasoning (Brennan, 1987). Models deriving from more complex taxometric methods have not, by and large, been favorably received. Brennan noted that

> acceptance is contingent on the presence of coherent interpretations of the classes and a clear nomenclature, on the face validity of the system, on its consistency with the intuitive experience of the practitioner, and on effective decision-making implications of the classification for the practitioner. (p. 239)

The responsibility for achieving these goals falls on the researcher. Unfortunately, the few attempts at introducing empiricism into taxonomic models for sex offenders have given only cursory attention to those goals.

From a practical standpoint, developing, testing, revising, and retesting classification models requires a substantial investment of time and money. It is no accident that the limited period of progress in developing empirically based models for classifying child molesters and rapists coincided with high priority funding at the National Institute of Justice. Although the work of Knight and Prentky focused exclusively on extrafamiliar child molesters and rapists, one could easily justify the need for similar research programs that targeted incest offenders, juvenile sex offenders, and, most recently, Internet offenders. An additional practical hurdle is the need for a close working relationship between the researchers and the practitioners and gatekeepers who are responsible for the offenders. Developing valid classification models requires a high degree of functional interactivity between researchers and practitioners. Researchers must be cognizant of and responsive to the needs of practitioners, and, for their part, practitioners must "buy in" to the need for valid classification and be committed to implement classification faithfully (i.e., precisely in accordance with the guidelines set forth by the researchers). In sum, the primary hurdles to developing and testing classification models with sex offenders are twofold: (1) the previously mentioned necessity of a collaborative working relationship between the researchers and the users, both in the development and testing phase and in the implementation phase, and (2) a funding priority that will support programmatic research on classification.

ETIOLOGY

Although there has been much speculation and clinical treatises on the etiology of sexual aggression, ranging from psychoanalytic theory to evolutionary theory, empirical research is actually quite limited. There is, however, a considerable body of science that has identified factors antecedent to or associated with sexual aggression against women, including histories of abuse in childhood; impulsive, antisocial behavior beginning in adolescence; misogynistic anger; negative or hostile masculinity; rape-related cognitive distortions (rape myths); sexual entitlement; and impersonal sex. Malamuth (2003) has persuasively argued that while general antisocial characteristics may indeed "set the stage" and contribute to a propensity to rape, they must be considered within the context of a hierarchical approach. Malamuth (2003) argued that the influence of general antisociality is mediated by risk factors more specific to rape. This is a critical theoretical and empirical step in the integration of risk factors for more general antisocial behavior with those relevant to rape, suggesting that although there may be some shared general "disturbances" to normative social behavior underlying a variety of antisocial outcomes, there are also *specific* pathways mediating particular antisocial behaviors. In focusing on risk factors predicting rape, researchers have sought to develop a useful, empirically testable model of risk and protective factors that can be used to predict which men have certain proclivities to aggress and which men *are relatively likely to actually aggress*.

This line of research has shown that the large number of risk factors reported in the literature (Prentky & Knight, 1991) may be reduced to a more manageable number of key factors that may be meaningfully organized into two main clusters labeled *hostile masculinity* and *impersonal sex* (e.g., Malamuth, 1998). The hostile masculinity path is described as a personality profile combining two interrelated components: (a) an insecure, defensive, hypersensitive, and hostile-distrustful orientation, particularly towards women, and (b) sexual gratification by controlling or dominating women. The impersonal sex pathway is characterized by a promiscuous, noncommittal, game-playing orientation towards sexual relationships. This model has yielded a wide range of predictions that have been tested in both cross-sectional and longitudinal studies (e.g., Dean & Malamuth, 1997; Malamuth, Linz, Heavey, Barnes, & Acker, 1995). Moreover, this model has been successfully shown to have wide general applicability to various ethnic populations and community samples in various countries throughout the world with both noncriminal and criminal samples (e.g., Abbey, 2006; Hall, Teten, DeGarmo, Sue, & Stephens, 2005; Martin, Vergeles, Acevedo, Sanchez, & Visa, 2005).

In another important contribution, Knight and Sims-Knight (2003) revised the Malamuth model, arguing that the important dimension of hostile masculinity was not univocal. The principal difference between these path models is the single dimension of hostile masculinity in the confluence model or a bifurcation into separate dimensions of antisocial behavior and callousness/unemotionality in the Knight model. This research, along with the models issuing from it, has been pivotal in providing sound evidence for a unified, theoretical explanation of sexual aggression against women. Thus far, all of the aforementioned research is based on self-report, usually from surveys or questionnaires, and from offender files. These data sources are subject to obvious criticisms, including the potential bias in offender disclosures of sensitive information and inherent bias of faulty memory in recalling long-distant events. The ideal solution would be a prospective, longitudinal study targeting a large, diverse sample of preadolescents and adolescents who have already evidenced sexually aggressive behaviors.

Another area of research on etiology is the one-time (now tarnished) silver bullet of childhood sexual victimization. The prevailing working hypothesis in the decade of the 1980s was that sexual offenses represented a "recapitulation" of the offender's own experience of sexual victimization (e.g., Finkelhor et al., 1986; Garland & Dougher, 1990; R. S. Kempe & Kempe, 1984; Lanyon, 1986; Rogers & Terry, 1984). It is clear that the predictive weight of childhood sexual victimization is a function of a number of "morbidity" factors (Kaufman & Zigler, 1987; Prentky, 1999), and that some factors, such as penetration (e.g., Burton, 2000) and co-occurrence of caregiver inconstancy along with sexual victimization (Prentky et al., 1989), can be potent aggravators of risk to engage in sexually aggressive behavior.

A related fruitful area of research on the contributory impact of child abuse is brain damage and its potential role in undermining attachment. Replicated studies on diverse samples have demonstrated that child abuse can cause permanent damage to the neural structure and functioning of the developing brain (e.g., DeBellis et al., 1999a,b; Teicher, 2000, 2002).

The theoretical importance of attachment for sex offenders would seem obvious. If there is *one* thing that can be said to characterize all sex offenders, it is their maladaptive interpersonal relationships. Although there has been considerable attention to attachment and intimacy deficits (e.g., Cortoni & Marshall, 2001; Marshall, 1993; Marshall, Hudson, & Hodkinson, 1993; Marshall, Serran, & Cortoni, 2000; Smallbone & Dadds, 2000; Ward, Hudson, & Marshall, 1996; Ward, Hudson, Marshall, & Siegert, 1995), it is not been formally incorporated into and tested in preexisting path models. The next generation of path models must include a more sensitive analysis of "initial life conditions," including early markers of malattachment, severity of malattachment, and morbidity factors associated with physical and sexual victimization (e.g., age of onset, duration, relationship to the perpetrator, and severity).

In sum, we have given short shrift to the critical importance and the often profoundly subtle effects of abuse and neglect in childhood. Among the numerous methodological problems, those that stand out include

1. The failure to take into account the age of onset and the duration of the abuse
2. The potential for hard-wired damage in cases of protracted abuse with early onset
3. Pre-natal *abuse* associated with exposure to licit as well as illicit drugs
4. The complex, possibly potentiating, role of concurrent aversive life experiences, such as chronic fear from observed violence, abuse perpetrated by multiple offenders, caregivers who fail to protect, and multiple types or forms of abuse (e.g., emotional and physical abuse)
5. Abuse perpetrated by individuals of varying attachment to the child, representing varying degrees of betrayal
6. Abuse that includes a wide range of acts perpetrated on the child and acts that the child is forced to perform, ranging from noninvasive acts (i.e., caressing and frottage) to frightening, degrading, and humiliating acts, leaving deep emotional scars
7. The nature, quality, and stability of caregivers in the child's life at the time of the abuse

Perhaps most glaring is the failure to address in any systematic way the role of caregiver attachments in the child's history and to regard severe fractures in attachments as a serious form of abuse. Such a detailed analysis of abuse history may reveal vastly more informative data about behavioral outcomes than the simple, categorical assessment that "the offender was sexually abused when he was 7 years old."

Such an analysis requires, however, a comprehensive protocol for gathering data on abuse history, data that will inevitably come from self-report, either in survey or structured interview format, raising all of the issues associated with anamnestic recall (e.g., the more remote the recalled events, the less accurate they may be; the more traumatic the event, the more it may be distorted or repressed; events may be created or exaggerated in the context of a forensic interview, etc.). Similar to an anamnestic assessment of risk (Otto, 2000), the offender's recollections of childhood abuse should include, whenever possible, detailed historical records (e.g., child welfare records; school records; and treatment, medical, and hospitalization records) and third-party reports (e.g., by family members, relatives, caseworkers, school nurses, or teachers). Although there are numerous available scales for assessing histories of childhood sexual abuse in adults, there are no standardized questionnaires, to the best of our knowledge, that are designed to capture the full gamut of abuse-related experiences described here. Ideally, to address social desirability response bias (cf. Saunders, 1991), a comprehensive self-report should be developed that has an embedded measure of social desirability or includes a standalone measure such as the Marlowe-Crowne (Crowne & Marlowe, 1964). This comprehensive self-report should also include embedded cross-checks using archival or third-party data.

Another theoretically interesting area of inquiry on etiology stems from the writings of Kafka (e.g., Kafka, 1997, 2003; Kafka & Hennen, 2003) on the pathophysiology of paraphilic and non-paraphilic-related disorders. Kafka's monoamine hypothesis, which targets the one segment of the sex offender population that is characterized by high sexual drive and deviant sexual interests, derives its supports from four sources:

1. Monoamine neurotransmitters that modulate human sexual motivation
2. Drugs that affect monoamine neurotransmitters and can have significant inhibitory and disinhibitory effects on sexual behavior
3. Paraphilias that have DSM-IV Axis I comorbid associations with non-sexual disorders that are also associated with monoaminergic dysregulation
4. Drugs that enhance central serotonergic function and mitigate paraphilic sexual arousal and sexual behavior (cf. Kafka, 2003)

Although the efficacy of medications, both antiandrogens as well as SSRI antidepressants, have a lengthy empirical track record of efficacy, no research to the best of our knowledge has incorporated "biology" into a unified theoretical model. Accomplishing this task does not require assaying hormones or other procedures that might be out of reach for some researchers. Much of Kafka's data comes from a detailed history that he gathers from his patients/clients at intake. Asking the right questions and probing for detailed answers can yield invaluable behavioral data on intensity of sexual drive, the range and quality of deviant sexual interests, characteristics of sexual fantasies (e.g., the degree to which fantasies are intrusive, recurrent, internally generated, and vivid (cf. Prentky and Burgess, 1991) and comorbid factors associated with changes in sexual drive.

RISK ASSESSMENT

In civil commitment trials, statutory language does *not*, in fact, refer to risk but rather uses terms translated to mean a statistical probability of sexual re-offense, typically "likely" (Mossman, 2008). The language in the current Washington state statute (Community Protection Act of 1990) defines a *sexually violent predator* as "a person who has been convicted of or charged with a crime of sexual violence and who suffers from a mental abnormality or personality disorder which makes the person *likely* to engage in predatory acts of sexual violence" (italics added); most states use the same or similar language (Prentky & Burgess, 2000).

Over 30 years ago, Monahan and Wexler (1978) addressed the probability standards used in civil commitment, distinguishing between a standard of proof and a standard of commitment, with the latter assessing the probability of being dangerous. The terms used were the same ones we see today, *likely* and *highly likely*. The "outcome variable" has changed, however. We have supplanted *dangerousness* with *risk* (cf. Borum, 1996; Grisso & Tomkins, 1996; Heilbrun, Nezu, Keeney, Chung, & Wasserman, 1998), bringing criminology "in line" with health care and environmental health risk-management models. Risk has clear conceptual and theoretical advantages. Risk implies the presence of a potential hazard and the probability of occurrence of that hazard; risk reduction implies reduction in the probability of the occurrence of the hazard, often using calculable probabilities for different health-care outcomes (Prentky & Burgess, 2000).

Researchers have responded to the statutory demand by developing, testing, and revising risk-assessment scales. When those risk-assessment scales include life tables, clinicians may opine about "likely to engage" using estimates extracted from the table associated with the scale they are using (e.g., the Static-99, Hanson & Thornton, 1999; or Static-2002, Hanson & Thornton, 2003), the Sex Offense Risk Appraisal Guide (Quinsey, Harris, Rice, & Cormier, 1998) and the Minnesota Sex Offender Screening Tool-Revised (Epperson, Kaul, & Hesselton, 1998). The aforementioned actuarial risk-assessment scales provide, as stated, life tables with probabilistic esti-mates of re-offense derived from reference groups, typically composed of heterogeneous samples of incarcerated sex offenders with known outcomes.

Of the numerous methodological challenges that arise in risk assessment research, we will limit our attention to the following six accounting for the passage of time, the effect of age, base rate information, offender heterogeneity, time frame for reoffending, and confidence intervals for risk predictions.

FAILURE TO ACCOUNT FOR THE PASSAGE OF TIME

Since civil commitment follows expiration of criminal sentence, the last known criminal behavior is often many years in the past. From the standpoint of assessing risk, however, failure to account for, or estimate the relevance of, the passage of time on risk may treat *current risk as equivalent to historical risk*

(risk at time of last offense). In a study that uniquely sought to test the assumption of risk stability over time among general offenders, police files for an entire birth cohort were examined to determine whether offenders who had criminal records from many years ago exhibited a higher risk of future criminal records than those with no criminal record at all (Kurlychek, Brame, & Bushway, 2007). Kurlychek et al. (2007) found that "there is little to no distinguishable difference between these groups," (p. 64). The critical issue, simply stated, has been articulated many times. Risk predictors that are useful for assessing risk *status* (i.e., the probabilistic estimate of the risk based primarily on historical factors) may be different from the risk predictors that are useful for assessing risk *state* (i.e., estimated risk posed in the future, over the short term, based primarily on dynamic factors) (e.g., Douglas & Skeem, 2005). Almost 15 years ago, Mulvey and Lidz (1995) presented a "conditional" model of risk that is fluid rather than fixed and capable of adjusting to changes in situations and circumstances. We find ourselves in a methodologically compromising bind. With civil commitment occurring *after* completion of the criminal sentence, an increasing number of respondents have already been incarcerated for a considerable length of time when assessed under the SVP law, and many others have been incarcerated for an even longer time when petitioning for release after commitment. Although a variant of the "conditional model" is imperative given the amount of elapsed time since risk *status* was assessed (20 to 30 years is not uncommon), there are obvious limitations on risk predictors that are sensitive to changes in situations and circumstances when the passage of time in prison often appears frozen. The methodological challenge will be to develop a risk model that incorporates institutional dynamic factors (e.g., anger management), protective factors (e.g., treatment), maturational factors (age related), and discharge/release-related dynamic factors (i.e., community based). The chief difficulty will be the paucity of reliable data to assess variables that fall outside the custodial mission of prisons, the potentially biased reporting of key information (e.g., progress in treatment) by clinicians who are employees of the prison, and the lack of resources and support within the prison for developing a comprehensive, implementable release plan.

Bechman (2001) cited a three-judge Florida panel that rendered a consolidated opinion in 14 SVP cases. The judges stated,

> the underlying assumption of these instruments is that human beings do not change but are programmed to act in the future in accordance with the manner in which they have acted in the past—an assumption which runs contra to the basic principles of our legal and penal system and contra to the premises of clinical psychology and psychiatry.
>
> (*In re Roberto Valdez, 2000*)

Lip service acknowledgment of *change* in risk status is reflected by some research attention to acute and stable dynamic risk factors and protective risk factors. Thus far, however, very little progress has been made in integrating such factors into risk-assessment scales. Knowing which acute and dynamic risk factors to use, how to assess them, and when to employ them are empirical questions. The integration between static and dynamic risk factors must also be accomplished and there must be a systematic, standardized procedure for *adjusting* static risk with dynamic risk. Adjustment should not be a matter of clinical opinion. The principal obstacle to developing a comprehensive risk model for sex offenders is the seeming absence of need (i.e., the *need* is to assess risk status for commitment using one of the existing actuarial scales). There does not appear to be an equivalent need to assess risk state for those who are committed and petition for release.

THE EFFECT OF AGE ON RISK ASSESSMENT

The most obvious, potentially risk-relevant change as a function of time is *age*. Failure to take into account the inverse relationship between risk and age, and, in particular, the attenuation in risk during the fifth or sixth decade of life, may overestimate risk (Barbaree, Blanchard, & Langton, 2003; Fazel, Sjostedt, & Langstrom, 2006; Hanson, 2002, 2006; Prentky & Lee, 2007; Thornton, 2006). Although some of the actuarial scales include items that are intended to reflect the aging of the offender, none reflect changes after the age of 30 (Barbaree & Blanchard, 2008). In fact, there is some evidence that part of the ability of actuarial items to predict recidivism is attributable to the relationship between those items and age at time of release (Barbaree, Langton, & Blanchard, 2007). Numerous risk-relevant questions emerge from this research, such as how and when to incorporate age-sensitive input, using a systematic procedure, into a comprehensive risk assessment. We must ultimately address one single question: at some point do we simply "bet age?" In other words, is the known base rate for a particular group of sex offenders so low after a particular age that we need consider nothing more than age itself? To examine these questions, a single-cohort, long-term longitudinal design has distinct advantages.

The disadvantages are equally distinct, however, including confounding aging and period effects, attrition, and continuity of funding, especially if the follow-up period is 15 to 20 years. Given the substantial empirical evidence supporting an age effect for sex offenders, gathering longitudinal data on multiple age cohorts (i.e., an accelerated longitudinal design) would permit examination of age-outcome trajectories and age x cohort interaction effects (cf. Miyazaki & Raudenbush, 2000).

FAILURE TO USE BASE RATES

By and large, risk-assessment schemes assume base rate homogeneity (i.e., the incidence of sexual re-offense is comparable among all offenders). This assumption is a fallacy. Failure to incorporate accurate estimates of base rates for sexual re-offense into a risk analysis is a mainstay of overprediction. Although the criticality of base rates has been known and underscored for over half a century (Meehl & Rosen, 1955), contemporary approaches to risk assessment largely ignore this message. Barbaree (1997) demonstrated that failure to take into consideration more reliable base rates among subgroups of sexual offenders severely undermines any attempt to demonstrate the efficacy of treatment.

Although determining more accurate re-offense base rates for homogeneous subgroups of offenders is critical, accomplishing this task is deceptively difficult. Assuming that we can reliably identify homogeneous subgroups, base rates will vary from sample to sample (of the same subgroup) due to a number of sources of methodological variability (Prentky, Lee, Knight, & Cerce, 1997), including length of exposure time, method of detecting recidivists, offenses included as *failures*, and legal definitions of failure (i.e., charge, arrest, conviction, reincarceration). In addition, other potentially critical risk-relevant sources of base rate variability include differences in age at release, exposure to institutional treatment, the depth and quality of the release plan, and the specifics of the state-enforced management plan (i.e., community notification).

Offender Heterogenity and Life Tables

Assumed taxonomic homogeneity extends to life tables. The accuracy of probabilistic estimates taken from actuarial life tables can be no better than the degree of similarity of the respondent to the offenders composing the reference groups used to derive the estimates. The more the respondent departs from the reference group in risk-relevant ways, the more unreliable and inaccurate the estimates are likely to be (Cohen, 1981). As Woodworth and Kadane (2004) noted,

> A probabilistic prediction is relevant to the fact-finders in a commitment hearing only if it is generalizable from the development data base to the respondent on trial. Generalizability depends on two elements—standardized ascertainment of risk factors and outcomes, and conditional exchangeability of the respondent with his matching subgroup of the development sample. (p. 237)

Estimates drawn from commonly used life tables and applied to juvenile sex offenders, female sex offenders, older sex offenders (e.g., over age 50), and exclusive, endogamous incest offenders are likely to overestimate risk, whereas life table estimates applied to highly psychopathic and/or serial sex offenders are likely to underestimate risk. This question of "match" is critical and is largely ignored.

Time Frame for Reoffending

Perhaps the single most assured source of methodological quicksand is the expectation of long-term forecast, occasionally expressed as "lifetime risk."

The "time frame problem" also happens to be the most elusive and least acknowledged problem. There is no statutory basis for lifetime risk, and it appears that courts have not clarified the time frame for prediction (Mossman, 2008). The *Ewoldt* case (*In re the Detention of Kenneth John Ewoldt*, 2001) addressed the question of a particular time frame for an offender's likelihood of re-offending, finding that the Iowa statute does not require proof that the respondent is likely to re-offend in any given time frame. Although the origin of "lifetime risk" is unclear, it appears that it was first raised in an article by Doren (1998), in which he finds that statutory silence around "time frames within which the prediction is to be confined, presumably [leaves] open the interpretation that the time frame of relevance is the offender's life time" (p. 100). Doren (2002) reasserted this position in his book, noting problems associated with a "purely actuarial model" of risk prediction, "since there are no actuarial instruments designed to assess people's lifetime sexual recidivism likelihood" (p. 113). Lifetime sexual recidivism can be estimated only with very long-term follow-up studies, which Doren (1998) favors over shorter follow-up studies, a position that was critiqued by Wollert (2001). The critical empirical question is whether "lifetime" risk can be assessed with any degree of reliability. Long-term risk places the predictive burden on the assumption of temporal stability of risk. Such an assumption is, for myriad reasons, highly questionable and must be scrutinized empirically.

Confidence Intervals and Prediction of Individual Cases

Researchers frequently use regression analysis to make specific predictions using a derived equation. Confidence intervals (CI) are used to quantify the uncertainty about such predictions. Although predictions can be made for individual values, they are typically made for the conditional mean. Simply stated, CIs are informative with respect to uncertainty of predictions made for the mean, not individuals. Statistical uncertainty about prediction increases as the squared distance between conditional mean and an individual value increases. For an individual case (i.e., when risk scales are used to inform an opinion about a respondent's relative degree of risk in a civil commitment trial), we must derive a *prediction interval*. A prediction interval will estimate the uncertainty of the prediction for one individual. Uncertainty of individual predictions is always larger than that for mean predictions (Kleinbaum, Kupper, Nizam, & Muller, 2008; Wittink, 1988). Mathematically, as well as intuitively, the population mean is more stable, more reliable, and more precise than the prediction of a single case. The use of CIs in supporting opinions in SVP cases is a matter of considerable debate within the field (Cooke & Michie, 2010; Hanson & Howard, 2010; Hart, Cooke, & Michie, 2007). Deriving, no less reporting, prediction intervals is not even visible on the radar screen. Clearly, the larger question concerning the statistical uncertainty of our predictions is an empirical issue that is both critical and urgent for the field.

We have reached something of an impasse with regard to risk assessment. The science of risk assessment is becoming increasingly inaccessible to most forensic clinicians. Partly due to the seemingly esoteric nature of much of the research and partly due to the narrow focus on risk assessment, we are returning to the halcyon days of clinical judgment, only now with a veneer of science (the Static-99). Although we agree with Thornton, Hanson, and Helmus (2010) that it is time to "move beyond the standard model" of actuarial risk assessment, we differ with regard to the end goal (Lamade, Coward, & Prentky, in press). Whereas Thornton et al. (2010) advocate incorporating long-term psychological risk factors, we have recommended a broader, structured idiographic approach that embraces a wider range of nomothetic input.

REMEDIATION AND MANAGEMENT

Remediation embraces a range of psychological and medical interventions designed to mitigate risk of sexual re-offense. Remediation includes conventional therapy provided both in prison and in the community, medication (typically in combination with therapy), and therapy in the context of after-care and release programs. Management includes statutory provisions, most notably civil commitment, registration, and community notification, as well as non-treatment components of release and aftercare programs, including polygraphy, random urine screens, surveillance (e.g., using GPS), and intensive probation with specially trained officers.

Polygraphy has been increasingly used during the past 40 years, primarily with sex offenders to deter re-offending and verify compliance with parole, and in treatment to overcome denial and encourage full disclosure of all victims. Given its widespread use, especially by agencies within the federal government, The National Research Council of the National Academy of Sciences initiated a Study to Review the Scientific Evidence on the Polygraph in January, 2001 and the final report was published in October, 2002 (Committee to Review the Scientific Evidence on the Polygraph, 2003). The Committee examined 57 studies to quantify the accuracy of polygraph testing, finding that "The quality of the studies varies considerably, but falls far short of what is desirable." The Committee further commented that "Polygraph research has not developed and tested theories of the underlying factors that produce the observed responses." The Committee concluded, however, that "Notwithstanding the limitations of the quality of the empirical research and the limited ability to generalize to real-world settings, we conclude that in populations of examinees such as those represented in the polygraph research literature, untrained in countermeasures, specific-incident polygraph tests can discriminate lying from truth telling at rates well above chance."

The Committee's recommendations included rigorous, empirical research that is *generalizable to real world applications*, national standards for training and certification, and national standardization of procedures. Moving from mock trials with non-offenders to "real-world" trials with known sex offenders is critical. One methodological hurdle in conducting such research, however, is that polygraph examinations will be done only by examiners who are already trained, imposing an added burden of controlling for procedures. The examiners should be "blind," and the subjects, both sex offenders and controls, should be randomly assigned.

Although conventional psychotherapy programs have been the focus of outcome studies, it must be emphasized that none of the aforementioned interventions, including therapy, are supported by clear evidence of efficacy. This can only be regarded as a yawning gap in the research. All of these interventions are used routinely, presumably as an article of faith that they must work. These interventions could easily be examined using randomized trials. It is reasonable to surmise that each of these interventions have variable efficacy under different conditions and when used with different types of offenders. Although we regard demonstrations of effectiveness to be essential for all interventions (e.g., GPS, polygraphy, different types of community notification, residency restrictions, intensive vs. conventional probation), we will focus our comments on what is arguably the most methodologically complex intervention: psychological treatment.

There are numerous factors that can influence the assessed effectiveness of treatment in lowering sexual recidivism rates, including the quality of the treatment program, treatment completion versus dropouts, provision of outpatient treatment, provision of a variety of other management strategies, and the age of the offenders. From a methodological standpoint, failure to resolve critical issues such as confidentiality, the mixed roles of clinicians as therapists and as "agents of the prison" (reporters of sensitive disclosures), and, as noted, the inability to evaluate effectively impact of treatment on offenders, severely undermine the reliability of a key piece of evidence that the courts appear to rely on (cf. Prentky, Gabriel, & Coward, 2011). How to detect treatment effects requires a rigorous research commitment. There is no alternative if we are to answer the most basic questions: Which offenders can most benefit from treatment? What are the optimal modes of treatment for different offenders? What are the optimal conditions for treatment to take place? The only answer, as Marques, Wiederanders, Day, Nelson, and van Ommeren (2005) would undoubtedly agree, is further research of uncompromising quality.

How such research on treatment efficacy should be carried out is itself methodologically challenging. We have elsewhere commented on the following methodological issues that are outlined in more detail including the following eight: In a prison environment (1) where the highest premium is placed on security, not therapy; (2) where the conditions for therapy are suboptimal (e.g., severe space limitations that often require relying on part-time staff, limited scheduling options, adapting to the ever-changing conditions of a prison environment, which may require canceling groups or other treatment activities on a moment's notice, maintaining staff morale in an environment that is often unsupportive of, or even hostile to treatment); (3) where it may be dangerous to be known in population as a sex offender (i.e., the "risk" for any offender to fully disclose or "come clean" around sensitive topics in a dangerous environment, wherein the process of treatment (opening up and becoming emotionally vulnerable) may be at odds with the process of survival); (4) where confidentiality cannot be assumed or ensured; (5) where the offenders are reluctant "customers;" (6) where therapists often are inadequately trained and supervised; (7) where program-related resources are limited and often restricted (e.g., inability to provide desired interventions, such as anti-androgen medication); and (8) where the "outcome" variable (survival after release) is determined only after a complex legal proceeding, *not* by programmatic considerations, the task of examining the efficacy of treatment services for sex offenders is *exceedingly* difficult (cf., Prentky, Gabriel, & Coward, 2011, pp. 126–127).

Of the numerous methodological challenges that arise, we will limit our attention to these: designing rigorous treatment programs, heterogeneity of sex offenders, relapse prevention programs, dialectical behavior therapy, the Risk-Needs-Responsivity model, restorative justice, and penile plethysmographic assessment.

DESIGNING RIGOROUS TREATMENT PROGRAMS

Given that most formal treatment programs for sex offenders are in prisons, the overarching task is to design a program, as well as its evaluation component, that at least minimally addresses the problems that may compromise efficacy. The program must comply with the standards for evidenced-based treatment (Prentky et al., in press a). Identifying such a program will prove very difficult, however, since programmatic needs are inversely related to custody needs (i.e., the higher the custody level, the lower the likelihood of compliance with treatment needs). Because sex offenders are invariably classified to medium, if not high, security, maintaining minimum standards of evidence-based treatment may prove daunting. At minimum, a treatment program must include the following elements: (a) it must be operated and run by staff that are empowered to make and to execute all programmatic decisions; (b) all service providers must be appropriately trained and supervised and not in dual or conflictual relationships with the men they treat; (c) the depth of resources must be adequate to respond to all the assessed needs of the men; (d) there must be independent, periodic appraisals of dynamic and protective risk; (e) there must be ongoing needs assessments that feed and adjust treatment plans; (f) treatment goals must be achievable and must be assessed with objective criteria; (g) program completion must be achievable within a reasonable time frame and must be determined with objective criteria. Arguably, community-based treatment may be the more likely venue to ensure the aforementioned elements. Designing rigorous treatment evaluation programs in the community is not only more feasible—it should be considered one of the highest priorities for researchers.

HETEROGENEITY OF SEX OFFENDERS

As discussed previously, the heterogeneity of sex offenders is well documented and widely accepted. The implications for treatment are obvious. It cannot be assumed that optimal treatment for sex offenders is, effectively, a one-size-fits-all program. Although any credible program will provide treatment plans for each offender that presumably addresses the needs of that offender, two obvious problems emerge. First, this "needs analysis" that leads to a treatment plan is typically accomplished by one or more clinical members of the treatment team and is often uninformed by the empiricism that taxonomic research could provide. Awareness of the "subtype" of sex offender (discussed previously) for whom a treatment plan is being drafted might inform that plan with objective feedback about what has worked for other members of that subgroup. Second, no matter how insightful and thoughtful the treatment plan, the interventions will be constrained by the limits of the program (e.g., no matter how much anti-androgen medication might help, if it is not offered by the program, the offender will not receive it). It is the first problem that we have control over and that must be addressed.

As we already noted, treatment for sex offenders generally takes one core form (relapse prevention or RP), and this model is applied across the boards to all offenders. This approach arguably yields suboptimal results. The ideal research agenda would tackle the question of taxonomic differentiation with regard to treatment. In other words, what are the optimal treatment interventions for each identified subtype of sex offender? This could be approached in two ways. A taxonomic model that has been designed and tested for other purposes (e.g., risk) could be tested for its utility in informing treatment. Alternatively, a taxonomic model could be constructed for the explicit purpose of informing treatment and tested accordingly.

RELAPSE PREVENTION PROGRAMS

Relapse prevention for use with sex offenders was adapted from an intervention intended for use with alcoholics (Marlatt & Gordon, 1985). The theory guiding its adaptation for sex offenders assumes that sexual offending behavior has identifiable triggers (with cognitive, emotional, and behavioral aspects) that must be identified and dealt with in healthy ways to interrupt the offense cycle (Pithers, Marques, Gibat, & Marlatt, 1983). Although the theory makes intuitive sense, there is an obvious need for research to investigate the utility of RP with this highly heterogeneous population. Ward and Hudson (1996) criticized the model for being too complex for use with many sex offenders and pointed out that the desire to change behavior is a necessary prerequisite for RP to be successful, which cannot be assumed to be the case with many sex offenders. In his review of RP programs with sex offenders, Launay (2001) made several suggestions to enhance efficacy: procedures should be in place to ensure that offenders are motivated for treatment at the outset, programs should be supplemented with additional behavioral therapy and drug treatment when indicated, offenders should be provided follow-up treatment upon release (ideally with the same therapists they saw during incarceration), and more information should be offered on how to deal with lapses should they occur (e.g., stress management training). Launay suggested finally that longitudinal research should be conducted to monitor problems that arise post-treatment.

The larger question, rather than focusing on RP, is whether the application of treatment services is in line with known standards for evidence-based clinical practice. Simply stated, can the threshold standards for effective therapy established in the general population be applied to sex-offender treatment programs? Although the answer, well beyond the scope of this chapter, was addressed in some detail in Prentky et al. (2011), the authors concluded that:

> application of an evidence-based metric to assess treatment of sex offenders in prison yields underwhelming results. The results are underwhelming principally because of (a) markedly suboptimal treatment conditions, and (b) failure to be empirically responsive by demonstrating the "evidence" part of evidence-based practice. . . . [F]or treatment to be effective in a prison environment, there must be a firewall separating the treatment program from security-related and court-related concerns. Evidence-based practice places emphasis on training. Specialized training and demonstrated areas of competency, unlike most other areas of clinical practice, have never been articulated for this niche of practice involving sex offenders. This, too, is a broad area of neglect. (p. 128)
>
> (*cf. Prentky, Gabriel, & Coward, 2011*).

DIALECTICAL BEHAVIOR THERAPY

A promising potential treatment modality is dialectical behavior therapy (DBT). DBT was originally developed by Linehan as a treatment for borderline personality disorder (BPD) and clients presenting with high-risk, self-harming behaviors. DBT goals have obvious applicability to use with a sex offender population. Shingler (2004) pointed out that both those diagnosed with BPD and sex offenders exhibit interpersonal, behavioral, emotional, cognitive, and self dysregulation. These overlapping etiological explanations lead to the logical conclusion that the therapy found to be most effective with a BPD population may translate to effective treatment of some sex offenders. Although DBT has been implemented with various populations, including forensic populations, few studies have examined the efficacy of DBT with sex offenders. The Twin Rivers Corrections Center (TRCC) (Monroe, WA) sex offender treatment program is one example of the adaptation of DBT for use with sex offenders. In the second phase of a two-phase treatment program, the TRCC implemented DBT group skills training in a community setting and found that it was effective in reducing impulsivity and increasing therapeutic alliance in high-risk offenders. These results did not translate to lower-risk offenders, and the authors cited various methodological confounds (Berzins &

Trestman, 2004). This study highlights the need for further research to test the potential efficacy of DBT, as well as other strategies for managing aversive affect and maladaptive affective responses in some sex offenders. The theoretical basis, empirical foundation, and clinical practice of DBT are supported by a voluminous literature. ScienceDirect lists no less than 659 articles in response to the key words *practice standards for DBT*. Procedures for establishing DBT interventions and methods for assessing the integrity of those interventions are well established, and researchers must implement them.

THE RISK-NEEDS-RESPONSIVITY MODEL

In a recent meta-analysis, Hanson, Bourgon, Helmus, and Hodgson (2009) reported that human service interventions that follow the principles of the risk-need-responsivity (RNR) model are "the most effective for general offenders" (p. 6) and that when treatment based on RNR principles is applied to sex offenders, recidivism rates (sexual and general) are significantly reduced. The RNR model, developed by Andrews and Bonta (Andrews & Bonta, 1998; Bonta & Andrews, 2007) for general offenders, proposes that the most intense treatment services be reserved for those at greatest risk (the risk), that treatment programs target those "criminogenic needs" with empirical support (the need), and that programs use only techniques with demonstrated responsivity (i.e., techniques that sex offenders are known to respond to). Hanson et al. (2009) reported that programs that adhered to RNR evidenced the largest reductions in both sexual and general recidivism and that effectiveness increased as the number of RNR principles adhered to increased. Hanson et al. (2009) noted, however, the weak design of the majority of studies used in their meta-analysis. Of the 23 studies included, 19 were rated "weak," 5 as "good," and only 1 as "strong," according to the Collaborative Outcome Data Committee (CODC) study quality guidelines for the evaluation of sex offender treatment outcome research (cf. Beech et al., 2007).

Hanson et al. further pointed out that there were no studies of medical interventions that met the criteria to be included in their analysis. Application of RNR principles in well-designed and well-executed treatment outcome studies would clearly be a high priority area for research. Treatment programs adhering to RNR principles have been adopted with successful outcomes in general prison populations around the world, and developing several large-scale applications of the model to sex offenders should be a high priority. Adherence to CODC guidelines is also recommended. The CODC guidelines, established by a committee of 12 clinical researchers, consist of 20 items organized into seven categories. The guidelines serve three purposes: (1) reviewing the quality of existing studies, (2) evaluating the quality of existing programs, and (3) designing new treatment outcome studies. CODC provides an excellent set of standards for anyone interested in designing a new study on treatment efficacy with sex offenders. The largest methodological obstacle will be institutional cooperation. As we have noted previously (item 1 in this list), the effective implementation of any non-custodial program in a custodial environment, including RNR, requires full "buy in" and cooperation on the part of the prison.

RESTORATIVE JUSTICE

A model that warrants attention with selected groups of sex offenders is restorative justice, which focuses on the harm caused by the crime primarily to the victim and secondarily to the community. Through mediation between victims and offenders, reparations, conferencing, and negotiation, restorative justice moves justice out of the courtroom and into the community (Rodriguez, 2007). The potential value of such a model for rehabilitating certain sexual offenders by requiring full accountability and full confrontation with victim impact needs to be explored. Moreover, the philosophy of restorative justice as applied to sexual offenses seeks justice for victims that would otherwise not be served by the traditional criminal justice system. Although Rodriguez (2007) points out that little is known about which offenders are likely to benefit from a restorative justice model, an innovative, victim-driven restorative justice program was developed for date and acquaintance rapists and non-penetration sex offenders (Koss, Bachar, & Hopkins, 2003). As noted, this is an expansive view of treatment that embraces the victim as well as the community, using community conferences to identify the harm and to develop plans to repair, rehabilitate, and reintegrate. For some offenders, such as juveniles, this may prove to be a far more effective intervention than community notification. Although clearly this is an area that merits empirical scrutiny, it will impose numerous challenges, primarily around galvanizing community support, securing "buy in" from all interested parties, and sustaining commitment, emotional as well as monetary, for a long time period.

PENILE PLETHYSMOGRAPHIC ASSESSMENT

We would be remiss if we neglected to comment on penile plethysmogaphic assessment (PPG). Although the forensic use of the PPG would have placed discussion in the section on risk assessment, the far more frequent use of the PPG is in the context of treatment. Indeed, there is a general consensus in the field that PPG assessments should *not* be done for forensic use (Murphy & Barbaree, 1994; Prentky & Burgess, 2000). The PPG is a medical device that quantifies an erectile response to auditory and visual stimuli depicting normative and deviant sexual themes. The PPG is used to assess sexual preference, primarily for child molesters, and sexual arousal to depictions of coercion and aggression in sexual acts, and sexual sadism. In the context of a treatment program, the PPG would be used to assess the presence of deviant sexual arousal and the changes in such arousal in response to covert sensitization and aversion therapy. Barker and Howell (1992) noted that the PPG is "the best objective measure of male sexual arousal, because blood flow to the genital area does not seem to be influenced by factors other than sexual eroticism" (p. 22).

The troubling downside to the PPG is the failure to adopt national standards. Although the Association for the Treatment of Sexual Abusers published *Guidelines for the Use of the Penile Plethysmograph* (ATSA, 1993), there is no evidence that these, or any other, standards have been widely adopted. From a methodological standpoint, we should be concerned about the lack of standardization of stimuli and procedures, the lack of standards for training and requirements for users, variable interpretations of the data, and the lack of norms, both for nonoffenders and subgroups of sexual offenders. When used in a forensic context, there are also serious ethical concerns, most notably, the overinterpretation of data and PPG-based predictions of a client's guilt or innocence.

COMMUNITY MANAGEMENT

Upon release from incarceration or the completion of remediation programs, most offenders will return to and reside in the community. Community-based management strategies include statutory provisions (e.g., registration, community notification, residency restrictions), treatment (typically sex offender group therapy, medication), and non-treatment components, such as polygraphy, random urine screens, surveillance (e.g., using GPS), and intensive probation monitoring with specially trained officers. Although the primary goal of prevention is the same in all states, methods for managing sex offenders vary by jurisdiction and local resources and practice. Not only will the program components (e.g., registration, community notification) and implementation of such components vary among programs, but there is also variation within programs, whereby components are used differently for different offenders. For example, although most jurisdictions employ some type of risk-classification system for community-notification purposes, how "low-risk" or "high-risk" offenders are treated may differ from state to state (Logan, 1999). All of these issues may pose challenges for researchers investigating management effectiveness, particularly in studies that seek to determine whether effectiveness results from particular characteristics of management programs or differences in consequence severity. Two primary issues for consideration in evaluating the effectiveness of outpatient management are community notification and residency restrictions.

COMMUNITY NOTIFICATION AND REGISTRATION

Schwartz (2003) summed up the problem succinctly by noting that, "Both public notification and involuntary commitment were passed with no thought to researching the effectiveness of such measures," (p. 377). Perhaps the single most urgent research question is whether civil commitment laws and community notification laws are effective in reducing recidivism and mitigating risk. A recent review by Cohen and Jeglic (2007) concluded,

> *Overall, the current legal methodologies for controlling sex offenders are unproven and very much under-researched. The notable lack of supporting research makes it difficult to discern the actual effectiveness of these methods, and it is clear that a great deal more research is necessary. . . . [T]he research on these methods has not been promising thus far. (p. 380)*

In addition, program variance across jurisdictions in terms of which offenders warrant community notification, how offenders are "tiered" (classified according to risk level), how risk level corresponds to the methods of notification imposed on the offender, the extent of disclosure, and the standards and procedures used to release the information, all undermine research efforts to examine efficacy. Moreover, community notification potentially leaves offenders vulnerable to harassment and victimization and heightened stress and substantially increases their difficulty reintegrating back into society (Levenson & Cotter, 2005). As Levenson and D'Amora (2007) cautioned, sex offender management policies, including community notification, "do not appear to be evidence based in their development and implementation because they are founded largely on myths rather than on facts" (p. 168). Since every state has a community-notification provision, it is imperative that these programs be empirically scrutinized with respect to efficacy.

RESIDENCY RESTRICTION

Several states have policies that prohibit sex offenders who have abused children from residing within close proximity to places where children congregate (e.g., schools, parks, day care centers, school bus stops, etc), with restrictions generally ranging from 500 to 2,000 feet (Levenson & Cotter, 2005). Although victim protection is paramount, concerns have been raised as to how these restrictions impact offenders' reintegration. For example, residency restrictions often result in limiting accessibility to treatment facilities, limiting employment options, limiting housing options, and increasing psychological isolation and distress (Levenson & Cotter, 2005), all of which may increase dynamic risk for further sexually deviant behavior. Levenson and Cotter (2005) examined a random sample of sex offenders drawn from two outpatient counseling centers in Florida and found that most sex offenders reported that residency restrictions increased isolation, created financial and emotional distress, and they did not perceive residency restrictions as helpful in risk management.

CONCLUSION

The current state of the art was summed up whimsically using Hans Christian Andersen's fable of *The Emperor's New Clothes*:

Like the king who appeared before his startled minions with transparent lack of attire, the fact finder is frequently confronted by expert testimony that is energetic in spirit but naked in substance. Like the king, the experts sport a well-tailored suit of opinions, which often are diaphanous. The net result is an expensive process that has a veneer of legal and scientific polish but ignores both the norms of a just society and the solid guidance that good science could furnish.

(Prentky, Janus, Barbaree, Schwartz, & Kafka, 2006, pp. 385–386)

Clearly, the enactment of statutory management strategies has far outpaced research. The research agenda that we have articulated is expansive but no more so than the magnitude of the problem. Sexual offenders will not disappear, nor will the problems associated with sexual aggression be assuaged by legislative fiat. The most productive and cost-efficient approach is one that will inform our interventions with empirical research. We have elsewhere recommended, and continue to recommend, a reconceptualization of the problem of sexual aggression and the adoption of a public health model (Prentky, 2003). Mercy and O'Carroll (1988) advised, over 20 years ago, "Injury resulting from interpersonal violence is now recognized as an important public health problem" (p. 285). Sexual aggression qualifies as *injury* resulting from *interpersonal* violence. A research program could be developed to design, implement, and pilot-test a public health model on a limited scale. Such an approach, although not as viscerally satisfying as a criminal model, may be more effective at addressing the root causes of sexual aggression, thereby reducing its incidence. Simply incarcerating and releasing known sex offenders will never achieve the ultimate goal of making society a safer haven for children and women.

REFERENCES

Abbey, A. (2006). Cross-sectional predictors of sexual assault perpetration in a community sample of single African American and Caucasian men. *Aggressive Behavior, 32*(1), 54–67.

American Psychiatric Association. (2000). *Diagnostic and Statistical Manual of Mental Disorders.* (4th ed.). Text Revision (DSM-IV-TR). Washington, DC: American Psychiatric Association.

Andrews, D. A., & Bonta, J. (1998) *The psychology of criminal conduct* (second edition). Cincinnati, OH: Anderson Publishing Co.

Association for the Treatment of Sexual Abusers (ATSA). (1993). The *ATSA practitioner's handbook.* Lake Oswego, OR: Author.

Barbaree, H. E. (1997). Evaluating treatment efficacy with sexual offenders: The insensitivity of recidivism studies to treatment effects. *Sexual Abuse: A Journal of Research and Treatment, 9*, 111–128.

Barbaree, H. E., & Blanchard, R. (2008). Sexual deviance over the lifespan: Reductions in deviant sexual behavior in the aging sex offender. In D. R. Laws & W. O'Donohue (Eds.), *Sexual deviance: Theory, assessment, and treatment* (2nd ed., pp. 37–60). New York, NY: Guilford Press.

Barbaree, H. E., Blanchard, R., & Langton, C. M. (2003). The development of sexual aggression through the lifespan: The effect of age on sexual arousal and recidivism among sex offenders. In R. Prentky, E. Janus, & M. Seto (Eds.), *Sexually coercive behavior. Understanding and management* (Vol. 989, pp. 59–71). New York, NY: Annals of the New York Academy of Sciences.

Barbaree, H. E., Langton, C. M., & Blanchard, R. (2007). Predicting recidivism in sex offenders using the VRAG and SORAG: The contribution of age-at-release. *International Journal of Forensic Mental Health, 6,* 29–46.

Barker, J. G., & Howell, R. J. (1992). The plethysmograph: A review of the recent literature. *Bulletin of the American Academy of Psychiatry and Law, 20,* 13–25.

Bechman, D. C. (2001, Summer). Sex offender civil commitments: Scientists or psychics? *Criminal Justice, 16*(24), 24–33.

Beech, T., Bourgon, G., Hanson, K., Harris, A., Langton, C., Marques, J., . . . Yates, P. (2007). *Sexual offender treatment outcome research: CODC guidelines for evaluation* (Cat. No.: PS4-38/1-2007E-PDF). Retrieved November 18, 2010, from http://www .publicsafety.gc.ca/res/cor/rep/codc-eng .aspx

Berzins, L. G., & Trestman, R. L. (2004). The development and implementation of Dialectical Behavior Therapy in forensic settings. *International Journal of Forensic Mental Health, 3*(1), 93–103).

Bonta, J., & Andrews, D. A. (2007). *Risk-need-responsivity model for offender assessment and rehabilitation* (Corrections Research User Report No. 2007-06). Ottawa, Ontario: Public Safety Canada.

Borum, R. (1996). Improving the clinical practice of violence risk assessment. *American Psychologist, 51,* 945–956.

Brennan, T. (1987). Classification: An overview of selected methodological issues. In D. M. Gottfredson & M. Tonry (Eds.), *Prediction and classification* (pp. 201–248), Chicago, IL: The University of Chicago Press.

Cohen, L. J. (1981). Are there any a priori constraints on the study of rationality? *Behavioral and Brain Sciences, 4,* 359–367.

Cohen, M., & Jeglic, E. L. (2007). Sex offender legislation in the United States: What do we know? *International Journal of Offender Therapy and Comparative Criminology, 51*(4), 369–383.

Committee to Review the Scientific Evidence on the Polygraph, National Research Council. (2003). *The polygraph and lie detection.* Washington, DC: The National Academies Press.

Community Protection Act of 1990. (Chapter 3, WA Laws of 1990).

Cooke, D. J., & Michie, C. (2010). Limitations of diagnostic precision and predictive utility in the individual case: A challenge for forensic practice. *Law and Human Behavior, 34,* 259–274.

Cortoni, F.A., & Marshall, W.L. (2001). Sex as a coping strategy and its relationship to juvenile sexual history and intimacy in sexual offenders. *Sexual Abuse: A Journal of Research and Treatment, 13,* 27–43.

Crowne, D. P., and Marlowe, D. (1964). *The approval motive: Studies in evaluation dependence.* New York, NY: Wiley.

Dean, K., & Malamuth, N. (1997). Characteristics of men who aggress sexually and of men who imagine aggressing: Risk and moderating variables. *Journal of Personality and Social Psychology 7,* 449–455.

DeBellis, M. D., Baum, A. S., Birmaher, B., Keshavan, M. S., Eccard, C. H., Boring, A. M., . . . Ryan, N. D. (1999a). Developmental traumatology. Part I: Biological stress systems. *Biological Psychiatry, 45*(10), 1259–1270.

DeBellis, M. D., Keshavan, M. S., Clark, D. B., Casey, B. J., Giedd, J. N., Boring, A. M., . . . Ryan, N. D. (1999b). Developmental traumatology. Part II: Brain development. *Biological Psychiatry, 45*(10), 1272–1284.

Doren, D. M. (1998). Recidivism base rates, predictions of sex offender recidivism, and the "sexual predator" commitment laws. *Behavioral Sciences and the Law, 16,* 97–114.

Doren, D. M. (2002). *Evaluating sex offenders. A manual for civil commitments and beyond.* Thousand Oaks, CA: Sage.

Douglas, J. E., Burgess, A. W., Burgess, A. G., & Ressler, R. K. (1992). *A crime classification manual: A standard system for investigating and classifying violent crime.* New York, NY: Simon & Schuster.

Douglas, K. S., and Skeem, J. L. (2005). Violence risk assessment: Getting specific about being dynamic. *Psychology, Public Policy, and Law, 11,* 347–383.

Epperson, D. L., Kaul, J. D., & Hesselton, D. (1998). *Final report on the development of the Minnesota Sex Offender Screening Tool-Revised (MnSOST-R).* St. Paul, MN: Minnesota Department of Corrections.

Fazel, S., Sjostedt, G., & Langstrom, N. (2006). Risk factors for criminal recidivism in older sexual offenders. *Sexual Abuse: A Journal of Research and Treatment, 18*(2), 159–167.

Finkelhor, D., Araji, S., Baron, L., Browne, A., Peters, S. D., & Wyatt, G. E. (1986).

A sourcebook on child sexual abuse. Newbury Park, CA: Sage.

Garland, R. J., & Dougher, M. J. (1990). The abused-abuser hypothesis of child sexual abuse: A critical review of theory and research. In J. R. Feierman (Ed.), *Pedophilia: Biosocial dimensions* (pp. 488–509). New York, NY: Springer-Verlag.

Gookin, K. (2007, August). *Comparison of state laws authorizing involuntary commitment of sexually violent predators: 2006 update* (Document No. 07-08-1101). Olympia, WA: Washington State Institute for Public Policy.

Grisso, T., & Tomkins, A. J. (1996). Communicating violence risk assessments. *American Psychologist*, 51, 928–930.

Hall, G. C. N., Teten, A. L., DeGarmo, D. S., Sue, S., & Stephens, K. A. (2005). Ethnicity, culture, and sexual aggression: Risk and protective factors. *Journal of Consulting and Clinical Psychology*, 73(5), 830–840.

Hanson, R. K. (2002). Recidivism and age: Follow-up data on 4,673 sexual offenders. *Journal of Interpersonal Violence*, 17, 1046–1062.

Hanson, R. K. (2006). Does Static-99 predict recidivism among older sexual offenders? *Sexual Abuse: A Journal of Research and Treatment*, 18(4), 343–355.

Hanson, R. K., Bourgon, G., Helmus, L., & Hodgson, S. (2009). The principles of effective correctional treatment also apply to sexual offenders: A meta-analysis. *Criminal Justice and Behavior*, 36(9), 865–891.

Hanson, R. K., & Howard, P. D. (2010). Individual confidence intervals do not inform decision-makers about the accuracy of risk assessment evaluations. *Law and Human Behavior*, 34, 275–281.

Hanson, R. K., & Thornton, D. (1999). *Static 99: Improving actuarial risk assessment for sex offenders* (User Report No. J2-165/1999). Ottawa, Canada: Public Works and Government Services Canada.

Hanson, R. K., & Thornton, D. (2003). *Notes on the development of Static-2002* (Cat. No. JS42-116/2002). Ottawa, Canada: Public Works and Government Services Canada.

Hart, S. D., Cooke, D. J., & Michie, C. (2007). Precision of actuarial risk assessment instruments: Evaluating the "margins of error" of group v. individual predictions of violence. *British Journal of Psychiatry*, 190, 60–65.

Heilbrun, K., Nezu, C. M., Keeney, M., Chung, S., & Wasserman, A. L. (1998).

Sexual offending: Linking assessment, intervention, and decision-making. *Psychology, Public Policy, and Law*, 4, 138–174.

In re the Detention of Kenneth John Ewoldt, State of Iowa, Appellee vs. Kenneth John Ewoldt, Appellant. No. 92/00-0792. Supreme Court of Iowa. (634 N.W.2d 622; 2001 Iowa Sup. LEXIS 180).

In re Roberto Valdez, Case No. 99-000045CI, et al., Cir. Ct. of the Sixth Judicial Cir. (Pasco and Pinellas Counties, Florida, August 21, 2000).

Kafka, M. P. (1997). Hypersexual desire in males: An operational definition and clinical implications for males with paraphilias and paraphilia-related disorders. *Archives of Sexual Behavior*, 26(5), 505–521.

Kafka, M. P. (2003). The monoamine hypothesis for the pathophysiology of paraphilic disorders: An update. In R. A. Prentky, E. S. Janus, & M. C. Seto (Eds.), *Sexually coercive behavior: Understanding and management* (pp. 86–94). Annals of the New York Academy of Sciences, Vol. 989. New York, NY: New York Academy of Sciences.

Kafka, M. P., & Hennen, J. (2003). Hypersexual desire in males: Are males with paraphilias different from males with paraphilia-related disorders? *Sexual Abuse: A Journal of Research and Treatment*, 15(4), 307–323.

Kaufman, J., & Zigler, E. (1987). Do abused children become abusive parents? *American Journal of Orthopsychiatry*, 57, 186–192.

Kempe, R. S., & Kempe, C. H. (1984). *The common secret: Sexual abuse of children and adolescents*. New York, NY: W. H. Freeman.

Kleinbaum, D. G., Kupper, L. L., Nizam, A., & Muller, K. E. (2008). *Applied regression analysis and other multivariable methods*. (4th Ed.) Pacific Grove, CA: Thomson Brooks/Cole.

Knight, R. A., Carter, D. L., & Prentky, R. A. (1989). A system for the classification of child molesters: Reliability and application. *Journal of Interpersonal Violence*, 4, 3–23.

Knight, R. A., & Prentky, R. A. (1990). Classifying sexual offenders: The development and corroboration of taxonomic models. In W. L. Marshall, D. R. Laws, & H. E. Barbaree (Eds.), *The handbook of sexual assault* (pp. 23–52). New York, NY: Plenum Press.

Knight, R. A., Rosenberg, R., & Schneider, B. (1985). Classification of sexual offenders: Perspectives, methods and validation. In A. Burgess (Ed.), *Rape and sexual assault: A research handbook* (pp. 222–293). New York, NY: Garland.

Knight, R. A., & Sims-Knight, J. E. (2003). The development antecedents of sexual coercion against women in adolescents. In R. Geffner & K. Franey (Eds.), *Sex offenders: Assessment and treatment*. New York, NY: Haworth Press.

Koss, M. P., Bachar, K. J., & Hopkins, C. Q. (2003). Restorative justice for sexual violence: Repairing victims, building community, and holding offenders accountable. *Annals of New York Academy of Science, 989*, 384–396.

Kurlychek, M. C., Brame, R., & Bushway, S. D. (2007). Enduring risk? Old criminal records and predictions of future criminal involvement. *Crime & Delinquency, 53*(1), 64–83.

Lamade, R., Coward, A., & Prentky, R. A. (in press). Optimizing risk mitigation in management of sexual offenders: A structural model. *International Journal of Psychiatry and the Law.*

Lanyon, R. I. (1986). Theory and treatment in child molestation. *Journal of Consulting and Clinical Psychology, 54*, 176–182.

Launay, G. (2001). Relapse prevention with sex offenders: Practice, theory and research. *Criminal Behaviour and Mental Health, 11*, 38–54.

Levenson, J. S., & Cotter, L. P. (2005). The impact of sex offender residency restrictions: 1,000 feet from danger or step from absurd? *International Journal of Offender Therapy and Comparative Criminology, 49* (2), 168–178.

Levenson, J. S., & D'Amora, D. A. (2007). Social policies designed to prevent sexual violence. The Emperor's New Clothes? *Criminal Justice Policy Review, 18*, 168–199.

Logan, W. A. (1999). Liberty interests in the preventive state: Procedural due process and sex offender community notification laws. *Journal of Criminal Law and Criminology, 89*(4), 1167–1231.

Malamuth, N. (1998). The Confluence Model as an organizing framework for research on sexually aggressive men: Risk moderators, imagined aggression and pornography consumption. In R. Geen & E. Donnerstein (Eds.), *Aggression: Theoretical and empirical reviews.* (pp. 229–245). New York, NY: Academic Press.

Malamuth, N. (2003). Risk assessment: Discussion of the section. In R. A. Prentky, E. Janus, & M. Seto (Eds.), *Understanding and managing sexually coercive behavior. Annals of the New York Academy of Sciences* (Vol. 989, pp. 236–238) New York, NY: New York Academy of Sciences.

Malamuth, N., Linz, D., Heavey, C., Barnes, G., & Acker, M. (1995). Using the confluence model of sexual aggression to predict men's conflict with women: A ten year follow-up study. *Journal of Personality and Social Psychology, 69*, 353–369.

Marlatt, G. A., & Gordon, J. R. (Ed.). (1985). *Relapse prevention: Maintenance strategies in the treatment of addictive behaviors.* New York, NY: Guilford Press.

Marques, J. K., Wiederanders, M., Day, D. M., Nelson, C., & van Ommeren, A. (2005). Effects of a relapse prevention program on sexual recidivism: Final results from California's Sex Offender Treatment and Evaluation Project (SOTEP). *Sexual Abuse: A Journal of Research & Treatment, 17*(1), 79–107.

Marshall, W.L. (1993). The role of attachment, intimacy, and loneliness in the etiology and maintenance of sexual offending. *Sexual and Marital Therapy, 8*, 109–121.

Marshall, W. L., Hudson, S. M., & Hodkinson, S. (1993). The importance of attachment bonds in the development of juvenile sex offending. In H. E. Barbaree, W. L. Marshall, & S. M. Hudson (Eds.), *The juvenile sex offender* (pp. 164–181). New York, NY: Guilford Press.

Marshall, W.L., Serran, G.A., & Cortoni, F.A. (2000). Childhood attachments, sexual abuse, and their relationship to adult coping in child molesters. *Sexual Abuse: A Journal of Research and Treatment, 12*, 17–26.

Martin, A. F., Vergeles, M. R., Acevedo, V. L., Sanchez, A. C., & Visa, S. L. (2005). The involvement in sexual coercive behaviors of Spanish college men: Prevalence and risk factors. *Journal of Interpersonal Violence, 20*(7), 872–891.

Meehl, P. E., & Rosen, A. (1955). Antecedent probability and the efficiency of psychometric signs, patterns, or cutting scores. *Psychological Bulletin, 52*, 194–216.

Mercy, J. A., & O'Carroll, P. W. (1988). New directions in violence prediction: The public health arena. *Violence and Victims, 3*, 285–301.

Miyazaki, Y., & Raudenbush, S. W. (2000). Tests for linkage of multiple cohorts in an accelerated longitudinal design. *Psychological Methods, 5*(1), 44–63.

Monahan, J., and Wexler, D. (1978). A definite maybe: Proof and probability in civil commitment. *Law and Human Behavior, 2*, 37–42.

Mossman, D. (2008). Analyzing the performance of risk assessment instruments: A response to Vrieze and Grove (2007). *Law and Human Behavior, 32*, 279–291.

Mulvey, E. P., and Lidz, C. W. (1995). Conditional prediction: A model for research on dangerousness to others in a new era. *International Journal of Law and Psychiatry, 18*, 129–143.

Murphy, W. D., & Barbaree, H. E. (1994). *Assessments of sexual offenders by measures of erectile response: Psychometric properties and decision making*. Brandon, VT: Safer Society Press.

Otto, R. K. (2000). Assessing and managing violence risk in outpatient settings. *Journal of Clinical Psychology, 56*, 1239–1262.

Pithers, W. D., Marques, J. K., Gibat, C. C., & Marlatt, G. A. (1983). Relapse prevention with sexual aggressive: A self-control model of treatment and maintenance of change. In J. G. Greer & I. R. Stuart (Eds.), *The sexual aggressor: Current perspectives on treatment* (pp. 214–239). New York, NY: Van Nostrand Reinhold.

Prentky, R. A. (1999). Child sexual molestation. In M. Hersen & V. Van Hasselt (Eds.), *Handbook of psychological approaches with violent offenders: Contemporary strategies and issues* (pp. 267–300). New York, NY: Kluwer.

Prentky, R.A. (2003). A 15-year retrospective on sexual coercion: Advances and projections. *Sexually Coercive Behavioral Understanding and Management, 989*. The New York Academy of Sciences, New York, NY.

Prentky, R. A., & Burgess, A. W. (2000). *Forensic management of sexual offenders*. New York, NY: Kluwer Academic/Plenum Press.

Prentky, R. A., & Burgess, A. W. (1991). Hypothetical biological substrates of a fantasy-based drive mechanism for repetitive sexual aggression. In A. W. Burgess (Ed.), *Rape and sexual assault III* (pp. 235–256). New York, NY: Garland.

Prentky, R. A., Coward, A., & Gabriel, A. (2008). Muddy diagnostic waters in the SVP courtroom: A reply to First & Halon. *Journal of the American Academy of Psychiatry and the Law, 36*(4), 455–458.

Prentky, R. A., Gabriel, A., & Coward, A. (2010). Sexual abuse. In J. C. Thomas & M. Hersen (Eds.), *Handbook of clinical psychology competencies. Vol. II: Intervention and treatment for adults* (pp. 1063–1094). New York, NY: Springer.

Prentky, R. A., Gabriel, A., & Coward, A. (2011). Sex offender services: Efficacy, obstacles, public policy. In J. W. White, M. P. Koss, & A. E. Kazdin (Eds.), *Violence against women and children: Navigating solutions*. (Vol. 2, pp. 115–135). Washington, DC: American Psychological Association.

Prentky, R. A., Janus, E., Barbaree, H., Schwartz, B., & Kafka, M. (2006). Sexually violent predators in the courtroom: Science on trial. *Psychology, Public Policy, & Law, 12*(4), 357–393.

Prentky, R. A., & Knight, R. A. (1991). Identifying critical dimensions for discriminating among rapists. *Journal of Consulting and Clinical Psychology, 59*(5), 643–661.

Prentky, R. A., Knight, R. A., Sims-Knight, J., Straus, H., Rokous, F., & Cerce, D. (1989). Developmental antecedents of sexual aggression. *Development and Psychopathology, 1*(2), 153–169.

Prentky, R. A., & Lee, A. F. S. (2007). Effect of age-at-release on long-term sexual re-offense rates in civilly committed sexual offenders, *Sexual Abuse: A Journal of Research and Treatment, 19*(1), 43–59.

Prentky, R. A., Lee, A. F. S., Knight, R. A., & Cerce, D. (1997). Recidivism rates among child molesters and rapists: A methodological analysis. *Law and Human Behavior, 21*, 635–659.

Quinsey, V. L., Harris, G. T., Rice, M. E., & Cormier, C. A. (1998). *Violent offenders: Appraising and managing risk*. Washington, DC: American Psychological Association.

Rodriguez, N. (2007). Restorative justice at work: Examining the impact of restorative justice resolutions on juvenile recidivism. *Crime Delinquency, 53*(3), 355–379.

Rogers, C. M., & Terry, T. (1984). Clinical interventions with boy victims of sexual abuse. In I. Stuart & J. Greer (Eds.), *Victims of sexual aggression* (pp. 91–104). New York, NY: Van Nostrand Reinhold.

Saunders, D. G. (1991). Procedures for adjusting self-reports of violence for social desirability bias. *Journal of Interpersonal Violence, 6*(3), 336–344.

Schwartz, B. K. (2003). Overview of rehabilitative efforts in understanding and managing sexually coercive behaviors. In R. Prentky, E. S. Janus, & M. C. Seto (Eds.), *Sexually coercive behavior: Understanding* and management (pp. 360–383). New York, NY: New York Academy of Sciences.

Shingler, J. (2004). A process of cross-fertilization: What sex offender treatment can learn from dialectical behaviour therapy. *Journal of Sexual Aggression*, 10(2), 171–180.

Smallbone, S. W., & Dadds, M. R. (2000). Child attachment & coercive sexual behaviors. *Sexual Abuse: A Journal of Research and Treatment*, 12(1), 3–15.

Teicher, M.H. (2000). Wounds that time won't heal: The neurobiology of child abuse. *Cerebrum: The Dana Farber Forum on Brain Science*, 2(4) 50–67.

Teicher, M. H. (2002). Scars that won't heal: The neurobiology of child abuse. *Scientific American*, 283(3), 68–75.

Thornton, D. (2006). Age and sexual recidivism: A variable connection. *Sexual abuse: A journal of research and treatment*, 18(2), 123–135.

Thornton, D., Hanson, R. K., & Helmus, L. (2010, Summer). Moving beyond the standard model for actuarial assessment for sexual offenders. *ATSA Forum*, XXII(3).

Ward, T., & Hudson, S. M. (1996). Relapse prevention: a critical analysis. *Sexual Abuse: A Journal of Research and Treatment*, 8, 177–200.

Ward, T., Hudson, S. M., & Marshall, W. L. (1996). Attachment style in sex offenders: A preliminary study. *Journal of Sex Research*, 33, 17–26.

Ward, T., Hudson, S. M., Marshall, W. L., & Siegert, R. (1995). Attachment style and intimacy deficits in sexual offenders: A theoretical framework. *Sexual Abuse: A Journal of Research and Treatment*, 7, 317–335.

Wittink, D. R. (1988). *The application of regression analysis*. Boston, MA: Allyn and Bacon.

Wollert, R. (2001). An analysis of the argument that clinicians under-predict sexual violence in civil commitment cases. *Behavioral Sciences and the Law*, 19, 171–184.

Woodworth, G. G., & Kadane, J. (2004). Expert testimony supporting post-sentence civil incarceration of violent sex offenders. *Law, Probablility and Risk*, 3, 221–241.

CHAPTER 20

Special Populations:
Juvenile Offenders

KEITH R. CRUISE AND EKATERINA PIVOVAROVA

INTRODUCTION

Since the inception of juvenile courts over 100 years ago, philosophical shifts reflecting rehabilitation and punishment have influenced the types of research conducted within the juvenile justice system. To illustrate, in the landmark case of *In re Gault* (1967), the U.S. Supreme Court called into question whether the broad goals of rehabilitation were being achieved by the juvenile justice system in extending key due process protections to juveniles during adjudication hearings. The Court's concern regarding the failure of the rehabilitation model was reflected in Martinson's (1974) review of juvenile justice rehabilitation programs, which exemplified the *nothing works* philosophy in stating "with few isolated exceptions the rehabilitative efforts that have been reported so far have no appreciable effect on recidivism" (p. 25).

Methodological criticisms (see Gendreau & Ross, 1979) served as a catalyst for a series of subsequent meta-analyses that have reached a more optimistic conclusion regarding the effectiveness of rehabilitation programs. In addition, the legislative shift toward a more punitive juvenile justice system in the 1980s, and the concomitant adultification of juvenile courts influenced a line of research addressing adolescent legal decision-making capacities in areas such as juveniles' understanding of rights in interrogation and juvenile competence to stand trial.

Current research with juvenile offenders continues to focus on rehabilitation. For example, major research efforts have focused on the development and validation of intervention programs tested via randomized clinical trials and effectiveness field trials, with models to guide program dissemination and transportability studies. Finally, in limiting the application of capital sentencing to criminal defendants above the age of 18, the Supreme Court's recent recognition that adolescents are "categorically less culpable" than adult offenders (see Roper v. Simmons, 2005), reflects the greater efforts being made in the field toward incorporating a developmental focus into research addressing forensic assessment issues, including studies investigating patterns of persistence and desistance of offending behaviors and maturational changes.

There are unique methodological challenges to overcome when conducting research with juvenile offenders. Despite these challenges, readers will find that incorporating research methods commonly used within studies of adult offenders (discussed elsewhere in this volume) are appropriate and effective with juvenile offenders (i.e., methods used to design prospective studies investigating the predictive utility of risk assessment procedures). Our goal in this chapter is to broadly address unique methodological issues that arise in the context of research with juvenile offenders. We have divided the chapter into sections that address broad sampling issues, consent and assent, assessment, treatment, and finally additional ethical issues that are commonly encountered within juvenile offender research. When possible, we offer illustrative studies that exemplify sound methodological standards that can guide navigating these issues in future studies.

THE JUVENILE JUSTICE SYSTEM AND SAMPLE SELECTION ISSUES

The juvenile justice system has been around for little more than 100 years, and the structure of the system has been driven by a combination of state and local statutory authority. As with the adult criminal justice system, there are multiple points of contact with progression through the juvenile justice system, driven by legal decision makers with unique diversionary routes out of the system. The process begins at referral, most commonly done by law enforcement (i.e., arrest), and moves to intake, detention, possible transfer (waiver), adjudication, disposition, and finally dispositional review. Studies with juvenile offenders are conducted across each point of the system (detention, community supervision/probation, residential/correctional treatment settings). The combination of state and local control and multiple decision makers (police, probation, courts) precludes uniform processing procedures across jurisdictions. As a result, failure to thoroughly investigate processing procedures within a given jurisdiction can result in well-meaning researchers ignoring a serious external validity threat that will limit the generalizability of study findings, given how processing decisions can impact sample selection.

For example, in 2005, approximately 1.7 million delinquency cases were processed in the juvenile courts in the United States, with formal filing of petitions in only 56% of the cases (Sickmund, 2009). Of petitioned cases, 623,900 (66%) cases were adjudicated with 140,100 (22%) resulting in placement, 373,400 (60%) resulting in probation, and 110,400 (18%) cases involving "other sanctions." Accordingly, sampling from juvenile offenders in placements is a gross misrepresentation of juvenile offenders across the system, as placed youth were only 8% of total cases, 15% of cases resulting in formal charges/petitions being filed, and 22% resulting in delinquent adjudications. Demographic differences involving gender, age, and race across processing points also impact sampling characteristics.

Proportionately, male youth represented 73% of all cases handled in 2005, compared to 27% for female youth (Sickmund, 2009). Despite the much smaller proportion of female youth (27% or 464,700 cases), the 2005 percentage is more than double the number of females involved in juvenile court cases in 1985, indicating that formal identification of female youth within the juvenile justice system is increasing at a higher rate than for male youth (32% increase in cases for males between 1985 and 2005). From 1985 to 2005, greater proportions of female youth were identified across person, property, drug, and public order offenses.

Historically, researchers have discounted female youth in studies of juvenile delinquency due to the "tyranny of small numbers"; however, via analysis of multiple juvenile crime data sets, Tracy, Kempf-Leonard, and Abramoske-James (2009) have concluded that despite differences in overall proportion within a given year, trends across time indicate that female and male juvenile offenders possess more similarities than differences in terms of arrest rates, juvenile court processing, and placement in juvenile corrections. Thus, given greater proportions of female youth within the system, researchers can neither ignore the sampling of gender nor consider delinquent acts committed by females to be categorically less serious than the behaviors of male youth.

Comparative studies and gender-specific investigations are warranted, particularly given the numerous questions that exist in the literature on issues related to the development of female aggression, risk assessment, and effectiveness of therapeutic interventions for female juvenile offenders (see Odgers & Moretti, 2002). However, greater gender consistency at the national level does not preclude gender disparity at the local level. Local processing practices may still differentially impact female versus male youth, preventing equal sampling of genders at specific points within the system. When considering the inclusion of both male and female youth in a particular sample, investigators need to thoroughly investigate the processing decision-points within the jurisdiction to ensure that any gender differences that emerge are not spurious findings that are attributed to system variables.

Investigators have long been aware of racial disparities within the juvenile justice system, with the term *disproportionate minority contact* (DMC) being used to describe the greater proportion of juvenile minorities within the system relative to the proportion found in the general population (Cabaniss, Frabutt, Kendrick, & Arbuckle, 2007). Black youth are especially at risk for being overrepresented within the system, representing 33% of juvenile court cases yet accounting for only 17% of the U.S. juvenile population (Sickmund, 2009).

Furthermore, the overall drop in crime rates since 1994 has not been reflected evenly across race groups, such that the number of cases processed for Black youth continue to be significantly higher than those for White and other racial groups.

The literature suggests that both differential involvement of minority youth in criminal activities and biased processing of minority juveniles by court officers are factors contributing to DMC (Leiber & Fox, 2005). A full examination of methodologies used to investigate DMC is beyond the scope of this chapter. However, researchers are encouraged to monitor research reports documenting the extent of DMC, including the effectiveness of strategies at the national and local levels to reduce DMC, as the ability to disentangle the source of race effects (i.e., true race differences versus system processing effects or a combination of both) within a given study is complicated. As noted by Kempf-Leonard (2007), convenience sampling that employs simple main-effect comparisons of juvenile offenders by race is insufficient, given what we know about DMC.

The age range of juvenile court jurisdiction is statutorily defined, can vary across states, and is impacted by mandatory waiver provisions for specific crimes that can influence the age range of juvenile offenders found in a given study. The typical age range of juvenile offender samples is 12 to 17 with a mean of 15. However, a significant proportion of youth also enter the system either before or after the general age range, which can vary across states and types of crimes. These unique state-level differences can impact the generalizability of study findings. For example, in 2004 data indicated that a small number of states including Maryland, Massachusetts, and New York consider children as young as 7 to be eligible for prosecution in juvenile justice courts. Alternatively, in the same year, 34 states had statutes extending juvenile jurisdiction over youths ages 18 and above, with some states (e.g., California, Montana, and Oregon) holding authority over offenders up to their 24th birthday.

Recent studies in legal decision-making capacities have consistently found important age differences, in that youth below age 13 performed significantly worse on measures of trial competence and decisions regarding Miranda rights (see Grisso et al., 2003; Viljoen, Zapf, & Roesch, 2007). Given these findings, it is critical to include adequate representation of youth in the lower age range to ensure the generalizability and stability of age-related findings across studies. Sampling strategies that employ over-sampling of juvenile offenders in the 11-to-13-year-old range will often be required to ensure balanced numbers of juvenile offenders across age groups such that age effects are not estimated on a small number of younger offenders relative to older juvenile offenders. Biased sampling of age groups is not limited to the lower age range of the juvenile justice system. Investigators must also be aware that youth "age out" of the system, with this age demarcation varying across jurisdictions. Longitudinal designs that rely on collection of official court records to obtain recidivism data need to take account of the maximum age of juvenile court jurisdiction, since obtaining outcome data may require establishing cooperative data access agreements with both the juvenile and adult court systems (see Schubert et al., 2004, for a thorough discussion of data tracking and retention strategies in longitudinal studies of juvenile offenders).

Just as there are unique points of processing that can influence sample generalizability, there are similar challenges to defining groups based on type of juvenile crime. For example, a unique element of the juvenile justice system is designation of status offenders referencing youth who are adjudicated for conduct that would not be considered a crime if committed by an adult (e.g., truancy, running away from home, curfew violations). Research samples of status offenders can imply a less serious form and course of delinquent behavior given that status offenders may be diverted out of traditional juvenile court processing, reside in community settings, and typically include a younger age range. The logical assumption is that samples of status offending youth differ from samples of other delinquent groups on emotional, behavioral, and familial characteristics.

However, Feld (2009) recently highlighted that the demarcation between status offenses and delinquency is imprecise and impacted by system-level decision making. Drawing on trends in arrest rates for assault, Feld's analysis revealed that jurisdictions appear to be circumventing federal status offense diversion mandates by redefining behaviors that traditionally were charged as status offenses to delinquent acts. Further, he found that this pattern disproportionately affects female youth in that intrafamilial conflicts that formerly would have resulted in an "incorrigible" status offense charge are more likely to be charged as simple or aggravated assault. Therefore, studies that seek to define sample groups based on the status offender/juvenile offender distinction may result in sampling groups with greater within-group heterogeneity and diminished between-group homogeneity that systematically varies by gender.

INFORMED CONSENT

There are a number of excellent resources that discuss both ethical principles and regulatory standards involving informed consent in social science research. When research involves children as participants, the informed consent process generally involves providing both parents and youth with information regarding the research procedures, addressing appropriate confidentiality protections, outlining risks and potential benefits, and allowing for an individual/voluntary choice regarding participation. Bruzzese and Fisher (2003) concluded that adolescents are more likely to be able to make competent decisions regarding research participation than preadolescent children; however, there are multiple challenges that arise in meeting the standard of full parental consent and youth assent in research involving juvenile offenders.

First, under the federal guidelines, investigators must carefully review multiple subsections for research with vulnerable populations including protections for children involved in research (see 45 CFR §§ 46.401–46.409; DHHS, 2005) and protections for research involving prisoners (45 CFR § 46.301–306; DHHS, 2005) when a study involves juvenile offenders who are involuntarily confined or detained. Disclosure of protected health information by covered entities under the Health Insurance Portability and Accountability Act (HIPAA: Public Law 104-191) must also be consulted to determine the types and level of informed consent and youth assent that will be required for a given study. Second, individual states may have varying statutory consent categories regarding adolescent health-care decision making (i.e., some states allow adolescents to seek specific forms of health care without parental consent) that may or may not address age standards for consenting to behavioral health research. For example, if a study with juvenile offenders involves access to substance abuse treatment services or testing for sexually transmitted diseases, relevant health-care decision-making statutes must be consulted to determine how such standards will inform the requirements for parental consent and youth assent procedures. Third, the researcher must consider the custodial status of youth participants and identify whether a parent/guardian or juvenile justice agency representative has the legal authority to provide permission for possible research involvement. Given the combination of federal and state law, researchers will find that designing and implementing informed consent procedures generally involves consultation and contact with juvenile justice administrators, child welfare agency representatives, and parent/guardians, with no uniform standards being applicable across types of studies.

Fourth, the level and extent of access to parents/guardians must also be considered. For example, brief lengths of stay (i.e., generally three to seven days in short-term detention centers) may not allow researchers enough time to obtain full parental consent and recruit youth participants prior to discharge. Even when lengths of stay are longer, samples obtained via other types of out-of-home placement settings (i.e., residential treatment centers or long-term secure custody institutions) will generally not facilitate direct contact between researchers and parents in order to obtain written parental consent. Barriers involving brief lengths of stay, extra effort required to obtain active parent consent, and additional recruitment strategies can increase the likelihood of sample selection bias and substantially raise study costs. Relative to youth in community settings, youth in the juvenile justice system also have a higher prevalence of mental health disorders (Shufelt & Cocozza, 2006) and higher rates of learning disabilities (Eggleston, 2008) that must be considered when developing youth assent procedures. These concerns, coupled with evidence suggesting that high-delinquent youths have diminished psychosocial maturity relative to low-delinquent youth (see Modecki, 2007), are all potential sources of additional vulnerabilities that must be considered in designing an ethical youth assent process. Given the discussion thus far, it is not unreasonable to consider whether the identified barriers and issues can be adequately addressed. The large number of studies conducted with juvenile offenders across different settings suggests that the clear answer to this is yes. However, we acknowledge that the typical length of text devoted to the "informed consent" process in most published research reports provides researchers with little guidance as to how this process is achieved. Therefore, we offer the following suggestions for developing informed-consent procedures.

First, given the youth vulnerabilities noted previously, it is critical that the length and reading level of youth assent forms are commensurate with the typical reading level and language capacities found in juvenile justice populations. We recommend writing assent forms between a third- and sixth-grade reading level to achieve maximum comprehension across possible participants. Most word processors can quickly and efficiently provide readability statistics, such as the Flesch Kincaid (Flesch, 1950). We know of no study that has documented average readability of either parental consent or youth assent forms used in research protocols with juvenile offenders. Readers might consider study results regarding capacities and comprehension of juvenile Miranda warnings to be an appropriate parallel when determining levels of reading comprehension appropriate for juveniles when creating youth assent forms (see Rogers, Hazelwood, Sewell, & Shuman, 2008; Viljoen et al., 2007). Even after careful construction of consent and assent form documents, researchers should plan to read out loud youth assent forms and allow time for questions during actual youth assent procedures.

Second, even when research involves adolescents, federal regulations allow for waiver or *modification* of standard written informed parental consent procedures under specific circumstances (see 45 CFR §§ 46.116c and 46.116d; 45 CFR § 46.408). In general, waivers or modifications in the standard parental consent requirement are directly tied to the definition and determination of the study as involving minimal risk (see 45 CFR §§ 46.102 and 46.303d).

Third, if parental permission is not a reasonable requirement to protect youth participants, parental permission can be waived as long as "an appropriate mechanism" for participant protection is provided that is consistent with any federal, state, or local laws (see 45 CFR § 116d). For example, Teplin, Abram, McClelland, Dulcan, and Mericle (2002) carefully documented the logic for obtaining a waiver of parental consent in their study of mental disorder prevalence conducted in a juvenile detention setting and discussed additional protections that were built into the consent procedures. Even with the waiver, the researchers made attempts to contact parents and documented that 43.8% of parent/guardians could not be reached despite multiple attempts. The use of a participant advocate is a viable option in such situations, as long as the advocate has adequate training in research protections and is independent of the research team and the institution (see procedures employed by Teplin et al., 2002). In most studies that involve direct contact with juvenile offenders, or their records, researchers should plan for documenting parental permission and active youth assent.

Given parent accessibility concerns in prospective studies determined to be minimal risk, we have used a process of telephonic consent with audio recordings of parental permission (with subsequent mailing of consent forms) in a series of studies conducted in juvenile detention and correctional centers. This is considered a modification of the written parental consent requirements under 45 CFR §§ 46.102 and 46.303d. Such modifications are reasonable given the broad concerns regarding passive parental consent procedures as well as the practical likelihood that mailing and subsequent return of parental consent forms via standard mail would result in a biased sample due to limited stays in certain juvenile facilities. Use of telephonic consent procedures with audio recordings provides a mechanism to obtain permission in a timely manner and directly review elements of a standard parental consent form with the parent; it also allows for the possibility of a meaningful dialogue between the researcher and parent regarding any concerns or questions about the study that would not be available if the parental consent procedure were handled via mail only.

Finally, given the multiple vulnerabilities referenced here and participant legal status, researchers must carefully consider the voluntary nature of the consent and assent process. This involves a careful delineation of confidentiality protections and providing direct language regarding the extent to which research data will be available to juvenile justice personnel. The "goodness of fit" approach to constructing the consent process (see Fried & Fisher, 2008) provides an appropriate decision-making framework to address these concerns. Readers will find that a recent study conducted by Langhinrichsen-Rohling, Arata, O'Brien, Bowers, and Klibert (2008) provides benchmarks for outcomes associated with various consent procedures employed with juvenile offender samples. This study also referenced self-reported distress across different samples when surveys of sensitive topics such as suicide behavior, abuse/neglect, and substance use were employed. Findings from this study considered within the "goodness of fit" model are excellent resources to guide the development of the consent process in juvenile justice studies. As a final note regarding informed consent, we encourage full disclosure by authors of the procedures employed and outcomes obtained via different informed-consent procedures in published reports. Consistent documentation of Institutional Review Board (IRB) determinations of minimal risk, delineating procedures used to obtain parental permission and youth assent, and documenting percentages of consent/assents obtained via the procedures (inclusive of refusal rates by parent and youth) will serve as valuable resources to fellow researchers in designing consent procedures across similar studies.

ASSESSMENT AND PREDICTION RESEARCH

Assessment research conducted with juvenile offenders has focused on developing and testing measures designed to guide clinical and judicial decision-making, establishing prevalence of mental disorders, and investigating the onset and trajectories of youth aggression/violence. One of the first challenges that investigators will face is selecting assessment measures that are appropriate for juvenile offenders. Grisso (2005) documented a number of important considerations involved in evaluating the psychometric properties of instruments for use in screening and assessment of juvenile offenders. These considerations are relevant and should serve as a guide to selecting measures for research purposes and when considering validation of new instruments. Here, we highlight relevant recommendations and offer some additional considerations based on current research findings.

First, researchers must be able to document that a given assessment measure has been adequately validated for use with juvenile offenders. The most obvious source of this information is the availability of a test manual that documents the validation procedures and juvenile offender normative samples. The age, gender, and race differences that impact sampling that were addressed previously must also be considered in determining whether adequate norms exist for the instrument under consideration for a particular study. It is simply not enough for an assessment to have been validated on samples of adolescents in either community or clinical settings. As mentioned previously, rates of psychopathology, learning disorders, and maturity differences exist between juvenile offender and community samples. Therefore, it is critical that adequate norms exist that encompass the age range, gender, ethnicity, and point of processing within the juvenile justice system, with such data mapping consistently onto the distribution of these characteristics within a given research sample.

Even when assessment measures were validated specifically for use with adolescent offending populations and have a published test manual, these concerns warrant careful review. For example, the Risk-Sophistication-Treatment Inventory (RSTI; Salekin, 2004) was developed via a rigorous test construction process in conceptualization, item development, and construct validation. Adequate sample representation of males and females ages 14 and above were included in the normative sample, but only 75 youth ages 9 to 13 were represented and only 19 were female. Similarly, the normative data published in the Youth Level of Service/Case Management Inventory (YLS/CMI; Hoge & Andrews, 2002) were based on 263 adjudicated youth in either probation or custody sentences, with neither the age distribution nor the raw score differences by setting reported in the manual. Adequate norms exist for older male youths across settings for both tests; however, in the absence of other published reports, these norms appear insufficient to support use of the RSTI with young females or the YLS/CMI in long-term correctional settings. Conversely, the test manual for the

Psychopathy Checklist: Youth Version (PCL:YV; Forth, Kosson, & Hare, 2003) delineates normative testing across 16 samples reflecting community/clinical, probation, and institutionalized settings. Distribution by gender and age within setting allows for efficient mapping of normative characteristics onto a potential research sample.

Second, assessment selection must also be informed by psychometric properties reflecting adequate reliability and validity. Estimates of reliability are fairly straightforward with numerous resources being devoted to this topic. With the field's growing interest in juvenile risk assessment and development of structured professional judgment tools for estimating risk and treatment needs, careful attention to inter-rater reliability is warranted when selecting assessment measures. Recent research establishing concerns regarding field inter-rater reliability of adult psychopathy measures (see Boccaccini, Turner, & Murrie, 2008) warrant attention in the juvenile-forensic arena as well. Many instruments designed for use with juvenile offenders purport that the instruments can be rated by juvenile justice personnel—for example, YLS/CMI and Structured Assessment of Violence Risk in Youth (SAVRY; Borum, Bartel, & Forth, 2002). When selecting such rating-based instruments, researchers need to determine the level of training and experience required to establish adequate inter-rater reliability and whether such information is to be based on field ratings or extracted from agency records. In addition, researchers should determine whether appropriate levels of inter-rater reliability have been established via prior research and incorporated into the design of a new study.

Research establishing the validity of assessment measures is also of critical importance when selecting assessment measures. Grisso (2005) articulated relevant questions to consider within this domain, including the quality and comprehensiveness of validity studies, the type of validity (concurrent, construct, predictive), and the research sample for which validity has been established. Just as inter-rater reliability is of chief concern regarding the dependability of measurement, predictive validity is often of paramount concern given that most studies incorporate measures to predict future behaviors. Regarding the latter, careful consideration of the predicted outcome base rate within a specific population, specificity of the outcome criterion, and the length of time between assessment and identification of the outcome are critical.

We encourage researchers to carefully consider additional sources of measurement bias that can impact the generalizability of results based on test scores. While expedient in terms of resources and time, the reliability and validity of self-report measures is contingent on juvenile offenders' willingness to self-disclose in an honest manner. Too often, investigators do not consider the impact of response styles that can bias assessment results. For example, Rogers et al. (2002) investigated social desirability and social nonconformity response styles via a within-subjects simulation design in a sample of detained juvenile offenders. Across both conditions, participants were able to significantly affect scores across interview and self-report psychopathy measures, with larger effect sizes for self-report measures.

A separate yet related issue is combining scores from multiple informants and determining to what extent developmental differences impact the use of individual test scores versus multiple informant scores. Chu (2008) noted that obtaining multiple informants can be valuable when there are concerns about limitations inherent in a single reporter (e.g., cognition, language, insight) and/or when measures require evaluation of emotions and behaviors across multiple contexts (e.g., community, home, school, treatment settings). However, as noted previously, obtaining multiple informants in juvenile justice settings can be problematic. Even when multiple reporters are available, lack of agreement across raters requires that a priori decisions be made on how to weigh multiple sources of information. There is no one accepted standard for combining scores but such decisions should be guided by empirical research.

For example, Roose, Bijttebier, Decoene, Claes, and Frick (2010) found evidence supporting a bi-factor structure with the Inventory of Callous-Unemotional Traits (ICU) across self-report and combined scores derived from parent and teacher reports. Using the same measure in a sample of juvenile sex offenders, White, Cruise, and Frick (2009) found that parent report and self-report ICU scores differentially predicted general and sexual risk factor scores such that each informant may provide unique information regarding risk in this context. However, evidence of convergent validity was maintained by combining scores (taking the higher of either self-report or parent-report scores). Given these concerns, it is critical that investigators carefully consider the extent to which measures are susceptible to response distortion and to what extent scores derived from multiple informants can compensate for any limitations inherent in the use of single-informant scores.

Finally, equivalence of measurement must also be considered via developmental differences. Too often, assessment studies with juvenile offenders assume that test scores will result in similar levels of criterion and predictive validity for the sample as a whole without considering differential associations or accuracy by gender, age, or other relevant factors. For example, while establishing no significant gender differences in risk assessment scores, Welsh, Schmidt, McKinnon, Chattha, and Meyers (2008) tested predictive accuracy in a combined sample of male and female youth despite drastic difference in base rates of detected general and violent recidivism for male and female youth. Using similar measures and methods, Viljoen et al. (2007) tested age-related differences in the predictive validity of multiple risk assessment tools via moderated hierarchical logistic regression analysis. By comparing younger (ages 12 to 15) to older male youth (ages 16 to 18), the researchers detected significant age differences, with more accurate results being obtained for older youth and unacceptably high rates of false positives (incorrectly predicting violence) found across measures predicting new offenses for younger males. To summarize, the field would greatly benefit from further empirical investigation of measurement bias with particular attention to developmental and gender differences.

Choice of research design within assessment studies also warrants careful attention. Given the challenges previously noted in participant recruitment and sample selection, it is not surprising that the most common research design is a cross-sectional study that compares one or more groups on a relevant emotional or behavioral outcome. Even when studies are designed to test the predictive validity of an assessment instrument, follow-up periods are typically short (12 to 24 months). The juvenile psychopathy research conducted during the past decade provides an excellent example of methodology issues inherent in assessment studies. In 2001, Edens, Skeem, Cruise, and Cauffman (2001) reviewed existent juvenile psychopathy studies and raised two methodological issues.

First, the authors questioned whether the existent literature allowed for accurate predictions of future violent behaviors, given that studies measuring the association between psychopathy and violence were a mix of postdictive and short-term prospective studies that failed to consistently control for potential demographic and development (i.e., age) differences. Second, they noted that due to developmental characteristics inherent to adolescents (e.g. impulsivity, egocentricity), research had not yet considered the extent to which the psychopathy/violence association is inflated by normative developmental characteristics and to what extent the construct is stable across the adolescence into adulthood. A follow-up review by Sharp and Kine (2008) found that not much has changed following the call for improved empirical investigations by Edens et al. (2001). The majority of studies considered to be longitudinal are in fact relatively short-term in scope and do not account for age differences. For example, Corrado, Vincent, Hart, and Cohen (2004) assessed the PCL:YV using a cross-sectional design of adolescent offenders, with follow-up evaluations being conducted anywhere from 1.2 to 27 months after intake.

A notable improvement in this cross-sectional design employed by Corrado et al. (2004) was controlling for age and race differences in isolating the association between PCL:YV scores and outcomes. However, the researchers did not address age as a potential moderator of these associations or consider the extent to which items or factor scores were invariant across age. Even if studies find significant differences between age groups, if the study employs a cross-sectional design, results cannot address the question of configural invariance across age groups or stability across ages (see Sharp & Kine, 2008). An exception is an exemplary study by Frick, Kimonis, Dandreaux, and Farell (2003). The researchers investigated a sample of community youths over the span of four years, conducting yearly follow-up investigations (years 2, 3, 4), and therefore were able to draw conclusions regarding the stability of psychopathy by repeated measurement within participants across time. Furthermore, this study accounted for a number of other potential limitations by incorporating a two-step stratified random sample with careful classification of groups in high/low callousness and conduct problems as well as stratifying by gender, ethnicity, and SES.

There are significant challenges to effectively conducting longitudinal studies with juvenile offenders (see Schubert et al., 2004) and as such, cross-sectional designs will likely continue to be the norm. However, given the greater emphasis on developmental differences among juvenile offenders, the field could benefit from greater use of accelerated longitudinal designs that involve simultaneous sampling of cohorts at different stages of development (i.e., age groups), observing groups over a shorter time frame, and incorporating growth curve analyses (Raudenbush & Chan, 1992). Such enhancements will allow for testing of cohort and cohort by age interactions to estimate change in a construct of interest across different developmental stages.

JUVENILE OFFENDER TREATMENT RESEARCH

The overarching philosophy of rehabilitation on which the juvenile court was founded has led to a focus on the development and evaluation of juvenile offender treatment programs. Just as in assessment research, a number of methodological issues are encountered in evaluating outcomes in juvenile offender treatment programs. As noted in the introduction to this chapter, early reviews of rehabilitation programs concluded that such programs did not produce reductions in future offenses. Recent reviews have been much more optimistic regarding both community-based and residential-based programs, particularly programs that incorporate cognitive-behavioral techniques (see Landenberger & Lipsey, 2005) and treatments that address juvenile offenders' social ecology within the community (see Henggeler, Schoenwald, Borduin, Rowland, & Cunningham, 2009). A great deal of progress has been made by researchers incorporating the methodological framework associated with evidenced-based practices or empirically supported treatments (see Weisz, Jenson-Doss, & Hawley, 2006).

To summarize briefly, empirically supported treatments are tested across multiple independent samples with clearly defined sample characteristics, incorporate a treatment manual, and show evidence of outcome change in the treatment group relative to a control/comparison group. Moreover, treatments are given greater overall support when similar results are obtained across randomized controlled trials and subsequently replicated via field-based studies (see Timmons-Mitchell, Bender, Kishna, & Mitchell, 2006). In general, community-based treatment outcome research has surpassed residential/corrections-based research in terms of adherence to the tenets of empirically supported treatments. Although methodological issues can arise across both contexts, the challenges of rigorous empirical testing within residential/correctional settings are more complex and difficult to overcome. Our goal within this section is to review some of the methodological issues that can arise across both settings when conducting treatment outcome research.

An overarching problem is that juvenile offenders do not self-select into the juvenile justice system nor is treatment considered voluntary, given that juveniles under court supervision will have disposition plans that can mandate participation in treatment programs as part of juvenile court supervision. Release from out-of-home placements or successful completion of probation supervision may be contingent on successful completion of mandated treatment programming. It is the case that testing service delivery within the system can enhance external validity; however, random assignment of juveniles into treatment versus control conditions, sample selection, and controlling the characteristics of comparison group are often not under the direct control of the investigators (see Chu, 2008). Simply put, research involving juvenile offenders under court supervision may not be able to incorporate a no-treatment control group. Even under situations where researchers are evaluating an experimental treatment versus "treatment as usual," the researchers may not be completely free to establish inclusion and exclusion criteria without the involvement of juvenile court personnel or facility administrators. These problems can create sample selection problems that jeopardize the internal validity of treatment outcome studies.

Just as in assessment studies, sample representativeness can also be an issue in treatment research. For example, early multisystemic therapy (MST) studies adopted restrictive exclusion criteria, eliminating youth with serious mental health problems and sexual offenses. Given what we currently know about the prevalence of mental health disorders among juvenile offenders across all levels of the juvenile justice system, adopting this stringent exclusion criteria likely resulted in a treatment group very different from the typical mental health profile found in juvenile offender samples. More recent MST studies have relaxed such exclusions to incorporate youth with significant physical and mental health problems into experimental groups (see Henggeler, Sheidow, & Lee, 2007) and/or modified and tested MST including juveniles with sex offenses (Letourneau et al., 2009). Another potential sampling problem occurs when treatment groups are formed based on legal charge or offense characteristics. This has been a significant problem in treatment research with juvenile sex offenders, the underlying assumption being that such offenders represent a homogeneous subgroup and/or that outcomes will vary based on characteristics such as victim gender, age, or type of offense (see Chaffin, 2008, for a comprehensive review of evidence debunking this assumption).

The inability to randomly assign offenders into treatment and control groups has often resulted in comparing known groups of treatment completers versus treatment refusers, unsuccessful discharges, or a group of offenders that dropped out of treatment prematurely. There are often numerous factors that may account for successful versus unsuccessful completion of treatment programs that have little to do with the actual treatment delivery (i.e., access/transportation in community-based programs, relocation, unexpected administrative transfers from one facility to another). Pre-treatment differences on important variables (i.e., prior histories of juvenile offending, risk, severity of mental health problems) must be examined between the attrition and treatment groups as such variables may result in a confound, with treatment effects being overestimated and/or masked depending on the availability and analysis of pretreatment information (see Worling & Curwen, 2000).

If pretreatment group differences are detected that are attributed to nonrandom assignment, one approach to controlling such differences is through the use of propensity analysis (see Caldwell, Skeem, Salekin, & Van Rybroek, 2006). One limitation of this approach is that the development of a composite "propensity score" to control for nonrandom assignment is only as effective as the comprehensiveness and quality of data available with which to compare the groups. Additionally, the reduction of multiple variables into a single composite does not allow for careful exploration of which specific demographic, clinical, legal, or other variables had the greatest impact on nonrandom assignment. Therefore, this approach can limit the overall generalizability of results, because such variables are likely to be sample dependent. At a minimum, we recommend that careful attention be devoted to specifying the inclusion and exclusion criteria involved in all treatment outcome studies regardless of design. When quasi-experimental designs are employed, careful description of referral procedures must be included, with particular emphasis placed on clinical, demographic, and legal variables that may differ across groups. In addition to simple testing of group differences and/or application of propensity scores, we encourage researchers to specify and test mediating or moderating factors that can account for mechanisms of change (see Kazdin, 2006).

Two final methodological issues that warrant mention in the context of juvenile offender treatment outcome research are outcome assessment and system-level confounds affecting outcome. As referenced in the section on assessment, adequate normative and psychometric properties are equally relevant when selecting measures to assess treatment outcomes. In addition, researchers must also carefully consider to what extent self-report versus multiple informant information will be used in outcome studies. Assessments of outcomes will also be influenced by the sensitivity of the selected measures to change. Effect sizes and "responsiveness" should be explored as additional indicators when selecting measures to monitor change over time (see Morlock, Williams, & Cappelleri, 2008, for an application of responsiveness indices to outcome research).

When official records are used to document outcomes, researchers must consider the extent to which these records are complete and thorough and reflect consistent operationalization of the outcomes of interest. Finally, in addition to the nonrandom assignment, there are a host of system-level confounds that can also serve as internal validity threats in treatment outcome research. Setting and length of follow-up time are of particular concern. Policies and procedures, ratio of staff to youth found in different juvenile justice settings, availability of crisis intervention, and strict protocols to accommodate emergency situations will all vary across settings and can influence differences between treatment and comparison groups during the course of a treatment study.

Moreover, juvenile justice settings are prone to staff turnover that may broadly impact the day-to-day functioning of facilities where interventions are being tested (security as well as treatment staff). It is critical that researchers carefully consider issues related to staff stability in terms of initial training in treatment protocols and what effect treatment/security staff turnover may have on outcomes. Finally, longer follow-up periods enhance ecological validity but are also prone to multiple internal validity threats. For example, day-to-day operations within facilities may change during the course of an intervention study as facility administrators adopt new programming within institutions. Changes in agency policies and procedures can inject a serious threat to internal validity, particularly when this involves alterations in the tracking of follow-up variables such as indicators of institutional maladjustment. Longer follow-up times will also involve broad changes in development/maturation of treated youth during follow-up periods as well as greater likelihood of multiple contextual changes that are outside the control of the youth or researchers (e.g., release from restrictive placement back into the community, changes in family functioning, exposure to changing community contexts).

ADDITIONAL ETHICAL CONSIDERATIONS

Mental health and juvenile justice professionals have long recognized the conflicting interests inherent in child mental health service delivery and have acknowledged that such services are inextricably linked to both the child protection and juvenile justice systems (see Melton, Ehrenreich, & Lyons, 2001). This linkage makes analysis of ethical considerations a complex endeavor, because individual rights of the adolescent may conflict with both parent and state interests. In the context of research design, the state has an interest in guaranteeing that specific juvenile offender programs are cost-effective and result in positive outcomes. Parents have a vested interest in the consent process and confidentiality protections when their child considers participating in experimental treatment programs or contributes data to a particular study. Of equal importance are the interests of the youth themselves, given the vulnerabilities of being in custody, the possibility of coercion regarding research involvement, and their legal capacity to provide research consent or assent. In addition to the Federal Code of Regulations, other federal law, and relevant state law, ethics codes adopted by professional disciplines address aspirational principles that must be considered in the context of studies with juvenile offenders. These principles include autonomy, beneficence and nonmaleficence, and justice.

Autonomy is the primary principle that underlies the informed consent process for parent and youth as well as the responsibilities of the researcher to consider the potential for coercion and exploitation within institutional settings. In his review, Grisso (1996) argued that "normative power residuals" influence interactions between officials and members of the institution and therefore impact possible coercion and the ability of those in custody to make an independent choice regarding research participation. Such dynamics call for careful consideration when conducting research with juvenile offenders. First, investigators must recognize that normative power residuals will differ across various types of institutions (community supervision/ probation, short-term detention, and long-term secure custody). Second, when conducting research within a juvenile justice facility, researchers must consider how their role vis-à-vis the institution will be perceived by the parent/guardians and youth. Confidentiality protections as well as mandated breaches of confidentiality (i.e., mandatory reporting of child abuse and neglect), perceptions of voluntary choice about participation, and use of incentives must be balanced against the potential for coercion.

Beneficence and nonmaleficence broadly encourage professionals to "do good" and avoid actions that can result in harm. In the context of research, these ethical principles relate to a careful examination of the potential risks and benefits that a research protocol presents to the study population. The application of this standard does not preclude research protocols involving some level of risk but requires that the presence of risk be carefully weighed against the likelihood that the study will produce meaningful results. Definitions of risk and "minimal risk" vary as a function of the vulnerability of the population. As previously discussed, a review of risks involved in research with juvenile offenders will necessitate consideration of additional protections for prisoners, protections for children, and in certain circumstances, protections applicable to state wards.

Direct versus indirect benefits must also be considered. Researchers must carefully plan in advance to have mechanisms for managing emergency and high-risk situations. In a juvenile justice setting, the availability of monitoring/supervision and accessibility to medical and mental health services following research participation may be more readily accessible than in similar research conducted in other contexts (i.e., community probation settings). However, researchers will find that accessing facility intervention services must be done while also protecting the confidentiality of information obtained as part of the research process. Safety precautions and interventions to manage distress, including decision-making criteria and referral mechanisms, must be addressed with facility administrators and explained to parents and youth participants as part of the consent and assent process.

Justice refers to equal access and equal benefit from professional knowledge and activities and, in the context of research, requires implementation of equitable inclusion and exclusion criteria, the possibility of equal benefits for all participants, and not exploiting unique characteristics or circumstances of special populations. In conducting research with juvenile offenders, the principle of justice relates to involving such youth only in projects that have a direct impact on factors contributing to involvement in the justice system. Such youth should not be used as a convenience sample when the research questions have little bearing on factors that contribute to juvenile delinquency. Selection criteria must guarantee that all youth have a similar chance of participation, unless valid reasons exist as to why specific groups of juveniles should not be included.

Additionally, research participation should not be linked to incentives such as cash payment, offers of reduction in community service, or changes in status within the facility; that negate choice about participation because the incentive is too desirable. Researchers also should be aware of indirect incentives (i.e., time out of dorm units or cells) that are unique to incarcerated juveniles and may represent incentives that negate individual and voluntary choice depending on how such incentives are employed.

CONCLUSIONS

The challenges researchers encounter in effectively designing and implementing studies with juvenile offender populations are diverse, with different challenges emerging at each stage of the research process. The overarching rehabilitation philosophy found within the juvenile justice system suggests that social scientists will continue to have an important role in developing and testing the efficacy of assessment and treatment techniques that are developed based in part on this philosophy. Additionally, empirical results generated from studies based on sound methodological principles will guide changes in the juvenile justice policy and practices. Careful consideration of the methodological issues presented here will enhance the likelihood that researchers can conduct studies that will have an impact on the juvenile offender policy and programming.

REFERENCES

Boccaccini, M. T., Turner, D. B., & Murrie, D. C. (2008). Do some evaluators report consistently higher or lower PCL-R scores than others? Findings from a statewide sample of sexually violent predator evaluations. *Psychology, Public Policy, and Law*, 262–283.

Borum, R., Bartel, P., & Forth, A. (2002). *Structured assessment of violence risk in youth: Professional manual.* Lutz, FL: Psychological Assessment Resources.

Bruzzese, J. M., & Fisher, C. B. (2003). Assessing and enhancing the research consent capacity of children and youth. *Applied Developmental Science, 7*, 13–26.

Cabaniss, E. R., Frabutt, J. M., Kendrick, M. H, & Arbuckle, M. B. (2007). Reducing disproportionate minority contact in the juvenile justice system: Promising practices. *Aggression and Violent Behavior, 12*, 393–401.

Caldwell, M., Skeem, J., Salekin, R., & Van Rybroek, G. (2006). Treatment response of adolescent offenders with psychopathic features: A 2-year follow-up. *Criminal Justice and Behavior, 33*, 571–596.

Chaffin, M. (2008). Our minds are made up—don't confuse us with the facts: Commentary on policies concerning children with sexual behavior problems and juvenile sex offenders. *Child Maltreatment, 13,* 110–121.

Chu, B. C. (2008). Clinical research with children and adolescents. In D. McKay (Ed.), *Handbook of research methods in abnormal and clinical psychology* (pp. 405–426). Thousand Oaks, CA: Sage.

Corrado, R. R., Vincent, G. M., Hart, S. D., & Cohen, I. M. (2004). Predictive validity of the Psychopathy Checklist: Youth Version for general and violent recidivism. *Behavioral Sciences and the Law, 22,* 5–22.

Department of Health and Human Services (2005). Title 45 Public Welfare, Part 46, *Code of Federal Regulations, Protection of Human Subjects.* Washington, DC: Government Printing Office.

Edens, J. F., Skeem, J. L., Cruise, K. R., & Cauffman, E. (2001). Assessment of "juvenile psychopathy" and its association with violence: A critical review. *Behavioral Sciences and the Law, 19,* 53–80.

Eggleston, C. (2008). Juvenile offenders with special education needs. In R. Hoge, N. Guerra, & P. Boxer (Eds.), *Treating the juvenile offender* (pp. 239–257). New York, NY: Guilford Press.

Feld, B. (2009). Violent girls or relabeled status offenders? An alternative interpretation of the data. *Crime & Delinquency, 55,* 241–265.

Flesch, R. (1950). Measuring the level of abstraction. *Journal of Applied Psychology, 34,* 384–390.

Forth, A. E., Kosson, D. S., & Hare, R. D. (2003). *Hare Psychopathy Checklist: Youth Version technical manual.* North Tonawanda, NY: Multi-Health Systems.

Frick, P. J., Kimonis, E. R., Dandreaux, D. M., & Farell, J. M. (2003). The 4 year stability of psychopathic traits in non-referred youths. *Behavioral Sciences and the Law, 21,* 713–736.

Fried, A. L., & Fisher, C. B. (2008). The ethics of informed consent for research in clinical and abnormal psychology. In D. McKay (Ed.), *Handbook of research methods in abnormal and clinical psychology* (pp. 5–22). Thousand Oaks, CA: Sage.

Gendreau, P., & Ross, R. R. (1979). Effective correctional treatment: Bibliotherapy for cynics. *Crime and Delinquency, 25,* 463–489.

Grisso, T. (1996). Voluntary consent to research participation in the institutional context. In B. Stanley, J. E. Sieber, & G. B. Melton (Eds.), *Research ethics: A psychological approach* (pp. 203–224). Lincoln: University of Nebraska Press.

Grisso, T. (2005). Evaluating the properties of instruments for screening and assessment. In T. Grisso, G. Vincent, & D. Seagrave (Eds.), *Mental health screening and assessment in juvenile justice* (pp. 71–96). New York, NY: Guilford Press.

Grisso, T., Steinberg, L., Woolard, J., Cauffman, E., Scott, E., Graham, S., Lexcen, F., . . . Schwartz, R. (2003). Juveniles' competence to stand trial: A comparison of adolescents' and adults' capacities as trial defendants. *Law and Human Behavior, 27,* 333–363.

Henggeler, S. W., Schoenwald, S. K., Borduin, C. M., Rowland, M. D., & Cunningham, P. B. (2009). *Multisystemic therapy for antisocial behavior in children and adolescents* (2nd ed.). New York, NY: Guilford Press.

Henggeler, S. W., Sheidow, A. J., & Lee, T. (2007). Multisystemic treatment of serious clinical problems in youths and their families. In D. W. Springer & A. R. Roberts (Eds.), *Handbook of forensic mental health with victims and offenders: Assessment, treatment, and research* (pp. 315–345). New York, NY: Springer.

Hoge, R. D., & Andrews, D. A. (2002). *Youth Level of Service/Case Management Inventory user's manual.* North Tonawanda, NY: Multi-Health Systems.

In re Gault 387 U.S. 1 (1967).

Kazdin, A. E. (2006). Mechanisms of change in psychotherapy: Advances, breakthroughs, and cutting-edge research (do not yet exist). In R. Bootzin, & P. McKnight (Eds.), *Strengthening research methodology: Psychological measurement and evaluation* (pp. 77–101). Washington, DC: American Psychological Association.

Kempf-Leonard, K. (2007). Minority youths and juvenile justice: Disproportionate minority contact after nearly 20 years of reform efforts. *Youth Violence and Juvenile Justice, 5,* 71–87.

Landenberger, N. A., & Lipsey, M. W. (2005). The positive effects of cognitive behavioral programs for offenders: A meta-analysis of factors associated with effective treatment. *Journal of Experimental Criminology, 1,* 451–476.

Langhinrichsen-Rohling, J., Arata, C., O'Brien, N., Bowers, D., & Klibert, J. (2008). Sensitive research with adolescents: Just how upsetting are self-report surveys anyway? *Violence and Victims, 21,* 424–444.

Leiber, M. J., & Fox, K. C. (2005). Race and the impact of detention on juvenile justice decision making. *Crime & Delinquency, 51,* 470–497.

Letourneau, E. J., Henggeler, S. W., Borduin, C. M., McCart, M. R., Saldana, L., Chapman, J. E., & Schewe, P. A. (2009). Multisystemic therapy for juvenile sex offenders: 1-year results from a randomized effectiveness trial. *Journal of Family Psychology, 23,* 89–102.

Martinson, R. (1974). What works? Questions and answers about prison reform. *The Public Interest, 35,* 22–54.

Melton, G. B., Ehrenreich, N. S., & Lyons, P. M. (2001). Ethical and legal issues in mental health services for children. In C. Walker & M. Roberts (Eds.), *Handbook of clinical child psychology* (3rd ed.) (pp. 1074–1093). New York, NY: Wiley.

Modecki, K. L. (2008). Addressing gaps in the maturity of judgment literature: Age differences and delinquency. *Law and Human Behavior, 32,* 78–91.

Morlock, R. J, Williams, V. S., & Cappelleri, J. C. (2008). Development and evaluation of the Daily Assessment of Symptoms—Anxiety (DAS-A) scale to evaluate onset of symptom relief in patients with generalized anxiety disorder. *Journal of Psychiatric Research, 42,* 1024–1036.

Odgers, C. L., & Moretti, M. M. (2002). Aggressive and antisocial girls: Research update and challenges. *International Journal of Forensic Mental Health, 1,* 103–119.

Raudenbush, S. W., & Chan, W. (1992). Growth curve analysis in accelerated longitudinal designs. *Journal of Research in Crime and Delinquency, 29,* 387–411.

Rogers, R., Hazelwood, L. L., Sewell, K. W., & Shuman, D. W. (2008). The comprehensibility and content of juvenile Miranda warnings. *Psychology, Public Policy, and Law, 14,* 63–87.

Rogers, R., Vitacco, M. J., Jackson, R. J., Martin, M., Collins, M., & Sewell, K. W. (2002). Faking psychopathy? An examination of response styles with antisocial youth. *Journal of Personality Assessment, 78,* 31–46.

Roose, A., Bijttebier, P., Decoene, S., Claes, L. & Frick, P. J. (2010). Assessing the affective features of psychopathy in adolescence: A further validation of the Inventory of Callous and Unemotional Traits. *Assessment, 17,* 44–57.

Roper v. Simmons, 543 U.S. 551 (2005).

Salekin, R. T. (2004). *Risk-Sophistication-Treatment Inventory professional test manual.* Lutz, FL: Psychological Assessment Resources.

Schubert, C. A., Mulvey, E. P., Steinberg, L., Cauffman, E., Losoya, S. H., Hecker, T., . . . Knight, G. P. (2004). Operational lessons from the pathways to desistance project. *Youth Violence and Juvenile Justice 2,* 237–255.

Sharp, C., & Kine, S. (2008). The assessment of juvenile psychopathy: Strengths and weaknesses of currently used questionnaire measures. *Child and Adolescent Mental Health, 13,* 85–95.

Shufelt, J. L., & Cocozza, J. J. (2006, June). *Youth with mental health disorders in the juvenile justice system: Results from a multi-state prevalence study.* National Center for Mental Health and Juvenile Justice Research and Program Brief. Retrieved March 15, 2009, from http://www.ncmhjj.com/pdfs/publications/PrevalenceRPB.pdf

Sickmund, M. (2009, June). Delinquency cases in juvenile court, 2005. *Office of Juvenile Justice and Delinquency Prevention Fact Sheet.* Retrieved March 15, 2009, from http://www.ncjrs.gov/pdffiles1/ojjdp/224538.pdf on 07/13/09

Teplin, L. A., Abram, K. M., McClelland, G. M., Dulcan, M. K., & Mericle, A. A. (2002). Psychiatric disorders in youth in juvenile detention. *Archives of General Psychiatry, 59,* 1133–1143.

Timmons-Mitchell, J., Bender, M. B., Kishna, M. A., & Mitchell, C. C. (2006). An independent effectiveness trial of multi-systemic therapy with juvenile justice youth. *Journal of Clinical Child and Adolescent Psychology, 35,* 227–236.

Tracy, P. E., Kempf-Leonard, K., & Abramoske-James, S. (2009). Gender issues in juvenile and criminal justice. *Crime & Delinquency, 55,* 171–215.

Viljoen, J. L., Scalora, M., Cuadra, L., Bader, S., Chavez, V., Ullman, D., & Lawrence, L. (2007). Assessing risk for violence in adolescents who have sexually offended: A comparison of the J-SOAP-II, J-SORRAT-II and SAVRY. *Criminal Justice and Behavior, 35,* 5–23.

Viljoen, J. L., Zapf, P. A., & Roesch, R. (2007). Adjudicative competence and comprehension of Miranda rights in adolescent defendants: A comparison of legal standards. *Behavioral Sciences and the Law, 25,* 1–19.

Weisz, J. R., Jenson-Doss, A., & Hawley, K. M. (2006). Evidence-based youth psycho-therapies versus usual clinical care. *American Psychologist, 61,* 671–689.

Welsh, J. L., Schmidt, F., McKinnon, L., Chattha, H. K., & Meyers, J. R. (2008). A comparative study of adolescent risk assessment instruments: Predictive and incremental validity. *Assessment, 15,* 104–115.

White, S. F., Cruise, K. R., & Frick, P. J. (2009). Differential correlates to self-report and parent-report of callous-unemotional traits in a sample of juvenile sexual offenders. *Behavioral Sciences and the Law, 28,* 910–928.

Worling, J. R., & Curwen, T. (2000). Adolescent sexual offender recidivism: Success of specialized treatment and implications for risk prediction. *Child Abuse & Neglect, 24,* 965–982.

CHAPTER 21

Research With Offenders With Intellectual Disability

DEBRA CHEN, KAREN SALEKIN, J. GREGORY OLLEY, AND SOLOMON M. FULERO

INTRODUCTION

In a seminal 2002 case, the U.S. Supreme Court ruled that executing individuals with mental retardation (aka intellectual disability) violates the Eighth Amendment prohibition against cruel and unusual punishment (*Atkins v. Virginia*, 2002). In explaining its opinion, the Court wrote:

> Because of their disabilities in areas of reasoning, judgment, and control of their impulses, however, they do not act with the level of moral culpability that characterizes the most serious adult criminal conduct. Moreover, their impairments can jeopardize the reliability and fairness of capital proceedings against mentally retarded defendants.
>
> *(Atkins v. Virginia, 536 U.S. 304, 2002, p. 1)*

The Court's decision in *Atkins* was the culmination of a growing recognition that individuals with intellectual disabilities have impairments that must be considered at every stage of criminal proceedings. For some defendants with intellectual disability (ID), these considerations begin with an assessment of whether their waiver of *Miranda* rights (*Miranda v. Arizona*, 384 U.S. 436, 1966) was valid; whereas, for others, the considerations begin with the question of whether they were capable of participating meaningfully in their defense (i.e., trial competence). As discussed throughout this chapter, impaired intelligence and problems in adaptive behavior invariably render an ID offender more vulnerable than a non-ID offender to problems in negotiating the legal system. These questions are the subject of a growing interest in ID individuals among the forensic mental health community. However, conducting valid and relevant research requires attention to several methodological challenges, some of which are reviewed in this chapter.

WHAT IS INTELLECTUAL DISABILITY?

Intellectual disability (ID) is a diagnostic term that refers to a significant impairment in the level at which an individual typically functions. Individuals with ID demonstrate limitations in one or more areas of day-to-day functioning and have a measured intelligence that is approximately two standard deviations or more below the mean of the general population. Deficits in measured intelligence and adaptive behavior must manifest before the age of 18 years. The two most commonly used definitions of ID are those of the American Association on Intellectual and Developmental Disabilities (AAIDD, 2010; formerly the American Association on Mental Retardation, 2002) and the American Psychiatric Association (APA; 2000).

Though similar in regard to age of onset and the requirement of deficits in both measured intelligence and adaptive behavior, the definitions put forth by the AAIDD and the APA differ in two ways. First, they view the construct of adaptive behavior differently; second, the AAIDD has focused its attention on systems of support and has removed the levels of ID (i.e., mild, moderate, severe, and profound) from its definition. Of note, the APA follows the 1992 definition put forth by AAIDD with the requirement that an individual demonstrate deficits in adaptive behavior in 2 of 10 categories (i.e., communication, self-care, home living, social/interpersonal skills, use of community resources, self-direction, functional academic skills, work, leisure, and health and safety). In contrast, the AAIDD no longer requires impairments in 2 of 10 categories, but instead requires that an individual display significant impairments that are at least two standard deviations below the mean in either (1) conceptual, social, or practical skills or (2) an overall score that includes the domains of conceptual, social, and practical skills (AAIDD, 2010; AAMR, 2002). With the exception of the Adaptive Behavior Assessment System-2nd Edition (ABAS-II; Harrison & Oakland, 2003), available measures of adaptive behavior do not provide a straightforward procedure for mapping the results of testing directly onto either definition.

When considering the characteristics of the ID offender, one should be aware that such individuals are likely to be functioning at the level of mild intellectual disability (with an IQ of approximately 55–70). It is this group of individuals who are more likely to live independently or with minimal supervision, to be employed in a community setting, and to participate in social activities outside of a structured environment. Thus, in comparison to their more severely disabled counterparts, individuals with mild ID have more opportunities to engage in criminal behavior and are more vulnerable to the negative influences of non–intellectually impaired offenders who reside in the community.

Given the lack of a bright-line distinction between the typical ID offender and the non-ID offender, it is not surprising that research has not borne out the previously held notion that ID offenders were fundamentally different from non-ID offenders. As noted in a recent review of the literature (Jones,

2007), the research indicates that the risk factors for offending are generally the same for individuals with ID as they are for the general offender population (e.g., familial offending, psychosocial disadvantage, unemployment). Similarly, the ID offender is no more or less likely to commit a particular type of offense than is a non-ID offender (Holland, Clare, & Mukhopadhyay, 2002).

USING APPROPRIATE DEFINITIONS

Although both the AAIDD's and the APA's definition of ID have been widely accepted and used in research with offenders with ID, when conducting research it is essential to identify the specific population to be studied. While the AAIDD has dispensed with labels, such as mild, moderate, and severe levels of disability, the functioning of individuals with ID varies widely, and it may be beneficial not only to specify which individuals are to be worked with but to adopt specific definitions of functioning for these individuals so that conclusions may be drawn about clearly delineated groups. It is recommended that researchers consider using the IQ and adaptive behavior delineations set forth by the APA for mild, moderate, severe, and profound ID in determining population groups.

Obtaining an Appropriate Sample

Prevalence rates for individuals with ID within the criminal justice system have varied over the years, with estimates of rates in the United States varying from 2.6% (MacEachron, 1979) to 39.6% (Holland, 1991). More recent research indicates that between 4% and 14% of offenders in a jail or prison population carry an ID diagnosis (Petersilia, 2000). Comparison of available research on the prevalence of ID in the criminal justice system is extremely difficult, because research samples are not always representative of "true" ID offenders. For example, some researchers err when they classify an individual as an ID offender solely on the basis of measured IQ (some of which use a cut score well above 70), and further inaccuracies result when the ID offender is classified based on the results of a short form or group IQ test rather than on a comprehensive measure of intelligence (Axelrod, 2002). As mentioned earlier, in addition to questions regarding the classification of an ID offender, prevalence rates can vary by setting and stage of criminal proceedings (see Holland et al., 2002; and Lindsay, Hastings, Griffiths, & Hayes, 2007 for comprehensive reviews of these issues). In general, however, it is safe to say that obtaining a sample of offenders with ID will be an arduous task, and decisions regarding acceptable limitations in diagnostic accuracy must be made in light of the focus of the study.

Obtaining a comparison sample of non-offenders with mild ID also presents significant problems. Individuals with mild ID are often not identified as such in school and do not receive professional services or supports in adulthood. Thus, there is often no systematic mechanism for finding such individuals. Even if located, people with mild ID typically resist being labeled with this disability (Edgerton, 1993).

ISSUES OF INFORMED CONSENT

In addition to the issues with sample size and type, research with ID offenders comes with at least one more large hurdle: that of guardianship and informed consent. For many studies, the appropriate comparison group is a non-offender ID sample. However, in many settings where persons with ID reside (i.e., residential programs, group homes, and even with family members), a formal guardianship has been put into place, and it is the guardian who must legally consent to participate in research. For residential programs, this may be a relatively painless procedure, because in many instances, a member of the program's administration has been appointed guardian. However, in circumstances where the guardian is in a different city or state, negotiating informed consent can be a difficult and lengthy process. Further, best practice indicates that the participating individual with ID give informed consent or assent for participation.

HOW TO DETERMINE THE APPROPRIATE SAMPLE

As previously mentioned, to be identified as having ID, an individual must have low IQ and deficits in adaptive behavior, both of which manifested prior to age 18. To determine whether individuals meet IQ requirements for ID, tests such as the Wechsler Adult Intelligence Scale-Fourth Edition (WAIS-IV; Wechsler, 2008) and the Stanford-Binet 5 (SB5; Roid, 2003) are well established and widely accepted. At the time of writing, the WAIS-IV is the most recently normed test, and because of this, people may choose to use it in studies that require diagnosis. However, the relative "newness" of the test means that for some time after initial publication, there are few, if any, data in existence beyond those provided by the publisher. In addition, concurrent validity studies were not completed using the SB5, so at present it is not known whether a person who meets the low-IQ prong using the WAIS-IV would do so on the SB5, and vice versa. Data from the WAIS-III validation studies demonstrated that the Full Scale IQ scores between these two measures were highly correlated ($r=.82$; Roid, 2003). Unfortunately, due to the restructuring of the WAIS-IV, it cannot be assumed that this level of concordance exists for the new measure. Because it is newly published, there is less research available regarding its concurrent validity. On a more positive note, the validation studies of the WAIS-IV have shown high concordance between the WAIS-III and the WAIS-IV ($r = .94$; Wechsler, 2008), suggesting that the two measures can be used interchangeably.

For research that requires a diagnosis of ID, the choice of an adaptive behavior measure is dictated by the sample on which it is normed.

Specifically, the measure must be one that is normed on the general population rather than a sample of individuals already diagnosed with ID or any other restricted sample (AAMR, 2002). Three commonly used tests that meet these criteria are (1) the Adaptive Behavior Assessment System-Second Edition (ABAS-II; Harrison & Oakland, 2002), (2) the Scales of Independent Behavior-Revised Full Scale (SIB-R; Bruininks, Woodcock, Weatherman, & Hill, 1996), and (3) the Vineland Adaptive Behavior Scales-Second Edition (VABS II; Sparrow, Cicchetti, & Balla, 2005). Of course, as with all tests, these measures have strengths and limitations, and the choice of which one to use is an important consideration when conducting research with this population. Researchers would be wise to peruse the literature regarding the pros and cons of each test and to review studies that have used them as dependent variables. It is here where the strengths and limitations may be most apparent. Of great import is the fact that measures of adaptive behavior are based on the report of collateral sources who can report on the day-to-day functioning of clients, rather than on information from the clients themselves (the ABAS-II being more flexible on this issue). As such, research can be seriously impeded by a lack of access to such collateral sources, extensive periods of no contact between a collateral source and the individual (e.g., if an offender has been in prison for a decade, the person would have to provide ratings based on memories that are at least 10 years old), and/or collateral sources who refuse to participate in the study.

For researchers interested in conducting studies in which making the diagnosis occurs within the confines of a correctional institution, it is strongly recommended that the researcher *not* consider correctional officers to be appropriate respondents on a measure of adaptive behavior. For many reasons these individuals are not appropriate, but two of the most important are their inability to provide ratings of typical functioning in a community setting and their inability to rate many abilities due to limitations inherent in the system (e.g., cooking a meal, using scissors). The difficulties associated with the assessment of adaptive behavior for research purposes are similar to those experienced in legal cases in which ID is an issue. At present, the field has not yet adopted a universally accepted method of assessing adaptive behavior in criminal defendants (see Widaman & Siperstein, 2009), though recommendations have been made. For example, Tassé (2009) recommended that researchers consider not only formal adaptive behavior measures, such as the three previously mentioned, but also collateral sources of data, including, but not limited to, school records, employment and medical records, and individuals who knew the person of interest well but not well enough to complete an entire adaptive behavior measure.

Studies that are designed to address questions regarding pre-trial competencies result in another dilemma for the researcher. To provide the most ecologically valid results, the researcher would want to include a sample of offenders awaiting trial; however, the administration of a full IQ test and/or measures of adaptive behavior could invalidate the results of a subsequent assessment. It has been well established that testees show increases in IQ scores due to the effect of practice that occurs with repeated administrations of a test over a short time (Catron & Thompson, 1979; Matarazzo, Carmody, & Jacobs, 1980), as well as with different tests that measure the same construct (e.g., the SB5 followed by the WAIS-IV). Perhaps most concerning about this situation is that counsel for the defendant and triers of fact are likely to be unaware that a test was given as part of a research study, and because of this, clinicians may interpret the subsequent scores as accurate, when in fact they might well be inflated.

There are a few suggestions the researcher may wish to consider when conducting research with pre-trial samples. One option would be to use a short-form IQ test, with the understanding that the results would not necessarily fulfill the criteria for a diagnosis. The results of this approach would be applicable to people with low intelligence, rather than those formally diagnosed ID, though for research purposes this may be sufficient. Another problem with some short-form intelligence tests is that the subtests closely resemble or are identical to one or more subtests of the parent test (e.g., the Abbreviated SB5 consists of the two routing subtests of the full test), resulting in the same dilemma just described. Three alternative strategies may work in the best interests of the ID offender and provide the researcher with a sample that is appropriate: (1) including only offenders who have already been identified as ID and are entering or reentering the system, (2) using a community sample of individuals who have been in trouble with the law but have never gone to trial or been incarcerated, and/or (3) using test scores that are available from records held at the institution. If available, records might also allow for assessment of adaptive behavior without tainting test results that might later be obtained from collateral sources in a legal matter.

To Flynn or Not to Flynn

In addition to considering the concurrent validity of various intelligence tests, it is also essential to understand and consider the "Flynn effect" when interpreting the data. In brief, the Flynn effect is the gradual increase in measured intelligence in the general population over time (Flynn, 1984). After analyzing thousands of studies, Flynn found that the rise in IQ was approximately .33 points per year, resulting in a 3-point inflation in a test for every 10 years after it was normed. The increase in scores has been found to be directly related to the norming sample, such that when a newer version of a test is published, the test scores are interpreted in comparison with peers of that cohort rather than a generation past. This is pertinent to researchers when they choose to use prior test scores for identifying participants, in that a full scale score of 73 might disqualify a person from inclusion in a study, when in fact an adjusted score of 70 might be closer to the ground truth.

The choice to adjust individual scores (i.e., to reduce scores commensurate with the amount of time elapsed from date of publication or the beginning of the norming cycle) or not to adjust scores is up to the researcher, but this choice is not trivial and should be informed by science. One option would be to include all participants using the Flynn adjustment (hence broadening the subject pool) and then conducting all analyses using Flynn corrected scores and noncorrected scores. A study such as this could produce very interesting results, since research has demonstrated that legal competencies are greatly affected by intellectual ability (see e.g., Fulero & Everington, 1995, discussed subsequently), and in some instances, Flynn adjustments can be more than 10 points, depending on which IQ measure was used.

COMORBID DISORDERS

Offenders with ID, like their non-offender counterparts, often meet criteria for other psychiatric disorders; however, research is limited with regard to the prevalence of dual diagnosis (Fletcher, Loschen, Stavrakaki, & First, 2007; O'Brien, 2002). Accordingly, researchers may be interested in measures that can determine the presence of psychiatric disorders in individuals with ID. There are several informant-based measures, such as the Assessment of Dual Diagnosis (Matson & Bamburg, 1998), the Prout-Strohmer Assessment System (Prout & Strohmer, 1989), and the Reiss Screen for Maladaptive Behavior (Reiss, 1988), which were developed specifically for use with individuals with ID and for which there is some evidence of their utility. There is also a variety of self-report measures available, such as the Psychiatric Assessment Schedule for Adults with a Developmental Disability (Moss et al., 1997), which is administered as a semi-structured clinical interview. It is important to note, however, that these measures were designed to be used with specific ID populations (i.e., mild to moderate, severe and profound) and special attention must be paid to the standardization procedures used with each instrument to determine whether it is appropriate for use with a particular sample. (For a more detailed description of specific measures that can be used as part of a battery for dual diagnosis, readers are directed to Hurley, Levitas, Lecavalier, & Pary, 2007).

Offenders with ID are similar to the general offender population with regard to the presence of substance use disorders, and these disorders have been found to play a role in their criminal actions. In a 2001 study, McGillivray and Moore compared the rate of self-reported substance use in a sample of 30 young adults with mild ID who were involved in the criminal justice system with a matched comparison group of 30 non-offenders. Among the findings, the authors found that substance use was more prevalent among offenders with ID than non-offenders and that more than 50% of the ID offenders were under the influence of alcohol and/or drugs at the time of the crime (McGillivray & Moore, 2001). Indeed, the link between substance use and crime has been well established in the non-ID offender population, but it becomes of heightened concern when one considers the potentially compounding effects of substances on individuals who have diminished abilities in the areas of judgment, reasoning, and impulse control (Meyers, Branch, & Lederman, 1988). It is, therefore, very difficult, if not impossible, to determine whether screening for substance abuse/use at the time of the crime would provide researchers with a more "typical" or "atypical" ID offender. Given the high prevalence of substance use in this population, it is recommended that researchers consider a variable they must measure and control for in designing their studies.

COMPETENCE TO WAIVE MIRANDA AND COMPETENCE TO STAND TRIAL

One area of particular concern for individuals with ID who are in the criminal justice system is pre-trial competency. Although there is a limited body of research in this area, the research that does exist indicates that many individuals with ID have impairments that interfere with their ability to competently proceed through adjudication. For example, Thomas Grisso (1981, 1998) created a set of scales to measure competence to waive interrogation and arrest rights as described by the U.S. Supreme Court in the *Miranda v. Arizona* case (1966). Although Grisso's scales were originally designed to measure competence to waive *Miranda* rights in youthful offenders, a line of research studying the validity of the use of these scales with individuals with ID emerged in the 1990s.

Fulero and Everington (1995) worked with two samples of individuals with ID; the first sample of 29 adult individuals had been diagnosed with mild and moderate ID and were living in community-based settings, and the second sample of 25 adult individuals with ID had also been diagnosed with mild and moderate ID and were offenders on probation living in a variety of housing situations. Both groups scored lower than the normative data of the adult and juvenile normative sample provided by Grisso in his manual. However, the investigators were unable to perform statistical analyses to determine significant differences in scores between the normative sample and the study's samples. In a later project, Everington and Fulero (1999) again studied Grisso's scales with 48 adjudicated male and female offenders (18 had been diagnosed with ID, with a mean IQ of 68 and a range of 59 to 75, and 30 had not been diagnosed with ID). Offenders with ID scored significantly lower than the non-ID offenders on all three subtests of the scales. They also discovered that the individuals with ID were significantly more likely than their non-ID counterparts to receive a score of zero on items in the Comprehension of Miranda Rights subtest.

Another competence measure, the Competence Assessment for Standing Trial for Defendants with Mental Retardation (CAST-MR; Everington & Luckasson, 1992), has been specifically developed for use with ID populations. Research with the CAST-MR has demonstrated strong psychometric properties (Everington, 1990) as well as adequate predictive utility (Everington & Dunn, 1995). For example, in a study of 35 adult offenders with ID who had been court-ordered for pre-trial evaluation of competence to stand trial (15 had been found competent and 20 had not), Everington and Dunn (1995) discovered that the CAST-MR has an overall agreement rate of 68.57% with the court-determined competence status of the participants. The CAST-MR has been used in studies examining restoring competency to stand trial in offenders with ID (Anderson & Hewitt, 2002) as well as other issues regarding competence to stand trial (Everington, DeBerge, & Mauer, 2000). Furthermore, in their survey of test usage ratings for forensic evaluations of competency or sanity in adults, Archer, Buffington-Vollum, Stredny, and Handel (2006) found that among forensic psychologists, the CAST-MR was the second most frequently used competency measure, after the MacArthur Competence Assessment Tool-Criminal Adjudication (MacCAT-CA; Poythress et al., 1990). Although the literature with both these measures of pre-trial competency is still limited, both the CAST-MR and scales for Miranda comprehension appear appropriate for use in research with individuals with ID.

THE ISSUE OF MALINGERING ID

Before the ruling in *Atkins v. Virginia* (2002), there was a virtual absence of discussion of the possibility of feigned ID in forensic evaluations. With the exception of faking a disability in order to collect Social Security benefits, it was believed that few people would want to feign this disorder, and thus, there was little interest in the topic. Whatever the cause, the oversight is surprising, because the presence of individuals with ID in the criminal justice system has been well documented, and the incentive to feign is readily apparent (e.g., having a confession suppressed).

Research on the use of existing measures of malingering to detect feigned ID has produced disappointing results. Overall, this literature has demonstrated that existing measures and methods, when used according to the current standards of practice, generally misclassify bona fide cases of ID as malingered (Graue et al., 2007). In their review of research examining the use of various cognitive effort, psychiatric feigning, and adaptive behavior measures in the study of malingering ID, Salekin and Doane (2009) concluded that there are specific measures that should certainly not be used, such as the Structured Interview of Reported Symptoms (Rogers, Bagby, & Dickens, 1992). Other measures warrant further study before conclusions can be drawn, such as the Test of Memory Malingering (Tombaugh, 1996) and the Advanced Clinical Solutions for the WAIS-IV and WMS-IV, which proffers to assess suboptimal effort (Holdnack & Drozdick, 2009). Due to the lack of comprehensive evidence available on this topic, it is recommended that researchers consider examining measures that have not been studied at the time of writing, continue to study the measures for which research is sparse, and work to develop malingering indexes specific for use with individuals with ID.

At the time of this writing, only one published study has examined whether adaptive behavior measures were resilient to college students' attempts at feigning adaptive behavior deficits (Doane & Salekin, 2008).

After the students were instructed to feign deficits they believed to be appropriate for individuals with ID, mild ID, and moderate ID, the two adaptive behavior measures used were administered to the college students as the respondents. This technique can guide researchers who are interested in learning about respondent malingering as well as the question of whether individuals with ID can successfully malinger lower FSIQ scores on intelligence tests.

A detailed discussion of methods for conducting malingering research is presented in Chapter 11 of this book, but specific issues relevant to ID are discussed in the following text. Identifying an appropriate population for studying malingering of ID can be complicated. For example, it is important to screen out individuals with traumatic brain injury (which can be costly and difficult to achieve) as the presence of a traumatic brain injury may confound a study that simply uses low IQ as a means of identifying ID. Second, a threshold for inclusion should be no higher than an IQ of 85, because these individuals are unlikely to have the collateral evidence required to support a diagnosis of ID before the age of 18 and, therefore, would not be likely to be subject to an evaluation of ID in a criminal proceeding. The ideal sample for research examining feigned ID would be those in the borderline intellectual functioning range (i.e., IQ of 71 to 84—or 75 to 89, if one includes the standard error of measurement) who could possibly have FSIQ scores below 70, may have been described as "slow" in the past, and may have adaptive behavior deficits. These individuals would be most likely to be motivated to malinger ID and have the appropriate collateral evidence to support it.

CONCLUSIONS

Research with ID samples is not an easy task. There are unique design and implementation issues, beginning with the selection of the sample (e.g., pre-adjudicated vs. post-adjudicated offenders, incarcerated or community resident samples, etc.), and including the measurement of ID and adaptive behavior itself, as well as the Flynn effect problem. Added to that is the difficulty of using ID samples within the context of a forensic population, with issues of potential malingering and the possible contamination of legal cases. This chapter is intended to provide the interested researcher with some guidance in conceptualizing the difficulties that this sort of research inevitably brings with it.

REFERENCES

American Association on Intellectual and Developmental Disabilities (2010). *Intellectual disability: Definition, classification, and systems of support* (11th ed.). Washington, DC: Author.

American Association on Mental Retardation (2002). *Mental retardation: Definition,* *classification, and systems of supports* (10th ed.). Washington, DC: Author.

American Psychiatric Association (2000). *Diagnostic and statistical manual of mental disorders—DSM-IV-TR* (4th ed.). Washington, DC: Author.

Anderson, S. D., & Hewitt, J. (2002). The effect of competency restoration training on defendants with mental retardation found not competent to proceed. *Law and Human Behavior*, *26*, 343–351. doi: 10.1023/A:1015328505884

Archer, R. P., Buffington-Vollum, J. K., Stredny, R. V., & Handel, R. W. (2006). A survey of psychological test use patterns among forensic psychologists. *Journal of Personality Assessment*, *87*, 84–94. doi: 10.1207/s15327752jpa8701_07

Atkins v. Virginia, 536 U.S. 304 (2002).

Axelrod, B. N. (2002). Validity of the Wechsler Abbreviated Scale of Intelligence and other very short forms of estimating intellectual functioning. *Assessment*, *9*, 17–23. doi: 10.1177/1073191102009001003

Bruininks, R. H., Woodcock, R. W., Weatherman, R. F., & Hill, B. K. (1996). *Scales of Independent Behavior-Revised: Comprehensive manual*. Chicago, IL: Riverside.

Catron, D. W., & Thompson, C. C. (1979). Test-retest gains in WAIS scores after four retest intervals. *Journal of Clinical Psychology*, *35*, 352–357. doi: 10.1002/1097-4679(197904)35:2<352::AID-JCLP2270350226>3.0.CO;2-2

Doane, B. M., & Salekin, K. L. (2008). Susceptibility of current adaptive behavior measures to feigned deficits. *Law and Human Behavior*, *33*, 329–343. doi: 10.1007/s10979-008-9157-5

Edgerton, R. B. (1993). *The cloak of competence: Revised and updated*. Berkeley, CA: University of California Press.

Everington, C. T. (1990). The Competence Assessment for Standing Trial for Defendants with Mental Retardation (CAST-MR): A validation study. *Criminal Justice and Behavior*, *17*, 147–168. doi: 10.1177/0093854890017002001

Everington, C. T., & Dunn, C. (1995). A second validation study of the Competence Assessment for Standing Trial for Defendants with Mental Retardation (CAST-MR), *Criminal Justice and Behavior*, *22*, 44–58. doi: 10.1177/0093854895022001004

Everington, C. T., DeBerge, K., & Mauer, D. (2000). The relationship between language skills and competence to stand trial abilities in persons with mental retardation. *Journal of Psychiatry and Law*, *28*, 475–492. Retrieved from www.jaapl.org

Everington, C. T., & Fulero, S. M. (1999). Competence to confess: Measuring understanding and suggestibility of defendants with mental retardation. *Mental Retardation*, *37*, 212–220. doi: 10.1352/0047-6765(1999) 037<0212:CTCMUA>2.0.CO;2

Everington, C. T., & Luckasson, R. (1992). *Competence Assessment for Standing Trial for Defendants with Mental Retardation (CAST*MR)*. Worthington, OH: IDS.

Fletcher, R., Loschen, E., Stavrakaki, C., & First, M. (Eds.) (2007). *Diagnostic manual--intellectual disability (DM-ID): A textbook of diagnosis of mental disorders in persons with intellectual disability* (pp. 63–68). Kingston, NY: NADD Press.

Flynn, J. R. (1984). The mean IQ of Americans: Massive gains 1932 to 1978. *Psychological Bulletin*, *95*, 29–51. doi: 10.1037/0033-2909.95.1.29

Fulero, S. M., & Everington, C. (1995). Assessing competency to waive *Miranda* rights in defendants with mental retardation. *Law and Human Behavior*, *19*, 533–543. doi: 10.1007/BF01499342

Graue, L. O., Berry, D. T. R., Clark, J. A., Sollman, M. J., Cardi, M., Hopkins, J., & Werline, D. (2007). Identification of feigned mental retardation using the new generation of malingering detection instruments: Preliminary findings. *The Clinical Neuropsychologist*, *21*, 929–942. doi: 10.1080/13854040600932137

Grisso, T. (1981). *Juvenile waiver of rights: Legal and psychological competence*. New York, NY: Plenum.

Grisso, T. (1998). *Instruments for assessing understanding and appreciation of Miranda rights*. Sarasota, FL: Professional Resource Press.

Harrison, P. L., & Oakland, T. (2003). *Adaptive behavior assessment system* (2nd ed.). San Antonio, TX: Psychological Corporation.

Holland, A. J. (1991). Challenging and offending behavior by adults with developmental disorders. *Australia and New Zealand Journal of Developmental Disabilities*, *17*, 119–126.

Holland, T., Clare, I. C. H., & Mukhopadhyay, T. (2002). Prevalence of ''criminal offending'' by men and women with intellectual disability and the characteristics of ''offenders'': Implications for research and service development. *Journal of Intellectual Disability Research*, *46*, 6–20. doi: 10.1046/j. 1365-2788. 2002.00001.x

Holdnack, J. A., & Drozdick, L. W. (2009). *Advanced Clinical Solutions for the WAIS-IV and WMS-IV*. San Antonio, TX: The Psychological Corporation.

Hurley, A. D., Levitas, A., Lecavalier, L., & Pary, R. J. (2007). Assessment and diagnostic procedures. In R. Fletcher, E. Loschen, C. Stavrakaki, & M. First (Eds.), *Diagnostic manual—Intellectual disability: A textbook of diagnosis of mental disorders in persons with intellectual disability* (pp. 11–31). Kingston, NY: NADD Press.

Jones, J. (2007). Persons with intellectual disabilities in the criminal justice system: Review of issues. *International Journal of Offender Therapy and Comparative Criminology, 51,* 723–733. doi: 10.1177/0306624X07299343

Lindsay, W. R., Hastings, R. P., Griffiths, D. M., & Hayes, S. C. (2007). Trends and challenges in forensic research on offenders with intellectual disability. *Journal of Intellectual and Developmental Disability, 32,* 55–61. doi: 10.1080/13668250701378520

MacEachron, A. E. (1979). Mentally retarded offenders: Prevalence and characteristics. *American Journal of Mental Deficiency, 84,* 165–176.

Matarazzo, J. D., Carmody, T. P., & Jacobs, L. D. (1980). Test-retest reliability and stability of the WAIS: A literature review with implications for clinical practice. *Journal of Clinical Neuropsychology, 2,* 89–105. doi: 10.1016/S0891-4222(97)00031-0

Matson, J. L., & Bamburg, J. W. (1998). Reliability of the assessment of dual diagnosis (ADD). *Research in Developmental Disabilities, 19,* 89–95. doi: 10.1016/S0891-4222(97)00031-0

McGillivray, J. A., & Moore, M. R. (2001). Substance use by offenders with mild intellectual disability. *Journal of Intellectual and Developmental Disability, 26,* 297–310. doi: 10.1080/13668250120087317

Meyers, A. R., Branch, L. G., & Lederman, R. I. (1988). Alcohol, tobacco, and cannabis use by independently living adults with major disabling conditions. *The International Journal of Addictions, 23,* 671–685.

Miranda v. Arizona, 384 U.S. 436 (1966).

Moss, S., C., Ibbotson, B., Prosser, H., Goldberg, D. P., Patel, P., & Simpson, N. (1997). Validity of the PAS-ADD for detecting psychiatric symptoms in adults with learning disability (mental retardation). *Social Psychiatry & Psychiatric Epidemiology, 32,* 344–354. doi: 10.1007/BF00805440

O'Brien, G. (2002). Dual diagnosis in offenders with intellectual disability: Setting research priorities: A review of research findings concerning psychiatric disorder (excluding personality disorder) among offenders with intellectual disability. *Journal of Intellectual Disability Research, 46,* 21–30. doi: 10.1046/j.1365-2788.2002.00002.x

Petersilia, J. (2000). *Doing justice? The criminal justice system and offenders with disabilities.* Irvine, CA: University of California.

Poythress, N. G., Nicholson, R., Otto, R. K., Edens, J. F., Bonnie, R. J., Monahan, J., & Hoge, S. K. (1999). *The MacArthur Competence Assessment Tool-Criminal Adjudication: Professional manual (MacCAT-CA).* Lutz, FL: Psychological Assessment Resources.

Prout, H. T., & Strohmer, D. C. (1989). *Prout-Strohmer Assessment System.* Schenectady, NY: Genium Publishing.

Reiss, S. (1988). *The Reiss Screen for Maladaptive Behavior test manual.* Worthington, OH: IDS.

Roid, G. (2003). *Stanford-Binet Intelligence Scales (5th ed.): Technical manual.* Itasca, IL: Riverside.

Rogers, R., Bagby, M. R., & Dickens, S. E. (1992). *SIRS-Structured Interview of Reported Symptoms: Professional manual.* Odessa, FL: PAR.

Salekin, K. L., & Doane, B. (2009). Malingering intellectual disability: The value of available measures and methods. *Applied Neuropsychology, 16,* 105–113. doi: 10.1080/09084280902864485

Sparrow, S. S., Cicchetti, D. V., & Balla, D. A. (2005). *Vineland Adaptive Behavior Scales: (2nd ed.) (Vineland II), Survey Interview Form/Caregiver Rating Form,* Livonia, MN: Pearson Assessments.

Tassé, M. J. (2009). Adaptive behavior assessment and the diagnosis of mental retardation in capital cases. *Applied Neuropsychology, 16,* 114–123. doi: 10.1080/09084280902864451

Tombaugh, T. N. (1996). *Test of Memory Malingering (TOMM).* New York, NY: Multi-Health Systems, Inc.

Wechsler, D. (2008). *Wechsler Adult Intelligence Scale-4th ed.* San Antonio, TX: The Psychological Corporation.

Widaman, K. F., & Siperstein, G. N. (2009). Assessing adaptive behaviors of criminal defendants in capital cases: A reconsideration. *American Journal of Forensic Psychology, 27,* 5–32.

PART V

CIVIL AND FAMILY LAW ISSUES

CHAPTER 22

Decisional Competence to Consent to or Refuse Mental Health Treatment

ERIC B. ELBOGEN

A FUNDAMENTAL ETHICAL value underlying mental-health care is that adults have the right to determine how to treat their own psychological conditions (Appelbaum & Grisso, 1995; Hoge, 1994). Self-determination of mental health care is only meaningful, though, when a patient has provided informed consent, meaning his or her decision was freely made, adequately informed, and based on sufficient ability or capacity to make treatment decisions (Grisso & Appelbaum, 1998a). In the United States, this capacity to make treatment decisions informs legal determinations of decisional "competence" to consent to or to refuse treatment (Wettstein, 2004). With respect to mental health care, decisional competence is, therefore, a necessary legal condition before a mental health professional can accept a patient's treatment consent or refusal (Berg, Appelbaum, & Lidz, 2001). In addition, ensuring decisional competence promotes respect for individual autonomy *and* facilitates shared decision making between mental health professionals and patients. As such, the process of obtaining informed consent and evaluating whether a client has decisional competence is grounded in ethics, law, and good clinical practice (Grisso & Appelbaum, 1998a).

The terms competence and autonomy are sometimes confused, but bioethicists clarify that "competence allows a person to exercise his or her autonomy" (Wettstein, 2004). Still, in the case of mental illness, a person's ability to exercise autonomous choice may be compromised at times because a mentally ill person's level of decisional competence can fluctuate as a result of the cyclical nature of the disorder (Grisso & Appelbaum, 1998a). For example, a person with schizophrenia who experiences commanding auditory hallucinations to use cocaine and stop taking medications may be unable to make treatment decisions competently. However, when this very same person is stabilized in the community, does not exhibit overt psychotic symptoms, and no longer hears voices, he or she may be able to competently consent to or refuse mental health treatment. Thus, a given individual at one time may have decisional competence to make mental health treatment decisions but at another time may not. It is also important to note that decisional competence as a legal term is task specific (Grisso & Appelbaum, 1998a). This means, for example, that if a person is competent to manage their finances, that same person may be not competent to make mental health treatment decisions. In other words, to assess decisional competence, it is necessary to focus on the functional abilities being assessed (as opposed to seeking some global determination that someone is "incompetent").

Several developments in the law inform assessments of decisional competence to make mental health treatment decisions. In *Schloendorff v. Society of New York Hospitals* (1914), Justice Benjamin Cardozo asserted that "every human being of adult years and sound mind has a right to determine what shall be done with his body." Judge Cardozo's maxim is frequently cited as providing key criteria for informed consent (namely, that treatment decisions be voluntary), but in addition, the statement raises the question about what constitutes a "sound" mind. In other words, while people in the United States are legally presumed to be competent to make treatment decisions, does this apply to people of "unsound" mind? Judge Cardozo thus foreshadowed that the voluntariness of a treatment decision is a necessary, but not a sufficient, condition for informed consent. In other words, additional components regarding a person's cognitive state would be needed to more comprehensively define informed consent.

The holding in *Canterbury v. Spence* (1972) helped define what has been called the "materiality" standard of informed consent, by which clinicians need to ask not what they think patients should know but what the "reasonable patient" would want to know. To meet this standard, patients should understand the medical condition, the specific problem to be addressed by treatment, proposed interventions, benefits, side effects and complications, and reasonable alternatives to the treatment. As a result, *Canterbury* and subsequent case law (e.g., *Truman v. Thomas*, 1980) has aimed to guarantee that patients receive sufficient information to make choices about treatment so as to form a reasonable basis to decide whether or not to refuse that treatment.

As applied to mental health care, these legal holdings indicate that for a person to make an informed choice about mental health treatment, the person would need to comprehend the mental illness, the specific psychological problem addressed by the treatment, proposed interventions, the risks and clinical benefits of each, and whether there were other therapeutic options available. Although not explicit, this formulation implies that the patient is not only making this decision freely and with adequate information but with sufficient decisional competence. In other words, if a patient does not have decisional competence, he or she cannot provide informed consent and thereby have his or her preferences honored.

Grisso and Appelbaum (1998a) posited four domains underlying decisional competence to make treatment decisions: understanding, appreciation, reasoning, and choice. First, *understanding* means that the patient comprehends the basic information and issues involved related to abilities assessed. In the case of making mental health treatment decisions, one would assess to what extent the patient is able to understand basic components of the mental disorder or to what extent the patient is able to understand the risks and benefits of different treatment modalities and options. Second is the domain of *appreciation*, which connotes acknowledging that the decision that must be made is relevant to the patient and that the patient believes that this decision relates to his or her own situation. For example, does the psychiatric patient believe that he or she has a mental disorder? Does the patient believe that the psychotropic medications or psychotherapy are relevant to him or her?

Third, decisional competence involves assessment of *reasoning* abilities. This involves determining whether a person can clearly weigh the pros and cons of the decision to consent to or refuse mental health treatment and focuses on the process by which the patient arrives at his or her ultimate decision. Can the patient compare different mental health treatment options in a rational and organized manner? Finally, the fourth dimension involves *choice*, which means that the individual can meet the demands involved in the decision-making context of making a mental health treatment decision and can arrive at a final choice among the different options available. Is the patient able to express a preference for a particular treatment that is consistent with the reasoning indicated previously? Or is the patient too ambivalent to select a final choice?

However, when psychiatric patients experience a crisis, they may or may not have sufficient decisional competence in these four domains to consent to or refuse mental health treatment. A treatment refusal can be especially relevant during these periods of crisis, since not being treated may increase a person's risk of harm to self or others. In general, courts have precluded the need for an assessment of decisional capacity when forced medication is medically appropriate, such as when a person with mental illness is at imminent risk of being dangerous (*Washington v. Harper*, 1990). In other situations, in which a psychiatric patient may not be imminently dangerous, case law in the United States has generally outlined two models for handling a patient's right to refuse psychiatric treatment (Wettstein, 2004). First is what has been called a "treatment-driven" model as exemplified in the case of *Rennie v. Klein* (1983). The court in *Rennie* mandated a medical review by independent psychiatrists determining whether a person is competent to make decisions before medications could be forced. Thus, forced medication occurs without judicial review and is left at the purview of clinicians. The second model, called the "rights-driven" model, does involve court intervention and is exemplified by *Rogers v. Commissioner* (1983). In *Rogers*, it was held that only a judge using substituted judgment could authorize involuntary administration of antipsychotic medication. In this model, a committed psychiatric patient is presumed competent and has a right to make treatment judgments until he or she is adjudicated incompetent by a judge.

Either way, forcing psychotropic medication potentially raises issues of coercion and undermines a person's autonomous choice (Wettstein, 2004). How can individuals with mental illness have their autonomy respected at the time they have lost decisional capacity? As a potential solution to this problem, legislation on advance-care planning for mental health treatment has proliferated in recent years with the goal of promoting greater self-determination among people with mental illness during periods of decisional incompetence. In the United States, psychiatric advance directive (PAD) laws have been passed in 25 states, allowing competent persons to document advance instructions for their future mental health treatment or to designate a health care agent to make decisions for them, in the event of an incapacitating psychiatric crisis (Swanson et al., 2006). In addition to recognizing the potential benefits of PADs, many states are beginning to recognize legal obligations under the federal Patient Self-Determination Act of 1991, which includes informing all hospital patients that they have a right to prepare advance directives and, with certain caveats, that clinicians are obliged to follow these directives (Hoge, 1994). As such, federal law helps ensure that people with mental illness, in whatever state they live, can use medical advance directives to specify mental health treatment preferences or to assign proxy decision makers for mental health decisions.

The presumption of competence to execute PADs is a controversial legal feature of these statutes. Some mental health professionals would argue that a clinical assessment of competence should be required for patients who want to complete PADs, in view of the fluctuating decisional capacity that often characterizes severe mental illness. However, mandatory screening for competence—placing the burden on people with mental illness to prove they are competent before completing a legal document—could be seen as a form of discrimination against adults with disabilities (Srebnik, Appelbaum, & Russo, 2004). Regardless, it is important to note that civil commitment criteria typically override patient treatment preferences and that doctors can override preferences in PADs if they do not comport with community standards of medical care (Swanson et al., 2006). As such, despite the intent of PADs to promote patient self-determination, it is important to recognize that PAD laws do not permit patients to write any preference they want "carte blanche."

Decisional competence to make mental health decisions is a prerequisite to self-determined mental health care, derives from case law on informed consent, and is a central focus of PAD statutes. Because it forms a cornerstone of mental health care, much empirical research conducted during the past two decades has focused on various facets of decisional competence to make mental health treatment decisions. In the following text, the predominant empirical methodologies are described by (a) sample population, (b) measurement of decisional capacity, (c) construct validity of decisional capacity tools, and (d) interventions to improve decisional capacity. In each, challenges faced by researchers are highlighted and avenues to expand scholarship are recommended. Methodological approaches used relatively less often in the forensic psychology literature are also pointed out, including (a) descriptive research on clinical practice of decisional competence assessment and (b) qualitative analysis of treatment decision making. Ultimately, the more we know about decisional competence to make mental health treatment decisions, the more we can help promote autonomy and self-determination and high quality mental health care among the millions of people who suffer from mental disorders.

SAMPLE POPULATION AND DECISIONAL COMPETENCE

Most research examining competence to consent to or refuse mental health treatment has been limited to patients with schizophrenia and major depression. The MacArthur Treatment Competence Study (Grisso, Appelbaum, Mulvey, & Fletcher, 1995) found that

- Only a minority of subjects with schizophrenia, depression, or no mental illness showed impaired decisional abilities.
- Patients with schizophrenia, followed by those with depression, showed the poorest understanding of treatment, the poorest reasoning in decision making regarding treatment, and the greatest likelihood of not appreciating their illness or potential benefits of treatment.
- Among hospitalized depressed patients (Grisso et al., 1995), only 25% showed some difficulties with decision making, and 14% typically failed to acknowledge the potential value of treatment.
- Among hospitalized patients with schizophrenia, only 25% met their definition of "impaired" on each of three domains (understanding, appreciation, and reasoning) and 48% showed adequate performance on all three domains.

Overall, the findings have helped to dispel the belief that having a serious mental illness automatically meant that someone lacked decisional competence.

There has also been research assessing decisional competence in middle-aged or older adults with schizophrenia (Palmer, Dunn, Appelbaum, & Jeste, 2004), ostensibly because this subgroup may suffer from a combination of psychiatric symptoms and cognitive deficits. With respect to PADs, research has also primarily focused on psychotic disorders. Srebnik et al. (2005) showed that those diagnosed with schizophrenia were competent to complete PADs and make treatment decisions, finding that most participants were able to understand, appreciate, and reason adequately about PADs and the treatment preferences within the documents. Elbogen, Swanson, Appelbaum, et al. (2007) found the same results in the same population using a different and larger sample. As with the findings previously cited by Grisso and Appelbaum, researchers have shown that with respect to PADs, most people with schizophrenia and other psychotic disorders are competent to write and document treatment preferences within these legal documents.

However, considerable heterogeneity exists within diagnosis regarding decisional capacity (Jeste, Depp, & Palmer, 2006). Jeste et al. (2006) evaluated the magnitude of differences across 12 published studies on competence to make treatment decisions and found substantial variation among people with schizophrenia. Srebnik et al. (2005) and Elbogen, Swanson, Appelbaum, et al. (2007) correspondingly found that diagnosis per se did not relate to competence to complete PADs but that within diagnosis, there existed a wide range of abilities. Indeed, most empirical studies (with only a few exceptions) have involved relatively stable outpatients with schizophrenia or depression rather than patients with these disorders who suffer from severe symptoms. It is this latter group that is likely at greatest risk for needing a competency evaluation in clinical practice, and yet it is these same individuals who may be most difficult to have consent to a study in the first place. Institutional review boards (IRBs) are often reluctant to grant approval for research involving participants who potentially cannot competently consent to the research itself. Thus, there is arguably a somewhat limited range in terms of severity, even within schizophrenia and depression spectrum disorders. One solution is to argue that a study of decisional capacity is "low risk" and therefore might not require a high level of consent such that "assent" could plausibly be the appropriate standard for such research.

Researchers have not yet fully explored decisional capacity with respect to other mental disorders. Outside of one case study (Byatt, Pinals, & Arikan, 2006), there appear to be no studies that enrolled patients with bipolar disorder to study their capacity to make mental health treatment decisions. Moreover, some other psychiatric disabilities and psychological problems for which people consent to or refuse treatment have not been thoroughly examined, including posttraumatic stress disorder, adjustment disorders, obsessive-compulsive disorder, generalized anxiety disorders, phobias, and dysthymia. Some scholars have argued about the need to examine decisional capacity in connection with anorexia and other eating disorders, arguing that many factors that influence competence in anorexia nervosa are different from those in schizophrenia and depression (Charland, 2006). Are patients with these disorders able to understand, appreciate, reason, and make choices about their treatments, and if so, what affects these decisions? Future research would investigate these dimensions of decisional competence for a greater variety of mental health problems. Access to these varying clinical populations is often a challenge for investigators. But colleagues conducting almost any type of clinical trial might be persuaded that their adding a measure of decisional capacity would enhance their study and address important clinical and ethical concerns about the intervention itself.

MEASUREMENT OF DECISIONAL COMPETENCE

A recent literature review (Sturman, 2005) showed that the MacArthur Competence Assessment Tool-Treatment (MacCAT-T) is currently the most widely used instrument to assess patients' competence to make treatment decisions, examining capacity in the four domains of understanding, appreciation, reasoning, and choice (Grisso & Appelbaum, 1998b). Grisso et al. (1997) reported that the MacCAT-T shows (a) a high degree of inter-rater reliability, (b) good construct validity, and (c) reasonable clinical feasibility, requiring about 15 to 20 minutes to administer.

Another instrument used to measure decisional competence to make mental health treatment decisions is the Hopkins Competency Assessment Test (HCAT), a brief instrument for evaluating the competency of patients to give informed consent or write advance directives (Janofsky, McCarthy, & Folstein, 1992). The HCAT consists of a short essay regarding the principles of informed consent and a questionnaire for determining patients' understanding of these principles. Research has shown that correct answers on the HCAT correlate significantly with forensic psychiatrists' assessments of decisional capacity. Consequently, the instrument has been used as a tool to screen patients for decisional competence to consent to or refuse treatment. An instrument focusing on just the appreciation domain of decisional competence is the California Scale of Appreciation (CSA) (Saks et al., 2002), which consists of 18 items rated according to the concept of what are called "patently false beliefs," sets of beliefs that are grossly improbable (Saks et al., 2002), and has been validated with patients with psychotic disorders and comparison subjects.

The Competence Assessment Tool for Psychiatric Advance Directives (CAT-PAD) was developed to mirror the structure of the MacCAT-T and was designed to assess competence to complete a PAD (Srebnik et al., 2004). From the perspective of the four domains of decisional competence, competence to complete a PAD is thought to involve two abilities: a capacity to write the PAD document and a capacity to make the treatment decisions recorded within the PAD. In other words, someone may understand, appreciate, and reason satisfactorily about what a PAD is and how to fill one out but may still be less competent with respect to the specific treatment preferences documented within, such as making choices about medications or hospital treatment. Thus, the CAT-PAD assesses decisional capacity regarding the nature and value of PADs *and* a specific treatment choice. A briefer version of the CAT-PAD is the Decisional Competence Assessment Tool for Psychiatric Advance Directives (DCAT-PAD) (Elbogen, Swanson, Appelbaum, et al., 2007). Both the CAT-PAD and DCAT-PAD have shown very good to excellent internal consistency and good construct validity in psychotic populations.

The majority of the aforementioned studies using decisional capacity tools have investigated consent to or refusal of antipsychotic or antidepressant medications. To our knowledge, only a few studies have examined decisional capacity with respect to electroconvulsive therapy (ECT) (Lapid et al., 2003; Westreich, Levine, Ginsburg, & Wilets, 1995). Even less has been studied regarding psychotherapeutic interventions, possibly because such interventions are perceived to have less potential harm to a patient than would side effects of medication. However, it is largely unknown how patients decide to enroll in dialectical behavior therapy (DBT), cognitive behavioral therapy (CBT), interpersonal therapies, and brief family interventions.

Consider a number of evidence-based practices for patients with severe mental illness, such as assertive community treatment, supported employment, family psychoeducation, integrated dual disorders treatment, and illness management and recovery. To what extent do patients who are beginning to use these interventions truly understand their benefits and risks and alternatives? The process of making decisions about these psychosocial treatments would, on the surface, seem quite different from the process of making decisions about psychotropic medications. Given that many of these evidence-based practices are framed as "client centered," it is surprising how little is known about the decisional competence of people with mental illness to consent to them. Failing to provide complete informed consent would both undermine the self-determination of the consumer and potentially undermine the effectiveness of the treatment, especially to the extent to which expectations are misunderstood.

CONSTRUCT VALIDITY OF DECISIONAL COMPETENCE TOOLS

Research confirms that increased psychiatric symptoms, usually assessed with the Brief Psychiatric Rating Scale (BPRS), relate to reduced decisional capacity on most domains of the MacCAT-T (Grisso & Appelbaum, 1998a; Grisso et al., 1995; Jeste et al., 2006; Palmer & Savla, 2007). Recent research has also confirmed the importance of neurocognition in assessing decisional competence; however, no particular cognitive tests have emerged as unique predictors of decisional capacity, and there is not yet sufficient empirical analysis to discern differential relationships between specific neuropsychological abilities and specific domains of decisional capacity (Palmer & Savla, 2007). Elbogen, Swanson, Appelbaum, et al. (2007) found that the understanding domain was predicted by estimated pre-morbid IQ, higher abstract thinking abilities, superior immediate memory, and delayed memory whereas appreciation was predicted by symptom severity on the BPRS. As a result, it may be that cognitive functioning relates to some domains of decisional competence (e.g., understanding) whereas psychiatric symptoms relate to other domains (e.g., appreciation).

One limitation in this literature, which involves a number of instruments used to measure construct validity of these decisional tools, is the difficulties inherent in measuring psychiatric symptoms. For example, the widely used BPRS has multiple versions, some anchored and others not, and requires rater training and assessment of inter-rater reliability. Other measures tapping symptoms of psychosis or depression (e.g., Beck Depression Inventory) may not have such requirements and may provide concurrent or divergent validity on current sets of findings. With regard to studies of cognitive functioning and decision making, investigations using a more comprehensive neuropsychological assessment battery would help elucidate cognitive mechanisms underlying the treatment decision-making process. One would assume that executive functioning would be associated with the reasoning section of the MacCAT-T, but research has not examined this possible association in any detail. Moreover, how does memory functioning relate to the treatment decision-making task? Expansion of the measures used to correlate with decisional competence instruments would lead to a richer and more in-depth understanding of decisional capacity.

Further, most studies have been cross-sectional; longitudinal research might help identify new variables associated with decisional competence. For example, might there be clinical benefits associated with higher levels of decisional competence? In the context of a facilitated PAD intervention, the exercise of sharpening and clarifying one's mental health treatment preferences and decision making was associated with enhanced therapeutic alliance, increased perceived self-determination of treatment, and reduced coercive interventions (Elbogen, Swanson, Appelbaum, et al., 2007; Elbogen, Swanson, Swartz, et al., 2007; Swanson et al., 2006). Perhaps similar benefits exist for those who have a high level of decisional competence to make mental health treatment decisions? Future research would therefore look at clinical outcomes associated with decisional competence to determine whether ethical practice (ensuring informed consent) relates to therapeutic benefit (enhanced treatment engagement).

INTERVENTIONS TO IMPROVE DECISIONAL COMPETENCE

Only a few studies have focused specifically on improving competence to make mental health treatment decisions. One intervention focused on antipsychotic medication decisions among people with schizophrenia and compared a single educational session alone with a single educational session followed later by distribution of printed information and review of patients' answers on a questionnaire testing their knowledge (Kleinman, Schachter, Jeffries, & Goldhamer, 1993). The authors found that knowledge increased for both groups at six months and two years but that there were no significant differences between two groups. A second study focused on ECT decision making for patients with depression (Westreich et al., 1995) in which participants in the control condition were given a standard informed consent and those in the experimental condition were given a video on ECT. However, the authors found no differences between the groups, indicating that the addition of an informational video to the consent process did not result in improved knowledge about ECT. Another study essentially replicated this finding (Lapid et al., 2003), showing that an educational intervention improved decisional competence but that no single intervention seemed better than any others, concluding that additional educational intervention may not result in measurable improvement in decisional competence.

In the area of PADs, the facilitated PAD is an intervention that encourages patients to think about past treatment experiences and provides education for participants about writing an advance instruction and designating proxy decision makers (Swanson et al., 2006). PAD facilitators (a) elicit preferences and advance consent or refusal for psychotropic medications, hospital treatment, or ECT and (b) gather information about crisis symptoms, relapse and protective factors, and instructions for inpatient staff (e.g., effective strategies to avoid use of seclusion and restraints). The facilitated PAD intervention bolstered subjects' competence to make mental health treatment decisions (Elbogen, Swanson, Appelbaum, et al., 2007). It was hypothesized that the facilitation process helped participants to actively think about their preferences for hospitalization in the event of a crisis as well as how they would want hospital staff to treat them if they were confined to an inpatient unit. As such, the facilitated PAD afforded participants an opportunity to consider consequences of hospital treatment. It was concluded that the facilitated PAD may therefore maximize the likelihood that PADs accurately reflect patients' preferences for future treatment and also increase the likelihood that clinicians would adhere to said requests.

A number of intervention modalities used in other areas of decisional capacity can be adapted by researchers for improving mental health treatment decision making. Dunn and Jeste (2001) reviewed the literature on interventions to improve informed consent for medical treatment and found that written, rather than oral, consent led to greater understanding and that shorter rather than longer consent forms were better. Further, visually based and multimedia presentations were helpful for understanding treatment-related consent information. Finally, interventions that involved more active patient participation improved understanding (Dunn & Jeste, 2001). However, there has been no application of these methods to improving competence to make mental health treatment decisions. Further, outside of the facilitated PAD, most research in this area has not been designed as a randomized clinical trial; thus, it is largely unknown which interventions best enhance decision making (although such studies are common among medically ill patients). A study comparing different types of multimedia presentations with a "usual-care" control group would help determine to what extent (or whether) psychiatric patients make gains in decisional capacity. Applying intervention research designs to this area of scholarship would contribute to the knowledge base on capacity to make mental health treatment decisions given the limited research in this area to date.

DESCRIPTIVE RESEARCH ON CLINICAL PRACTICE OF DECISIONAL COMPETENCE ASSESSMENT

Without a closer examination of how competence to make mental health treatment decisions occurs in actual practice, it will be difficult to pinpoint strategies for improving the assessment in "real-world" clinical settings. In other words, while clinicians may be aware of, or even use, the MacCAT-T, it is unknown how they use the MacCAT-T to arrive at final decisions of decisional competence. Are the results of these measures ignored (i.e., used only when they concur with the clinician's opinion)? Are the results being used incorrectly to determine competence? Might other dimensions, such as a patient's behavior, override the findings of the MacCAT-T? Are there certain clinical circumstances in which the MacCAT-T is perceived by mental health professionals as more or less useful? Without descriptive research into the process of how decisional competence is actually assessed, the science of assessing decision making will not be effectively integrated into practice at the bedside.

Several methodologies could be employed to help describe the process of how (or whether) decisional capacity is assessed in clinical practice. One approach is to use surveys to gather data from clinicians about how they make decisions when they conduct capacity assessments. One study surveyed psychiatrists in Canada about attitudes and behaviors with respect to obtaining informed consent for antipsychotic medications (Schachter & Kleinman, 2004). The authors found that 78% of those surveyed routinely disclosed information about tardive dyskinesia when prescribing antipsychotic medications. They found that positive attitudes toward informed consent were a strong predictor of whether psychiatrists disclosed information about antipsychotic medications and the risk of tardive dyskinesia. It should be noted, however, that most questions asked in the survey concerned disclosure of information rather than whether and how clinicians assessed decisional capacity specifically. To our knowledge, there have been no surveys of clinicians' usual practice in assessing decisional capacity.

Another approach to descriptive research involves direct observation of the assessment process itself. The frequency of assessment of decisional capacity has been addressed in the context of research that focuses on informed consent in outpatient medical care. In an analysis examining the process of informed consent in 1057 audiotaped encounters containing 3552 clinical decisions (Braddock, Edwards, Hasenberg, Laidley, & Levinson, 1999), only 9% of treatment decisions met the authors' definition of completeness for informed consent. Basic decisions were completely informed 17% of the time, whereas less than 1% of complex decisions were considered completely informed. Among the elements of informed consent most often present was discussion of the nature of the intervention (71% of the time); the element least often present was assessment of patient's decisional competence (observed only 1.5% of the time). It is important to recognize, however, that this finding about the infrequency of the decisional competence assessments may indicate that competency is a very rare issue in clinical practice, not that it was insufficiently assessed. It is also unknown how these findings would compare to informed consent in mental health treatment decisions.

A final methodology for analyzing in decision making would be through archival record review, to determine how or whether a decisional competence evaluation was documented and to what extent the circumstances surrounding the referral influenced the assessment. For decisional competence for mental health treatment, no empirical research has been conducted examining this to our knowledge. Record reviews, direct observation, and surveys could help address questions such as what facilitates or thwarts decisional competence assessment in practice. Why might the process of informed consent be incomplete and the use of PADs be uncommon in mental health practice?

Commentators have identified a number of objections to informed consent that serve as barriers to regular assessments, including the concern that consent cannot be truly informed, that patients do not wish to be involved in decision making, that there may be harmful effects from informing patients, and that informed consent takes too much time, especially in the current environment of managed care (Berg et al., 2001). With respect to PADs, people with mental illness report difficulty in understanding advance directives, skepticism about their benefit, and lack of contact with a trusted individual who could serve as proxy decision maker. The sheer complexity of filling out these legal forms, obtaining witnesses, having the documents notarized, and filing the documents in a medical record or registry may pose formidable barriers (Elbogen, Swanson, Appelbaum, et al., 2007). Moreover, surveys of mental health professionals' attitudes about PADs suggest that they are generally supportive of these legal instruments but have significant concerns about some features of PADs and the feasibility of implementing them in usual care settings. Clinicians are concerned, for example, about following PADs that contain treatment refusals or medically inappropriate instructions. They also worry about lack of access to PAD documents in a crisis, lack of staff training on PADs, lack of communication between staff across different components of mental health systems, and lack of time to review the advance directive documents (Van Dorn et al., 2006).

A number of descriptive research questions about implementation remain. How frequently do psychiatrists go through all the elements of informed consent with their patients when helping them to decide to take psychotropic medications? How often does this happen when an outpatient psychotherapist first meets with a client or when people with mental illness are enrolled in psychosocial recovery and rehabilitation programs? And when informed consent does happen, is decisional competence considered? Questions about rates with which informed consent occurs in practice can help identify potential barriers to its use. Do clinicians' perceptions about the usefulness of informed consent affect frequency, or are systemic time constraints the real barrier to informed consent? Do any factors appear to be related to increased use of informed consent with people of mental illness?

It may be hypothesized that clinicians who perceive the usefulness of shared decision making or psychosocial recovery may be more likely to engage a patient in the process of informed consent. Future research is needed to detail how best to increase the use of this ethical and arguably clinically necessary practice. Similar research is needed to identify barriers to an increased frequency of PADs for the same reasons. Without more knowledge about what obstacles get in the way of clinicians using PADs or helping patients go through the process of informed consent, there will be little chance of developing empirically based strategies for enhancing and increasing their use.

QUALITATIVE ANALYSIS OF MENTAL HEALTH TREATMENT DECISION MAKING

Despite decisional competence tools prompting participants to answer open-ended questions, virtually all studies described involve quantitative but not qualitative understanding of what participants say. Rich data on the process of decision making have not been tapped into in the forensic psychology literature. Qualitative research on PADs has yielded important insight into how patients make mental health treatment decisions. One study examined content of 80 PADs and found 81% of mentally ill participants provided advance consent to medications, most often antidepressants and second-generation antipsychotics, and 64% documented advance refusal of medications, usually first-generation antipsychotics (Srebnik et al., 2005); 68% preferred hospital alternatives to hospitalization, 89% specified methods of de-escalation during a psychiatric crisis, and 72% indicated that they would refuse ECT. Instructions were rated as feasible, useful, and consistent with practice standards for the vast majority of the PADs (>95 %). Results from both studies suggest that people with mental illness can provide clinically useful mental health treatment preferences.

Qualitative analysis of the kinds of mental health treatment decisions in 125 PADs created by patients with psychotic disorder showed that while the majority (75%) of people with mental illness refused at least one psychotropic medication, all of the subjects consented to at least one psychotropic medication as well; in other words, no one refused all medications (Elbogen, Swanson, Swartz, et al., 2007). Instead, people with mental illness provided reasons why they refused psychiatric treatment, usually due to unfavorable side effects. For example, people wrote, "I refuse Haldol or Thorazine, because they make me stiff, I get blurred vision, and feel like a zombie," "I don't want Depakote, because one time I had it and I got pancreatitis," and "They've given me Ativan before, but I absolutely do not want any medications I could become addicted to."

Patients preferred atypical antipsychotics to conventional antipsychotic medications. Half the sample refused electroconvulsive therapy (ECT) under any circumstance, and again, people with mental illness were generally able to state the reasons behind these ECT treatment decisions. Psychiatrists blindly rated these PAD documents and found medication preferences were rated as feasible and consistent with community practice standards (90.5%) (Swanson et al., 2006). Similarly, hospital preferences were rated as feasible (83.1%) and clinically useful (94.1%). Global ratings of the PADs showed high feasibility and consistency with community practice standards in mental health care (90.5%).

However, what patients say they want in terms of mental health treatment may be different from what they actually do with respect to the mental health treatment. In particular, treatment and medication non-adherence remains commonplace in the treatment of schizophrenia, bipolar disorder, and depression. For example, the CATIE study showed 64% to 82% discontinuation rates of antipsychotic medications over a year and a half among people with schizophrenia (Lieberman et al., 2005). However, treatment non-adherence and psychiatric disorders may be intentional—when patients choose not to take their medications—or inadvertent—when patients forget to take their medications as prescribed. It is also possible that patients demonstrate intermittent adherence, especially among those who are experiencing uncomfortable or even painful side effects from psychotropic medications. There has been very little research examining the interrelationships between decisional competence, treatment preferences, and adherence to mental-health service.

SUMMARY

This chapter describes main areas of empirical research on decisional competence to consent to or to refuse mental health treatment; however, other methodologies relevant to advancing the field should be mentioned. For example, ethical and philosophical inquiry into the four criteria of decisional capacity posited previously has received only a little emphasis in mainstream forensic psychology and forensic psychiatry literature, despite the fact that most of the aforementioned research explicitly or implicitly relies on this conceptualization of decisional capacity. Might there be other definitions of decisional capacity that could be considered? Are the four domains required? There has been some debate about the necessity of the "appreciation" component of decisional capacity (Saks et al., 2002). But in general, significantly more attention is needed to sharpen definitions of the understanding, reasoning, appreciation, and choice domains and to question and clarify the boundaries of these domains.

In terms of law and policy, research has yet to analyze how each of the 50 states in the United States defines decisional capacity. How many use the four criteria outlined? Or some subset of these? Or none at all? If these criteria are not used in statutory language of decisional competence, what is substituted instead? A review of 25 PAD statutes shows considerable variability across jurisdictions for defining decisional capacity. Future work might involve a content analysis of such statutory language to better learn how the law generally defines decisional competence to consent to or refuse treatment. Currently, this is unknown.

Despite the numerous questions raised, empirical research has made significant progress in understanding and improving decisional competence to make mental health treatment decisions. This research has dispelled the myth that people with mental illness are simply unable to competently make mental health treatment decisions or write PADs. With the development of more sophisticated instruments of measuring decisional competence has come the insight that people with mental illness are able to understand, appreciate, reason, and make choices about their mental health treatment to a level of sufficient decisional capacity. In other words, mental illness does not necessarily imply incompetence to make mental health treatment decisions.

At the same time, this research has revealed risk factors that may decrease a patient's ability to make treatment decisions confidently, including psychiatric symptoms and neurocognitive deficits. Further, this research has sought to increase decisional competence to make treatment decisions, including among patients with severe cognitive deficits. Promising interventions, including multimedia approaches and the facilitated PADs, have revealed statistically significant improvements in various domains of decisional competence over the short term and for even the most impaired patients. Research also reveals that, when asked about advance treatment preferences, people with mental illness are able to make reasonable choices and provide good reasons behind those choices.

In sum, decisional capacity to make health treatment decisions is a cornerstone of every single clinical encounter with patients suffering from mental illnesses. In addition to obtaining informed consent to meet ethical and legal standards, mental health professionals have long recognized the therapeutic value for their clients and patients to be involved in their treatment, to share in decision making, and to understand what treatment goals are. The importance of this has been underscored by a tremendous amount of empirical research during the past decades on the topic, but this research is merely the first step in understanding and improving a phenomenon that is essential to mental health practice. In the end, efforts to increase understanding of decisional competence to make mental health decisions and to enhance clients' decisional competence to make those decisions will ultimately lead to better quality of care, improved therapeutic alliance, and better ability of mental health clients to determine their own care—and hopefully, their own lives.

REFERENCES

Appelbaum, P. S., & Grisso, T. (1995). The MacArthur Treatment Competence Study: I. Mental illness and competence to consent to treatment. *Law and Human Behavior, 19*(2), 105–126.

Berg, J. W., Appelbaum, P. S., & Lidz, C. W. (2001). *Informed consent: Legal theory and clinical practice* (2nd ed.). New York, NY: Oxford University Press.

Braddock, C. H., Edwards, K. A., Hasenberg, N. M., Laidley, T. L., & Levinson, W. (1999). Informed decision making in outpatient practice: Time to get back to basics. *JAMA, 282*, 2313–2320.

Byatt, N., Pinals, D., & Arikan, R. (2006). Involuntary hospitalization of medical patients who lack decisional capacity: An unresolved issue. *Psychosomatics: Journal of Consultation Liaison Psychiatry, 47*(5), 443–448.

Canterbury v. Spence., 464 F.2d 772 (D.C. Cir. 1972).

Charland, L. C. (2006). Anorexia and the MacCAT-T Test for mental competence: Validity, value and emotion. *Philosophy, Psychiatry, & Psychology, 13*(4), 283–287.

Dunn, L. B., & Jeste, D. V. (2001). Enhancing informed consent for research and treatment. *Neuropsychopharmacology, 24*(6), 595–607.

Elbogen, E. B., Swanson, J. W., Appelbaum, P. S., Swartz, M. S., Ferron, J., Van Dorn, R. A., & Wagner, H. R. (2007). Competence to complete psychiatric advance directives: Effects of facilitated decision making. *Law and Human Behavior, 31*(3), 275–289.

Elbogen, E. B., Swanson, J. W., Swartz, M. S., Van Dorn, R., Ferron, J., Wagner, H. R., & Wilder, C.W. (2007). Effectively implementing psychiatric advance directives to promote self-determination of treatment among people with mental illness. *Psychology, Public Policy, and Law, 13*(4), 273–288.

Grisso, T., & Appelbaum, P. S. (1998a). *Assessing competence to consent to treatment: A guide for physicians and other health professionals.* New York, NY: Oxford University Press.

Grisso, T., & Appelbaum, P. S. (1998b). *MacArthur Competence Assessment Tool for Treatment (MacCAT-T).* Sarasota, FL: Professional Resource Press/Professional Resource Exchange.

Grisso, T., Appelbaum, P. S., Mulvey, E. P., & Fletcher, K. (1995). The MacArthur Treatment Competence Study: II. Measures of abilities related to competence to consent to treatment. *Law and Human Behavior, 19*(2), 127–148.

Hoge, S. K. (1994). The Patient Self-Determination Act and psychiatric care. *Bulletin of the American Academy of Psychiatry & the Law, 22*(4), 577–586.

Janofsky, J. S., McCarthy, R. J., & Folstein, M. F. (1992). The Hopkins Competency Assessment Test: A brief method for evaluating patients' capacity to give informed consent. *Hospital & Community Psychiatry, 43*(2), 132–136.

Jeste, D. V., Depp, C. A., & Palmer, B. W. (2006). Magnitude of impairment in decisional capacity in people with schizophrenia compared to normal subjects: An overview. *Schizophrenia Bulletin, 32*(1), 121–128.

Kleinman, I., Schachter, D., Jeffries, J., & Goldhamer, P. (1993). Effectiveness of two methods for informing schizophrenic patients about neuroleptic medication. *Hospital & Community Psychiatry, 44*(12), 1189–1191.

Lapid, M. I., Rummans, T. A., Poole, K. L., Pankratz, V. S., Maurer, M. S., Rasmussen, K. G., ... Applebaum, P. S. (2003). Decisional capacity of severely depressed patients requiring electroconvulsive therapy. *Journal of ECT, 19*(2), 67–72.

Lieberman, J. A., Stroup, T. S., McEvoy, J. P., Swartz, M. S., Rosenheck, R. A., & Perkins, D. O. (2005). Effectiveness of antipsychotic drugs in patients with chronic schizophrenia. *New England Journal of Medicine, 353*, 1209–1223.

Palmer, B. W., Dunn, L. B., Appelbaum, P. S., & Jeste, D. V. (2004). Correlates of treatment-related decision-making capacity among middle-aged and older patients with schizophrenia. *Archives of General Psychiatry, 61*(3), 230–236.

Palmer, B. W., & Savla, G. N. (2007). The association of specific neuropsychological deficits with capacity to consent to research or treatment. *Journal of the International Neuropsychological Society, 13*(6), 1047–1059.

Rogers v Commissioner, 390 Mass. 489, 458 NE2d 308 (1983).

Rennie v Klein, 720 F2d 266 (3rd Cir 1983).

Saks, E. R., Dunn, L. B., Marshall, B. J., Nayak, G. V., Golshan, S., & Jeste, D. V. (2002). The California Scale of Appreciation: A new instrument to measure the appreciation component of capacity to consent to research. *American Journal of Geriatric Psychiatry, 10*(2), 166–174.

Schachter, D. C., & Kleinman, I. (2004). Psychiatrists' attitudes about and informed consent practices for antipsychotics and tardive dyskinesia. *Psychiatric Services, 55*(6), 714–717.

Schloendorff v. Society of New York Hospital, 211 N.Y. 125, 105 N.E. 92 (1914),

Srebnik, D., Appelbaum, P. S., & Russo, J. (2004). Assessing competence to complete psychiatric advance directives with the competence assessment tool for psychiatric advance directives. *Comprehensive Psychiatry, 45*(4), 239–245.

Srebnik, D., Rutherford, L. T., Peto, T., Russo, J., Zick, E., & Jaffe, C. (2005). The content and clinical utility of psychiatric advance directives. *Psychiatric Services*, *56*(5), 592–598.

Sturman, E. D. (2005). The capacity to consent to treatment and research: A review of standardized assessment tools. *Clinical Psychology Review*, *25*(7), 954–974.

Swanson, J. W., Swartz, M. S., Elbogen, E. B., Van Dorn, R. A., Ferron, J., Wagner, H. R., McCauley, B., . . . Kim, M. (2006). Facilitated psychiatric advance directives: A randomized trial of an intervention to foster advance treatment planning among persons with severe mental illness. *American Journal of Psychiatry*, *163*(11), 1943–1951.

Truman v. Thomas, 611 P.2d 902 (Cal. 1980).

Van Dorn, R. A., Swartz, M. S., Elbogen, E. B., Swanson, J. W., Kim, M., Ferron, J., . . . Scheyett, A. M. (2006). Clinicians' attitudes regarding barriers to the implementation of psychiatric advance directives. *Administration and Policy in Mental Health and Mental Health Services Research*, *33*(4), 449–460.

Washington v Harper, 494 US 210 (1990).

Westreich, L., Levine, S., Ginsburg, P., & Wilets, I. (1995). Patient knowledge about electroconvulsive therapy: Effect of an informational video. *Convulsive Therapy*, *11*(1), 32–37.

Wettstein, R. M. (2004). Competence. In S. G. Post (Ed.), *Encyclopedia of bioethics* (3rd ed., Vol. 3, pp. 488–494). New York, NY: Macmillan Reference.

CHAPTER 23

Methodological Issues in Divorce Mediation Research

ROBERT E. EMERY AND DAVID A. SBARRA

M EDIATION IS A method of dispute resolution in which the disputing parties meet with a neutral third party who facilitates the process of negotiation and, to varying degrees, offers guidance regarding the content of a settlement. Unlike arbitration or adjudication, in mediation the mediator holds no authority to make a decision if the parties fail to reach their own agreement. Mediation is typically confidential, so the parties are free to discuss a range of issues and options without fear that, if the process breaks down, the mediator will offer an opinion about a preferred settlement in a subsequent forum. Some forms of mediation are explicitly *not* confidential, however, and the mediator will make a written or oral recommendation to subsequent decision makers (arbiters, judges). In what is sometimes called "muscle mediation," the mediator will share his or her recommendation with the parties, particularly if the mediation process is bogging down, as a way of "encouraging" them to reach a mediated settlement. Mediation that is not confidential approximates a dispute resolution process called "med-arb," where the mediator becomes an arbiter (whose recommendation may be binding or nonbinding) if the parties fail to reach a mediated agreement.

Mediation has roots in ancient Greek and Chinese traditions and has been practiced informally in the United States since colonial times (Folberg, Milne, & Salem, 2004). Divorce mediation has a far more recent history, dating only to the 1970s. Divorce mediation became increasingly widespread in the United States in the 1980s, particularly following the implementation of California's mandatory custody mediation law in 1981, the first in the country (Emery & Wyer, 1987a). "Mandatory" mediation generally means that parties must attend at least one educational session about mediation, separately or together. Contrary to common belief, there is no obligation to reach an agreement in mandatory mediation, nor is there any obligation to continue beyond the first educational appointment.

Divorce mediation may attempt to help the parties resolve both financial disputes (property, alimony, child support, tax issues), childrearing issues (legal custody, physical custody, shared parental decision making or time scheduling), and often issues outside of the traditional scope of the law, such as how to coordinate co-parenting in two households or planning for children's college education (Emery, 2004). Most research, however, has focused on what is often called custody mediation—attempts to resolve only issues concerning the children (often including child support).

Various models of divorce and custody mediation have been developed by different experts. Some types of divorce mediation are explicitly problem focused, a model often preferred by attorney mediators (Lowry, 2004). Other types of divorce mediation are more therapeutic, explicitly adopting the goal of transforming the parents' relationship during the process of negotiating a settlement (Bush & Pope, 2004). Still other types of divorce mediation are a hybrid, primarily devoted to agreement-focused negotiations but with the mediator remaining keenly aware of, sensitive to, and periodically educating parents about the emotional dynamics of separation (Emery, 1994).

Custody mediation may be court connected, perhaps literally housed in the courthouse. It may be conducted by a social service agency independent of the court. Or custody mediation may take place in a private center or independent private practice, perhaps on a contract basis with a court. The duration of mediation, particularly public court-connected mediation, may be limited to an hour or some similarly short period of time. In other forums, particularly private practice, divorce mediation may involve perhaps 10 to 20 one- or two-hour meetings lasting over a period of several months.

The parties in mediation may be limited to the partners/parents, who may or may not be married, or may include key third parties such as step-parents, grandparents, children, and the lawyers representing each side. Potential clients may be routinely screened *out* of mediation, such as when a history of serious partner violence creates fear and/or power imbalances between the parties. Clients also may be screened out of mediation based on their inability to represent themselves, particularly due to serious mental illness or substance abuse.

Mediators may be mental health professionals or attorneys, though in many states, a mediator may simply be someone who meets minimal training requirements, perhaps as little as completing 40 hours of mediation training. Finally, some mediators work in pairs, often male-female and ideally mental health professional–attorney pairs. Other mediators work alone. This chapter describes the range of methodological issues that pertain to divorce mediation research.

INDEPENDENT VARIABLES

Defining Mediation

As the reader grappling with our extended definition of mediation may now appreciate, one huge methodological issue in mediation research is the definition of mediation. The topics discussed previously are not just methodological issues in evaluating and conducting mediation research, but they are also issues of serious debate in the world of divorce dispute resolution. Carefully defining mediation procedures, processes, and screening criteria and investigating important alternatives on these variables are the obvious methodological answers to the wide-ranging and substantively important variations in mediation. Researchers have varied in how much attention they have paid to defining the approach to mediation under investigation. Moreover, we are aware of only one systematic study that has investigated variations in mediation methods (McIntosh, Wells, Smyth, & Long, 2008). In our view, therefore, the most basic methodological issue is the need for more research, especially high-quality research.

Defining Adversary Procedures

Defining mediation is only half the problem. Mediation and other less formal methods of dispute resolution are often labeled alternative dispute resolution (ADR)—that is, as alternatives to traditional dispute resolution, namely attorney negotiations and litigation. Methodologically and substantively, this means that researchers must carefully define the experimental group and what they mean by mediation or some other form of ADR, and they must also define (and study) the control group or traditional adversary settlement processes. We can define the *theory* behind legal dispute resolution procedures. The core philosophy of procedural justice in the United States is that legal opponents are adversaries whose interests are in complete conflict. In terms of game theory (which we review briefly later in this chapter), legal disputes are viewed as zero-sum games; whatever one side wins, the other side loses by the same amount. The sale of a house is a good illustration of a zero sum game; if the buyer pays more, the seller gains by exactly that amount.

The theory of legal representation that follows from the assumption of perfectly competing interests is the *adversary system*, a system of legal representation in which disputants and their legal advocates are viewed as opponents. For lawyers, this means that their most important and their ultimate ethical responsibility is "vigorous representation," representing their client's interests, and only their client's interests, to the utmost of the attorney's ability (while the other side does the same for the opposing client). Neither side has any obligation to take interests of neutrals into account—for example, children. In fact, lawyers are prohibited from representing anyone's interests other than their client's. To fail to do so would be considered dual representation, a basic ethical violation.

Conflict is expected in the adversary system. In fact, conflict is a formalized part of the adjudication process and is an informal expectation in attorney negotiations. Perhaps the best evidence of the conflict inherent in traditional attorney negotiations is the growing movement to change the way in which lawyers negotiate divorce disputes, particularly collaborative law (Tesler & Thompson, 2007) and cooperative law (Lande, 2008). As their names imply, both of these relatively new approaches seek to remove acrimony from attorney negotiations.

As we discuss shortly, the potential for adversary procedures to create or exacerbate conflict between separating partners who remain parents, hopefully two involved parents, is one of the main reasons why mediation and other forms of ADR have been promoted in custody disputes. In fact, 90% or more of divorce cases are settled outside of trial (Maccoby & Mnookin, 1992). Why is out-of-court settlement the rule when the theory of the law outlines a series of formalized, adjudicative procedures? A key reason is that *no* legal dispute is, in fact, a purely zero-sum game. If nothing else, both sides benefit by reducing the transaction costs—that is, the time, effort, cost, and uncertainty that go into a trial. Of critical importance, custody disputes are quite obviously a non–zero-sum game, because both parents hopefully share common interests in their children's well-being.

We know that practice differs from theory. What we do *not* know is what happens in cases where parents obtain a pro se (unrepresented) divorce, as occurs perhaps 40% of the time (Schepard, 2004); what happens during attorney negotiations about divorce and custody matters; or even what happens during custody trials. Anecdotally, we know there is great variation. Some lawyers are negotiators; others are litigators. Some attorneys attend to the emotions of divorce when interviewing their clients; others insist on only hearing facts. Some counsel their clients to consider the children's or even their former partner's point of view; others offer their clients one thing—vigorous representation to their utmost.

To social scientists, how the adversary system works in practice is a black box. In studying ADR, researchers also obtain data at least on the outcome if not much on the processes of their control group, adversary settlement procedures. For example, we recently documented how adversary procedures (mostly litigation) *increase* conflict between parents in the first year following their custody dispute whereas mediation *decreases* conflict. For a small percentage of cases, adversary procedures reduce conflict over the course of 12 years, however, perhaps by encouraging one parent to drop out of children's lives, while mediation tends to keep both parents involved (Sbarra & Emery, 2008).

METHODOLOGICAL CONSEQUENCES OF LEGAL THEORY–PRACTICE DICHOTOMY

Methodologically, variation in adversary settlement procedures, and in the theory versus the practice of the law, has two major consequences. First, when comparing mediation to adversary settlement, researchers usually can define the treatment they gave to their experimental group (even though some fail to do so), because the investigators often have some control over the mediation service. In our research, for example, we developed, implemented, and executed a somewhat unique mediation service, because no mediation program existed in the court or in the region that we studied (Emery, 1994).

However, our adversary settlement control group was much harder to define, as it is for other researchers. We documented that 75% of contested cases were decided in court by a judge (Emery, Matthews, & Wyer, 1991; Emery & Wyer, 1987b). What we do not know is what procedures came before this or led to settlement in 25% of the cases, whether or in what way other actors became involved (custody evaluators, attorneys for the children), or what steps attorneys took toward litigation (e.g., whether settlement was reached "on the courtroom steps"). We also do not know what happened in court, other than the actual decisions the judges reached. Still, researchers can conduct fair and methodologically sound comparisons of mediation and adversary settlement procedures. In doing so, however, we must acknowledge the likely wide variations in the litigation control group. This means that critics can fairly ask: Mediation compared to what (Levy, 1984)?

This last observation brings us to our second point. Because there is so little evidence on the actual practice of the law versus the theory behind it and because the philosophy of the adversary system is embedded in the American consciousness and embraced (if also derided) by American culture, even empirically oriented psychologists can end up comparing mediation in practice with adversary settlement in theory. For example, citing a string of non-empirical law review articles about procedural justice while ignoring the empirical literature, law professor Penelope Bryan argues,

> At mediation's inception, proponents promised that it would fulfill many procedural and substantive justice criteria better than courts. . . . Few of these claims, however, withstand close scrutiny. . . . Frustration with the current state of affairs, however, should not drive us to uncritically implement seriously flawed alternatives.
>
> (Bryan 2006, p. 205)

Not only are such comparisons unfair, but the winner also is predetermined. Facts about ADR inevitably pale against the theory of adversary procedures, just as the reality of adversary procedures looks dreadful when compared with lofty ADR theories of cooperation, common goals, and always putting children first. What both sides need is more evidence, and the defenders of adversary procedures are well behind in the data race.

More Independent Variables: Other Forms of ADR

We do not want to belabor the point, so we will only note briefly that the whole independent variable definition story includes much more than detailing and studying variations on mediation and traditional adversary settlement procedures in divorce and custody cases. Many forms of alternative dispute resolution procedures address these problems and merit careful study, including parenting education, collaborative law, parenting coordination, and custody evaluations (which sometimes are used explicitly for dispute resolution purposes and always constitute an implicit form of arbitration). There is plenty of research to do, and many great reasons to do it, including the facts that children are involved and custody actions are one of the most common sources of litigation in the United States today.

INDEPENDENT VARIABLES STUDIED IN RESEARCH TO DATE: A LIMITED DOMAIN

As we have noted, ADR and traditional adversary procedures for divorce and custody matters need more research. By far, most of the research conducted in this general area to date has been on mediation, and we credit mediation researchers with beginning to open the black box. But mediation research is limited. Like our studies, most investigations have been court based and have studied problem-focused custody mediation (rather than more therapeutic approaches). Many of these studies involve evaluation research, where there is no attempt to manipulate an independent variable, but a handful of studies use either randomized designs or quasi-experimental methods. We are aware of only one quasi-experimental study that compared alternative forms of mediation, specifically "child-focused mediation" (only the parents were involved but the rationales for mediation focused on the children's needs) versus "child-inclusive mediation" (a psychologist had a single, separate interview with the children and offered a feedback session to the parents in mediation) (McIntosh et al., 2008).

This is a sparse offering, but the list of research studies of mediation is long relative to studies of other interventions in the divorce and child custody area. We are aware of a small handful of primarily evaluation studies that have been conducted of parent education (e.g., Devlin, Brown, Beebe, & Parulis, 1992) and only one study of divorce that attempted to assess the use of adversary procedures in any detail (Maccoby & Mnookin, 1992). We also know of only one study of custody evaluations that was based on an actual analysis of evaluations rather than self-reports about the process (Levy, 1985). Again, the list of topics for which further research is needed is extensive.

INTERNAL VALIDITY

Internal validity is, of course, essential to experimental designs, and internal validity is notoriously difficult to achieve and maintain in field research. We view our own research as probably the most successful in this area to date, but our design necessitated randomly approaching parents about entering into mediation or participating in our assessment of adversary settlement rather than first securing their permission for random assignment (a procedure that many or most families surely would have refused). Fortunately, we achieved very high acceptances of our random offer. Yet, we also faced the inevitable issue of attrition over time, particularly over the long course of the 12 years we followed families in our research (Emery et al., 2001).

These issues of internal validity are familiar and pervasive, so we will not elaborate further. Instead, it may be helpful to point out a few problems that are unique to this particular area of research. For one, some investigators have used clearly confounded independent variables. For example, one research group repeatedly compared three groups following (not very successful) random assignment to mediation versus adversary settlement. These groups included (1) all families in the adversary settlement group, (2) families that reached an agreement in mediation, and (3) families that failed to reach an agreement in mediation (Pearson & Thoennes, 1984). Not surprisingly, the families who reached an agreement in mediation were the most satisfied. The surprise (and note of caution) is that the obvious methodological explanation of this outcome—non-random assignment to groups (agreement versus no agreement) was confounded with satisfaction—was not immediately seized upon, perhaps because the research was disseminated in legal rather than social science journals. We make the case for peer review, even when an audience other than peers may be most interested in the substance of research on divorce and custody.

Achieving pure random assignment to mediation versus adversary settlement is certainly much more difficult to achieve today than it was in the 1980s when we began our research, because mediation was new then while ADR is widespread today. Investigators are more likely to have success comparing alternative forms of mediation or perhaps alternative types of ADR (e.g., mediation versus collaborative law). Offering services otherwise unavailable (e.g., to low income clients) is another approach that should allow for randomized trials. Furthermore, comparisons between different forms of ADR will serve to increase internal validity by comparing two known procedures, which bypasses another problem inherent in the mediation/litigation comparison—namely, it is often difficult to ascertain whether the outcomes of interest are due to the success of mediation or the failure of adversarial procedures.

Before leaving the topic, we should note one last issue related to independent variables: treatment fidelity. Psychotherapy researchers today almost invariably use treatment manuals as a key part of ensuring treatment integrity and fidelity; yet, as other methodological critics have noted, this practice generally has not been adopted in mediation research. Our own studies did include the development and publication of treatment manuals (Emery, 1994; Emery, Shaw, & Jackson, 1987), and McIntosh and Moloney (e.g., McIntosh, Long, & Moloney, 2004) have developed extensive written and video materials describing child-focused and child-inclusive mediation. These are positive steps, although we have a hard time envisioning a study of adversary settlement where lawyers follow a detailed treatment manual guiding their counsel, negotiations, and litigation strategies.

EXTERNAL VALIDITY

External validity is a final but very important methodological issue to address in relation to independent variables and experimental design. To what extent do the results of any given study of mediation apply to mediation offered in other settings, by mediators with different backgrounds and training, clients with different backgrounds, variations in mediation procedures, methods, and goals, and so on? In publishing our research, we have consistently cautioned that the answer to this question is, "No one can know." This is true for all the usual reasons that make experimental interventions unusual, including relatively small sample sizes, enthusiastic and relatively well-trained mediators, and the effects of data collection on the mediators and clients. Research tells us what mediation *can* do in practice—specifically, what the type of mediation studied can do under the conditions it was studied. However, experimental research cannot tell us what mediation *does* do in practice. This is the reason why we have combined the results of small-scale experimental studies with larger-scale evaluation studies in reviewing the substantive support for mediation (see Emery, Sbarra, & Grover, 2005).

One specific concern is worth noting in addition to the variety of general concerns that apply across different areas of intervention research. Mediation programs sometimes are poorly supported and poorly funded in practice. Judges, particularly those in under-resourced or rural jurisdictions, may designate a relatively untrained probation officer to be the court's mediator, for example, giving the mediator perhaps an hour or two to work with contested cases with an emphasis on "getting agreements." Or well-meaning volunteers may mediate custody disputes in a community mediation center, perhaps one that accepts court-ordered referrals, but their educational and professional background may not have prepared them for the legal, interpersonal, or emotional disputes they quickly encounter. We would not expect mediation in these settings to produce results like those identified in research any more than we would expect calling some untrained but well-intentioned health care professional "doctor" would make that person an effective surgeon.

DEPENDENT VARIABLES

Conceptualizing and assessing outcomes that might be affected by mediation, some other form of ADR, or by adversary processes also poses methodological concerns and challenges. These dependent variable issues are not nearly as extensive or as potentially problematic as the independent variable concerns just discussed. For those reasons, we will consider this topic only briefly within the context of the three major sets of dependent variables investigators need to assess: (1) measures related to the speed and cost of dispute resolution, including the administration of justice; (2) party satisfaction with dispute resolution; and (3) broader effects on relationships between members of the divorced family and individual psychological outcomes.

COST AND SPEED OF DISPUTE RESOLUTION

A number of concerns about traditional adversary settlement relate to the cost to the parties and to the court, in terms of time, money, and human resources. Similarly, mediation and other forms of ADR have been promoted, in part, based on claims that they will relieve a burden on courts, lead to more timely settlements, cost the parties less money, and lead to greater compliance and fewer future legal action.

These claims (or hypotheses) require a wide-ranging assessment, one that includes some dependent variables that social scientists (particularly psychologists) do not typically assess (e.g., financial effects) along with others that are not readily available (e.g., lawyers' fees). As we have reviewed elsewhere, different researchers, including ourselves, have done at least a passing job of assessing outcomes in this domain. It seems fairly well established, for example, that mediation produces high enough settlement rates (50% or more), even among high-conflict couples who seem otherwise destined for litigation, to conclude that quality mediation significantly alleviates the burden on courts (Emery et al., 2005). Mediation also appears to lead to more rapid agreements, but whether it saves money has yet to be clearly documented. Importantly, mediation may lead to more formal compliance with agreements (e.g., making child support payments as ordered) but also to more informal changes in the agreement (e.g., informally making a significant change or two in children's living arrangements during the course of their childhood). We found both outcomes in our research (Emery, Matthews, & Wyer, 1991; Emery et al., 2001), suggesting that research needs to study not only whether a change was made but how and why it was done.

PARTY SATISFACTION

The extent to which parties are satisfied following dispute resolution is another important area of measurement, although this topic is fairly well covered by mediation researchers who consistently find generally high levels of satisfaction in evaluation research and greater satisfaction with mediation than with adversary settlement (Emery et al., 2005). In assessing satisfaction, it is important to use multiple items/scales to assess a range of content domains that include purported strengths of both mediation (e.g., protecting children's interests) and of legal representation (e.g., protecting parties' rights). We also have found gender differences in satisfaction with mediation in comparison with adversary settlement, apparently reflecting the relatively strong position of mothers in Virginia courts during the time period of our studies (Emery et al., 1991; Emery, 1994). Similar gender differences were not found in California (Kelly & Duryee, 1992), but from a methodological perspective, these are the kinds of potential differences that remain important to consider.

FAMILY RELATIONSHIPS AND INDIVIDUAL MENTAL HEALTH

Whether mediation positively impacts on family relationships and individual mental health is the final area where investigators need to think carefully about dependent variables. There are many measures of family relationships, but there is no gold-standard assessment, a circumstance that makes the choice of measures challenging. In our research, the measures that showed the most dramatic effects due to mediation, and some effects were quite large—were those specifically developed by researchers studying the quantity of contact and quality of relationships between children and parents in divorced families.

Importantly, we also found that time is a critical factor to consider. In our studies, the benefits of mediation for family relationships grew notably stronger over time, so much so that an average of about 6 hours of mediation produced dramatic benefits for nonresident parent-child relationships fully *12 years later*. Our results strongly suggest the need for more longitudinal assessment.

While researchers have come to expect mediation to have only a limited, if any, effect on the individual mental health of children or parents, this remains an important area to continue to assess. We offer two methodological considerations in this regard. First, new, more subtle measures of psychological outcome/adjustment are being developed—for example, assessment of young adults' experience of psychological pain (versus psychopathology) (Laumann-Billings & Emery, 2000). Second, we urge investigators to include theoretically based, multi-construct assessments akin to our focus on assessing partners/parents feelings of love (non-acceptance of the marital termination), anger (co-parenting conflict), and sadness (depression). These measures yielded some important differences in outcome 12 years after dispute settlement (Sbarra & Emery, 2005, 2008), but perhaps more importantly, they provided data consistent with some of our clinical hypotheses about divorce adjustment and how this is affected by different forms of dispute resolution (Sbarra & Emery, 2008). We believe theory is always a good thing, even when working out the details of dependent variables and outcome measures.

LINKING INDEPENDENT AND DEPENDENT
VARIABLES: PROCESS RESEARCH

An important goal of intervention research is to identify specific processes that produce desired change. In broadest terms, game theory (discussed subsequently) offers a theoretical basis for what makes mediation more effective than competitive, adversary processes in resolving non–zero-sum games. Cooperation allows the parties to choose outcomes that maximize joint utility over the long run even if competition would (appear to) maximize individual utility in the short run.

Divorce disputes are emotional, however, and in our view offer one of the clearest examples of the limits of the economic model of rational actors maximizing utility. Rather than maximizing, divorcing partners sacrifice money (e.g., lawyers' fees) and sadly sometimes harm their own children (e.g., openly deriding the other parent to the children) in an economically irrational, emotionally charged effort to hurt their former partner. In our view, the ability to address emotional issues is what makes divorce and custody mediation more effective, on average, than adversary alternatives.

In the present context, our concern is not which theoretical model is correct (both surely contribute to divorce mediation's success) but to underscore the need to link processes to outcomes. One of the very few studies to do so in the mediation context is Bickerdike and Littlefield's (2000) analysis of 112 Australian couples. These investigators assessed premediation levels of attachment, anger, and sadness, videotaped mediation sessions, and obtained data on mediation outcome. Consistent with our hypothesis that adults whose partner wanted the separation will resist settlement in order to contest the end of the marriage (Emery, 1994; Sbarra & Emery, 2008), these investigators found that differences in the partners' acceptance of the end of the marriage predicted failure to reach agreement in divorce mediation. Differences in acceptance also predicted less problem solving in actual mediation sessions, suggesting that the interactions were less rational and objective when the partners were in emotional dispute (Bickerdike & Littlefield, 2000). We find these results fascinating and perfectly consistent with our conceptualizations, but for present purposes this study illustrates another, much needed method of mediation research.

ANALOG RESEARCH

Mediation research (and mediation researchers) will benefit greatly by considering the wealth of *analog research* being conducted in the fields of social psychology, organizational behavior, and behavioral economics. By analog research, we mean empirical studies that are not focused on child custody mediation per se but have implications for an improved understanding of how mediation is conducted and the processes that may promote or hinder positive outcomes for families. Depending on one's point of view, it is either surprising or obvious that custody mediation research has not drawn on the work in these fields. Mediators are typically trained as clinical/family psychologists, or they are family law attorneys or members of an allied health profession (e.g., clinical social work) or sometimes even people who hold a bachelor's degree and have pursued certificate-level training in advanced family mediation. None of these fields provide extensive training in digesting basic research on bargaining or procedural justice, yet these are precisely the topics that mediators need to understand and research when working with families in emotionally heated, high-stakes custody situations. An exhaustive literature review of all the analog topics germane to contemporary custody mediation is beyond the scope of this chapter; instead, a series of illustrative studies from different fields are discussed that we hope can spark interest in new ways of studying mediation. Because the balance between internal and external validity is a central concern of this chapter, this section concludes with a brief discussion of the limits of analog research and potential extensions designed to increase the generalizability of the findings.

Game Theory and Behavioral Economics   Game theory has a rich tradition in psychology (Camerer, 2003), and we noted previously that in the court system, legal disputes are typically conceptualized as zero-sum games, where whatever is won by another person is lost by the adversary. In general, game theory research seeks to build mathematical models that will explain how people will interact with each other in a decision-making context. Classical game theory analysis predicts that people will act as rational, self-maximizers until they reach a position where they can no longer improve their outcome, yet evidence from thousands of studies indicates that people deviate quite substantially from this strategy. In social decision-making situations, a partner's reciprocity and one's own emotional state play a large role in how people respond to specific decisions.

Interesting neuroscientific evidence suggests that the striatum, a brain region within the meso-limbic dopamine system that is associated with reward processing, tracks partners' reciprocation of offers and that activity in this region can predict increased cooperation in subsequent rounds of social decision-making games (see Sanfey, 2007). A similar approach provided one of the first illustrations of the way in which emotional responding impacts social decisions. Sanfey and colleagues (Sanfey, Rilling, Aronson, Nystrom, & Cohen, 2003) demonstrated that activity in the anterior insula, a brain region associated with the detection of noxious physical stimuli, varied with acceptance/rejection of offers in a social decision-making game. Specifically, greater insula activity was observed when actors rejected unfair offers and predicted decreased probability of future cooperation, which suggests that emotional responses—especially disgust and anger spurred by unfair offers—act to override the rational, cognitive processing of social decisions (Sanfey et al., 2003).

While imaging studies of the anterior insula and meso-limbic dopamine system are not likely to be immediately adopted by mediation researchers, these game theory findings have direct relevance to how mediation is studied. There are few contexts in which reciprocity and fairness matter as much as in the give-and-take decisions needed to derive satisfying custody resolutions. This brief review of relevant neuroeconomic findings suggests that these processes unfold in an automatic manner that is not necessarily conscious. Studying reciprocity and people's perceptions of the fairness of their partner's offers will be a challenge for process-oriented mediation research, but it is a task that has the potential to yield insight into why and how successfully mediated agreements emerge.

Procedural Justice Research   While a portion of game theory research addresses how decision makers view each others' offers and responses, procedural justice (PJ) focuses on the fairness of the decision-making process (Thibaut & Walker, 1975). Because custody mediation often involves extensive compromise for both parties (assuming both parties are interested in fully engaging the process of mediation), understanding the ways in which PJ is achieved is a critical task for future mediation research. The PJ effect, which is well-replicated across legal, industrial, political, and interpersonal contexts, refers to the fact that people care about the justice of allocation and decision-making processes and that people will report satisfaction with a less than desirable outcome if they feel the decision was made in a just and fair manner.

Thibaut and Walker's (1975) initial model of PJ centered on control—whether participants can control the presentation of evidence and the actual decisions that are made. Lind and Tyler (1988) extended this model in several ways by suggesting that when decisions involve group membership (including family-related decisions), PJ is impacted by perceptions and actual control as well as by people's assessments of neutrality in the decision-making environment, their trust of the authority figure making the decisions, and their standing in the decision-making context. Thus, from this perspective PJ is achieved not only when parties feel they have a sense of control in how they present their side of the story and how the decisions are made, but when these outcomes are coupled with participants' feeling that the decision-making context did not undermine their social standing.

Kitzmann and Emery (1993) found support for these ideas in a custody mediation context. Relative to parents mediating their custody dispute, procedural factors (e.g., perceived control over decisions, feeling that one's rights were protected) were more important for parents litigating their custody dispute as well as for parents who perceived the divorce as high conflict and for men (who were at a decided disadvantage in the custody settlements, where nearly all physical custody was assigned to mothers).

Although a surge of basic research on procedural justice has occurred during the past two decades, a central question remains for mediation research: Does procedural fairness predict custody-related outcomes that matter for children and families? Some authors have argued that this is indeed the case (Bryan, 2006), but we are aware of no empirical assessments of the components of PJ on mediation settlement rates, agreement adherence, child or adult functioning, or parental relationships. We encourage mediation researchers to ground their studies in contemporary PJ research, then seek to determine whether elements of PJ predict these critical outcomes.

The Role of Power in Negotiation Research We have long held that a central psychological dynamic relevant to divorcing parents is the renegotiation of power boundaries (Emery & Dillon, 1994). Gaining power—that is, the unfettered ability to control one's ex-partner by controlling decisions about the children—is an unstated goal of many parents who pursue custody litigation, often as a means of retaliating against or punishing one's ex-partner. There is a relatively large social psychology literature on the role of power in negotiation settings (Howard, Gardner, & Thompson, 2007), and one of the more interesting angles of this work is understanding negotiation contexts in which power does not corrupt. In other words, in what situations will someone with power work toward a cooperative agreement?

A key finding from this literature is that, in most situations, interdependence construals promote the benevolent use of power; when negotiating disputants feel connected via a common goal, they are more likely to act cooperatively and generously (Howard et al., 2007). These findings have important implications for custody mediation. Process-oriented research that measures how well mediators frame the superordinate goal of child welfare may redress why some power imbalances are maintained or overcome in different practice settings. Furthermore, the basic research in this area may be used to better understand how interdependence, or other-oriented construals are promoted. In the often heated context of mediation practice, we doubt it is possible to move a rejected, angry, and generally disaffected parent from a power-seeking position to a more other-oriented, benevolent decision-making frame, but it is likely that self–other goals rest on a continuum that can be measured and, ultimately, used as a predictor of mediated outcomes.

SUMMARY: PROMISES AND PERILS OF ANALOG RESEARCH

We have argued that a great deal of contemporary mediation research can gain by considering the larger corpus of work on game theory, procedural justice, and power-based negotiating strategies. The most compelling reason for appreciating and drawing from analog studies is their internal validity. Many of the studies reviewed here provide exquisite experimental control, which allows for a high degree of confidence in the observed findings. This is something to like and applaud about this research; we know what is manipulated and the precise reason for the observed outcomes. At the same time, caution is needed when seeking to generalize from this work to the large practice and study of custody mediation.

Consider, for example, the decision-making games used in the neuro-economic studies previously described. One commonly used tool is the ultimatum game (UG; see Sanfey, 2007), which pits two players against each other in a series of simple monetary exchanges. It is clear that emotion plays a large role in the UG decision strategies, but simple economic decisions vastly underestimate the complicated features of custody decisions that are *defined by* the emotional nature of divorce. (In their defense, behavioral economists are aware of the simplicity of their models, and they have not set out to inform complicated clinical practice situations.) The applicability of many of these concepts to contemporary mediation research remains to be determined. At the very least, mediation researchers should look outside their own (relatively small) field of study and invoke many of the potentially useful constructs and paradigms being used elsewhere. This will certainly involve sacrificing some of the internal validity of well-controlled laboratory studies, but drawing on analog research in this way is something that must occur for the field to advance by any substantial measure.

SUMMARY AND RECOMMENDATIONS

Mediation research can be rightly criticized on methodological grounds, particularly when compared with the far more extensive and sophisticated literature on psychotherapy process and outcome (Beck & Sales, 2001). Despite the various methodological limitations that we have outlined, however, research provides at least tentative support for the benefits of quality divorce mediation. Perhaps more importantly, mediation research gives us possibly the best look into the black box of the complicated process of resolving divorce and custody disputes.

Still, the black box has only been cracked open. Among the most pressing substantive and methodological research needs are the following:

- Quality empirical research of all kinds on mediation, adversary processes, custody evaluations, and the many newer forms of alternative dispute resolution in divorce and custody disputes. At the top of our wish list would be making research on dispute resolution in divorce and custody disputes a major priority of a private or public funding agency—an obvious need given the costs, the range of professionals involved, and especially the large number of adults and children involved in custody disputes in the United States today.
- Randomized trials comparing alternative forms of dispute resolution (e.g., mediation versus collaborative law; collaborative law versus traditional legal practice), as well as comparing alternative models of a

given form of dispute resolution (e.g., facilitative versus transformative mediation; confidential versus non-confidential mediation).

- The inclusion of a range of carefully measured dependent variables, including measures of the cost, time, and speed of dispute resolution; party satisfaction; family relationships; and individual well being.
- Longitudinal follow-up studies.
- Research linking actual dispute resolution processes to outcomes.
- Analog research that is more closely linked to substantive questions relevant to field research (e.g., the influence of emotion in dispute resolution) and that uses methods more closely related to field research (e.g., analog studies of people who have an ongoing relationship such as dating couples).
- Simply better baseline data—that is, more careful, extensive, and representative court records providing aggregate information on custody disputes, who is involved, the processes used to reach resolution, and the substantive decisions reached using different dispute resolution alternatives.

REFERENCES

Beck, C. J. A., & Sales, B. D. (2001). *Family mediation: Facts, myths, and future prospects.* Washington, DC: American Psychological Association.

Bickerdike, A. J., & Littlefield, L. (2000). Divorce adjustment and mediation: Theoretically grounded process research. *Mediation Quarterly, 18,* 181–201.

Bryan, P. E. (2006). *Constructive divorce: Procedural justice and sociolegal reform.* Washington, DC: American Psychological Association.

Bush, R. A. B., & Pope, S. G. (2004). Transformative mediation: Changing the quality of family conflict interaction. In J. Folberg, A. L. Milne, & P. Salem (Eds.), *Divorce and family mediation: Models, techniques, and applications* (pp. 53–71). New York, NY: Guilford Press.

Camerer, C. F. (2003). *Behavioral game theory: Experiments in strategic interaction.* New York, NY: Sage.

Devlin, A. S., Brown, E. H., Beebe, J., & Parulis, E. (1992). Parent education for divorced fathers. *Family Relations, 41,* 290–296.

Emery, R. E. (1994). *Renegotiating family relationships: Divorce, child custody, and mediation.* New York, NY: Guilford Press.

Emery, R. E. (2004). *The truth about children and divorce: Dealing with the emotions so you and your children can thrive.* New York, NY: Viking/Penguin.

Emery, R. E., & Dillon, P. (1994). Conceptualizing the divorce process: Renegotiating boundaries of intimacy and power in the divorced family system. *Family Relations, 43,* 374–379.

Emery, R. E., Laumann-Billings, L., Waldron, M., Sbarra, D. A., & Dillon, P. (2001). Child custody mediation and litigation: Custody, contact, and co-parenting 12 years after initial dispute resolution. *Journal of Consulting and Clinical Psychology, 69,* 323–332.

Emery, R. E., Matthews, S., & Wyer, M. M. (1991). Child custody mediation and litigation: Further evidence of the differing views of mothers and fathers. *Journal of Consulting and Clinical Psychology, 59,* 410–418.

Emery, R. E., Sbarra, D. S., & Grover, T. (2005). Divorce mediation: Research and reflections. *Family Court Review, 43,* 22–37.

Emery, R. E., Shaw, D. S., & Jackson, J. A. (1987). A clinical description of a model of child custody mediation. In J.P. Vincent (Ed.), *Advances in family intervention, assessment and theory* (Vol. 4, pp. 309–333). Greenwich, CT: JAI.

Emery, R. E., & Wyer, M. M. (1987a). Divorce mediation. *American Psychologist, 42,* 472–480.

Emery, R. E., & Wyer, M. M. (1987b). Child custody mediation and litigation: An experimental evaluation of the experience of parents. *Journal of Consulting and Clinical Psychology, 55,* 179–186.

Folberg, J., Milne, A. L., & Salem, P. (Eds.). (2004). *Divorce and family mediation: Models, techniques, and applications.* New York, NY: Guilford Press.

Howard, E. S., Gardner, W. L., & Thompson, L. (2007). The role of the self-concept and the social context in determining the behavior of power holders: Self-construal in intergroup versus dyadic dispute resolution negotiations. *Journal of Personality and Social Psychology, 93,* 614–631.

Kelly, J. B., & Duryee, M. A. (1992). Women's and men's views of mediation in voluntary and mandatory mediation settings. *Family and Conciliation Courts Review, 30,* 34–49.

Kitzmann, K. M., & Emery, R. E. (1993). Procedural justice and parents' satisfaction in a field study of child custody dispute resolution. *Law and Human Behavior, 17,* 553–567.

Lande, J. (2008). Practical insights from an empirical study of cooperative lawyers in Wisconsin. *Journal of Dispute Resolution, 2008,* 203–266.

Laumann-Billings, L & Emery, R.E. (2000). Distress among young adults from divorced families. *Journal of Family Psychology, 14,* 671–687.

Levy, R. J. (1984). Comment on the Pearson-Thoennes study on mediation. *Family Law Quarterly, 17,* 525–533.

Levy, R. J. (1985). Custody investigations in divorce cases. *American Bar Foundation Research Journal, 10,* 713–797.

Lind, E. A., & Tyler, T. R. (1988). *The social psychology of procedural justice.* New York, NY: Plenum Press.

Lowry, R. L. (2004). Evaluative mediation. In J. Folberg, A. L. Milne, & P. Salem (Eds.), *Divorce and family mediation: Models, techniques, and applications* (pp. 72–91). New York, NY: Guilford Press.

Maccoby, E. E., & Mnookin, R. H. (1992). *Dividing the child: Social and legal dilemmas of custody.* Cambridge, MA: Harvard University Press.

McIntosh, J. E., Wells, Y. D., Smyth, B. M., & Long, C. M. (2008). Child-focused and child-inclusive divorce mediation: Comparative outcomes from a prospective study of postseparation adjustment. *Family Court Review, 46,* 105–124.

McIntosh, J., Long, C., & Moloney, L. (2004). Child-focused and child-inclusive mediation: A comparative study of outcomes, *Journal of Family Studies, 10,* 87–96.

Pearson, J., & Thoennes, N. (1984). *Final report of the divorce mediation research project.* (Available from authors, 1720 Emerson St., Denver, CO 80218.)

Sanfey, A. G. (2007). Social decision-making: Insights from game theory and neuroscience. *Science, 318,* 598–602.

Sanfey, A. G., Rilling, J. K., Aronson, J. A., Nystrom, L. E., & Cohen, J. D. (2003). The neural basis of economic decision-making in the Ultimatum Game. *Science, 300,* 1755–1758.

Sbarra, D. S., & Emery, R. E. (2005). Coparenting conflict, nonacceptance, and depression among divorced adults: Results from a 12-year follow-up study of child custody mediation using multiple imputation. *American Journal of Orthopsychiatry, 75,* 63–75.

Sbarra, D. S., & Emery, R. E. (2008). Deeper into divorce: Using actor-partner analyses to explore systemic differences in coparenting following mediation and litigation of custody disputes. *Journal of Family Psychology, 22,* 144–152.

Schepard, A. (2004). *Children, courts, and custody: Interdisciplinary models for divorcing families.* New York, NY: Cambridge University Press.

Tesler, P. H., & Thompson, P. (2007). *Collaborative divorce: The revolutionary new way to restructure your family, resolve legal issues, and move on with your life.* New York, NY: HarperCollins.

Thibaut, J., & Walker, L. (1975). *Procedural justice: A psychological analysis.* Hillsdale, NJ: Lawrence Erlbaum.

CHAPTER 24

Research on Intimate Partner Violence in Forensically Relevant Contexts: Methodological Challenges and Controversies

MINDY B. MECHANIC

THE CASE OF Beverly Ibn-Tamas (*Ibn-Tamas v. United States*, 1979) was the first to address the admissibility of expert testimony on battered woman syndrome (BWS). Beverly Ibn-Tamas was a pregnant nurse from the Washington, D.C. area who attempted to defend herself from an impending assault by her physician husband, who had previously battered her. According to Ms. Ibn-Tamas's account of the offense, she witnessed her husband walking down the stairs in their home while swinging at her and threatening to kill her, as he had previously done. Believing her life and that of her unborn child was endangered, she recalled grabbing a gun and crouching down and hiding from her husband in an effort to seek safety. When he entered the room where she hid, Ms. Ibn-Tamas shot her husband once, killing him.

At her trial in 1977, Ms. Ibn-Tamas argued that the lethal act of killing her husband was committed in self-defense; however, she was convicted of second-degree murder. Because the trial judge in the case ruled that expert testimony on BWS did not fall within the province of traditional medical or scientific testimony, the jury was not permitted to hear testimony from a defense expert prepared to offer it. The expert in the case, Dr. Lenore Walker, nevertheless provided testimony that was heard only by the judge outside the presence of the jury. Ms. Ibn-Tamas appealed her conviction, in part based on the exclusion of expert evidence from the jury. In the first evidentiary ruling governing expert testimony on BWS, the appeals court opined that expert testimony on BWS is admissible, albeit conditionally.

The court outlined three conditions necessary for the admissibility of BWS testimony (Walker & Shapiro, 2003). The conditions are as follows: First, the information had to be "beyond the ken" of the average layperson, consistent with the Frye standard. Second, the expert offering testimony had to be qualified in his or her field. Third, the testimony had to be accepted as valid by the relevant scientific community. The Ibn-Tamas case is notable for being the first case governing the admissibility of expert testimony on BWS. This seminal ruling opened the doors to increased use of expert testimony on BWS in the defense of battered women charged with crimes—initially, crimes committed against their abusive partners. Since that landmark case, social science literature on intimate partner violence (IPV) has proliferated, resulting in significant shifts in the content and nature of expert testimony in battered women's criminal cases. Similarly, the legal landscape governing the use of expert evidence in battered women's criminal cases has also evolved, both independent of the developments in the social science literature and along with it.

Social science research on IPV and its effects has witnessed a meteoric rise in the scope and volume of research generated across a variety of social science (e.g., psychology and sociology), health care (e.g., medicine and nursing), public health (e.g., epidemiology and prevention), and legally oriented disciplines (e.g., law, criminology, and criminal justice). The content of IPV-related topics studied is almost as varied as the methods employed to study them. While not claiming to be exhaustive, this chapter addresses salient methodological issues and challenges to conducting forensically relevant IPV research on a range of topics related to IPV victimization and perpetration.

Setting the stage, the chapter opens with a brief overview of IPV research topics relevant to forensic practice. Next, the chapter discusses methodological and measurement challenges to conducting IPV-related research. For ease of discussion, these topics are categorized methodologically as follows: (a) epidemiological approaches, (b) clinical/convenience approaches, and (c) intervention/prevention studies. Within topics, major methodological challenges are discussed. The measurement of IPV using existing standardized or structured scales is then presented. The chapter concludes with a presentation of ethical considerations unique to conducting IPV-related research.

FORENSICALLY RELEVANT IPV TOPICS

Expert evidence on IPV may find its way into courtrooms in civil, criminal, juvenile, or family court proceedings. In the criminal context, battered women charged with crimes might introduce expert evidence on "intimate partner battering and its effects," formerly known as battered woman syndrome (BWS), to support claims of justification (i.e., self-defense) or duress/coercion. For example, a battered woman defendant alleged to have assaulted or murdered her abusive intimate partner might introduce expert evidence to support a claim that her harmful/lethal actions were self-defensive rather than primarily aggressive in nature, even though her behavior might not fully comport with the traditional legal requirements for self-defense (i.e., the use of equal force in the face of a *reasonable* belief that one faces *imminent* death or serious bodily harm at the hands of an adversary).

In such a case, psychological research on battered women's responses to partner violence, including appraisal of risk of harm and deployment of coping strategies, both distal and proximal to the event, might be relevant in explaining how a battered woman defendant may have *perceived* herself as threatened with imminent death or serious bodily injury, even in the face of objective evidence suggesting otherwise, (e.g., her partner was unarmed whereas she possessed a weapon, or her lethal actions occurred within hours, rather than seconds or minutes of her partner's most recent threat against her life or physical integrity). Thus, such research can be useful in explaining a battered woman's subjective perceptions of risk at the time she took lethal action, even when objectively they may not fully align with the legal requirements for self-defense.

Battered women charged with crimes committed by or at the behest of their abusive intimate partners might also seek to introduce evidence to support claims that their behaviors were not the product of volition (i.e., free will), which is the underlying philosophical basis for attaching criminal liability. Instead, it might be argued that their actions were committed under conditions of duress or coercion (e.g., fear that if they failed to comply with their abuser's demands, serious harm to them would result), conditions vitiating the ability to exercise volition. Duress/coercion cases might involve a variety of potential charges, including forgery, robbery, drug sales, or a range of other criminal acts in which the defendant alleges that her participation was coerced rather than voluntary. Despite the specific criminal charge, in such cases battered women defendants claim that their volition was compromised based on their beliefs that serious harm to them would result from failure to comply with their batterer's demands for their participation in the criminal acts.

Coercion/duress cases include criminal acts committed by battered women (acts of commission) as described here, but also include acts of omission (i.e., liability for *failure to act* in expected or appropriate ways). Examples include a battered woman's failure to protect her child from being harmed or killed by her abusive partner (e.g., failure to protect cases) or a battered woman who is complicit in hiding the dead body of a victim murdered by her abusive partner instead of refusing to participate in an act she knows is criminal. Thus, expert evidence can be used to frame battered women's overt actions as well as their failure to act in ways they would otherwise be expected to.

Prosecutors charging batterers with crimes committed against their abusive partners might also seek to introduce expert psychological evidence to support the effective prosecution of their cases. In the prosecution context, there are three primary goals for the introduction of expert evidence on battering and its effects:

1. To rebut commonly held myths and misconceptions about battered women that might hinder successful prosecution (e.g., that leaving is always a safe and viable option or that all battered women are economically or socially disadvantaged and lack access to resources to extricate them from the abuse).
2. To bolster the credibility of a battered woman witness, who might appear impaired or whose behavior might appear confusing or irrational as a consequence of the violence in her life (e.g., she might use substances as a coping mechanism or she might engage in behavior that is protective of her abuser while perilous to herself).
3. To explain the contradictions in some battered women's behavior, such as initially filing a police report but subsequently recanting her statements or refusing to cooperate in the prosecution of the case against her batterer. Thus, research pertaining to a wide range of IPV topics, such as the public's endorsement of myths about intimate partner violence or the contradictions in battered women's behavior, might be introduced in the prosecution context to bolster the credibility of a battered woman witness.

Finally, expert evidence on IPV might be introduced in a variety of other types of (noncriminal) legal contexts, including (a) child custody and visitation, (b) battered women immigrants seeking asylum in the United States to get away from abusive partners in their native countries, (c) battered women suing their batterers for monetary damages in tort actions, or (d) battered women bringing actions against individuals or corporate entities for discrimination in housing, the workplace, or other settings. Thus, it is clear from this non-exhaustive review that research on some aspect of intimate partner violence is relevant to cases tried in a variety of criminal, civil, and family court settings. The next section proceeds to examine methodological considerations within several IPV-related topics.

METHODOLOGICAL CHALLENGES

Although research on the nature, dynamics, and consequences of IPV is critically important, the lynchpin of research is the reliable and valid assessment of IPV (Bachman, 2000; Saltzman, 2004). Plaguing all types of research on IPV are issues of definition, operationalization, and measurement of the IPV construct. The absence of standardized definition and measurement of IPV has hampered research on the topic (Saltzman, 2004), leading to unnecessary acrimony among scholars when conflicting data are reported. Data documenting rates, impact, dynamics, or any other aspect of IPV are inextricably bound with the ways in which IPV has been defined and operationalized. For example, in epidemiological studies, broader, more inclusive definitions of IPV naturally result in higher prevalence estimates than narrower, more restrictive definitions (DeKeseredy, 2000). In addition, the specific *wording* of questions posed to respondents is critical in terms of whether they endorse specific victimization experiences.

For example, studies relying on behaviorally specific questions generally document higher rates of violence against women compared with those relying on descriptive labels such as battered, raped, assaulted, or stalked (Hamby & Koss, 2003). Similarly, inclusion/exclusion criteria defining "battering," in clinical/convenience samples of battered women or perpetrators, undoubtedly influence the nature of study findings. For example, in a research study using a large sample of help-seeking battered women in which the author participated, inclusion criteria restricted the sample to women who had experienced recent and severe IPV. This meant that victims who experienced only minor aggression or emotional abuse only and/or those whose violence occurred more than 12 months ago were not eligible for study participation (Mechanic, Weaver, & Resick, 2008). Because of limits imposed by this restrictive definition, less severe cases of IPV were screened out, thus influencing study findings of both high levels of violence exposure and high rates of consequent psychopathology. Thus, it is critical to consider the ways in which IPV has been defined and operationalized in any given research study when interpreting conclusions.

Equally crucial are the methods by which potential participants are identified, selected, or recruited for research participation. In prospective studies, methods for participant retention during the course of the study timeline are also important considerations. Sample selection strategies can impose serious constraints on the generalizability of findings, which may be more or less problematic depending on the design and goals of a particular research study. An important caveat to remember is that there is no single *best method* for conducting research in this area, only the best method to answer the specific question posed by the research study. The following section of this chapter explores several methodological challenges to conducting research, in the context of specific IPV research approaches.

EPIDEMIOLOGICAL RESEARCH

Epidemiological research documents the prevalence of IPV victimization or perpetration, along with identification of correlates such as perpetrator gender, help seeking, police reporting, receipt of injuries or other victimization-related behaviors, and consequences.

Because the goals of epidemiological research are to capture prevalence or incidence data documenting IPV perpetration and/or victimization rates, studies in this category rely on *representative* samples of the general population rather than specialized samples recruited from police or court dockets, batterer intervention programs, battered women's residential and non-residential agencies, medical contexts, or other settings unique to IPV victims or perpetrators (generally referred to as convenience samples). Examples of research fitting within this genre include the family violence survey (Straus & Gelles, 1990) and other national surveys relying on the Conflict Tactics Scale or its revision (CTS-2: Straus, Hamby, Boney-McCoy, & Sugarman, 1996) and the National Violence Against Women Survey (NVAW: Tjaden & Thoennes, 1998; 2000a; 2000b). Not surprisingly, even with carefully controlled and executed research methodologies, epidemiological studies frequently report discrepant rates of IPV victimization or perpetration, often triggering formidable academic controversies in the research literature as to what the discrepancies are attributable to and their implications for interpreting the meaning and accuracy of obtained prevalence rates.

Because epidemiological studies endeavor to identify IPV rates in the general population, the issue of *sampling* is of critical importance because samples that do not accurately reflect the socio-demographic characteristics of the population will under- or over-represent actual victimization/perpetration rates in the population. Through the use of samples that accurately represent the socio-demographic characteristics of the general or a specific population (e.g., such variables as age, gender, race, ethnicity, socioecomonic status, rural vs. urban location), it is possible to obtain generalizable knowledge about IPV prevalence and its correlates.

GENERALIZABLE KNOWLEDGE AND SAMPLING ISSUES

Stratified random sampling procedures are employed to identify and recruit participants for epidemiological studies. By recruiting samples reflecting the population of interest in terms of relevant socio-demographic characteristics, these sampling techniques enable researchers to identify study samples from which generalizable knowledge may be obtained. Thus, for example, if one were conducting a study to assess IPV rates in the general population and the general population was 52% female, the study sample should reflect the sex distribution proportionately.

Similarly, other socio-demographic characteristics of the population relevant to the research need to be proportionately reflected in the study sample, which can be a procedural challenge for sample selection when multiple socio-demographic characteristics have to be accounted for in the right proportions. If a study sample fails to accurately reflect the socio-demographic characteristics of the population, it is quite likely that the obtained IPV estimates will be biased in ways that limit the generalizability of obtained data. Hypothetically speaking, if IPV victimization rates varied significantly as a function of gender, race, ethnicity, socioeconomic status, or urban/rural location, and if the study sample failed to match the population in terms of these characteristics, the obtained estimates of victimization/perpetration may significantly over- or under-represent the actual rates in the general population. Thus, careful attention to sampling procedures is critical in epidemiological studies of IPV.

Because of the need to procure representative samples, epidemiological studies do not use participants from specialized populations of IPV victims or perpetrators. Individuals seeking refuge in battered women's shelters or those whose cases are processed through the criminal justice system, for example, are not representative of the general population in many key ways. For example, most battered women do not seek formal help, and those that do typically report more severe violence exposure (Gleason, 1993; Gondolf & Fisher, 1988; Saunders, 1994) and fewer economic and social resources compared with those who do not seek help (Sackett & Saunders, 2001). If prevalence data were drawn from such restricted samples, compared with nationally or regionally representative community-based samples, artificially elevated rates of IPV exposure and help-seeking behavior would be reported, but they would be an artifact of the sample, rather than a true reflection of prevalence rates or of help-seeking behavior because of the biased nature of the sample.

It is important to remember that the issue is not that data drawn from representative samples of the general population are necessarily "better" than those derived from clinical or other convenience samples; rather, the quality of the sampling strategy can be evaluated only in the context of a particular study's research goals. For example, a study whose aim is to identify the prevalence of IPV and corresponding rates of criminal justice system use by battered women would be best accomplished by using a representative sampling strategy. In contrast, a study whose aim is to understand the factors influencing battered women's decisions to extend or drop protective orders would be best accomplished by using a convenience sample of battered women who obtained protective orders, identified through criminal justice system agencies, and followed prospectively. Thus, research methods are only as good as the questions they are designed to answer, so that a particular method might be a poor choice for some research question but an excellent choice for addressing others.

THE GENDER SYMMETRY DEBATE AS AN EXAMPLE IN METHODOLOGY

One recent research area that has been the subject of considerable controversy in the literature on IPV is the issue of gender symmetry of IPV perpetration. Specifically, some researchers (Archer, 2000; Dutton & Nicholls, 2005; Straus, 2006) argue that IPV perpetration is not gendered; that males and females perpetrate IPV at equivalent rates, and in some cases females perpetrate higher rates of IPV compared to males. This is referred to as the gender symmetry perspective. In contrast, other researchers (White, Smith, Koss, & Figueredo, 2000; Swan, Gambone, Caldwell, Sullivan, & Snow, 2008) contend that IPV is gendered—that males are the primary perpetrators and females are the primary victims of IPV (the gender asymmetry view). Bridging this contentious divide, researchers such as Johnson (1995; 2006) adopt the position that variations in conceptualization and methodological approaches account for the divergence in findings, creating something of an artifact based on research methodology rather than a true phenomenon of gender symmetry in IPV perpetration. In essence, Johnson argues that IPV is not a unitary phenomenon; various qualitatively distinct forms of IPV exist, but certain research approaches are more likely to identify one over another type of IPV, leading to potentially spurious conclusions about gender and IPV perpetration.

Specifically, Johnson (1995, 2006) maintains that data supporting the gender symmetry view of IPV perpetration were often obtained from nationally representative samples interviewed via telephone surveys, using the CTS or its progeny. Several potential conceptual and methodological issues might explain why epidemiological studies using the CTS, often with large representative, national samples, might find relatively equal rates of IPV perpetration across gender.

First, the CTS queries participants about *tactics* they have used to deal with conflicts in their relationship with their spouses, thus providing the framework for respondents conceptualizing aggressive acts as tactics used to resolve conflicts rather than as acts perpetrated with other motives (e.g., use of violence to control, threaten, or otherwise manipulate a partner) or in other contexts. The CTS assesses aggressive acts in a decontextualized manner that fails to provide a motive or context (such as self defense) for aggressive acts (outside of conflict tactics), thus obscuring the nature and meaning of those acts. Some argue that IPV cannot be assessed in a valid manner absent the assessment of context (Lindhorst & Tajima, 2008). Self-defensive, offensive, or retaliatory acts of aggression vary in terms of their nature, consequences, and meaning. The prevalence of each type of aggressive act also varies as a function of gender, with women tending to report greater use of self-defensive than offensive aggression, as compared with men. Thus, limitations associated with the measurement of IPV via the CTS might partially account for discrepant findings in the gender symmetry debate by failing to identify some acts of female-perpetrated violence as self-defensive and/or retaliatory, thus leading to inaccurate conclusions about equal rates of aggression perpetration. The frequency, nature, and meaning of battered women's use of self-defensive, retaliatory, or offensive force may be crucial in the context of battered women's criminal cases, and research conducted with large population samples surveyed with the CTS may fail to accurately document them.

Johnson (2006) argues that epidemiological studies finding gender symmetry in perpetration do so because they assess primarily minor rather than severe forms of aggression, which are in fact perpetrated at different rates by men and women. Specifically, Johnson maintains that the more severe and injurious forms of IPV, characterized by high levels of coercive control, fear, and receipt of injuries, are perpetrated primarily, if not exclusively, by males against their female partners, yet data documenting severe forms IPV are not obtained via large-scale telephone studies using the CTS for a variety of methodological and sampling reasons. Instead, such data tend to be obtained primarily from relatively small, in-depth studies of battered women, relying on convenience samples of victims seeking services at domestic violence agencies, medical settings, or law enforcement and criminal justice system contexts. From these samples, more severe cases of IPV are drawn, and detailed, nuanced questions are asked of participants in ways that provide greater explication of the context and nature of IPV acts perpetrated.

Thus, from Johnson's perspective, discrepant findings and divergent interpretations of gender symmetry findings are attributable to major methodological differences in sampling and measurement approaches between two different approaches to research (i.e., epidemiological vs. clinical) such that each captures a veridical, yet unique component of the IPV landscape. Thus, a more accurate interpretation of those data might be that men and women perpetrate relatively equal rates of minor aggression, whereas more severe, injurious forms of aggression accompanied by high levels of coercive control, are more often perpetrated by men than women (Johnson, 2006). Finally, Johnson (1995, 2006) maintains that the large representative samples using the CTS actually had refusal rates of 40%, rather than the reported 18%, thereby biasing the results in ways that suggested gender symmetry. Thus, the lesson here underscores the importance of understanding the methodological basis for interpretation of data in this area.

Sample Selection Issues and Limitations

Selection of sample participants in epidemiological surveys is most often accomplished through random digit dialing procedures in which representative geographic regions are mapped out and potential households for recruiting study participants are identified via landline telephone numbers. Through random selection procedures, potential households are identified, and within those households a protocol is used to select study participants. However, there are several potential threats to generalizability study findings from the use of such procedures. First, reliance on the use of household telephones to screen potential study respondents is problematic, because the most economically disadvantaged members of the population are omitted from potential participation due to lack of home telephones. Given that IPV disproportionately affects individuals of lower socioeconomic status (Benson & Fox, 2004), this might produce artificially depressed IPV rates, both in terms of frequency and severity of violence perpetration. Moreover, in recent years, many individuals have opted to forgo landline phones in favor of cell phone service.

This trend is particularly evidenced in younger segments of the population. Because IPV tends to be disproportionately high among young couples (Tjaden & Thoennes, 2000a), studies recruiting participants on the basis of landline phones may fail to capture this important segment of the population. Similarly, individuals living in college dorms and those in prisons or other institutionalized settings are also excluded from potential inclusion in such studies. Thus, the many limitations to sample selection and measurement in large-scale epidemiological studies may limit generalizability, sometimes resulting in divisiveness and political rancor when those findings are interpreted.

Other important sample-selection issues include the methods by which potential study participants are recruited from within a household. In the IPV research context, one concern is that potential survey respondents might be excluded from participation by an abusive partner monitoring, controlling, or otherwise interfering with autonomy such that an abused partner is prohibited from participating or must provide false data because the abuser is listening in on her conversation. In a study in which the author was a co-investigator, a representative sample using random digit dialing procedures was used to identify potential female survey respondents in a research project assessing IPV in the context of a natural disaster. Of the 31 refusals, 14 (45%) declined to participate due to their male partners' request or restriction of their activities (Mechanic, Griffin, & Resick, 2000). It is possible that these potential respondents were battered women whose partners controlled their activities, preventing their participation, thus potentially biasing the sample in ways that underestimate IPV rates.

Thus, the strengths of epidemiological studies in the context of IPV research include the capacity to obtain generalizable knowledge from representative populations as well as the reliance on structured and standardized approaches for collecting data. As described previously, there are several unique challenges posed by epidemiological studies of IPV that must be considered when interpreting findings derived from them.

CLINICAL/CONVENIENCE SAMPLES

Many studies of IPV victims or perpetrators use specialized populations with known exposure to IPV. These samples are typically recruited in clinical, criminal justice, forensic, or medical settings and are generally on the smaller side, especially as compared with large-scale epidemiological studies that collect data from thousands of participants. While epidemiological studies of IPV most often opt for breadth, asking abbreviated questions about IPV exposure (and sometimes its correlates or consequences), studies using clinical/convenience samples most often opt for depth, typically assessing IPV phenomenology, clinical symptomatology, and many other relevant dimensions in greater detail than can be assessed in telephone-based population surveys.

While epidemiological studies typically rely on highly structured surveys for data collection, more clinically oriented studies employ a diverse range of methods for data collection, incorporating both quantitative and qualitative approaches either exclusively or in tandem. These data collection methods include (a) structured, semi-structured, and unstructured questionnaires or surveys; (b) structured, semi-structured, and unstructured interviews either individually or group-administered; (c) archival data; and (d) behavioral observation methods, including physiological recording devices. Given inherent limitations to the reliability and validity of any single data-collection strategy, many clinical studies adopt a multi-method approach, one that maximizes the validity of findings by limiting reliance on any single strategy, a method that is inherently flawed. Studies relying on convenience or clinical samples of victims or perpetrators pose unique methodological challenges that diverge from those specific to conducting epidemiological research. First, because samples are drawn from clinics or other agencies, they are not representative of the general population of IPV victims or perpetrators in various ways, thus posing constraints on generalizability. For example, battered women seeking medical or mental health services or those seeking criminal justice remedies are likely to be significantly different in many ways from battered women in the community who do not elect to seek assistance from formal sources, such as help providers. Similarly, batterers who are involved in the criminal justice system and/or those participating in court-ordered batterer intervention programs are also not representative of the general population of batterers.

Whereas epidemiological studies select participants randomly and query them about their experiences with violence victimization and/or perpetration, convenience/clinical studies identify individuals already known to be victims or perpetrators and query them in depth about the nature and consequences of those experiences. Because samples of known victims/perpetrators are used, sample selection concerns revolve around the nature of recruitment strategies for the study, including inclusion/exclusion criteria, participant identification, recruitment and retention procedures, and compensation for participation. Concerns about recruitment procedures are necessary to understand the nature of the sample, as well as any limits to generalizability imposed as consequences of the procedures used to identify, select, retain, and compensate participants.

Various strategies might be used to recruit participants for a study of battered women. For example, researchers might place advertisements in local newspapers or post flyers in laundromats, day care centers, and other general community venues catering to women. Such a study might then have potential participants contact researchers to set up a telephone appointment to explain more about the study and to screen potential participants using inclusion/exclusion criteria. There must be a mechanism in place to record the proportion of individuals who are screened, including information about how they came to know about the study, as well as data on (a) proportion screened out of the study for each of the specified criteria; (b) proportion of participants who met screening criteria yet declined to participate, ideally along with reasons why; and (c) proportion of participants that met screening criteria and agreed to participate, ideally broken down by those who actually completed participation and those who were unable to do so.

These criteria describe the larger pool of potential participants from which the final sample was drawn, allowing researchers to make some statements about the representativeness of their sample vis-à-vis their potential pool of participants. For example, if a very high proportion of potential participants declined to continue after being screened, one might wonder if there was something problematic about the screening procedures. Similarly, it would be important to know whether there were significant socio-demographic or violence-exposure differences between participants recruited from each of the various locations, or whether there were differences among those who agreed to participate and actually did so and those who either did not agree or agreed but failed to complete participation.

Whether the sample is recruited through general non-victim or perpetrator-related community venues or directly through victim assistance or other agencies, researchers must spell out the specific mechanisms employed to "advertise" the study to prospective participants. Imagine that researchers obtain cooperation from a battered woman's shelter to recruit participants for a project and that staff at the shelter have agreed to inform potential participants about the study. Questions arise as to whether the procedures used for staff recruitment of participants is *standardized*, such that *all* women entering the shelter are apprised and screened for participation and all are informed and evaluated in the same fashion. Problems arise if there are lapses in the implementation of these standardized recruitment and screening procedures, especially when lapses are either non-random or idiosyncratic.

For example, imagine that researchers are conducting a study of the mental health consequences of IPV exposure and that agency staff agreed to inform and screen each new resident of the shelter at the intake interview. However, if for example, one or more staff members conducting the screening interviews believed that some new residents were simply "too fragile" to make a decision about research participation or that they were "too distraught" to participate in a study, the sample would be potentially biased, and some of the most severe cases would have been screened out by non-random procedures, posing a threat to the study's validity and generalizability. Similarly, if participants were recruited without using standardized procedures, such that shelter intake workers used their own idiosyncratic procedures to inform potential participants about the study or to screen them, threats to validity and generalizability would be paramount. It should be noted that while these concerns are not entirely unique to convenience/clinical samples, they are more likely to be problematic in these settings compared with epidemiological studies employing paid, trained telephone interviewers using standardized procedures from participant recruitment and assessment.

Issues regarding compensation are also important insofar as they might have implications for the generalizability of the sample. For example, if a sample of very poor battered women is offered high sums of money to participate in a study, not only is the sample potentially limited by that fact, but depending on the nature of the study, the validity of the data might be compromised.

Treatment or intervention studies of IPV victims or perpetrators of violence pose a unique set of challenges to contend with, the biggest of which is participant recruitment and retention during the course of the study. One of the major challenges to the successful completion of intervention studies is the retention of participants throughout the duration of the intervention and throughout the multiple follow-up assessments, if those are part of the study design. If the study uses more than one active treatment/intervention, it is critical that participants be randomly assigned to intervention conditions, even when one of the treatments is believed to be more desirable, more effective, or more potentially beneficial to a particular participant (e.g., treatment matching). For example, if the study screener completes the screening process for a potential participant and deems that individual eligible to participate and the individual agrees to participate after completing informed consent procedures, the participant must be assigned to the condition through random assignment. If, however, the screener believes that this individual would benefit more from intervention A than intervention B and proceeds to assign that individual accordingly, there is a threat to the validity of the findings based on non-random assignment of participants to conditions.

Other problems with intervention studies include participant dropout during the intervention or the follow-up window. This is especially challenging if there is differential dropout between treatment conditions in a study. These issues with retention pose serious threats to the validity of study findings. Research assessing treatment outcomes for men enrolled in batterer intervention programs is often limited because of problems associated with participation dropout (Gondolf, 2001). For example, if study findings show that batterer intervention programs significantly reduce IPV perpetration but the most severely abusive men dropped out of the study before data on outcomes could be collected, the validity of study findings are threatened by differential dropout.

It is important to note that the problem with participant retention is not unique to intervention research but also plagues longitudinal studies that aim to track participants over time to follow the natural course of various behaviors, symptoms, or engagement in formal help-seeking systems. While issues of retention are problematic with *any* longitudinal or intervention study, unique issues with battered women and IPV perpetrators add additional challenges to retention concerns. For example, battered women who have left their abusive partners are generally living in a state of flux that often involves fear of future violence from their abusive partners, such that they are on the move, in hiding, or otherwise difficult for researchers to track. In addition, leaving an abusive relationship is more of a process than an event, involving multiple attempts to leave and then returning to the relationship before successfully extricating oneself from it.

The author conducted a small pilot study of acutely and severely battered women followed up over six months (Taft, Resick, Pannuzio, Vogt, & Mechanic, 2007). In an effort to retain participants over the six-month period, they were tracked and followed using intensive biweekly tracking procedures. In addition, contact information of several individuals who would always know how to reach the participant was obtained. Despite extensive efforts to track and retain participants, a sizable percentage was lost to follow up often because they were unable to be found. Perhaps, more interestingly, a significant percentage was located but was unwilling to participate. We were able to briefly interview the unwilling participants to find out why they refused to complete the follow-up portions of the study. Interestingly, the most common reason reported was that the women had reunited with their abusive partners and felt too much shame to face the research staff, because their initial participation occurred at a time when they had found the courage to leave. Thus, this information was helpful in discovering valuable information about how to improve future retention procedures through the use of "motivational" interviewing methods (e.g., Miller & Rollnick, 1991, 2002; Murphy & Maiuro, 2009) such as those used for substance abuse interventions in which relapse is expected and procedures to handle it are built in by design. Future prospective studies of battered women might build in a protocol that discusses these potential issues with participants at the outset to reduce the risk of dropout at subsequent follow-up periods.

With the popularity of perpetrator-intervention studies and the pressing social need to document the effectiveness (or lack thereof) of such studies, researchers have discussed a host of methodological problems plaguing this area of research (Babcock, Green, & Robie, 2004; Feder & Wilson, 2005)—problems that pose serious threats to the validity of conclusions regarding problems with sample recruitment, retention, and so on. Interested readers are referred to those articles for additional information. For more information on recruitment and retention of participants in a variety of IPV-related research areas, the interested reader is referred to a paper by Dutton et al. (2003) that discusses many issues related to participant recruitment and retention.

MEASURES

IPV is a multidimensional construct comprising various topographical acts united by a common thread. All aggressive acts, while superficially unique, function as a form of coercive control (Beck & Raghavan, 2009; Dutton & Goodman, 2005; Johnson, 2006; Mechanic, Weaver, & Resick, 2008; Stark, 2006). A range of behaviors, including physical aggression, sexual coercion and violence, stalking, and psychological abuse comprise intimate partner abuse (Mechanic, Weaver, & Resick, 2008). Depending on the goals of the research, it may be important to consider including measurement of all relevant dimensions of the IPV construct instead of measuring only physical aggression.

From an assessment perspective, sound measurement development practices ought to include an articulation of the theoretical and/or conceptual specification of the construct being assessed (Groth-Marnat, 2003), but measures of IPV often fail to specify the underlying conceptual or theoretical underpinnings for the assessment tool (for exceptions, see Beck & Ragavan, 2009; Tanha, Beck, Raghavan, & Figueredo, 2010). Critiques of the CTS, including the revised version (the CTS-2) are numerous, including the oft-cited criticism that the CTS fails to measure the situational or motivational context for violence, thus obscuring the meaning of the acts, which are measured as simple frequency counts of aggressive actions perpetrated by an aggressor or experienced by a victim (DeKeseredy, 2000; 2006). A more thorough critique of the CTS is beyond the scope of this chapter.

There are many existing standardized or structured measures for assessing IPV. An exhaustive review of them is beyond the scope of this chapter, but the interested reader is referred to the following sources for comprehensive information about extant IPV measures: (Rathus & Feindler, 2004; Thompson, Basile, Hertz, & Sitterle, 2006).

Finally, while the majority of research covered in this chapter describes survey or clinical research with general or specialized populations primarily using survey or questionnaire approaches, it is also worth noting that some research on IPV is laboratory based, using experimental methods (usually in combination with survey or questionnaire administration) for assessing relationship conflict and aggression. Experimental studies of marital violence typically employ behavioral observation and physiological assessment measures (e.g., Babcock, Jacobson, Gottman, & Yerington, 2000) administered to samples of maritally violent and nonviolent couples.

SAFETY AND ETHICAL CONCERNS

This chapter would be remiss if it did not address the multitude of safety and ethical issues involved in conducting research in this area. When dealing with battered women, procedures must be in place to protect their safety and well-being. This entails the development of safety protocols regarding whether and how participants are contacted via mail or telephone and what written information is to be used. The protocol should include procedures for what messages, if any (and in what form), can be left for a battered woman and how the research staff member will identify herself when contacting the participant, in case the batterer answers the phone, is monitoring the call, or is listening in. It is critical that research participation does not further jeopardize a battered woman's safety.

In addition, the physical safety of battered women must be considered. For example, concerns that battered women might be followed or stalked by their abusive partner led the author's research team to install security devices at the location where the research was conducted in order to enhance participant safety. Other concerns include the format of referrals or informed consent documents participants are provided with after leaving the study session, because such things can trigger aggressive or menacing responses by the batterer if he finds them. Thus, it is often necessary to discuss safety concerns with each battered woman participant to reduce the risk of harm. Davies, Lyon, and Monti-Catania (1998) provide extensive information on safety planning with battered women. For additional detailed information about safety issues in conducting research with battered women, the interested reader is referred to Campbell and Dienemann, 2001; Ellsberg and Heise, 2002; Ellsberg, Heise, Pena, Arguto, and Winkvist, 2001; and Sullivan and Cain, 2004.

Finally, ethical concerns have been raised about the potentially re-traumatizing effects of victim participation in research by concerned researchers, clinicians, and even institutional review boards (IRBs). While a complete discussion of this interesting and complex issue is beyond the scope of this chapter, it is important to consider and recognize the vulnerability of traumatized individuals and the ways in which research participation might affect them. The interested reader is referred to several recent studies that have addressed the issue empirically in the context of research of IPV and sexual assault (Griffin, Resick, Waldrop, & Mechanic, 2003; Grubaugh, Frueh, & Magruder, 2005; Johnson & Benight, 2003).

SUMMARY/CONCLUSIONS

This chapter describes a range of relevant forensic contexts in which research on IPV might be introduced. Given the proliferation of research on this topic and the interest of the legal profession on battering and its effects, the chapter endeavors to describe some of the most important methodological and measurement issues relevant to conducting and consuming research on IPV. Among the most important concerns are sampling issues, operationalization and measurement of IPV, and recruitment and retention of study participants in treatment along with prospective studies of victims or perpetrators. Finally, because of the very sensitive nature of the topic, ethical and safety issues relevant to conducting research with battered women were discussed.

REFERENCES

Archer, J. (2000). Sex differences in aggression between heterosexual partners: A meta-analytic review. *Psychological Bulletin*, 126, 651–680.

Babcock, J. C., Green, C. E., & Robie, C. (2004). Does batterers' treatment work? A meta-analytic review of domestic violence treatment. *Clinical Psychology Review*, 23, 1023–1053.

Babcock, J. C, Jacobsen, N. S., Gottman, J. M., & Yerington, T. P. (2000). Attachment, emotional regulation, and the function of marital violence: Differences between secure, preoccupied, and dismissing violent and nonviolent husbands. *Journal of Family Violence, 15*, 391–409.

Bachman, R. A. (2000). Comparison of annual incidence rates and contextual characteristics of intimate-partner violence against women from the National Crime Victimization Survey (NCVS) and the National Violence Against Women Survey (NVAWS). *Violence Against Women, 6*, 839–867.

Beck, C. J. A., & Raghavan, C. (2009, in press). Intimate partner violence screening in custody mediation: The importance of assessing coercive control. *Family Court Review.*

Benson, M. L., & Fox, G. L. (2004). *When violence hits home: How economics and neighborhood play a role.* Washington, DC: National Institute of Justice. NCJ 205004

Campbell, J. C., & Dienemann, J. D. (2001). Ethical issues in research on violence against women. In C. M. Renzetti, J. L. Edleson, & R. K. Bergen (Eds.), *Sourcebook on violence against women.* Thousand Oaks, CA: Sage.

Davies, J., Lyon, E., & Monti-Catania, D. (1998). *Safety planning with battered women: Complex lives/difficult choices.* Thousand Oaks, CA: Sage.

DeKeseredy, W. S. (2000). Current controversies on defining nonlethal violence against women in intimate heterosexual relationships. *Violence Against Women, 6*, 728–746.

DeKeseredy, W. S. (2006). Future directions. *Violence Against Women, 11*, 1078–1085.

Dutton, D., & Nicholls, T. (2005). The gender paradigm in domestic violence research and theory: Part I—the conflict of theory and data. *Aggression and Violent Behavior, 10*(6), 680–714.

Dutton, M. A., & Goodman, L. (2005). Coercion in intimate partner violence: Toward a new conceptualization. *Sex Roles, 52*, 743–756.

Dutton, M. A., Holtzworth-Munroe, A., Jouriles, E., McDonald, R., Krishnan, S., McFarlane, J., & Sullivan, C. (2003). *Recruitment and retention in intimate partner violence research.* (NCJ 201934). Washington, DC: U.S. Department of Justice.

Ellsberg, M., & Heise, L. (2002). Bearing witness: Ethics in domestic violence research. *The Lancet, 359*, 1599–1604.

Ellsberg, M., Heise, L., Pena, R., Arguto, S., & Winkvist, A. (2001). Researching domestic violence against women: Methodological and ethical considerations. *Studies in Family Planning, 32*(1), 1–16.

Feder, L., & Wilson, D. B. (2005). A meta-analytic review of court-mandated batterer intervention programs: Can courts affect abusers' behavior? *Journal of Experimental Criminology, 1*, 239–262.

Gleason, W. J. (1993). Mental disorders in battered women: An empirical study. *Violence and Victims, 8*, 53–68.

Groth-Marnat, G. (2003). *Handbook of psychological assessment,* 4th ed. New York, NY: Wiley.

Gondolf, E. W. (2001). *Batterer intervention systems: Issues, outcomes, and recommendations.* Thousand Oaks, CA: Sage.

Gondolf, E. W., & Fisher, E. R. (1988). *Battered women as survivors: An alternative to treating learned helplessness.* Lexington, MA: Lexington Books.

Griffin, M. G., Resick, P. A., Waldrop, A. E., & Mechanic, M. B. (2003). Participation in trauma research: Is there evidence of harm? *Journal of Traumatic Stress, 16*(3), 221–227.

Grubaugh, A. L., Frueh, C. B., & Magruder, K. M. (2005). Research participants and questions about sexual trauma. *American Journal of Psychiatry, 162*(9), 1757–1758.

Hamby, S. L., & Koss, M. P. (2003). Shades of gray: A qualitative study of terms used in the measurement of sexual victimization. *Psychology of Women Quarterly, 27*, 243–255.

Ibn-Tamas v United States, 407 A.2d 626 (1979).

Johnson, L. E., & Benight, C. C. (2003). Effects of trauma-focused research on recent domestic violence survivors. *Journal of Traumatic Stress, 16*(6), 567–571.

Johnson, M. P. (1995). Patriarchal terrorism and common couple violence: Two forms of violence against women. *Journal of Marriage and the Family, 57*, 283–294.

Johnson, M. P. (2006). Conflict and control: Gender symmetry and asymmetry in domestic violence. *Violence Against Women, 12*, 1003–1018.

Lindhorst, T., & Tajima, E. (2008). Reconceptualizing and operationalizing. *Journal of Interpersonal Violence, 23*, 362–388.

Mechanic, M. B., Griffin, M. G., & Resick, P. A. (2000). *The effects of intimate partner abuse on women's psychological adjustment to a major disaster* (unpublished manuscript).

Mechanic, M. B., Weaver, T. L., & Resick, P. A. (2008). Mental health consequences of intimate partner abuse: Assessment of four different forms of abuse. *Violence Against Women, 14*, 634–654.

Miller, W. R., & Rollnick, S. (1991). *Motivational interviewing: Preparing people to change addictive behavior.* New York, NY: Guilford Press.

Miller, W. R., & Rollnick, S. (2002). *Motivational interviewing: Preparing people for change* (2nd ed.). New York, NY: Guilford Press.

Murphy, C. M., & Maiuro, R. D. (2009) (Eds.). *Motivational interviewing and stages of change in intimate partner violence.* New York, NY: Springer.

Rathus, J. H., & Feindler, E. L. (2004). *Assessment of partner violence: A handbook for researchers and practitioners.* Washington, DC: American Psychological Association.

Sackett, L. A., & Saunders, D. G. (2001). The impact of different forms of psychological abuse of battered women. In K. D. O'Leary & R. D. Maiuro (Eds.), *Psychological abuse in violent domestic relations.* (pp. 197–211). New York, NY: Springer.

Saltzman, L. E. (2004). Definition and methodological issues related to translational research on intimate partner violence. *Violence Against Women, 10,* 812–830.

Saunders, D. G. (1994). Posttraumatic stress symptom profiles of battered women: A comparison of survivors in two settings. *Violence and Victims, 9,* 31–44.

Stark, E. (2006). Commentary on Johnson's "Conflict and control: Gender symmetry and asymmetry in domestic violence." *Violence Against Women, 12,* 1019–1025.

Straus, M. A. (2006). Future research in gender symmetry of assaults on intimate partners. *Violence Against Women, 12,* 1086–1097.

Straus, M. A., & Gelles, R. J. (1990). *Physical violence in American families.* New Brunswick, NJ: Transaction Publishers.

Straus, M. A., Hamby, S. L., Boney-McCoy, S., & Sugarman, D. B. (1996). The revised conflict tactics scales (CTS2): Development and preliminary psychometric data. *Journal of Family Issues, 17*(3), 283–316.

Sullivan, C. M., & Cain, D. (2004). Ethical and safety considerations when obtaining information from or about battered women for research purposes. *Journal of Interpersonal Violence, 19*(5), 603–618.

Swan, S. C., Gambone, L. J., Caldwell, J. E., Sullivan, T. P., & Snow, D. L. (2008). A review of research on women's use of violence against male intimate partners. *Violence Against Women, 23,* 301–314.

Tanha, M., Beck, C. J. A., Figueredo, A. J., & Raghavan, C. (2010). Sex differences in intimate partner violence and the use of coercive control as a motivational factor for intimate partner violence. *Journal of Interpersonal Violence, 25,* 1836–1854.

Taft, C. T., Resick, P. A., Pannuzio, J., Vogt, D. S., & Mechanic, M. B. (2007). Coping among victims of relationship abuse: A longitudinal examination. *Violence and Victims, 22,* 408–418.

Thompson, M. P., Basile, K. C., Hertz, M. F., & Sitterle, D. (2006). *CDC measuring intimate partner victimization and perpetration: A compendium of assessment tools.* Atlanta, GA: Centers for Disease Control and Prevention, National Center for Injury Prevention and Control.

Tjaden, P., & Thoennes, N. (1998). *Stalking in America: Findings from the national violence against women survey* (NCJ Report No. 169592). Washington, DC: U.S. Department of Justice.

Tjaden, P., & Thoennes, N. (2000a). *Full report of the prevalence, incidence, and consequences of violence against women: Findings from the national violence against women survey.* (NCJ Report No. 183781). Washington, DC: U.S. Department of Justice.

Tjaden, P., & Thoennes, N. (2000b). *Extent, nature, and consequences of violence against women: Findings from the national violence against women survey.* (NCJ Report No. 181867). Washington, DC: U.S. Department of Justice.

Walker, L. E. A., & Shapiro, D. L. (2003). *Introduction to forensic psychology: Clinical and social psychological perspectives.* New York, NY: Springer.

White, J. W., Smith, P. H., Koss, M. P., & Figueredo, A. J. (2000). Intimate partner aggression—what have we learned? Comment on Archer (2000). *Psychological Bulletin, 126,* 697–702.

CHAPTER 25

Research on Child Abuse and Neglect

CATHY SPATZ WIDOM AND ELISE C. LANDRY

INTRODUCTION

In the early 1960s, the groundbreaking work of Kempe and his colleagues (Kempe, Silverman, Steele, Droegemueller, & Silver, 1962) called attention to the "battered child syndrome" in an article in the *Journal of the American Medical Association*. Since that time, there has been increased attention to all forms of child maltreatment by policy makers and the general public as well as by juvenile court judges, child protection service workers, mental health professionals, teachers, and law enforcement personnel. Childhood maltreatment remains a serious public health concern, with an estimated 3.3 million referrals to child protective agencies for suspected child maltreatment in 2005 and 899,000 cases substantiated after investigation (U.S. Department of Health and Human Services, 2007). However, unlike many other research areas, the field of child maltreatment is faced with a number of statutory, methodological, and ethical challenges that make it "one of the most difficult types of research to undertake" (Runyan & English, 2006, p. 255).

Child maltreatment encompasses any acts of commission or omission by a parent or other caregiver that result in harm, potential for harm, or threat of harm to a child, even if harm is not the intended consequence (Leeb, Paulozzi, Melanson, Simon, & Arias, 2008). Four forms of maltreatment are widely recognized: (a) physical abuse, (b) sexual abuse, (c) neglect, and (d) psychological abuse (sometimes referred to as emotional abuse). Definitions typically place responsibility for safeguarding children from maltreatment on all caregivers, including parents, relatives, teachers, babysitters, clergy, and coaches. However, with the exception of sexual abuse, 80% or more of maltreatment is perpetrated by parents or parent substitutes (U.S. Department of Health and Human Services, 2007).

In this chapter, we address some of the challenges facing researchers in the field of child abuse and neglect and suggest ways to overcome these hurdles with hopes of enhancing child maltreatment research. We begin with a brief historical review of child protection laws and then discuss methodological and ethical issues, including mandatory reporting of child abuse and neglect.

A BRIEF HISTORICAL REVIEW OF CHILD PROTECTION LAWS

To begin, there is an inherent conflict in the legal response to child maltreatment: protecting the child from harm versus the privacy rights of the family. The societal responsibility to protect children from harm has emerged in the legal constructs of the best interests of the child standard and *parens patriae*, both of which require states to act in the best interests of children and protect them. In contrast to this responsibility is the belief that the privacy rights of the family are of utmost importance. When addressing state intrusions into privacy matters, the state's interest must outweigh the privacy interest at stake. However, in the realm of child abuse and neglect, this has typically been interpreted to signify the state's willingness to intrude into the privacy of family life only when there is "the imminent threat to the life or health of a minor child"(Zimring, 1989). To understand what constitutes an imminent threat to the life or health of a child, it is necessary to understand how society's views of children have changed over the years.

From the 1600s to the early 1800s, children were viewed as the property of their parents, particularly the father. Children had no legal rights and could be severely punished for failing to obey their parents. The Stubborn Child Law of 1646 provides a startling example of the absolute power parents were believed to have over their children. Under this law, parents could seek state punishment of disobedient children, including capital punishment in cases of severe disobedience (Ichikawa, 1997). As property, parents could treat their children as they saw fit. During this time period, children were removed from their parents only if the state viewed the parents as neglecting a child's moral development. The Elizabethan Poor Law of 1601 provides a vivid illustration of early "child protection" laws (M. J. Cox & Cox, 1985). This law granted the state the right to remove children from parents who permitted them to grow up in "idleness or ignorance," placing them in settings in which they would learn the value of hard work (Bremner, 1970).

The identification of child maltreatment as a significant social problem in the United States emerged during the industrialization period of the 1800s. This period was marked by child labor and increased poverty in urban areas, which made the issue of child suffering increasingly visible and harder to ignore (Giovannoni, 1989). In an early attempt to improve the moral development of children being raised in these impoverished circumstances, states developed institutions and orphanages for their care.

The year 1874 is generally recognized as the year in which child maltreatment first became an issue of national concern (Peled & Kurtz, 1994).

The case of Mary Ellen, a 10-year-old child who was found beaten and chained by her parents, was widely publicized that year and led to the first organized response to child maltreatment. There were no laws in existence addressing the abuse of children by their parents. Although the Society for the Prevention of Cruelty to Animals attempted to prosecute Mary Ellen's parents under animal cruelty laws (Peled & Kurtz, 1994), the court held that her parents had not committed any prosecutable crime. Mary Ellen's case led to the establishment of the Society for the Prevention of Cruelty to Children, which eventually was incorporated into a national organization focused on raising awareness of child abuse as a social problem—the American Humane Association. Although child abuse remained a concern of the child welfare system and research on learning and attachment theories began to highlight the importance of nurturing children, the public and political focus retreated until the 1960s.

Motivated by the work of Kempe and his colleagues (Kempe et al., 1962), the Children's Bureau turned its focus to the creation of child-protection laws and mandatory reporting obligations. Furthermore, scholars and practitioners called attention to child maltreatment as a legitimate problem with severe consequences for the victims (Roche, Labbe, Brown, & Chadwick, 2005). Not only did this work establish the need for clear definitions of various forms of maltreatment, it also cemented society's recognition of maltreatment as a problem occurring within families.

In 1967, the landmark Supreme Court decision in *In re Gault* that children are protected by the same constitutional rights as adults did not specifically address child maltreatment but represented a tremendous advance in children's rights. By 1974, Congress had passed the first key federal legislation addressing child abuse and neglect: the Child Abuse Prevention and Treatment Act (CAPTA; PL 97-247). CAPTA included provisions to charge the states with the responsibility to develop standards for defining abuse (a minimum definition); to require the states to establish mandatory reporting of suspicions of maltreatment; and to require the states to identify the state agency responsible for investigating abuse allegations. CAPTA also provides federal funding to states in support of prevention, assessment, investigation, prosecution, and treatment activities and to public agencies and nonprofit organizations for demonstration programs and projects.

Since its initial passage in 1974, the scope of CAPTA legislation has been expanded with amendments to allocate additional federal funds for research on child abuse (Title I of the Child Abuse Prevention and Treatment and Adoption Reform Act of 1978, PL-266 and Child Abuse Amendments of 1984, PL 98-457). The Child Abuse Prevention, Adoption, and Family Services Act of 1988 (PL100-294) established both the National Center on Child Abuse and Neglect and a national clearinghouse designated to serve as a repository for information related to child abuse. CAPTA was later amended and reauthorized by the Keeping Children and Families Safe Act of 2003 (PL 108-36). In sum, a federal commitment to child abuse and neglect as a social problem was solidified through the passage of CAPTA and regularly recurring amendments. At the same time, research examining child maltreatment has faced major methodological and ethical challenges.

METHODOLOGICAL ISSUES

DEFINITIONAL ISSUES

The first challenge in the field of child maltreatment research is basic: there is no "gold standard" to determine whether child abuse or neglect has occurred. As Knutson and Heckenberg (2006) noted, "the field has not achieved a gold standard against which operational definitions of physical abuse and other forms of maltreatment can be judged." Similarly, in a discussion of neglect, Dubowitz (2006), a pediatrician, has suggested that there may never be a single definition of neglect, given the multiplicity of purposes for its definition. The pediatrician may have a rather low threshold for considering a situation as neglect, being primarily concerned with the health of the child. In contrast, the child protection service (CPS) worker, bound and guided by state laws and limited agency resources, typically has a higher threshold. Finally, a prosecutor may have the highest threshold for considering something neglect, pursuing only the most serious cases.

For researchers, there is the additional problem of the equivalence of definitions used and, thus, the comparability of populations covered by the studies. While nominal definitions are often similar, operational definitions frequently differ. From a scientific perspective, one would not expect convergence in findings (although it may occur) unless studies use the same or similar definitions.

The broadest definition of physical abuse places it within a continuum of parental behavior that ranges from mild physical punishment at one end to extreme violence at the other (broken bones or severe physical trauma). However, this breadth of definitions directly influences research findings. Weis (1989) noted that varying definitions have led to estimates ranging from 1% to 30% of all children in the United States suffering from physical abuse. The low estimates depend on narrower criteria, whereas higher estimates are based on broader, more encompassing definitions. Similarly, a definition of childhood sexual abuse that includes any unwanted sexual experiences (e.g., unwanted touching that occurred from childhood through age 18) leads to high prevalence rates.

Over 90% of parents report spanking of children or some form of corporal punishment, although some parents report spanking young children only rarely (Gallup Organization, 1995; Straus & Donnelly, 1994/2001; Straus, Gelles, & Steinmetz, 1980/2006; Straus & Stewart, 1999). According to The Center for Effective Discipline (2008), 29 states have banned corporal punishment in schools along with numerous school districts in areas without statewide laws; however, no state has firm legislation controlling corporal punishment in the home. The complexity of definitional issues in child maltreatment research is illustrated by the variations in cultural acceptance of physical punishment in child-rearing practices and regional differences in these practices (Korbin, 2002).

MEASUREMENT

Four basic sources of information are typically used in child abuse and neglect research. The most common involves information obtained from studies based on self-reports from victims old enough to comply with surveys or on parents reporting severe physical punishment or patterns of care. A second source of information is based on official statistics from agencies investigating victims (e.g., child protection services) or police (investigating victims and offenders). Some studies use samples drawn from treatment or other specialized groups, whereas others depend on analyses of case files of samples not specific to abuse or neglect. All of these sources of information have biases, which produce uncertainty in estimates of prevalence.

Self-Reports of Child Maltreatment   Obtaining information about child maltreatment through the use of self-reports is the most frequently used method. In an excellent discussion of self-report approaches to child abuse research, Portwood (2006) noted: "At their best, standardized self-report questionnaires address wide range of potentially abusive and neglectful experiences, employ clear and specific definitions, and produce normative data that researchers can then use to make meaningful comparisons between groups" (p. 236). In addition, self-reports are relatively easy to use, can be brief and inexpensive, are administered by a broad range of staff, offer the possibility of wide geographic coverage and group administration, and are not subject to the biases of official reporting agencies (discussed subsequently).

However, there are a number of concerns about sole reliance on self-report data from surveys or interviews. One difficulty is ensuring that the same question means the same thing to respondents in different contexts. People from different backgrounds may interpret events or experiences in different ways, and responses to these questions may represent a person's cognitive appraisal of the event or experience. Asking people retrospectively about their adverse childhood experiences is limited by how good their memories are, how they evaluated the experience initially and when they looked back on it, and what they are willing to say now. Relatively few child-maltreatment assessment instruments contain measures of validity (e.g., lie scales), and response biases are rarely assessed. When reporting current events, parents and other family members may be concerned that the self-report of some acts might place them in legal jeopardy and may, therefore, be more likely to deny, minimize, or reframe their reports (Degarmo, Reid, & Knutson, 2006).

Although the most obvious way to determine whether child abuse and/or neglect has occurred would be to ask children, few studies have directly asked children about abuse (Amaya-Jackson, Socolar, Hunter, Runyan, & Colindres, 2000; Portwood, 2006). Not surprisingly, there are a number of reasons for the paucity of this type of research: Children may distort their responses to avoid stigma, to protect their abuser, or to avoid the possibility of removal from their home.

Research by Bower and Knutson (1996) showed that individuals who report having experienced certain behaviors that would be labeled as abusive tend not to characterize themselves as abused. Other work suggests that victims of sexual abuse may not identify themselves as victims of abuse, despite endorsing items that would be legally defined as rape (Koss, Gidicz, & Wisniewski, 1987).

Scholars have pointed out that information we remember from childhood may be heavily dependent on information told to us in childhood or later and/ or constructed by a parent (Radke-Yarrow, Campbell, & Burton, 1970). For research purposes, it is difficult to determine whether a person is recalling the objective details of a particular experience or recollecting details of what occurred based on other knowledge. One study of a large sample of 18-year-old youths who had been studied prospectively from birth found no evidence to support the validity of retrospective measures of subjective psychological states and processes (e.g., recollections of childhood experiences) (Henry, Moffitt, Caspi, Langley, & Silva, 1994). In another study, Offer, Kaiz, Howard, and Bennett (2000) examined autobiographical memory in a longitudinal study of mentally healthy adolescent males who were then re-interviewed at approximately age 48. These authors found substantial differences between adult memories of adolescence and what was actually reported during adolescence, including questions about parental discipline. This reliance on retrospective self-reports makes it difficult to know whether any consequences might be due to the actual abuse experience or the person's cognitive appraisal of the experience.

Another problem in making inferences about the association between retrospectively assessed childhood maltreatment and later outcomes is recall bias (Raphael, 1987). The net effect of recall bias is to inflate measures of association, by creating differential accuracy in reports of childhood experiences that differ as a function of current physical or psychological status. A classic example is provided by Brown and Harris (1978) in describing a study by Stott (1958), who found that mothers of "mongoloid" children reported more shocks during pregnancy than mothers of children without Down syndrome, concluding that socio-emotional factors played a role in the etiology of Down syndrome. Since research later identified chromosomal abnormalities as the cause, it is possible that these mothers used extra effort to recall pregnancy-related events. Another possibility is that ordinary events were redefined as traumas by mothers of affected children in an effort to explain their child's condition. A more recent example is provided in White, Widom, and Chen (2007), where current life status, including depression, drug problems, and life dissatisfaction, was related to adult retrospective reports of physical abuse for both men and women.

It is frequently forgotten in the debate about the accuracy of reports of child abuse that it is virtually impossible to determine the extent of false positives—that is, whether there is "over-reporting." For example, some individuals who report a given form of abuse in childhood misrepresent some or all of their childhood experiences (Rich, 1990). Short of following an individual child throughout the course of every day of his or her entire life, no one has yet been able to determine a way to make this assessment accurately.

Reliance on Official Reports of Child Abuse and Neglect   Because of the multiple potential methodological problems associated with self-reports of child maltreatment, researchers in the field have often turned to administrative data to determine child abuse and/or neglect. Research using child protective services (CPS) data to identify and measure maltreatment has become a common practice. All 50 states, the District of Columbia, and the U.S. territories have mandatory child abuse reporting laws that require certain professionals and institutions to report suspected maltreatment to a CPS agency. The initial report is called a referral, and about one-third of referrals are screened out each year and do not receive further attention from CPS. The remaining referrals are "screened in," and an investigation or assessment is conducted by the CPS agency to determine the likelihood that child abuse or neglect has occurred or that the child is at risk. After conducting interviews with family members, the alleged victims, and other people familiar with the family, the CPS agency makes a determination, or finding, about whether the child is a victim of abuse or neglect or is at risk of abuse or neglect. Each state establishes rules for the determination of a finding and terminology. National Child Abuse and Neglect Data System (NCANDS) is a federally sponsored effort that collects and analyzes data on child maltreatment and publishes an annual report (for more information on NCANDS, see U.S. Department of Health and Human Services, 2007).

Although records of official agencies, such as CPS, do not suffer from the problems associated with self-reports of child abuse, a different set of problems confronts researchers who rely solely on the use of administrative record data to operationally define child maltreatment. Legal definitions of maltreatment vary from state to state. State and local practices and policies that affect how child abuse and neglect cases are identified also vary. Information on child maltreatment derived from police, court, or social service agencies misses out on some unknown number of cases of abuse that are not reported to authorities. Rates of maltreatment substantiated by child protection agencies are dramatically lower than rates reported by victims or parents. For example, one study found evidence of contact with child protection services in only 5% of physically abused and 8% of sexually abused children (MacMillan, Jamieson, & Walsh, 2003). Another study showed that even children under scrutiny by agencies report 4 to 6 times more lifetime abuse experiences than recorded in official records (Everson et al., 2008). Some of these discrepancies may be due to differences in definitions and criteria for abuse. But these limitations of administrative record data have provoked researchers to attempt to improve on the use of this information.

Thus, recognizing the limitations of administrative record data, attempts have been made to develop standard definitions and coding schemes to categorize child maltreatment experiences. Two examples are briefly mentioned. The National Incidence Studies (NIS; Sedlak & Broadhurst, 1996) was designed to estimate the incidence of child abuse and neglect, beyond the estimates provided by CPS, by including information from a sample of professionals who are mandated reporters of child maltreatment (e.g., police, health care professionals, hospital personnel, teachers, day care workers, etc.). The Maltreatment Classification System (MCS; Barnett, Manly, & Cicchetti, 1993), a standardized coding scheme for use with administrative data, was designed as a systematic framework for coding aspects of children's abuse and/or neglect experiences across multiple dimensions thought to be related to developmental outcomes across multiple domains of functioning. In addition, the MCS was designed to add "depth and breadth to maltreatment assessment that is lacking in use of CPS labels alone" (Manly, 2005, p. 426). The MCS has also been applied to other case record data, such as treatment records, medical records, and foster care placement histories (Manly, 2005).

In studies of child abuse and neglect that rely exclusively on administrative data, it is important to consider factors that lead families to be identified as abusive or neglectful as distinct from those factors related to child abuse and neglect. Official records may represent the more serious and extreme cases, cases that pass thresholds put in place by CPS or prosecutors. Where substantiation and validation are important, dependence and use of official agency records may be the most appropriate method.

Ultimately, since all current methods suffer manifest limitations, the researcher is confronted with fundamental questions: To what extent do these different methods of ascertainment influence the results of research? To what extent do different methods of ascertainment of child maltreatment limit the generalizability of findings?

SAMPLING

Another challenge in child maltreatment research is assessing the representativeness of samples—that is, generalizing from a particular sample to the broader population. This is a concern when researchers use non-representative, specialized, or convenience samples, including in-patients, clients in therapy groups, prisoners, college students, or members of HMOs. Researchers need to ask how these groups may differ from individuals abused or neglected in childhood but not in such circumstances. Not all abused and neglected children end up in treatment for psychiatric or substance abuse problems; conversely, not all abused and neglected children are able to go to college. If the "survivors" are the ones who attend college or university and the non-survivors are those who end up in prison or hospitalized, this important characteristic needs to be taken into account when interpreting findings (cf. Rind, Tromovich, & Bauserman, 1998). This is one important advantage of prospective longitudinal studies, since they permit the researcher to follow groups of children into the future and to document their successes, failures, and other outcomes along the way.

Researchers often need to make decisions about when and whether to include different types of child abuse and neglect. These decisions influence the kinds of samples studied and, therefore, results. Some studies distinguish between abused and neglected children, treating them as separate groups. Others combine them into a single category, arguing that it is difficult to isolate cases of pure abuse from pure neglect. In many studies, sexual abuse is treated as a separate entity, excluded from studies of physical abuse or neglect. There is some evidence to suggest that different forms of child maltreatment may have different causes and/or consequences, leading some researchers to argue that the effects of different types and subtypes of maltreatment should be examined separately (e.g., Kinard, 2001; Lau et al., 2005; Manly, Cicchetti, & Barnett, 1994). However, these findings may be confounded by differences in the characteristics of the samples being studied (e.g., more females experience sexual abuse).

The problem with looking at the effects of different types or subtypes of maltreatment is that it ignores the comorbidity among different types of maltreatment. There is considerable discussion about the extent to which children experience multiple forms of maltreatment over the course of their lives (Finkelhor, 2008; Widom, Czaja, & Dutton, 2008). Retrospective self-report studies find that many children report being exposed to more than one type of maltreatment (Finkelhor, Ormrod, Turner, & Hamby, 2005). In one examination (Lau et al., 2005), high rates of multiple types of maltreatment were found in narratives of child protection reports in the United States. Exposure to multiple types of abuse contributes to high rates of repeated referrals to child protection services: 22% of children with substantiated maltreatment in the United States were re-reported within 24 months (Fluke, Shusterman, Hollinshead, & Yuan, 2008). Re-reports may also indicate increased surveillance (Drake, Jonson-Reid, & Sapokaite, 2006; Finkelhor, 2008). Researchers need to ask, What are the effects of studying individuals who have experienced multiple types of abuse and/or neglect? To what extent does the aggregation of cases of multiple types of abuse and neglect obscure important behavioral or psychological differences?

Despite the knowledge that child maltreatment may be perpetrated by multiple types of caregivers, researchers often limit inclusion criteria to victims of abuse or neglect by caretakers, usually in the home environment. Abuse outside the home is rarely addressed, and in some jurisdictions it is treated differently. While parents and caretakers may represent the most frequent perpetrators, the exclusion of abuse by others provides a less than complete understanding of the problem. Are the causes of abuse by non-parent or caretakers different from those of others? While this requirement is appropriate for some studies and for some research questions, the exclusion of abuse from other sources limits the generalizability of the findings. Furthermore, the relationship of the perpetrator to the victim varies with the age of the child. Infants and toddlers are more likely to be victimized by parents, whereas for older children, the percentage of parent perpetrators decreases and the role of people outside the home increases (U.S. Department of Health and Human Services, 2007). If research is restricted to abuse by caretakers only, this practice places limits on the ability to assess etiological factors.

A number of studies have restricted their samples to abused children who are currently living with their biological parents. How representative are samples of abused children who remain in the homes of their biological parents? To what extent are findings generalizable to children not living with their biological parents? This is particularly of concern in studies of children in foster care.

A related issue is the extent to which samples are restricted to child abuse among intact families. Children living with single parents appear to be at higher risk of experiencing physical and sexual abuse and neglect than children living with two biological parents (Boney-McCoy & Finkelhor, 1995; Finkelhor, Moore, Hamby, & Straus, 1997; Sedlak & Broadhurst, 1996)—that is, the rate of child abuse in single-parent households is 27.3 children per 1,000, nearly twice the rate of child abuse in two-parent households (15.5 children per 1,000) (Child Welfare Information Gateway, 2003). This means that one must use caution in interpreting the results of studies or surveys that are restricted to intact families, since these experiences may not be generalizable to a substantial portion of children growing up in abusive or neglectful home environments. Conversely, it is necessary to understand the role of family structure on the etiology and consequences of child abuse and neglect.

In certain fields, studies routinely recognize the importance of excluding children with evidence of neurological impairment, particularly in research assessing aspects of cognitive or intellectual functioning. However, since abused and neglected children have been shown to have lower intellectual skills than their non-abused peers (Perez & Widom, 1994) and are more likely to be placed in special education classes (Jonson-Reid, Drake, Kim, Porterfield, & Han, 2004), the elimination of these children from research may provide an incomplete picture of consequences. This potential consequence of child abuse and neglect is relevant in determining a child's ability to understand questions in the context of forensic investigations. Thus, for public policy purposes, it would seem important to have information on such impairments among maltreated children.

DESIGN

Most of the literature on child abuse and neglect relies on cross-sectional designs, providing snapshots of people at one point in time. Many of these studies use retrospective self-reports to define child maltreatment and, therefore, exhibit many of the problems of self-reports discussed earlier. In addition, these cross-sectional studies are limited in their ability to assess outcomes or consequences of child abuse or neglect because they do not account for the temporal ordering of maltreatment and subsequent outcomes. There is little possibility of examining causal relationships. Cross-sectional studies cannot demonstrate that child maltreatment causes some particular outcome—only that child abuse is associated with a certain outcome. Thus, from a scientific perspective, there is considerable ambiguity in the meaning of relationships or associations based on cross-sectional designs.

The discrepancy between retrospective reports of child abuse and neglect with findings from prospective longitudinal data is illustrated in the findings of three direct comparisons. In these studies, researchers have found major differences in consequences of child abuse depending on the design utilized: for pain (Raphael, Widom, & Lange, 2001); for drug abuse (Widom, Weiler, & Cottler, 1999); and for other childhood adversity with pain in adulthood (McBeth, Macfarlane, Benjamin, Morris, & Silman, 1999). Retrospective self-reports of child abuse showed strong relationships for these outcomes (pain, drug abuse), whereas when abused and neglected children were followed up into adulthood, they did not differ from control children on these outcomes.

ETHICAL ISSUES IN CHILD MALTREATMENT RESEARCH

Although research in child maltreatment often uses official records of child abuse and neglect, designs that are not limited to official data may discover unreported incidents of abuse and neglect. Such discoveries require consideration of mandated reporting requirements. Furthermore, child maltreatment research often involves topics of an embarrassing or upsetting nature. Federal regulations require that researchers protect participants against potential harm—that is, against anything that might "reasonably place [the individual] at risk of criminal or civil liability or be damaging to the subjects' financial standing, employability, insurability, reputations, or be stigmatizing." (45 C.F.R. 46 § 101). Research in the area of child maltreatment may involve a number of potential risks, including those that involve social stigma and/or legal consequences. In completing institutional review board (IRB) applications, researchers need to anticipate potential harms that might occur as a result of taking part in a particular piece of research and should develop plans to minimize such risks.

INFORMED CONSENT

Federal regulations require researchers to obtain informed consent from human research participants. Informed consent is intended to assure that research participants are aware of the potential risks and benefits involved in participating in the research so that participants can make an informed decision about whether or not to participate. Consent forms provide information about the nature and/or purpose of the research, a description of what participation requires, potential risks and benefits, the voluntary nature of participation, and protections of confidentiality of the information collected.

In the case of child maltreatment research, one question sometimes asked is how explicit the informed consent needs to be? For example, in a study that focuses on child abuse, researchers might provide accurate but incomplete descriptions of the purpose of the research, so that potential participants might be told that they are participating in a study of "family interaction styles" or "how parents punish misbehaving children" (National Research Council, 1993). In this case, the researcher would have to convince the IRB that this language was not deceptive, but necessary to obtain unbiased information from the participants. At the same time, such research would have to inform potential participants of possible risks that might be involved in participating and what exceptions to confidentiality might be made (i.e., if the researcher determines that the participant or someone else is in danger of imminent harm) and to whom the information would be reported. In addition, participants would need to be told about safeguards to protect them against unnecessary harm.

INFORMED CONSENT WITH SPECIAL POPULATIONS: MINOR CHILDREN

When conducting research with minors, researchers are required to obtain written consent from the legal guardian of the minor child. The minor child will provide verbal (if ages 8 to 11) or written (12 to 18 years old) assent, on the assumption that minor children cannot truly provide informed consent. The federal regulations assume that parents will make decisions in the children's best interests, but the regulations also recognize that some parents (e.g., those who abuse or neglect their children) may have conflicting interests (45 C.F.R. 46 § 408).

Standard informed-consent procedures are based on the presumption that a parent or guardian will protect his or her child's interests. However, in the case of child maltreatment research, the consenting parent may be the perpetrator of the alleged abuse or neglect or may have conflicted allegiances because of the relationship between the child and the alleged abuser. In these cases, the U.S. Department of Health and Human Services (2004) regulations state that an IRB "may waive the [parent/guardian] consent requirements . . . provided an appropriate mechanism for protecting the children who will participate as subjects in the research is substituted." The regulations do not provide specific guidance as to what these mechanisms are, instead indicating that the decision "would depend upon the nature and purpose of the activities described in the protocol, the risk and anticipated benefit to the research subjects, and their age, maturity, status, and condition" (45 C.F.R § 46.408[c]). In such cases, researchers need to apply to their IRBs for a waiver of written parental permission.

When children have been removed from the homes of their biological or adoptive caregivers, obtaining consent from a legal caregiver becomes even more complex. In most cases where a child has been removed from the home, the parents are no longer able to give legal consent. Therefore, the question arises over who holds legal authority over the child and whether that person is familiar enough with the child to act in the child's best interests. Researchers need to make certain that consent is obtained by an individual capable of making such determinations for the child. Liss (1994) and Sieber (1994) suggest that researchers become familiar with the legal requirements of the state in which their research is conducted to determine who has the legal authority to designate an adult who can authorize a foster child's participation in research. In some states this might be a child welfare worker, a guardian ad litem (or child advocate), or a judge. In other states, researchers may be required to obtain consent from the biological parents, even if they do not hold legal custody. Researchers also need to be sensitive to the power differential between the child and the researcher and recognize the possibility that these children may be at risk for coercion due to their previous victimization. Researchers need to make sure that abused and neglected children understand that they have the freedom to choose to participate or not to participate in the research (Kinard, 1985).

MANDATORY REPORTING OF CHILD ABUSE AND NEGLECT

In the context of their research, researchers may discover information that indicates that participating children are at risk for abuse and/or neglect. In this situation, researchers need to be aware of their obligation to report such abuse, as well as the potential consequences that the child and family may face as a result of such a report.

The standard for what constitutes an abusive act varies among the states (NCCAN/NAIC: http://nccanch.acf.hhs.gov). State-by-state child protective regulations are updated annually on the NCCAN Web site. Many states define abuse in terms of *harm* or *threatened harm* to a child's health or welfare. Other states use standards that include such language as *acts or omissions, recklessly fails or refuses to act, willfully causes or permits, and failure to provide.* These state-by-state standards guide mandatory reporters in their decision on whether to make a report to child protective services.

In addition to defining the acts or omissions that constitute child abuse or neglect, several states provide specific definitions of the persons who are reportable under the civil child abuse reporting laws to child protective services as perpetrators of abuse. These are persons who have some relationship or regular responsibility for the child. This generally includes parents, guardians, foster parents, relatives, or other caretakers responsible for the child's welfare.

A number of states provide exceptions in their reporting laws, which exempt certain acts or omissions from their statutory definitions of child abuse and neglect. For example, in six states (Arkansas, Florida, Louisiana, Pennsylvania, West Virginia, and Wisconsin) and the District of Columbia, financial inability to provide for a child is exempted from the definition of neglect. In 14 States[1], the District of Columbia, American Samoa, and the Northern Mariana Islands, physical discipline of a child, as long as it is reasonable and causes no bodily injury to the child, is an exception to the definition of abuse.

The Child Abuse Prevention and Treatment Act (CAPTA) Amendments of 1996 added new provisions specifying that nothing in the Act be construed as establishing a federal requirement that a parent or legal guardian provide any medical service or treatment that is against the religious beliefs of the parent or legal guardian (42 U.S.C.A. § 5106i). At the state level, civil child abuse reporting laws may provide an exception to the definition of child abuse and neglect for parents who choose not to seek medical care for their children due to religious beliefs.

A question frequently raised in child maltreatment research is whether researchers are mandated to report child abuse. Although all 50 states require mandated reporting of suspected child abuse, the states differ in terms of who is identified as a mandatory reporter. In some states the obligation to report abuse extends to anyone in the general citizenry having reason to suspect maltreatment. Nineteen states[2] and the Commonwealth of Puerto Rico stipulate that *all persons* are required to report known or suspected cases of child abuse or neglect or to report when they have reason to believe or there is reasonable cause to believe or suspect that maltreatment is happening. Other states enumerate specific lists of mandated reporters, such as health professionals, teachers, and child care providers (Liss, 1994; Margolin et al., 2005; Socolar, Runyan, & Amaya-Jackson, 1995; Steinberg, Pynoos, Goenjian, Sossanabadi, & Sherr, 1999). Furthermore, some states have identified discretionary reporters, who have the option (not the requirement) to report suspected abuse (Margolin et al., 2005).

Although no state specifically enumerates researchers as mandated reporters, Liss (1994) suggests that researchers are clearly mandated reporters in states that give the general citizenry the broad mandate of reporting abuse and neglect. However, in states with enumerated lists of reporters, researchers must consider their particular discipline in assessing whether or not they are mandated to report abuse and neglect. Liss (1994) suggests that this decision is obvious for physicians, who are always mandated reporters regardless of their status as practitioners or researchers but less obvious for social scientists. This is particularly true for psychologists, who can hold multiple roles, including clinician, teacher, and researcher. Many states use

---

1. Arkansas, Colorado, Florida, Georgia, Indiana, Minnesota, Mississippi, Missouri, Ohio, Oklahoma, Oregon, South Carolina, Texas, and Washington.

2. Alabama, Delaware, Florida, Idaho, Indiana, Kentucky, Maryland, Mississippi, Nebraska, New Hampshire, New Jersey, New Mexico, North Carolina, Oklahoma, Rhode Island, Tennessee, Utah, and Wyoming.

terms such as *mental health professional* when defining mandated reporters, but do not specify who is considered a mental health professional (Liss, 1994). In a field with numerous specialties, it is not always clear who is considered a "mental health professional." Therefore, researchers should become familiar with the reporting laws in the states in which they conduct research in order to determine whether their profession falls under the requirements. If there is any question, the state child protective services should be consulted to evaluate whether a report should be made (Margolin et al., 2005).

For researchers engaged in child maltreatment research or contemplating research involving child abuse or neglect, mandatory reporting requirements are viewed as a major challenge. Potential risks that might result from reporting child abuse and neglect discovered in the course of research include loss of participation of subjects at the consent stage (refusals to participate), attrition in longitudinal studies, legal risks to the family, and legal liability of researchers as a result of reporting (Socolar et al., 1995). To avoid these consequences, some researchers avoid mandatory reporting by limiting response options, using anonymous data collection, or transmitting data to a state in which reporting abuse discovered in the course of research is not mandated (Socolar et al., 1995).

Another approach is to obtain a *Certificate of Confidentiality* from the federal government for the research. A Certificate of Confidentiality from the federal government protects the individual's privacy and personal information from being disclosed, even if ordered by a court. However, according to federal guidelines, personally identifiable information protected by a Certificate of Confidentiality may be disclosed under the following circumstances, among other limited categories: "information on such things as child abuse, reportable communicable diseases, possible threat to self or others . . . provided that such disclosures are spelled out in the informed consent form." (http://grants.nih.gov/grants/policy/coc/faqs.htm).

It is argued that Certificates of Confidentiality circumvent state mandatory reporting laws and provide researchers with an opportunity to conduct more valid, generalizable research on child maltreatment. However, while some believe that federal Certificates of Confidentiality should preempt state mandatory reporting laws, it is unclear whether these certificates in fact do so (Socolar et al., 1995). According to Knight et al. (2000), child maltreatment researchers generally agree (although not unanimously) that even the federal Certificate of Confidentiality does not relieve researchers of either the ethical or the legal duty to report suspected maltreatment (Melton, 1990; Putnam, Liss, & Landsverk, 1996; Runyan, 2000). In addition, a number of federal institutes and funding agencies will not fund research if the researchers indicate an interest in avoiding mandated reporting through the use of Certificates of Confidentiality (Margolin et al., 2005; Socolar et al., 1995). Similarly, some IRBs require consent forms to include language in compliance with mandatory reporting laws even if they accept the research project's Certificate of Confidentiality (Margolin et al., 2005). Even if no legal obligation for child maltreatment researchers to report abuse exists, many in the research and legal fields argue that there is a moral and ethical obligation, particularly when a child is at risk of current or imminent harm (Liss, 1994; Margolin et al., 2005; Socolar et al., 1995).

Fear of having to report child abuse and neglect cases has exerted a chilling effect on many researchers, leading them to avoid questions about these important childhood experiences or asking these questions only of study participants who are over age 18 (not minors). However, a body of empirical evidence is developing regarding researchers' experiences with mandatory reporting of child abuse and neglect that is informative. Researchers involved in the LONGSCAN consortium (Knight et al., 2000) have described their experiences in reporting research participants to child protective services. In their work across the five sites involved in the consortium, Knight et al. (2000, p. 10) found:

> [A] total of 17 CPS reports on 15 children were made by study staff from among a total of 4,078 interviews conducted with the 1,354 participants. This constitutes 1.1% of study subjects and 0.42% of the research interviews. . . . Researchers shared their decision to report with the primary caregiver prior to reporting in 15 of the 17 reports. CPS accepted nine of the 17 reports, or slightly more than half, for investigation, while five were not accepted for investigation. The CPS status of the remaining 3 referrals is unknown.

CONCLUSIONS

Although the issues discussed here are challenging, researchers should not be deterred from incorporating questions about childhood maltreatment in their research and furthering our knowledge of the causes and consequences of child abuse and neglect. In contrast to research in the physical or natural sciences where it may be possible to measure objects with great precision, it is virtually impossible to establish absolute rates of child abuse and neglect or to be confident that every person who reports abuse or does not report abuse was in fact abused or not. Given these complex and inherent methodological challenges, researchers need to recognize the effects of the choices they make in conducting their research and should attempt to minimize bias whenever possible.

- Researchers need to ask what information is included or excluded as a result of decisions made about definitions, criteria, or methods employed in research.
- While not all researchers will or should define child abuse and neglect in identical ways, the rationale and decisions about the criteria for labeling a case of child abuse or neglect must be explicit, and the implications of these decisions must be taken into account in evaluating and discussing the findings.

- Systematic comparisons of types of abuse and neglect are necessary to understand the representativeness and generalizability of samples. Further research is needed to determine the usefulness and necessity of conceptualizing and empirically distinguishing between types of child abuse and neglect.
- Greater efforts are needed to validate information used in research, using reverse and forward record checks whenever possible. Efforts to assess family histories should not rely solely on single-person reports but should include information from multiple sources.
- There is a continued need to develop reliable and valid measures to assess different types of child maltreatment across diverse populations and for use with children, adolescents, adults, and parents or caregivers.
- Researchers should not be deterred from engaging in studies of child abuse and neglect because of fears of mandatory reporting laws.

REFERENCES

Amaya-Jackson, L., Socolar, R. R. S., Hunter, W., Runyan, D. K., & Colindres, R. (2000). Directly questioning children and adolescents about maltreatment: A review of survey measures used. *Journal of Interpersonal Violence, 15*, 725–759.

Barnett, D., Manly, J. T., & Cicchetti, D. (1993). Defining child maltreatment: The interface between policy and research. In D. Cicchetti & S. J. Toth (Eds.), *Advances in applied developmental psychology: Child abuse, child development and social policy* (pp. 7–73). Norwood, NJ: Ablex Publishing.

Boney-McCoy, S., & Finkelhor, D. (1995). Psychosocial sequelae of violent victimization in a national youth sample. *Journal of Consulting and Clinical Psychology, 63*(5), 726–736.

Bower, M. E., & Knutson, J. F. (1996). Attitudes toward physical discipline as a function of disciplinary history and self-labeling as physically abused. *Child Abuse & Neglect, 20*, 689–699.

Bremner, R. H. (1970). *Children and youth in America* (Vol. 1). Cambridge, MA: Harvard University Press.

Brown, G. W., & Harris, T. O. (1978). *Social origins of depression: A study of psychiatric disorder in women.* New York, NY: Free Press.

Center for Effective Discipline. (2008). Discipline and the law. Retrieved November 15, 2010, from http://www.stophitting.com/index.php?page=statelegislation

Child Welfare Information Gateway (2003). Retrieved November 15, 2010, from http://www.childwelfare.gov/.

Cox, M. J., & Cox, R. D. (1985). *A brief history of policy for dependent and neglected children.* Norwood, NJ: Ablex Publishing.

Degarmo, D. S., Reid, J. B., & Knutson, J. F. (2006). Direct laboratory observations and analog measures. In M. M. Feerick, J. F. Knutson, P. K. Trickett, & S. M. Flanzer, (Eds.), *Child abuse and neglect: Definitions, classifications, and a framework for research* (pp. 293–328). Baltimore, MD: Brookes.

Drake, B., Jonson-Reid, M., & Sapokaite, L. (2006). Re-reporting of child maltreatment: Does participation in other public sector services moderate the likelihood of a second maltreatment report? *Child Abuse & Neglect, 30*, 1201–1226.

Dubowitz, H. (2006). Defining child neglect. In M. M. Feerick, J. F. Knutson, P. K. Trickett, & S. M. Flanzer, (Eds.), *Child abuse and neglect: Definitions, classifications, and a framework for research* (pp. 107–128). Baltimore, MD: Brookes.

Everson, M. D., Smith, J. B., Hussey, J. M., English, D., Litrownik, A. J., & Dubowitz, H. (2008). Concordance between adolescent reports of childhood abuse and child protective service determinations in an at-risk sample of young adolescents. *Child Maltreatment, 13*, 14–26.

Finkelhor, D. (2008). *Childhood victimization. Violence, crime and abuse in the lives of young people.* New York, NY: Oxford University Press.

Finkelhor, D., Moore, D., Hamby, S. L., & Straus, M. A. (1997). Sexually abused children in a national survey of parents: Methodological issues. *Child Abuse & Neglect, 21*(1), 1–19.

Finkelhor, D., Ormrod, R., Turner, H., & Hamby, S. L. (2005). The victimization of children and youth: A comprehensive national survey. *Child Maltreatment, 10,* 5–25.

Fluke, J. D., Shusterman, G. R., Hollinshead, D. M., & Yuan, Y. Y. (2008). Longitudinal analysis of repeated child abuse reporting and victimization: Multistate analysis of associated factors. *Child Maltreatment, 13,* 76–88.

Gallup Organization. (1995). *Disciplining children in America: A Gallup poll report.* Princeton, NJ.: Gallup Organization.

Giovannoni, J. (1989). Definitional issues in child maltreatment. In D. Cicchetti & V. Carlson (Eds.), *Child maltreatment: Theory and research on the causes and consequences of child abuse and neglect* (pp. 3–37). New York, NY: Cambridge University Press.

Henry, B., Moffitt, T. E., Caspi, A., Langley, J., & Silva, P. A. (1994). On the "remembrance of things past": A longitudinal evaluation of the retrospective method. *Psychological Assessment, 6,* 92–101.

Ichikawa, D. P. (1997). An argument on behalf of children. *Child Maltreatment, 2,* 202–211.

In re Gault. 387 U.S. 1. (1967).

Jonson-Reid, M., Drake, B., Kim, J., Porterfield, S., & Han, L. (2004). A prospective analysis of the relationship between reported child maltreatment and special education eligibility among poor children. *Child Maltreatment, 9,* 382–394.

Kempe, C. H., Silverman, F. N., Steele, B. F., Droegemueller, W., & Silver, H. K. (1962). The battered-child syndrome. *Journal of American Medical Association, 181,* 17–24.

Kinard, E. M. (1985). Ethical issues in research with abused children. *Child Abuse and Neglect, 9,* 301–311.

Kinard, E. M. (2001). Characteristics of maltreatment experience and academic functioning among maltreated children. *Violence and Victims, 16,* 323–337.

Knight, E. D., Runyan, D. K., Dubowitz, H., Brandford, C., Kotch, J., Litrownik, A., & Hunter, W. (2000). Methodological and ethical challenges associated with child self-report of maltreatment. *Journal of Interpersonal Violence, 15,* 760–775.

Knutson, J. F., & Heckenberg, D. (2006). Operationally defining physical abuse of children. In M. M. Feerick, J. F. Knutson, P. K. Trickett, & S. M. Flanzer, (Eds.), *Child abuse and neglect: Definitions, classifications, and a framework for research* (pp. 69–106). Baltimore, MD: Brookes.

Korbin, J. E. (2002). Culture and child maltreatment: Cultural competence and beyond. *Child Abuse & Neglect, 26,* 637–644.

Koss, M., Gidicz, C., & Wisniewski, N. (1987). The scope of rape: Incidence and prevalence of sexual aggression and victimization in a national sample of higher education students. *Journal of Consulting and Clinical Psychology, 55,* 162–170.

Lau, A. S., Leeb, R. T., English, D., Graham, J. C., Briggs, E. C., Brody, K. E., & Marshall, J. (2005). What's in a name? A comparison of methods for classifying predominant type of maltreatment. *Child Abuse and Neglect, 29,* 533–551.

Leeb, R. T., Paulozzi, L. J., Melanson, C., Simon, T. R., & Arias, I. (2008). Child maltreatment surveillance. *Uniform definitions for public health and recommended data elements.* Atlanta, GA: Centers for Disease Control and Prevention.

Liss, M. (1994). Child abuse: Is there a mandate for researchers to report? *Ethics & Behavior, 4,* 133–146.

MacMillan, H. L., Jamieson, E., & Walsh, C. A. (2003). Reported contact with child protection services among those reporting child physical and sexual abuse: Results from a community survey. *Child Abuse & Neglect, 27,* 1397–1408.

Manly, J. T. (2005). Advances in research definitions of child maltreatment. *Child Abuse & Neglect, 29,* 425–439.

Manly, J. T., Cicchetti, D., & Barnett, D. (1994). The impact of subtype, frequency, chronicity, and severity of child's maltreatment on social competence and behavior problems. *Development & Psychopathology, 6,* 121–143.

Margolin, G., Chien, D., Duman, S. E., Fauchier, A., Gordis, E. B., Oliver, P. H., . . . Vickerman, K. A. (2005). Ethical issues in couple and family research. *Journal of Family Psychology, 19,* 157–167.

McBeth, J., Macfarlane, G. J., Benjamin, S., Morris, S., & Silman, A. J. (1999). The association between tender points, psychological distress, and adverse childhood experiences: A community-based study. *Arthritis & Rheumatism, 42*(7), 1397–1404.

Melton, G. B. (1990). Certificates of Confidentiality under the Public Health Service Act: Strong protection but not enough. *Violence & Victims, 5,* 67–71.

National Research Council (1993). *Understanding child abuse and neglect.* Washington, DC: National Academies Press.

Offer, D., Kaiz, M., Howard, K. I., & Bennett, E. S. (2000). The altering of reported experiences. *Journal of the American Academy of Child & Adolescent Psychiatry, 39*(6), 735–742.

Peled, T., & Kurtz, L. (1994). Child maltreatment: The relationship between developmental research and public policy. *The American Journal of Family Therapy, 22,* 247–262.

Perez, C., & Widom, C. S. (1994). Childhood victimization and long-term intellectual and academic outcomes. *Child Abuse and Neglect, 18*(8), 617–633.

Portwood, S. G. (2006). Self-report approaches. In M. M. Feerick, J. F. Knutson, P. K. Trickett, & S. M. Flanzer (Eds.), *Child abuse and neglect: Definitions, classifications, and a framework for research* (pp. 233–254). Baltimore, MD: Brookes.

Putnam, F. W., Liss, M. B., & Landsverk, J. (1996). Ethical issues in maltreatment research with children and adolescents. In K. Hoagwood, P. S. Jensen, & C. Fisher (Eds.), *Ethical issues in mental health research with children* (pp. 113–129). Mahwah, NJ: Lawrence Erlbaum.

Radke-Yarrow, M., Campbell, J. D., & Burton, R. V. (1970). Recollections of childhood: A study of the retrospective method. *Monographs of the Society for Research in Child Development, 35*(5), 1–83.

Raphael, K. G. (1987). Recall bias: A proposal for assessment and control. *International Journal of Epidemiology, 16*(2), 167–169.

Raphael, K. G., Widom, C. S., & Lange, G. (2001). Childhood victimization and pain in adulthood: A prospective investigation. *Pain, 92*(1–2), 283–293.

Rich, C. L. (1990). Accuracy of adults' reports of abuse in childhood. *American Journal of Psychiatry, 147*(10), 1389–1390.

Rind, B., Tromovich, P., & Bauserman, R. (1998). A meta-analytic examination of assumed properties of child sexual abuse using college samples. *Psychological Bulletin, 124*(1), 22–53.

Roche, A. J., Labbe, J., Brown, J., & Chadwick, D. (2005). The work of Ambroise Tardieu: The first definitive description of child abuse. *Child Abuse & Neglect, 29,* 325–334.

Runyan, D. K. (2000). The ethical, legal, and methodological implications of directly asking children about abuse. *Journal of Interpersonal Violence, 15*(7), 675–681.

Runyan, D. K., & English, D. J. (2006) Measuring child abuse and neglect using child protective service records. In M. M. Feerick, J. F. Knutson, P. K. Trickett, & S. M. Flanzer (Eds.), *Child abuse and neglect: Definitions, classifications, and a framework for research* (pp. 255–292). Baltimore, MD: Brookes.

Sedlak, A. J., & Broadhurst, D. D. (1996). *Third national incidence study of child abuse and neglect, final report.* Washington, DC: U.S. Department of Health and Human Services, Administration for Children and Families, Administration on Children, Youth and Families, National Center on Child Abuse and Neglect.

Sieber, J. E. (1994). Issues presented by mandatory reporting requirements to researchers of child abuse and neglect. *Ethics & Behavior, 4,* 1–22.

Socolar, R. R., Runyan, D. K., & Amaya-Jackson, L. (1995). Methodological and ethical issues related to studying child maltreatment. *Journal of Family Issues, 16,* 565–586.

Steinberg, A. M., Pynoos, R., Goenjian, A. K., Sossanabadi, H., & Sherr, L. (1999). Are researchers bound by child abuse reporting laws? *Child Abuse & Neglect, 23*(8), 771–777.

Stott, D. H. (1958). Some psychosomatic aspects of casualty of reproduction. *Journal of Psychosomatic Research, 3,* 42–45.

Straus, M. A., & Donnelly, D. A. (1994/2001). *Beating the devil out of them: Corporal punishment in American families and its effects on children.* San Francisco, CA: Jossey-Bass/Lexington Books.

Straus, M. A., Gelles, R. J., & Steinmetz, S. K. (1980/2006). *Behind closed doors: Violence in American families.* New Brunswick, NJ: Transaction Publishers.

Straus, M. A., & Stewart, J. H. (1999). Corporal punishment by American parents: National data on prevalence, chronicity, severity, and duration in relation to child and family characteristics. *Clinical Child and Family Psychology Review, 2*(2), 55–70.

U.S. Department of Health and Human Services. (2007). *Child maltreatment 2005* (Administration for Children and Families). Washington, DC: Government Printing Office.

U.S. Department of Health and Human Services Protection of Human Subjects Regulations, 45 C.F.R § 46.408 (2004).

Weis, J. G. (1989). Family violence research methodology and design. In L. Ohlin & M. Tonry (Eds.), *Family violence* (pp. 296–321). Chicago, IL: University of Chicago Press.

White, H. R., Widom, C. S., & Chen, P. H. (2007). Congruence between adolescents' self-reports and their adult retrospective reports regarding parental discipline practices during their adolescence. *Psychological Reports, 101*, 1079–1094.

Widom, C. S., Czaja, S. J., & Dutton, M. A. (2008). Childhood victimization and lifetime revictimization. *Child Abuse & Neglect, 32*, 785–796.

Widom, C. S., Weiler, B. L., & Cottler, L. B. (1999). Childhood victimization and drug abuse: A comparison of prospective and retrospective findings. *Journal of Consulting and Clinical Psychology, 67*(6), 867–880.

Zimring, F. E. (1989). *Toward a jurisprudence of family violence*. (Vol. 11). Chicago, IL: University of Chicago Press.

Author Index

Subject Index